$s_{\overline{X}}$	An estimate of the standard error of the mean
H_0	Statistical hypothesis, or null hypothesis
p	Probability of occurrence if H_0 were true
α	Level of significance
β	Probability of a type-II error (accepting a false H_0)
t	Student t-ratio
ν	Degrees of freedom
s_{W}^2	Pooled within—group variance based on both samples
$\hat{\Delta}$	Estimate of effect size based on sample data
$s_{\overline{X}_1 - \overline{X}_2}$	Estimate of the standard error of the difference between two means
σ_p	Standard error of a proportion for infinite populations
χ^2	*Chi*—square statistic
s_r	Estimate of σ_r
σ_Z	Standard error of the Fisher Z transformation
Z_r	Fisher Z-transformation of r
MS_{B}	Mean square between groups estimate of the population variance, σ^2
MS_{W}	Mean square within groups estimate of σ^2
q	Studentized range statistic
HSD	Honest significant difference
$A \times B$	Interaction of factors A and B
$MS_{A \times B}$	Mean square for interaction of factors A and B estimate of σ^2
$\overline{X}_{j\cdot}$	Mean score of row j in a two-way ANOVA
$\overline{X}_{\cdot k}$	Mean score of column k in a two-way ANOVA
$\overline{X}_{\cdot\cdot}$	Grand mean for the total sample in a two-way ANOVA
$\overline{X}_{jk}$	Mean score of the cell in row j and column k in a two-factor ANOVA

❖ Basic Statistics for the Behavioral Sciences

Third Edition

Kenneth D. Hopkins
University of Colorado, Boulder

B. R. Hopkins

Gene V Glass
Arizona State University, Tempe

Allyn and Bacon
Boston • London • Toronto • Sydney • Tokyo • Singapore

Copyright © 1996, 1987, 1978 by Allyn & Bacon
A Simon & Schuster Company
Needham Heights, MA 02194

Editor-in-Chief, Education: Nancy Forsyth
Editorial-Production Administrator: Joe Sweeney
Editorial-Production Service: Walsh Associates
Composition Buyer: Linda Cox
Manufacturing Buyer: Megan Cochran
Cover Administrator: Suzanne Harbison

Library of Congress Cataloging-in-Publication Data

Hopkins, Kenneth D.
     Basic statistics for the behavioral sciences / Kenneth D. Hopkins,
   B.R. Hopkins, Gene V Glass. — 3rd ed.
          p.   cm.
     Includes bibliographical references and index.
     ISBN 0-205-16086-7
     1. Social sciences—Statistical methods.   I. Hopkins, B. R.,
   1932-   . II. Glass, Gene V, 1940-   .   III. Title.
   HA29.H734   1995
   519.5—dc20   95-32847
                                                              CIP

Printed in the United States of America

10 9 8 7 6 5 4 3 2 1   00 99 98 97 96 95

❖ Contents

❖ PREFACE

The third edition of this textbook is designed for a one- or two-semester course in applied statistics. The methods and concepts are applicable to empirical research in all behavioral disciplines.

The approach of this text is conceptual, not mathematical; it is not a "cookbook." Although the mathematical derivation of a formula reinforces its validity, it does not necessarily insure a real understanding of its meaning or application. Indeed, the number of formulas used in the text is kept to a minimum; the ratio of words to mathematical symbols of text material would rank high among statistics texts. We have stressed the understanding, application, and interpretation of concepts rather than derivation and proof or hand-computation. Examples with computational requirements are kept short so as not to divert attention from the concepts to computational details. However, we do believe that one's understanding of statistics is enhanced by working through a few examples by hand. For students whose knowledge of elementary algebra has faded through disuse, we have provided a set of MATH NOTES in the Appendix to allow a quick concise review of the needed algebraic skills. Whenever statistical topics are introduced in the text that involve these math skills, students are directed to the relevant math note for additional clarification and practice if they so desire. The math notes also include practice exercises to illustrate and reinforce the process at hand. No assumption is made that most students will need to attend to all of the math notes; they can be skipped without distraction if not needed.

We have pruned away much deadwood found in some other statistics texts, and earlier editions of this book. Although every text claims to reflect the latest influences of computers and calculators, obsolete techniques of calculating certain statistics can still be found in some recently published texts. On the other hand, useful procedures that were excluded in previous editions because of the heavy computational labor costs are now included because of the painless functions provided by spreadsheets. Statistical power and type II errors continue to be emphasized. Unlike many texts, we emphasize interval estimation and effect size of statistical measures, not just hypothesis testing.

We have tried to be sensitive to changes in statistical pedagogy occasioned by the widespread availability of spreadsheets (which now come with many available statistical functions, including multiple regression and factorial analysis of variance). We strongly recommend their use for statistical computations, along with the use of the increasing number of their built-in statistical functions for measures of central tendency, variability, correlation, regression, t-test, and the analysis of variance.

Our selection of topics has been guided by three considerations: (1) What are the most useful statistical methods? (2) Which statistical methods are the most widely used in scholarly journals in the behavioral and social sciences? (3) Which statistical methods are fundamental to further study? Most of the statistical techniques that are used in doctoral dissertations in the behavioral sciences are treated in this text. This text provides a more thorough coverage of analysis of variance (ANOVA) techniques than usually found in introductory statistics texts for social sciences because ANOVA continues to be the most widely used statistical method in psychological and educational research.

The third edition of *Basic Statistics for the Behavioral Sciences* differs from the previous edition in several respects, paramount among which are the following:

1. It incorporates a unique "case method" approach. The data set used in this case study approach is from the High School and Beyond study (HSB) and gives data on a representative sample of 200 U.S. high school seniors, including five academic achievement measures along with several demographic and personological variables. This data set was selected to provide a widespread exposure to a variety of statistical measures in a realistic application and to enhance the understanding and meaningfulness of their use. Suggested computer exercises are also included for each chapter, although many instructors will wish to tailor their own assignments, using this and/or other data sets suited to their course emphases.* The HSB file is given in various formats, some of which are readable by SPSS, SAS, BMDP, SYSTAT, MINITAB, EXCEL, LOTUS, QUATTRO PRO, and virtually any other statistical or spreadsheet software that you have available. It is anticipated that the case study analyses will be useful in providing the kind of experience in data analysis that the typical researcher goes through in analyzing and understanding real data: frequency distributions and matters of normality and skewness, outlier identification, central tendency, variability, correlation, multiple regression, confidence intervals, hypothesis testing, and so on. It is anticipated that the continuous involvement with these data sets will help the student experience a unified "big picture" of statistical analysis, sometimes lost when there is no continuity across the various chapters. It is anticipated that many, if not most, students will become sufficiently confident to pursue other challenging and interesting questions they may have pertaining to these data beyond those included in the chapter's Suggested Computer Activities.
2. The pedagogical features of this new edition include an expanded selection of diagnostic mastery test items and problems and exercises following each chapter. In addition, an abundant number of context-relevant quiz items have been embedded throughout the several sections of each chapter so that the reader may check and reinforce his or her understanding of the current content prior to proceeding to subsequent sections. We believe that the immediate feedback from these embedded quizzes will enhance content mastery to a significant degree.

In this edition, we have tried to maintain the high professional standards of the previous two editions of *BSBS*. The goal of technical accuracy was paramount, while maintaining a minimum requisite of mathematical skills. We believe the sequence of topics is appropriate for undergraduate and graduate work, and that the text has an orientation that is appropriate for both research consumers and producers. Chapters have been written to be as self-contained as possible to provide more instructional options in course content and emphasis.

During the time this text was being revised, our colleagues and students contributed in innumerable ways to our efforts. We cannot name them all here, but the following colleagues deserve special thanks for contributing recently to our education in statistical methods: Julian Stanley deserves credit for his influence as mentor. Richard Jaeger, Jason Millman, and Lorrie Shepard have made several suggestions based on extensive classroom experience that improved its instructional quality. Many others made technical or pedagogical contributions. We are indebted to Grace Vrell and Donna Hopkins for their careful proofing and many excellent editorial suggestions.

---

*The data files are on the accompanying diskette in ASCII (HSB200.TXT), SPSS (HSB200.SAV), and EXCEL (HSB200.XLS) formats. Macs that can covert files to Mac format are common.

1

Introduction: Why Study Statistical Methods?

❖ 1.1 THE "IMAGE" OF STATISTICS

Popular attitudes toward statistics often include a mixture of anxiety, cynicism, fear, and contempt. "Freudian slips" have sometimes turned statisticians into "sadisticians." The warning "Don't become a statistic" is taken to mean "Don't let something evil befall you." Statisticians have been disparagingly placed in the company of both liars and crafty politicians, and therefore accused of "statisticulation," that is, the art of lying with numbers while appearing objective, rational, and scientific.

W. H. Auden apparently felt that the Biblical ten commandments should be expanded to eleven when he wrote, "Thou shalt not sit among statisticians, nor commit a social science." The remark that "If all the statisticians in the world were laid end to end, it would be a good thing." has its adherents even among students! However, it is probably an exaggeration to suggest that if a statistician were compelled to stand in boiling water with ice packs on his head, he would conclude that, "On the average, I feel fine."

The use of statistics may or may not be numerical "hocus pocus." In their attempt to promote their self-interest, liars may misrepresent numbers and statistics, but they also misuse words as well. On the other hand, people of integrity attempt to use words and statistics to honestly communicate with one another. Advertisers and the media constantly bombard the audience with claims and reports that are blatantly false or grossly distorted. Increasingly, people are learning to be wary of "scientific" reports because they often have been distorted by half-truths into propaganda for some point of view. The educated layman, not just the professional man, needs statistical literacy to have the critical knowledge and skills needed to assess the credibility of information given via numbers as well as via words. Logical thinking is a good safeguard against the uncritical acceptance of verbal hogwash, while a working knowledge of statistics makes us less vulnerable to quantitative rubbish. Hopefully, you will discover that a study of statistics will not only improve your ability to read and evaluate research literature, but help you to become a more competent and confident consumer or producer of quantitative evidence used to support claims and conclusions.

We expect, given a bit of willingness on your part, that you will find your exploration of statistics to be not only rewarding but—well, dare we say—enjoyable!

It is increasingly recognized that experimental research can make important contributions to our lives by giving us more effective medicines, diets, treatments, materials, and curricula, to mention a few. Consider the following quote by T. M. Porter (1986) in this regard:

> Statistics has become known in the twentieth century as the mathematical tool for analyzing experimental and observational data. Enshrined by public policy as the only reliable basis for judgments as to the efficacy of medical procedures or the safety of chemicals, and adopted by business for such uses as industrial quality control, it is evidently among the products of science whose influence on public and private life has been most pervasive. Statistical analysis has also come to be seen in many scientific disciplines as indispensable for drawing reliable conclusions from empirical results. . . . Not since the invention of the calculus, if ever, has a new field of mathematics found so extensive a domain of application.

Statistics is a basic tool for empirical research in education and the behavioral and social sciences. Some knowledge of statistical methods is a virtual necessity to pursue a career of scholarship in many empirical disciplines. Within the last three decades, graduate schools have appropriately acknowledged its importance as a research tool by accepting course work in statistics as a substitute for one of the two foreign language requirements that were traditionally required for the Ph.D. degree. This substitution is strikingly apt: Statistics is an increasingly important language for communicating information based on quantitative data.

❖ 1.2 TWO TYPES OF STATISTICS

Two streams of influence have led to the development of statistical methods. One branch was dedicated to keeping orderly government records (*state* and *statistics* come from the same Latin root, *status*). From this branch evolved the activities of counting, measuring, describing, tabulating, ordering, and census-taking, all of which eventually led to *descriptive* statistics. The second stream of influence originated in the mathematics of games of chance and led to the development of *inferential* statistics, that is based squarely on mathematical probability. This text offers an introduction to the most widely used descriptive and inferential statistics in behavioral research (Willson, 1980; Goodwin & Goodwin, 1985; Elmore & Woehlke, 1988). The emphasis in Chapters 2 through 8 is on commonly used descriptive statistics; whereas, the dominant theme in Chapters 9 through 16 is inferential statistics.

❖ 1.3 DESCRIPTIVE STATISTICS

Descriptive statistics involves tabulating, depicting, and describing sets of data. These data may be from quantitative variables, such as height, intelligence, or grade level (variables that are characterized by an underlying continuum), or from categorical variables, such as gender, college major, or occupation. Very large sets of data must generally undergo a process of organization and summarization before they are readily intelligible by mere mortals. The human mind cannot easily extract the full import of an array of unorganized data without the aid of special techniques. Thankfully, descriptive statistics provides tools for organizing, simplifying and summarizing basic information from an otherwise unwieldy mass of data.

❖ 1.4 INFERENTIAL STATISTICS

Inferential statistics provides methods to estimate characteristics of a total group (population) based on data from a smaller set (sample) of observations. For example, a school administrator may wish to determine the proportion of children in a large school system who come to school without breakfast (use drugs, are latch-key kids, qualify for a special program, carry handguns, or whatever). With a little knowledge of statistics, the administrator would know that it is unnecessary and inefficient to question each child. The proportion for the entire district who come to school without breakfast could be estimated fairly accurately (with a margin of error of about 5%) from a sample of as few as 400 children. The primary purpose of inferential statistics is to estimate population attributes from just a sample of cases. Descriptive statistics often serves as a springboard for inferential statistics.

❖ 1.5 THE INTERDISCIPLINARY NATURE OF STATISTICS

All empirical disciplines make extensive use of statistical methods. A joint committee of the American Statistical Association and the National Council of Teachers of Mathematics produced a very readable book, *Statistics: A Guide to the Unknown* (Tanur, Mosteller, Kruskal, Link, Pieters, Rising, & Lehmann, 1978) that gives many interesting applications of statistics in the fields of public health, political science and government, semantics, law, business, demography, anthropology, economics, sociology, geology, astronomy, genetics, accounting, agriculture, business, psychology, and education. Scanning these studies will help you appreciate the broad applicability and practical utility of statistical methods.

❖ 1.6 STATISTICS AND MATHEMATICS

The discipline of statistics is a branch of applied mathematics, and, when taught in departments of mathematics, courses in statistical methods are usually taught such that formal proofs of mathematical theorems and the derivation of statistical formulas are the major foci. Such statistics courses require considerable proficiency in college level mathematics. On the other hand, if the primary objective of a course in statistics pertains to the appropriate use, understanding and interpretation of statistics, advanced mathematics is of minor importance. In this book, we make extensive use of intuition, common sense, and logical reasoning. Most of the rationale of applied statistics and their appropriate use can be mastered without reference to advanced mathematical skills.

While writing this book, we have borne in mind that the principal function of a textbook is to serve as an instructional resource. We have endeavored to present the concepts and techniques of statistics conceptually without extensive use of mathematics. The mathematics that you will encounter in this text does not go beyond what you enjoyed years ago in Algebra I. However, since some of you have had little occasion to use those math skills in recent years, we have provided explanatory Math Notes with practice exercises in Appendix A. As they are needed, these exercises are referenced in the text to provide you with a little review to polish mathematical skills that may have grown dull from disuse.

Unlike some areas of study that are characterized by vague verbal discourse, statistical terms are defined, unambiguously and precisely. A speaker for some political action group might receive an enthusiastic reaction to some string of words such as, "Viable, democratic, and synergistic alternatives are critical to bring the unique needs of the whole child into creative homeostasis with his ecological environment." If the statement is scrutinized, however, its meaning is so ambiguous and imprecise that it is essentially meaningless. If you are inclined toward critical and precise thought, the restrictive and confining mantle of statistics will soon begin to feel comfortable and reassuring. We think that you will agree that the satisfying confidence of knowing that you are mastering a logical and unambiguous language will outweigh the effort involved in learning the language.

❖ 1.7 CASE STUDY WITH COMPUTER APPLICATIONS

A special feature of this text is that the data from an actual study (Rock, Hilton, Pollack, Ekstrom, & Goertz, 1985) will be used chapter by chapter to illustrate and reinforce the related concepts and procedures. The data are from a large national sample of high school seniors (the High School and Beyond study, HSB) who were measured on five achievemental variables (reading, writing, math, science, and civics) and who were categorized according to sex, race (Hispanic, Asian, Black, or White), socio-economic level (low, middle, high), type of school (public or private), and choice of a high school program (general, academic, or vocational). Our case study for this text is based on a random sample of 200 seniors from the HSB study.

The data for the 200 students of this case study are included as a data file on the diskette provided with this text. The data are also listed in Table I of Appendix B. Hopefully you have access to statistical (such as SPSS) or spreadsheet (such as EXCEL) software, and can use them to serve your computational needs.

We believe that using the case study method provides an ideal practicum for learning statistics since it allows you to "role-play" the activities and procedures that researchers follow in seeking to understand and interpret their data. You will be guided through the same decision-making and interpretation activities that behavioral researchers go through, and hopefully will emerge with a more comprehensive overview of the role of various statistical processes in research investigations than would otherwise be the case. This approach is designed to enable you to experience how various statistical procedures facilitate a proper understanding of what the data do, and do not, say.

❖ 1.8 SECRETS OF SUCCESS

Based on our many years of experience from having taught this course, the authors would like to suggest that you consider the following learning strategies for mastering statistics—to minimize needless confusion and frustration.

1. Try to set aside a block of time for study each day at a time when you are alert and rested. The superiority of "spaced versus massed" practice is especially true in statistics.
2. Do not allow yourself to fall behind since future topics build on the past (see Figure A in the Preface). The study of statistics is like building a skyscraper, where each chapter is a floor—one weak floor and subsequent floors will have a shaky foundation.
3. "Be ye doers of the word, and not hearers only, deceiving your own selves" (James 1:22). Do yourselves a favor—carefully work out some simple problems and test items using only paper, pencil, and hand calculator before using the computer. If you rely solely on the computer for all computational tasks, your understanding of the process will be impoverished. (In addition, your appreciation of your predecessors, who persevered through statistics using only pencils, tablets, and lots of erasers, will be deficient!) On the other hand, once your confidence has been gained through brute mental force, let the

computer handle the computational details while you concentrate on more important aspects of research, such as comprehension and interpretation.

4. Periodically review and reinforce important concepts. Appendixes C, D, and E have been assembled to assist you in this effort. Appendix C lists the statistical symbols, ordered as encountered in the text, along with their definitions and some descriptive information. Appendix D lists the statistical formulas also ordered as encountered in this text. Appendix E is a rather comprehensive glossary of important statistical terms and their definitions as used in this text. We think you will find these glossaries helpful in your goal of statistical mastery.

The Mastery Tests and Problems and Exercises that follow the subsequent chapters can be a valuable learning aid. These items have been designed to assess a basic mastery of all fundamental concepts introduced in the chapter and will enhance your understanding and retention of important concepts and techniques. Resist the temptation to skip the Mastery Tests and Problems and Exercises; they will help you diagnose areas in need of further review.

5. Discipline yourself to read each chapter at least once before and after the related lecture. A single reading is not sufficient for most students.

❖ 1.9 THE REWARDS OF YOUR LABOR

No doubt you will want to make a vigorous effort to master the content of this course in order to gain the following salubrious fruits from your labors:

1. a better understanding of information expressed quantitatively,
2. a considerable knowledge of statistical terms, concepts, and rationale—as a consequence, you should be able to better evaluate research with respect to implications for practice and theory,
3. a foundational knowledge of statistical terms, concepts, analyses, and methods,
4. increased confidence in your ability to achieve worthwhile goals (and more fun than you ever expected).

❖ 2

Frequency Distributions: Statistical Tables and Graphs

❖ 2.1 VARIABLES

Personal characteristics such as height, age, gender, IQ, GPA, self-concept, reading ability, and class size are known as *variables,* or more explicitly, *personological* variables—variables on persons. These characteristics are called variables because, when observed, the observations differ among persons. Birth weight is a variable because weights vary among newborns. Attitude toward statistics among college students is a variable also and probably runs the gamut from strongly negative (not you, of course) to strongly positive. In contrast, the number of nickels equivalent to a quarter is not a variable since the answer is always five—the number of nickels in a quarter is therefore not a variable, but a *constant*.

One class of variables, such as height, intelligence, or grade level, is characterized by an underlying continuum, and the variables are termed *quantitative* or *continuous* variables. Another class of variables, known as *qualitative* or *categorical* variables, represents difference, not in degree but in kind—variables like gender, college major, or occupation.

❖ 2.2 MEASUREMENT OF VARIABLES

Before a variable can be treated statistically, it must be observed/measured for a set of observational units. *Observational units* are those entities that are observed. In this book, most of our examples are drawn from the fields of education and the behavioral and social sciences—hence, the most common observational unit will be persons; schools, zip codes, and states, among others, are also common observational units. When observations are quantified (expressed numerically), the numbers are said to be measurements—a *measurement* is an *observation* that is *expressed numerically*. In this book, observation, measurement, and score have essentially the same meaning.

Variables can be measured in several different ways. For example, teaching effectiveness could be assessed by student performance, student course evaluation questionnaires, teacher self-evaluations, supervisor ratings, or peer evaluations. Some of these methods of assessment could yield quantitative data (e.g., scores or ratings) while others could be expressed in words. It does not necessarily follow that just because some approaches are quantifiable and amenable to statistical analysis that they are necessarily superior to approaches that are not. The credibility of the research findings and generalizations are no better than the accuracy, appropriateness and meaningfulness of the measures from which the conclusions were derived. Statistical analyses, however, are only applicable when information is expressed numerically—numbers are the only language that statistics understands.

❖ 2.3 USE OF SYMBOLS

To expedite communication, variables are represented by italicized uppercase letters (e.g., X, Y, Z). When only one variable is under consideration, the italicized upper case symbol X is used to denote that variable. When two variables are being studied (such as the relationship between IQ and spelling ability), X represents one of the variables and Y the other. If three variables are under consideration, they will be labeled as X, Y, and Z, and so on.

To specify a particular observation in a given set (list or array) of observations, subscripts are used. Subscripts are "name tags." The first observation listed for variable X is denoted as X_1, the third observation in the list of X-observations is represented by X_3, and so on. If for variable X, the set of observations is listed as: 96, 102, 111, 79, 90, . . . ; it follows that $X_1 = 96$, $X_2 = 102$, $X_3 = 111$, et cetera.

Immediate clarification and reinforcement of new information is a helpful step in the process of learning new material. To this end, we have often interspersed quiz questions in this text so that you can readily assure yourself that the current content has been mastered. Suggestion: For maximum benefit, respond to these quiz items without first peeking at the appended answers.

> **Quiz:** Refer to the above list of X-observations: (a) What is the symbol for 79? (b) What observation corresponds to X_5? (c) $X_2 + X_3 =$ _____ (d) Does X_1 imply the highest score?
>
> **Answers:** (a) X_4, (b) 90, (c) $102 + 111 = 213$, (d) No, it specifies the first score listed in the array of scores.

❖ 2.4 FREQUENCY DISTRIBUTIONS

The use of visual representations for communicating quantitative information has been a neglected facet of statistics. Fortunately, the widespread availability of microcomputers and graphic software is helping to correct this situation. In this text, we will often include printouts of graphs, tables, and statistical results from some of the most widely used computer software packages to illustrate their suitability for statistical and communication purposes.

Statistical information can be more easily communicated if it is organized into tables and displayed in graphs. In this chapter, we will use several techniques and approaches to illustrate how to arrange and portray a set of data so that important characteristics of the data set are readily apparent.

❖ 2.5 ORGANIZING DATA FOR MEANING

Unless a large set of data is systematically organized, it is difficult to assimilate and interpret. Procedures for organizing, summarizing, and simplifying data are fundamental to statistical methods. The burgeoning use of quantification and statistical analyses in the social and behavioral sciences has dramatically underscored the need for organizing data to communicate meaning. If a huge set of numbers is not summarized and simplified, we can quickly become overwhelmed by the plethora of numerical data. On the other hand, when data are organized and presented graphically, communication, comprehension, and interpretation are facilitated.

❖ 2.6 AN EXAMPLE

For instructional purposes, examples using smaller sets of data have certain advantages over larger sets of data. They allow most of your attention to be focused on the procedures involved and their meanings, with a minimum of repetitious mechanical/computational details. On the other hand, larger sets of data give more realistic and trustworthy information about interesting characteristics of the population from which the data are drawn. Throughout this text, we will use, as a case study, a sample of data from the monumental High School and Beyond (HSB) study to illustrate most of the statistical procedures. Our case study consists of data on a representative national sample of 200 high school senior students who were measured on five achievemental variables (reading, writing, math, science, and civics) and who were classified by sex, race (Hispanic, Asian, Black, White), socioeconomic (SES) level (low, middle, high), type of school (public or private), and choice of high school program (general, academic, vocational).[1]

To make the illustrations of the statistical processes less cumbersome, Table 2.1 displays only a small sample ($n = 40$) of math scores—scores that were randomly selected[2] from the larger HSB data set of 200. Suppose you are in this group and your score was 56. How do you go about evaluating your performance relative to the other examinees?

As you scan the array of math scores in Table 2.1, you unconsciously try to see whether your score is high or low—you try to get a sense of what is a typical score, and discover a pattern to the distribution of scores. As you peruse the data in Table 2.1, notice that the highest score (X_{max}) is 71 and the lowest score (X_{min}) is 38. This information helps to interpret your score of 56, that is, your score is about midway between X_{max} and X_{min}. However, this visual scanning process is not very precise and can easily result in errors, especially as

❖ **TABLE 2.1** An unordered sample of 40 math scores randomly selected from the HSB data set.

61	67	56	64	71	38	61	63
43	58	46	49	50	50	55	47
50	52	51	56	53	54	51	51
39	50	40	41	58	42	40	41
55	42	61	52	42	59	45	56

---

[1]The data for the 200 students of this case study are listed in Table I of Appendix B. When the purpose is to focus attention on techniques, we often use only a small sample of data. To further illustrate statistical procedures, computer output, and discuss statistical findings and interpretations, we often use larger samples such as the HSB data set.

[2]Random sampling occurs when each of the students has the same independent probability of being selected as a sample participant—sampling methods are discussed in Chapter 9.

the number of scores (n) increases. Statistics gives us systematic ways to organize otherwise unwieldy quantities of data that will facilitate our efforts to understand and interpret the data. In Table 2.1, there are only 40 observations—imagine the difficulty in trying to grasp a distribution in which that are hundreds of unordered scores! The good news is that the interpretation of even massive amounts of data is greatly facilitated by well designed tables and graphs.

❖ 2.7 UNGROUPED FREQUENCY DISTRIBUTIONS

Certain important features of a set of scores are illuminated if the scores are merely organized into an ungrouped frequency distribution. An ungrouped frequency distribution is comprised of two columns: (1) a listing of every possible score arranged in reverse rank-order from high to low, and (2) a frequency (f) column listing the number of times each score was obtained.

> **Quiz:** With reference to Table 2.1, would the score of 75 appear in the ungrouped frequency distribution?
>
> **Answer:** No, because 75 is greater than X_{max} (71).

In Table 2.2, the leftmost two columns (panel A) illustrate an ungrouped frequency distribution of the sample of math data found in Table 2.1. The number of times a score is obtained is the frequency (f) of that score and is shown just to the right of the score tabular entry. The sum of the frequencies is the total number of observations (n). Notice that you can now observe your score of 56 relative to the other 39 scores and more accurately interpret your performance on the math test.

❖ 2.8 GROUPED FREQUENCY DISTRIBUTIONS

Unless the range of scores (i.e., $X_{max} - X_{min}$) is small, the ungrouped frequency distribution spreads out the scores so much that the shape of the distribution is not readily apparent. If similar scores are grouped together into an interval, the pattern of the distribution of scores will become more evident. This loss of information pertaining to individual scores is sacrificed in order to gain information about the entire distribution of scores. The span (width) of the class intervals and, consequently, the number of intervals are somewhat arbitrary, but the decision should be influenced by the number of observations in the sample. With larger samples of $n = 200$ or more, 20 or more intervals may be suitable; whereas with a smaller sample of 50 or so, perhaps 10 intervals would be appropriate.

Figure 2.1 gives a procedural flowchart outlining the procedures for constructing a grouped frequency distribution. Although, in practice, computers do most of the work for us, an understanding of the process is needed to make good choices in depicting data graphically. To organize data into a grouped frequency distribution: (1) Compute the range. (2) Determine the interval width. (3) Specify the interval limits. (4) Tally the scores to find the frequency for each interval. These four steps are visually represented in Figure 2.1.

The data of Table 2.1 will be used to illustrate this four step procedure to construct a grouped frequency distribution.

1. *Compute the range.* The *range* is the difference between the largest score, X_{max}, and the smallest score, X_{min} (see Panel B of Table 2.2):

$$\text{range} = X_{\max} - X_{\min} \qquad\qquad \textbf{(2.1)}$$

In Table 2.2, $X_{\max} = 71$, $X_{\min} = 38$, and range $= 71 - 38 = 33$.

2. *Determine the interval width.* The interval width (w) is computed by dividing the range by the desired number of intervals. In this case (since n is rather small), we will use 10 as the desired number of intervals:

$$w = \text{range}/10$$

❖ **TABLE 2.2** Ungrouped frequency (Panel A) and grouped frequency and percentage (Panel B) distributions.

Panel A		Panel B

X	f
71	1
70	0
69	0
68	0
67	1
66	0
65	0
64	1
63	1
62	0
61	3
60	0
59	1
58	2
57	0
56	3
55	2
54	1
53	1
52	2
51	3
50	4
49	1
48	0
47	1
46	1
45	1
44	0
43	1
42	3
41	2
40	2
39	1
38	1
$n = 40$	

To make a grouped frequency distribution:

Step 1. *Compute the range.*
   range $= X_{\max} - X_{\min}$
   range $= 71 - 38 = 33$

Step 2. *Determine the interval width, w.*
   $w = \text{range}/10$
   $w = 33/10 = 3.3$, rounded to 3

Step 3. *Specify the interval limits.*
   Lower limits are multiples of w
   that is, 36, 39, 42, 45, 48, …
   Upper limits = lower limits + 2,
   that is, 38, 41, 44, 47, 50, …

Step 4. *Tally the data.*

Interval	Tally	f	%
69–71	I	1	2.5
66–68	I	1	2.5
63–65	I I	2	5.0
60–62	I I I	3	7.5
57–59	I I I	3	7.5
54–56	┼┼┼ I	6	15.0
51–53	┼┼┼ I	6	15.0
48–50	┼┼┼	5	12.5
45–47	I I I	3	7.5
42–44	I I I I	4	10.0
39–41	┼┼┼	5	12.5
36–38	I	1	2.5
		$n = 40$	100.0

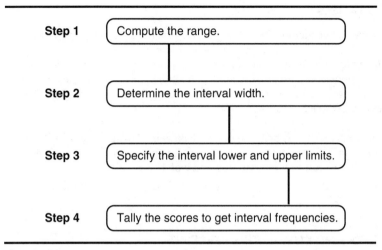

Step 1 — Compute the range.

Step 2 — Determine the interval width.

Step 3 — Specify the interval lower and upper limits.

Step 4 — Tally the scores to get interval frequencies.

❖ **FIGURE 2.1** Flowchart to construct grouped frequency distributions.

In Table 2.2, $w = 33/10 = 3.3$ rounded to 3. When w is not a whole number, it should be rounded to arrive at a whole number. (Odd numbers have certain advantages when the data are graphed, as you will see later in the chapter.)

3. *Specify the interval limits.* To avert the probability of grouping the data in a way most favorable to the researcher's personal biases, the procedure for assigning the interval limits should be standardized. Each interval should begin with a multiple[3] of w (i.e., $1w = 3$, $2w = 6$, $3w = 9$, $4w = 12$, etc.). The first interval begins with (i.e., has a lower limit of) the greatest multiple of w that is less than or equal to X_{min}; thus, for the data of Table 2.1, the first interval begins with $(12)(3)$ or 36—36 is the largest multiple of 3 that is less than X_{min} (38). The first interval will contain three score values: 36, 37, and 38; thus the interval is 36–38. The next interval begins with $36 + 3$ or 39; each interval's lower limit is w greater than the lower limit of the preceding interval. Likewise, the upper limit of each interval is found by adding w to the upper limit of the preceding interval. Intervals are defined sequentially until the interval is reached that contains the highest score, X_{max} (71 in Table 2.2). In Table 2.2, the first (or lowest) interval is 36–38, then 39–41, 42–44, et cetera.

4. *Tally the scores.* For each score place a tally mark by the interval containing that score. For the fifth tally for an interval, a line through the first four tallies organizes the tallies into convenient counting groups of five. A grouped frequency distribution of the math scores listed in Table 2.1 is given in panel B of Table 2.2 using the common picket-fence method of tallying described above.

The specified interval limits that appear in Table 2.2 are referred to as *apparent* interval limits. The *exact* interval limits, however, extend .5 units to either side of the apparent interval limits, that is, the exact lower limit is .5 units less than the apparent lower limit, and the exact upper limit is .5 units greater than the apparent upper limit. For the first interval in Table 2.2, the apparent limits are 36–38, but the exact limits are 35.5–38.5—a span or width of 3 units.

---

[3]See Math Note 1 in Appendix A for a review of multiples.

❖ 2.9 TUKEY'S TALLIES

When *n* is large, an alternative method for tallying the observations was suggested by Tukey (1977). Tukey's method tallies the scores into convenient counting groups of ten: The first four tallies are denoted by dots forming the corners of a square; the next four tallies are line segments forming the sides of the square; the ninth and tenth tallies are indicated by diagonal lines inside the square. The Tukey method of tallying data is illustrated in Table 2.3 for the 200 math scores from the HSB data set.

> **Quiz:** (1) Which tally method, picket-fence or Tukey, is your favorite? (2) What are the exact interval limits for the interval whose apparent limits are 60–62 in Table 2.3? (3) The Tukey tally result for an interval frequency of 17 would be ____.
>
> **Answers:** (1) Preferred answer is "I like them both." (2) The exact limits are 59.5–62.5. (3) ⊠ ⊔

❖ 2.10 PERCENTS AND CUMULATIVE PERCENTS

Table 2.3 displays not only the intervals with their associated frequencies, but it also lists the "%" and "Cumulative %" (cumulative percent) columns, which are used later in this

❖ **TABLE 2.3** A grouped frequency distribution of the 200 math scores of the High School and Beyond Case Study (HSB) data set illustrating the Tukey tally method.

Interval	Tukey Tally	f	%	Cumulative %
75-77		2	1.0	100.0
72-74		4	2.0	99.0
69-71	⊔	7	3.5	97.0
66-68	⊔	7	3.5	93.5
63-65	⊠	13	6.5	90.0
60-62	⊠ ∟	16	8.0	83.5
57-59	⊠ ⊠	21	10.5	75.5
54-56	⊠ ⊠	22	11.0	65.0
51-53	⊠ ⊠	21	10.5	54.0
48-50	⊠ ⊠	22	11.0	43.5
45-47	⊠ ⊿	19	9.5	32.5
42-44	⊠ ☐	18	9.0	23.0
39-41	⊠ ⊠	23	11.5	14.0
36-38		3	1.5	2.5
33-35		2	1.0	1.0
		$n = 200$	100.0	

chapter. These columns can be constructed rather simply: to *obtain the % and Cumulative % columns* of a frequency distribution:

Step 1:	To find the "%" column, convert the frequencies into percents—divide the frequency in the interval by n to get the proportion of scores in the interval, then convert to percent by multiplying by 100:[4] % = $100 \times (f/n)$ or % = $100f/n$.
Step 2:	To find the "Cumulative%" for an interval, add the percent for the interval to the cumulative percent entry of the preceding interval. (For the first interval, the "%" column entry is also the "Cumulative %" column entry.)

For example, the 42–44 interval of Table 2.2 shows $f = 4$. For step 1, since $n = 40, f/n = 4/40 = .10$, and .10 multiplied by 100 = 100(.10) = 10.0%. For step 2, to find the cumulative percent for this interval, add its interval percent (10.0%) to the cumulative percent of the preceding interval (2.5% + 12.5% = 15.0%) to get 25.0%.

Quiz: Suppose you have a grouped frequency distribution of $n = 50$ scores and the beginning (i.e., lowest scores) four interval frequencies are 2, 5, 6, and 11. (1) Convert these frequencies to percents for the first four intervals. (2) Use these percents to compute the cumulative percents for the first four intervals.

Answers: (1) Interval percents: 4%, 10%, 12%, and 22%. (2) Cumulative percents: 4%, 14%, 26%, and 48%.

❖ 2.11 GRAPHS OF FREQUENCY DISTRIBUTIONS

A distribution of observations can more easily be conceptualized if it is depicted graphically. We can gain important information concerning a set of scores merely by glancing at a visual display of the data. Three common types of graphs are histograms (bar graphs), frequency polygons (line graphs), and ogive (cumulative percentage) curves. Also, pie charts, box-and-whisker plots, and time-series graphs can often be used advantageously.

❖ 2.12 THE HISTOGRAM OR BAR GRAPH

A histogram is a graph of a frequency (or percentage) distribution using bars whose lengths correspond to the frequency (or percentage) of observations for each interval. This type of graph can be used for both quantitative and categorical data. Unlike the frequency polygon (Section 2.13), it can be used to display categorical data such as occupation, religious affiliation, race, et cetera—variables whose observations cannot be meaningfully ranked from less to more. The vertical axis (the ordinate or Y-axis of your high school algebra course) of the histogram is labeled "Frequency" so that the heights of the rectangular bars indicate the interval frequencies.

A *frequency* histogram of the 200 math scores in Table 2.3 is displayed as the middle figure in Figure 2.2. Two other frequency histograms of these same data using interval widths of 2 and 5 are also included in Figure 2.2 for comparative purposes. Notice that as

---

[4]See Math Note 2 in Appendix A for a review of percentage.

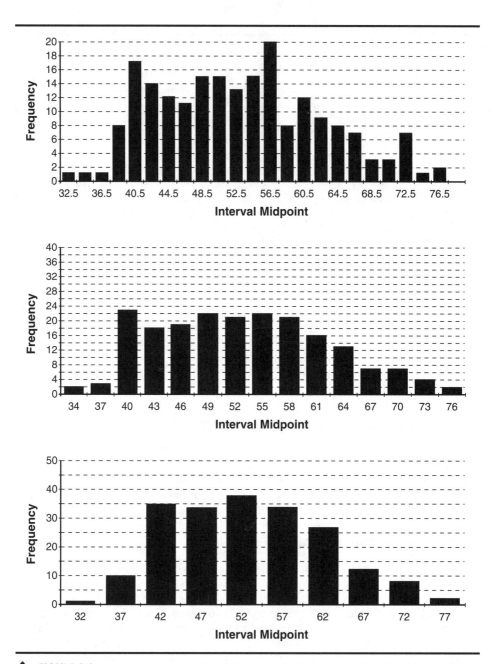

❖ **FIGURE 2.2** Frequency histograms of the 200 math scores with interval widths of 2 (top), 3 (middle), and 5 (bottom) using the EXCEL spreadsheet.

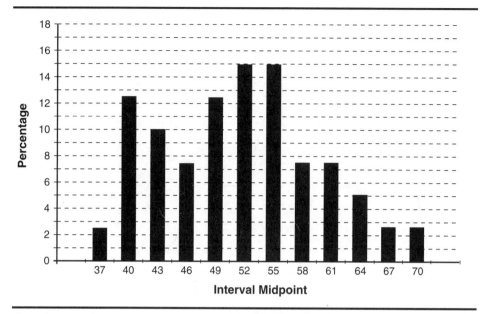

❖ **FIGURE 2.3** Percentage histogram of the sample of 40 HSB math scores using the EXCEL spreadsheet.

the number of intervals is decreased, by increasing the interval width from $w = 2$ to $w = 5$, the jaggedness and irregularities of the distributions decrease and the overall pattern of the scores becomes more evident. Of course, it would be possible to increase the interval width to the extent that the shape of the distribution would be obscured. The researcher hopes to find the middle ground between an interval width either too large or too small so that the overall pattern of the data is most apparent.

Observe that in Figure 2.2, the midpoint of each interval is given along the horizontal baseline (the X-axis or abscissa). For example, the 36–38 interval in the middle chart in Figure 2.2, has a midpoint of 37. For simplicity, only the interval midpoints are displayed along the abscissa to avoid a more crowded and cumbersome appearance. Note the advantage of interval widths that are odd numbers—the midpoints when $w = 2$ are not whole numbers. Your score of 56, when viewed with Figure 2.2 as a backdrop, takes on greater meaning, that is, your score is in the upper half, but not far from the center of the distribution.

The rectangular bars comprising histograms may depict (1) frequencies, (2) percentages, or (3) both frequencies and percentages simultaneously. It is usually easier to understand and to communicate information using percentages rather than using only frequencies. Figure 2.3 portrays a *percentage* histogram of the 40 math scores of Table 2.1; the height of a bar reflects the percentage of the sample falling within that interval—the "%" column in Table 2.2. Of course, the shape of the distribution is portrayed equally as well via percentage histograms as with frequency histograms.

❖ 2.13 FREQUENCY POLYGONS

A second widely used method to depict numerical information graphically is the line graph or frequency polygon. The process of constructing a frequency polygon is similar to that of

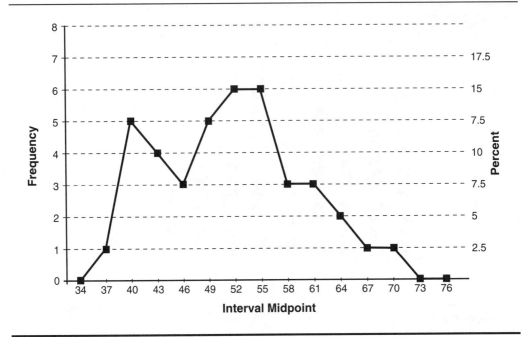

❖ **FIGURE 2.4** Sample of 40 HSB math scores frequency and percentage polygon.

the histogram except that only a point above the midpoint of each interval is used to indicate frequency. For a given histogram, if a point is placed at the midpoint of the top of each rectangular bar, and adjacent points are connected by line segments, the resulting figure is a frequency polygon. If frequencies are transformed to percents, the figure is described as a percentage polygon. Frequency/percentage polygons are particularly appropriate for quantitative variables such as age, test scores, income, et cetera.

The polygon of Figure 2.4 and the histogram of Figure 2.3 graphically display the same data—the sample of 40 math scores listed in Table 2.1. It is interesting to compare the two figures and to note their similarity. Note that Figure 2.4 is both a percentage (right-hand axis) and a frequency (left-hand axis) polygon.

❖ 2.14 POLYGONS VERSUS HISTOGRAMS

Of course, it would be misleading to construct a frequency polygon for categorical variables such as college major or ethnic group. Frequency/percentage polygons are appropriate only for quantitative variables like test scores, income, et cetera—variables that have an underlying continuum (i.e., can be arranged in order from high to low). Histograms, on the other hand, are appropriate for both quantitative and categorical variables.

For categorical data, it is best to leave larger gaps between the bars of a histogram to illustrate the absence of an underlying continuum. For continuous data, it seems best to minimize the intervening gaps between the bars to reflect the continuous nature of the data.

Frequently, it is informative to display two or more distributions in the same figure to

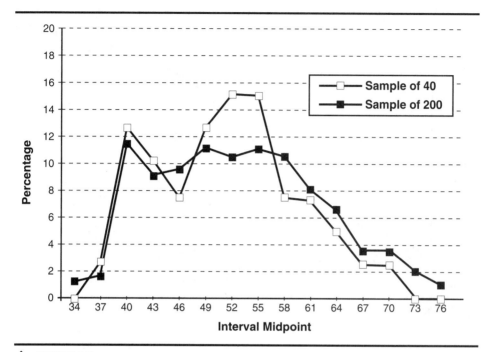

❖ **FIGURE 2.5** Percentage polygons of the 40 math scores of Table 2.2 and the 200 math scores of Table 2.3 using Quattro Pro computer software.

allow visual comparability and differentiation. When presenting two or more distributions of scores on the same graph, percentage polygons are usually preferable to histograms. By using color or other graphic distinctions (dashed lines, solid lines, dotted lines, etc.), you can display two or more distributions simultaneously in the same figure. In Figure 2.5, a percentage polygon for the random sample of the 40 math scores of Table 2.2 and a percentage polygon for the 200 math scores of Table 2.3 are simultaneously displayed. It is interesting to peruse Figure 2.5 to note the similarities and dissimilarities of the two polygons and to ponder how, and to what extent, a small sample ($n = 40$) may be expected to differ from a larger sample ($n = 200$) due to chance alone. Questions of this sort are the essence of inferential statistics—a foretaste of delicacies to come (Chapters 9–16).

> **Quiz:** A percentage polygon would be an appropriate way to display which of the following variables? gender, race, annual salary, IQ
>
> **Answers:** annual salary and IQ

❖ 2.15 THE OGIVE CURVE

A line graph using the cumulative percent table entries is called an *ogive* or a *cumulative percentage curve*. Figure 2.6 is an ogive curve based on the 200 math scores in Table 2.3. Note that the vertical axis represents cumulative percentage—the percent of scores falling at or below each interval (see Table 2.3). The upper value of each interval (not the midpoint)

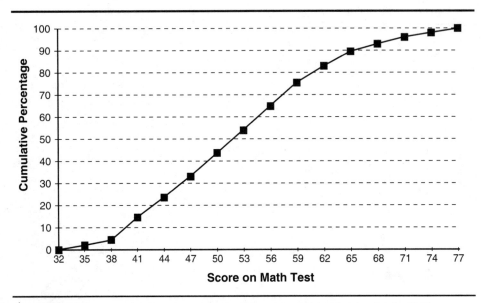

❖ **FIGURE 2.6** Ogive curve of the sample of 200 HSB math scores of Table 2.3 (using the EXCEL spreadsheet).

is ordered along the baseline. To construct an ogive, place a point above the apparent upper limit of each interval to indicate the cumulative percentage of that interval, and connect the points with line segments.

❖ 2.16 MEDIAN, QUARTILES, AND PERCENTILES

Ogive curves are particularly useful for finding specific points in the distribution of scores. One of the most interesting points is the *median*, which is the 50th percentile—the point below which 50% of the scores fall. The median is easy to estimate from an ogive: (1) Locate "50" on the vertical axis; (2) from "50", move horizontally to intersect the ogive curve; (3) then move vertically down to intersect the baseline and read the median of the distribution.

Quiz: Using Figure 2.6, estimate the median of the HSB data set.

Answer: The median is about 52.

Three additional important points in a distribution are the *quartiles*—the points that partition the distribution into fourths or quarters. These quartiles (Q_1, Q_2, and Q_3) can be estimated from the ogive curve by finding the scores that correspond to the cumulative percentage values of 25, 50, and 75. The point that divides the bottom quarter (25%) from the upper three-quarters of the distribution is the *first quartile* (Q_1); the *second quartile* (Q_2) is identical with the median and is the 50th percentile; the *third quartile* (Q_3) divides the upper quarter from the lower three-quarters of the distribution.

Quiz: Using Figure 2.6: (1) Estimate Q_1; (2) estimate Q_3.
Answers: (1) 45, (2) 59

Percentiles partition a distribution into hundredths. The 70th percentile (P_{70}) exceeds 70 percent of the scores in the distribution; P_{30} exceeds 30 percent; et cetera. Percentiles are points in a distribution below which a given percent, P, of the cases lie. We have noted that P_{50} is equivalent to both the median and Q_2. P_{25} and P_{75} are aliases for Q_1 and Q_3, respectively. Percentiles easily convert into percentile rank, which is a very popular and useful way to communicate a score's relative standing within a given distribution. The *percentile rank* of a point is the percent of cases falling below that point. If your score corresponds to P_{90}, your percentile rank is 90 and your score is exceeded by only 10 (i.e., $100 - 90 = 10$) percent of the cases. This would place you near the top of the distribution, which is quite good if the variable under consideration is a desirable outcome, for example, statistical achievement, skill, chronological age, et cetera. A percentile rank of 48 would place one near the center of the distribution, and a percentile rank of 8 would place one near the bottom.

Let us use the ogive in Figure 2.6 to estimate the percentile rank of your score of 56. This procedure is the reverse of the procedure followed for estimating the median of a distribution. First, locate your score of 56 along the baseline; then move vertically up until you intersect the ogive curve; then turn left and move horizontally to the left margin and read the cumulative percent (percentile rank) of your score (about 65).

Quiz: Using Figure 2.6, estimate the percentile rank of the following math scores: (1) 40, (2) 56, (3) 64
Answers: (1) 10, (2) 65, (3) 88

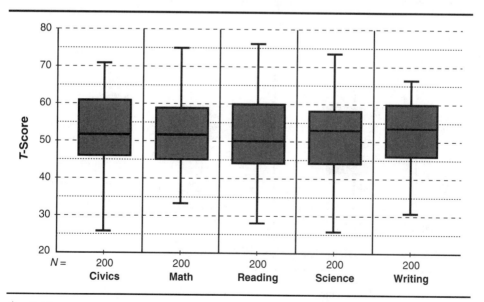

❖ **FIGURE 2.7** Box plots of 200 HSB students in five achievement areas. (These box plots were produced using SPSS Windows software.)

❖ 2.17 BOX-AND-WHISKER PLOTS

The box-and-whisker plot (or box plot for short) is a simple and useful graph for displaying a distribution. In recent years, it has become widely used, largely as a result of the influence of Tukey (1977). Vertical box plots of the HSB distributions of five subject areas for the sample of 200 students are given in Figure 2.7 using SPSS software (Box plots can also be oriented in a horizontal format). The box extends from Q_1 to Q_3 (termed "hinges" by Tukey) and defines the middle 50% of the distribution. The lower whisker ordinarily extends from Q_1 down to X_{min}, and the upper whisker ordinarily extends from Q_3 up to X_{max}. If, however, X_{min} or X_{max} had deviated too markedly from the rest of the scores, the whiskers would have stopped at the smallest and largest scores that seemed to belong with the data set. Very extreme scores are described as *outliers* and should always be double-checked for accuracy; often outliers merely represent measurement or data entry errors. Statistical criteria (Glass & Hopkins, 1996, Section 3.9) for designating observations as outliers are built into computer software that produces box plots.

From the ogive of Figure 2.6, Q_1 is estimated to be 45, and Q_3 is estimated to be about 59. Therefore, the bottom side of the math box coincides with $X = 45$, and the top side of the box coincides with $X = 59$. The vertical line crossing the box at 52 defines the median (Md). For precisely symmetrical distributions, the median falls midway between Q_1 and Q_3, and the whiskers are equal in length. It is immaterial as to whether the box plots are displayed vertically or horizontally.

> **Quiz:** Based on the information presented in Figure 2.7, how would you answer the following questions? Which subject area: (1) had the highest median, (2) had the least median, (3) had the smallest range, (4) contained the highest score?
>
> **Answers:** (1) writing, (2) reading, (3) writing, (4) reading

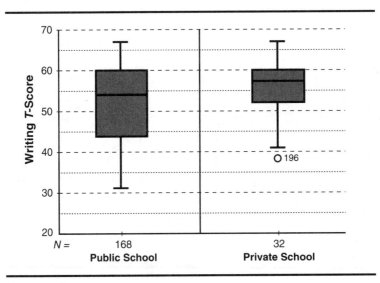

❖ **FIGURE 2.8** Box plots of Writing by School type for 200 HSB students. (These box plots were produced by SPSS Windows software)

Box plots are also especially useful for comparing the distributions of two or more groups on some variable of interest. Figure 2.8 gives box plots depicting the distributions of the HSB data set achievement scores in writing for students from public schools versus students from private schools. Peruse the box plots of Figure 2.8 to observe in what ways the plots differ. Would you like a little more practice in analyzing comparative box plots?

Quiz: (1) As a group, which tends to have the higher scores? (2) The range of scores is greater in which group? (3) The interquartile range (i.e., from Q_1 to Q_3) is greatest in which group? (4) Which group has the greater proportion of low scoring students? (5) How does the top 25 percent (upper whisker) for public schools compare to that for private schools?

Answers: (1) private schools, (2) public schools, (3) public schools, (4) public schools, (5) apparently the same

❖ 2.18 TIME-SERIES GRAPHS

A time-series graph is a line graph in which the baseline represents time. It can be very informative about trends in ways that no static representation of data can be. Familiar examples of time-series graphs include the Dow-Jones stock prices, the Consumer Price Index, new claims for unemployment insurance, et cetera. Figure 2.9 is illustrative of time-series graphs depicting the patterns of changes in food stamp participation in relation to poverty rates (top) and high school GPA and ACT college admission test scores (bottom) over the last two to three decades.

Time-series data are interesting, and provide information pertaining to changes that have been reported over a period of time. The infinitely more difficult challenge of attempting to explain how and why such changes occur is the source of numerous heated debates in the political, social, educational, and religious communities.

❖ 2.19 PIE CHARTS

You are no doubt familiar with pie charts; a pie chart is a circle graph with sectors drawn proportional to the frequencies making up the categories comprised by the variable being graphed. It is particularly suited to display the categorical frequencies in relation to each other and in relation to the whole, especially when the number of categories is not large.

Figure 2.10 presents pie charts depicting the racial and socio-economic level composition of the HSB data set. Although unnecessary, the 3-dimensional aspect adds spice to the pie.

The race pie (top figure) is partitioned into four slices, each of which is given a unique pattern to identify the segment.[5] Note how small the non-White group slices are (12%, 5.5%, 10%) in comparison to the White segment (72.5%); whereas, the sizes of the slices comprising the SES pie do not differ as much.

❖ 2.20 DESCRIBING DISTRIBUTIONS

A specific statistical vocabulary is used for describing various types of distributions such as those depicted in Figure 2.11. The bell-shaped distribution in panel A of Figure 2.11 illus-

---

[5]If you have access to a color printer, you can create even more attractive and illuminating figures through the use of both color and geometric patterns to differentiate various facets of a graph.

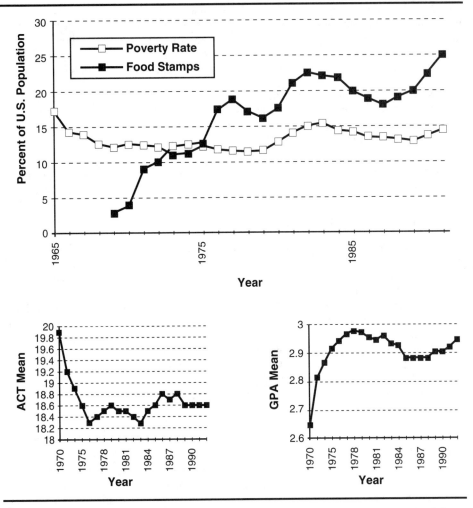

❖ **FIGURE 2.9** Time-series graphs portraying patterns of changes in food stamp participation in relation to poverty rates (top) and high school GPA and ACT college admission test scores (bottom) over the last two to three decades.

trates a *normal* curve (also referred to as a normal distribution). The normal curve is symmetrical about a vertical line at the median, that is, each half of the curve is the mirror image of the other. In a normal distribution, the median is also the mode—the most frequent score. The normal distribution is the most important distribution in statistics, and one that you will encounter throughout your study of statistics.

The curve in panel B of Figure 2.11 has two distinctly different points about which the scores tend to cluster. It is termed a *bimodal* distribution (i.e., a distribution with two modes). If the heights of all U.S. adults were plotted, a bimodal distribution would result. The heights of females would cluster around their mode of approximately sixty-four inches, and the male heights would cluster around their mode of about sixty-nine inches. When the

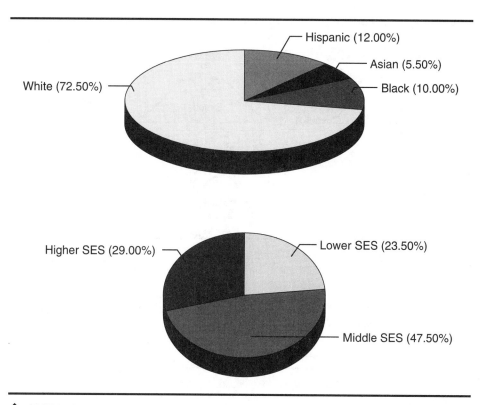

❖ **FIGURE 2.10** Pie charts of the race (top) and socio-economic level (bottom) of the 200 students of the HSB case study data set (using the Quattro Pro spreadsheet).

frequencies clustering around the two modes differ substantially, the more popular value is said to be the major mode, and the smaller hump represents the minor mode. The bimodal type of distribution might also occur when the population is polarized into two opposing camps with little agreement between them, for example, attitude toward abortion.

Panel C in Figure 2.11 illustrates a *rectangular* distribution—a symmetrical distribution with a constant frequency for all values of *X*. Perhaps the variable "weekday of birth" (M, T, W, Th, F, Sa, Su) would have a distribution that is approximately rectangular, since the number of births is approximately the same for each day of the week.

Panels D and E of Figure 2.11 represent *skewed* distributions, that is, curves that are not symmetrical. Skewness can be of any degree, from very slight to very extreme. The direction of skewness is labeled as *positive* when the distribution "tails off" toward the right or high scores in the distribution, and is labeled as *negative* when the distribution elongates toward the left or low-scoring end of the range. Do not be confused by the terms negative or positive in reference to skewness; the terms positive and negative have nothing to do with desirable or undesirable performance; they refer instead to the algebraic sign (+ or –) of the result when the degree of skewness is quantified using an index of skewness (see Glass & Hopkins, 1996, section 6.9). Negative skewness is illustrated in panel E of Figure 2.11, since most score toward the high end and the curve trails off toward the left or low end. The distribution of the number of days absent for students in a class during the school year

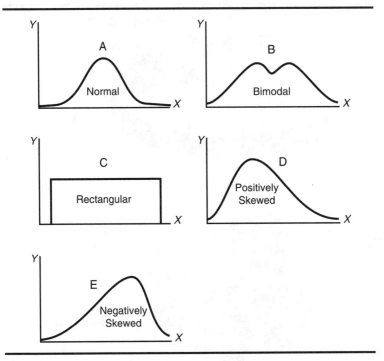

❖ **FIGURE 2.11** Common types of frequency distributions. The vertical axis (Y) represents the frequency of occurrence, and the horizontal axis (X) represents the numerical value of the observations.

would be expected to be positively skewed—most students would miss only a few days, but a few individuals would miss many days. Scores on a very easy test will tend to be negatively skewed.

Quiz: Make your best guess as to the distribution shapes of the following variables for the population of the U.S. adult female citizens: (1) height, (2) number of siblings, (3) score on a twenty-five word spelling test designed for fifth grade students.

Answers: The shapes would probably be: (1) normal, (2) positively skewed, (3) negatively skewed.

❖ 2.21 MISLEADING GRAPHS: HOW TO LIE WITH STATISTICS

The ability to interpret properly—and not be misled by—information that is presented graphically is an important type of literacy for both the layman and the professional. The popular media continually bombard the public with a plethora of data-based figures. Textbooks in all empirical disciplines are filled with numerous graphs. Standardized achievement tests and university entrance tests are heavily weighted with graphic information that must be read critically. Just as words can be misused to distort the facts (e.g., "politicalese"), so can pictures. At times, self-interest tempts one (including researchers) to use literal facts in such a way that the message received is ambiguous, that is, lying with impunity (at least in the legal sense). Graphs and charts can be organized to propagandize rather than to illuminate. Tufte (1983) gives many flagrant examples in his excellent book. Many, if not most, figures in the popular media are constructed to be as remarkable as possible; journalists often compromise accuracy to maximize the shock value of a story, irrespective of whether words or pictures are used to portray the story. It behooves us to be on our toes so that we are not numbered among the credulous victims of misinformation.

❖ 2.22 DISTORTED REPRESENTATION

A common, but not very subtle, error evident in many pictographs (histograms that use pictures to represent frequencies) found in the popular media is the linear versus area fallacy. To get "more bang for the buck," graphic artists often represent the frequency of a category by the height of the figure (linear distance), yet make only one figure per category. This lack of uniform representation of a frequency conveys a distorted picture of the data. Figure 2.12 presents two graphs of the identical data. The simple histogram at the bottom gives the appropriate representation of the comparative differences in the data pertaining to the inflation in the dollar from 1958 to 1978. Notice in Figure 2.12 how the top pictograph figure exaggerates the amount of inflation across the five presidencies. The data are scaled by the length of the dollar bill, but it is the area of the bills that carries the perceptual weight for the reader. The area of the Carter dollar is less than 20 percent that of the Eisenhower bill; whereas, the proper area is 44 percent. If the bills were of the same width as the Eisenhower dollar, but were fragments of different lengths, the representation would be fair and accurate. (Is the result not dramatic enough without fudging?)

❖ 2.23 MISLEADING SCALING AND CALIBRATION

A more common shortcoming of graphs appears in Figure 2.13—the use of an arbitrary beginning scale value on the vertical axis. Figure 2.13 (top) is a common method of a perceptual exaggeration—the change over time is made to appear much larger than it is. Notice how different the magnitude of the change appears in a proper figure like the lower graph of the figure. Many graphs (e.g., stock prices) typically ignore the zero point, and thus perceptually exaggerate the magnitude of changes. The calibration of the graph should generally include zero for quantitative variables having an absolute zero point (i.e., where zero means none) such as income, years of experience, height, et cetera. For variables in which zero is meaningless or arbitrary, such as standardized measures of achievement, aptitude, affective and psychological variables, et cetera, the graph should generally include the full range of potential scores with room to spare in either direction.

❖ 2.24 COMBINATION GRAPHS

Combination graphs can be one of the most subtle ways of giving unwarranted credibility to graphic propaganda. All three graphs in Figure 2.14 use the same identical data, but note that the top and middle graphs lead to opposite conclusions! This is possible by an inappropriate scaling of both variables. Combination graphs need to be carefully scrutinized (Wainer, 1992).

Purchasing
Power
of the
Diminishing
Dollar

Source: Labor Department

1958 – Eisenhower: $1.00

1963 – Kennedy: 94¢

1968 – Johnson: 83¢

1973 – Nixon: 64¢

1978 – Carter: 44¢
(August)

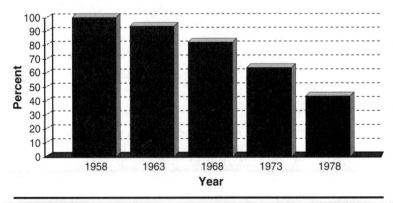

❖ **FIGURE 2.12** Two graphs of the same data. The upper pictograph uses the linear versus area fallacy to exaggerate differences in the inflation rate. A more appropriate representation of the data comparison is displayed by the lower histogram.

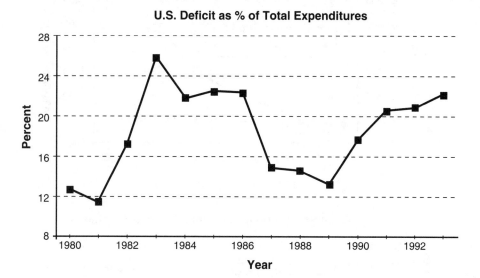

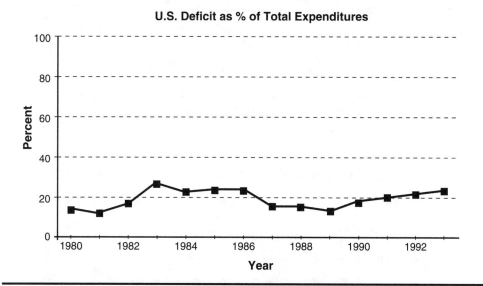

❖ **FIGURE 2.13** Two time-series graphs of the same data. The upper figure uses inadequate vertical scaling to exaggerate changes in the deficit as a percentage of the total federal expenditures. (*Source:* New York Times, March 19, 1993)

Public School Funding Soars; No Payoff in SAT Scores

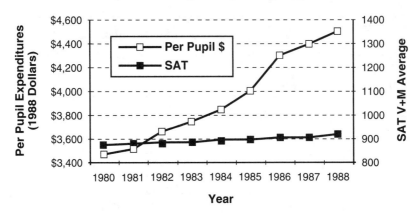

SAT Scores Soar Despite Minimal Gains in Funding

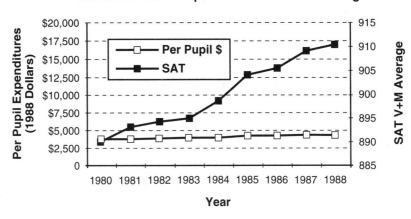

Trends in Public School Funding and SAT Scores

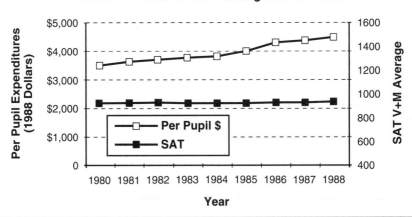

❖ **FIGURE 2.14** Three graphs using the same data. The top graph exaggerates the per pupil expenditure, whereas the middle graph exaggerates the SAT gains: these two graphs seem to warrant opposite conclusions. The lower figure is a more appropriate display of the data.

The lower graph in Figure 2.14 gives a more credible display of the same data used in the upper and middle graphs. The left margin includes zero and has a range of $5,000 which gives a reasonable ceiling for expenditures per pupil. The right margin scaling seems fair also since 400 is the lowest possible score and 1,600 the highest possible score for these instruments.

❖ CHAPTER SUMMARY

Before a variable can be studied statistically, it must be measured; measurement is a process of assigning numbers to observations of a variable. Statistical methods are tools for organizing, summarizing, and simplifying a set of data. One characteristic of interest in a set of data is the shape of its frequency distribution. Distributions can be normal, skewed (positively and negatively), rectangular, or bimodal. Tables and graphs can illuminate an otherwise unwieldy quantity of data. The form or shape of a distribution becomes evident if the observations are represented graphically by frequency/percentage histograms, and frequency/percentage polygons. Ogive (cumulative percentage) curves are especially useful for determining percentiles, such as the first quartile (Q_1 or P_{25}), the median (Q_2 or P_{50}), and the third quartile (Q_3 or P_{75}). Box-and-whisker plots are simple and effective graphs for conveying the salient features of a distribution. Time-series graphs reveal changes in a variable over a given time interval.

Graphs can be a weapon as well as a tool—they can inform, but also distort. When pictures are used to represent frequencies, all should be the same size in at least one dimension. Scales that have a true zero point should begin with zero to avoid exaggerating effects. Combination graphs can be particularly effective for propaganda, leading to false cause and effect relationships.

MASTERY TEST

1. If an IQ score of 115 is at P_{84}, what percent of scores exceed 115?

2. Which one of these types of distribution is best for conveying the shape of the frequency distribution of 600 test scores?
   (a) rank-order distribution   (b) ungrouped frequency distribution   (c) histogram

3. Consider the following set of math scores from the HSB data set:
   43 58 46 49 50 50 55 47 50 52 51 56
   53 54 51 51 39 50 40 41 58 42 40 41
   (a) Find X_{max}.   (b) Find X_{min}.   (c) Compute the range.

4. The range in a set of observations can be most accurately determined from which of the following?
   (a) ungrouped frequency distribution
   (b) grouped frequency distribution

5. Guess whether each of the following distributions is positively or negatively skewed.
   (a) family income in dollars per year
   (b) age at graduation from college
   (c) populations of cities in the United States
   (d) scores on a very easy test

6. Given: $X_{min} = 42$ and the interval size (w) is 5. What are the apparent lower and upper score limits of the lowest three intervals?

7. What do you call a score that deviates markedly from all other scores in the distribution?

8. If the baseline (X-axis or abscissa) variable represents a categorical variable (such as nationality or gender), are histograms preferred to frequency polygons?

9. Can a percentage polygon and a frequency polygon be represented in the same figure?

10. Which one of the following four terms differs most from the other three?
(a) X-axis   (b) Y-axis   (c) horizontal axis   (d) abscissa

In questions 11–16, match the verbal and graphic descriptions:

11. rectangular distribution

    (a)

12. bimodal distribution

    (b)

13. normal distribution

    (c)

14. positively skewed distribution

    (d)

15. negatively skewed distribution

    (e)

16. Which of the above curves (a–e) are approximately symmetrical?

17. For visually representing data in a grouped frequency distribution, how many classes are generally recommended for sample sizes of about
(a) 60?   (b) 1,000?

18. Which of these graphs is best for determining percentiles?

(a) histogram   (b) percentage polygon   (c) ogive curve

19. Which one of the following four terms differs most from the other three?
(a) Q_1 (b) Median   (c) P_{50} (d) Q_2

20. The number of eggs in a dozen is a
(a) variable.   (b) constant.

21. In a box-and-whisker plot, what percent of the cases fall within the box?

22. In a vertical box-and-whisker plot, if the lower whisker is longer than the upper whisker, the distribution would appear to be
(a) normal.   (b) bimodal.   (c) positively skewed.   (d) negatively skewed.

23. The HSB data set includes data on 10 different variables. For each variable listed below, decide whether the variable is (a) categorical or (b) continuous.
(a) type of school   (e) type of school program   (h) writing score
(b) gender   (f) reading score   (i) science score
(c) race   (g) math score   (j) civics score
(d) SES

24. Consider the following variables and hypothesize about the approximate shape of their distributions in the United States. Answer (N) for normal, (B) for bimodal, (R) for rectangular, (PS) for positively skewed, and (NS) for negatively skewed.
(a) weight of males at age 20   (d) month of birth
(b) weight of females at age 20   (e) days from conception to birth
(c) weight of persons at age 20   (f) age at first marriage

ANSWERS TO MASTERY TEST

1. 16%
2. (c)

3. (a) 58 (b) 39 (c) 19
4. (a)

5. (a) positively (b) positively (c) positively (d) negatively
6. 40–44, 45–49, 50–54
7. outlier
8. yes
9. yes
10. (b)
11. (e)
12. (d)
13. (b)
14. (c)
15. (a)
16. (b), (d), and (e) (Note: As drawn, the bimodal curve appears to be symmetrical. However, bimodal curves are usually *not* symmetrical since the two peaks may differ in height, and are distinguished by "major" mode and "minor" mode.)
17. (a) 10 (b) 15 or 20
18. (c)
19. (a)
20. (b)
21. 50%
22. (d)
23. (a) a (b) a (c) a (d) b (e) a (f) b (g) b (h) b (i) b (j) b
24. (a) N (b) N (c) B (d) R (e) NS (f) PS

PROBLEMS AND EXERCISES

1. Suppose that the following data set is a random sample of 40 self-concept scores.

100	112	88	105	100	102	98	113
102	87	93	93	117	100	98	92
100	117	97	100	83	67	76	100
106	117	89	83	100	109	109	93
105	108	104	63	81	109	100	98

(a) Determine X_{max}, X_{min}, and the range.
(b) About how many intervals would you suggest to display the distribution?
(c) Determine the interval width, w, to allow for about 10 intervals.
(d) If $w = 5$, what is the first (lowest scores) interval?
(e) If $w = 5$, list the intervals.
(f) Construct a grouped frequency distribution for the 40 scores. (Use the picket-fence tally method.)
(g) Construct percentage and cumulative percentage columns of these data.
(h) Would a frequency polygon be an appropriate graph for these data? Why?
(i) Construct a polygon like Figure 2.4 of these data.
(j) Construct an ogive of these data.
(k) Estimate P_{10}, P_{50}, and P_{90} using the ogive.
(l) Construct a horizontal box-and-whisker plot for these data. (Note: Box plots can have either a vertical or a horizontal orientation. For the horizontal orientation, the whiskers extend to the left and to the right of the box.)
(m) Comment upon the apparent symmetry or asymmetry of these data.
(n) How would an ogive of a positive skew differ from that of a negative skew?
(o) Can you surmise how the ogive of a rectangular distribution would appear?

2. The following data set is from a random sample of 50 cases from the HSB data set. In this case, the numerals represent the race of the individuals, where: 1 = Hispanic, 2 = Asian, 3 = Black, 4 = White.

4	1	4	4	1	1	4	4	4	2
4	4	2	4	4	4	3	4	4	4
1	4	4	4	1	4	4	3	4	4
4	3	1	4	4	4	1	3	4	4
4	3	3	4	4	3	3	4	4	4

(a) Is a frequency polygon appropriate to graph these data? Why?
(b) Is a bar graph appropriate to graph these data? Why?
(c) Construct a grouped frequency distribution for these data. (Use the Tukey tally method.)
(d) Construct a percentage column of these data.
(e) Construct a frequency histogram of these data.
(f) Label the vertical axes of the figure in (e) to indicate both frequency and percentage.
(g) Should there probably be gaps between the columns of the histogram? Why?

ANSWERS TO PROBLEMS AND EXERCISES

1. (a) $X_{max} = 117$, $X_{min} = 63$, range = 54
   (b) about 10 intervals unless n is quite large
   (c) w = range/10 = 54/10 = 5.4, round to 5.
   (d) The least multiple of 5 that is less than 63 is 60: 60–64.

   (e)   (f)   (g)

Interval	Tally	f	%	Cum.%
60–64	I	1	2.5	2.5
65–69	I	1	2.5	5.0
70–74		0	0.0	5.0
75–79	I	1	2.5	7.5
80–84	III	3	7.5	15.0
85–89	III	3	7.5	22.5
90–94	IIII	4	10.0	32.5
95–99	IIII	4	10.0	42.5
100–104	₩₩ ₩₩ I	11	27.5	70.0
105–109	₩₩ II	7	17.5	87.5
110–114	II	2	5.0	92.5
115–119	III	3	7.5	100.0
		$n = 40$	100.0	

(h) Yes, frequency polygons are excellent for continuous variables.

(i)

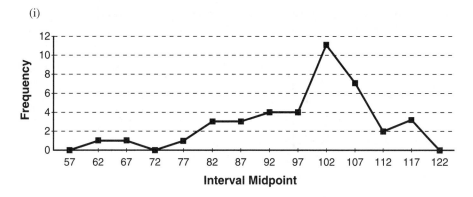

(j)

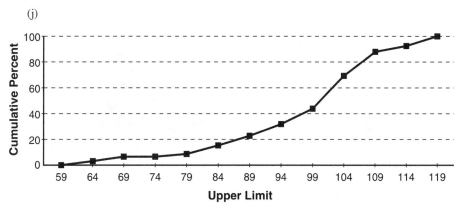

(k) $P_{10} = 80$; $P_{50} = 100$; $P_{90} = 110$

(l)

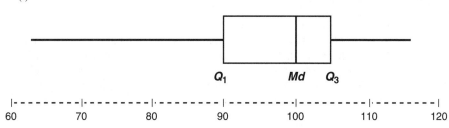

(m) It appears that the distribution is asymmetric and skewed to the left.

(n) The ogive of a positively skewed distribution would rise very quickly from the baseline on the left side of the ogive due to the mass of scores in the lower regions. On the other hand, the ogive of a negatively skewed distribution would not begin to rise quickly until it reached the higher scores on the right side of the figure.

(o) a straight line sloping up from bottom left to top right.

2. (a) no, since these data are categorical rather than quantitatively continuous.

(b) an excellent move, since the data have no underlying continuum.

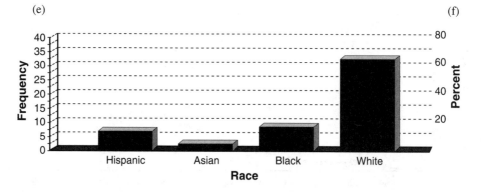

	(c) Code	Tally	(d) Code	Percent
Hispanic	1		7	14.0
Asian	2		2	4.0
Black	3		8	16.0
White	4		33	66.0
			$n = 50$	100.0

(e)   (f)

(g) Yes, since it is consistent with categorical nonrankable data.

 SUGGESTED COMPUTER EXERCISE

We strongly recommend that computer software be used throughout the various chapters. You may wish to use a spreadsheet to do your computational exercises, but do some by hand first to insure that the process is understood. The popular software spreadsheets (e.g., EXCEL, LOTUS, QUATTRO PRO) have built in statistical functions for most of the statistical analyses covered in this book. If available, you may wish to use special statistical software that is widely used in educational and behavioral research (e.g., SPSS, SAS, BMDP, SYSTAT).

3

Measures of Central Tendency and Scales of Measurement

❖ 3.1 MEASUREMENT SCALES

Many people have erroneous notions about the nature of measurement. *Measurement* involves *assessment*, a process by which *things* are *differentiated*. It is not limited to the use of highly developed and refined instruments. Certainly, thermometers, yardsticks, and stopwatches can be used to precisely measure temperature, distance, and time. However, these variables can also be measured informally by observation—by the "trained eye." Skilled printers using only sight and touch are said to be able to assess (measure) the thickness of a film of ink to an incredible degree of precision—millionths of an inch! Our senses are our yardsticks for assessing the environment around us. When these observations are expressed using the language of numbers, the process of measurement has been completed. Indeed, there is a close correspondence between the scientific maturity of a discipline and the degree to which the relevant variables in that discipline can be measured objectively and accurately.

Measurement in the social sciences and education usually produces numbers, but such numbers are without some of the mathematical properties of numbers for the measurement of such variables as time, distance, area, weight, and cost. For example, the scale of measurement for assessing IQ differs in significant ways from that for measuring height. This is important because the interpretation given to a "score" is influenced by the scale of measurement involved. Four scales or levels of measurement are commonly distinguished: nominal, ordinal, interval, and ratio scales.

❖ 3.2 NOMINAL SCALES

Nominal measurement is the most rudimentary form of measurement. It is the process of grouping units (objects, persons, etc.) into categories based on one or more observed attributes or properties. With nominal (categorical) scales, the assigned numbers define each distinct grouping and serve merely as labels or names (i.e., nominal—using a number as a name tag). The numbers make categorical rather than quantitative distinctions; each distinct numeral represents a different category. The magnitude of the numbers do not reflect any inherent ordering of the things to which they are assigned, but serve only as identity codes. The observations cannot be ordered from little to much or from less to more. Any question pertaining to the magnitude of the underlying variable is irrelevant to nominal measurement. The only comparative question relevant for nominal data pertains to whether two observations are the same or different. Examples of nominal measurement are political party (1 = Republican, 2 = Democrat; or 1 = Democrat, 2 = Republican—with nominal scales the numerical codes are arbitrary), ethnicity (1 = Black, 2 = Asian, 3 = Hispanic, etc.), and college major (1 = education, 2 = mathematics, 3 = English, 4 = fun and games, etc.). Nominal variables having only two categories, such as gender and type of school (private or public), are termed *dichotomous* variables.

Quiz: Measurement of which of the following variables would result in nominal scales: occupation, type of school program, reading score, height in inches?

Answer: Occupation and type of school program are nominal variables.

❖ 3.3 ORDINAL SCALES

An ordinal scale of measurement is achieved when the observations can be placed in a rank order with respect to the characteristic being assessed. The magnitude of the numbers is not arbitrary (as it is with nominal scales), but represents the rank-order of the attribute observed. A continuum underlying the numbers is assumed. Social class, rank-in-class, beauty contests (indeed, all variables expressed as ranks), and percentile norms are examples of ordinal scales.

Quiz: Measurement of which of the following variables could be expressed as ranks and represent ordinal measurement: (1) degree objective (BA, MA, or PhD), (2) gender, (3) favorite sport?

Answer: degree objective

❖ 3.4 INTERVAL SCALES

Interval scales are more highly refined, so much so that consecutive numbers mark off equal intervals, that is, equal quantities of the variable being measured. A given numerical difference represents the same magnitude of the attribute (or trait, or property, or characteristic) at all points along the scale. The difference between the temperatures (kinetic energy) of 50° and 51° is identical in magnitude to the difference between 70° and 71°. With interval scales, however, the zero point is arbitrary and does not represent "none" or "empty" or "zilch"; that is, zero does not represent the absence of the characteristics measured; it represents a convenient point from which to mark off intervals of equal magnitude. For the centigrade temperature scale, the temperature at which water freezes is assigned to 0°C; for the Fahrenheit scale, the point at which a saturated saline solution freezes is assigned 0°F. Each time we write the date, the number used for the year (A.D.—number of years since the birth of Christ) represents an interval scale.

Quiz: Measurement of which of the following variables could be expressed using an interval scale: (1) career objective, (2) social class, (3) self-concept score, (4) water temperature in Kealakekua Bay?

Answer: water temperature in beautiful Kealakekua Bay! (The water temperature could also be expressed as a ratio scale if the temperature is expressed using the absolute [Kelvin] scale.)

❖ **TABLE 3.1** Scale of measurement in relation to the relevancy of questions pertaining to the relationship between two observations, X_1 and X_2.

	Is this question relevant for:			
Question pertaining to two observations	*Nominal Data?*	*Interval Data?*	*Ordinal Data?*	*Ratio Data?*
Is X_1 different from X_2?	Yes	Yes	Yes	Yes
Is X_1 greater than X_2?	No	Yes	Yes	Yes
X_1 exceeds X_2 by how many units?	No	No	Yes	Yes
X_1 exceeds X_2 by what percentage?	No	No	No	Yes

❖ **3.5 RATIO SCALES**

Ratio scales have the properties of ordinal and interval scales, but, in addition, the zero number represents an absence of the characteristic in question (i.e., the scale has an absolute zero point); consequently, numbers can be compared as ratios. Measures of length using a ruler or tape measure exemplify ratio measurement. If Sue is 60 inches tall and Carmen is 50 inches tall, then Sue is 120% (60/50 = 1.20) as tall as Carmen, or Sue is 20% taller than Carmen. The assessment of IQ, however, does not have the ratio quality—if Toni has an IQ score of 125 and Jack has an IQ of 100, one cannot say than Toni is 25 percent more intelligent than Jack. Measures of time, distance, weight, area, and cost usually represent ratio scales. Well-developed measures of scholarship, aptitude, social and psychological concepts are often *assumed* to have at least ordinal or quasi-interval qualities.

> **Quiz:** Which of the following variables have measures that probably represent ratio scales: (1) cost per student, (2) distance from school, (3) weight?
>
> **Answer:** all of the above

❖ **3.6 MEASUREMENT SCALES AND STATISTICS**

In the late 1950s and for about two decades thereafter, the importance of levels of measurement scales for statistical applications was exaggerated. Many textbooks unfortunately contended that most conventional statistics are inappropriate unless the measurements represent an interval or a ratio scale. Since most measurements in the behavioral sciences lack interval scale properties, considerable attention was turned away from classical statistical methods toward *non-parametric* statistics—statistics that are less efficient, but make fewer assumptions pertaining to the population parameters. It has now been shown that the disenchantment with classical statistics was unwarranted.[1] Nevertheless, awareness of the level of measurement represented is important for a correct interpretation of the statistical

---

[1]The principal papers and studies on this issue are given by Heerman and Braskamp (1970, pp. 30–110), Borgatta & Bohrnstedt (1980), Townsend & Ashby (1984), Mitchell (1986), Luce, Krantz, Suppes & Tversky (1990), and especially Velleman & Wilkinson (1993) who state: "Unfortunately, the use of Steven's categories in selecting or recommending statistical analysis methods is inappropriate and can be wrong. They do not describe the attributes of real data that are essential for good statistical analysis. Nor do they provide a classification scheme appropriate for modern data analysis methods."

measures of the data set involved. For examples if an increase in GPA from 2.0 to 3.0 were described as a 50% gain, this would imply that GPA is a ratio scale, which is preposterous. Again, if the difference in GPA from 2.0 to 3.0 were described the same as the difference between 3.0 and 4.0, this would imply that GPA is an interval scale; this is also obviously false, since the performance levels required for letter grades differ markedly. However, one could defensibly conclude that a GPA of 3.0 is better than a GPA of 2.0 since GPA clearly constitutes an ordinal scale of measurement.

❖ 3.7 MEASURES OF CENTRAL TENDENCY

In our daily lives, the most common encounter we have with a statistical concept pertains to "average." We all have been using "averages" since elementary school. We are continually exposed to reports of averages—average salary, average rainfall, average weight, even batting averages. Perhaps you have noticed that the term "average" is somewhat ambiguous. We hear about the average housewife, the average voter, the average family, even an "average Joe"; average is used in so many different ways that the term is rarely used in scientific communication, unless the context makes its meaning clear. In this chapter, we will distinguish among the three common measures of so-called "average" (or more precisely, measures of central tendency)—the mean, median, and mode.

When you scan an unordered array of test scores to see if your score is high or low, or above or below average, you are seeking relevant statistical information that will enable you to interpret and evaluate your performance with more accuracy and meaning. Your informal method of organizing the information (i.e., eyeballing) may not be systematic, but your behavior aptly illustrates the need for the data to be organized, digested, and summarized so that correct interpretations of the data can be drawn.

A measure of central tendency or middle-location of data sets is far and away the most widely used type of statistical index; ordinarily, it is the single most important description of a distribution. This is true not only in empirical research but also in quantitative information designed for the general public.

❖ 3.8 THE MEAN

The mean,[2] or arithmetic average, of a set of observations (X) is simply its sum (ΣX) divided by the number of observations (n). (See Math Note 3 in the Appendix to review simple summation and Σ.) For statistical purposes, the mean of a sample ($\bar{X}$) is distinguished from the mean of the population (μ). A *population mean* (μ) is a *parameter* and is based on the *complete* set of observational units (N) in the population as defined by the researcher, for example, all principals in California, all Colorado students enrolled in bilingual programs, all public elementary schools in the United States, et cetera. A *sample mean* ($\bar{X}$) is an inferential statistic; it is based on a subset, preferably a random sample, of observational units (n) selected from the entire population. In Chapter 9, we will learn how the accuracy with which $\bar{X}$ estimates μ can be determined.

Formulas are used in mathematics and science because they are precise and succinct. A formula is a sentence expressed mathematically. Contrast the number of words in a narra-

---

[2]The term "mean," without modifier, always denotes the arithmetic mean. There are, however, other kinds of means—the harmonic mean, the geometric mean, and the trimean—that have occasional application in applied statistics. Brief discussions of these measures can be found in Glass & Hopkins (1996).

❖ **TABLE 3.2** An unordered distribution of $n = 11$ scores.

8	3	7	4	11	2	9	4	10	11	4

tive definition of the mean to the concise definition of the sample mean, $\overline{X}$, expressed in Equation 3.1:

$$\overline{X} = \frac{\Sigma X}{n} \tag{3.1}$$

where the summation symbol denotes "the sum of"; thus, ΣX means the sum of all scores: $\Sigma X = (X_1 + X_2 + \ldots + X_n)$, and n is the number of scores (sample size).

The set of 11 scores given in Table 3.2 will be used to illustrate the computation of the mean. From Table 3.2: $X_1 = 8, X_2 = 3, X_3 = 7, \ldots, X_{11} = 4$. $\Sigma X = 8 + 3 + 7 + \ldots + 4 = 73$, and $n = 11$; thus, $\overline{X} = 73/11 = 6.63636^3$ or 6.64.

> **Quiz:** (1) Suppose you find an error in scoring: The score of 9 in Table 3.2 should be corrected to 13. (1) Would the mean of the distribution change? (2) Find the mean of the corrected distribution of the 11 scores.
>
> **Answers:** (1) yes, (2) 77/11 = 7

If the 11 observations in Table 3.2 represented the entire population, the procedures would be the same, but the mean would be represented by μ, rather than $\overline{X}$. For example, the mean score of students in a class on an examination is not ordinarily used to make an inference about some other group, but is a descriptive statistic for the class; thus, the appropriate symbol for the mean would be μ and the number of scores would be designated by N (see Equation 3.2).

$$\mu = \frac{\Sigma X}{N} \tag{3.2}$$

❖ 3.9 THE MEDIAN

The median (Md) is another common measure of central tendency. In Chapter 2, we saw that the median is the middle score in a set of ordered scores—the point below (and above) which an equal number of observations fall; the median is the fiftieth percentile (P_{50}) or the second quartile (Q_2).

---

[3]For most purposes, answers with three or four figures convey the appropriate degree of precision. Do not be concerned if your answers differ slightly from those in the book; small discrepancies will result from intermediate points at which rounding takes place. Certain hand-calculators are accurate to more decimal places than others. Round only after you have the final answer. The mean should be carried to one or two more decimal places than the individual observations. Math Note 4 pertains to rounding of numbers.

Quiz: (1) If 37 students score above the median, how many students score below the median? (2) If a score of 29 has a percentile rank of 41, what can you infer about the value of the median?

Answers: (1) 37, (2) The median will be larger than 29.

To find the median of a group of scores:

Step 1.	Arrange the scores in rank-order.
Step 2.	Count down to the middle score in the ordered distribution.

As an example, find the median for the data of Table 3.2. For step 1, place the 11 scores in Table 3.2 in rank order, that is, 2, 3, 4, 4, 4, 7, 8, 9, 10, 11, 11. For step 2, the middle score of these 11 ordered scores is the 6th score, that is, the median is 7.

For distributions like Table 3.2, with an odd number of observations, the middle observation is the median. By glancing at the ordered distribution above, you will notice that the median (*Md*) is the 6th score from the top (or the 6th score from the bottom). The 6th score is 7; there are 5 scores greater than the median value of 7 and 5 scores smaller than the median. (Since the score 7 that coincides with the median point is viewed as spanning the entire interval from 6.5 to 7.5, half of the score of 7 can be thought of as falling below the point 7.0 and the other half of 7 above 7.0.)

Quiz: If, in Table 3.2, the score of 9 were changed to a 12, what is the median of the revised distribution?

Answer: The median would remain the same; *Md* = 7.

For a distribution comprised of an even number of observations, the median falls midway between the middle-most pair of scores. Consider the 11 scores in Table 3.2, and suppose, because of some irregularity, we had to throw out the 2 and were left with only $n = 10$ scores: 3, 4, 4, 4, 7, 8, 9, 10, 11, 11. The median is midway between the 5th (7) and 6th (8) scores; *Md* = 7.5.

Quiz: If a score below the median of a distribution is changed to a smaller value, (a) will the value of the median change? (b) will the value of the mean change?

Answers: (a) no; (b) yes, the mean will decrease.

The median can be found for any distribution that can be ordered—that is, only an ordinal scale of measurement is required. For example, if you like large numbers, suppose members of Congress are ranked on an economic irresponsibility scale (e.g., the number of votes for bills that will increase the national debt); the huge irresponsibility score of the middle-most member represents the median with respect to this scale, even though only a rank order is involved.

When *n* is very small, ranking the observations can be done quickly and determining the median is simple. When *n* is very large, however, the process of determining the median by hand is time-consuming. In the past, approximate methods for estimating the median from grouped frequency distributions were often included in statistics textbooks. These methods were less than accurate, nonintuitive and tedious. Fortunately, the availability of inexpensive microcomputers has rendered these procedures and formulas unnecessary.

Quiz: How can students' thankfulness for computer technology be enhanced?

Answer: Have them rank a set of 600 scores.

❖ 3.10 THE MODE

The mode is the most frequently occurring observation—the most common or popular score. In Table 3.2, the mode is 4, because 4 is the observation with the greatest frequency. What is the mode score when a pair of dice are tossed many times? Since 7 occurs more frequently than any other result (actually in the long run, one toss in six yields a 7), 7 is the mode. The modal grade given in a freshman chemistry course may be C. The modal nationality in the world is Chinese. Notice that, unlike the median and the mean, the mode can be employed even with categorical variables—data that represent only a nominal scale of measurement. There are about 100 females to every 95 males in the United States; so, the modal sex is female. The concepts of mean and median are virtually meaningless with categorical variables.

Quiz: What are the mean and median of ethnicity in the United States?

Answer: I do not answer stupid questions!

The mode, however, has meaning with data at all levels of measurement. Notice, in Table 2.2, the ease with which the mode can be identified ($Mo = 50$) from an ungrouped frequency distribution (Section 2.7). With grouped frequency distributions (Section 2.8), the midpoint of the interval with the largest frequency can be used to estimate the mode. In Table 2.3, the mode is estimated to be 40—the midpoint of the (39–41) interval—the interval with the greatest frequency (23). Please do not bother to do it by hand, but if an ungrouped frequency distribution of the 200 math scores of the HSB data set in the Appendix Table I were developed, its mode would be 57. As you can observe, the mode based on a grouped frequency distribution may differ markedly from the actual mode. As you might suppose, the mode varies a lot from sample to sample, and it cannot be depended upon to give a good estimate of the mode of the population, especially if n is not huge.

❖ 3.11 MEAN, MEDIAN, AND MODE OF COMBINED SUBGROUPS

Suppose the mean, median, and mode of test scores for each of three separate schools (subgroups) are known, but we wish to find the three measures of central tendency for the composite group (i.e., all three schools combined into one large group). Given the three subgroup means and their respective n's, we can compute the composite mean (the so-called *grand mean* symbolized by $\bar{X}_{.}$) using Equation 3.3.

Caution: The grand mean is not merely the mean of the subgroup means unless the subgroup sample sizes are identical. The grand mean ($\bar{X}_{.}$) of unequal sized groups is computed by dividing the sum of the subgroup sums by the sum of the group n's, as is implicit in Equation 3.3. This can be quickly accomplished by completing the following steps:

To find the composite mean for all data in two or more subgroups (J):

Step 1.	Compute the sum of the scores (ΣX) for each subgroup, $\Sigma X = n\,\overline{X}$. Add these subgroup sums to obtain the total sum of all scores in all subgroups.
Step 2.	Find the total number of scores ($n.$) in all subgroups combined: $n. = \Sigma n_j$. That is, add up all the subgroup n's.
Step 3.	Divide the grand sum by $n.$—this quotient is the grand mean, $\overline{X}.$, for the aggregated data set.

For three groups ($J = 3$):

$$\overline{X}. = \frac{\Sigma X_1 + \Sigma X_2 + \Sigma X_3}{n_1 + n_2 + n_3}$$

The more general formula to find the grand mean for any number of subgroups (J) is:

$$\overline{X}. = \frac{\Sigma X_1 + \Sigma X_2 + ... + \Sigma X_J}{n_1 + n_2 + ... + n_J} \qquad \textbf{(3.3)}$$

The mode or median of the composite data set cannot be computed from the subgroup modes or subgroup medians. For both the mode and median, we must have the original data in hand and form a single combined frequency distribution before the mode or median of the aggregated data can be found.

Quiz: The scores, sample sizes and measures of central tendency are given for each of three subgroups of a small data set:

Subgroup 1 (2, 3, 3, 3, 4, 7, 7, 8, 8); $n = 9$; $Mo = 3$, $Md = 4$, $\overline{X} = 5$.
Subgroup 2 (1, 1, 4, 6, 6, 6, 8, 8); $n = 8$; $Mo = 6$, $Md = 6$, $\overline{X} = 5$.
Subgroup 3 (2, 2, 2, 7, 8, 8, 13); $n = 7$; $Mo = 2$, $Md = 4$, $\overline{X} = 6$.

(1) Compute ΣX for each of the three subgroups. (2) Find the sum of all scores in the composite distribution. (3) Find the total number of scores in the composite distribution. (4) Compute the grand mean, designated by the appropriate symbol. (5) Find the median of the aggregated data set. (You will need to combine all observations into a single ungrouped frequency distribution.) (6) Find the mode of the composite distribution.

Answers: (1) 45, 40, 42, (2) 127, (3) 24, (4) $\overline{X}. = 5.29$, (5) 6, (6) 8

With small subgroup samples, the composite group mean, mode, and median are simple to determine. However, when large sets of data are involved, only the grand mean is reasonably simple to compute. Only the mean is algebraically defined (i.e., by an equation: $\overline{X} = \Sigma X/n$); one advantage of an algebraically defined statistic is that it is, therefore, amenable to further mathematical development and manipulation.

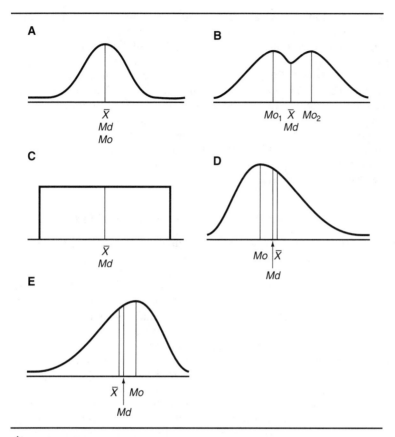

❖ **FIGURE 3.1** The relationship between measures of central tendency with various types of distributions.

❖ 3.12 CENTRAL TENDENCY AND SKEWNESS

In symmetrical distributions with just one mode, such as the normal curve in Figure 3.1A, the mean ($\overline{X}$), median (Md), and mode (Mo) have the same value. For example, the mean, median, and mode of the population of IQ scores are all 100 because the distribution of IQ scores is quite accurately represented by the normal curve.

For bimodal and rectangular distributions as in Figure 3.1B and Figure 3.1C, only the mean and median are identical. Note that a perfectly rectangular distribution would not have a mode, since all X-values have the same frequency.

In skewed distributions like Figures 3.1D and 3.1E, the mean, being sensitive to the magnitude of each score, is "pulled" toward the extreme scores in the "tail" of the distribution. Consequently, the mean has the largest value of the three measures of central tendency in a positively skewed distribution, and the smallest value in a negatively skewed distribution. Contrary to popular opinion, it is not always the case that 50% of cases are above average (the mean). Observe in Figure 3.1D that it is quite possible for 70% or more of the scores in a distribution to be below average (or above average as in Figure 3.1E).

The median is expected to fall between the mean and mode in skewed distributions; theoretically, in large, smooth, skewed distributions, the median is expected to be about twice as far from the mode as it is from the mean (see Figures 3.1D and 3.1E). However, with small data sets, the mode is very erratic and its relation to the mean and median is quite unpredictable. In extremely skewed distributions, the mean may be influenced to such an extent that it is no longer a good *descriptive* measure of the central tendency of a distribution. In severely skewed distributions, the median is preferable to the mean for descriptive purposes; indeed, only in symmetrical distributions is the mean easy to interpret (and that is because it is equal to the median). For example, if we determine the mean contribution to philanthropic purposes by U.S. households in 1995, 90% of households could be below the mean! The mean, however, remains the measure of choice for most *inferential* statistical purposes, as we shall see in later chapters.

❖ 3.13 MEAN, MEDIAN, OR MODE—WHICH MEASURE IS BEST?

The mode is applicable for each of the four scales of measurement. Only the mode is meaningful for categorical variables such as political affiliation, religious affiliation, ethnicity, college major, or occupation. However, for inferential purposes, the mode has a distinct disadvantage—the mode of a sample is not a very reliable estimate of its population mode unless the size of the random sample is extremely large. *Reliability* in statistics represents the accuracy with which the statistic estimates the corresponding population parameter. Stated differently, there is a large *sampling error* associated with the sample mode; sampling error is the difference between the sample statistic and the corresponding population parameter. The sample median is more reliable (i.e., has less sampling error) than the sample mode—the sample mean has less sampling error than either the mode or the median, which is one reason why it tends to be preferred for inferential purposes.

As an example, suppose a class were randomly divided into two subgroups, A and B, and the same test was given to both subgroups. The difference between the two means would be expected to be less than that between the two medians, which, in turn, would be expected to be less than the difference between the two modes. Stated another way, in the long run, the sample mean gives a closer estimate of its population parameter than does the median or the mode. The concept of sampling error is a fundamentally important consideration in inferential statistics and will be developed more fully in later chapters.

For descriptive purposes, the median is often the preferred measure of central tendency. As the 50th percentile of the distribution, it communicates "average" well for both symmetrical and asymmetrical continuous distributions. The median of a distribution also has an interesting mathematical characteristic—it is the point from which the sum of the distances (absolute values)[4] to all other scores in the distribution is a minimum.

In terms of absolute values, $\Sigma|X-Md|$ is less than either $\Sigma|X-\bar{X}|$ or $\Sigma|X-Mo|$, in fact, $\Sigma|X-Md|$ is less than $\Sigma|X-k|$ where k is any other conceivable point of reference. That is, the cumulative distance from the median point to all scores in the group is less than that from any other point. To give an example, suppose that the scores 1, 3, 6, 7, and 8 are placed along a number line as illustrated in Figure 3.2. Now let us calculate the absolute deviation of each score from the median: $|1-6| = 5$, $|3-6| = 3$, $|6-6| = 0$, $|7-6| = 1$, $|8-6| = 2$; so

---

[4]Math Review: The absolute value of a number refers to its numerical value (ignoring its sign). Absolute values are denoted by vertical bars, for example, $|-7| = 7$; $|-2.8| = 2.8$, $|.04| = .04$. (Math Note 8 in Appendix A discusses absolute values.)

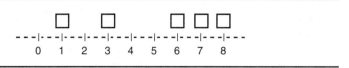

❖ **FIGURE 3.2** A set of five scores on a number line.

$\Sigma|X–Md| = 11$. This sum is smaller than that generated from deviating about any point other than the median. Find the sum of the absolute deviations from the mean and compare the two sums. $\Sigma|(X– \overline{X})| = \Sigma|(X–5)| = (4 + 2 + 1 + 2 + 3) = 12$, which, as predicted, exceeds the sum of the absolute deviations from the median. Try any other point from which to deviate to confirm that, indeed, the median tends to be closer to the other scores in a distribution than any other score or point—the cumulative distance from the median point to all scores in the group is less than from any other point. This is congruent with the preference for the median as a descriptive measure of central tendency.

Quiz: For the scores in Figure 3.2, find the (1) median, (2) mean, and (3) mode.

Answers: (1) 6, (2) 5, (3) no mode exists since f = 1 for each score.

The mean or arithmetic average is the most common measure of central tendency. In addition, researchers tend to use means more than any other measure of central tendency. As noted previously, the mean is a more reliable statistic (i.e., has less sampling error) than either the mode or the median. Furthermore, the mean also lends itself more readily to further statistical treatment than does the median or mode since it is algebraically defined.

The mean is also the measure of central tendency that satisfies the least-squares criterion; that is, the sum of squared[5] deviations of a set of scores is less from the mean than from any other point. That is, $\Sigma(X– \overline{X})^2$ is less than $\Sigma(X–Md)^2$, less than $\Sigma(X–Mo)^2$, and less than $\Sigma(X–k)^2$ where k is any other conceivable point. Strange as it may seem, although the sum of the absolute deviations from the median is less than from any other point, when the deviations are squared, the sum is least from the mean—statistical facts are sometimes counterintuitive.

Although the least-squares criterion seems a bit odd, it turns out to be of major importance and use in inferential statistical procedures. Statistics that satisfy the least-squares criterion (as does the mean) usually are superior for purposes of statistical inference (Section 1.4) than statistics that do not, such as the median and the mode. Inferential statistics will be studied in Chapters 9–16.

Quiz: For the scores in Figure 3.2, confirm that the mean meets the least-squares criterion: Compare the sum of the squared deviations from the mean with that for the median.

Answer: The sum of the squared deviations from the mean, $16 + 4 + 1 + 4 + 9 = 34$, is less than that from the median, $25 + 9 + 0 + 1 + 4 = 39$.

The following situation summarizes several of the issues that arise in the use of measures of central tendency. Suppose that a school district employs 1,000 persons, all of whom

---

[5]Math Review: "*X*-squared" or X^2 means *X* multiplied by itself, that is, $(X)(X)$; $3^2 = (3)(3)$ or 9, $(–5)^2 = (–5)(–5) = 25$. See Math Note 9 for a review of squaring and exponents.

earn between \$25,000 and \$45,000 per year, except for 50 administrators, who each earn more than \$50,000. The *mean* salary for the district personnel is likely to be misleadingly high, since it does not adequately characterize the 950 nonadministrators. However, the *median* will not be sensitive to the values of the very high salaries. In fact, the median can be determined without even knowing the actual salaries of the administrators—the top interval of "more than \$50,000" will have a frequency of 50. In such instances, it is highly desirable to report both the median and the mean. It would probably be even more meaningful to exclude the 50 administrators from the distribution and to report their salaries separately. The 950 teachers represent a more homogeneous group, yet even the teacher distribution would probably be skewed to the right, with new teachers near the bottom of the salary schedule far outnumbering old-timers who are receiving the maximum salary. A devious school superintendent might use the mean as the "average" at professional meetings or when negotiating with teachers' groups, but would use the mode as the "average" when trying to obtain public support for an increase in taxes. In skewed distributions, the median is usually the best single descriptive measure, although each of the various "averages" convey some complementary information.

❖ CHAPTER SUMMARY

The numbers in a set of data have different properties depending on the nature of the variable being measured and the precision involved in the assessment procedures. The four basic types of measurement scale or level of measurement are described as nominal, ordinal, interval, and ratio scales. With *nominal* scales, the numbers are used only as name tags, and do not represent values or amounts. With *ordinal* scales, the numbers can be placed in rank order by amount or degree. With *interval* scales, the numbers represent equal units along a continuum, but have an arbitrary zero point. A *ratio* scale is an interval scale, but also has an absolute zero. The measurement scale represented by a set of data depends in part on the nature of the variable in question and partly on the quality of the assessment procedures. Measures of categorical variables remain nominal scales regardless of how carefully they are assessed. Measures of continuous variables that theoretically can be measured by interval or ratio scales may represent only ordinal scales if crude measurement procedures are employed.

There are three common measures of central tendency: the mean, median, and mode. The *mean* is the most widely used measure of "average" both in communicating information to the general public and in empirical research. Of the three, the sample mean is the most precise (i.e., has less sampling error) and tends to be better for inferential purposes, that is, making inferences about population parameters. The numerical value of the mean is influenced by the value of every score. Consequently, in skewed distributions, it is "drawn" toward the elongated tail more than is the median or mode. In positively skewed distributions, the mean is expected to exceed both the median and mode; the reverse is true for negatively skewed distributions. For continuous distributions, the median is usually the most meaningful indicator of central tendency for descriptive purposes.

The *median* is the 50th percentile of a distribution (P_{50}), and partitions a set of scores at the midpoint. The median is also the point in a distribution from which the sum of the absolute deviations of all scores is at a minimum. If these differences are squared, however, the total would be least from the mean, not the median. The mean, therefore, is the measure of central tendency that satisfies the surprisingly important least-squares criterion.

The *mode*, unlike the mean and median, can be used even with nominal scales. The mode is the most frequently occurring observation, but it is less reliable than either the

❖ **TABLE 3.3** Characteristics of the mean, median, and mode.

Characteristic	Mean	Median	Mode
Most reliable*	✔		
Least reliable			✔
Requires only nominal scale			✔
Requires only ranked observations		✔	
The point below and above which half of the observations fall		✔	
The "center of gravity" of a distribution	✔		
Influenced by the specific value of every observation	✔		
Will be equal in a symmetrical distribution	✔	✔	
Will be equal in a normal distribution	✔	✔	✔
Will have the largest value in a positively skewed distribution	✔		
Will have the largest value in a negatively skewed distribution			✔
Its value is neither the largest nor the smallest in skewed distributions		✔	
Lends itself best to other arithmetic operations	✔		
Is most widely used in more advanced statistical methods	✔		
Can be estimated graphically from ogive curves		✔	
Can be most quickly estimated from histograms or frequency polygons			✔
Best for continuous variables for descriptive purposes		✔	
Is equal to P_{50} and Q_2		✔	

*For normal and most other empirical distributions

mean or the median. In symmetrical, unimodal distributions, the mode, median, and mean have the same value. Other information is summarized in Table 3.3.

ACTIVE REVIEW—A CLOZE[6] EXERCISE

Three commonly used measures of __(a)__ are the mean, the mode, and the __(b)__. Usually the scores will cluster around the most frequently occurring score, the __(c)__. The midpoint that separates the distribution into equal-sized halves is the __(d)__. The most dependable, stable, or reliable measure of central tendency tends to be the __(e)__. The __(f)__ is sensitive to the value of every score in the distribution; this is not true of the __(g)__ or the __(h)__. Distributions that are precisely symmetrical and have a certain mathematically specified bell shape are termed __(i)__ distributions. In a true normal distribution, the mode, median, and mean have the same __(j)__. All normal distributions are __(k)__, but some symmetrical distributions are not __(l)__. A test may be so difficult that there are many __(m)__ scores and few extremely __(n)__ ones. Such a distribution would be described as being skewed __(o)__. In skewed distributions, the __(p)__ is often the preferred descriptive measure of cen-

---

[6]The cloze exercise is a common measure of reading comprehension. Because of the redundancy in language, if the reader is understanding what is being read, the blank word can usually be anticipated (if the blank word is selected appropriately). Thus, the cloze exercise is a mastery test using a different format.

tral tendency, but for inferential purposes the __(q)__ has the smallest sampling error. On a very easy test, the __(r)__ will be greater than the __(s)__, but less than the __(t)__. If the mean IQ for a class is found to be 110 and the median 100, the distribution is probably skewed __(u)__. If a class had a mean of 89.3 and a median of 90.1, skewing appears to be __(v)__. If this class were combined with a gifted class, the shape of the distribution of the composite IQ scores would probably be __(w)__. If a test could be developed so that each score was obtained with equal frequency, the shape of the distribution would be both __(x)__ and __(y)__, and there would be no __(z)__.

Expected answers to this cloze test are given below.

(a) central tendency	(h) median	(o) positively	(v) negligible
(b) median	(i) normal	(p) median	(w) bimodal
(c) mode	(j) value	(q) mean	(x) symmetrical
(d) median	(k) symmetrical	(r) median	(y) rectangular
(e) mean	(l) normal	(s) mean	(z) mode
(f) mean	(m) low	(t) mode	
(g) mode	(n) high	(u) positively	

MASTERY TEST

1. Are there usually several ways of measuring the same variable?
2. Will different ways of measuring the same variable result in equally accurate observations?
3. Can observations on an interval or ratio scale be converted to an ordinal scale (ranks)?
4. What level of measurement is required for each of the following statements?
   (a) X is 25% greater than Y.
   (b) X is greater than Y.
   (c) X is not the same as Y.
   (d) X is 7 points less than Y.
5. Suppose a variable is measured using an interval, an ordinal, and a ratio scale. Order the measures, from least to most desirable.
6. If $X_1 = 20$, $X_2 = 14$, and $X_3 = 8$, what is the value of (a) $X_1 + X_3$, and (b) ΣX?
7. When persons are measured on an interval scale are *differences* between persons measured on a ratio scale?
8. If student achievement is measured by the number of library books read, does this represent a true ratio scale?

Questions 9–12 refer to the following array of observations:

$$0, 0, 0, 1, 1, 2, 4, 7, 11$$

9. What is the numerical value of the mode?
10. What is the numerical value of the median?
11. What is the numerical value of: (a) ΣX, (b) n, (c) the mean?
12. Describe the shape of the distribution.
13. In a negatively skewed distribution, which measure of central tendency tends to have the smallest value? The largest value?

14. Which sample statistic ($\overline{X}$, *Md*, or *Mo*) is expected to differ least from its corresponding population parameter? These differences are described as ____.

15. Which measure of central tendency is the most reliable? Which is least reliable?

16. Which measure of central tendency would be preferred with categorical variables such as ethnicity or marital status?

17. Which one term *least* belongs with the others?
(a) $\overline{X}$　　(b) P_{50}　　(c) Q_2　　(d) median

18. Which option *least* belongs with the others?
(a) mode　　(b) median　　(c) most popular score　　(d) most frequent score

19. If the mean salary of teachers in public elementary and secondary schools in the United States was $38,000 and if the median salary was $34,000, the distribution would appear to be
(a) symmetrical.　　(b) bimodal.　　(c) skewed positively.　　(d) skewed negatively.

20. In a large county mental health clinic, a group of eight client-centered counselors see an average of five clients per day, while twelve behavior-modification therapists see an average of ten clients per day. What is the mean number of clients seen by the twenty therapists in the clinic?

21. If the mean and median are equal, we would not expect the distribution to be
(a) normal.　　(b) rectangular.　　(c) bimodal.　　(d) symmetrical.　　(e) skewed.

22. In a distribution of scores for which $\overline{X} = 65.5$, $Md = 64$, and $Mo = 60$, it was found that a mistake had been made on one score. Instead of 70, the score should have been 90. Consequently, which one of the above measures of central tendency would *certainly* be incorrect?
(a) mean　　(b) mode　　(c) median

23. If there were 40 observations in the distribution in question 22, what would be the correct value for the mean?

24. If the mean salary for 100 older employees of a Veterans Administration Hospital was $39,000 and for 50 younger employees was $30,000, find the mean salary for all employees combined.

25. If the majority of the students in your statistics class have read and studied this chapter so carefully that they know the answers to almost all questions on this Mastery Test, the distribution of Mastery Test scores would probably be
(a) normally distributed.　　(b) skewed negatively.　　(c) skewed positively.

26. If $n_1 = 7$, $n_2 = 7$, $\overline{X}_1 = 8.0$, and $\overline{X}_2 = 12.0$,
(a) $n_{total} = n. = $ _?_　　(b) $\overline{X}_{grand} = \overline{X}. = $ _?_

27. Given *X*: 6, 10, 2, 6.
(a) $\Sigma X = $ _?_　　(b) $n = $ _?_　　(c) $\overline{X} = $ _?_

ANSWERS TO MASTERY TEST

1. yes
2. probably not
3. yes
4. (a) ratio, (b) ordinal, (c) nominal, (d) interval
5. ordinal, interval, ratio
6. (a) 28, (b) 42
7. yes
8. Probably not, since books would vary in length and difficulty, the measure would lack equal units of measurement.
9. 0
10. 1
11. $\Sigma X = 26$; $n = 9$; $\overline{X} = 2.89$
12. skewed positively
13. mean, mode
14. mean, sampling errors
15. mean, mode
16. mode
17. (a), because (b), (c), and (d) are synonymous
18. (b)
19. (c)

20. 8 clients per day	**24.** $36,000	
21. (e)	**25.** (b)	
22. (a)	**26.** $n. = 14$, $\overline{X}. = 10$	
23. 66	**27.** $\Sigma X = 24$, $n = 4$, $\overline{X} = 6$	

PROBLEMS AND EXERCISES

Items 1–10 are based on the following data:

In a sixth-grade class of 36 students, a "guess who" sociometric technique was administered to assess the degree of positive peer relationships for each student. The scores for the 36 students were:

22	3	12	2	0	7	1	9	1	28	5	2
2	2	33	4	8	13	2	3	1	28	10	14
22	1	4	15	1	52	5	8	3	11	17	1

1. What is the range?

2. Construct an ungrouped frequency distribution.

3. Construct a grouped frequency distribution, with $w = 5$.

4. Construct a histogram of these data and comment upon the type and shape of the distribution.

5. Construct an ogive.

6. Estimate Q_1 and Q_3.

7. Compute the mean.

8. Determine the median.

9. Determine the mode.

10. Compare the distance from Q_1 to Q_2 with the distance from Q_2 to Q_3. The pattern suggests _____ skewness.

11. For a recent decade, the increase in mean income in the south was 74% for Whites and 113% for Nonwhites. What was the mean increase for both groups combined if among every 100 workers 82 were White?

12. Suppose seven friends live along a highway and they want to meet together at one of their homes for tacos and to discuss measures of central tendency and their favorite types of graphs. If their homes along the highway are situated from east to west in this order: A, B, C, D, E, F, and G, where should they meet to minimize the sum of the distances travelled? (*Hint:* From what point is the sum of the deviations minimized?)

13. Suppose a distribution has a mean of 70, a median of 65, and a mode of 55. The distribution is skewed in which direction?

14. If you gave an IQ test to a class on two separate occasions, as a general rule, comment upon the relative differences between the two means, the two medians, and the two modes.

Items 15–16 pertain to the data presented in Table 2.2.

15. $Mo = ?$

16. $Md = ?$

ANSWERS TO PROBLEMS AND EXERCISES

1. Range $= X_{max} - X_{min} = 52 - 0 = 52$

2.

X	f	X	f	X	f	X	f	X	f	X	f	X	f
52	1	44	0	36	0	28	2	20	0	12	1	4	2
51	0	43	0	35	0	27	0	19	0	11	1	3	3
50	0	42	0	34	0	26	0	18	0	10	1	2	5
49	0	41	0	33	1	25	0	17	1	9	1	1	6
48	0	40	0	32	0	24	0	16	0	8	2	0	1
47	0	39	0	31	0	23	0	15	1	7	1		
46	0	38	0	30	0	22	2	14	1	6	0		
45	0	37	0	29	0	21	0	13	1	5	2		

3.

Interval	f	Interval	f	Interval	f
50–54	1	30–34	1	10–14	5
45–40	0	25–29	2	5–9	6
40–44	0	20–24	2	0–4	17
35–39	0	15–19	2		

4. The distribution is asymmetrical and highly positively skewed.

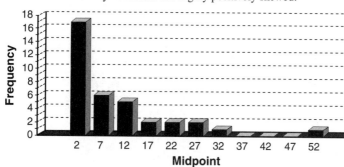

5.

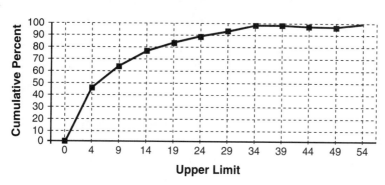

6. $Q_1 = 2$ or 3, $Q_3 = 13.5$

7. 9.78

8. 5
9. 1
10. $Q_3 - Q_2$ is greater than $Q_2 - Q_1$. Positive
11. $\overline{X}_{grand} = \overline{X}. = (n_1 \overline{X}_1 + n_2 \overline{X}_2)/(n_1 + n_2) = [82(74) + 18(113)]/100 = 81\%$.
12. Md at point D. (The sum of the absolute deviations is a minimum about the median.)
13. It is skewed to the right, that is, positively.
14. It is expected that the means differ least and that the modes differ most.
15. Mode = 50
16. Median = 51

 SUGGESTED COMPUTER EXERCISE

1. For the reading scores of the HSB data set:
   (a) Find the reading mean and median.
   (b) Find the reading mode.
2. For the other curricular variables of the HSB data set (writing, math, science, and civics) find the mean, median, and mode.

4

Measures of Variability:
How Different Are the Observations?

❖ 4.1 INTRODUCTION

The two most important statistical characteristics of any data set are (1) its central tendency and (2) its variability. These concepts are very helpful in summarizing the main features of a bewildering mass of data. Measures of central tendency pertain to the average or typical or representative score for the distribution. A second important consideration pertains to the *variability* among the scores, that is, how large are the differences among the scores. Measures of variability quantify the degree of dispersion or the extent of individual differences evidenced in the distribution. To properly interpret an observation, we need measures of central tendency and variability. In this chapter, we consider three measures of variability: one old friend (the range), and two new friends (the variance and the standard deviation). As was the case in Chapter 3 concerning means (μ versus $\overline{X}$), it will be necessary to make distinctions between measures of variability based on population data and measures based on sample data—population parameters versus sample statistics.

Quiz: Try this analogy: Sample is to Statistic as Population is to " ? ".

Answer: Parameter

The need for measures of variability (or dispersion or heterogeneity or scatter or spread or individual differences) to complement measures of central tendency is apparent from Figure 4.1, where the figures portray the distributions of IQ scores of three hypothetical schools. Although each of the three distributions is normally distributed, and the means, medians, and modes are equal, the schools are obviously dissimilar with respect to the variable being measured.

School A typifies a relatively homogeneous group of students; there are few very bright students (note the small portion of scores above 120) and few very dull students (few scores below 80). School B illustrates a school in which the distribution of IQ scores is similar to that of the nation as a whole. Individual differences are greater among students in school B

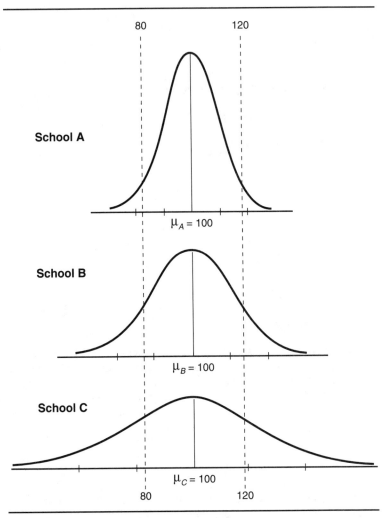

❖ **FIGURE 4.1** Distributions of IQ scores from three hypothetical schools that are identical with respect to measures of central tendency, but that differ greatly in variability.

than in school A; school B has more bright *and* more dull students than school A. School C is quite heterogeneous; the scores indicate greater individual differences than in schools A or B. Which school has the largest percentage of gifted children (i.e., IQ ≥ 130)? Which has the most low-scoring children? It should be apparent from Figure 4.1 that school C is the answer to both questions. Individual differences are least in school A, and greatest in school C. The point to underscore is that measures of central tendency *and* measures of variability are needed to describe important characteristics of distributions. For example, Oklahoma City and San Francisco both have annual mean temperatures of 57°F, but what about January or July?

Quiz: Which school in Figure 4.1 would have the greatest need for teachers who are skilled in working with students who have exceptional abilities and needs?

Answer: School C since it has more low-scoring and more high-scoring pupils.

❖ 4.2 ASSESSING VARIABILITY

In Figure 4.1, the differences in the spread of scores are obvious. But how is the degree of heterogeneity in a distribution described? Expressed descriptions such as "very much," "considerable," and "little" are verbal attempts to communicate variability, but are subjectively interpreted and, therefore, somewhat lacking in precision. Statistical indices are needed that objectively quantify the degree of variability in the distribution. Such measures have been developed and are available for your research needs.

❖ 4.3 DEVIATION SCORES

For variability, the differences between the mean and each score are considered. These differences from the mean are referred to as *deviation* scores and are symbolized by lower-case letters: x when considering one variable (and x and y when considering two variables as in Chapter 7). For population data, the general formula for a deviation score is presented as Equation 4.1:

$$x = X - \mu \qquad \qquad (4.1)$$

Quiz: Given a very small population comprised of only $N = 3$ scores, X: 5, 9, 4.
(a) $\mu = $ __?__ , (b) $x_1 = $ __?__ , $x_2 = $ __?__ , $x_3 = $ __?__
Answers: (a) 6, (b) –1, 3, –2

As you can deduce from Equation 4.1, raw scores above the mean have positive deviation scores, and raw scores below the mean have negative deviation scores. Typically, roughly half of the deviation scores are positive and half are negative, and their sum is always zero. Whether the distribution is markedly heterogeneous or markedly homogeneous, the sum of its deviation scores from the mean is zero. This is true for all distributions of all different shapes and of all sizes, that is, $\Sigma x = 0$. Obviously, Σx cannot be used to reflect variability.

❖ 4.4 SUM OF SQUARES

What if each deviation score is squared (i.e., multiplied by itself)? You may recall that any number, positive or negative, when multiplied by itself, is a positive product; therefore, the sum of all the squared deviation scores in a distribution (Σx^2) is a positive number. Σx^2, the sum of squares (*SS*), can never be negative. This sum of squares can be interpreted as one way of quantifying the totality of variability in a set of scores. If two groups of the same size take the same test, the group with the greater *SS* has the greater variability, that is, it is more heterogeneous and is characterized by greater individual differences. The sum of squares is used in several statistical procedures in subsequent chapters. The definitional formula for the sum of squares can be expressed as:

$$\text{Sum of Squares} = SS = \Sigma x^2 = \Sigma(X - \mu)^2 \qquad \textbf{(4.2)}$$

Since the value of the sum of squares is strongly affected by the number of observations in the data set, it is not a useful measure of variability.

Quiz: (1) Given a population of $N = 3$, with the following *deviation* scores, x: -1, 3, -2, find the sum of squares, and express this result using a mathematical expression. Thor computed $SS = -239$ for his data; what do you know for certain?

Answers: (1) $\Sigma x^2 = 1 + 9 + 4 = 14$. (2) Thor made an unforgivable error—SS cannot be a negative number since it sums the *squares* of the deviation scores, and squared scores are always positive.

❖ 4.5 THE POPULATION VARIANCE

The purpose of a measure of variability is to quantify the extent of variation among the set of scores of a distribution. We used one measure of variability, the range, in Chapter 2; recall that the range considers only one difference—the difference between X_{min} and X_{max}. The variance is a more refined measure of dispersion than the range.

When all N observations in the population are included in the data set, the variance, σ^2, is found by dividing the sum of squares by N, as defined by Equation 4.3.

$$\sigma^2 = \frac{\Sigma(X - \mu)^2}{N} = \frac{\Sigma x^2}{N} = \frac{\text{sum of squares}}{N} = \frac{SS}{N} \qquad \textbf{(4.3)}$$

where $\Sigma(X - \mu)^2 = (X_1 - \mu)^2 + (X_2 - \mu)^2 + \ldots + (X_N - \mu)^2$. Equation 4.3 defines the population variance, σ^2, as the sum of the squared deviations divided by the total number of observations, so σ^2 is the average squared deviation. Note that, like the mean, the variance is influenced by the numerical value of every score in the distribution. The variance of a population of scores can be computed as indicated below:

To compute σ^2 for a population of scores:

Step 1.   Find the deviation of each score from the mean: Equation 4.1: $x = X - \mu$.

Step 2.   Square each deviation score: $x^2 = (x)(x)$.

Step 3.   Add all x^2's to find the sum of squares: $SS = \Sigma x^2$.

Step 4.   Find the variance by dividing SS by N: $\sigma^2 = SS/N$.

❖ 4.6 AN EXAMPLE

Assume that we have a shockingly small population consisting of only $N = 3$ persons whose heights are measured as: $X_1 = 61$ inches, $X_2 = 63$ inches, and $X_3 = 71$ inches. To find the variance, we must first find the value of μ: $= \Sigma X/N = (61 + 63 + 71)/3 = 65$.

Step 1. $x_1 = (61 - 65) = -4; x_2 = (63 - 65) = -2; x_3 = (71 - 65) = 6.$

Step 2. $x_1^2 = 16; x_2^2 = 4; x_3^2 = 36.$

Step 3. $16 + 4 + 36 = 56 = $ sum of squares or SS.

Step 4. $\sigma^2 = SS/N = 56/3 = 18.67.$

Now we know that σ^2 is 18.67, that is, the average squared deviation score is 18.67 square inches. The variance, like the sum of squares, does not have much direct descriptive meaning. If your instructor were to inform your class that the class variance for exam 1 was 275 square percentage points, it is not likely that the class would glow with illumination. One problem with the variance is that it is expressed in *squared* units rather than the original units. However, it is a measure of variability of a set of scores and can be used to compare the relative heterogeneity among samples. If your instructor reported that, on the math review test given on the first day of class, the mean and variance were 72 and 275, respectively, but last year's class on the same exam had a mean and variance of 72 and 125, respectively, there are interesting implications for the design of instruction. Your instructor would have a greater challenge this year—meeting the needs of the slow starters while maintaining the interest of the math whizzes.

The average squared deviation score, the variance, is also more descriptively called the "mean square," and this is the terminology that will be used repeatedly in Chapters 14–16 as well as in more advanced statistics courses. As budding statisticians, you will want to add "mean square" to your statistical vocabulary.

Quiz: Suppose that the same spelling test was given to three different classes and that the three class variances were computed to be: $\sigma_1^2 = 100$, $\sigma_2^2 = 0$, $\sigma_3^2 = 400$. (1) Individual differences were greatest in which class? (2) Is it mathematically possible for $\sigma_2^2 = 0$ in class 2?

Answers: (1) Class 3, (2) Yes, if all students get the same score (e.g., 100%), all deviation scores are zero.

❖ 4.7 THE STANDARD DEVIATION OF A POPULATION

The standard deviation (σ) is simply the square root[1] of the variance. The standard deviation (Eq. 4.4) returns the metric to that of the original scores, thus it has more direct descriptive value.

$$\sigma = \sqrt{\sigma^2} = \sqrt{\frac{SS}{N}} \qquad \textbf{(4.4)}$$

The variance of the three observations of height (61″, 63″, 71″) in Section 4.6 was found to be 18.67 square inches. Therefore, the standard deviation of height for that popu-

---

[1]Math Note 12 reviews the meaning of square roots, not the calculation. Your hand calculators give the square root of a number quickly and accurately. The square root of a number ($\sqrt{n}$) is that positive number that multiplied by itself equals the original number. Since $(3)(3) = 9$, $(\sqrt{9}) = 3$.

lation of three observations is the square root of 18.67 or 4.32 inches. (Be grateful for your calculator—in the old days we had to do the barbarous square root computations by hand while walking miles to school in the snow.) The standard deviation is more useful for *describing* the variability of a data set than is the variance (although the variance has properties that are superior for use in inferential statistics). The standard deviation carries the same units as the original scores. Approximately two-thirds of the scores are expected to be within one (+ or −) standard deviation from the mean. For normal distributions, about one-third of the scores deviate more than one σ from μ. Chapter 5 gives several interesting applications of μ and σ!

> **Quiz:** In Chapter 5, we will see that there are important reasons for transforming raw scores into "standard" scores; this involves adding, subtracting, multiplying, or dividing the original scores by constants. (1) In the population of observations, 61, 63, and 71, if the constant of 100 is added to each observation, the transformed values would be 161, 163, and 171. Compute the mean, SS, variance, and standard deviation of this population of transformed values. (2) If each original observation is multiplied by 2, the transformed observations would be 122, 126, and 142. Compute the mean, SS, variance, and standard deviation of this transformed distribution. (3) Study your results and express a generalization about adding or multiplying by a constant k and its effect upon the mean and standard deviation.
>
> **Answers:** (1) $\mu = 165$, $SS = 56$, $\sigma^2 \approx 18.67$,[2] $\sigma \approx 4.32$, (2) $\mu = 130$, $SS = 224$, $\sigma^2 \approx 74.67$, $\sigma \approx 8.64$, (3) By adding a constant, k, to each score, the mean will increase by k, but the standard deviation is unaffected. By multiplying by a constant, k, the mean and standard deviation of the transformed values will be k multiplied by the original values of μ and σ.
>
> (If a constant, k, is subtracted from each observation, the mean is decreased by k, but the measures of variability are unaffected. If each score is divided by a constant, k, both the mean and the standard deviation are divided by k, and the variance and SS are divided by k^2.)

❖ 4.8 PARAMETERS VERSUS STATISTICS

The distinction between population parameters and sample statistics (i.e., estimates of population parameters) will become increasingly important in subsequent chapters. One of the first tasks of the researcher is to define a population of interest, for example, all third graders in a school district, all Hispanic principals in California, et cetera. The entire set of persons or things that the researcher wishes to describe is the population of interest. Recall that we use the symbol, N, to denote the total number of persons, elements, or observational units in the researcher's population. If the researcher has data for each of the N units in the population, the entire population has been included, and the statistical measures that are computed are called parameters for that population. Lower-case Greek letters are used as symbols for parameters (e.g., μ represents the population mean, and σ represents the population standard deviation). Sample statistics are denoted by corresponding Roman letters (e.g., s stands for the sample standard deviation). For example, if *all N* observations in the population are used in the computation of the mean, the mean is designated by μ (not $\overline{X}$).

---

[1] Symbol definition: The symbol "$\approx$" stands for "approximately equal to."

Quiz: (1) What term denotes the entire set of persons that meet the conditions and descriptions stated by the researcher? (2) Quantified attributes of a researcher's *sample* group are called what?

Answers: (1) population (2) statistics (or estimates of parameters)

❖ 4.9 SAMPLING ERROR AND THE SAMPLE VARIANCE

Data sets usually do not contain all the observations in the population. Equations 4.3 and 4.4 are appropriate only when we are working with the entire population of observations. If one has IQ scores from a random sample of 80 persons from the general population, the mean of the 80 observations is symbolized by $\overline{X}$, not μ. Obviously, we do not expect the values of $\overline{X}$ and μ to be exactly the same; there is going to be some *sampling error* (chance differences) associated with the selection of the sample of persons that will cause the value for the sample mean, $\overline{X}$, to differ to some extent from that of the population mean, $\mu = 100$. Would you be surprised if $\overline{X}$ was 98 or 101, rather than 100? Probably not, since 98 and 101 are in the ballpark of 100. Would you be surprised if $\overline{X}$ were 80 or 125? Probably so (unless the sample is ridiculously small), since 80 and 125 differ greatly from the parameter of 100. Intuitively, we know that sample statistics will differ somewhat from their corresponding parameters. Statisticians (and embryonic statisticians) call this type of difference *sampling error*.

$$\text{Sampling error} = \text{the Statistic} - \text{the Parameter} \qquad \textbf{(4.5)}$$

Since $\overline{X}$ is expected to differ a bit from μ, would the difference $(X - \overline{X})$ equal the difference $(X - \mu)$ for each X? Obviously not. Consequently, the sum of squares, SS, based on $(X - \overline{X})$ will differ from the sum of squares based on $(X - \mu)$. Therefore, Equation 4.3 ($\sigma^2 = SS/N$) would give a slightly different answer for variance if differing values of SS were used.

In Chapter 3, we saw that the mean satisfies the least-squares criterion—that the sum of squares for any set of scores is least when deviating about its own $\overline{X}$ than deviating from any other point. Hence, the sample SS from $\overline{X}$ will be less than the sum of the squares from μ (except in the rare event when $\overline{X} = \mu$). When μ is unknown, the use of the estimate, $\overline{X}$, rather than μ to compute the sum of squares, SS, results in a value for the sum of squares that is too small, and Equation 4.3 would give a biased underestimate of the population variance. Thankfully, the mathematical statisticians have solved this difficulty for us—they have proved, amazingly enough, that the bias in SS resulting from the use of $\overline{X}$ rather than μ, is precisely compensated for by replacing the denominator n by $(n - 1)$ (see Eq. 4.6)! Using the divisor $(n - 1)$ results in an unbiased estimate of the population variance from the random sample of n observations; $n - 1$ has the nonintuitive name of *degrees of freedom*, and is represented by ν (the Greek letter pronounced as "new," that corresponds to our letter n). You will encounter the expressions "degrees of freedom" and "ν" throughout the book; think of degrees of freedom as sample size, adjusted to compensate for bias. The sample variance, s^2, defined by Equation 4.6, is an unbiased *inferential statistic*; it is the unbiased estimate of σ^2:

$$s^2 = \frac{\Sigma(X - \overline{X})^2}{n-1} = \frac{\Sigma x^2}{n-1} = \frac{\Sigma x^2}{\nu} = \frac{SS}{\nu} \qquad \textbf{(4.6)}$$

The sample variance, s^2, has a property that is very important in statistical inference—the statistic s^2 is an *unbiased* estimate of the parameter σ^2. An unbiased estimate is one in which the overestimates and underestimates tend to balance out in the long run.

> **Quiz:** (1) If the value of SS is obtained by using μ as the point of reference and we divide SS by N, the result is the variance of the __?__, symbolized by __?__. (2) When the value of SS is obtained by deviating the scores from $\overline{X}$ and this sum of squares is divided by $(n-1)$, the result is an unbiased estimate of σ^2, symbolized by __?__. (3) What is the name and symbol for $(n-1)$?
> **Answers:** (1) population, σ^2, (2) s^2, (3) degrees of freedom, ν

The sample standard deviation is simply the square root of the sample variance, as "explicified" in Equation 4.7:

$$s = \sqrt{s^2} = \sqrt{\frac{SS}{\nu}} \qquad \textbf{(4.7)}$$

❖ 4.10 EXPECTED VALUES

If a statistic is unbiased, its "expected value" is equal to the parameter it estimates. The expected value of a sample statistic is its mean value "in the long run." Statisticians have esoteric ways of describing the meaning of "in the long run," but it is the same concept as "in the long run, 50% of the tosses of a fair coin will be heads" and "in the long run, one-sixth of the tosses of a pair of dice will yield a seven." Unbiased means that there is no systematic tendency for the statistic to be either larger than or smaller than its corresponding parameter:

$$E(\text{unbiased statistic}) = \text{parameter} \qquad \textbf{(4.8)}$$

Equation 4.8 states that, in the long run, the mean value of an unbiased statistic (i.e., its expected value) is the parameter it estimates. Another way of saying this is that, in the long run, the algebraic sum of the sampling errors for that statistic is zero. The sample variance, s^2, is just as likely to be greater than σ^2 as it is to be less than σ^2. Equation 4.9 indicates that the expected value of the sample variance is equal to the variance in the population; that is, s^2 is an unbiased estimator of σ^2:

$$E(s^2) = \sigma^2 \qquad \textbf{(4.9)}$$

It is also true that $E(\overline{X}) = \mu$ and that $\overline{X}$ is an unbiased estimator of μ. Other things being equal, unbiased statistics are preferred over those that are biased.

❖ 4.11 THE SAMPLE STANDARD DEVIATION, s, AS AN ESTIMATE OF THE PARAMETER, σ

It may intuitively appear that if $E(s^2) = \sigma^2$, then s should also be an unbiased estimate of σ. This is not the case—a square root of an unbiased statistic is not an unbiased estimate of the

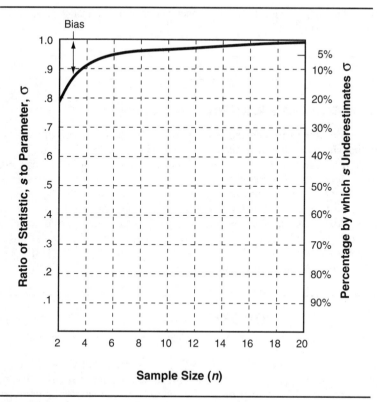

Bias

Ratio of Statistic, *s* to Parameter, σ

Percentage by which *s* Underestimates σ

Sample Size (*n*)

❖ **FIGURE 4.2** The amount of bias in *s* in estimating σ as a function of sample size *n*.

square root of the parameter, for example, $E(s) \neq \sigma$. Fortunately, the error that results by using *s* as an estimate of σ is negligible unless *n* is small. Figure 4.2 illustrates that the bias in *s* decreases as sample size increases.

Notice that *s* tends to underestimate σ, but that the bias is small—only about 5% [i.e., $E(s) = .95\sigma$] when $n = 6$, and only about 1% [i.e., $E(s) = .99\sigma$] when $n = 20$. Since published research usually involves *n*'s larger than 20, the degree to which *s* underestimates σ is usually of little consequence.

Quiz: (1) Are s^2 statistics from larger samples better estimates (i.e., have less sampling error) of σ^2 parameters than s^2 statistics from smaller samples? (2) Are s^2 statistics computed from larger samples less *biased* than s^2 statistics from smaller samples?

Answers: (1) Yes, the sample variances based on larger samples tend to have smaller sampling errors—that is, they are expected to differ less from σ^2. (2) No, the sample variance is unbiased for all samples sizes.

❖ 4.12 RANGE

In Chapter 2, the *range* was used in determining the size of the interval to be used in constructing grouped frequency distributions. The range is easy to understand—the simplest measure of variability. The range is simply the difference between the largest (X_{max}) and the smallest (X_{min}) observations (Eq. 4.10):

$$range = X_{max} - X_{min} \qquad \textbf{(4.10)}$$

❖ 4.13 THE H-SPREAD AND THE INTERQUARTILE RANGE

Although not as important as the variance and standard deviation, there are two other measures of variability that should be in our statistical vocabulary, the *interquartile range* and the *semi-interquartile range*. In Section 2.16, the quartiles of a distribution of scores were defined. The first quartile, Q_1, is the point on the scale below which 25% of the scores lie—it is the 25th percentile. Q_2 is equivalent to the median or the 50th percentile. The point below which 75% of the scores lie defines Q_3. The difference (interquartile range) between the first and third quartiles of a group of scores, that is, $Q_3 - Q_1$, is the interquartile range. A synonym for $Q_3 - Q_1$ is H-spread (Tukey, 1977), the difference between Q_1 (Tukey's "lower hinge") and Q_3 (Tukey's "upper hinge"). The *semi-interquartile range*, Q, is one-half the distance between the third and first quartiles, that is:

$$Q = \frac{Q_3 - Q_1}{2} \qquad \textbf{(4.11)}$$

Q can be a useful descriptive measure of variability. If two groups of scores have the same value of Q, they are likely to possess similar patterns of heterogeneity. In distributions that are not severely skewed, $Md \pm Q$ can be used to reconstruct the approximate score limits within which the middle-most fifty percent of the scores fall. In Section 5.12 we will see that in a normal distribution $Q = .674\sigma$, or σ equals $1.5Q$; in other words, when a distribution is approximately normal one can estimate σ from Q, or vice versa.

Quiz: In the population of normally distributed IQ scores, $\sigma = 15$. Estimate the 25th and 75th percentiles in this distribution.

Answers: $Q_1 = P_{25} = 90$, and $Q_3 = P_{75} = 110$. (Q is about 10—two-thirds of σ.)

❖ 4.14 THE INFLUENCE OF SAMPLE SIZE ON THE RANGE

A major shortcoming of the range as an *inferential statistic* is that its value is greatly affected by sample size. The range is determined by only two atypical (the largest and smallest) observations, and as the sample size is increased, the range tends to increase. This is not the case with s^2; the expression $E(s^2) = \sigma^2$ does not depend on n; it is true regardless of sample size.

Table 4.1 shows the influence of sample size on the expected value of the sample range. The comparisons of the range with the variance and the standard deviation are given. The IQ scale is used as an example to illustrate the trends and relative magnitudes of these measures of variability. Table 4.1 gives the range, s^2, and s in IQ scores that are expected in random samples from the population ($\mu = 100$, $\sigma = 15$) for selected sample sizes ranging from 2 to 1,000. Note that the expected value of the range varies markedly with sample size,

❖ **TABLE 4.1** The effect of sample size on the expected value of the range, variance, and standard deviation.

		IN IQ UNITS $(\mu = 100, \sigma = 15)$		
n	*Range/σ*	*Expected Value of the Range*	*Expected Value of s^{2*}*	*Expected Value of $s^{\dagger}$*
2	1.1	17	225	12
5	2.3	35	225	14.1
10	3.1	46	225	14.6
20	3.7	56	225	14.8
50	4.5	68	225	14.92
100	5.0	75	225	14.96
200	5.5	83	225	14.98
500	6.1	92	225	14.99
1,000	6.5	98	225	14.996

*i.e., $E(s^2)$

†i.e., $E(s)$

while the expected value of the sample variance remains constant for all values of *n* since it is an unbiased estimator. The expected value of the sample standard deviation rapidly approaches the parameter, σ, as *n* increases—there is little bias in *s* unless *n* is very small. Notice that with a random sample of $n = 20$, the expected value of the range (56) is 3.7 times the value of σ (15); but with a sample of $n = 100$, the expected value of the range increases to 75, or 5 times σ. The range has very limited value as an inferential statistic because its value is so dependent on sample size. The range is, however, useful as a descriptive statistic, and should be considered a complement to, not a substitute for, s^2 and *s*.

Like the range, the interquartile range and *Q* have limited value as inferential statistics.

❖ 4.15 RELIABILITY AND CONSISTENCY OF ESTIMATORS

Reliability in statistics represents the stability and consistency of the statistic as an estimate of the corresponding population parameter. The mean is more reliable than the median or the mode; this indicates that sample means from the same population are more alike (have less variability) than are sample medians or sample modes. Similarly, the sample variances (and standard deviations) are more reliable and stable than are sample ranges and interquartile ranges.

The fact that a statistic is unbiased [e.g., $E(s^2) = \sigma^2$] for every value of *n* does not imply that the statistic based on 10 observations will be as *accurate* as an estimate based on 100 observations. With all statistical measures, as *n* increases, the sampling error decreases and the estimate is expected to approach the parameter in numerical value. This characteristic, that a statistic approaches the parameter as *n* increases, is called *consistency*.

All applied statistics have the consistency property, but not all are unbiased—and of those that are unbiased, not all are equally efficient. *Efficiency* pertains to the amount of sampling error expected in a given statistical measure—more efficient indices tend to have less sampling error, that is, give estimates closer in value to their corresponding parameters. Statisticians' preference for certain inferential statistics over others is based on unbiasedness and reliability since all are consistent, for example, the mean is preferred over the median and the mode for inferential purposes because it is more reliable (or efficient).

❖ CHAPTER SUMMARY

Measures of variability are needed to quantify the degree of dispersion in a distribution. The variance, standard deviation, and range are common measures of variability. If a distribution contains all of the observations in the population, the statistical measures are parameters. The variance and standard deviation for the population are symbolized by σ^2 and σ, respectively. If the distribution contains only a sample of observations from the population, the statistical measures are called statistics (or inferential statistics). Estimates of the population variance and standard deviation are symbolized by s^2 and s, respectively. The difference between a statistic and the relevant parameter is *sampling error*.

Statistical measures are evaluated in terms of reliability, consistency, and unbiasedness. Consistency means that the sampling error in a statistic decreases as n increases—all statistical measures are consistent. Reliability is the extent to which sample estimates of a parameter tend to have less sampling error. More reliable statistics have relatively less sampling error for competing statistical indices—the mean is preferred to the other measures of central tendency because in the long run it has less sampling error for any value of n; it is more reliable and efficient. Unbiased statistics are those for which the expected value of the statistic equals the parameter, regardless of n. The expression, $E(s^2) = \sigma^2$, states that the variance of a sample is an unbiased estimate of the population variance. The sample standard deviation, s, is slightly biased—it tends to underestimate the parameter σ although the degree of bias is negligible unless n is quite small. The range can be meaningful as a descriptive statistic, but has limited use in inferential statistics because it is greatly influenced by n, the larger the n, the larger the range.

MASTERY TEST

1. Complete the analogy: _____ is to a sample as parameter is to _____.

Answer questions 2–10 with one of the following measures of variability:

               (a) range   (b) standard deviation   (c) variance

When obtained for a random sample of observations:

2. Which is completely unbiased?
3. Which contains the most bias?
4. Which is least reliable (stable)?
5. Which is greatly influenced by sample size?
6. Which contains bias that is negligible if n is 20 or more?
7. Which is easiest to calculate?
8. Which has the same expected value regardless of sample size?
9. Do all have the property of consistency?
10. Which is not expressed in the same units as the original observations?
11. If all scores are not equal, is the range always larger than the variance and standard deviation?
12. To obtain the sample variance, will the sum of squares be divided by the sample size, n, or by the degrees of freedom, $v = n - 1$?

13. Which symbol represents the sample estimate of variance?
14. Which symbol represents the population standard deviation?
15. Which symbol represents the size of the sample?
16. Which symbol represents the mean of the population?
17. If the variance is found to be 100, what is the standard deviation?
18. Using Table 4.1, and assuming that a sample of 100 observations is randomly drawn from a population with $\sigma = 10$, estimate the range.
19. In question 18, which has the larger value, the range or the variance?

Which measure of central tendency would:

20. be most appropriate for nominal data?
21. fit best with the term "middle score"?
22. be sensitive to the numerical value of each score?
23. vary least from sample to sample?
24. be expected to be least in a negatively skewed distribution?

The same spelling test was given to a random sample of students from three different schools and the results for each school, when charted, approximated a bell-shaped curve. The summary results were as follows:

	School A	*School B*	*School C*
$\bar{X}$:	40	50	50
s:	5	10	20
n:	10	100	50

Which school would seem to:

25. be most homogeneous?
26. have more students scoring above 75?
27. have the greatest range?
28. have the lowest average spelling score?
29. Which of the school $\bar{X}$'s probably comes closest to its corresponding μ?
30. Find s^2 for (a) School A; (b) School B;(c) School C.
31. Rearrange Equation 4.6 and compute SS for School A.
32. If all three schools were pooled together, find the grand mean (Eq. 3.3).

ANSWERS TO MASTERY TEST

1. statistic, population
2. variance
3. range
4. range
5. range (see Table 4.1)
6. standard deviation
7. range
8. variance
9. yes
10. variance
11. range $> \sigma$, but range not always $> \sigma^2$
12. $n - 1$
13. s^2
14. σ
15. n
16. μ
17. 10
18. $5(10) = 50$

19. variance, 100 vs. 50
20. mode
21. median
22. mean
23. mean
24. mean
25. A

26. C
27. C
28. A
29. B
30. 25, 100, 400
31. $9(25) = 225$
32. 49.375

PROBLEMS AND EXERCISES

1. A random sample of six honor students was selected and given a memory span test. These data are listed below. For these data, compute the (a) median, (b) mode, (c) range, (d) degrees of freedom, (e) mean, (f) sum of squares ($SS = \Sigma x^2$), (g) sample variance, and (h) sample standard deviation.

X	x	x^2
6	—	—
9	—	—
5	—	—
4	—	—
7	—	—
5	—	—

$\Sigma X =$ ___

2. A random sample of 10 first-semester Typing IA students were given a 5-minute typing test at the semester's end. The WPM score for each was determined, and the scores are presented below. For these data, find the (a) median, (b) mode, (c) range, (d) degrees of freedom, (e) mean, (f) sum of squares, (g) sample variance, and (h) sample standard deviation.

X: 22, 21, 29, 22, 27, 25, 25, 25, 30, 24

3. Calculate (a) $\overline{X}$, (b) SS, (c) s^2, and (d) s for the following data.

			Pupils			
X: 5	2	8	5	4	3	8

4. For the following data, compute (a) $\overline{X}$, (b) SS, (c) s^2, and (d) s.

		Respondent		
X: 6	2	7	1	4

5. For the following data, compute (a) $\overline{X}$, (b) SS, (c) s^2, and (d) s.

			Observers				
X: 8	3	6	1	4	2	5	3

Exercises 6–9. Occasionally, summary statistics like n, $\overline{X}$, and s are given, but the researcher needs to work the formulas "backwards" to determine ΣX and SS. For each of the following exercises, work backwards to find both ΣX and SS.

6. $\overline{X} = 25$, $s = 10$, $n = 11$.
7. $\overline{X} = 82.4$, $s = 8$, $n = 10$.
8. $\overline{X} = 110.5$, $s = 20$, $n = 40$.
9. $\overline{X} = 28.4$, $s = 3$, $n = 41$.

The following information applies to problems 10–15. Each student in a 6th-grade class was asked to list his or her best friend (anonymously). The scores of a representative sample of eleven students is given below. The scores indicate the number of times each of the eleven students was listed as "best friend" by a classmate.

$$1, \quad 0, \quad 2, \quad 1, \quad 0, \quad 0, \quad 1, \quad 0, \quad 2, \quad 4, \quad 0$$

10. Calculate the range.
11. Compute $\overline{X}$.
12. Calculate the sum of squares using deviation scores.
13. Calculate *SS* using an alternate formula: $(SS = \Sigma X^2 - n\,\overline{X}^2)$.
14. Calculate s^2 and s.
15. If 10 points were added to each score, indicate whether the value of each of the following would change:
    (a) $\overline{X}$ (b) range (c) s^2 (d) s
16. With respect to sampling error, what is the essential difference between parameter and statistic?
17. What is the essential difference between sample and population?
18. What is the essential difference between n and N?
19. Find $\overline{X}$, SS, s^2, s and the range for the following grade-placement scores from a standardized reading test.
    $$6.8, \quad 6.7, \quad 6.5, \quad 6.4, \quad 6.4, \quad 6.3, \quad 6.1, \quad 6.0$$
20. Why do basketball teams from large high schools tend to be taller than teams from small high schools?

Test data from the HSB data set were processed by a computer software program and the output is displayed below (N = 200).

Variable	Mean	s	s^2	Range
Reading *T*-score	52.23	10.25	105.12	48.00
Writing *T*-score	52.78	9.48	89.84	36.00
Math *T*-score	52.64	9.37	87.77	42.00
Science *T*-score	51.85	9.90	98.03	48.00
Civics *T*-score	52.40	10.74	115.26	45.00

21. If a constant of 100 is added to each of the reading scores, what would be the mean, standard deviation, and variance of the revised distribution?
22. Find the sum of scores (ΣX) for the civics data.
23. Hassan's *deviation* score for his science *T*-score was 6.65. (a) What was his science score? (b) Estimate his percentile rank in the distribution of science scores.
24. Do you like big numbers? Using Equation 4.6, work backwards to find *SS* for the reading data.
25. Actually the HSB data set is a sample for a much larger set of data in which all five tests were transformed so that the mean of each was 50, and the variance was 100. The mean of which of the five tests has the least sampling error? If you compared the five ranges in the HSB data set with the corresponding ranges in the entire data set, what would you expect to find?

ANSWERS TO PROBLEMS AND EXERCISES

1. (a) $Md = 5.5$, (b) $Mo = 5$, (c) range = 5,
   (d) $V = 5$, (e) $\overline{X} = 6$, (f) $SS = 16$,
   (g) $s^2 = 3.2$, (h) $s = 1.79$
2. (a) $Md = 25$, (b) $Mo = 25$, (c) range = 9,
   (d) $V = 9$ (e) $\overline{X} = 25$, (f) $SS = 80$,
   (g) $s^2 = 8.89$, (h) $s = 2.98$
3. (a) $\overline{X} = 5$, (b) $SS = 32$, (c) $s^2 = 5.33$,
   (d) $s = 2.31$
4. (a) $\overline{X} = 4$, (b) $SS = 26$, (c) $s^2 = 6.5$,
   (d) $s = 2.55$
5. (a) $\overline{X} = 4$, (b) $SS = 36$, (c) $s^2 = 5.14$,
   (d) $s = 2.27$
6. $\Sigma X = 275$, $SS = 1,000$
7. $\Sigma X = 824$, $SS = 576$
8. $\Sigma X = 4,420$, $SS = 15,600$
9. $\Sigma X = 1164.4$, $SS = 360$
10. Range = $4 - 0 = 4$
11. $\overline{X} = X/n = 11/11 = 1.0$
12. $SS = 16$
13. $SS = 27 - 11(1.0)^2 = 16.0$
14. $s^2 = 1.60$, $s = 1.2649$ or 1.26
15. (a) $\overline{X}$ would increase by 10; (b) unchanged,
    (c) unchanged, (d) unchanged

16. Parameters are error-free; inferential statistics contain sampling errors.
17. A sample is selected from the larger population. A sample is to the population as a part is to the whole.
18. N and n are the number of observations in a population and a sample, respectively.
19. Range = $6.8 - 6.0 = .8$, $\overline{X} = 6.4$, $SS = .52$,
    $\sigma^2 = .52/7 = .0743$, $\sigma = \sqrt{.07428} = .273$
20. The range is a function of sample size. On the average then, small high schools will have very tall students much less frequently (see Table 4.1).
21. $\overline{X} = 152.23$; s and s^2 are unchanged.
22. $200(52.4) = 10,480$
23. (a) 58.5, (b) Hassan is about two-thirds of a standard deviation above the mean; hence, he is expected to be near the 75th percentile.
24. $SS = s^2(n - 1) = 105.12(199) = 20,918.88$
25. Science. The ranges in the HSB data set would all be expected to be smaller than in the entire data set.

 ## SUGGESTED COMPUTER EXERCISE

For the reading, writing, and math tests in the HSB data set:

(a) find the standard deviation, variance, range, and Q_1 and Q_3 for each.

(b) compute the semi-interquartile range, $Q = (Q_3 - Q_1)/2$, and

(c) find the ratio of the standard deviation to Q, s/Q, for each variable. Does $s/Q \approx 1.5$?

5

The Normal Distribution and Standard Scores

❖ 5.1 INTRODUCTION

The normal distribution[1] is a critical concept in statistics. It is used in all but the introductory chapter of this book. In this chapter, we will become more familiar with the normal curve and use it to describe and evaluate the performance of individuals and groups. Even more fundamentally important applications of the normal curve in inferential statistics will become evident in subsequent chapters.

The normal distribution is approximated by many empirical distributions. It is the most important distribution in statistics. The study of the normal distribution dates back at least to the eighteenth century. It was observed, for example, that if an object was weighed repeatedly, the observed weights were not identical; there was some variation among the measurements. If enough measurements were taken, the distribution of the observations displayed a regular pattern; a pattern now recognized to be the normal distribution. Errors of observation of many kinds were found to follow this same pattern; in fact, the distribution was initially referred to as the "normal curve of errors." It was soon discovered that many observations other than measurement error are normally distributed. If ten fair coins are flipped randomly, the number of heads recorded, and the procedure repeated many, many times, the distribution in Figure 5.1 will result.

Note that the expected value for the number of heads (the mean of the theoretical distribution shown in Figure 5.1) is 5. In normal distributions, the mean is also the mode and occurs more frequently than any other value. Figure 5.1 shows that almost 25 percent of the sets of ten tosses result in 5 heads. However, for 75 percent of the sets of ten flips, the number of heads is not 5 but deviates systematically from 5, for example, 4 and 6 heads

---

[1]The term normal distribution is often used as synonymous with normal curve, normal probability curve, or the Gaussian curve. Bell-shaped curve and bell curve are also used to signify a normal distribution, but many bell-shaped curves are not true normal distributions. We will use the terms normal curve and normal distribution interchangeably.

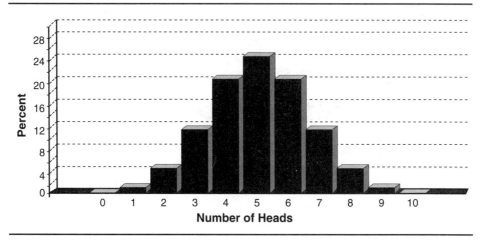

❖ **FIGURE 5.1** The binomial distribution of the number of heads observed when ten fair coins are tossed an infinite number of times.

were each observed in 20 percent of the sets. The distribution is approximately normal, but note that it does not result from errors of measurement but from the "laws of chance."

❖ 5.2 DISCRETE AND CONTINUOUS MEASURES

No real set of actual data is ever perfectly described by the normal curve—every sample of data contains some sampling error. For example, the empirical distribution for the coin-tossing illustration will approximate the distribution in Figure 5.1 if ten fair coins are tossed 1,000 times;[2] an even closer approximation will occur if the distribution is based on 1,000,000 tosses. In addition, the distribution in Figure 5.1 has gaps—there are no points between 4 and 5, between 5 and 6, et cetera. This type of distribution represents a *discrete* measure—the "scores" change by jumps. The true normal distribution is *continuous*—any fractional value is possible. Height, weight, time, and temperature are continuous variables, whereas number of siblings, credit hours acquired, and number of correct answers on a test represent discrete variables. The normal curve can be used as a model to represent discrete measures with negligible error if the range of "scores" is fairly large. If a distribution like the one in Figure 5.2 were constructed on the number of heads observed when 100 fair coins (rather than ten) are randomly tossed many, many times, the normal curve would be sliced into 101 strips (rather than the eleven in Fig. 5.1) and the resulting gaps would be rather small.

> **Quiz:** Use Figure 5.1 to answer these questions. If you were to put ten coins into a container, shake the box, and empty the coins on a table, what is the probability that you will get: (1) exactly 7 heads, (2) get 7 or 8 heads, (3) 7 or more heads, and (4) 3 or fewer heads?
>
> **Answers:** (1) approximately .12, (2) approximately .16 (.12 + .04) (3) approximately .17, (4) approximately .17

---

[2]The binomial distribution is used to construct Figure 5.1 (see Glass & Hopkins, 1996, Section 9.10).

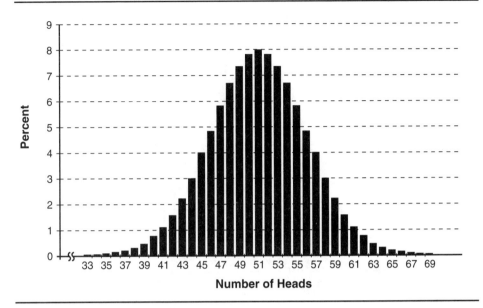

❖ **FIGURE 5.2** The binomial distribution of the number of heads observed when 100 fair coins are tossed an infinite number of times.

❖ 5.3 GOD LOVES THE NORMAL CURVE

Late in the nineteenth century, the Englishman Francis Galton took systematic measurements of a number of physical, psychological, and psychomotor variables on large numbers of persons. Figure 5.3 illustrates his findings using the heights of 8,585 adult men born in Great Britain. Galton observed that this distribution and many others were very close approximations to the normal distribution.

The measurement of many variables in all disciplines have distributions that are good approximations of the normal distribution: kernels per ear of corn, weight of trout at one year of age, leaf thickness for a given variety of plants, the distribution of daily high temperatures on July 4 in Boulder, Colorado for the past 100 years, your reaction time plotted by several days in succession, size of hands, et cetera. Stated differently, "God loves the normal curve!" Even though no set of empirical data is ever perfectly described by the normal distribution, the fit is often extremely close to the theoretical normal curve, especially if the number of observations is large. Even for variables that are perfectly normally distributed, the distributions of sample data are never perfectly normally distributed because of measurement imperfections and sampling error.

In Chapter 9, Panel A of Figure 9.2 gives a perfectly normal theoretical distribution of IQ scores (within the limits imposed by the discrete nature of IQ scores), and Panel B gives the distribution of a random sample of 10,000 scores. Notice that even with a very large sample, there are some trivial discrepancies. Although the curve is straining to become normal—yearning for perfection, it still has some ragged edges. A curve based on 1,000 scores would likely be much more irregular; but with a sample of 1,000,000 the sampling error would be so small that the sample distribution would be virtually indistinguishable from the theoretical curve.

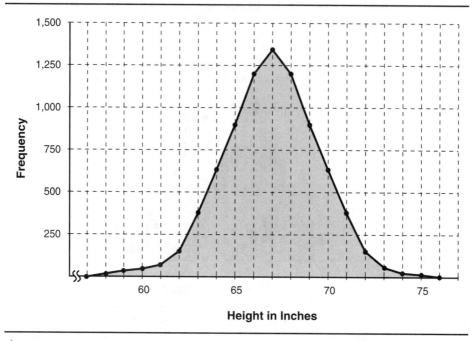

✦ **FIGURE 5.3** Frequency polygon of the heights of 8,585 nineteenth-century Englishmen.

Quiz: If a population is normally distributed, what will be the effect on the following if the size of the random sample is increased: (1) ($\overline{X} - \mu$), (2) (s − σ), and (3) the non-normality of the distribution of sample scores?

Answers: (1) This sampling error of the mean is expected to decrease in magnitude as sample size increases. (2) This sampling error of the standard deviation is expected to decrease in magnitude as sample size increases. (3) The degree of non-normality is expected to decrease as sample size increases.

Although the commonly observed empirical bell-shaped curves (e.g., height, IQ, and other variables) have piqued the curiosity of scientists from several disciplines, the prominence of the normal distribution in statistics is primarily due to its mathematical properties. No other distribution has such desirable properties with which mathematical statisticians can work magic. Many technical and practical problems in statistics have been solved mathematically only by assuming the observations in the population are normally distributed. Specific instances will appear in later chapters.

✦ 5.4 CHARACTERISTICS OF THE NORMAL CURVE

A mathematically perfect, normal distribution is given in Figures 5.4 and 5.5. Recall from Chapter 2 that two important characteristics of the normal curve are that it is unimodal and that it is symmetrical about its mean. Notice that the right half of the distribution is the mirror image of the left half; the symmetry is perfect; the skewness of the distribution is

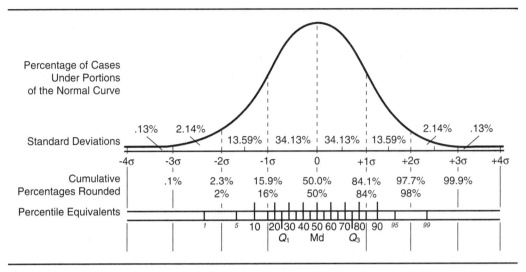

Percentage of Cases
Under Portions
of the Normal Curve

Standard Deviations

.13%   2.14%   13.59%   34.13%   34.13%   13.59%   2.14%   .13%

-4σ   -3σ   -2σ   -1σ   0   +1σ   +2σ   +3σ   +4σ

Cumulative
Percentages Rounded

.1%   2.3%   15.9%   50.0%   84.1%   97.7%   99.9%
         2%   16%   50%   84%   98%

Percentile Equivalents

1   5   10   20 30 40 50 60 70 80 90   95   99
                     Q_1 Md Q_3

❖ **FIGURE 5.4** The normal curve with percentile equivalents and cumulative percentages.

zero. Notice that as the distance from the mean increases, the tails of the curve more closely approach, but never quite touch, the horizontal axis. The theoretical normal distribution has an infinite range, but all empirical distributions have finite ranges. Table 4.1 (Section 4.14) shows that for samples of 100 observations or fewer, the range is expected to be about five standard deviations or less; if $n = 500$, the range is expected to be about 6σ.

In Chapter 4 it was noted that in a normal distribution roughly two-thirds of the observations are within 1σ of μ. We will now be more precise: 68 percent (.6826) of the observations (or equivalently, 68% of the area under any true normal curve) fall between a point one standard deviation below the mean ($\mu - \sigma$) and a point one standard deviation above the mean ($\mu + \sigma$) in a perfectly normal distribution (see Figure 5.4). Approximately 16 percent of the scores exceed μ by more than 1σ, and about 16 percent of the scores are more than 1σ less than μ. Only about 2 percent of the scores exceed μ by more than 2σ; also, about 2 percent fall below μ by more than 2σ.

The Wechsler intelligence tests yield IQ scores that have a mean of 100 and a standard deviation of 15. Assuming these IQ scores are normally distributed, what percentage of persons would have IQ scores in the "very superior" range, that is, above 130? Since 130 is 2 standard deviations (2σ) above the mean and corresponds to the 98th percentile (P_{98}, see Figure 5.4), only about 2 percent of the scores would be expected to exceed 130. This is very close to the empirically determined percentage of 2.32 percent. Also, about two percent of the IQ scores would be expected to fall in the "mentally deficient" range, that is, below 70.

Quiz: Assume that the Wechsler intelligence tests are normally distributed with $\mu = 100$ and $\sigma = 15$. Sonya scored 1σ above the mean. (1) What was her score? (2) What was her deviation score? (3) Jali scored two standard deviations below the mean; what was his deviation score? (4) What was his IQ score?

Answers: (1) $100 + 1\sigma = 115$, (2) 15, (3) $(-2)(15) = -30$, (4) $100 - 2(15) = 70$

Although the values of μ and σ will change depending on the variable observed and the units employed, each normal curve is symmetrical and always has the same percentage of the observations falling between the mean and points equidistant from μ in σ-units—such as $+1\sigma$ and -1σ from μ, as shown in Figure 5.4. Several fascinating topics in subsequent chapters assume a good working knowledge of the general characteristics of a normal distribution.

❖ 5.5 STANDARD SCORES

An effort to interpret and compare the performances of an individual on two or more variables is difficult when the data distributions have differing means and standard deviations. This problem can be overcome by tranforming the data so that all variables have identical means and the same standard deviations, that is, by "standardizing" the parameters of the distributions—transforming raw scores to standard scores. *Standard score* distributions have values for the mean and standard deviation that are fixed, known, and never vary. Since the parameters are always the same, interpretations and comparisons among standard scores are made more effortlessly.

❖ 5.6 THE BASIC STANDARD SCORE, THE z-SCALE

The most basic and useful standard score is the z-score scale. When observations are expressed in standard deviation units from the mean they are z-scores. The z-score distribution has fixed parameters: $\mu = 0$, $\sigma = 1$. The following formula defines a z-score:

$$z = \frac{X - \mu}{\sigma} = \frac{x}{\sigma} = \frac{\text{deviation score}}{\text{standard deviation}} \qquad \textbf{(5.1a)}$$

Algebraically rearranging[3] Eq. 5.1a gives Eq. 5.1b:

$$X = \mu + z\sigma \qquad \textbf{(5.1b)}$$

Whatever the mean and standard deviation of the original raw scores may have been, when transformed to z-scores, the mean is 0 and the standard deviation is 1. The shape of the distribution, however, remains intact—only the parameters have been changed to $\mu = 0$ and $\sigma = 1$. You may find that you have a score of 42, but this means little unless you know the group mean and standard deviation. A z-score, however, can easily be interpreted relative to the entire distribution since its parameters are always known and never vary. If we know that Jill's z-score is 1.5, we know that she scored 1.5 standard deviations above the mean, and, consequently, her score is quite high relative to the others in the distribution. A Wechsler IQ score of 130 is equivalent to a z-score of 2—it is two standard deviations above the mean and a very superior score. A z-score of -2 is two standard deviations below the mean and is equivalent to an IQ score of 70. A negative z-score indicates a score falling

---

[3]See Math Note 13 to review operations with fractions, and Math Note 16 for formula rearrangement.

below the mean; scores above the mean equate to positive z-scores, and a z-score of 0 coincides with the mean.

To convert a raw score, X, to a z standard score, we need only know X, μ, and σ and apply Equation 5.1a. Specifically, to convert a Wechsler IQ score of 90 to a z-score, given that $\mu = 100$ and $\sigma = 15$, we use Equation 5.1a: $z = (90 - 100)/15$, or $z = -.67$ (z-scores are often rounded to two decimal places). In other words, an IQ of 90 is 67% of a standard deviation below the mean.

Conversely, if we want to find out what IQ score, X, corresponds to a z-score of $z = 1.6$, we use Equation 5.1b: $X = 100 + 1.6(15)$, or $X = 124$. That is, a z-score of 1.6 has an IQ equivalent of 124.

Quiz: (1) A normal distribution with $\mu = 50$, and $\sigma = 10$ is transformed to z-scores. For the z-score distribution: (1) What is its mean? (2) What is its standard deviation? (3) Find the z-score equivalent of a score 2σ below the mean and (4) 1.5σ above the mean. (5) The z-score that corresponds to $X = 50$ is ____. (6) $X = 62$ is equivalent to a z-score of ____.

Answers: (1) zero, (2) 1, (3) $z = -2$, (4) $z = 1.5$, (5) $z = 0$, (6) $z = 1.2$

❖ 5.7 OTHER STANDARD SCORES

The z-scale ($\mu = 0$, $\sigma = 1$) is the most basic and widely used standard score, and is the basis for all other standard scores. In order to avoid negative numbers and decimal fractions, other standard score scales have been devised. Their parameters for μ and σ are "standardized"—as with all standard scores, the mean and standard deviation are set to some designated *standard*. When raw scores from different variables are transformed to the same standard score scale, the comparison and interpretation of the performances is facilitated. A newborn is frequently measured in length, weight, and head circumference. If these measures are converted to z-scores or some other standard score, they can be easily and accurately compared. To learn that your scores on the Verbal and Quantitative scales of the Graduate Record Examinations are 615 and 525 means little unless you know that both use a standard score scale with $\mu = 500$ and $\sigma = 100$. Most standardized tests of intelligence, achievement, interest, and personality report performance in standard scores. Such measures rarely report z-scores, however, but transform the z-scores to other standard-score scales that do not involve negative numbers or decimals and are thus easier to use.

You can convert a z-score to any other standard score (A) with any mean you choose (μ_A) and with any σ you choose (σ_A) using the general formula in Equation 5.2:

$$A = \mu_A + z(\sigma_A) \qquad\qquad \textbf{(5.2)}$$

where A is the standard score on the new scale that is equivalent to z, μ_A is the mean for the new standard-score scale, and σ_A is the standard deviation for the new standard-score scale. Suppose you have a set of z-scores and wish to transform them to a new standard score scale that has a $\mu = 100$ and $\sigma = 15$. Applying Equation 5.2, the specific transforming formula would be: $A = 100 + 15z$. A z of 1.8 corresponds to a standard score of $A = 100 + 15(1.8) = 127$; a z of $-.60$ converts to $A = 100 + 15(-.60) = 100 - 9 = 91$. Did you notice anything familiar about the new standard score scale? It is the common (Wechsler) IQ scale, IQ scores are standard scores on a scale with a mean of 100 and a standard deviation of 15.

Quiz: (1) Write a standard score conversion formula that will give a standard score distribution with $\mu = 20$ and $\sigma = 5$. Use the conversion formula in (1) to convert the following z-scores to the new standard scores: (2) $z = 1$, (3) $z = -.6$, (4) $z = 2.2$

Answers: (1) $A = 20 + 5z$, (2) $A = 20 + 5 = 25$, (3) $A = 20 + (-.6)(5) = 17$, (4) $A = 20 + 2.2(5) = 31$ (This is the standard score scale used by the ACT, a widely used college admissions test.)

❖ 5.8 *T*-SCORES

The most commonly used standard score for reporting test performance is the T standard-score scale[4] that has a mean of 50 and a standard deviation of 10. To convert z-scores to T-scores, Equation 5.2 becomes:

$$T = 50 + 10z \hspace{3cm} \textbf{(5.3)}$$

For reporting purposes, T-scores should probably be rounded to the nearest whole number.

Quiz: Assume the Stanford-Binet IQ scores are distributed normally with $\mu = 100$ and $\sigma = 16$. A Stanford-Binet IQ of 68 equates to a z-score of ___(1)___, and a T-score of ___(2)___. A Stanford-Binet IQ of 138 equates to a z-score of ___(3)___, and a T-score of ___(4)___.

Answers: (1) $(68 - 100)/16 = -2$, (2) $50 - 2(10) = 30$, (3) $z = 2.38$, (4) $T = 74$

Figure 5.5 shows the relation of z-scores, T-scores, and several other standard scores. Observe that *converting raw scores to standard scores does not alter the shape of the distribution or affect the percentile equivalent of any observation.* Standard scores have the advantage of having a known and constant mean and standard deviation. The Wechsler IQ scale is a widely used standard-score scale with $\mu = 100$ and $\sigma = 15$. The standard score scale employed by the classic Stanford-Binet Intelligence Scale has the same mean, $\mu = 100$, but a different standard deviation, $\sigma = 16$.

Quiz: A Wechsler IQ score of 145 has a z-score of ___(1)___. A z-score of 3 corresponds to a Stanford-Binet IQ score of ___(2)___.

Answers: (1) $z = 3$, (2) Stanford-Binet IQ $= 100 + 3(16) = 148$

❖ 5.9 PERCENTILE VERSUS STANDARD SCORE UNITS

You may wonder why statisticians bothered to invent standard scores since they appear to provide only percentile information that is readily obtained from the simple calculation of percentiles. For all the clarity and simplicity of the percentile scale, it is an ordinal scale

---

[4]The T-scale was originally proposed as a "normalized" standard score, but in current practice T-scores are not ordinarily normalized. Normalized T-scores are obtained by first converting the scores to percentiles, then converting the percentiles to the T-score associated with that percentile in a normal distribution.

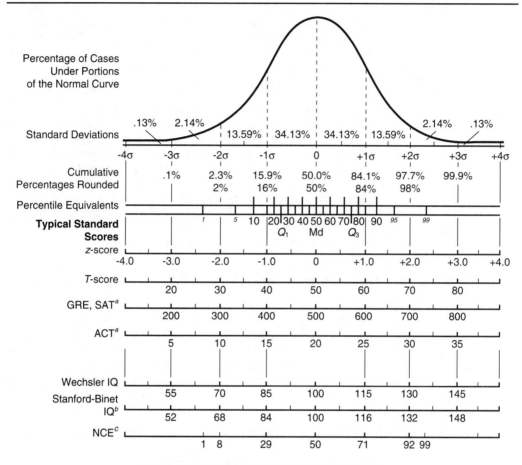

THE NORMAL CURVE, PERCENTILES, AND STANDARD SCORES

Distribution of scores of many standardized educational and psychological tests approximate the form of the normal curve shown at the top of this chart. Below it are shown other standard scores that are used by certain tests.

The zero (0) at the center of the baseline shows the location of the mean (average) raw score on a test, and the symbol σ (sigma) marks off the scale of raw scores in standard deviation units.

Most systems are based on the standard deviation unit. Among these standard score scales, the z-score and the T-score are general systems that have been applied to a variety of tests. The others are special variations used with College Entrance Examination Board tests the Graduate Records Examination, and other intelligence and ability scales.

Tables of norms, whether in percentile or standard score form, have meaning only with reference to a specified test applied to a specified reference population. The chart does not permit one to conclude, for

instance, that a percentile rank of 84 on one test necessarily is equivalent to a z-score of +1.0 on another; this is true only when each test yields essentially a normal distribution of scores and when both scales are based on identical or very similar groups of people.

[a]Score points (norms pertain to university students and not the general population). (GRE = Graduate Record Examination, SAT = Scholastic Aptitude Test of the College Entrance Examination Board, ACT = American College Testing Assessment.)

[b]Standard-score IQ's with $\sigma = 16$ are also used on certain other intelligence tests.

[c]The NCE ("Normal Curve Equivalent") scale is an ill-conceived normalized scale used in the evaluation of certain federally funded educational programs. The NCE scale has $\mu = 50$ and $\sigma = 21$; and the NCE unit is 1/98 of the distance between the 1st and 99th percentiles, expressed in z-score units. The NCE scale invites the confusion of NCE standard scores with percentiles.

❖ **FIGURE 5.5** Illustrations of various standard score scales. (Adapted from Test Service Bulletin No. 48. The Psychological Corporation, New York, by permission of The Psychological Corporation.)

with very unequal units. In addition, it does not lend itself to arithmetic operations such as averaging, consequently it has limited usefulness in inferential statistics and research. In Figure 5.5, observe that the percentile units near the mean are extremely narrow, whereas the percentile units near the tails are much wider. This illustrates that the actual measured raw score difference between the 50th and 53rd percentiles is much smaller than the raw score difference between the 95th and 98th percentiles, although both span precisely three percentile units. Specifically, for P_{50}, $z = 0.0$; for P_{53}, $z = .075$ (a z-score difference of only .075). However, for P_{95}, $z = 1.645$ and for P_{98}, $z = 2.054$, a z-score difference of .41—more than five times the difference between P_{50} and P_{51}! Expressing these z-score differences in IQ units: $.075z$ corresponds to a difference of $.075(15) = 1.1$ IQ units near the mean, but $.41z$ corresponds to a difference of $.41(15) = 6.1$ IQ units near the extremes. Stated differently, if Sally's IQ score increased by one point from 100 to 101, her percentile rank increased by three units (from 50 to 53); if Mary's IQ score increased by six points from 125 to 131, her percentile rank also changed by just three points (from 95 to 98). Percentile units distort the true magnitude of differences. Unlike percentile units, standard scores units are uniform throughout the range of the distribution, and thus avoid this problem of unequal units; they lend themselves more readily to meaningful comparisons and statistical computations.

❖ 5.10 PROPORTIONS AND AREAS WITHIN THE NORMAL CURVE

To more precisely determine the percent of the distribution falling below any point of a normal distribution, additional information is needed beyond that given in Figures 5.4 or 5.5. Table A in Appendix B gives the correspondence between z-scores and areas (proportions) of the normal curve below the z-scores. Using Table A, you can find the area below any z-score listed. You can also use this table to find the z-score corresponding to any desired percentile rank. This table will often be used in one of two ways: (1) to find the percentile equivalent of a known z-score, (2) to find the z-score equivalent of a known percentile rank.

❖ 5.11 DETERMINING THE PERCENTILE RANK OF OBSERVED SCORES

Complete the following steps to find the percentile equivalent ("area below") of a score in a normal distribution in which μ and σ are known.

To find the percentile equivalent of a raw score from a normal distribution:

Step 1.	Convert X to z using Equation 5.1a: $z = (X - \mu)/\sigma$.
Step 2.	Enter Table A Appendix B; find z in z-column; read out the percentile equivalent from the adjacent "area below" column.

For the normally distributed Wechsler IQ distribution with a mean of 100 and a standard deviation of 15, let us find the percentile equivalent of an IQ of 150:

For step 1, $z = (150 - 100)/15 = 50/15 = 3.33$ (rounded).

For step 2, enter Table A Appendix B with $z = 3.33$; read the "area below" (.99957), thus $P_{99.96}$. Only about 4 scores in 10,000 would be so high.

Suppose a basketball coach wants to find out the proportion of adult males who are 76″ (64″) or taller. (Assume for adult males, $\mu = 69.7″$ and $\sigma = 2.6″$) In this case, the area above the z-score is needed rather than the area below. To find the area above a given observation, find its z-score, access Table A, and subtract the "area below" column from 1.0000—this difference corresponds to the area above the z-score:

For step 1, $z = (X - \mu)/\sigma = (76 - 69.7)/2.6 = 6.3/2.6 = 2.423$ or 2.42.

For step 2, enter Table A with $z = 2.42$; read out the "area below" of .9922. Area above $= 1.0000 - .9922$, or .0078, or about 78 in 10,000. Approximately 8 men in 1,000 are expected to be 6'4″ or taller given these parameters for the height of adult males. As we mentioned earlier, no known traits are perfectly normally distributed, but the approximation is sufficiently accurate to be very useful for many purposes.

Quiz: Some police departments have required their male applicants to be at least 5'10″ tall. Using the normal distribution of adult male height norms (parameters) of $\mu = 69.7$ inches and $\sigma = 2.6$ inches, what proportion of the male population would be excluded by this requirement?

Answer: $z = (70 - 69.7)/2.6 = .12$. From Table A, the area (proportion) below $z = .12$ is .5478, so approximately 55% of the adult males would fail to meet this criterion.

❖ 5.12 DETERMINING THE RAW SCORE EQUIVALENT OF PERCENTILES

Table A can also be used to find the raw score equivalent of a given percentile rank for a normal distribution with known parameters.

To find the score equivalent of a given percentile in a normal distribution:

Step 1.	Enter Table A Appendix B in the "area below" column and locate the entry that corresponds to the desired percentile, then read the associated z-score equivalent from the adjacent z-score column.
Step 2.	Use Equation 5.1b: $X = \mu + z\sigma$.

As an example, suppose you want to know what Wechsler IQ score ($\mu = 100$, $\sigma = 15$) in a normal distribution has the percentile rank of 75:

For step 1, locate .75 in the "area below" column of Table A, and retrieve its z-score equivalent, $z = .674$.

For step 2, $X = 100 + .674(15)$, or about 110; an IQ of 110 corresponds to a percentile rank of 75.

Quiz: (1) In a normal curve, find the z-score equivalent of the 25th percentile, P_{25}. (2) What Wechsler IQ score equates to a percentile rank of 95?

Answers: (1) Find .25 in the "area below" column; read out $z = -.674$. (2) Find .95 in the "area below" column; read out $z = 1.645$. From Equation 5.1b, $X = 100 + 15(1.645) = 124.675$, or the IQ equals about 125.

❖ 5.13 DETERMINING THE AREA BETWEEN TWO z-SCORES

Table A is also used to find the area or proportion of a normal distribution that falls between any two z-values.

To find the area between two z-scores in a normal distribution:

> **Step 1.**   Find the "area below" for the first z-score (z_1).
>
> **Step 2.**   Find the "area below" for the second z-score (z_2).
>
> **Step 3.**   Subtract the smaller "area below" from the larger "area below."

This difference is the proportion of the normal distribution that lies between the two given z-scores. Figure 5.6 illustrates the procedure of finding the proportion of IQ scores between z-scores of –1.27 and .50. Note that the area below z = –1.27 was found (step 1), the area below z = .50 was found (step 2), and the difference in these areas was computed (step 3) to specify the proportion between them.

As an example, let us find the proportion of the normal distribution that falls between z_1 = –1.282 and z_2 = 1.282.

For step 1, enter Table A with z_1 = –1.282, and read out "area below" of .1000.

For step 2, enter Table A with z_2 = 1.282, and read out "area below" of .9000.

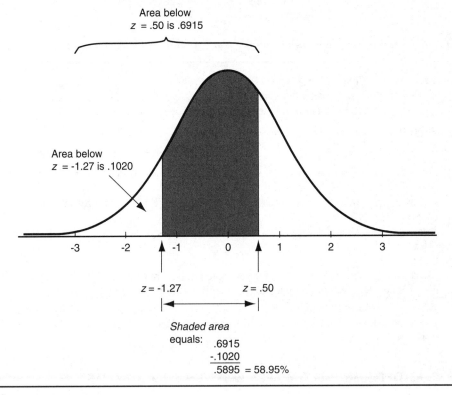

Area below
z = .50 is .6915

Area below
z = -1.27 is .1020

z = -1.27 z = .50

Shaded area
equals: .6915
           -.1020
           .5895 = 58.95%

❖ **FIGURE 5.6** The area between two z-scores in a normal distribution.

For step 3, compute $(.9000 - .1000) = .8000$ or 80 percent.

The middle-most 80 percent of the normal curve falls between the two z-scores: $z = -1.282$ and $z = 1.282$.

Quiz: What percent of Wechsler IQ scores fall between $X_1 = 110$ and $X_2 = 120$?

Answer: For IQ = 110, $z = .67$, and area below = .7486. For IQ = 120, $z = 1.33$, and area below = .9082. Area between = $(.9082 - .7486) = .1596$ or 16 percent.

❖ 5.14 USE OF STANDARD SCORES WITH SAMPLES

Throughout this chapter, we have been dealing with the situation in which the population of observations is known to be normally distributed with known parameters μ and σ. Where μ and σ are unknown, and the sample $\overline{X}$ and s are used as estimates of μ and σ, the values in Appendix B Table A are only approximations; the accuracy of the approximation depends upon the accuracy of the statistics $\overline{X}$ and s. When n is 100 or more, the z-value for an observation using $\overline{X}$ and s will probably differ from the z-value using μ and σ by .1 or less in most situations. When based on larger samples, the degree of precision using $\overline{X}$ and s is adequate for most purposes . However, we should be wary of making inferences based on Table A when $\overline{X}$ and s are based on small samples, or when we are uncertain that the distribution is normal.

❖ CHAPTER SUMMARY

The normal distribution has some important mathematical properties that make it very useful in inferential statistics. Fortunately, the distributions of many variables in the social and behavioral sciences are closely approximated by the normal distribution.

The normal distribution is symmetrical, unimodal, and bell-shaped. There is a fixed and known proportion of the curve below any point expressed in σ-units or z-scores. The z-score transformation, $z = (X - \mu)/\sigma$, converts an array of scores to a distribution with $\mu = 0$ and $\sigma = 1$, but does not change the shape of the distribution. There is a fixed and known proportion of the normal curve below each z-score, and these proportions can be found from the Appendix B Table A (and certain software such as EXCEL). Table A specifies exact proportions when μ and σ are known, but gives approximations when the z-score is computed using $\overline{X}$ and s. The accuracy of the approximations is probably adequate for most purposes with sample sizes of 100 or larger when the distribution is known to be approximately normal.

In addition to z-scores, there are other widely used standard-score scales; the most popular is the T-scale that sets $\mu = 50$ and $\sigma = 10$. Performances on many variables can be easily compared if each variable is expressed on the same standard-score scale.

MASTERY TEST

Information on the Wechsler intelligence and ITBS achievement tests is given below. The ITBS achievement parameters are expressed as grade-equivalent (GE) scores. Answer questions 1–10 assuming all the distributions are normal.

	Iowa Test of Basic Skills			
	Reading			Arithmetic
Wechsler IQ	Grade 3	Grade 5	Grade 8	Grade 5
μ 100	3.0	5.0	8.0	5.0
σ 15	1.0	1.4	1.9	1.1

1. Jeri's IQ score was 115. (a) Jeri's deviation score, $x =$ __?__; (b) Jeri's z-score is __?__; (c) Jeri's percentile rank is __?__. (d) What percent of the population scores higher?

2. Upon entering grade 3, Bob obtained a reading score of 2.0. (a) Bob's deviation score, $x =$ __?__; (b) Bob's z-score is __?__; (c) Bob's percentile rank is __?__; (d) Bob's score converted to a T-score is __?__.

3. If an entering fifth-grade pupil obtains a percentile rank of 84 in reading, (a) her reading z-score = __?__, and (b) her reading grade-equivalent (GE) score is __?__.

4. What GE score for grade 5 arithmetic equates to the 84th percentile point?

5. June was reading at GE 6.1 when she entered grade 8. (a) Her z-score = __?__. (b) Her percentile rank = __?__. (c) If her Wechsler IQ has the same percentile rank, what is her IQ score?

6. June (see item 5) scored as well or better than about what percentage of the children in her grade?

7. Upon entering grade 3, approximately what percent of the 3rd graders read as well as the average 4th grader (GE of 4.0)? About what percent read as well as the average 5th grader?

8. At grade 5, does a GE score of 6.0 have a higher percentile rank in arithmetic than in reading?

9. In reading, what percentage of entering 8th graders score below the average entering 5th grader?

10. What percentage of the entering 5th graders score between GE scores of 4.0 and 6.0?

11. The score, $X = 176$, is from a normal distribution with $\mu = 163$ and $\sigma = 26$; express X as a: (a) z-score, (b) T-score, and (c) percentile equivalent.

12. Which of these is not characteristic of a normal distribution?
    (a) symmetrical   (b) unimodal   (c) skewed   (d) bell-shaped   (e) beautiful

13. Which of these reflects the poorest performance on an academic test?
    (a) P_{10} (b) $z = -1.5$ (c) $T = 30$

14. With a sample of 1,000 representative observations, which of these is probably *least* accurately characterized by the normal distribution?
    (a) scores on a musical aptitude test
    (b) number of baby teeth lost by age 8
    (c) size of reading vocabulary of 12-year-old children
    (d) number of times attended a religious service in the past year
    (e) scores on an inventory measuring interest in politics

15. If raw scores are changed to z-scores, does the shape of the distribution change?

16. If z-scores are multiplied by 10, σ increases from __?__ to __?__.

17. What is the variance in a distribution expressed as:
    (a) z-scores?   (b) T-scores?

18. If a random sample is taken from a normally distributed population, will the frequency distribution of the sample data appear to be normally distributed if: (a) $n = 50$? (b) $n = 50,000$? Verbalize the relationship between sample size and sampling error.

19. If scores from a skewed distribution are converted to z-scores, will the z-distribution be normal? Could you use Table A to get accurate percentile ranks for the z-scores?

20. Zenat's z-score on the Graduate Record Exam (GRE) was 1.8, what was her GRE score? (Refer to Figure 5.5 for GRE parameters.)

21. Write a standard score conversion formula that will give a standard score distribution with $\mu = 20$ and $\sigma = 4$, and use it to convert $z_1 = -.75$ and $z_2 = 1.25$ to the new standard scores.

22. If some industry required their female applicants to be between $5'6''$ and $5'10''$ in height, and if the normal distribution of adult female height had parameters of $\mu = 65''$ inches and $\sigma = 2.6''$, what proportion of the female population will:
    (a) be too short to qualify?   (b) be excluded by this requirement?

23. P_{67}, in a normal curve, equates to what: (a) z-score? (b) T-score? (c) Wechsler IQ score? (d) GRE score? (Refer to Figure 5.5 for parameters.)

ANSWERS TO MASTERY TEST

1. (a) $x = 15$, (b) $z = 1$, (c) percentile rank $= 84$, (d) 16%
2. (a) $x = -1.0$, (b) $z = -1.0$, (c) percentile rank $= 16$, (d) 40
3. (a) $z = 1.0$, (b) GE $= 5.0 + 1(1.4) = 6.4$
4. GE $= 5.0 + 1(1.1) = 6.1$
5. (a) $z = -1$, (b) P_{16}, (c) IQ $= 100 + 15(-1)$ $= 85$
6. 16%
7. (a) $z = (4.0 - 3.0)/1.0 = 1$, area above $=$ $(100 - 84) = 16$ percent
   (b) $z = 2.0$, area above $= 2$ percent
8. yes, since $z_{arith} = .91$ and $z_{read} = .71$
9. $z = (5 - 8)/1.9 = -1.58$, area below $= 5.7$ percent
10. $z_1 = (4 - 5)/1.4 = -.71$, area below $=$ $.2389$.
    $z_2 = (6 - 5)/1.4 = .71$, area below $= .7611$; area between $= 52$ percent.
11. (a) .5, (b) 55, (c) P_{69}
12. (c)
13. (c)
14. (d)
15. no, just the parameters change
16. from $\sigma = 1$ to $\sigma = 10$
17. $1^2 = 1$; $10^2 = 100$
18. (a) Not likely, since n is small; (b) Very nearly, since n is large. As n increases, sampling error decreases.
19. No, the shape remains unchanged. No, Table A is only appropriate for normal curves.
20. GRE $= 500 + 100(1.8) = 680$
21. $A = 20 + 4z$. $A_1 = 20 + 4(-.75) = 17$; $A_2 =$ $20 + 4(1.25) = 25$.
22. (a) $z = (66 - 65)/2.6 = .38$, area below $=$ .648; approximately 65% are too short;
    (b) $z = (70 - 65)/1.92$; area below $=$ .9726, area above $= (1.0 - .9726) = .0274$, or approximately 3% are too tall; and 68% (65% + 3%) are excluded.
23. (a) $z = .44$, (b) $T = 54$, (c) IQ $= 107$, (d) GRE $= 544$

PROBLEMS AND EXERCISES

Suppose Brea obtained the following percentiles on five subtests on the McCarthy Scale of Children's Abilities:

Subtest	Percentile
Verbal	98
Perceptual	99.9
Quantitative	50
Memory	84
Motor	16

Use Figure 5.4 or Figure 5.5 to answer exercises 1–3.

1. If Brea's Motor performance improved by 1σ, the percentile equivalent would increase from 16 to __?__, or a gain of __?__ percentile units.

2. If the Verbal score improved by 1σ, the percentile equivalent on the Verbal tests would increase from 98 to __?__, or a gain of __?__ percentile units.

3. In standard deviation units, is the size of the difference between Brea's performance on the Verbal and Perceptual tests the same as the difference between her Motor and Quantitative scores?

4. On occasion, you might encounter a measure of variability, Q, the semi-interquartile range (or quartile deviation): $Q = (Q_3 - Q_1)/2$ or, equivalently, $(P_{75} - P_{25})/2$. Estimate Q on the Wechsler IQ scale ($\mu = 100$, $\sigma = 15$).

Grading on the normal curve was popular in some circles a few decades ago. The most common method used the following conversion:

Grade	z-Score
A	above 1.5
B	.5 to 1.5
C	−.5 to .5
D	−1.5 to −.5
F	below −1.5

5. Using this system, what percent of A's, B's, C's, D's, and F's are expected with a normal distribution of scores?

6. For persons who know nothing about the content, but guess randomly at each of 100 true-false items, what percent will receive passing scores if 65 is required for passing? (For "know-nothing" examinees, $\mu = 50$ and $\sigma = 5$.)

7. Suppose we want to find the middle-most z-score interval for a normal curve that includes 80 percent of the scores, that is, exclude the bottom 10% as well as the top 10%. Using Table A, what are the two z-scores that include the middle-most 80 percent of the distribution?

8. For normal curves, find the middle-most z-score interval that includes: (a) 50% of the scores, (b) 75% of the scores, and (c) 95% of the scores.

9. If scores from the HSB data set for Civics and Reading are assumed to be normally distributed with a mean of 50 and a standard deviation of 10 in the national population, find the z-score and national percentile rank of the following scores.
   (a) Reading = 57   (b) Civics = 45

10. What is the minimum T-score that is required to place an examinee in the top 10 percent of a normal distribution of T-scores ($\mu = 50$, $\sigma = 10$)?

11. What percent of the scores in a normal distribution have z-scores between the following pairs of points?
    (a) $z_1 = -1.96$, $z_2 = 1.96$
    (b) $z_1 = -2.58$, $z_2 = 2.58$
    (c) $z_1 = -1.65$, $z_2 = 1.65$

12. Stanford-Binet IQ scores are normally distributed with a mean of 100 and a standard deviation of 16, the middle 90 percent fall between what two IQ scores?

13. (Refer to item 12 above.) What is the probability that a randomly selected Stanford-Binet IQ score will be:
    (a) 110 or higher?

(b) 124 or lower?

(c) between 92 and 116?

14. Suppose a researcher who was interested in creativity and its relationship to right-handedness or left-handedness administered his creativity test to 1,000 randomly selected high school seniors who were right-handed and to 1,000 high school seniors who were left-handed. Interestingly enough, both sets of data were normally distributed. For group 1 (right-handed), the computed stats were: $\overline{X}_1 = 80$, $s_1 = 12$, and for group 2 (left-handed), $\overline{X}_2 = 90$ and $s_2 = 20$.

(a) Which group was most homogeneous with respect to creativity?

(b) What percent of the group 1 (right-handed) pupils were more creative than the "average" left-handed pupil?

(c) What percent of the left-handed pupils were more creative than the "average" right-handed pupil?

(d) If scores of 100 or above qualify a student for a special curriculum, what percent and how many students of each group would qualify?

Items 15–18. Descriptive summary statistics for the quantitative variables of the HSB data set are displayed below. Assume all variables are approximately normally distributed.

Variable	Mean	s	s^2	Range
Reading T-score	52.23	10.25	105.12	48.00
Writing T-score	52.78	9.49	89.84	36.00
Math T-score	52.64	9.37	87.77	42.00
Science T-score	51.85	9.90	98.03	48.00
Civics T-score	52.41	10.74	115.26	45.00

15. Suppose your score on the math test was $T = 56$. Compared to those students in the HSB data set, what would be your (a) deviation score, (b) z-score, and (c) percentile rank?

16. Suppose a student had a percentile rank of 33 in math based on the national norms of $\mu = 50$ and $\sigma = 10$. (a) Find his T-score for math, and (b) convert this Math T-score to a percentile rank as compared to his peers in the HSB data set.

17. Based on the national norms ($\mu = 50$, $\sigma = 10$), one participant had the following scores: Reading $z = -.6$, Writing $T = 41$, and Math = 84th percentile rank. Convert these data to a new standard score with $\mu = 500$ and $\sigma = 100$, and comment upon their relative rankings.

18. These descriptive summary statistics for the subject matter variables may suggest that this sample differed slightly from the general population. Can you specify this evidence?

ANSWERS TO PROBLEMS AND EXERCISES

1. 50, 34

2. 99.9, 1.9

3. yes, 1σ in each instance

4. $P_{75} = 100 + .6745\sigma = 110.12$, $P_{25} = 100 - 10.12 = 89.88$;
   $Q = (110.12 - 89.88)/2 = 10.12$ or about 10 points

5. A = 7%; B = 24%; C = 38%; D = 24%; F = 7%

6. $z = (65 - 50)/5 = 3.0$, area above = 1.000 $- .9987 = .0013$ or about 1 in 1,000

7. $z_1 = -1.28$, $z_2 = 1.28$; 80% of the z-scores lie between $z = -1.28$ and $z = +1.28$.

8. (a) .50 interval: $z_1 = -.68$, $z_2 = .68$; 50% of the z-scores lie between $z = -.68$ and $z = .68$.
   (b) .75 interval: $z_1 = -1.15$, $z_2 = 1.15$; 75% of them lie between $z = -1.15$ and $z = 1.15$.
   (c) .95 interval: $z_1 = -1.96$, $z_2 = 1.96$; 95% of them lie between $z = -1.96$ and $+1.96$.

9. (a) $z = (57 - 50)/10 = .7$, which corresponds to a percentile rank of 76.

(b) $z = (45 - 50)/10 = -.5$, which corresponds to a percentile rank of 31.

10. From Table A, $P_{90} = z = 1.28$; $T = 50 + 10(1.28) = 63$.

11. (a) 95% (b) 99% (c) 90%

12. $z_1 = -1.65$; IQ $= 100 + 16(-1.65) = 74$; $z_2 = 1.65$; IQ $= 100 + 16(1.65) = 126$.

The middle-most 90 percent of the Stanford-Binet IQ's lie in the interval from 74 to 126.

13. (a) 16%, (b) 93%, (c) 53%

14. (a) group 1, (b) $z = .83$, 20%, (c) 69%, (d) For group 1: $z = 1.67$; area $= .0475$ (4.75%); about 47 qualify. For group 2: $z = .5$; area $= .3085$ (30.85%); about 308 qualify.

15. (a) $x = 56 - 52.64 = 3.36$, (b) $z = 3.36/9.37 = .36$, (c) from Table A, percentile rank = 64

16. (a) $z = -.5$ and $T = 45$, (b) $z = (45 - 52.64)/9.37 = -.82$ and the percentile rank is 21.

17. $A_{read} = 500 + 100(-.6) = 440 = P_{27}$; $A_{writing} = 500 + 100(-.9) = 410 = P_{18}$; $A_{math} = 500 + 100(1) = 600 = P_{84}$. This person ranks rather highly in math, but much lower in reading and writing.

18. The means for the subject matter variables are a bit higher than 50, which is the national population parameter. Also, this group seems to be a bit more homogeneous than the national population since their standard deviations seem somewhat less than the national population parameter of 10. Also, the ranges for these variables seem depressed—the range/s ratios tend to be less than the expected value of 5.5 (see Table 4.1 for $n = 200$).

SUGGESTED COMPUTER EXERCISE

1. Transform the math scores in the HSB data set to z-scores and T-scores (using their own mean and standard deviation), and get a frequency distribution of the math T-scores.

2. Do the same as in exercise 1 for civics. From the frequency distribution of z-scores for civics, find the percentage of the civics z-scores falling into the A, B, C, D, and F categories for grading on the normal curve (see problem 5 above). Why do the percentages differ from those found in problem 5?

6

Correlation: Concept and Computation
Relationships between Two Variables

❖ 6.1 INTRODUCTION

In addition to measures to describe the central tendency and variability of distributions, there is a need for measures that describe the degree of relationship between two variables. Chapter 6 is the first of two chapters on correlation. In this chapter, we will study the meaning, use, and computation of the correlation coefficient, r, the common measure of relationship. In Chapter 7 attention is given to factors that influence the magnitude and interpretation of correlation coefficients.

❖ 6.2 THE NEED FOR A MEASURE OF RELATIONSHIP

We are often curious about whether two variables are related; and if they are, the strength of the relationship. For example, is absenteeism related to grades? Is class-size associated with gains in achievement? Is fluency in speaking related to vocabulary size? Are cranial capacity and IQ related? Is there a correlation between musical ability and intelligence? To answer questions such as these, measures of relationship or correlation are needed.

Most people have a general understanding of correlation. Two variables, X and Y, are correlated if they tend to "go together." We can verbally describe the degree of association between variables by such verbal descriptions as strong, low, positive, negative, or moderate, but these terms lack precision. A quantification of the degree of correlation between two variables is needed to maximize precision and objectivity.

The coefficient of correlation was derived to be a statistical summary of the degree of relationship or association between two variables. As examples: (1) The higher the aptitude test scores, the higher the college grades tend to be; the lower the test scores, the less likely that the student will obtain good marks in college. (2) Husbands and wives tend to be more alike with respect to the social class of their families (and many other factors) than are people in general. (3) Children resemble their parents in IQ more closely than they resemble cousins, and they resemble cousins more than unrelated adults. Some degree of positive correlation between members of families is usually found for almost any characteristic, such as personality, attitude, interest, or ability.

Pearson derived a measure of relationship, the product-moment coefficient of correlation to quantify the degree of relationship between variables; this measure is signified by r for the inferential statistic and by ρ (the lowercase Greek letter "rho") for the parameter. Since about 1900, this correlation coefficient has been a widely employed statistic in virtually all empirical disciplines; well over 90% of all correlation coefficients reported in research literature in the behavioral sciences are Pearson correlations.

You may recall that a z-score indicates a raw score's position within the distribution of scores relative to μ in σ-units. A z-score of 1.5 is 1.5 σ above μ and a z-score of $-.44$ is $.44\sigma$ below μ. When a population has been measured on two variables, X and Y, each person has two z-scores, the z_X-score for the X-variable and the z_Y-score for the Y-variable. If persons who score high on X tend to also score high on Y, both z-scores will be positive and their product will also be positive—if persons who score low on X tend to also score low on Y, both z-scores will be negative but their product will be positive. The average z-score product, as indicated in Equation 6.1, is a measure of the relationship between two variables in the population:

$$\rho = \frac{\Sigma z_X z_Y}{N} \tag{6.1}$$

Notice that the sum of all the z-score products are divided by N, which yields an average z-score product as a measure of relationship. When those who score high on X tend to score low on Y, the z-score products tend to be negative and the correlation coefficient is negative.

Quiz: (1) When most of the high scorers on variable X are also high scorers on variable Y, r_{XY} would be ___?___ .

(2) When most of the high scorers on X are low scorers on Y, r_{XY} would be ___?___ .

(3) When about half of the high scorers on variable X are also high scorers on variable Y, r_{XY} would be ___?___ .

Answers: (1) positive, (2) negative, (3) near zero

The correlation coefficient provides an objective means for examining a relationship; it is a safeguard to protect us from our own strong proclivity for "confirming" our preconceived notions based on intuition or unsystematic observation. (Even Aristotle believed that a positive correlation existed between the age of a mother and the proportion of male children.)

❖ 6.3 HOW CORRELATION IS EXPRESSED

Pearson's correlation coefficient (along with several other less common measures of association) summarizes both the *magnitude* and the *direction* of a relationship. The variables being correlated can be any two quantitative variables, such as history achievement (X) and reading achievement (Y), speed of running the 100-yard dash (X) and skill in playing the violin (Y), or political conservatism (X) and age (Y). In all such situations, the correlation coefficient can have values that range from the minimum value, $\rho = -1.0$, for a perfect inverse (negative) relationship, up through $\rho = 0$ for no relationship, and up to the maximum value, $\rho = +1.0$, for a perfect direct (positive) relationship. For perfectly correlated variables, a score on one of the variables will give a perfectly accurate prediction of the score on the other variable. For strongly correlated variables, a score on one of the variables gives a fairly accurate prediction of the score on the other variable. For weakly correlated variables, a score on one of the variables gives a prediction of the score on the other which is little better than an outright guess.

The correlation coefficient is sometimes confused with percentage. An r of .60 means that there is a tendency for the pairs of z-scores for each unit to be somewhat similar but with many exceptions—it does not mean that there is 60 percent agreement, conformity, correspondence, congruity, or consistency among the z-scores, nor that the two variables are 60 percent related, nor that 60 percent of what X measures is also measured by Y.

The algebraic sign (+ or −) of the computed correlation coefficient indicates the direction of the relationship. When low scores on X tend to be associated with low scores on Y, and high scores on X with high scores on Y, the correlation between X and Y is positive. If high scores on X are associated with low scores on Y and vice versa, the correlation is negative. If the exceptions to the rule are few and small, the magnitude of r will be high, perhaps .90 or above. When there are often substantial exceptions to the rule, the magnitude of r will be moderate, perhaps in the neighborhood of .50 or below. When there are many glaring exceptions to the rule, the magnitude of r may be quite small, perhaps only .30 or below.

Quiz: The Pearson correlation coefficients between Science and the other four subjects of the HSB data pool are listed below.

	Writing	Math	Reading	Civics
Science	.57	.63	.63	.47

Science seems to be least strongly correlated with (1). Complete the following summary statement: Students who score above the mean in science tend to score (2) the mean in math, but with some (3).

Answers: (1) Civics, (2) above, (3) exceptions

Correlation coefficients allow us to compare the strength and direction of the relationship between different pairs of variables. For example, the very low relationship between musical and psychomotor abilities ($\rho \approx .2$)[1] is less than the moderate relationship between verbal and mathematical abilities ($\rho \approx .6$).

❖ 6.4 THE USE OF CORRELATION COEFFICIENTS

A classic example of the use of correlation coefficients is illustrated in the "nature-nurture" studies of intelligence measures. Table 6.1 gives correlation coefficients between intelligence (measured by IQ from an individually administered intelligence test) and varying degrees of genetic and environmental similarity. Data on academic achievement, height, and weight are also given in Table 6.1. The correlation coefficients in Table 6.1 are r's (not ρ's)—sampling error will cause some degree of irregularity in the results. The accuracy with which the r for the random sample estimates ρ for the population is determined largely by the size of n. The inferential precision in a sample r is treated in Chapter 13.

---

[1]The symbol, $\approx$, indicates "is approximately equal to."

❖ **TABLE 6.1** Correlation coefficients of intelligence (IQ), academic achievement, height, and weight, for persons of varying genetic and environmental similarity.

	Identical Twins Reared		Fraternal Twins Reared	Siblings Reared		Unrelated Children Reared	
	Together	*Apart*	*Together*	*Together*	*Apart*	*Together*	*Apart*
Intelligence	.91	.67	.64	.50	.40	.23	0.0
Achievement	.96	.51	.88	.81	.53	.52	0.0
Height	.96	.94	.47	.50	.54	.00	0.0
Weight	.93	.88	.59	.57	.43	.24	0.0

Data from Erlenmeyer-Kimling & Jarvik (1963); see also Hopkins & Stanley (1981, p. 366).

Notice in Table 6.1 that home environment is associated more strongly with scholastic achievement than measures of scholastic aptitude. For example, in Table 6.1 the computed correlation between the scholastic achievement of pairs of unrelated children reared together is $r = .52$, but the correlation between their IQ scores is only $r = .23$. Further, siblings reared together are much more similar in scholastic attainment ($r = .81$) than they are in IQ ($r = .50$). Observe also in Table 6.1 that, although height is less related to environment than is weight, a strong hereditary factor is evident in weight for identical twins reared apart ($r = .88$).

❖ 6.5 SCATTERPLOTS

An intuitive understanding of the meaning of correlation coefficients (such as those given in Table 6.1) is illuminated by studying some illustrative *scatterplots* (also called scatter diagrams and scattergrams). In a scatterplot, each mark (dot or tally) represents the intersection of two scores—there is one mark for each subject's *pair* of observations. The chief purpose of the scatterplot is to display graphically the relationship between two variables—to portray the nature of the relationship between the two variables. The relationship between two variables, *X* and *Y,* is *linear* if the elliptical swarm of points tends to fall along a straight line. The relationship is not linear but *curvilinear* if the points tend to hover along a curved line. As the magnitude of the coefficient approaches zero, the swarm of points loses its elliptical shape and becomes more circular; as the magnitude of *r* increases in absolute value toward 1.0, the elliptical swarm of points becomes more and more narrow and shrinks to form a straight line at $r = 1.0$ or $r = -1.0$. It is important to remember, however, that the relationship between two variables is accurately summarized by the Pearson's *r* and ρ only when the relationship is linear.

A perfect positive linear relationship ($r = 1.0$) is shown in Panel A of Figure 6.1; the dots fall on a straight line from (lower *X*, lower *Y*) to (higher *X*, higher *Y*). All points fall along the same straight line, but not necessarily from corner to corner of the scatterplot. Perfect correlation affords perfect predictability—for example, if $r = 1$ and if Jo's z_X score is also 1.23, we would know that her z_Y score is 1.23. Mental ages correlate 1.0 with IQ's for persons of the same chronological age and either variable could be predicted from the other without error. Height expressed in inches obviously correlates 1.0 with height expressed in centimeters.

A perfect negative relationship ($r = -1.00$) is illustrated in Panel B of Figure 6.1. If every student attempts all items on an objective test, the number of right answers will corre-

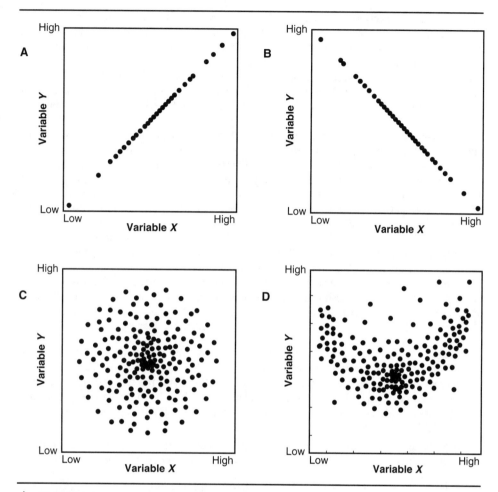

❖ **FIGURE 6.1** Scatterplots depicting linear relationships of $r = +1$ (Panel A), $r = -1$ (Panel B), $r = 0$ (Panel C), and a curvilinear relationship (Panel D).

late -1.0 with the number of wrong answers. Empirical relationships between variables are rarely perfect (r's of exactly -1 or 1), but values of .90 and above are not rare (as evident in Table 6.1).

In Panel C of Figure 6.1, there is no relationship between variables X and Y ($r \approx 0$). A knowledge of Jo's X-score does not improve the prediction of her Y-score over chance—no matter what the value of X, the best prediction of Y for all persons would be identical, $\overline{Y}$ when $r = 0$.

❖ 6.6 LINEAR AND CURVILINEAR RELATIONSHIPS

The value of r describes the degree of *linear* relationship between X and Y. If X and Y are perfectly linearly related (i.e., $r = 1.0$ or $r = -1.0$), the points in the scatterplot will form a straight line, as illustrated in Panels A and B of Figure 6.1. If the points in a scatterplot are evenly dispersed above and below a straight line that could be drawn through the swarm of points, a linear relationship of some degree exists between X and Y. If the points in a scatterplot appear to be clustered about a curved line rather than a straight line, the relationship between the two measures is nonlinear or curvilinear. Since r (or ρ) expresses only the linear relationship between X and Y, it would be inappropriate for use with curvilinear data—if substantial curvilinearity exists, the Pearson r will seriously underestimate the degree of relationship.

Panels C and D of Figure 6.1 illustrate two different kinds of scatterplots in which the numerical value of r is approximately zero. It is obvious, however, that there is a definite relationship between X and Y in Panel D (e.g., X = room temperature, Y = comfort level), but no systematic relationship in Panel C. A major purpose of scatterplots is to ensure that the relationship is roughly linear before assuming that r is an accurate indication of the degree of relationship between X and Y. A substantial, but curvilinear relationship, can exist, and yet the computed value of r could be quite small or even 0. If we know that X and Y are linearly related, the meaning of r is unequivocal. Although there are statistical tests for linearity (Glass & Hopkins, 1996, Chapter 17), unless n is small, the "eyeball" check is sufficient to detect any substantial degree of nonlinearity.

Fortunately, most variables in the behavioral sciences and education are linearly related. However, curvilinear relationships are not uncommon when studying affective, sociological, and economic variables, but are rare between cognitive and psychomotor variables. There is one variable, age, that has a curvilinear relationship with many other variables.

> **Quiz:** (1) When age (ages 6 through 96) is correlated with muscular strength, the nature of the relationships is typically ___?___. (2) Is it appropriate to use the Pearson r to examine the relationship between race and IQ? (3) If the left half of a swarm of points appears to indicate a positive relationship, but the right half of the swarm appears to indicate a negative relationship, what is the nature of the correlation between the variables?
>
> **Answers:** (1) curvilinear, (2) No, since race is a categorical rather than a quantitative variable. (3) Apparently there is a curvilinear correlation between the two variables.

Spurious curvilinearity can result from poorly developed assessment measures. For example, educational and psychological test scores can be curtailed by "ceiling" effects, that is, the test is too easy for the particular group of examinees involved, with the result that the scores are negatively skewed and the test fails to discriminate between the individuals in the top score range. Of course a test can also be too difficult for a group of examinees, and yield a positively skewed distribution of scores and fail to differentiate between individuals in the low score range. Suppose, for example, that a large group of fourth graders took a sixth-grade math test (Test X) and a second-grade spelling test (Test Y). As displayed in Figure 6.2A, scores for test X are skewed positively because the test is too difficult for these examinees; scores on test Y are negatively skewed because of an inadequate test "ceiling." The nonlinearity in Figure 6.2A is an artifact of the inappropriate measurement; the relationship is said to be an artifact because it is an artificial result due to inadequate measurement. Tests of appropriate difficulty reveal a linear relationship between cognitive abilities such as math and spelling.

The curvilinearity between the variables in Figure 6.2B is real and not due to faulty measures. Note that r gives a conservative, minimum estimate of the relationship between

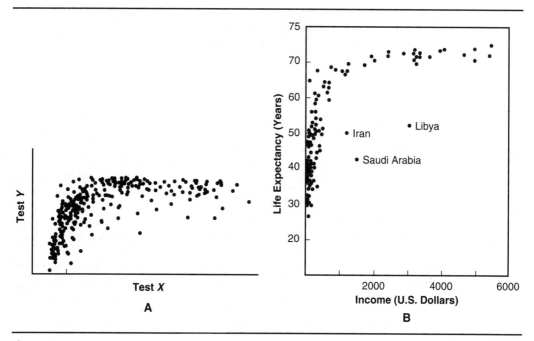

❖ **FIGURE 6.2** Spurious (panel A) and genuine (panel B) curvilinear relationships.

two variables; a curvilinear correlation coefficient[2] will never be less than r for any set of data.

The value of r for the data in Figure 6.2A is small; it is probably only about $r = .30$. It appears, however, that if the spelling test (Test Y) were made more difficult and the math test (Test X) easier, the relationship would become linear and the value of r_{XY} for these persons would increase substantially.

> **Quiz:** Describe the scatterplots for the following variables: (1) X: age in months, Y: age in years; (2) X: age of Celica, Y: assessed value of Celica; (3) among adults in their 30s, X: age, Y: height.
>
> **Answers:** (1) The swarm of points form a straight line from lower-left to upper-right, indicative of a perfect positive correlation. (2) The elliptical swarm of points is oriented from upper-left toward lower-right, indicative of a negative correlation. (3) A "blobical" swarm of points is formed without apparent orientation or directionality.

❖ 6.7 THE PEARSON PRODUCT-MOMENT CORRELATION COEFFICIENT

Before calculating the Pearson correlation coefficient, we want to become familiar with a close statistical relative, the *covariance*. We are interested in the covariance because it is a

---

[2]See Glass & Hopkins (1996, Section 8.7) for computation of nonlinear correlation coefficients. The usual measure is η ("eta"); in all instances, $\eta \geq r$. Occasionally, a nonlinear relation can be made linear if one (or both) of the variables is subjected to certain mathematical transformations.

stepping stone to expedite the computation of the correlation coefficient. Since we are now dealing with two variables, X and Y, subscripts are needed to distinguish s_X from s_Y. Notice that the formula (Eq. 4.6) for the sample variance in X can be written as:

$$s_X^2 = \frac{\Sigma x^2}{n-1} = \frac{\Sigma(X - \bar{X})^2}{n-1}$$

The covariance, s_{XY}, is defined similarly, as shown in Equation 6.2:

$$s_{XY} = \frac{\Sigma xy}{n-1} = \frac{\Sigma(X - \bar{X})(Y - \bar{Y})}{n-1} \qquad \textbf{(6.2)}$$

If there is no association between X and Y, the covariance, s_{XY}, will be zero; but unlike the correlation coefficient, it has no numerical upper limit and consequently is rarely used as a descriptive measure.

The Pearson r between variables X and Y specifically is denoted by r_{XY}, or simply r if there is no ambiguity in identifying which two variables are being correlated. The procedural steps for the calculation of r are listed below.

To compute r, the Pearson correlation coefficient:

Step 1.   Compute the standard deviations, s_X and s_Y, using Equations 4.6 and 4.7.

Step 2.   Compute the covariance using Equation 6.2.

Step 3.   Use Equation 6.3 to determine r:

$$r = \frac{s_{XY}}{s_X s_Y} \qquad \textbf{(6.3)}$$

With algebraic manipulation, this computational formula, Equation 6.3, for r is readily modified by making three replacements to show its relationship to z-scores: (1) Replace s_{XY} by $\Sigma xy/(n-1)$, (2) then replace x/s_X by z_X, and (3) replace y/s_Y by z_Y (see Math Note 16 to review formula rearrangement). After these replacements, the equation for r is expressed in the z-score format:

$$r = \frac{\Sigma z_X z_Y}{n-1} \qquad \textbf{(6.4)}$$

The z-score format (Eq. 6.4) is useful for conceptualizing the rationale underlying the correlation coefficient, but Equation 6.3 is preferable for the computation of r.

❖ 6.8 ANOTHER ALTERNATE FORMULA FOR *r*

With a little more algebra, the formula for the Pearson product-moment correlation coefficient given in Equation 6.3 can be shown to be equivalent to Equation 6.5:

$$r = \frac{\Sigma xy}{\sqrt{(SS_X)(SS_Y)}} = \frac{\Sigma XY - n\overline{X}\,\overline{Y}}{\sqrt{(\Sigma X^2 - n\overline{X}^2)(\Sigma Y^2 - n\overline{Y}^2)}} \qquad \textbf{(6.5)}$$

Except for rounding error, Equations 6.3, 6.4, and 6.5 yield identical values for *r*. Since we almost always want to know s_X and s_Y as well as *r*, Equation 6.3 is particularly useful.

The computation of *r* is illustrated in Table 6.2 for a sample of $n = 20$ students in a statistics course where $X =$ Exam I scores and $Y =$ Final Exam scores. Using Equation 6.3, the Pearson correlation coefficient, the ratio of the covariance to the product of the two standard deviations, was found to be $r = .29$ (see columns 6–9 and rows 22–27). All procedures for calculating *r* by hand are very time-consuming and highly vulnerable to computational error. Happily, calculations when *n* is large are now performed using spreadsheets or statistical software, and even some hand calculators yield *r* with a touch of a key after the data have been entered (it is still difficult to enter large data sets without data entry errors). However, avail yourself of the opportunity of working through at least one or two examples by hand, to better understand the meaning of the correlation coefficient. (In addition, your empathy for the previous generation of statistics students, who survived statistics using only pencils, tablets, and erasers, will be enhanced!)

> **Quiz:** Consult Table 6.2. (1) Compute *r* using Equation 6.4. (2) Compute the numerator of Equation 6.5, $\Sigma XY - n\,\overline{X}\,\overline{Y}$, using raw scores (reference columns 1–3). (3) The sum of squares for Test 1 was ___?___ and the sum of squares for the Final Exam was ___?___ (see columns 8–9). (4) Compute *r* using Equation 6.5.
>
> **Answers:** (1) $r = 5.501/19 = .29$, (2) $\Sigma XY - n\,\overline{X}\,\overline{Y} = 123{,}759 - 20(80.2)(76.9)$ $= 411.4$, (3) $SS_X = 1{,}483.2$, $SS_Y = 1{,}359.8$, (4) $r = 411.4/1{,}420.16 = .29$

Note in Table 6.2 that the relationship between Test I and the Final Exam is very low ($r = .29$); the modest relationship is further illuminated by the scatterplot given in Figure 6.3. There were several "slow starters" who finished strong and others who "peaked" prematurely. Notice that the highest score on the Final (94%) was earned by student #17 who scored only 75% on Test I; on the contrary, student #6 who was in the stratosphere with Test I (96%) came back to earth on the Final (81%). Stated differently, after the first test there remains a sufficient basis for hope, and an insufficient reason for overconfidence!

❖ 6.9 CORRELATION IS NOT CAUSATION

The relationship between the number of storks sighted for a seven-year period and the size of the population in a community in Germany is given in Figure 6.4—the relationship is extremely high ($r = .95$). Was your initial hypothesis regarding the origin of babies right after all?!

Correlation per se does not establish causation. The fact of a relationship between two variables does not necessarily imply that there exists a causal link between them. Even

❖ TABLE 6.2 A computational illustration of r between the Test I (X) and Final Exam (Y) for 20 students in applied statistics.

Person	TEST I X	FINAL Y	XY	x	y	xy	x^2	y^2	z_x	z_y	$z_x z_y$
1	84	66	5544	3.8	-10.9	-41.42	14.44	118.81	0.4299	-1.2884	-0.5538
2	70	77	5390	-10.2	0.1	-1.02	104.04	0.01	-1.1538	0.0118	-0.0136
3	87	84	7308	6.8	7.1	48.28	46.24	50.41	0.7692	0.8392	0.6456
4	68	56	3808	-12.2	-20.9	254.98	148.84	436.81	-1.3801	-2.4704	3.4094
5	81	86	6966	0.8	9.1	7.28	0.64	82.81	0.0905	1.0757	0.0973
6	96	81	7776	15.8	4.1	64.78	249.64	16.81	1.7873	0.4846	0.8662
7	90	79	7110	9.8	2.1	20.58	96.04	4.41	1.1086	0.2482	0.2752
8	82	82	6724	1.8	5.1	9.18	3.24	26.01	0.2036	0.6028	0.1227
9	89	81	7209	8.8	4.1	36.08	77.44	16.81	0.9955	0.4846	0.4824
10	70	84	5880	-10.2	7.1	-72.42	104.04	50.41	-1.1538	0.8392	-0.9684
11	88	81	7128	7.8	4.1	31.98	60.84	16.81	0.8824	0.4846	0.4276
12	65	74	4810	-15.2	-2.9	44.08	231.04	8.41	-1.7195	-0.3428	0.5894
13	87	74	6438	6.8	-2.9	-19.72	46.24	8.41	0.7692	-0.3428	-0.2637
14	89	74	6586	8.8	-2.9	-25.52	77.44	8.41	0.9955	-0.3428	-0.3412
15	69	74	5106	-11.2	-2.9	32.48	125.44	8.41	-1.2670	-0.3428	0.4343
16	80	71	5680	-0.2	-5.9	1.18	0.04	34.81	-0.0226	-0.6974	0.0158
17	75	94	7050	-5.2	17.1	-88.92	27.04	292.41	-0.5882	2.0213	-1.1890
18	84	83	6972	3.8	6.1	23.18	14.44	37.21	0.4299	0.7210	0.3099
19	76	68	5168	-4.2	-8.9	37.38	17.64	79.21	-0.4751	-1.0520	0.4998
$n = 20$	74	69	5106	-6.2	-7.9	48.98	38.44	62.41	-0.7014	-0.9338	0.6549
Sum:	1604	1538	123759	Sum:		411.4	1483.2	1359.8			$\Sigma z_x z_Y$: 5.5010
				Div. by $n - 1$:		21.652632	78.063158	71.568421			
				Rounded:		$s_{XY} = 21.65$	$s_X^2 = 78.06$	$s_Y^2 = 71.57$			
							$s_X = 8.84$	$s_Y = 8.46$			
Mean:	80.2	76.9				$r = 21.65/(8.84)(8.46) = .29$					

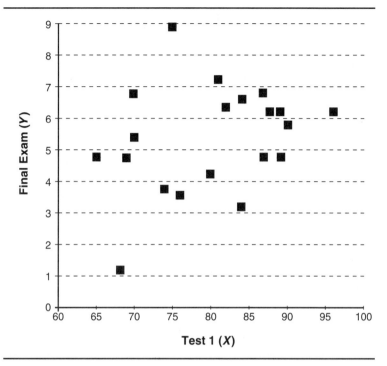

❖ **FIGURE 6.3** Scatterplot depicting the relationship between Test I and the Final Exam for 20 students in a statistics course.

though correlations between variables can be useful in investigating causal relationships when coupled with other information, it is a dangerous and potentially misleading criterion for causation when used alone. Many superstitions are probably explained by the correlation = causation fallacy. It is understandable why some babies think that a parent's kiss makes pain go away, because after the immediate kiss on the hurt finger, indeed, the pain goes away.

1. Even when one can presume that a causal relationship does exist between the two variables being correlated, r, by itself, can prove nothing about whether X causes Y or Y causes X.
2. A variable (or variables) other than the two being correlated is sometimes responsible for the observed correlation.
3. The relationships that exist among variables in behavioral and social sciences are almost always too complex to be explained in terms of a single cause.

Let us examine some examples of the problems that arise in attempts to discover causal relationships using correlation coefficients. For example, it is true that in high schools in the United States there is a positive correlation between the average teacher's salary and students' scores on achievement tests. Does this indicate that salary differences *cause* higher achievement? Would the scores be higher if the pay of teachers were increased? Affirmative answers to these questions are not justified by the correlation alone. A prominent third

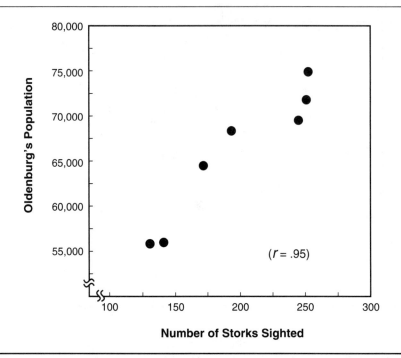

❖ **FIGURE 6.4** Scatterplot of the population of Oldenburg, Germany with the number of storks observed for years, 1930–1936. (These data, along with primary sources, can be found in Box, Hunter, & Hunter, 1978.)

variable is the financial and economic condition of the community that may largely influence both its ability to pay teachers' salaries and the students' achievement. Moreover, the economic and financial condition of the community is in part dependent upon the cognitive abilities and values of its citizens, another variable that may contribute to both higher teachers' salaries and higher academic achievement.

It has been found that the percentage of dropouts in each of a number of high schools is negatively correlated with the average number of books per pupil in the libraries of those schools. However, common sense tells us that piling more books into the library will not affect the dropout rate any more than a tougher attendance policy will bring about a magical increase in the number of volumes in the school library. If only common sense always served us so well!

Numerous studies have found correlation coefficients of $r \approx -.2$ or so between test anxiety (X) and performance on achievement and other cognitive tests (Y). Does this prove that high anxiety has, to some degree, interfered with the students' performance on the tests, and that examinees with less anxiety (not being handicapped by fear and worry) were able to perform up to a fuller measure of their ability? This conclusion may be attractive because it may fit our expectation. Is it not also plausible that achievement differences cause anxiety? Might not unprepared pupils become anxious when their knowledge is tested, while well-prepared students find the testing experience pleasant and less anxiety producing? What is involved here is the question of whether X can be said to cause Y or Y to cause *X*—a simple correlation coefficient between *X* and *Y* cannot decide the matter. Studies of association alone, without other controls, are often impossible to interpret causatively.

Failure to point out that a correlation does not prove causation is a widespread error in the interpretation of data. Of course, it is not the statistic, *r*, that is at fault. Have you noticed how readily we tacitly infer causation to correlations that support our beliefs, or how adroitly we detect this *post hoc* fallacy (i.e., correlation = causation) when the stated relationship contradicts our core beliefs? For example, Sunday school attendance is generally believed to be valuable in many ways (and it may be), but a positive relationship between Sunday school attendance and honesty, for example, cannot imply that children are honest because they attend Sunday School. Underlying and causing both attendance and honesty may be, for example, training in the home. Definite scientific evidence regarding causation requires experimental studies—studies in which persons are randomly assigned to treatment experimental and control groups. Statistics for this type of study are considered in Chapter 10.

> **Quiz:** How can the following relationships be explained other than causation? There is a substantial correlation between: (1) water temperature of the ocean and the number of drownings at nearby beaches, and (2) the number of handguns in cities and the number of murders in cities.
>
> **Answers:** (1) Warmer water probably attracts more swimmers, and thus more drownings. (2) Population figures would probably account for the correlation.

While correlation does not directly establish a causal relationship, it may furnish clues to causes (Cronbach, 1982; Smith & Glass, 1986). When it is feasible, these clues can be formalized as hypotheses that can be tested in other studies in which control, either direct or statistical, can be exerted over other influences.

❖ 6.10 ZERO CORRELATION AND CAUSATION

Just as a positive correlation cannot be said to represent causation, so a zero correlation does not necessarily rule out a causal relationship. For example, some studies with college students have found no correlation between hours of study for an examination and test performance. If you believe that the amount of study is unrelated to test performance, we have some nice bridges for sale that might interest you! Actually, some gifted students study little and still achieve as well as some of their less gifted classmates who study more. A well-designed study that controls for aptitude and background would no doubt show that hours of study do in fact influence test performance to some extent.

From the above discussion, it should be clear that we must be very careful not to infer causation solely on the basis of a correlation coefficient. Likewise, we cannot conclude with certainty that there is no causative relationship between two variables just because some correlation coefficient from some ill-designed "study" fails to show a relationship between the two variables.[3] Nonzero correlation coefficients do indicate that *Y* can be pre-

---

[3]It is useful to keep distinct (1) the relation between two variables, as measured, and (2) the actual relation between two variables. Mere mortals can compute the first; only God knows the second. This chapter, as well as Chapter 7, details several reasons why a measured relationship may be an incomplete indication of the true or actual relationship between two variables.

dicted more accurately if we know X than if we do not know X, but prediction per se does not necessarily presuppose a causal relationship. In one of our best chapters, Chapter 8, we will deal more fully with the topic of prediction.

❖ CHAPTER SUMMARY

An objective and precise measure to describe the degree of relationship between two variables is highly desirable in scientific inquiry. The Pearson product-moment correlation (r for a sample, and ρ for the population) is the usual measure of correlation. The degree of linear relationship can vary from a perfect negative correlation of $r = -1.0$ up to a perfect positive correlation of $r = +1.0$. The magnitude of the relationship is indicated by the absolute value of the correlation coefficient—the greater the magnitude of r, the stronger the relationship and the greater the predictability of Y from X or X from Y. The sign (+ or –) of a coefficient only indicates the direction of the relationship. A coefficient of 0 indicates no correlation between two variables was detected. A strong positive correlation indicates that there is a tendency for persons to maintain similar z-scores on the two measures, that is, persons who have high numbers on X tend to also have high numbers on Y, and that low numbers on Y are associated with low numbers on X. A negative relationship indicates that high scorers on variable X tend to be low scorers on variable Y and vice versa.

The correlation coefficient accurately describes the degree of association between two variables only when they are linearly (straight-line) related. If a curvilinear (curved-line) relationship exists between X and Y, the Pearson r should not be used to quantify the relationship since the actual degree of association would be spuriously underestimated by r. Statistical measures for curvilinear relationships can be found in more advanced texts. Scatterplots adequately allow a visual check of the linearity or nonlinearity question.

Correlation must be carefully distinguished from causation. There can be correlation without causation, and vice versa.

MASTERY TEST

1. Which correlation coefficient below indicates the strongest relationship?
   (a) .55   (b) .09   (c) –.77   (d) .1

2. With which of the coefficients given as options to question 1 do the X-observations below $\overline{X}$ tend to be associated with Y-scores above $\overline{Y}$?

3. If IQ scores correlate .5 with "% right" on a test for a group of third-grade pupils, then what is the correlation between IQ scores and "% wrong"?

4. Suppose a measure of political conservatism is given to representative samples of persons of ages 15, 20, 30, 45, and 60 and that the respective means were 60, 85, 80, 70, and 65. The correlation between age and political conservatism is which of the following?
   (a) 1.0   (b) –1.0   (c) linear   (d) curvilinear

5. If the Pearson r were calculated between age and political conservatism in question 4, the obtained coefficient would be
   (a) an underestimate of the true relationship.
   (b) an overestimate of the true relationship.
   (c) an accurate estimate of the true relationship.

In questions 6–10, select the scatter diagram that best matches the relationship described.

6. $\rho = +1.00$ Perfect direct relationship

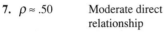
(a)

7. $\rho \approx .50$ Moderate direct
relationship

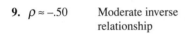

8. $\rho = .00$ No relationship (i.e., 0
covariation of X with Y)

(b)

9. $\rho \approx -.50$ Moderate inverse
relationship

(c)

10. $\rho = -1.00$ Perfect inverse
relationship

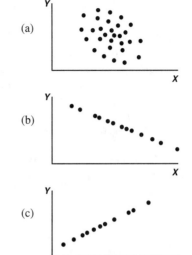

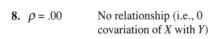

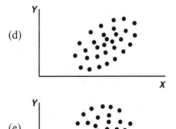

(d)

(e)

11. Indicate whether the expected correlation between the two designated variables would be positive, negative, or zero. (Assume the population for items a–i below is made up of all persons in grade 12 in the United States.)
(a) X, height in inches; Y, weight in pounds
(b) X, age in months; Y, time in seconds required to run 50 yards
(c) X, reading achievement in grade-placement units; Y, arithmetic achievement in grade-placement units
(d) X, shoe size; Y, "citizenship" rating of student on a 10-point scale by his or her teacher
(e) X, arithmetic achievement in T-score units; Y, number of days absent from school during the year
(f) X, social security numbers; Y, IQs (ignore persons without social security numbers)
(g) X, interest in sports; Y, interest in politics
(h) X, total miles traveled by a car; Y, year in which the car was manufactured
(i) X, maximum daily temperature; Y, amount of water used by residents

12. If $r_{XY} = -.80$ in part h of question 11, what would the value of r_{XY} be if Y was changed from "year in which the car was manufactured" to "age of vehicle"?

13. The correlation of X with Y is $r = .60$; the correlation of X with W is $r = -.80$. Is X more closely linearly related to Y or to W?

14. If $r_{XY} = .50$, what is r_{YX}?

15. If $r_{AB} = 1.0$ and $r_{AC} = -1.0$, what is r_{BC}?

16. If the number of correct answers to questions 1–15 above was correlated with the number of incorrect answers, what would r be? (Assume no omitted answers.)

17. If you computed r and obtained $r = -1.3$, you would know for certain that
    (a) the relationship is extremely strong.
    (b) the relationship is certainly negative.
    (c) both of the above
    (d) a computational error has been made.

18. Which of these is not a parameter?
    (a) σ (b) r (c) ρ (d) σ^2 (e) μ

19. Which symbol in question 18 would be used to describe the relationship between two variables for a sample of observations?

20. One study on heart attacks reported that persons who attend church regularly had a lower risk of heart attacks than nonattenders. Assuming the information is true, which one of the following statements is correct?
    (a) If you start attending church more regularly, your chances of a heart attack are *certain* to be reduced.
    (b) There is definitely no causal relationship between the two variables.
    (c) If you are a regular churchgoer, you are less likely to have a heart attack than if you are a nonchurchgoer.
    (d) The correlation provides definitive information pertaining to causation.

21. A researcher correlated the MTAI scores of a group of 100 experienced secondary school teachers with the number of students each teacher failed in a year. He obtained an r of $-.39$. He concluded that teachers tend to fail students because they do not have "accepting" attitudes toward students. Comment on the researcher's conclusions.

ANSWERS TO MASTERY TEST

1. (c)
2. (c)
3. $-.5$
4. (d)
5. (a)
6. (c)
7. (d)
8. (e)
9. (a)
10. (b)
11. (a) positive, (b) zero, (c) positive, (d) zero, (e) negative, (f) zero, (g) zero, (h) negative, (i) positive

12. $r = .80$
13. W
14. $.50$
15. $r_{BC} = -1.0$
16. -1.0
17. (d)
18. (b)
19. (b)
20. (c)
21. The researcher mistakenly assumed that correlation implies causation.

PROBLEMS AND EXERCISES

1. Compute the Pearson product-moment correlation coefficient between the 10 pairs of arithmetic and IQ scores below. (Use Eq. 6.3.)

Pupil	IQ	Arithmetic
A	105	15
B	120	23
C	83	11
D	137	22
E	114	17
F	96	10
G	107	4
H	117	30
I	108	18
J	130	14

2. Using Equation 6.5, compute the Pearson r for the data in problem 1 after subtracting 80 from every IQ score and after adding 10 to each Arithmetic score. How does this value of r compare with the value of r obtained in problem 1?

3. The numerator of Equation 6.5 is Σxy or $\Sigma(X - \bar{X})(Y - \bar{Y})$, that is, the sum of the products of the deviation scores. Which two individuals (in problem 1 above) contributed most to the positive correlation coefficient, $r = .52$, and which two individuals most diminished the correlation coefficient? ($\bar{X}_{IQ} = 111.7$ and $\bar{X}_{arith} = 16.4$)

4. A group of 10 students were given two forms of a typing test, and the number of errors that were made by each student on each test was determined. Find the sum of the z-score products and the Pearson correlation coefficient between the number of errors on test 1 and the number of errors on test 2. The means and standard deviations are given, so it is convenient to use the standard z-score formula for r (Eq. 6.4).

Student	Test 1	Test 2	z_1	z_2	$z_1 z_2$
a	8	10	___	___	___
b	7	7	___	___	___
c	4	8	___	___	___
d	4	6	___	___	___
e	4	6	___	___	___
f	4	4	___	___	___
g	3	7	___	___	___
h	3	4	___	___	___
i	2	3	___	___	___
j	1	5	___	___	___
	$\bar{X}_1 = 4$	$\bar{X}_2 = 6$		$\Sigma z_1 z_2 =$ ___	
	$s_1 = 2$	$s_2 = 2$			

5. One study reported the importance of eight morale factors for employees and employers as indicated below.

	Importance	
Factor	Employees	Employers
A. Credit for work done	1	7
B. Interesting work	2	3
C. Fair play	3	1
D. Understanding and appreciation	4	5
E. Counseling on personal problems	5	8
F. Promotion based on merit	6	4
G. Good working conditions	7	6
H. Job security	8	2

(a) Compute Pearson r using Equation 6.5.

(b) Which two factors contributed most to the negative correlation?

6. Researchers demonstrated a correlation of $r = -.52$ between average teacher's salary (X) and the proportion of students who drop out of school before graduating (Y) across 120 high schools in a state. They concluded that increasing teachers' salaries would reduce the dropout rate. Comment on their conclusions.

7. Compute r for the following data:

	Rodent Identification						
	a	b	c	d	e	f	g
Hours of Deprivation, X	2	3	4	5	6	7	8
Time to Learn Maze, Y	9	7	8	4	4	5	2

(a) Compute r.

(b) Construct a scatterplot of these data.

(c) Comment upon the relationship between r and the shape of the plot of points.

8. The data given in the table below show the relationship between verbal and nonverbal IQs from the Lorge-Thorndike Intelligence Test (LT) and the reading and arithmetic achievement as measured by the Iowa Test of Basic Skills (ITBS). At each grade level, each correlation is based on approximately 2,500 nationally representative pupils.

	Verbal IQ			Nonverbal IQ		
Grade Level	3	5	7	3	5	7
Reading	.68	.76	.81	.53	.65	.67
Arithmetic	.66	.72	.74	.61	.68	.71

On the basis of the above data, are the following statements true or false?

(a) The correlation between the intelligence and achievement measures appears to increase with grade level.

(b) The nonverbal IQs correlate as highly with achievement as do verbal IQs.

(c) Verbal and nonverbal IQs tend to correlate slightly higher with reading than with arithmetic.

(d) The correlation between both measures of achievement and both measures of intelligence is substantial at each of the three grade levels.

9. Compute r for the following pairs of scores:

	Student Identification					
	a	b	c	d	e	f
Hours Employed, X	40	0	28	15	44	8
Hours of Study, Y	20	24	16	30	18	28

10. Compute r for the following pairs of scores:

	Student Identification						
	a	b	c	d	e	f	g
Attitude Scores, X	9	4	6	2	8	4	2
Aptitude Scores, Y	4	7	8	3	6	2	4

11. A random sample of 6 students was selected to do a pilot run of a study to investigate the relationship between speed of reading an essay (X) measured in minutes required to read the essay, and the recall of content detail (Y) as measured by a quiz over the material presented in the essay. Compute the Pearson r based on the data as recorded below.

	Student Identification					
	a	b	c	d	e	f
Speed of Reading, X	10	8	15	12	14	16
Recall of Content, Y	17	17	13	16	15	12

ANSWERS TO PROBLEMS AND EXERCISES

1. $s_X = 15.73$, $s_Y = 7.412$, $s_{XY} = 60.36$; $r = .52$

2. $SS_X = 2,228$, $SS_Y = 494.4$, $\Sigma xy = 543.2$; $r = .52$ (Linear transformations do not alter the value of r since the shapes of the distributions remain intact.)

3. Pupils C ($xy = 154.98$) and D ($xy = 141.68$) contributed most. Pupils I ($xy = -5.92$) and J ($xy = -43.92$) diminished the computed r the most.

4. $\Sigma z_1 z_2 = 7.25$; $r = .81$.

5. (a) $r = -.095$ (b) A and H

6. The researcher is inferring a causal relationship solely from correlational evidence. He has no justification for doing so. It may well be the case—and probably is—that teachers' salaries and the dropout rate are *both* functions of the social and economic status of the community, and that increasing teachers' salaries in a given school would not bring about a decrease in the dropout rate.

7. (a) $\Sigma X^2 = 203$, $SS_X = 28$; $s_X = 2.16$; $\Sigma Y^2 = 255$, $\Sigma Y^2 = 255$, $SS_Y = 37.71$; $s_Y = 2.51$; $\Sigma XY = 166$; $\Sigma XY = 166$; $s_{XY} = -4.83$; $r = s_{XY}/(s_X s_Y) = -4.83/5.42$; $r = = -.89$

(b)

Time to Learn (vertical axis) vs *Hours of Deprivation* (horizontal axis)

(c) The narrow elliptical scatterplot indicates a strong negative relationship be-

tween time to learn and hours of deprivation.

8. (a) true
   (b) false
   (c) false (true only with verbal IQs, not
   with nonverbal IQs)
   (d) true

9. $\Sigma X^2 = 4609$; $SS_X = 1571.5$; $s_X = 17.73$;
   $\Sigma Y^2 = 3240$; $SS_Y = 157.33$; $s_Y = 5.61$;
   $\Sigma XY = 2714$; $s_{XY} = -69.2$;

$r = s_{XY}/(s_X s_Y) = -69.2/99.47$; $r = -.70$

10. $\Sigma X^2 = 221$; $SS_X = 46$; $s_X = 2.77$;
    $\Sigma Y^2 = 194$; $SS_Y = 28.86$; $s_Y = 2.19$;
    $\Sigma XY = 182$; $s_{XY} = 2$;
    $r = s_{XY}/(s_X s_Y) = 2/6.07$; $r = .33$

11. $\Sigma X^2 = 985$; $SS_X = 47.5$; $s_X = 3.08$;
    $\Sigma Y^2 = 1372$; $SS_Y = 22$; $s_Y = 2.10$;
    $\Sigma XY = 1095$; $s_{XY} = -6$;
    $r = s_{XY}/(s_X s_Y) = -6/6.47$; $r = -.93$

 COMPUTER CHALLENGE

1. Complete the correlation matrix printed below giving the Pearson correlation coefficients for the
   curricular variables of the HSB data set.

	Reading	Writing	Math	Science	Civics
Reading	1.00				
Writing		1.00			
Math			1.00		
Science				1.00	
Civics					1.00

2. When one variable is a dichotomy (e.g., sex) and the other variable is continuous (e.g., reading
   scores), the Pearson formula for r results in the point-biserial correlation coefficient (see Glass
   & Hopkins, Section 7.15, 1996). Find the point-biserial correlation coefficients between sex and
   each of the five curricular variables of the HSB data set.

7

Interpreting Correlation Coefficients:
Factors That Influence the Value of *r*

❖ 7.1 INTRODUCTION

Correlational analyses are among the most frequently used statistical procedures in the behavioral sciences. Correlation coefficients abound in academia and professional research, and occasionally find their way into the popular media. Proper interpretation of correlation coefficients requires an understanding of factors that can substantially influence the value of *r*.

Correlation coefficients are not only frequently used in research, they would appear high in the list of "The Top 10 Most Frequently Misinterpreted Statistics." Correlation coefficients are often confused with causation (Section 6.9) or misinterpreted as percentages. The effects of dissimilar distributions, range-restriction, and measurement error are often unrecognized and ignored. Sophisticated-sounding jargon such as "highly statistically significant" can give a gross exaggeration of the importance or practicality of the findings in the ears of the statistically illiterate. In this chapter, special attention is given to factors that influence the numerical value and interpretation of *r*.

❖ 7.2 LINEAR TRANSFORMATIONS AND CORRELATION

When raw scores are converted to percentages, the raw scores have been *transformed* into percentages; a transformation converts one set of numbers into a different set of numbers. Any transformation of scores (e.g., subtracting a constant from each score) that does not change the shape of the distribution is a *linear* transformation. Such transformations as raw scores into percentage scores (or to *z*-scores or *T*-scores) are termed linear transformations; there is a perfect linear correlation $|r| = 1.0$ between the raw scores and the transformed scores. Adding, subtracting, multiplying, and dividing by a constant are all linear transformations. Thus, the correlation between one measure (*X*) and any other measure (Y) will be identical in absolute value regardless of whether r is computed using raw scores, percent-correct scores, z-scores, T-scores, or any other linear transformation of X or Y. These are all linear transformations that alter only the mean and/or standard deviation, but leave the shape of the distribution intact—they do not affect skewness, outliers, et cetera. For example, in Table 6.2 (Section 6.8) a correlation of .29 was found between scores on Test I and scores on the Final Exam. This $r = .29$ would remain if the Test I scores were converted to z-scores, or the Final Exam scores were converted to T-scores. Linear transformations do not affect the correlation between two sets of measures obtained on a sample or population.

However, the use of exponents, such as squaring each score or taking the square root of each score, is a *nonlinear* transformation, and will alter the shape of the distribution. This alteration will change several aspects of the distribution—central tendency, variability, and skewness. Unlike linear transformations, the z-score for a given value of X will differ depending on the particular nonlinear transformation employed. If z-scores change on a variable, then the correlations between that variable and all other variables will also change.

> **Quiz:** Using raw scores $r_{XY} = .77$. Would r_{XY} change when: (1) each X-score was changed to a z-score? (2) 100 was added to each Y-score? (3) each X-score was changed to percent-correct? (4) each Y-score was squared?
>
> **Answers:** (1) no, (2) no, (3) no, (4) yes, squaring (or taking the square root) is a nonlinear transformation and may alter the shape of the distribution and all its parameters.

❖ 7.3 SCATTERPLOTS

In Chapter 6, we made use of scatterplots to see if a relationship appeared to be linear or curvilinear—the nature of the relationship between two measures is often illuminated if their scatterplot is studied. Scatterplots also can identify many computational errors in r, that is, is the visual check of the scatterplot commensurate with the computed value of r? From Figure 7.1, it is seen that the correlation is substantial, linear, and positive; hence, the computed value of $r = .612$ appears reasonable.

> **Quiz:** (1) If the swarm of points in a scatterplot is oriented from lower-left to upper-right, r is expected to be ___?___ (positive or negative). (2) As the elliptical swarm of points becomes more and more narrow, the absolute value of r gets ___?___. (3) If r is near zero and the relationship is not curvilinear, the swarm of points could be described as ___?___.
>
> **Answers:** (1) positive, (2) larger and closer to 1.0, (3) roughly circular or "blobical"

Computer software is readily available for computers and microcomputers that computes correlation coefficients and produces scatterplots like those in Figures 6.3 and 7.1. Figure 7.1 depicts the relationship ($r = .612$) between scores on a standardized reading readiness test given to 157 kindergarteners and scores on a standardized reading test administered one year later to the same students. By studying the scatterplot, it is evident that reading "failure" can be predicted more accurately than reading "success;" no pupil with very low scores on the reading readiness test obtained a high score on the reading test, yet some pupils with high reading readiness scores obtained low scores on the reading test. This kind of information is not revealed by a correlation coefficient.

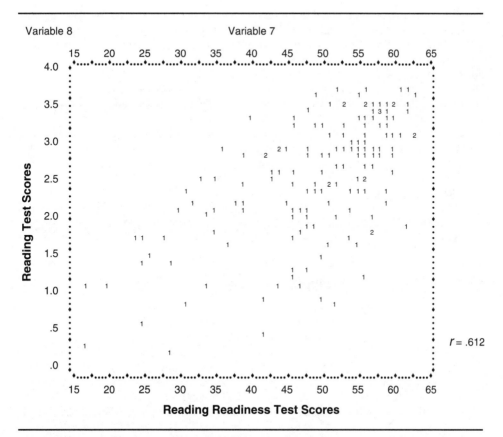

FIGURE 7.1 A computer-produced scatterplot of 157 raw scores on a standardized kindergarten reading readiness test with subsequent grade-equivalent scores on a standardized reading test administered at the end of grade 1. (The "2s" in Figure 7.1 indicate that two students with identical X-scores also had Y-scores that were equal—that is, two "dots" are represented by the "2.")

❖ 7.4 THE PEARSON CORRELATION COEFFICIENT AS AN INFERENTIAL STATISTIC

If all N observations in the population are used in the computation of the correlation coefficient, the resulting coefficient is the parameter, ρ ("rho"), not an inferential statistic, r. As is the case with the mean, whether the formulas result in a parameter (ρ) or a statistic (r) is not a computational matter, but depends on whether the coefficient is based on the population of observations or only on a sample of observations. If the entire population of observations is used, the covariance is symbolized by σ_{XY} (rather than s_{XY}) and the standard deviations by σ_X and σ_Y (rather than s_X and s_Y). Occasionally, observations in the population are available, and ρ is used to symbolize the population correlation coefficient. For example, if the median income and median years of schooling were correlated for all states, the obtained correlation should be designated ρ rather than r. However, since all observations in the population are rarely represented in the set of data on which the correlation coefficient is based, r (not ρ) is ordinarily obtained. In Chapter 13, the interesting procedures for determining how accurately r estimates ρ are developed. The accuracy of r as an estimate of ρ depends largely on how the sample is selected and on n—estimates of ρ are quite erratic and crude with small n's.

Like all statistical measures in this book, r has the *consistency* property (Section 4.15)—as the size of the random sample (n) increases, the absolute difference between the inferential statistic r and the parameter ρ decreases, that is, the sampling error, $|r - \rho|$, decreases as n increases. However, the statistic r is not an unbiased estimate of ρ; the expected value of r is slightly less than ρ, but (like s) the amount of bias is negligible unless n is quite small.

Quiz: Complete the analogies: (1) Population is to ρ as sample is to ___?___ . (2) r is to statistic as ρ is to ___?___ . (3) If you were to describe the degree of relationship between quiz #1 and quiz #2 for *this* statistics class, which symbol for the correlation coefficient is appropriate? (4) Under what conditions is $|r - \rho|$ expected to be very small?

Answers: (1) r, (2) parameter, (3) ρ, (4) when n is very large

❖ 7.5 EFFECT OF MEASUREMENT ERROR ON r

In the social and behavioral sciences, variables of interest are often very difficult to assess, for example, personality, adjustment, attitudes, aptitudes, achievement, classroom climate, et cetera. Different measures of the same variable or the same measure administered on different occasions may reveal considerable discrepancies. In measurement theory, these differences are described as *measurement error*. Measurement error stems from a number of sources—different samples of test items, different test lengths (short tests are notoriously inconsistent), different observers, different scoring strategies, different levels of subjectivity (subjective tests usually contain substantial measurement error), different assessment procedures, good or bad luck in guessing, differences in levels of concentration or functioning, and so on. A fact of human experience is that we do not always function at a uniform level. Sometimes, admittedly and with all humility, we are remarkable; other days, however, and in all honesty, we are pathetic—if it is "one of those days," we need to invoke all our forces of rationalization to discredit the authenticity of the data at hand.

Since correlations are based on obtained scores that contain measurement error, the correlation coefficients of these scores with other variables are influenced by measurement error. Unfortunately, the effects of measurement error are often ignored; the correlation between measures X and Y is not distinguished from the correlation between variables X and Y. A surprising number of researchers are unaware of the influences of measurement error on the computed value of r. Measurement error in X or Y or both X and Y can greatly reduce the numerical value of r. Other things being equal, the greater the measurement error in X or Y, the lower will be the absolute value of the computed r; the smaller the measurement error, the larger the $|r|$. The weight and height for kindergarteners, when carefully measured, are substantially related, but we can imagine flawed ways of measuring each of these variables (e.g., by "eyeball" guessing or self-report) that contain so much measurement error that weight and height measures could show little or no correlation.

You have probably encountered "reliability" coefficients—reliability is the opposite of measurement error: the higher the reliability coefficient, the smaller the measurement error; the greater the measurement error, the smaller the reliability coefficient. If a measure has a reliability coefficient of 1.0, it is said to have perfect reliability. Measures of distance, weight, and time can have near perfect reliability. Independent estimates of character based on photographs would probably have a reliability coefficient near zero. If the quality of one's teaching were measured by a supervisor's ratings (which have been shown to have enormous measurement error), the correlation between teaching performance with any other variable is seriously diminished by the measurement error in the performance ratings. Without a reliable measure of teaching performance, teaching ability cannot be predicted very well regardless of any available relevant data.

As another example, suppose that cognitive aptitude and achievement were estimated from very short and inadequate measures (e.g., ten-item assessments). The computed *r* between them, instead of being substantial ($r \approx .6$), would be quite low ($r \approx .3$). If we reduce the measurement error, the obtained *r* will increase accordingly. In interpreting any correlation coefficient, we must bear in mind how and how well *X* and *Y* were measured.[1]

Quiz: Figure 6.3 is a scatterplot of scores on Test 1 and the Final Exam for a group of statistics students in which $r = .29$. (1) If only the odd-numbered items were scored, and *r* were recomputed, can you predict the direction of the change? (2) If Test 1 had been lengthened from 40 items to 80 items, the new *r* would be expected to be ____ (<, =, >) .29.

Answers: (1) Since shorter measures (i.e., smaller samples of items) have greater measurement error, the *r* would be expected to be less than .29.   (2) >

❖ 7.6 THE PEARSON *r* AND MARGINAL DISTRIBUTIONS

Mathematically, the maximum computed value of *r* under the most favorable circumstances is 1.0. However, *r* can attain the value of 1.0 only when both frequency distributions have precisely the same shape. (The marginal distribution of *X* is simply the frequency distribution of the measure represented on the baseline of a scatterplot; the marginal distribution of *Y* (the measure represented by the vertical axis) is the frequency distribution of *Y*—these two frequency distributions in a scatterplot are called *marginal distributions*.) If *X* is normally distributed and *Y* is skewed negatively, the maximum value for *r* is somewhat less than 1. The more dissimilar the shapes, the lower the maximum value for *r*. If one measure is dichotomous (e.g., dead or alive) and the other is normally distributed, the maximum value of the correlation can drop to .7 or even lower. In Figure 6.2A (Section 6.6), where one variable (Test *Y*) is skewed negatively and the other variable (Test *X*) is skewed positively, the maximum positive value for *r* would be considerably less than 1.0—perhaps $r \approx .8$ or so.

With a little practice, you can surmise what the approximate shape of the marginal frequency distributions would be from studying the data in the scatterplot. If you scrutinize the scatterplot of Figure 7.1, you will notice the preponderance of points in the upper right quadrant. Think of collapsing all the points, first down along the baseline to assess the shape of the *X*-variable. Can you see that most of the points would cluster in the higher scores regions of reading readiness. Next, mentally collapse the data over along the right margin to assess the shape of the *Y*-variable. Can you surmise that reading readiness and reading scores both appear to be skewed negatively? The shapes of the marginal distributions of *X* and *Y* should be borne in mind when interpreting correlation coefficients.

---

[1]Methods for estimating these reliability coefficients can be found in Chapter 5 of Hopkins, Stanley, & Hopkins (1990). There is a procedure to estimate the correlation between two variables assuming that each variable is measured free of measurement error—to correct *r* for the "attenuation" due to measurement error (Section 7.5). This "correction for attenuation" requires the obtained correlation coefficient and the reliability coefficients for *X* and *Y*.

Quiz: Study panel B of Figure 6.2 (Section 6.6); what is the shape of the distribution of measure X (Income)?

Answer: X is skewed positively.

❖ 7.7 EFFECTS OF HETEROGENEITY ON CORRELATION

Another major, and often ignored, influence on r results from the degree of heterogeneity of the sample. Other things being equal, the greater the variability of the sample data, the greater the value of r. With low variability among the observations, measurement errors may obscure whatever relationship might exist. For example, in a school having students of relatively homogeneous socioeconomic status (SES), the correlation between SES and achievement (or between SES and any other variable) will be much lower than in a school that is more heterogeneous in SES.

Figure 7.2 illustrates the common phenomenon of range restriction and its consequences on computed correlation coefficients. Notice that when the entire range in included, the scatterplot has a long narrow elliptical shape indicative of a very strong positive correlation coefficient. However, if only the upper region of X is selected, the scatterplot is

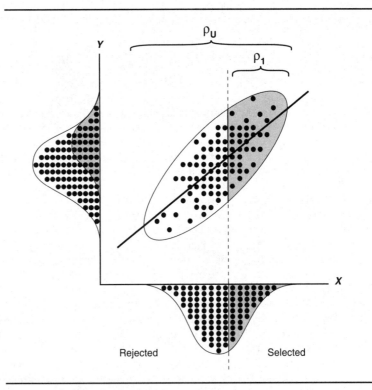

❖ **FIGURE 7.2** An illustration of the effect of restricted variability on the correlation between X and Y. The correlation coefficient *within* the selected and more homogeneous group (ρ_1) underestimates the magnitude of the relationship for the unrestricted range (ρ_U).

as wide as it is long—indicative of a modest value for r. There is only a slight relationship remaining between the two variables within the selected group, yet a substantial relationship exists for the total group.

> **Quiz:** If in Lincoln School each student's IQ score is multiplied by 10, (1) would the standard deviation be increased by a factor of 10? (2) Would this make the sample more heterogeneous and therefore enhance the correlations between IQ and other variables such as reading? (3) If only high ability students were used in the sample, the correlation between IQ and reading would ___?___ (increase, decrease, remain unchanged).

> **Answers:** (1) yes, (2) no, r is the average z-score product and all z-scores would remain unchanged by this linear transformation. (Note that when raw scores are converted to percentages, the raw scores are divided by a constant—the maximum score—to obtain a proportion, which is then multiplied by the constant 100 to obtain the percentage.) (3) decrease

Consider the scatterplot in Figure 7.1, which depicts the relationship between reading readiness test scores (X) in kindergarten and reading achievement test scores (Y) one year later at the end of the first grade for a large group of pupils. Suppose (to make the illustration dramatic) that all pupils with reading readiness test scores below the minimal criterion of 45 had not been promoted to grade one (but were required to spend another year in kindergarten). Obviously, then there would be no grade one reading test (Y) scores for the pupils who repeated kindergarten, hence scores for these children would be unavailable in the computation of r. Notice how much more nearly circular the scatterplot becomes when the range has been decreased and the lower-scoring pupils (below 45) on the reading readiness test are "erased." The r would drop from .61 to perhaps .20 or so.

The reading variable of the original ($n = 600$) HSB data set (from which our case study sample of $n = 200$ is a random sample) is substantially correlated to the other four subject matter variables as shown in line 1 of Table 7.1 where no selectivity was imposed on the data. However, when increasingly restrictive criteria were imposed, the correlations were diminished accordingly. When the bottom 20 percent who had reading z-scores less than -1.0 were eliminated, the r's between reading and the other variables dropped .05 to .10 points (see row 2 of Table 7.1). When only those whose reading score exceeded $\overline{X}_{reading}$ were selected ($n = 315$), the r's dropped .20 to .25 points (see row 3 in Table 7.1). When only the top 128 readers were selected (those with z-scores greater than 1.0), the r's dropped .32 to .45 points (see row 4 in Table 7.1). It is clear that the more the range of one of the variables is restricted, the greater the diminishing effect upon r. When a severe selec-

❖ **TABLE 7.1** The correlation of reading with four variables from the original HSB data set ($n = 600$) under differing selection criteria for restricting the range of the reading scores.

		Reading Correlated With			
Selection Criterion	Number	Writing	Math	Science	Civics
Total Group	$n = 600$	.63	.68	.69	.59
Reading Scores $z > -1$	$n = 480$	.54	.58	.62	.49
Reading Scores above $\overline{X}$	$n = 315$	.38	.45	.49	.36
Reading Scores $z > +1$	$n = 128$	.18	.31	.26	.24
Reading and Math $z > +1$	$n = 61$	.03	.06	.03	.14

tion criterion for both reading and math was imposed (students whose z-scores for reading and math exceeded 1.0), the original substantial correlation of $r = .63$ was almost completely washed out, $r = .03$.

Much misinterpretation of correlation has resulted from the failure to consider this important delimiting factor. The correlation between achievement and IQ will be seriously underestimated if based on a class of slow learners, since the ranges of both IQ and achievement have been curtailed. The correlation between performance in the long jump and the 100-yard dash will be much lower using only the members of the track team than it would be if a more heterogeneous group were sampled. A common example of restricted variability, and hence an underestimated relationship, is the correlation between college admission tests (SAT, ACT, GRE) and subsequent college grade-point averages. Since the tests are used in the selection and rejection of applicants, the correlation of test scores using only the selected students with a subsequent criterion (such as GPA) will underestimate the relationship and the test's predictive value for the total population. The degree of underestimation is related to the degree of selectivity; the more homogeneous the group, the lower the correlation. In a classic study, Thorndike (1949) found that the correlation between test performance and job performance was $r = .64$ for a total group of applicants ($n = 1,031$), but the correlation dropped to only $r = .18$ for the $n = 136$ who eventually qualified.

> **Quiz:** There is a subtle form of range restriction in Figure 6.3 (Section 6.8); a few students who did poorly dropped the statistics class after Test 1, and consequently were not included in the computation of r. How does the observed r of .29 of Figure 6.3 compare to the value of r expected if the low-scoring students had not dropped the course? Why?
>
> **Answers:** If there had been no loss of students, r would be expected to be greater than .29. When the range of either X or Y is restricted, the resulting computed correlation coefficient is diminished.

❖ 7.8 CORRECTING FOR RESTRICTED VARIABILITY

If we know the correlation for the homogeneous or restricted group (ρ_1) and the standard deviations of X for the restricted (σ_1) and the unrestricted population (σ_U), the correlation for the unrestricted population (ρ_U) can be estimated from Equation 7.1. The importance of Equation 7.1 for the purpose of correcting r's for distortions resulting from heterogeneity or homogeneity in the measures is obvious. However, understanding the concept of Equation 7.1 to illuminate the consequence of restricted (or exaggerated) variability on the magnitude of the observed correlation coefficient is much more important:

$$\rho_U^2 = \frac{\rho_1^2 \left(\dfrac{\sigma_U}{\sigma_1}\right)^2}{1 + \rho_1^2 \left(\dfrac{\sigma_U}{\sigma_1}\right)^2 - \rho_1^2} \tag{7.1a}$$

$$\rho_U = \sqrt{\rho_U^2} \tag{7.1b}$$

where ρ_1 and σ_1 are obtained on the restricted group 1, and σ_U and ρ_U are for the unrestricted population, group U.

Suppose all applicants for Whiz College with a score below 600 on the College Board SAT were rejected, and all those with scores of 600 or higher were accepted. For the selected applicants, the correlation between the SAT and GPA scores was .5. Estimate the correlation if all applicants had been admitted. The standard deviation in the selected group is 50, half the value of $\sigma = 100$ for the unselected group. Therefore, from Equation 7.1:

$$\rho_U^2 = \frac{(.5)^2\left(\dfrac{100}{50}\right)^2}{1+(.5)^2(2)^2-(.5)^2} = \frac{(.25)(2)^2}{1+(.25)(4)-.25} = \frac{1.00}{1.75} = .5714$$

$$\rho_U = \sqrt{.5714} = .76$$

The validity of Equation 7.1 rests on two assumptions that are represented in Figure 7.2: (1) that there is a linear relationship between X and Y throughout the entire range of X-values, and (2) that the scatterplot possesses *homoscedasticity*; in other words, that the standard deviation of Y is uniform at all points along the X-axis. (We will have more interesting things to say about homoscedasticity in Chapter 8.) Both these assumptions appear to be credible in Figure 7.2. In many instances, however, these assumptions are suspect; as, for example, in our illustration with SAT scores and college GPA. In instances where linearity is known from previous research, Equation 7.1 has been shown to be quite accurate. The homoscedasticity condition is suspect in Figure 7.1 where there appears to be more variation in Y's for high X's than for low X's; that is, no "low scorers" on X received good scores on Y, yet some "good scorers" on X received poor scores on Y.

Notice, however, Equation 7.1 pertains to parameters. Its use should be limited to large samples where the s and r are accurate estimates of σ_1 and ρ_1, respectively, and where the conditions of linearity and homoscedasticity are met (Gullicksen & Hopkins, 1976). To interpret correlation coefficients properly, it is important to realize that r is seriously affected by the heterogeneity of the sample.

❖ CHAPTER SUMMARY

The magnitude of the correlation coefficient between two variables is not influenced by a linear transformation of one or both variables. Linear transformations such as adding, subtracting, multiplying or dividing by a constant, do not alter the shape (e.g., skewness, etc.) of a distribution, the percentile rank of any observation, the number of standard deviations any observation deviates from the mean (i.e., the corresponding z-score), or the correlation of a measure with any other variable.

The true relationship between two variables will be stronger than the observed relationship because of the influence of measurement error. The greater the measurement error (i.e., the lower the reliability coefficient of one or both measures), the more the value of r is attenuated.

Sampling error in r is apt to be large when n is small; sampling error can seriously distort the actual correlation which exists between the variables. The effect of sampling error on r will be considered in more detail in Chapter 13.

The value of r is seriously influenced by the heterogeneity of the sample; the more homogeneous the sample, the lower the value of the correlation coefficient, and vice versa. Restricting the range of scores in X or Y or both X and Y will severely diminish the computed correlation coefficient. The formula to correct r for restricted variability can be useful for linear relationships characterized by homoscedasticity when the sample size is sufficiently large so that accurate estimates of σ_1 and ρ_1 are available.

For two variables with similar distributions, the computed value of r may range from -1 to $+1$. However, when the marginal distributions of the two variables differ markedly, the maximum value for $|r|$ may be substantially less than 1.0.

MASTERY TEST

1. If it is known that $r_{XY} = .50$, what will the correlation be if the X-values are multiplied by 100 and the Y-scores are divided by 10?
   (a) 5.00   (b) .50   (c) .05   (d) .005   (e) indefinite

2. If $r = 1.0$ and $z_X = -1.3$, what is z_Y? (Hint: $r = 1.0$ only when all pairs of z-scores are identical.)

3. If $r = -1.0$ and $z_Y = .70$, what is z_X?

4. If the IQ scores for test A are consistently precisely 10 points higher than the IQs using test B, what is the largest possible value for r between these two tests?

5. Ingrid calculated the covariance of height (X) in feet (e.g., 67″ becomes 5.58′) and running speed in seconds (Y) and obtained a covariance of 2.30 with a sample of 50 students. From the same original data, Shane calculated the covariance of height in inches, and running speed in minutes (e.g., 69 seconds becomes 1.15 minutes). Ingrid obtained a value of $r = .46$. If Shane is careful, he should find $r =$ __?__ .

6. For a particular set of data, $s_X = 5$ and $s_Y = 4$. What is the largest that s_{XY} could possibly be? [Hint: $r = s_{XY}/(s_X s_Y)$ and r cannot exceed 1.0.]

7. In which of the situations described below, would you expect the value of r to be greatest (other things being equal)?

Shape of X	Shape of Y
(a) rectangular	skewed negatively
(b) bimodal	normal
(c) normal	normal
(d) skewed negatively	skewed positively

8. In which of the situations in question 7, would it be impossible for r to equal $+1.0$?

9. If the correlation between IQ and reading was known to be .5 ($\rho_1 = .5$) for a homogeneous population ($\sigma_1 = 4$), estimate the correlation (ρ_U) for a representative population ($\sigma_U = 16$).

10. Suppose by observation alone, you estimated the heights (X) and weights (Y) of each of your classmates and that you calculated the correlation coefficient (r_1) between these observations. How would this coefficient compare with the coefficient (r_2) using data from a scale and tape measure to determine X and Y? Why?

11. Other things being equal, in which college would you expect the highest correlation between SAT scores and GPA?

		College	
IQ	*A*	*B*	*C*
$\overline{X}$	508	475	600
s	90	100	80

12. Which college in question 11 would you expect to have the lowest value for r?

13. Assume you found a correlation of .4 for a random sample of ten state universities between size of library (number of books) and prestige (rating by a panel of experts). The best estimate of ρ would be which of the following?
    (a) slightly less than .4   (b) .4   (c) slightly larger than .4

14. Would the estimate from question 13 be quite accurate? Why?

15. One study reported the correlation between IQ and creativity as being quite low ($r = .2$). The standard deviation of the IQ scores of the sample was approximately 5. What would be the effect on r if the sample did not have restricted variability in IQ?

16. Most creativity tests contain substantial measurement error. If some measurement error were removed from the creativity test (e.g., by increasing its length), how would the value of r between creativity scores and IQ scores be altered?

ANSWERS TO MASTERY TEST

1. (b), $r = .50$ is unaffected by linear transformations.

2. $z_Y = -1.3$

3. $z_X = -.70$

4. 1.0, adding a constant is a linear transformation not affecting r.

5. $r = .46$ since the relative standings and corresponding standard scores of the X's and Y's are unaffected; r is unaffected by the metric employed.

6. Maximum covariance is $s_{XY} = 5(4) = 20$.

7. (c)

8. (a), (b), and (d)

9. From Equation 7.1:
$$\rho_U^2 = \frac{(.5)^2 \left(\dfrac{16}{4} \right)^2}{1 + (.5)^2 (4)^2 - (.5)^2} = \frac{4.00}{4.75} = .8421$$
$$\rho_U = \sqrt{.8421} = .92$$

10. r_2 would be higher since it would contain less measurement error.

11. College B, because s is greatest

12. College C because s is least

13. (c)

14. No; n is too small—the sampling error may be huge.

15. The r would increase considerably.

16. The r would increase.

PROBLEMS AND EXERCISES

1. (a) When heights of girls or boys at ages 3 and 20 are expressed as T-scores, the covariance is approximately 70. What is the correlation coefficient between heights at the two ages?
   (b) What is the covariance if the two variables are expressed as z-scores?
   (c) If, at age 3, height is expressed in inches, but at age 20 it is expressed in centimeters, would the value of r be affected?
   (d) If shoes are removed before taking measurement at age 3 but not at age 20, what would be the effect on r?
   (e) If the subjects were measured with and without shoes on both occasions, which correlation would be slightly higher?

2. In question 15 of the Mastery Test, assume the statistics are parameters, assume a linear and homoscedastic relationship between IQ and creativity, and estimate the correlation of the population (ρ_U) using $\sigma_U = 15$ and Equation 7.1.

3. For the unrestricted population, $\rho_U = .8$ and $\sigma_U = 10$. For which of the following circumstances would the restricted correlation coefficient (ρ_1) be least?
   (a) $\sigma_1 = 8$ (b) $\sigma_1 = 5$ (c) $\sigma_1 = 3$

4. Examine the scatterplot at the beginning of the Problems and Exercises section in Chapter 8. The scatterplot shows the relationship between IQ scores at grades 5 and 7 for 354 students on the California Test of Mental Maturity.
   (a) Does the relationship appear to be linear?
   (b) Does the scatterplot appear to have the property of homoscedasticity?
   (c) Does the reported r of .83 appear to be reasonable according to the scatterplot?

5. Problem 7a of Chapter 6 pertained to the rodent-maze data below, and for these data, $s_X = 2.16$, $s_Y = 2.51$, $s_{XY} = -4.83$, and $r = -.89$.

<table>
<tr><td></td><td colspan="7">Rodent Identification</td></tr>
<tr><td></td><td>a</td><td>b</td><td>c</td><td>d</td><td>e</td><td>f</td><td>g</td></tr>
<tr><td>Hours of Deprivation, X</td><td>2</td><td>3</td><td>4</td><td>5</td><td>6</td><td>7</td><td>8</td></tr>
<tr><td>Time to Learn Maze, Y</td><td>9</td><td>7</td><td>8</td><td>4</td><td>4</td><td>5</td><td>2</td></tr>
</table>

If we restrict the range of Hours of Deprivation by eliminating the first and last entries, the restricted range problem would be as follows:

<table>
<tr><td></td><td colspan="5">Rodent Identification</td></tr>
<tr><td></td><td>b</td><td>c</td><td>d</td><td>e</td><td>f</td></tr>
<tr><td>Hours of Deprivation, X</td><td>3</td><td>4</td><td>5</td><td>6</td><td>7</td></tr>
<tr><td>Time to Learn Maze, Y</td><td>7</td><td>8</td><td>4</td><td>4</td><td>5</td></tr>
</table>

   (a) Compute s_X and s_Y.
   (b) Compute s_{XY}.
   (c) Compute r.
   (d) Compare your results for (a), (b), and (c) with the original statistics.

6. For this problem, let us consider the HSB data set in Appendix B as the population of interest ($N = 200$). Using SPSS computer software, a random sample of $n = 4$ students was selected from the HSB data set population and their Math and Reading T-scores are listed below.

X (Math)	Y (Reading)
42	47
52	55
41	57
56	47

   (a) Compute s_X and s_Y and compare your statistics to the parameters as listed in the table of results in Chapter 4 for problems 25–31.
   (b) Compute the covariance, s_{XY}.
   (c) Compute r.
   (d) Compute the sampling error for this sample ($r - \rho$).
   (e) Given the formula for ρ, $\rho = \sigma_{XY}/(\sigma_X\sigma_Y)$, rearrange this formula to solve for the covariance, σ_{XY}.

(f) Use the formula you derived in (e) above to solve for the covariance in the HSB data set, σ_{XY}. (Hint: The table of results in Chapter 4 for problems 25–31 and Table 7.1 provide useful information.)

(g) When you decrease the sample size, do you also decrease the magnitude of the correlation coefficient and decrease the sampling error?

7. Given: X is negatively skewed and Y is positively skewed.
   (a) Are there more positive z_X-scores than negative z_X-scores?
   (b) Are there more positive z_Y-scores than negative ones?
   (c) Why could r_{XY} never be 1.0?

ANSWERS TO PROBLEMS AND EXERCISES

1. (a) For T-scores, $\sigma_X = \sigma_Y = 10$; $r = 70/(10)(10) = .7$.
   (b) .7
   (c) no
   (d) very little, since roughly a constant heel height was added to height at age 20.
   (e) without shoes, because heel thickness would introduce a small amount of uncontrolled and irrelevant variation (measurement error).

2. $\rho_U = .52$

3. (c), as variability decreases, ρ is expected to decrease.

4. (a) yes, (b) yes, (c) yes

5. (a) $s_X = 1.58$, $s_Y = 1.82$
   (b) $s_{XY} = -2.0$
   (c) $r = -.70$
   (d) The variabilities of X and Y were restricted, and the r was reduced substantially. This is consistent with the principle that as the variability is curtailed, the obtained correlation coefficient is diminished.

6. (a) $s_X = 7.41$, which is less than $\sigma_X = 9.37$ for the population standard deviation for math; $s_Y = 5.26$, which is less than the $\sigma_Y = 10.25$ for the population.
   (b) $s_{XY} = -11.17$
   (c) $r = -.29$
   (d) $(r - \rho) = (-.29 - .68) = -.97$
   (e) $\sigma_{XY} = \rho\sigma_X\sigma_Y$
   (f) $(.662)(10.25)(9.37) = 68.07$
   (g) No, almost half of the time the statistic r will exceed the parameter ρ by a certain amount (sampling error), and with small samples, the sampling errors tend to be larger than with large samples.

7. (a) Yes, since $\overline{X} < Md$ in a negatively skewed distribution.
   (b) No, there are more negative z-scores in a positively skewed distribution.
   (c) Since if $r = 1.0$, all pairs of z-scores are identical, and since there are more positive z-scores in X than in Y, it is impossible for all pairs of z-scores to be identical.

 COMPUTER CHALLENGE

Let us perform several transformations of the HSB data and note their effects on the correlations among these variables.

1. For the variables reading and writing:[2]
   (a) Find r.
   (b) Transform the reading scores to z-scores and find r.

---

[2]Hint for EZQNT users: (b) Cursor over to the reading column, and from the SPREADSHEET menu choose TRANSFORM and BY FUNCTION and STANDARDIZE. (c) Move the cursor to the writing column, and from the SPREADSHEET menu choose TRANSFORM and ARITHMETICALLY and BY ADDITION.

    (c) Transform the writing scores by adding 100 to each and find r.

    (d) Based on these findings, what is the effect upon r when the data are transformed by adding or subtracting a constant or by multiplying or dividing by a constant?

2. For the variables math and science:[3]

    (a) Find r.

    (b) Use the square root transformation on the math scores and find r.

    (c) Multiply the science score by itself and find the r.

    (d) What is the effect upon r when the data are transformed by squaring or by taking the square root or by multiplying or dividing by a variable?

---

[3]Hint for EZQNT users: (b) Cursor over to the math column, and from the SPREADSHEET menu, choose TRANSFORM and BY FUNCTION and SQUARE ROOT. (c) Cursor over to the science column, and from the SPREADSHEET menu, choose TRANSFORM and MULTIPLY A VAR.

8

Prediction and Regression

❖ 8.1 PURPOSES OF REGRESSION ANALYSIS

How can information on one variable be used to predict an outcome on another variable? What is the margin of error in this prediction? One major use of statistical methods is to forecast. Insurance companies set their premiums on the basis of statistical predictions. The cost of automobile insurance for minors is greater than that for adults because age correlates with (and can predict) accident frequencies. Colleges admit and reject applicants primarily on the basis of predictions about their probable future scholastic performance, predictions that are made from scholastic aptitude tests and academic performance in high school. Delinquency and dropout prevention programs frequently use early indicators (predictors) to identify persons likely to become delinquents or dropouts. In vocational counseling and personnel selection, implicit or explicit predictions of various job-related criteria are made from variables such as age, interests, aptitudes, sex, and experience. Even the forecast of tomorrow's temperature is a prediction based on its relationship to other variables with which it is correlated, such as today's temperature.

❖ 8.2 INDEPENDENT AND DEPENDENT VARIABLES

Statisticians use mathematics to maximize the accuracy of predictions of a *dependent variable*, Y, (a criterion or outcome variable) from one or more *independent variables* or predictors, X. In statistical parlance, the dependent (predicted) variable, Y, is said to be a function of the independent (predictor) variable, X. No causal association is assumed. Knowledge about causation is critical for many purposes, but it is irrelevant to forecasting.

Insurance companies lower the premiums for minors who have taken driver training because they can predict that students who have taken such a course have fewer accidents (but note that this does not prove that the students have fewer accidents *because* of the training, i.e., correlation does not imply causation). Insurance companies also lower premiums for students who have good grades, but this only means good students cost them less in claims—that GPA (*X*) and cash outflow (*Y*) are correlated. The insurance premiums for adolescent males are also higher because sex (*X*) is correlated with expected cost to the company.[1]

Correlation is both *necessary* and *sufficient* for prediction. The higher the correlation, the better the prediction; the lower the correlation, the greater the margin of error in the predictions. In this chapter, we treat the simplest type of prediction: predicting the dependent variable, *Y*, from one independent variable, *X*, when both *X* and *Y* represent variables that are normally distributed and linearly related. Procedures for predictions involving curvilinear relationship or categorical variables are treated in more advanced texts (e.g., Glass & Hopkins, 1996, chapter 8). The underlying concepts and rationale of simple regression do extend, however, to these more complex applications.

❖ 8.3 THE REGRESSION EFFECT

Unless $r = |1.0|$ *all predictions* of *Y* from *X* evidence a regression toward the mean. Francis Galton first documented this regression effect in studying the relationships between the characteristics of parents and their children about a century ago. The heights of 192 father-son combinations are tallied in Figure 8.1, in which a scatterplot (also called a *bivariate* distribution) is displayed. Grouped frequency distributions of *X* (father's height—horizontal axis) and *Y* (son's height—vertical axis) are also portrayed in Figure 8.1 using the Tukey tally method (see Section 2.9). Notice that the means and standard deviations appear to be approximately equal for both *X* and *Y*, and that both variables appear to be normally distributed when allowance is made for sampling error (chance fluctuations).

If all sons had exactly the same height as their fathers, all tallies in Figure 8.1 would fall in the shaded squares, and *r* would be 1.0. Study Figure 8.1 and observe, as Galton did, that the sons of tall fathers *tend to be* taller than average, but not quite as tall as their fathers, that is, the sons regress toward the mean. Similarly, there is a trend for the sons of short fathers to be taller than their fathers, but shorter than average, that is, they also regress toward the mean.[2]

The mean height of the sons for each father-height is plotted within each column of Figure 8.1, and connected by the broken line. For example, for fathers who were 63 inches tall, the mean height of the sons was 66.5 inches; fathers who were 73 inches tall had sons whose mean height was 72 inches. Notice that, on average, the more a father's height deviates from its mean, the greater the difference between father's height and the son's height—the more *X* deviates from $\overline{X}$, the greater the amount of regression. This is illustrated in Figure 8.1 by the solid and dotted lines; the solid line just smooths out the raggedness of the dotted line—it is called the regression line or the line of best fit.

---

[1]The ethics of many statistical applications has been frequently ignored. Should a law-abiding male adolescent be required to pay more for automobile insurance because of the sins of his sex—isn't that guilt by association? Is he not denied equal opportunity under the law? This type of statistical stereotyping is very different from the use of one's own driving record (for which one is personally responsible) to adjust premiums. It is this type of myopic cost-benefit statistical application and reasoning that at one time made it more difficult for females to be accepted into certain careers such as medicine (the statistical data showed that on the average, females practiced fewer years and were more apt to marry and leave their career).

[2]Apparently, Galton did not initially recognize the ubiquity of this phenomenon and termed it "the law of filial regression." Actually, there is a regression effect (in terms of *z*-scores or percentiles) when any two variables are not perfectly correlated.

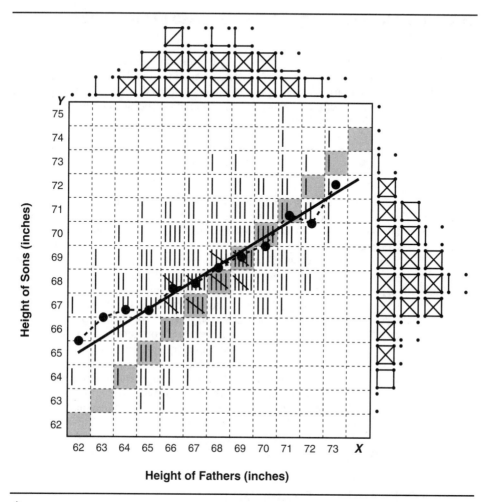

Y

Height of Sons (inches)

Height of Fathers (inches)

❖ **FIGURE 8.1** An illustration of the regression effect—a scatterplot of the heights of fathers and sons ($n = 192$), with marginal distributions for X and Y given at the top and to the right, respectively.

Regression toward the mean is expected whenever the absolute value of r is less than 1.0. Note that in Figure 8.1 the central tendency and variability of the distribution of X (fathers' heights) are approximately equal to those for distribution Y (sons' heights); the distributions of X and Y are comparably heterogeneous. It is counterintuitive, but nevertheless true, that, although the sons' heights tend to regress toward their mean, the sons are not more homogeneous in height than were their fathers. Stated differently, the percentile ranks for the sons tend to be closer to 50 than those of the fathers.

Quiz: Can you explain the fact that the range of sons' heights is comparable to the range of fathers' heights even though statistical regression is operating?

Answer: Ask again after I finish my study of this chapter and ponder the matter.

❖ 8.4 THE REGRESSION EQUATION EXPRESSED IN STANDARD z-SCORES

One of the most illuminating ways of statistically expressing the regression phenomenon can be seen when both X and Y are expressed as z-scores. Equation 8.1 is the simplest form of the regression (prediction) equation; it shows that the predicted z-score on the dependent variable, $\hat{z}_Y$, is the product of the z_X-score and the correlation coefficient between X and Y (the caret, "^", denotes "the predicted value of"):

$$\hat{z}_Y = rz_X \tag{8.1}$$

For examples, if $r = .6$ and $z_X = 1.0$, then $\hat{z}_Y = .6$; and if $r = .6$ and $z_X = -2.0$, then $\hat{z}_Y = -1.2$. Notice that when $|r| < 1$, $|\hat{z}_Y|$ is always less than $|z_X|$—the z_Y-value is predicted to regress toward the mean. How much closer to the mean of 0 is $\hat{z}_Y$ than z_X? If Equation 8.1 is rearranged, it is apparent that r is the ratio of $\hat{z}_Y$ to z_X (i.e., $r = \hat{z}_Y/z_X$), and r can be seen as the "slope" or average "rate of change" in z_Y per unit change in z_X. (Be grateful to your Algebra I teacher if you remember the meaning of the slope of a line.)

Square the equation $r = \hat{z}_Y/z_X$ to get $r^2 = \hat{z}_Y^2/z_X^2$. Since the variance of a distribution expressed as z-scores is always 1 ($s_{z_X}^2 = 1$), the variance of the $\hat{z}_Y$-values is r^2. Therefore, we see that r^2 is the proportion of variance in the criterion, Y, that is predictable from the independent variable, X. Unfortunately, r^2 has been dubbed the "coefficient of determination," which incorrectly encourages the fallacy that correlation equals causation.

The correlation coefficient between X and Y in Figure 8.1 is approximately $r = .50$. Hence from Equation 8.1, it is evident that, on the average, sons tend to deviate only half (.5) as far from $\overline{Y}$ (their mean) as their fathers do from $\overline{X}$ (the fathers' mean). For example, fathers who are two standard deviations below their mean ($z_X = -2.0$) tend to have sons who average only one standard deviation below the sons' mean ($z_Y = -1.0$); thus, given $r = 1/2 = .50$, fathers who are at the 98th percentile ($z_X = 2$) have sons who are at the 84th percentile ($z_Y = 1$), on the average.

❖ 8.5 CORRELATION AS PERCENTAGE

One should resist the initial inclination to interpret the values of r as a proportion in the usual sense. If $r = .80$, one should not say that "X and Y are 80% related" or "what X measures is 80% the same as what Y measures." Since $r = \hat{z}_Y/z_X$, we can see the sense in which the correlation coefficient can be directly interpreted as a proportion or a percentage. If $r = .8$ and X and Y are expressed as z-scores or T-scores, the expected z-score on the dependent variable ($\hat{z}_Y$) is only .8 (or 80%) as far from the mean of the Y-variable as z_X is from the mean of the X-variable. In other words, $100(1 - r)$ gives the percent of regression toward the mean (on the average) when X and Y are expressed as standard scores.

As an example, the correlation between IQ scores of a child and either parent is about .5. If Beulah's IQ score ($\mu = 100$, $\sigma = 15$) is 124, her z-score is $(124 - 100)/15$ or $z_X = 1.8$. We can predict that the IQ z-score of her son, Walter, is $\hat{z}_Y = .5(1.6)$ or $\hat{z}_Y = .8\sigma$ above the mean. Since IQ is a standard score ($\mu = 100$, $\sigma = 15$), Walter's predicted IQ score is $100 + .8(15)$ or 112—he is expected to be only .5 or 50% as far from the mean as is his mother. Even though 112 is our best prediction, this does not mean that the prediction is extremely accurate. In Section 8.8, we will deal with the accuracy and error in these predictions.

Quiz: If $r = 1.0$ and $z_X = 1.2$, $\hat{z}_Y$ is ___(1)___. If $r = 0$ and $T_X = 62$, $\overline{T}_Y =$ ___(2)___. Mrs. Miller's IQ score is 130, and since $r_{XY} = .5$, her children are expected to have an average IQ score of about ___(3)___. Stated differently, Mrs. Miller's IQ score places her at the ___(4)___ percentile, whereas her children are predicted to be at the ___(5)___ percentile.

Answers: (1) 1.2, (2) 50, (3) 115, (4) 98th, (5) 84th

❖ 8.6 USE OF REGRESSION EQUATIONS

It may seem peculiar that we talk about predicting Y from X, since we must have both X and Y in order to compute the r, required in Equation 8.1. Obviously, if we have the actual heights of fathers and their sons (as in Figure 8.1), Equation 8.1 would not be used to predict these same sons' heights. These particular sons' heights are known, and it would make no sense to predict them. However, if the correlation coefficient between X and Y is known, it can be used to predict the heights of sons ($\hat{Y}$'s) not represented in the data in Figure 8.1. Indeed, the data in Figure 8.1 allow us to predict even the eventual adult heights of the unborn sons from the height of any adult male. (You see how socially relevant statistics can be! Actually most applications have more importance than adult height; but this is the classic example, and one that we can get our teeth into.) The purpose of a regression equation is to make predictions for a new, but comparable, sample for which scores on the independent variable are available.

An Illustration. Seymour's grade-point average (GPA) is predicted from his test score on the ACT (see Figure 5.5 for the test parameters); the prediction is based on the relationship between GPA and ACT scores that was determined from some previous study. His predicted GPA can be viewed as the mean GPA obtained by the population of students having his same ACT score. The ACT correlates approximately .5 with GPA and has a mean (μ_X) of 20 with a standard deviation (σ_X) of 5. If the mean college GPA (μ_Y) is 2.6, and if the standard deviation (σ_Y) is .4, and if Seymour's ACT score (X) is 30, then his ACT score expressed as a z-score is: $z_X = (X - \mu_X)/\sigma_X = (30 - 20)/5 = 2.0$. His predicted z-score on Y is: $\hat{z}_Y = (.5)(2.0) = 1.0$; that is, his predicted GPA is one standard deviation above the mean GPA. Since $\mu_Y = 2.6$ and $\sigma_Y = .4$, Seymour's predicted GPA is: $\hat{Y} = 2.6 + (1)(.4) = 3.0$.

Quiz: It is given that $r = .80$ between first-year college GPA ($\overline{X} = 2.6$ and $s_X = .4$) and second-year college GPA ($\overline{Y} = 2.8$ and $s_Y = .3$). Yolanda's first-year GPA was 3.4, $z_X =$ ___(1)___, and her predicted z-score for her second-year GPA is $\hat{z}_Y =$ ___(2)___; her predicted second-year GPA = ___(3)___.

Answers: (1) $(3.4 - 2.6)/.4 = 2$, (2) $.8(2) = 1.6$, (3) $2.8 + 1.6(.3) = 3.28$

❖ 8.7 THE REGRESSION LINE

Any real set of data will have some irregularities due to sampling error like the dotted line in Figure 8.1. Figure 8.2 illustrates the relationship between two normally distributed variables, expressed as z-scores, that are linearly related and correlate .5 ($n = 300$). If the 300 dots were collapsed along the X-axis, they would form the normal curve as depicted. Similarly, if collapsed along the vertical axis, the observations would follow a normal curve.

When both X and Y are normally distributed and linearly related (i.e., a bivariate normal distribution), and when the mean scores on Y for each value of X are connected, theoretically, the straight line shown in Figure 8.2 would result. This line is termed the

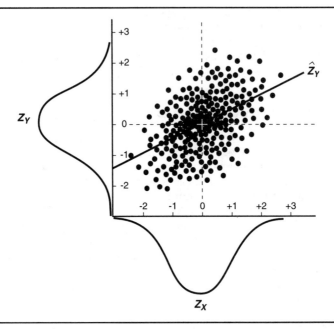

❖ **FIGURE 8.2** Scatterplot and regression line in which *X* and *Y* are normally distributed with $\rho = .5$.

regression line—it gives the predicted scores on the dependent variable, *Y*, for all points along the *X*-axis. Of course, when only a sample has been measured, the *Y*-means for the individuals at each *X*-score may differ a bit from the regression line due to sampling error (as we saw in Figure 8.1). It is assumed that the distribution of *Y*-scores, for the population of individuals at each *X*-score, are normally distributed about the predicted *Y*-score. For this reason, the density of the points is greatest near the regression line, as is evident in Figure 8.2. Conversely, the density between the points decreases as we move away from the regression line. In Figure 8.1, the regression line (the straight line) and the actual means of the observed *Y*-values (the broken line) are given for each reported value of *X*. Notice that these column means (shown by the broken line) do not deviate greatly from the regression line. If the sample were very large, the differences (sampling errors) would be expected to be smaller—if the total population were measured, it is assumed that the differences would disappear. When the line segments connecting the actual *Y*-means for points all along the *X*-axis remain in the proximity of a straight line, the regression is said to be *linear*.

Quiz: A bivariate normal distribution consists of two variables that are __(1)__ distributed. If the *Y*-means for individuals at each reported *X*-score follow along a straight line, the relationship is said to be __(2)__. The straight line connecting the predicted scores is called the __(3)__ line. It is assumed that, if the total population were measured, the *Y*-means for the population at each *X*-score would fall on the __(4)__ line. It is also assumed that the population of individuals at each *X*-score have *Y*-scores that are __(5)__ distributed about the __(6)__ line.

Answers: (1) normally, (2) linear, (3) regression, (4) regression, (5) normally, (6) regression

❖ 8.8 RESIDUALS AND THE CRITERION OF BEST FIT

Notice in Figures 8.1 and 8.2 that the prediction is rarely perfect. The *difference* between the predicted value on Y ($\hat{Y}$) and the Y-value actually observed is an "*error of estimate*" and is termed a *residual*:

$$residual = Y - \hat{Y} \qquad (8.2)$$

When the observed score on the criterion exceeds the predicted score, the residual will be positive. In Figures 8.1 and 8.2, all dots or tallies above the regression line have positive residuals; points below the regression line have scores below what was predicted and have negative residuals. Indeed, the mean of the residuals about the regression line will be zero.

> **Quiz:** In a previous quiz we predicted Walter's IQ score to be 112, but when tested he earned a score of 117. The residual for Walter is ___(1)___. (2) Are negative residuals just as common as positive residuals?
>
> **Answers:** (1) residual = 117 – 112 = 5, (2) yes

A regression line always passes through the *centroid* (i.e., the point of intersection of $\overline{X}$ and $\overline{Y}$) of the swarm of observations, but its *slope* (i.e., the angle of inclination from the horizontal or X-axis) depends on the value of r. Notice in Figure 8.2 that the centroid is indicated by a cross ("+") where the two means intersect ($z_X = 0$, $z_Y = 0$). The regression line is sometimes described as the "line of best fit," but "best" with respect to what? We have already seen that the mean of the residuals about the regression line is 0. However, it is best in another sense: The sum of *squared* residuals is less for the regression line than for any other straight line that could be drawn through the swarm of data. Recall (Section 3.13) that the mean is that point in a distribution about which the sum of squared deviations, Σx^2 or SS, is least; hence, the mean is the measure of central tendency that meets the *least-squares criterion*. The least-squares criterion applied to predicting Y from X requires that the sum of the squared residuals be as small as possible. In other words, the *regression line* is the straight line that defines the *best* prediction of Y from X—"best" in the sense that the sum of the squared residuals is less about that line than about any other straight line that can be drawn through the scatterplot.

> **Quiz:** Answer the following, based on Figure 8.1. Father Fred is 71 inches tall; his son Sam is predicted to be ___(1)___ tall, but Sam is actually taller than his dad—he is 73 inches tall. The difference between Sam's predicted height and his actual height is termed a ___(2)___, which in Sam's case is ___(3)___ inches. If this procedure were repeated for all father/son pairs, the mean of the residuals would be ___(4)___.
>
> **Answers:** (1) about 70.5 inches, (2) residual, (3) about 2.5, (4) 0

❖ 8.9 HOMOSCEDASTICITY

Observe in Figures 8.1 and 8.2 that the standard deviation of the residuals ($\sigma_{Y.X}$) is about the same for all columns (i.e., all values of X). The statistical term for a uniform vertical spread about the regression line for each X-value is quite impressive, *homoscedasticity* (i.e., equal spread). Homoscedasticity means that, in the population, the variance in the heights of the sons of short fathers who are 62 inches tall will be the same as the variance in the heights of sons whose fathers are 72 inches tall, and so forth. It is important to note that, even when homoscedasticity prevails in the population, because of sampling error one should not expect exact equality in sample standard deviations of residuals for all values of X, especially if n is not large. Sampling error will, of course, decrease as the size of the sample increases.

Note that the greater range in the residuals near the mean of the independent variable, X, in Figure 8.2 does not suggest a lack of homoscedasticity. Recall from Table 4.1 (Section 4.14) that, other things being equal, the greater the n, the greater the range is expected to be. Since there are more observations near the mean of X, the ranges of the residuals in this region tend to be greater even though the variance of the residuals will be about the same.

Quiz: Evaluate the scatterplot of Figure 7.1 (Section 7.3) with respect to (1) linearity, and (2) homoscedasticity.

Answers: (1) The $r = .612$ appears to be linear. (2) Since the reading test scores of the low-readiness region appear to be less variable than those of the high-readiness region, it appears that heteroscedasticity (flex those vocabulary muscles!) prevails rather than homoscedasticity.

❖ 8.10 THE RAW-SCORE REGRESSION EQUATION

The standard z-score form of the regression equation ($\hat{z}_Y = rz_X$) is best for conceptual purposes, but for practical applications, it is more efficient to use raw-score regression equations. Equation 8.3 is the regression equation in raw-score form, and, unlike Equation 8.1, it does not require the transformation of X to z_X or $\hat{z}_Y$ to $\hat{Y}$. The predicted criterion score, $\hat{Y}$, is the product of the regression coefficient, b, and the raw score on X, plus a constant, c (the *intercept*).

$$\hat{Y} = bX + c \tag{8.3a}$$

where
$$b = r(s_Y/s_X) \tag{8.3b}$$

and
$$c = \bar{Y} - b\bar{X} \tag{8.3c}$$

An Illustration.   How accurately can the reading scores in the HSB data set be predicted from math scores? To calculate the regression equation for predicting a person's score on the dependent variable, Y, from the score on the independent variable, X, we must know $\bar{X}$, $\bar{Y}$, r, s_X, and s_Y, as specified in Equation 8.3. To obtain these statistics, data must be gathered on a sample of students who have taken both tests. For the statistics pertaining to the HSB data set, (see the table preceding problem 15 of Chapter 5), we see that: for math, $\bar{X} = 52.64$, $s_X = 9.37$; and for reading, $\bar{Y} = 52.23$, $s_Y = 10.25$; and we found that $r = .662$ between reading and math. Using Equation 8.3b, we find that the regression coefficient is:

$$b = r(s_Y/s_X) = .66(10.25/9.37) = .724$$

It is no coincidence that r and b are so close in value in this instance; if $s_X = s_Y$, then $r = b$. When s_X and s_Y differ little, r and b will also differ little. The intercept, c, is found using Equation 8.3c:

$$c = \overline{Y} - b\overline{X} = 52.23 - .724(52.64) = 14.12$$

Substituting our values for b and c into Equation 8.3a, we have the raw-score regression equation for predicting reading scores from math scores:

$$\hat{Y} = .724X + 14.12$$

If Bertha's math score is 65, her predicted reading score is:

$$\hat{Y} = .724(65) + 14.12 = 61.18$$

Note the regression toward the mean. Figure 8.3 gives a scatterplot depicting this result graphically. A vertical line is drawn from the math score of 65 to intersect the regression line. At this point a horizontal line is drawn to intersect the left vertical axis, which gives a predicted reading score of 61. In like manner for any value of X, the predicted Y-score can be quickly determined. Predictions obtained graphically can be quite accurate.

Quiz: In the regression equation for predicting reading scores from math scores, $\hat{Y} = .724X + 14.12$, X stands for ___(1)___ scores, Y stands for ___(2)___ scores, and the

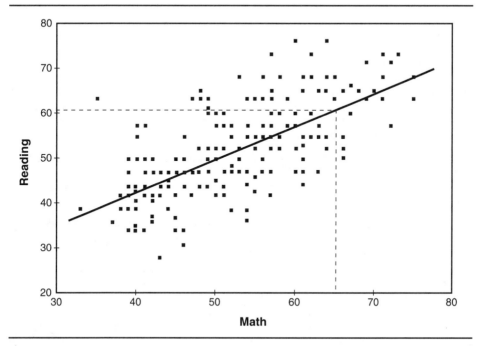

❖ **FIGURE 8.3** Scatterplot of HSB math and reading scores. A math score of 65 gives a predicted reading score of 61.

predicted score is designated by ___(3)___. If Jesse's math score is 40, his $\hat{Y}$ = ___(4)___. Find out how Jesse's z-score for math compares to his predicted z-score for reading. If $X = 40$, z_X = ___(5)___; for $\hat{Y}$ = 43.08, $\hat{z}_Y$ = ___(6)___; and the ratio of $\hat{z}_Y/z_X$ = ___(7)___, which is the value of ___(8)___.

Answers: (1) math, (2) reading, (3) $\hat{Y}$, (4) .724(40) + 14.12 = 43.08, (5) $(40 - 52.64)/9.37 = -1.35$, (6) $(43.08 - 52.23)/10.25 = -.89$, (7) $(-.89)/(-1.35) = .66$, (8) r

❖ 8.11 THE STANDARD ERROR OF ESTIMATE

The standard error of estimate simply is the standard deviation of the *residuals*—the errors of estimate in predicting Y from X. The standard error of estimate is denoted by the symbol $s_{Y.X}$ for sample estimates and $\sigma_{Y.X}$ for the parameter. The standard error of estimate can be described as "the standard deviation of the observations, Y's, when X is held constant," that is, "the standard deviation in Y when X is fixed." Figure 8.4 reproduces Figure 8.2, but has dashed lines drawn at $\pm 1s_{Y.X}$ and $\pm 2s_{Y.X}$ above and below the regression line. The residuals are normally distributed about the regression line; they have a mean of 0 and a standard deviation of $s_{Y.X}$. Note that about two-thirds (actually 68%) of the data points fall within the shaded area, the area within $\pm 1s_{Y.X}$ of the regression line. The upper line defines the 98th percentile for the residuals; the bottom line defines P_2.

The standard error of estimate can be used to set limits around a predicted score within which a person's actual score is likely to fall if the relationship is linear and has homoscedasticity. The standard error of estimate (standard deviation of the residuals) is given by Equation 8.4:

$$s_{Y.X} = s_Y \sqrt{1 - r^2} \tag{8.4}$$

The following statements can be made when the raw-score regression equation (Eq. 8.3a) is applied when the correlation is linear and the residuals are normally distributed about the regression line and have equal variability throughout the range of X. These conditions are sometimes described as bivariate normality.

1. Approximately 68% of the observed Y-scores will deviate less than one $s_{Y.X}$ from their predicted score, $\hat{Y}$.
2. Approximately 95% (actually 96%, but 95% is a nice round number) of the observed Y-scores will deviate less than two $s_{Y.X}$ from $\hat{Y}$.

Notice that, for homoscedastic scatterplots, although the value of $\hat{Y}$ differs for every unique value of X (except when $r = 0$), the slope of the regression line and the standard error of estimate do not depend on the value of X or on the range of X-values. This can best be seen by referring to Figure 8.4. Note that if only the treated group (or the untreated group) is considered, the regression line would still occur in the same place—hence predictions and the standard error of estimate would remain the same. Although the variability of X influences r (Section 7.7), it does not alter $\hat{Y}$ or $s_{Y.X}$.

The standard error of estimate in predicting reading scores from math scores (Figure 8.3) is estimated from Equation 8.4:

$$s_{Y.X} = 10.25\sqrt{1 - (.66)^2} = 10.25\sqrt{.5644} = 7.70$$

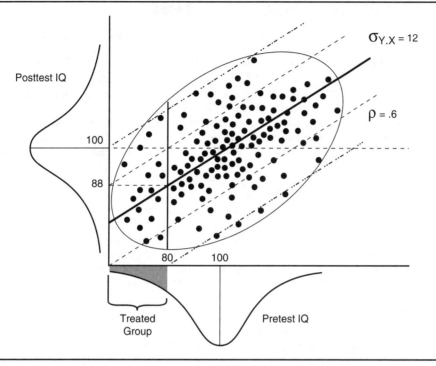

❖ FIGURE 8.4 Scatterplot with broken lines marking off $1s_{Y.X}$ and $2s_{Y.X}$ above and below the regression line.

The standard deviation of the reading scores for the total group was $s_Y = 10.25$, but for students whose math scores were identical, the standard deviation of their reading scores, $s_{Y.X}$, is expected to be 7.7. The standard deviation of the residuals will be less than s_Y except when r is 0.

Quiz: This item refers to the example above (i.e., predicting reading scores from math scores). Assume bivariate normality, a linear relationship with normally distributed residuals and homoscedasticity. Students whose math score is 33.9 ($2s_X$ below $\overline{X} = 52.64$) have a mean reading score of __(1)__; the standard deviation of their reading scores ($s_{Y.X}$) is __(2)__. What percent of the students are expected to have reading scores: (3) above 38.66? (4) between 38.66 ± 7.7? (5) between $38.66 \pm 2(7.7)$? Challenge item: (6) What percent of the students are expected to have reading scores below their math score of 33.9?

Answers: (1) .724(33.9) + 14.12 = 38.66, (2) 7.7, (3) 50%, (4) about 68%, (5) 95% or 96%, (6) In the distribution of residuals, a score of 33.9 has a residual of 33.9 − 38.66 = −4.76, which falls $z = -4.76/7.7 = -.62$ standard errors below the mean of the residuals. From Table A, find that the area below $z = -.62$ is .27; about 27 percent of the students with math scores of 33.9 are expected to score lower in reading than in math, even though the regression phenomenon occurs for the majority of the students. (By the way, is this your answer to the quiz item in Section 8.3?)

❖ 8.12 DETERMINING PROBABILITIES OF PREDICTIONS

Given bivariate normality, what percent of students whose math scores were 40 (rather low) will receive a reading score equal to or greater than the mean, 52.23? Stated differently (to illustrate a different facet of the same concept), what is the probability that Phil, who scored $X = 40$ in math, will earn a score $Y = 52.23$ or above in reading? Since $\hat{Y} = .724X + 14.12$, $\hat{Y} = .724(40) + 14.12$ or $\hat{Y} = 43.08$, which is the mean of the distribution of reading scores for students who scored 40 in math. We have previously found that $s_{Y.X} = 7.70$, which given homoscedasticity, is their standard deviation. That is, we have a normal distribution of Y-scores with a mean of 43.08 and a standard deviation of 7.70, and we want to know what proportion of *this* normal curve exceeds $Y = 52.23$. To do this we need to find the z-score of 52.23 in *this* distribution ($\overline{Y} = 43.08$, $s_{Y.X} = 7.7$) and cleverly use Table A in the Appendix to find the area above. In this distribution, a score of 52.23 as a z-score is $z = (52.23 - 43.08)/7.70 = 1.19$, that is, 1.19 standard deviations ($s_{Y.X}$) above its mean of 43.08. Entering Table A with $z = 1.19$, we see that .883 or about 88% of students who scored 40 on math will score below 52.23 on reading; about 12 percent of the students who scored 40 on math will earn a score of at least 52.23 in reading. Stated differently, for persons scoring 40 on math, the mean for reading is predicted to be 43.08. 34% of them will earn scores between 43.08 and 50.78 (43.08 + 7.70), and another 34% will score between 43.08 and 35.38; 16% will score above 50.78, and 2% will score above 43.08 + 2(7.70) = 58.48.

Quiz: Hoage's math score was 30; his goal is to score higher than 30 in reading—let us work out his chances of success. Using the regression equation above, Hoage's predicted score for reading is ___(1)___. The normal distribution of reading scores from all those who scored 30 on the math test has a mean of ___(2)___ and a standard deviation of ___(3)___; this standard deviation is called the ___(4)___. For a normal distribution with a mean of 35.84 and a standard deviation of 7.70, the z-score of a reading score of 30 is ___(5)___. Using Table A, the area below $z = -.80$ is ___(6)___. As a proportion, Hoage's chances of scoring 30 or higher in reading is about ___(7)___. (8) Why is Hoage expected to score higher in reading than in math?

Answers: (1) .724(30) + 14.12 = 35.84, (2) 35.84, (3) $s_{Y.X} = 7.70$, (4) standard error of estimate, (5) (30 – 35.84)/7.70 = –.76, (6) .2236, (7) 1.0 – .2236 = .7764 or about .78, (8) Regression to the mean tends to occur unless the correlation = |1|.

❖ 8.13 REGRESSION AND PRETEST-POSTTEST GAINS

One of the most subtle sources of invalidity in behavioral research results from the elusive phenomenon of regression toward the mean, "the regression effect." Even seasoned researchers have frequently failed to detect its presence; it has spoiled many otherwise commendable research efforts. Discussions of studies of atypical and special groups have frequently been flawed by a failure to consider the regression phenomenon. It is a statistical truism that, when subjects are selected because they deviate markedly from the mean on some measure (e.g., diagnosed as "learning disabled," dyslexic, underachieving, or retarded), regression toward the mean will occur on subsequent dependent measures unless $r = |1|$.

Many studies on academic remediation and treatment of the handicapped and other deviant groups follow this pattern: Those in greatest need are identified using a selection criterion such as a pretest, a remediation treatment is administered, and a reassessment on a posttest (outcome measure) then follows. For example, suppose among a group of young school children, all those who obtained IQ scores below 80 were given a special treatment (e.g., "cognitive enrichment") for one year and were then retested. Assume a correlation of .6 between pretest and posttest IQ scores, and assume that there was no practice effect (both assumptions are reasonable in this situation). If the treatment had absolutely no effect, how would the treated group fare on the posttest? Figure 8.4 represents the illustrative situation—the scatterplot depicts $r = .6$ and no treatment or practice effects. The means and variances are identical in both distributions (as they are when standard scores are employed). Figure 8.4 portrays a definite and pronounced tendency for subjects to regress toward the mean—on the average, subjects are only six-tenths ($r = .6$) as far from the posttest mean as they were from the pretest mean; that is, examinees tend to deviate only 60% as far from the posttest mean as they did from the pretest mean. Those examinees with pretest IQ scores of 80 deviate 20 points below the pretest mean ($x = -20$), and they would, on the average, deviate only 60% as much from the posttest mean ($y = -12$). They would be expected to have an average posttest score of 88 ($100 - 12 = 88$), an apparent "gain" of 8 points! Those initially having IQ scores of 70 ($x = -30$) would appear to have made even greater "growth," a gain of 12 points ($y = -18$), because their posttest mean is predicted to be 82 ($100 - 18 = 82$).

The standard error of estimate (Eq. 8.4) gives the standard deviation of posttest scores for persons having the same pretest score; in this example, $s_{Y.X} = 15\sqrt{1 - r^2} = 12$ IQ points. Using the standard error of estimate, we can predict the proportion of those with a given pretest score who will fall above (or below) any IQ score on the posttest (provided the assumptions of homoscedasticity and linearity between the two variables are met and that the residuals are normally distributed about the regression line).

Quiz: Assuming bivariate normality of the IQ scores ($\mu = 100$, $\sigma = 15$) in Figure 8.4, students scoring $X = 70$ on the pretest, that is, Group "70," had a deviation score of $x =$ ___(1)___ and a z_X score of ___(2)___. Given that $r = .6$, the predicted z-score on the posttest is $\hat{z}_Y = rz_X =$ ___(3)___); this is equivalent to an IQ score of ___(4)___ on the posttest. The distribution of IQ scores for Group "70" is normally distributed and has a mean of ___(5)___ and a standard deviation (i.e., $s_{Y.X}$) of ___(6)___. ___(7)___ percent of Group "70" is expected to have a posttest IQ-score of 82 or above, thus showing a "gain" of ___(8)___ IQ points.

Answers: (1) –30, (2) –2, (3) –1.2, (4) (–1.2)(15) or 18 points below the mean: $100 - 18 = 82$, (5) 82, (6) 12, (7) 50%, (8) 12

Is it surprising that about 84% of those scoring 70 on the pretest will regress and receive higher IQ scores on the posttest even without any treatment or practice effect? It is expected that one-half will "gain" 12 or more IQ points, and about one-sixth are expected to show a "phenomenal gain" of 24 or more IQ points (i.e., receive an IQ score of 94 or more)! Further, even *without* any treatment or practice effect, about 7 ($z = 1.5$) percent of those with an initial IQ of 70 are expected to obtain the population mean IQ score of 100 or more on the second test! Obviously, what may appear to an enthusiastic investigator to be a striking improvement in a deviant population, in fact, may result solely from the regression phenomenon.

Let us work out a second example to further illustrate the problem of statistical regression. One study treated infants born to mentally retarded mothers with an extensive regimen of sensory stimulation. The offspring were found to have much higher IQ scores than their mothers, and the authors uncritically attributed the increase to the sensory stimulation experiences. However, let us check out what increase in IQ would be expected due to statistical regression alone. The parent-child correlation coefficient between IQ scores is known to be approximately .5. For mothers with an IQ score of 70 (z-score = −2), we would predict the children to have a $\hat{z}_Y = .5(−2) = −1$, that is, a mean IQ of 85—an increase of 15 IQ points even without any special treatment. For numerous other examples of studies in which the regression effect was erroneously interpreted as a treatment effect, see Hopkins, 1969, and Shepard & Hopkins, 1977.

❖ 8.14 MULTIPLE CORRELATION

Thus far we have considered the prediction of a dependent variable from one independent variable. In many applications, however, two or more predictor variables are used. *Multiple regression* is the statistical term for predicting performance on Y from two or more *optimally weighted* independent variables. For example, most colleges use two predictor variables (high school percentile rank-in-class and ACT or SAT score) to predict GPA in college. The method of determining the multiple regression equation is explained in Glass & Hopkins (1996, Chapter 8), but, as with practically all statistical tasks, in practice it is virtually always obtained through spreadsheet or statistical software.

Equation 8.5b gives the correlation, R, of variable Y with an optimally weighted combination of variables X and Z:

$$R^2_{Y.XZ} = \frac{r^2_{YX} + r^2_{YZ} - 2r_{YX}r_{YZ}r_{XZ}}{1 - r^2_{XZ}} \tag{8.5a}$$

$$R_{Y.XZ} = \sqrt{R^2_{Y.XZ}} \tag{8.5b}$$

For example, rank in high school graduating class (X) and SAT scores (Z) correlate approximately .55 and .50, respectively, with college GPA (Y), and .50 with each other. If a multiple regression equation is developed which uses both predictors optimally and simultaneously, what would be the correlation between the predicted and actual GPA's?

$$R^2_{Y.XZ} = \frac{(.55)^2 + (.50)^2 - 2(.55)(.50)(.50)}{1 - (.50)^2} = \frac{.2775}{.75} = .37$$

$$R^2_{Y.XZ} = \sqrt{.3700} = .61$$

Notice that the $R^2_{Y.XZ}$ of .61 is not greatly different from the r of .55. This is because the correlation between the two predictor variables, X and Z, was $r = .50$. Other things being equal, if r_{XZ} had been 0, the multiple correlation would have risen to .74. To maximize predictive accuracy, it is desirable to have predictors that correlate highly with the criterion, but do not correlate highly with each other; the correlation between the predictors represents redundant, not unique, information.

Multiple regression and multiple correlation are not limited to only two predictors. With the help of computers, any number of independent variables can be employed for predicting a dependent variable, but typically the point of diminishing returns is rapidly reached.

Quiz: Let us use the HSB case study data to compute the multiple correlation of writing (Y) with the composite combination of reading (X) and math (Z). The following correlation matrix is based on the HSB case study data:

Correlation Matrix

	X	Z
Y	.60	.62
X	1.00	.66

From the correlation matrix, r_{YX} = ___(1)___ , r_{YZ} = ___(2)___ , and r_{XY} = ___(3)___ . The numerator of Equation 8.5a for R^2 = ___(4)___ , the denominator = ___(5)___ , and $R^2_{Y.XZ}$ = ___(6)___ ; $R_{Y.XZ}$ = ___(7)___ .

Answers: (1) .60 for writing and reading, (2) .62 for writing and math, (3) .66 for reading and math, (4) $.60^2 + .62^2 - 2(.60)(.62)(.66) = .2534$, (5) $1 - (.66)^2 = .5644$, (6) .4490, (7) .67

❖ 8.15 PARTIAL CORRELATION

At times we would like to know the relationship between two variables, X and Y, with the influence of a third variable, Z, controlled. For example, if we correlate high jump (H) and long jump (L) performance for all pupils in an elementary school, a very high correlation between H and L would be obtained since both are substantially correlated with age (A) in this heterogeneous population. Using partial correlation we can estimate the correlation between high jump and long jump for persons of the same age.

We saw in Chapter 6 that, other things being equal, the more heterogeneous the group of observations, the higher the correlation between them. It would be far more interesting to know what the correlation between H and L is with the contaminating effects of age removed—the partial correlation, $r_{HL.A}$. Equation 8.6 gives the correlation of variables Y and X with variable Z "partialed out." A partial correlation is actually the correlation of residuals on variables Y and X, using variable Z as the predictor in both instances:

$$r_{YX.Z} = \frac{r_{YX} - r_{YZ}r_{XZ}}{\sqrt{(1 - r_{YZ}^2)(1 - r_{XZ}^2)}} \tag{8.6}$$

In our example involving high jump (H) and long jump (L) and age (A), suppose we found the following: $r_{HL} = .8$, $r_{HA} = .7$, and $r_{LA} = .7$. Hence, the correlation of high jump and long jump for persons of the same age is estimated using Equation 8.6 as follows:

$$r_{HL.A} = \frac{.8 - (.7)(.7)}{\sqrt{[1 - (.7)^2][1 - (.7)^2]}} = \frac{.31}{.51} = .6078 \text{ or } .61$$

In other words, the correlation between H and L dropped from .8 to .61 when the effects of age were eliminated from both variables.

Suppose an investigator found that the number of "Sesame Street" television programs watched during the three months prior to entering the first grade correlated .4 with a reading readiness test administered at the beginning of grade one. Even the cautious researcher would be tempted to conclude that viewing "Sesame Street" programs improves performance on the reading readiness test. It may be, however, that parents of higher socioeconomic status (SES) have higher achievement motivation and see to it that their children view the programs more regularly. That is, perhaps SES (S) correlates with both the television viewing (T) and the readiness scores (R), and hence much of the apparent effect of "Sesame Street" may be shown to be superficial. Thus, if $r_{RT} = .40$, $r_{RS} = .50$, and $r_{TS} = .60$, then:

$$r_{RT.S} = \frac{.40 - (.5)(.6)}{\sqrt{[1 - (.5)^2][1 - (.6)^2]}} = \frac{.10}{.693} = .144 \text{ or } .14$$

The partial correlation, $r_{RT.S}$, estimates the correlation between television viewing and reading readiness scores for children of the same socioeconomic level, that is, SES is statistically controlled. In our hypothetical example, the very low partial correlation casts doubt on the impact that "Sesame Street" viewing has on reading readiness scores.

Quiz: With reference to the HSB data set, let us find the correlation between math (M) and science (S) with the influence of reading (R) controlled. The correlation matrix below is based on the HSB case study data:

Correlation Matrix

	S	R
M	.63	.66
S	1.00	.63

$r_{MS} = \underline{\quad(1)\quad}$, $r_{MR} = \underline{\quad(2)\quad}$, $r_{SR} = \underline{\quad(3)\quad}$, the numerator of Equation 8.6 = $\underline{\quad(4)\quad}$, the denominator = $\underline{\quad(5)\quad}$, and $r_{MS \cdot R} = \underline{\quad(6)\quad}$.

Answers: (1) $r_{MS} = .63$ for math and science, (2) $r_{MR} = .66$ for math and reading, (3) $r_{SR} = .63$ for science and reading, (4) $.63 - (.66)(.63) = .2142$, (5) $\sqrt{.3410} = .5840$, (6) $.2142/.5840 = .3668$ or $.37$

❖ CHAPTER SUMMARY

Correlation and regression are opposite sides of the same coin. If $r = |1.0|$, there is no regression toward the mean; if $r = .6$, scores tend to regress 40% ($1.0 - .6$) of the distance to the mean.

The expression $\hat{z}_Y = r z_X$ is the simplest form of the regression equation predicting the standard z-score on Y from the z-score on X. Equivalently $r = \hat{z}_Y / z_X$ shows r can be viewed as an expected rate of change in z_Y per unit z_X. The difference between an observed score, Y, and the predicted score, $\hat{Y}$, is called a residual. The regression line is defined by the least-squares criterion. It is the straight line that reduces the sum of the squared residuals to a minimum. The standard deviation of residuals is the standard error of estimate, $s_{Y \cdot X}$. It can be used with $\hat{Y}$ to determine the proportion of Y-values that are expected to fall in any given Y-score range assuming bivariate normality (homoscedasticity, linear relationship, and normally distributed residuals).

In multiple regression, two or more predictors are used to predict a dependent variable. The resulting correlation between the predictors (optimally weighted to yield the highest possible correlation) and Y is termed the multiple correlation, R. Partial correlation can be useful to estimate the correlation between two variables with the effects of one (or more) other variable(s) statistically removed.

Although the degree of variability in the predictor variable greatly influences the correlation coefficient, it does not affect the predicted values of the dependent variable or the standard error of estimate.

In a sense, Chapter 8 is an interesting excursion off the main road of Statistics I. Although the concept of correlation is a prerequisite for subsequent chapters of this book, you will not encounter regression equations again until you enroll in the next course in statistics. In Chapter 9, we will return to the main highway to view the statistics and parameters of central tendency and variability with a new and refreshing perspective!

MASTERY TEST

For the Mastery Test items, assume linear homoscedastic relationships with normally distributed residuals about their regression line.

1. Which type of variable *least* belongs with the other three?
   (a) independent   (b) predictor   (c) X-variable   (d) criterion

2. Which type of variable *least* belongs with the other three?
   (a) dependent   (b) independent   (c) predicted   (d) criterion

3. Which term *least* belongs with the other three?
   (a) percentile   (b) correlation   (c) regression   (d) prediction

4. If $r = .5$ and $z_X = 2.0$, what is the predicted z_Y score ($\hat{z}_Y$)?

5. The $\hat{z}_Y$ from question 4 would be expected to correspond to what percentile in a normal distribution of Y?
   (a) P_{50} (b) P_{75} (c) P_{84} (d) P_{98}

6. If $r = .5$ for persons at P_{98} on X, what is their average percentile on Y? (*Hint:* Using Table A, convert P_{98} to a z_X-score, compute rz_X, and cleverly use Table A again.)
   (a) P_{50} (b) P_{75} (c) P_{84} (d) P_{98}

7. If $r = -.6$ and $z_X = 1.5$, what is $\hat{z}_Y$?

8. If $r = 1.0$, are raw scores on X and Y identical for all pairs of scores?

9. If r is less than 1.0, is the variance in predicted z_Y scores ($\hat{z}_Y$) less than 1.0?

10. Do persons who score below the mean on X tend to have higher z-scores on Y than on X?

11. If $\hat{z}_Y = .75$, for $z_X = 1.0$, is $r = .75$?

12. Other things being equal, as the correlation increases, does the standard error of estimate increase?

13. For the raw-score regression equation, if $s_X = s_Y = 15$, does $r = b$?

14. In a bivariate normal distribution, is the regression of Y on X always linear?

15. In z-score units, will $s_{Y.X}$ always equal $s_{X.Y}$?

16. If $s_Y = 10$ and $r = .6$, what is the value of $s_{Y.X}$? (*Note:* $s_{Y.X} = s_Y \sqrt{1 - r^2}$)

17. (a) If $s_{Y.X} = 8$, what percentage of the actual Y-scores will be within 8 points of the predicted values?
    (b) What percentage of the observations on Y will be more than 8 points higher than predicted?
    (c) Will the percentage underpredicted by more than 8 points be expected to be the same as in part b?

18. Assume that the correlation between a parent's IQ score and the IQ score of an offspring is about $r = .5$; moreover, suppose we know that $\mu_X = \mu_Y = 100$ and that $\sigma_X = \sigma_Y = 15$. Estimate the average IQ of children of mothers with
    (a) IQ = 130.   (b) IQ = 90.   (c) IQ = 100.

19. The average IQ of both parents correlates approximately .6 with their offspring's IQ (Y). What is the value of the standard error of estimate for predicting Y if $\sigma_X = 15$?

20. If $s_{Y.X} = 12$, the observed IQ scores will be within 12 points of the predicted IQs for what percentage of the children?

21. For high multiple correlations, one wants independent variables that correlate (high or low?) with the dependent variable and correlate (high or low?) with each other.

22. To estimate the correlation between variables Y and X with the effects of variable Z removed, one would use
    (a) partial correlation.   (b) multiple correlation.   (c) linear correlation.

23. Match the term in the left-hand column with its definition in the right-hand column.
    A. $r_{XY.Z}$ (a) regression coefficient
    B. b (b) Pearson correlation coefficient
    C. r (c) standard error of estimate
    D. $s_{Y.X}$ (d) multiple correlation coefficient
    E. $R_{Y.XZ}$ (e) partial correlation coefficient
    F. $\hat{Y}$ (f) predicted z-score on Y
    G. $\hat{z}_Y$ (g) predicted score on Y

ANSWERS TO MASTERY TEST

1. (d)
2. (b)
3. (a)
4. $\hat{z}_Y = 1.00$
5. (c)
6. (c)
7. −.9
8. Not necessarily, but each pair would have identical z_X and z_Y scores.
9. yes
10. Yes, unless $r_{XY} = 1.0$.
11. yes
12. No, as r increases, $s_{Y.X}$ decreases.

13. Yes, since $b = r(s_Y/s_X) = r(15/15) = r$.
14. yes
15. In z-score units, yes, but not in raw-score units.
16. $s_{Y.X} = 10\sqrt{1-.36} = 8$
17. (a) 68%, (b) 16%, (c) yes
18. (a) 115, (b) 95, (c) 100
19. $s_{Y.X} = 15\sqrt{1-.36} = 15(.8) = 12$
20. 68%
21. high, low
22. (a)
23. A-e, B-a, C-b, D-c, E-d, F-g, G-f

PROBLEMS AND EXERCISES

For the problems and exercises, assume bivariate normality (linear relationship with homoscedasticity, and normally distributed residuals about the regression line).

For exercises 1–17, use Figure 8.5, a computer-produced scatterplot of IQ scores from the California Test of Mental Maturity obtained by 354 children tested at grade 5 (X) and two years later in grade 7 (Y). We will determine the regression equation $\hat{Y} = bX + c$ for predicting Y from X. The essential information is given in the figure.

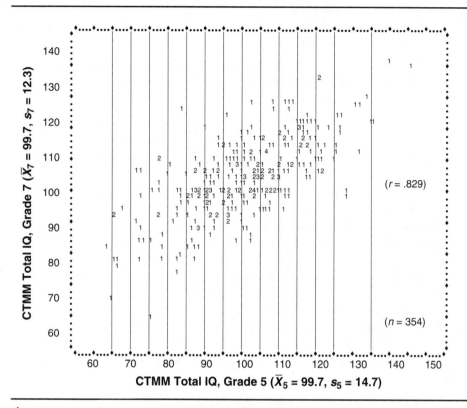

❖ **FIGURE 8.5** The regression effect in pretest-posttest designs.

1. What were the lowest and highest IQ scores obtained at grade 5?
2. What were the lowest and highest IQ scores obtained at grade 7?
3. Compute the regression coefficient for the raw-score regression equation: $b = r(s_Y/s_X)$.
4. Compute the constant for the raw-score regression equation: $c = \overline{Y} - b\,\overline{X}$.
5. Write the raw-score regression equation for predicting grade 7 IQ scores from grade 5 IQ scores.
6. Bobbie Jo obtained an IQ score of 140 at grade 5. Predict her grade 7 IQ score.
7. Thor's IQ score at grade 5 was 70. Predict his grade 7 IQ score.
8. Draw in the regression line in the figure (use the two points $[X, \hat{Y}]$ from exercises 6 and 7).
9. Compute the standard error of estimate ($s_{Y.X}$).
10. What percentage of the grade 7 predictions will be within 7 points of the observed values?
11. Draw in dotted lines one $s_{Y.X}$ above and one $s_{Y.X}$ below the regression line.
12. Chances are about 2 in 3 that Bobbie Jo's IQ score at grade 7 (see exercise 6) will be between __?__ and __?__, and that Thor's IQ score (see exercise 7) will be between __?__ and __?__.
13. Does the regression appear to be linear?
14. Does the scatterplot appear to possess homoscedasticity?
15. Does the scatterplot appear to be approximately bivariately normal (i.e., both X and Y normally distributed)?

16. What percentage of those who score 140 at grade 5 will score *at least* that high at grade 7?

17. For every 1,000 persons scoring 70 at grade 5, how many would be expected to receive "average" scores of 100 or better at grade 7? (See exercise 7.)

For exercises 18–26: In the national standardization of the Lorge-Thorndike Intelligence Test and the Iowa Test of Basic Skills, nonverbal IQ scores correlated .82 with reading scores at grade 8.

	IQ	Reading
μ	100	8.0
σ	15	2.0
	$\rho = .82$	

18. Determine the regression equation to predict grade-equivalent (GE) scores in reading from the IQ scores.

19. What is the average reading grade-equivalent score for persons with IQ scores of 100 at grade 8?

20. Persons with IQ scores of 90 have what average reading GE score at grade 8?

21. Compare the percentile equivalents in exercise 20 for X and $\hat{Y}$.

22. What percentage of the pupils with IQ = 90 read at grade level 8.0 or above? What is the value of $s_{Y.X}$?

23. What percentage of persons with IQ = 90 score 9.1 or higher on the reading test?

24. What is the average reading GE score for persons at P_{98} on the intelligence test?

25. What is this reading GE score in percentile units? (See exercise 24.)

26. What percentage of students with IQ scores of 130 obtain reading GE scores below grade level 8.0?

For exercises 27–31: The correlation of the mother's height is about r = .50 with the height of her sons or daughters. The correlation of the father's height with his offspring is the same. Assume that the correlation of the heights of husbands and wives is r = .30.

27. How accurately can children's height be predicted (that is, what is the multiple correlation coefficient) using the height of both parents as predictors?

28. Other things being equal, what would be the multiple correlation if $r = 0$ (not .3)?

29. Other things being equal, what would be the effect on R if the husband-wife correlation were greater than .3?

30. Estimate the correlation between heights of mothers (M) and of daughters (D) with no variation in fathers' heights (F). For example, for 1,000 daughters whose fathers are 5'8", what is the correlation between the daughters' heights with their mothers' heights?

31. Why is $r_{DM.F}$ less than r_{DM} in exercise 30?

32. Commercial speed-reading clinics often quote research showing the correlation of reading speed (S) with reading comprehension (C), suggesting that if speed is improved, comprehension will also be enhanced. The partial correlation between speed and comprehension drops to nearly zero when intelligence is partialed out. Explain.

For exercises 33–36: One large remedial reading study selected seventh-grade students who were reading 2.0 or more grades below grade level (7.0) on a standardized reading test. These students were then given a special reading program and tested one year later with a standardized reading test.

The mean scores of the treated groups increased 1.4 grade equivalents from 4.5 to 5.9 during the one-year interval between the pretest and posttest. Answer the remaining exercises using the information given below from the test manual; assume these "norms" were based on a large representative sample that was tested at the beginning of grade 7 (7.0) and again one year later (8.0).

Grade 7	Grade 8
$\bar{X} = 7.0$	$\bar{Y} = 8.0$
$s_X = 1.8$	$s_Y = 1.9$
$r = .8$	

33. What is the regression coefficient, b?
34. What is the intercept, c?
35. What is the predicted score on the posttest for the mean pretest score of $X = 4.5$ for the treated group?
36. How does the actual gain compare with the predicted gain?

ANSWERS TO PROBLEMS AND EXERCISES

1. 64 and 146
2. 56 and 138
3. $b = [.83(12.3)/14.7] = .69$
4. $c = 99.7 - .69(99.7) = 30.9$
5. $\hat{Y} = .69X + 30.9$
6. $\hat{Y} = .69(140) + 30.9 = 128$
7. $\hat{Y} = .69(70) + 30.9 = 79$
9. $s_{Y.X} = 12.3\sqrt{1 - (.83)^2} = 12.3(.558) = 6.9$ or about 7 points
10. approximately 68%
12. (128 ± 7) or $[121, 135]$, (79 ± 7) or $[72, 86]$
13. yes
14. yes
15. yes
16. $z = (140 - 128)/7 = 1.71$, from Appendix B Table A: only 4%
17. $z = (100 - 79)/7 = 3$, from Appendix B Table A: only about 1 person per 1,000
18. $b = .82(2.0)/15 = .11$, $c = 8.0 - .11(100) = -3$, $\hat{Y} = .11X - 3$
19. 8.0
20. $\hat{Y} = .11(90) - 3 = 9.9 - 3 = 6.9$
21. An IQ of 90 is equivalent to $z = (90 - 100)/15 = -.67$; from Appendix B Table A, this is P_{25}. A reading score of 6.9 is equivalent to $z = -.55$ and P_{29}.
22. $\hat{Y} = 6.9$; $s_{Y.X} = 2.0\sqrt{1 - (.82)^2} = 1.1$; thus,

$z = (8.0 - 6.9)/1.1 = 1.0$; hence, only 16% read at this level.
23. $z = (9.1 - 6.9)/1.1 = 2.0$, hence about 2%
24. $P_{98} = $ IQ of 130, $\hat{Y} = .11(130) - 3 = 11.3$
25. $z = (11.3 - 8.0)/2.0 = 3.3/2.0 = 1.65$ or P_{95}
26. $z = (8.0 - 11.3)/1.1 = -3$ or .13%
27. $R^2 = [.5^2 + .5^2 - 2(.5)(.5)(.3)]/(1 - .3^2) = .3846$, $R = .62$
28. $R^2 = .5/1 = .5$, $R = .71$
29. R would decrease.
30. $r_{DM.F} = [.5 - (.3)(.5)]/\sqrt{(.91)(.75)} = .42$
31. Since r_{MF} is not zero, if we hold the father's height constant, we restrict the variance in the mother's height; and, other things being equal, the smaller the variance in X, the lower the correlation.
32. The correlation between speed and comprehension appears to result from the correlation of each with IQ. For persons of the same IQ, there is little correlation between speed and comprehension. Hence, since an increase in reading speed will not increase cognitive ability, it would be expected to have little effect on comprehension.
33. $b = r(s_Y/s_X) = .8(1.9/1.8) = .84$
34. $c = \bar{Y} - b\bar{X} = 8 - .84(7) = 2.1$
35. $\hat{Y} = bX + c = .84(4.5) + 2.1 = 5.9$
36. They are equal: 1.4 grade equivalents.

 SUGGESTED COMPUTER EXERCISE

1. (a) In Section 8.10 the regression equation to predict reading scores from math scores was developed. Use spreadsheet or statistical software to find the regression equation to predict reading (the dependent variable) from writing (the independent variable).
   (b) The histogram of the residuals is approximately what shape?
   (c) How many, and what percent, of the errors of estimate (residuals) were in the interval above $+1s_{Y.X}$? below $-1s_{Y.X}$?

2. Use a spreadsheet to compute predicted reading scores from the math scores. The regression equation of Section 8.10 for this task was: $\hat{Y} = .724X + 14.12$.

9

Statistical Inference:
Sampling and Interval Estimation

❖ 9.1 THE FUNCTION OF STATISTICAL INFERENCE

In the preceding chapters, statistical inference has been a minor theme; descriptive statistics was the major focus. The principal objectives of statistics courses, however, belong to the realm of statistical inference; descriptive statistics serve as a necessary prerequisite. From this point on, we will be concerned with estimating and making statements about population parameters using inferential statistics. The *principal purpose of statistical methods* is to legitimize generalizations about populations using data from samples. This chapter introduces concepts that are fundamentally important in helping you to gain mastery of inferential statistics. As you master the content of this chapter, you will be laying a firm foundation for unfettered progress in the subsequent chapters of this book, as well as more advanced statistical methods.

In rare cases, all members of a population are observed, and in these cases only descriptive statistics are appropriate. However, the vast majority of surveys, such as the Gallup poll, involve identifying a population, selecting a representative sample, obtaining data on that sample, performing appropriate statistical analyses, and making inferences about the entire population from which the sample was selected. Usually the sample includes only a small fraction of the total population; for example, the Neilson ratings of the popularity of TV programs are based on the viewing habits of a sample of less than one in 10,000 homes (.01%) in the population. The computerized projections of winners in political elections are sophisticated applications of the concepts of this chapter. Before considering the theory underlying statistical inference, perhaps we should review and clarify some fundamental definitions and concepts.

❖ 9.2 POPULATIONS AND SAMPLES: PARAMETERS AND STATISTICS

The principal use of statistical inference in behavioral research is to make inferences about a large group of persons, or other observational units, from data on a relatively small group of persons. *Inferential statistical methods* employ inductive reasoning, that is, reasoning from the particular to the general, reasoning from the observed sample statistics to the unobserved population parameters. Inferential statistics addresses such questions as "What do I know about the average reading speed (μ, the parameter) of U.S. ten-year-olds (the population) after having learned that these 100 ten-year-olds (the representative sample) averaged 84.8 ($\overline{X}$, the statistic) words per minute?" The difference in the value for the sample and the value for the population is sampling error; other things being equal, the larger the sample, the smaller the sampling error.

Any defined aggregation of units (persons, books, schools, etc.) may be selected as a *population* (parent population, target population, or universe), while a *sample* is a part, or subset, of a population. The concept of a population is so all-inclusive that it may be difficult to grasp initially. In common parlance the term "population" usually refers specifically to the total number of persons residing in a given geographical area, but in behavioral research, researchers delimit the units of a population as they choose—hospitals, schools, research universities, businesses with fewer than twenty-five employees, kindergarten teachers, female elementary principals, and the like.

> **Quiz:** Complete the analogies: (1) "Part" is to "Sample," as "Whole" is to "__?__".
> (2) If a high school principal interviews a random sample of twenty students in Jefferson High School, what is the population in this instance?
>
> **Answers:** (1) Population, (2) all students in Jefferson High School

❖ 9.3 INFINITE VERSUS FINITE POPULATIONS

If it is conceivable that the process of counting the units comprising the population could be completed, and the numerical value for N be found, then the *population is finite*—if not, it is infinite. The truly infinite populations that come easily to mind are somewhat uninteresting or contrived, for example, the collection of all positive numbers, the collection of all possible measurements of your weight, the collection of tosses of a pair of dice which could be made throughout eternity, et cetera. Almost all populations that are studied are *finite* in size, for example, all persons living in the Western Hemisphere, all refrigerators manufactured in Canada in the last decade, all possible orderings of ten stimuli, the 181 school districts in Colorado, all social workers in Florida, or all books in the Chicago Public Library. A finite population may be extremely large—the proverbial "grains of sand in the sea," the number of census tracts in the United States, all first-grade children in California, or all unkept campaign promises by elected politicians in the decade of the 1990s.

The statistical techniques for making inferences for infinite populations are simpler than those for finite populations. The good news is that, in practice, it is generally unnecessary to bother about the distinction between finite and infinite populations in statistical applications. Unless the proportion of the population sampled (the *sampling fraction*, n/N) is .05 or greater, the techniques for making inferences to finite populations and those to infinite populations give essentially the same results. For most studies, the sampling fraction (n/N) is very small; hence, the less cumbersome statistical formulas for infinite populations are used. Even if the sampling fraction is as large as .05, the results from using the simpler methods (which assume that N is infinitely large) are only slightly less precise and efficient (and slightly more conservative) than the results from using procedures that take the sampling fraction into account.

In summary, most of the statistical techniques that are used in behavioral research were developed based on the assumption that an infinite population is being sampled, even though this is rarely the case. However, if the population is quite large and the sample from the population constitutes only a small proportion of the population (i.e., $n/N < .05$), it is of little concern that the parent population is not actually infinite. It is common to speak of a large population as being "virtually infinite;" that is, the finite population is sufficiently large so that statistical techniques that assume infinite populations can be used. In the illustrations and applications of this chapter, the populations are deemed virtually infinite in size. The slight inaccuracies resulting from this assumption are trivial, and conservative at that—sampling error will be a bit smaller than estimated.

Quiz: For a defined population, the $N = 1,200$ member faculty at the University of Colorado, Boulder, what are the sampling fractions for the following sample sizes? (1) $n = 30$ (2) $n = 12$ (3) $n = 240$ (4) The simpler statistical procedures (developed for infinite populations) would probably give satisfactory estimates of sampling error for which of the above sample sizes?

Answers: (1) 30/1,200 = .025, (2) 12/1,200 = .01, (3) 240/1,200 = .10, (4) $n = 30$ and $n = 12$ since these two sampling fractions are quite small (less than .05).

❖ 9.4 THE NEED FOR REPRESENTATIVE SAMPLES

The *method used to select the sample is of utmost importance* in judging the validity of the inferences made from the sample to the target population. The sample should be selected in a deliberate fashion from the parent population so that it is *representative* of the population, that is, the characteristics of the sample approximate those of the population within a known margin of error. The novice is often more concerned about the size of a sample rather than its representativeness—a very serious mistake. A representative sample of 100 is preferable to an unrepresentative sample of 12,000,000! The classic illustration of this point (and of how not to select a sample) occurred in the 1936 presidential preference poll conducted by the now-defunct periodical, *The Literary Digest*. Penny postcards were sent to an unrepresentative sample of 12,000,000 persons selected from telephone directories and automobile registration lists. Even though the response rate was poor (21%), the 2,500,000 who returned the postcards constitute one of the largest samples on record. Although 57% of the respondents indicated a preference for the Republican candidate, Alf Landon, to the chagrin of the magazine, Franklin Roosevelt was elected by the greatest majority in history up to that time, carrying all states except Maine and Vermont.

What went wrong? How can George Gallup's polls be presumed to be fairly accurate with samples of fewer than 2,000 persons when the *Literary Digest* was woefully misled by a sample that was more than 1,000 times as large? Hopefully, it is clear that *the size of a sample can never compensate for a lack of representativeness*. Obviously, automobile owners and people from homes with telephones were not a representative sample of voters in 1936. In addition, the 21% who returned the questionnaire probably were not a representative sample even of the 12,000,000 who received the postcards. (The possible self-selection bias in those persons who return questionnaires continues to this day to be the single greatest threat to plague the validity of mail surveys.)

Quiz: Please answer TRUE or FALSE. (1) A smaller representative sample is almost always preferable to a larger unrepresentative sample. (2) If a researcher is not confident that a sample is representative of the population, the sample size should be expanded to compensate for the doubts.

Answers: (1) True, but a larger representative sample is even better. (2) False, an increase in sample size will not insure representativeness; sampling procedure should be altered.

The *Literary Digest* survey, apart from the biased sampling plan, utilized an extremely inefficient strategy. To the trained eye of the statistician, it would have been evident that a sample only one-tenth of one-percent (.1%) as large as that used by the *Literary Digest* would have been *exceedingly* precise. Even in the era of the penny postcard, the postage for 12,000,000 postcards would have been $120,000! Any statistician would have known that $120 ($n = 12,000$) in postage would have done as well.[1]

❖ 9.5 TYPES OF SAMPLES

Statistical calculations from samples serve to give information about the characteristics of the target population. There are several appropriate ways in which samples can be selected from a population, but, unfortunately, there are even more inappropriate sampling methods. Appropriate sampling methods are those methods which maximize the probability that (1) the resulting sample will be adequately representative of the population, and (2) the resulting sample statistics will provide adequately precise estimates of the population parameters. Systematic sampling and random sampling are two of the most acceptable and widely recommended sampling methods. Other appropriate but more elaborate sampling methods are discussed in more advanced texts of survey research.[2] Unrepresentative samples often result from accidental, convenient, haphazard, or self-selected volunteer samples; generalizations based on such data are almost never valid and cannot be given much credibility. No information is usually better than misinformation.

❖ 9.6 RANDOM SAMPLES

In random sampling, *every unit* in the population has an *equal and independent chance* of being selected for the sample. The sampling units may represent persons such as nurses, marriage counselors, math teachers, first-grade pupils, welfare recipients, college graduates, or books in a library.

Random sampling criteria:

1. The probability of selecting any individual (or unit) in the target population as a sample participant must be the same as for selecting any other individual in the defined target population.
2. The probability of selecting any given person must not be affected by (i.e., must be independent of) whether or not any other person is selected.

---

[1]Another common misapplication of surveys, especially political polls, is to use present findings to make inferences about the future, for example, to project the results of an election. During the course of a campaign, voter preferences can vacillate considerably as issues and positions are clarified, "mud" is slung, performance in a debate registers, and so forth. A poll per se is not necessarily invalid just because it disagrees with the election outcome unless it was an "exit poll" of voters. In forecasting an election, it is the population of actual voters (those who in fact vote, not just the registered voters) that is the relevant population for the question at hand. Pollsters often try to identify probable voters within their sample, but this always remains to some extent uncertain (due to weather, health, etc.). The population of actual voters is never the same as the population of registered voters, which in turn is never the same as the population of persons who meet the criteria for being registered voters. In interpreting findings from any poll, one must bear in mind the pollster's definition of the population. In addition, one must remember that the inferential statistics are strictly generalizable only to the population surveyed at that particular time in the campaign, and not to how the population will respond at some time in the future.

[2]More complex sampling plans, such as stratified random sampling, cluster sampling, and two-stage sampling are treated in textbooks on sampling such as Cochran (1977), Jaeger (1984), or Kish (1965).

For example, if a school attitude inventory is to be given to fifty students at Lincoln School and two of the twenty classes (of twenty-five pupils each) are selected at random from among all classes in the school, the sampling unit would be classes, not pupils. Hence, the fifty students (in the two classes selected) cannot be viewed as a random sample of the pupils at Lincoln School. Although the probability of being included in the sample may have been approximately the same for each pupil (assuming all classes were of comparable size), the pupils' chances of being selected were not independent of one another (if one student in a class was selected, all students in that class were selected). In random sampling, the probability of selecting each unit is the same as for all other units, and the selection of one unit is independent of all other units.

As in all texts on statistical methods, the primary emphasis in this and subsequent chapters is on simple random sampling. The statistical formulas that have been derived have assumed random sampling procedures. In this text the term "sample," unless indicated otherwise, implies a "simple random sample."

Before a sample can adequately serve as a basis for making estimates of population parameters, it must be *representative* of the population, that is, its characteristics must adequately mirror those of the parent population. The criterion of representativeness, however, presents a problem. How can we be confident that the sample characteristics reflect those of the population unless the characteristics of the population are known? And if the characteristics of the entire population are known, it makes no sense to use a sample to estimate them. This quandary is resolved through the properties of randomness—random sampling of a population produces samples which, in the long run, are representative of the population. If a sample is randomly drawn, it is representative (within a known margin of error) of the population in all respects. A representative sample differs from the population only by chance amounts for any variable, whether measured or unmeasured, whether desirable or undesirable, or whether physical or metaphysical. Through the magic of statistical theory, the estimated magnitude of the sampling error (the statistic minus the parameter) can be quantified mathematically. *Random sampling* will ensure the representativeness of the samples, and hence will legitimize establishing estimates for the population parameters, within a certain calculable margin of error.

The ability to quantify the expected sampling error in representative samples is essential in inferential statistics. It is impossible to estimate the extent of sampling error with unscientific sampling strategies because they contain unidentified types and degrees of bias, in addition to chance differences. For example, one study compared the cognitive abilities of a sample of American Indian children with those of non-Indian children. The sample of Indian children was composed of those children who had been tested individually by school psychologists in one Indian community. Moreover, these children were tested because of poor academic performance! Obviously, this sample is biased and not representative of the relevant population of American Indian children; indeed, even a representative sample from this community would not provide an adequate basis for generalizing to other Indian communities or tribes. If, however, the children were selected randomly from the population of all Indian children in the United States, by using the procedures of this chapter we could estimate, within a known margin of error, the results that would have been obtained if all Indian children in the population had been tested.

Quiz: What sampling method is most likely to obtain samples in which the proportions of gender, socio-economic levels, age groups, culture groups, and achievement levels are comparable to the population proportions of these variables?

Answer: selection of a random sample from the defined population

❖ 9.7 RANDOM SAMPLING USING A TABLE OF RANDOM NUMBERS

Drawing names from a hat only roughly approximates randomness. The classic method of drawing a random sample is to use a table of random numbers (a table of randomly ordered digits, 0 through 9). If we select our sample by properly using such a table (for example, Table B in Appendix B), we will have a random sample.

The process of random sampling using a random number table is summarized in the four steps below:

Step 1.	Assign a unique number from 1 to N to the population units. For a population with $N < 100$, only 2-digit numbers are required, for example, 01, 02, 03, et cetera. For populations with $N < 1,000$, only 3-digit numbers are required, for example, 001, 002, 003, et cetera.
Step 2.	Decide the direction in which you will read the table (downward, upward, to the right, even diagonally); then "blindly" drop a pencil on the random number table and begin reading.
Step 3.	From the starting point, begin selecting successive random numbers which may potentially be matched to population units; for $N < 100$, select 2-digit numbers; for $N < 1,000$, select 3-digit numbers, et cetera. Select more random numbers than you think you will need to allow for duplicate numbers and numbers without a population match. (The spacing between columns of the random number table are merely for readability and can be ignored when selecting random numbers.)
Step 4.	Population units whose assigned numbers match the obtained random numbers constitute the random sample. Duplicate random numbers and random numbers which exceed N are ignored.

Let us work through an example of selecting a random sample using a table of random digits to clarify the steps above. We will consider the 200 students in the HSB data set (see Table I of Appendix B) as the parent population and select a 5% random sample ($n = 10$).

Step 1.	A unique three-digit ID number from 001 (C1) to 200 (C200) has been assigned to each student and is listed in the first column of Table I.
Step 2.	Let us decide to read the random number table horizontally, and then we let our pencil fall on the random number table. Suppose the point landed on row 6 near the second 1 in that row.
Step 3.	We begin our random sample selection process in Table B by mentally grouping the numbers into sets of three digits (ignore the spacing between pairs of digits). We move across to form successive 3-digit numbers: 157, 260, 689, 800, 533, 915, 470, 483, and so on. (All of the random numbers > 200 do not have an HSB match, but just keep going until you have matched 10 HSB cases.)
Step 4.	Thus, we select students numbered 157, 122, 045, 042, 009, and so on until we have our random sample of $n = 10$ students.

What about the random numbers specified by the table which do not match any student in the HSB data set, such as 260, 689, 800, and so on? Such unmatchable random numbers are simply discarded along with any duplicate random numbers which may appear.

Quiz: (1) What is the sampling fraction of the preceding random sample of $n = 10$ students? (2) Do statistical formulas that assume an infinitely large population give satisfactorily accurate results in this case? Why? (3) List the $n = 10$ student ID numbers comprising the random sample described above.

Answers: (1) 10/200 = .05, (2) Yes, since the sampling fraction is $\leq$ 5 percent. (3) 157, 122, 45, 42, 9, 183, 52, 121, 74, 49

If n is large, the process becomes tedious even though it is simple in theory. The process of selecting a random sample is greatly simplified if one has access to a personal computer. All computers have a random-number generating function that can be directed to select a random sample of n persons from a population of N persons and print them out quickly and accurately.

Suppose a superintendent wishes to interview ten teachers to obtain feedback about teacher morale. Why should he go through the process of randomly selecting a sample? Why not just select the ten "representative" teachers, teachers that the superintendent opines would be representative of the entire district? Such judgmental samples are notoriously biased. Numerous factors can operate on one's judgment to make the selection nonrepresentative. The superintendent might tend to select those who first came to mind, and hence the judgmental sample might have a greater proportion of very vocal, popular, bright, cooperative, or hostile teachers. If the selection of the sample is random, systematic biases cannot enter into the selection process; hence, it is more probable that the sample would be representative of the parent population and that the inferences derived from the sample statistics would have greater credibility.

❖ 9.8 SYSTEMATIC SAMPLES

If, from a list of all units in the parent population, every kth unit (e.g., every 10th, or every 40th, etc.) in the list is selected, the resulting sample is known as a systematic sample. Like random sampling, systematic sampling tends to result in representative samples; indeed, the statistical results from systematic samples tend to be slightly more precise than results from simple random samples, but to an inconsequential degree.

To draw a systematic sample of $n = 10$ students from the $N = 200$ HSB data set population, we could complete the following three steps.

> **Step 1.** Determine the step-size or "hop-size"—the reciprocal of the sampling fraction: $h = N/n$, rounded upward to the nearest whole number, if necessary. For this example, $h = 200/10 = 20$; thus, once the initial case has been identified, every 20th student in the HSB file will be selected for the sample (each successive case will "hop over" 19 intervening cases).
>
> **Step 2.** Determine the starting case by selecting a random number, between 1 and h. For this example, let us suppose that we used the random number table and selected 15.

> **Step 3.**   Select the systematic sample beginning with the 15th case and every *h*th (20th) student thereafter. For this example, students numbered 15, 35, 55, 75, 95, 115, 135, 155, 175, and 195 comprise the systematic sample of $n = 10$ students from the $N = 200$ students in the HSB data set population.

Quiz: Suppose you wish to develop a measure to estimate the size of one's vocabulary. There are 190,000 words in *Webster's Unabridged Dictionary*. Each of the 2,128 pages contains approximately 90 words. You design your measure to have about 100 words. You could take every $190,000/100 = 1,900$th word, but all that counting would be more than your psyche could withstand. You decide to strike a reasonable compromise by assuming that each of the pages has the same number of words, 90; you can then get a systematic sample of pages, and select one word from each page. (1) For the 2,128 pages, what is the hop size (h)? (2) How will you determine the starting page number? (3) What will be the 2nd, 3rd, and 4th page numbers that you will select? (4) How will you decide on which word to select from each of these pages? (5) Will your procedure give you a random sample? (6) Will your sample be a representative sample? (7) What is the population? (8) Margie knows 21% of the words on your vocabulary test—can you estimate the size of her vocabulary? (9) Can you estimate the margin of error in your estimate?

Answers: (1) $h = 2,128/100 = 21.28$ or 22. (2) We will select a random number between 1 and 22; assume this number is 15. (3) 2nd: $15 + 22 = 37$, 3rd: $37 + 22 = 59$, 4th: $59 + 22 = 81$, (4) You will select a random number between 1 and 90; assume this number is 13; thus, you will select the 13th word on each of the pages selected. (5) No, it is a "quasi-systematic" sample. (6) almost certainly, (7) the words defined in *Webster's Unabridged Dictionary*, (8) Yes, 21% of $190,000 = 39,900$. (9) No, but ask me again after I have studied Chapter 12!

The practical advantage of systematic samples is that they are often easier to obtain than random samples. Untrained workers in the field can be told to take every 5th student on the list, but could not be expected to select a 5% random sample. The availability of spreadsheet software has decreased the use of systematic samples, since obtaining a random sample of observations out of the N observations in the population is almost effortless. A disadvantage of systematic sampling is that there is no statistical theory that precisely determines the accuracy of the estimates. What is ordinarily done with systematic samples is to treat them as if they were random samples; the consequence of which is to obtain very slight underestimates of the accuracy of the statistics. Properly employed, findings from random and systematic samples are representative and generalizable; that is, we can be confident that the findings based on the sample are unbiased and can be applied to the population within a specified margin of error.[3]

---

[3]Systematic sampling is hazardous only if the list of population units is cyclically ordered. For example, if boys and girls were required to sit in alternate seats and a roster based on seating was used to select the sample, sampling fractions of 1/2, 1/4, 1/6, et cetera would result in a sample having either no boys or no girls.

❖ 9.9 ACCIDENTAL SAMPLES

Accidental sampling is the most prevalent, and most inappropriate, method of obtaining a sample. Convenient but haphazard collections of observations cannot be viewed as representative; consequently, the findings based on such data often distort more than they inform. Contrary to common practice, results from street corner polls, selected callers who respond to a TV or radio poll, or persons who agree to answer the questions of a telephone survey cannot legitimately be generalized to the desired populations, and generalizations from such surveys can mislead the unwary. Commercial advertisements often report "rose-colored" data on their products obtained on samples of unknown representativeness (or of known unrepresentativeness). You have wisdom above your years if you view conclusions based on accidental samples with vigorous skepticism and incredulity.

❖ 9.10 POINT AND INTERVAL ESTIMATES

In previous chapters, all statistical measures are *point estimates*; that is, a single numerical value served to estimate the parameter. The expression $E(\overline{X}) = \mu$ denotes that $\overline{X}$ is an unbiased point estimate of μ.

As the term suggests, an *interval estimate* is a range or band of values within which the parameter is said to lie with a stated level of probability. Interval estimates build on the value of point estimates by conveying the degree of precision in the estimates. Interval estimation is a valuable, but much underused, inferential statistical method in behavioral and social research.

For an example, suppose that, for a sample of children born to mothers who were heavy drug users, the mean IQ score at age two is 86. The point estimate of the parameter is 86, but if the n is small (e.g., 10), the interval estimate for the parameter μ might extend from 76 to 96. The interval estimate (76 to 96) tells us that the point estimate ($\overline{X} = 86$) is not very precise, and that the actual mean IQ score is probably somewhere in the defined interval. On the other hand, if n were large (e.g., 225), the interval estimate of the mean IQ score in this population would be approximately 84 to 88, and it would be evident that the parameter μ was estimated with considerable precision.

Understanding the rationale for interval estimates requires a grasp of *the most fundamentally important concept of inferential statistics—the concept of a sampling distribution.* A mastery of this challenging concept will likely require your undivided attention and your clearest thinking. However, the reward is worth the investment; the concept of the sampling distribution is a prerequisite to an understanding of all subsequent chapters of this book as well as almost all advanced statistical methods.

❖ 9.11 SAMPLING DISTRIBUTIONS: THE SAMPLING DISTRIBUTION OF THE MEAN

The concept of a sampling distribution is fundamental in inferential statistics. In this chapter, the concept is illustrated using the most common sampling distribution of all—the sampling distribution of the mean. Once you grasp this sampling distribution, the concept can easily be extended to other sampling distributions, such as the sampling distributions of proportions (Chapter 12) and the sampling distributions of the correlation coefficient (Chapter 13). A *sampling distribution of the mean* is simply a frequency distribution, not of raw scores (X's), but of sample means ($\overline{X}$'s), where each sample mean is based on a random sample of n raw scores. In other words, the sampling distribution of the mean is the frequency distribution of sample means that would result if we drew a random sample of size n from the parent population, computed its mean, and then repeated the process many times. The frequency distribution of these many $\bar{X}$-values is the sampling distribution of the mean.

Let us do a mental experiment to illustrate the sampling distribution of the mean. Suppose each student-researcher in a surprisingly large measurement class is assigned to draw a random sample of twenty-five children from the target population and find the mean IQ of these $n = 25$ children. Each of these many student-researchers then returns and reports the mean ($\bar{X}$) for the sample. The frequency distribution of these many $\bar{X}$'s is an approximation of the sampling distribution of the mean. (Assuming that the number of student-researchers in the class was enormous and that all children of the population were included, the frequency distribution would be the actual sampling distribution of the mean for $n = 25$, and the distribution curve would be nice and smooth.)

❖ 9.12 THE STANDARD ERROR OF THE MEAN

Let us pursue the illustration, now assuming that the observations (X's) in the population are normally distributed, and in which μ and σ are known. Please note that our purpose at this point is conceptual; by specifying these conditions, we are able to illustrate important concepts about sampling distributions without distracting qualifying statements. In a later section, we will consider the more typical situation in which μ and σ are unknown.

Assume that IQ scores are normally distributed with $\mu = 100$ and $\sigma = 15$. Recall that each of the student-researchers has randomly drawn twenty-five children, obtained their IQ scores, and computed $\bar{X}$; thus, many estimates of μ (sample means) are obtained. Assume that we have made a frequency distribution of these sample means, that is, we have constructed the sampling distribution of the mean. Thanks to the mathematician and the power of deductive logic, it has been proved that this sampling distribution has three very interesting characteristics:

1. The distribution of the $\bar{X}$'s is normally distributed.
2. Like the X's, the mean of the $\bar{X}$'s is equal to μ.
3. The standard deviation of the $\bar{X}$'s is given by Equation 9.1:

$$\sigma_{\bar{X}} = \frac{\sigma}{\sqrt{n}} \qquad (9.1)$$

For the above example, $\sigma_{\bar{X}} = 15/\sqrt{n}$, or $\sigma_{\bar{X}} = 3$. This sampling distribution is normally distributed with a mean of 100 and a standard deviation of 3.

The standard deviation of the sampling distribution of the mean is termed the *standard error of the mean*. You will be pleased to know that much of what you learned previously pertaining to areas under the normal curve can now be applied to sampling distributions. In fact, many questions pertaining to sampling distributions are quite similar to questions you encountered in Chapter 5.

Quiz: Given the sampling distribution of the mean IQ's described above, about what percent of the sample means would: (1) exceed 100? (2) fall between 100 and 103? (3) exceed 97? (4) be less than 94? (5) have a value between 94.12 and 105.88?

Answers: (1) 50%, (2) $z = (103 - 100)/3 = 1$; so the area between the mean ($z = 0$) and $z = 1$ is about 34%. (3) $z = -1$; so the area above is about 34% + 50% = 84%. (4) $z = -2$; so the area below is about 2% (more precisely, 2.14%). (5) In this distribution, the z-scores for 94.12 and 105.88 are -1.96 and 1.96; the area between $z = -1.96$ and $z = +1.96$ is 95%.

Recall that the sampling error pertaining to a sample mean is the ($\overline{X} - \mu$) difference. When $\sigma_{\overline{X}}$ is 3, 68 percent of the sampling errors are less than |3|; and about 95 percent of them are less than |6|. Please observe that, in Equation 9.1 when n is small, $\sigma_{\overline{X}}$ is large and, consequently, the sampling errors are large. When n is large, $\sigma_{\overline{X}}$ is small and, consequently, the sampling errors are small. In previous chapters you learned that, as the sample size *increases*, the magnitude of the sampling error *decreases*. This inverse relationship between sample size and the magnitude of sampling errors is extremely important.

Quiz: Given that the population of IQ's is normally distributed with $\mu = 100$ and $\sigma = 15$, compute the standard error of the mean, $\sigma_{\overline{X}}$, if: (1) $n = 4$, (2) $n = 16$, (3) $n = 25$, and (4) $n = 100$. (5) Notice that when n is quadrupled, $\sigma_{\overline{X}}$ is __?__.
Answers: (1) $15/2 = 7.5$, (2) $15/4 = 3.75$, (3) $15/5 = 3$, (4) $15/10 = 1.5$ (5) halved

❖ 9.13 CONFIDENCE INTERVALS

In our previous illustrations of IQ scores, both μ and σ of the parent population were known. For theoretical purposes, imagine for the moment the situation in which the population standard deviation is known ($\sigma = 15$), but the population mean, μ, is not known. How accurately does $\overline{X}$ estimate μ—how much sampling error is associated with estimates of μ? We know that the sampling distribution of the mean is normally distributed (Section 9.12) and has a standard deviation of $\sigma_{\overline{X}}$ (Eq. 9.1). Consequently, 68 percent of the $\overline{X}$'s are within one $\sigma_{\overline{X}}$ (above or below) of μ; if we place a band of one $\sigma_{\overline{X}}$ above and below each $\overline{X}$-value, μ would lie within that interval for 68 percent of the sample means. In other words, the .68 confidence interval (CI) for μ is [$\overline{X} \pm \sigma_{\overline{X}}$] as shown in Equation 9.2. (Recall that the symbol "±" is read "plus or minus"; i.e., [$\overline{X} \pm \sigma_{\overline{X}}$] indicates the range between $\overline{X} - \sigma_{\overline{X}}$ and $\overline{X} + \sigma_{\overline{X}}$.) The lower limit of the .68 confidence interval for μ is $\overline{X} - \sigma_{\overline{X}}$; the upper limit of the interval is $\overline{X} + \sigma_{\overline{X}}$. The width of a confidence interval refers to the range covered by the interval—the distance between the lower limit and the upper limit. For the .68 CI, the width is $2\sigma_{\overline{X}}$. The ".68" is referred to as the "confidence coefficient" of the confidence interval:

$$.68 \text{ CI} = [\overline{X} \pm \sigma_{\overline{X}}] = [\overline{X} - \sigma_{\overline{X}}, \overline{X} + \sigma_{\overline{X}}] \qquad \textbf{(9.2)}$$

Equation 9.2 indicates that, if we take each $\overline{X}$-value in the sampling distribution and form an interval that extends from one $\sigma_{\overline{X}}$ below to one $\sigma_{\overline{X}}$ above each $\overline{X}$, the parameter μ will fall within 68% (or .68) of such intervals. For example, if $\overline{X}$ is 98 and $\sigma_{\overline{X}} = 3$, .68 CI = [95, 101].

In actual practice, the researcher has just the one mean, $\overline{X}$, which is based upon the one sample of n observations. We have no way of knowing whether the particular mean is one of the 68% that falls within one standard error of μ. We do know, however, that in the long run 68% of the confidence intervals formed in this way will accomplish their mission, but 32% will not. We usually wish to be more than "68% confident" that we have achieved our goal of capturing μ within our interval. A wider confidence interval is needed so that we can be more confident that the specified range includes the parameter. The .95 confidence interval is commonly used. In the long run, the parameter μ will be contained within 95% (19 out of 20) of the .95 CI's:

$$.95 \text{ CI} = [\, \overline{X} \pm 1.96\sigma_{\overline{X}}\,] \tag{9.3}$$

Recall from the normal curve table (Appendix B Table A) that a z-score of -1.96 corresponds to $P_{2.5}$ (the 2.5th percentile), and that $z = 1.96$ corresponds to $P_{97.5}$. Equation 9.3 shows that we can be "95% confident" that the parameter, μ, is somewhere within the $[\,\overline{X} \pm 1.96\sigma_{\overline{X}}\,]$ interval. For example, if $\overline{X}$ is 98 and $\sigma_{\overline{X}} = 3$, .95 CI = [92.12, 103.88]. If greater confidence is desired, the .99 confidence interval can be determined by the formula: .99 CI $= [\,\overline{X} \pm 2.58\sigma_{\overline{X}}\,]$.

Quiz: The .90 CI $[\,\overline{X} \pm 1.65\sigma_{\overline{X}}\,]$ includes the middle-most 90% of the distribution. In the long run, the population mean will fall below the lower limit in __(1)__ percent of .90 CI's, and above the upper limit of __(2)__ percent of the .90 CI's. If $\overline{X} = 57.7$ and $\sigma_{\overline{X}} = 2$, the .90 CI for μ extends from __(3)__ to __(4)__ or (5) .95 CI = [___, ___].
Answers: (1) 5%, (2) 5%, (3) 54.4, (4) 61.0, (5) [54.4, 61.0]

❖ 9.14 CONFIDENCE INTERVALS WHEN σ IS KNOWN: AN EXAMPLE

In virtually all instances, μ and σ are either both known or both unknown. However, to illustrate the theory, we are assuming that σ is known but μ is unknown. (In the next section, we will deal with the more typical situation in which both μ and σ are unknown.)

Suppose as researchers we set out to determine the average IQ score of the approximately 500,000 American Indian children in the United States using the Wechsler Intelligence Scale for Children (WISC). The WISC is an individually-administered verbal and performance intelligence test that requires no reading, but must be administered by a trained examiner, and therefore is quite expensive. The available funds for this study will cover 100 test administrations, but no more.

Suppose also we have good reason to believe that the Indian children are as heterogeneous as the children that were used to norm the WISC. Hence, we use $\sigma = 15$ as the parameter for the standard deviation of the WISC IQ scores.

We take a random sample of 100 children and obtain the WISC IQ scores. We will calculate $\overline{X}$ as a point estimate of the parameter, μ, but we also wish to establish a confidence interval around $\overline{X}$ to establish lower and upper limits for μ. Not being unduly rebellious in nature, we behave conventionally and decide to use the .95 confidence interval.

With samples as large as 100, we can be confident that the sampling distribution is very nearly normal with $\sigma_{\overline{X}} = 15/\sqrt{100} = 1.5$. From Equation 9.3, we know that the middle-most 95 percent of the area under the unit normal curve lies within ± 1.96 standard deviations of the mean. The sampling distribution of $\overline{X}$ for samples of 100 from a population with $\sigma = 15$ appears in Figure 9.1, where distance along the baseline is in units of $\sigma_{\overline{X}} = 1.5$. Thus, 95% of the area under this curve lies within $[\mu \pm 2.94]$ because $z(1.5) = 1.96(1.5) = 2.94$.

Suppose we computed the mean of the $n = 100$ IQ scores and found that $\overline{X} = 105$. The .95 confidence interval is [105.0 + 2.94] or from a lower limit of 102.06 to an upper limit of

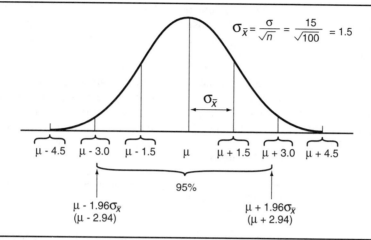

$$\sigma_{\bar{x}} = \frac{\sigma}{\sqrt{n}} = \frac{15}{\sqrt{100}} = 1.5$$

$\sigma_{\bar{x}}$

$\mu - 4.5 \quad \mu - 3.0 \quad \mu - 1.5 \quad \mu \quad \mu + 1.5 \quad \mu + 3.0 \quad \mu + 4.5$

95%

$\mu - 1.96\sigma_{\bar{x}}$
$(\mu - 2.94)$

$\mu + 1.96\sigma_{\bar{x}}$
$(\mu + 2.94)$

❖ **FIGURE 9.1** Sampling distribution of $\bar{X}$ for random samples of $n = 100$ from a parent population with unknown mean μ and $\sigma = 15$.

107.9, that is, [102.06, 107.9)]. In other words, we conclude that the value of μ for the population of Indian children in the United States is probably at least 102.06 and perhaps as high as 107.94. If more precision (i.e., a narrower confidence interval) is desired while holding the confidence coefficient at .95, the sample size must be increased. Use Equation 9.1 and confirm the fact that, if the sample size is quadrupled, the standard error of the mean will be cut in half; if $\sigma_{\bar{x}}$ is reduced by one-half, the width of the confidence interval will also be only half as wide.

> **Quiz:** From Equation 9.1, compute the standard error of the mean WISC IQ score if:
> (1) $n = 225$, and (2) $n = 900$. (3) What n is required to reduce $\sigma_{\bar{x}}$ to .25?
> **Answers:** (1) $15/15 = 1.0$, (2) $15/30 = .50$, (3) $n = 3,600$ (i.e., 4×900).

Confusion will result if you fail to distinguish between $\mu \pm 1.96\sigma_{\bar{x}}$ and $\bar{X} \pm 1.96\sigma_{\bar{x}}$. It is true that 95% of the sample means are included in the range, $\mu \pm 1.96\sigma_{\bar{x}}$, but it is not true that 95% of the sample means would fall in [$\bar{X} \pm 1.96\sigma_{\bar{x}}$] since $\bar{X}$ probably differs from μ to some extent.

❖ 9.15 CONFIDENCE INTERVALS WHEN σ IS UNKNOWN

It is very important to understand the theory that underlies the above example. Regardless of n, the .95 confidence interval is [$\bar{X} \pm 1.96\sigma_{\bar{x}}$]. Note, however, that Equations. 9.1–9.3 require the value of the parameter, σ (not an estimate, s). When σ is unknown, $\sigma_{\bar{x}}$ cannot be precisely determined but must be estimated from s. The estimate of the standard error of the mean, $s_{\bar{x}}$, is given by Equation 9.4:

$$s_{\bar{X}} = \frac{s}{\sqrt{n}} \tag{9.4}$$

Somewhat wider confidence intervals are expected when using $s_{\bar{X}}$ rather than the error-free $\sigma_{\bar{X}}$ when forming confidence intervals. For example, the .95 confidence interval is $[\bar{X} \pm 1.96\sigma_{\bar{X}}]$ when σ (and hence $\sigma_{\bar{X}}$) is known, and this is true for all sample sizes—the multiplier of $\sigma_{\bar{X}}$ is always 1.96 for the .95 confidence interval. However, when σ is unknown and must be estimated from the statistic s, the .95 confidence interval for μ requires a somewhat larger multiplier than 1.96 to compensate for the sampling error in s. When n is small, the sampling error tends to be large; consequently, the multiplier becomes much larger than 1.96; but as n gets larger and larger, the sampling errors diminish and the multiplier of $s_{\bar{X}}$ rapidly approaches (but never quite reaches) 1.96. This multiplier, the number of $s_{\bar{X}}$-values required, is termed the "critical value of t." Equation 9.5 is the general expression for a confidence interval when σ is unknown:

$$\text{CI} = [\bar{X} \pm ts_{\bar{X}}] \text{ or } [\bar{X} - ts_{\bar{X}}, \bar{X} + ts_{\bar{X}}] \tag{9.5}$$

In Equation 9.5, $s_{\bar{X}} = s/\sqrt{n}$ and the critical value of t depends on n and the level of confidence desired. Table 9.1 gives the critical values of t (the multiplier)—the number of $s_{\bar{X}}$'s (standard errors of the mean) that must be added and subtracted from $\bar{X}$ for the .90, .95, and .99 confidence intervals for various values of n.[4] For example, when $n = 20$, the .95 confidence interval when σ is known is $[\bar{X} \pm z\sigma_{\bar{X}}] = [\bar{X} \pm 1.96\sigma_{\bar{X}}]$; but when σ is unknown, the .95 confidence interval is $[\bar{X} \pm ts_{\bar{X}}] = [\bar{X} \pm 2.09s_{\bar{X}}]$. (Notice that $t = 2.09$ for $n = 20$ with a confidence coefficient of .95 in Table 9.1.) Since σ and hence $\sigma_{\bar{X}}$ are rarely known, the procedure involving t is the usual method used in setting confidence intervals.

Quiz: Other things being equal, as the sample size gets larger and larger, the sampling __(1)__ becomes smaller and smaller; $\bar{X}$ becomes a better estimate of __(2)__ ; $s_{\bar{X}}$ becomes a better estimate of __(3)__ ; the critical t-value becomes __(4)__ ; and the width of the .95 confidence interval gets __(5)__ .
Answers: (1) error, (2) μ, (3) $\sigma_{\bar{X}}$ (4) smaller, (5) smaller

In summary, by using the critical value of t (rather than z), confidence intervals can be constructed for the parameter μ using the values of $\bar{X}$ and s based on a single random sample from a population in which σ is unknown. With respect to the *construction of confidence intervals*, the *t-distributions* provide the multipliers of $s_{\bar{X}}$ for populations with unknown σ, whereas the *z-normal distribution* provides the multipliers of $\sigma_{\bar{X}}$ for populations in which σ is *known*.

An Example.   Consider again the problem of estimating the mean IQ for American Indian children. Recall that we had a random sample of 100 IQ scores and $\bar{X} = 105$. Instead of

---

[4]Both n and v are included in Table 9.1. For good reasons that need not concern us now, most t-tables (like Table C in the Appendix) are not based on n, but on a double cousin, the "degrees of freedom" for t ($v = n - 1$) rather than n. The expression "degrees of freedom" (or "df" or v) will be encountered many times in subsequent chapters. It is a statistical concept that has to do with the number of observations free to vary after allowance is made for the number of mathematical restrictions imposed on a set of data. For example, if the sum of 10 scores is computed, this is one mathematical restriction imposed on the data since only 9 of the scores are now free to vary—the 10th score is mathematically determined by the sum. Usually v is just slightly less than n. Unfortunately, degrees of freedom does not have a rich intuitive meaning.

❖ **TABLE 9.1** The critical value of *t* for various confidence coefficients, sample sizes (*n*), and degrees of freedom (*v*).

		t-Values for Confidence Coefficients		
n	*v*	*.90*	*.95*	*.99*
2	1	6.31	12.71	63.82
3	2	2.92	4.30	9.93
5	4	2.13	2.78	4.60
10	9	1.83	2.26	3.25
15	14	1.76	2.15	2.98
16	15	1.75	2.13	2.95
20	19	1.73	2.09	2.86
25	24	1.71	2.06	2.80
30	29	1.70	2.04	2.76
40	39	1.69	2.02	2.71
60	59	1.67	2.00	2.66
80	79	1.67	1.99	2.64
100	99	1.66	1.98	2.63
200	199	1.65	1.97	2.60
500	499	1.65	1.97	2.59
∞	∞	1.645	1.960	2.576

making the gratuitous assumption that $\sigma = 15$ as we did before, the standard deviation, s, of the 100 X's is computed and is found to be $s = 15.6$; hence, $s_{\bar{X}} = 15.6/10 = 1.56$. From Table 9.1, for $n = 100$, the appropriate critical t-value is 1.98; hence, the limits for the .95 confidence interval for μ extend $\pm 1.98 s_{\bar{X}}$ from $\bar{X}$. Equation 9.5 for this example with $n = 100$ becomes:

$$.95 \text{ CI} = [\bar{X} \pm 1.98 s_{\bar{X}}]$$
$$= [\bar{X} \pm 1.98(1.56)]$$

$$= [105.0 \pm 3.09], \text{ or } [101.91, 108.09]$$

The .95 confidence interval ranges from 101.91 to 108.09. Therefore, we can be fairly confident that the mean IQ of the population of American Indian children in the United States has a value greater than 101.91 but less than 108.09. If we replicated this research project, it is almost certain that the newly-computed $\bar{X}$ and s would differ somewhat from the original values, but we can be confident that the newly-constructed .95 confidence interval would probably also include μ. The two confidence intervals would probably have slightly different widths, and different lower and upper limits, but since both probably include μ, the two confidence intervals would probably overlap substantially.

The steps in determining a confidence interval for μ when s is unknown are presented below. These steps are illustrated using the following example. A medical researcher wishes to estimate the mean age of menarche in the United States. From a random sample of twenty-five females, she obtains a mean age of 12.8 years with a standard deviation of 1.1 years.

Step 1. Compute $s_{\overline{X}} = s/\sqrt{n}$ For this example:

$s_{\overline{X}} = 1.1/\sqrt{25} = .22$

Step 2. For the desired confidence coefficient, find the critical value of t (the multiplier of $s_{\overline{X}}$) by using $V = n - 1$ (Appendix B Table C) or by using n in Table 9.1.

For this example, with $n = 25$ and a .95 confidence coefficient, $t = 2.06$.

Step 3. Using Equation 9.5, compute $[\overline{X} \pm ts_{\overline{X}}]$. For this example:

.95 CI for $\mu = [12.8 \pm (2.06)(.22)] = [12.8 \pm .45] \approx [12.35, 13.25]$

We can be confident that the mean age of menarche, therefore, probably lies somewhere between 12.35 and 13.25 years. If more precision is needed for the .95 CI, a larger sample would be required. Increasing n serves to reduce the *width* of the CI (upper limit minus lower limit) in two ways, (1) a larger n results in a smaller $s_{\overline{X}}$, and (2) a larger n results in a smaller multiplier (t-value). For this reason, other things being equal, quadrupling the sample size results in a confidence interval that is slightly less than half as wide when σ is unknown. As we saw earlier, if σ were known, quadrupling the sample size would result in a confidence interval precisely half as wide since z for a given confidence coefficient is constant for all values of n.

Quiz: When σ is unknown, write the equation for the .90 CI if:
(1) $n = 10$, (2) $n = 30$, and (3) $n = 100$.
Answers: (1) $[\overline{X} \pm 1.83 s_{\overline{X}}]$, (2) $[\overline{X} \pm 1.70 s_{\overline{X}}]$, (3) $[\overline{X} \pm 1.66 s_{\overline{X}}]$

❖ 9.16 SAMPLING DISTRIBUTIONS AND CONFIDENCE INTERVALS WITH NON-NORMAL DISTRIBUTIONS

Although the frequency distributions of many populations are approximately normal in shape, non-normal distributions are also quite common. As defined by sociologists, measures of "social class" are extremely positively skewed. If the number of days present during the school year were graphed for a large representative group of students, the distribution would be negatively skewed. Annual gross family income is very skewed. The number of births on each day of the year is roughly rectangular in shape. Tests that are too easy or too difficult for a group of examinees will result in skewed distributions even if the underlying variable being measured is normally distributed. Experience shows that non-normal distributions are common.

❖ 9.17 THE ASSUMPTION OF NORMALITY AND THE CENTRAL LIMIT THEOREM

In the statistical theory that underlies the computation and use of confidence intervals, the assumption is made that the shape of the frequency distribution of the parent population is normal. What does one do when it is known or suspected that the parent population is not normal? Fortunately, mathematical statisticians have proved that, *regardless of the shape of the distribution of observations having a finite range in the parent population, the sampling distribution of the mean approaches normality as n increases*. This phenomenon is known as the *central limit theorem*; the distribution of sample means ($\overline{X}$'s) approaches a normal distribution as the sample size, n, increases. The central limit theorem has been called "the most important theorem in statistics from both the theoretical and applied points of view" (Snedecor & Cochran, 1980) and "one of the most remarkable theorems in the whole of mathematics" (Mood & Graybill, 1963).

Note that the theorem says nothing about the shape of the distribution of the observations in the parent population. Regardless of the form of the observations in the population distribution, the shape of the sampling distribution of the mean ($\overline{X}$) closely approximates the normal distribution if n is sufficiently large. How large is "sufficiently large"? The answer depends upon the distribution shape of the parent population. Except for extremely bizarre distributions, samples of $n = 25$ or more can be relied on to yield a very nearly normal sampling distribution of the mean, as will now be demonstrated.

❖ 9.18 A DEMONSTRATION OF THE CENTRAL LIMIT THEOREM

Since the central limit theorem is vital for a proper use and understanding of statistical methods, we will illustrate it extensively with actual sampling distributions in which n and the shape of the parent population are varied. The primary purpose of all the figures to follow (Figure 9.2) is to illustrate the validity of the central limit theorem. Random samples of n observations were drawn from three different parent populations: normal, rectangular, and skewed. The effect of n and non-normality on the sampling distribution is illustrated using sample sizes (n's) of 1, 2, 5, 10, and 25. As you peruse Figure 9.2, confirm the following two generalizations:

1. Even for non-normal parent populations, the shape of the sampling distributions rapidly approaches normality as n increases.
2. As n increases, the variability of the sampling distribution of $\overline{X}$ decreases; the decrease is accurately described by Equation 9.1, $\sigma_{\overline{X}} = \sigma / \sqrt{n}$ even if the parent population is non-normal.

Three parent populations are defined such that all have equal means ($\mu_1 = \mu_2 = \mu_3 = 100$) and equal standard deviations ($\sigma_1 = \sigma_2 = \sigma_3 = 15$). However, the populations differ in shape: one is normal, another rectangular, and the third is highly skewed. These three parent populations are shown in Panel A of Figure 9.2. Each bar in the histograms gives the percentage of the sample means having a particular IQ value. For example, the percentage of IQ scores of 100 with $\mu = 100$ and $\sigma = 15$ was 2.66% for the normal distribution (see Panel A of Figure 9.2), 1.89% for the rectangular distribution, and 2.58% for the skewed distribution.

Note that Panels B, C, and D of Figure 9.2 are *empirical* sampling distributions in which $n = 1$, 2, and 5, respectively. For example, in the first column of Panel D, a sample of five observations was selected randomly from the normal parent population; the mean of these five observations was computed; and this process was repeated 10,000 times.[5] The left-most figure in Panel D is the frequency distribution of these 10,000 means; that is, the figure is an empirical sampling distribution of the mean when the parent population is nor-

---

[5]The authors are indebted to George Kretke for this demonstration obtained via computer simulation. It is estimated that this project done by hand with only the aid of a table of random numbers and a hand calculator would have required approximately 2,500 hours—approximately a full working year!

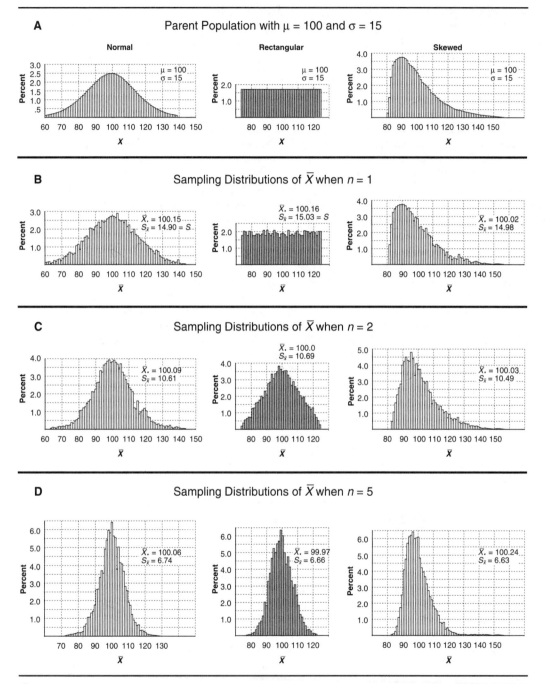

❖ **FIGURE 9.2** Percentage polygons of empirical sampling distributions of 10,000 means of *n* observations drawn randomly from normal, rectangular, and skewed distributions in which $\mu = 100$ and $\sigma = 15$. Sample size (*n*) is 1, 2, and 5 in Panels B, C, and D, respectively. Panels E and F give sampling distributions for $n = 10$ and $n = 25$, respectively.

E   Sampling Distributions of $\overline{X}$ when $n = 10$

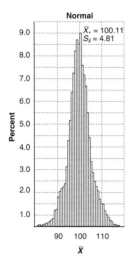

Normal

$\overline{X}_* = 100.11$
$S_{\overline{x}} = 4.81$

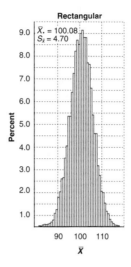

Rectangular

$\overline{X}_* = 100.08$
$S_{\overline{x}} = 4.70$

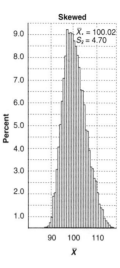

Skewed

$\overline{X}_* = 100.02$
$S_{\overline{x}} = 4.70$

F   Sampling Distributions of $\overline{X}$ when $n = 25$

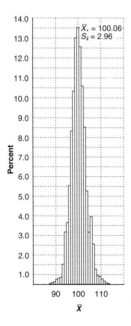

$\overline{X}_* = 100.06$
$S_{\overline{x}} = 2.96$

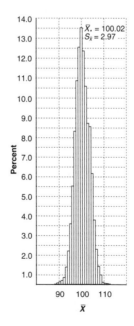

$\overline{X}_* = 100.02$
$S_{\overline{x}} = 2.97$

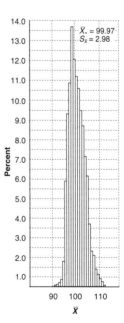

$\overline{X}_* = 99.97$
$S_{\overline{x}} = 2.98$

mal, $\mu = 100$, $\sigma = 15$, and $n = 5$. If the process had been continued until there were 1,000,000 or so $\overline{X}$'s, the empirical sampling distribution would have become almost perfectly symmetrical and normal; the small amount of irregularity evident in Figure 9.2D would virtually disappear and the empirical sampling distribution would coincide with the theoretical sampling distribution. In other words, the figure would become virtually perfectly normal if the number of samples drawn (not the number of observations per sample) was extremely large.

Observe that the mean of the sampling distributions (the mean of the $\overline{X}$'s) is approximately $\mu = 100$ in each figure. Indeed, the expression $E(\overline{X}) = \mu$ is another way of saying that the mean of the sampling distribution of an infinite number of samples (not just 10,000 as in Fig. 9.2) is the parameter, μ. In Panels B, C, and D of Figure 9.2, the sample sizes are small; hence, some degree of non-normality in the parent population continues to be evident in the sampling distributions, but progressively less so as n increases. Note, however, that as n increases from 1 to 5, the sampling distributions from the three different populations become more similar, and more nearly normal, because the central limit theorem is beginning to take effect with the two non-normal parent populations. The figures in Panel D of Figure 9.2 differ less than those in Panels B or C.

In Panel E, n has been increased to 10; the corresponding empirical sampling distributions of 10,000 means are given for the normal, rectangular, and skewed parent populations with $\mu = 100$ and $\sigma = 15$. Panel F gives the three corresponding empirical sampling distributions when n was increased to 25; notice that the sampling distributions are virtually identical in Panel F. If the distributions in Panels E and F do not appear to be normal, it is only because the vertical (Percent) axis has been scaled uniformly in all panels so that the decrease in the variability of the sampling distribution would be evident. If we compressed and rescaled the Y-axis so that the height of each column was only one-fourth its present size, the virtual normality of the three curves in Panel F would be apparent.

The sampling distributions in Figure 9.2 also demonstrate that, even in non-normal distributions, the standard deviation of the $\overline{X}$'s (the standard error of the mean) equals the standard deviation of the parent population divided by the square root of the sample size: $\sigma_{\overline{X}} = \sigma / \sqrt{n}$. In Table 9.2, the standard error of the mean, $s_{\overline{X}}$, based on 10,000 means of the various sampling distributions is reported along with the theoretical value, $\sigma_{\overline{X}} = \sigma / \sqrt{n}$. For example, when samples of $n = 25$ were drawn from a skewed parent population, the resulting 10,000 sample means had a standard deviation of 2.98, which agrees nearly perfectly with the theoretical standard error of the mean, $\sigma / \sqrt{n} = 15 / \sqrt{25} = 3$. In other words, even when the parent population is non-normal, the

❖ **TABLE 9.2** A comparison of observed values of $s_{\overline{X}}$ and theoretical values of $\sigma_{\overline{X}}$ for various sample sizes when the three parent populations (normal, rectangular, and skewed) sampled have equal means and standard deviations ($\mu = 100$ and $\sigma = 15$).

	Sample Size					
Parent Population	*n = 1*	*n = 2*	*n = 5*	*n = 10*	*n = 25*	*n = 100*
Normal, $s_{\overline{X}}$	14.90	10.61	6.74	4.81	2.96	1.498
Rectangular, $s_{\overline{X}}$	15.03	10.69	6.66	4.70	2.97	1.487
Skewed, $s_{\overline{X}}$	14.98	10.49	6.63	4.70	2.98	1.479
$\sigma_{\overline{X}} = \sigma / \sqrt{n}$	15	10.61	6.71	4.74	3.00	1.500

❖ **TABLE 9.3** Proportion of .68 confidence intervals that include the value of μ in 10,000 samples from normal, rectangular, and skewed parent populations.

Sample Size	Parent Population	Proportion of .68 Confidence Intervals Capturing μ
n = 2	Normal	.682
	Rectangular	.667
	Skewed	.714
n = 5	Normal	.686
	Rectangular	.679
	Skewed	.695
n = 10	Normal	.674
	Rectangular	.681
	Skewed	.689
n = 25	Normal	.682
	Rectangular	.678
	Skewed	.704
n = 100	Normal	.679
	Rectangular	.687
	Skewed	.690

formula $\sigma_{\bar{X}} = \sigma / \sqrt{n}$ *accurately* depicts the degree of variability in the sampling distributions of the mean.

❖ 9.19 ACCURACY OF CONFIDENCE INTERVALS

The data in Figure 9.2 also allow us to demonstrate empirically the validity of confidence intervals. Table 9.3 gives the percentage of sample means which produced a .68 confidence interval that included the parameter μ. It is evident from Table 9.3 that the .68 confidence intervals are quite accurate for non-normal distributions, even for samples as small as n = 5.

Three important concepts are illustrated and reinforced in Figure 9.2 and in Tables 9.2 and 9.3.

1. As n increases, sampling error decreases and sample means become increasingly more accurate estimates of μ. Equation 9.1 indicates that the standard deviation of the sampling distribution, $\sigma_{\bar{X}}$, is only one-tenth the value of s when $\bar{X}$ is based on samples of 100 cases (e.g., $\sigma_{\bar{X}} = 15 / \sqrt{100} = 1.5$). In Panel F of Figure 9.2, about 95% of the sample $\bar{X}$'s differ by less than 3.0 points from $\mu = 100$.
2. As n increases, all sampling distributions approach normality. The approximation is quite good with rectangular and skewed distributions if $n \geq 25$.
3. Confidence intervals using Equations 9.1–9.3 are also quite accurate with non-normal distributions, even with small n's.

❖ 9.20 THE CONCEPT OF THE SAMPLING DISTRIBUTION

The sampling distribution concept is used by the mathematical statistician to derive the techniques of inferential statistics. Of course, researchers do not seek to create their own sampling distribution by repeatedly drawing samples from a population (as we did in Figure 9.2). In practice, only one sample of n cases is drawn; then the theoretical concept of the sampling distribution is used to make inferences from that one sample to the population. For example, Jones might draw a sample of $n = 200$ cases and establish a single confidence interval (say, the .95 CI) around $\overline{X}$. Jones does not draw many samples or attempt to construct an actual sampling distribution of $\overline{X}$. Instead, a single interval is constructed, extending perhaps from 46.5 to 51.5. Is μ in this interval? It is impossible to know for certain. Is it rational to act or think as though μ is in this interval? Indeed it is, since in the long run μ would be found in ninety-five percent of the intervals constructed in such a manner. The technique of interval estimation is based on the theoretical concept of the sampling distribution, the validity of which was illustrated in Figure 9.2.

❖ CHAPTER SUMMARY

Most applications of inferential statistics involve populations of finite size, not infinite populations. The ratio of the sample size, n, to the size of the population, N, is known as the sampling fraction, n/N. For finite populations, unless the sampling fraction exceeds .05, negligible differences result by using the simpler inferential techniques which assume that N is infinite.

The most important characteristic of a sample is representativeness, that is, the sample characteristics approximately mirror those of the population. Representativeness is characteristic of random and most systematic samples. In random sampling, each unit in the population (person, school, city, etc.) has an equal and independent probability of being selected for the sample. In systematic sampling, every hth ($h = N/n$ rounded up) unit in the population list is selected after randomly selecting the initial unit. Most well-designed systematic samples and random samples differ inconsequentially with respect to representativeness and the accuracy of their derived statistics. Accidental samples should never be used for inferential purposes because of their (almost certain) non-representativeness.

Point and interval estimation are both useful. If $\overline{X} = 56.0$, 56.0 is a point estimate of μ. If the .95 confidence interval is [54, 58], then [54 to 58] is an interval that estimates the value of μ. When used appropriately, 95% of the .95 confidence intervals around $\overline{X}$ will include the value of the parameter, μ.

Sampling distributions are frequency distributions of statistics (such as $\overline{X}$), not individual observations (X). In this chapter, we have considered the sampling distribution of the mean and the associated confidence intervals. By using statistical theory, we can estimate the standard error of the mean, $s_{\overline{X}}$, from n and s. Unless n is very small, the .95 CI around $\overline{X}$ extends approximately two $s_{\overline{X}}$'s above and below $\overline{X}$. The precise number of $s_{\overline{X}}$'s that extend up and down from $\overline{X}$ are termed critical values of t.

The central limit theorem states that, even if the parent population of observations is non-normal, the sampling distribution will be approximately normal unless n is extremely small.

MASTERY TEST

1. Which (if any) of the following conditions would be essential to achieve randomness in sample selection? (Answer essential or nonessential.)
   (a) The observations must be normally distributed.
   (b) Each observation must have an equal chance of being chosen for the sample.
   (c) The selection of any one unit must be independent of that for all other units.

2. In a mail survey of the randomly sampled 400 social workers who were sent questionnaires, 240 returned them.
   (a) Can the 240 be considered a random sample of the population of social workers?
   (b) Can the 240 be considered a representative sample of the 400?
   (c) Can the 60% of the sample who responded be considered to represent approximately 60% of the population—the 60% who would have responded had they been sent questionnaires?

3. A sample of 100 families was randomly selected for a structured interview survey. Interviews with 38 of the families were not conducted because of unwillingness to cooperate, incorrect addresses, vicious dogs, or nobody home. Can the 62 be viewed as a random sample of the original population sampled?

4. A follow-up study was made of a group of chronic alcoholics who had undergone two weeks of intensive therapy. Only 36 of the 108 could be located eight weeks after treatment. Twenty-five of the 36 were coping satisfactorily. Can it be concluded that about two-thirds (i.e., 25/36 = .69) of those treated appear to be getting along adequately? Why?

For questions 5–10: A sample of seniors at Lincoln High School is to be tested. Classify the following procedures designed to obtain a sample of 100 students from the 1,000 seniors at the school? (Answer random, nonrandom, or systematic.)

5. Test 20 seniors in each of five randomly selected classes.

6. Select the first 100 seniors who arrive at school on a given day.

7. Use a table of random numbers and select 100 seniors from those who volunteered to participate.

8. Randomly select 100 seniors from those present on a given day.

9. Randomly draw 100 seniors from an alphabetical listing of all students.

10. Every tenth name on the roster of senior students was selected after randomly selecting the initial name.

For questions 11–18: Assume that the IQ's are normally distributed with $\mu = 100$ and $\sigma = 15$. Suppose a random sample of 9 was tested, the mean computed, and this process repeated 1,000 times.

11. Can we compute $\sigma_{\bar{X}}$, or must we estimate it from the 1,000 $\bar{X}$'s?

12. What is the value of $\sigma_{\bar{X}}$?

13. About what percentage of the means from the 1,000 random samples of $n = 9$ would exceed 105? 110?

14. About what percentage of the sample means would be between 95 and 105? Between 90 and 110?

15. Would the sample means be normally distributed?

16. What is the variance of this distribution of sample $\bar{X}$'s?

17. If $n = 225$ rather than 9 (i.e., 25 times as large), what would be the value of $\sigma_{\bar{X}}$?

18. If $n = 225$ what percentage of the $\bar{X}$'s would deviate by more than 1 point from 100—i.e., would fall outside the interval [99.0, 101.0]?

19. If the observations in a frequency distribution of X are not normally distributed, will the sampling distribution of the mean tend to be normally distributed?

20. Will the sampling distribution of the mean for $n = 25$ tend to be more nearly normally distributed than when $n = 10$?

21. What mathematical theorem states that the sampling distribution of the mean will approach normality as n increases, irrespective of the shape of the frequency distribution of raw scores?

22. If a mail questionnaire was sent to a random sample of 400 physicians and 200 were returned, the results on these 200 can be generalized
    (a) to all physicians in the population.
    (b) to half the population of physicians (i.e., the responding type).
    (c) to no other physicians.

23. Suppose that, instead of selecting a truly random sample, for convenience the last name on each page of a telephone directory was selected. Would this sample probably be quite representative of the population of listings in the telephone directory?

24. Assuming that σ is known but μ is unknown, is it true that $\overline{X} \pm 1.96\sigma_{\overline{X}}$ yields a .95 CI for any value of n?

25. If σ were known but μ were unknown, would two random samples of 100 observations result in two identical .95 CI's?

26. Is the width of the two confidence intervals in question 25 exactly the same?

27. For the same n, and when σ is not known, is the width of all .68 CIs exactly the same?

For questions 28–36: Are the following pairs of terms synonymous and equivalent?

28. (a) the standard error of $\overline{X}$
    (b) the standard deviation of the sampling distribution of $\overline{X}$

29. (a) σ^2/n (b) the standard error of $\overline{X}$

30. (a) $\sigma_{\overline{X}}^2$ (b) the variance of the sampling distribution of $\overline{X}$

31. (a) the population variance, σ^2 (b) n times the $\sigma_{\overline{X}}^2$

32. (a) the mean of the sampling distribution of the mean (b) $\sigma_{\overline{X}}^2$

33. (a) $E(\overline{X})$ (b) μ

34. (a) μ (b) $(\Sigma X)/n$

35. (a) $\overline{X}$ (b) $(\Sigma x)/n$

36. (a) s^2 (b) $\Sigma x^2/(n-1)$

37. If you conducted many studies on many different topics, in the long run, what percentage of your .95 CI's would be expected to contain the related parameter?

38. Given that $n = 60$ and σ is unknown, which of the three CI's, the .99 CI, the .95 CI, or the .90 CI,
    (a) would have greatest width?
    (b) would have the smallest width?
    (c) would be about twice as wide as the .68 CI?

39. Where would an increase in n of 20 have the greatest effect on reducing the width of the confidence interval?
    (a) increasing n from 5 to 25
    (b) increasing n from 10 to 30
    (c) increasing n from 40 to 60

40. Which type of estimates, point or interval estimates, more properly convey the degree of accuracy in the estimate?

MASTERY TEST ANSWERS

1. (a) nonessential, (b) essential, (c) essential
2. (a) no, (b) no, (c) yes
3. no

4. No, the 36 are probably not a representative sample of the 108.
5. nonrandom

6. nonrandom
7. nonrandom
8. nonrandom
9. random
10. systematic
11. We can compute the parameter $\sigma_{\bar{X}}$ because σ is known; $\sigma_{\bar{X}} = \sigma/\sqrt{n}$.
12. $\sigma_{\bar{X}} = 15/\sqrt{9} = 5$
13. $z = (105 - 100)/5 = 1.0$, giving about 16%; $z = (110 - 100)/5 = 2.0$, giving about 2%.
14. 68%, 95%
15. yes, approximately
16. $\sigma_{\bar{X}}^2 = (5)^2 = 25$
17. $\sigma_{\bar{X}} = 15/\sqrt{225} = 1.0$
18. 32%
19. Yes, unless n is very small.
20. Yes, but probably not importantly so.
21. the central limit theorem
22. b
23. Yes, but not of homes with telephones due to unlisted numbers.
24. Yes, but if σ were known, almost certainly μ would also be known.

25. No, since the values of $\bar{X}$ will probably differ.
26. Yes, the widths would be $4\sigma_{\bar{X}}$ (upper limit–lower limit).
27. No, since s, and hence $s_{\bar{X}}$, will vary somewhat.
28. yes
29. No, σ^2/n equals $\sigma_{\bar{X}}^2$, not $\sigma_{\bar{X}}$.
30. yes
31. Yes, $\sigma_{\bar{X}}^2 = \sigma^2/n$, so $\sigma^2 = n\sigma_{\bar{X}}^2$.
32. No, $\mu \neq \sigma_{\bar{X}}^2$.
33. yes
34. No, rarely is $\bar{X}$ precisely equal to μ.
35. No, $\bar{X} = \Sigma X/n$, not $(\Sigma x)/n$ $(\Sigma x = 0)$.
36. yes
37. 95%
38. (a) .99 CI, (b) .90 CI, (c) The width of the .95 CI is about twice that of the .68 CI.
39. a
40. interval estimates

PROBLEMS AND EXERCISES

1. By using the table of random digits (Table B in the Appendix B), draw a random sample of 5 students from the following set of 10:

Marlo	Tricia	Seiko	Paui	Moses
Alice	Maurice	Martha	Edith	Kim

2. Enter the table of random numbers and select two random single-digit numbers (0 through 9). Determine the mean of these two numbers and repeat the process until you have 25 means. Tally the 25 means into a (sampling) distribution.
   (a) Does the distribution appear to be approximately normal?
   (b) Compute the mean of these 25 means. What parameter is estimated by this value?
   (c) If you computed the standard deviation of the set of 25 means, what is the appropriate symbol?
   (d) What is the parameter being estimated in question c above?
   (e) In this situation do you know the value of μ?
   (f) Compare the mean of your means with μ.
   (g) If you continued finding means for pairs of random numbers until you had 100 means, would the sampling distribution be expected to appear more symmetrical? Would the sampling distribution be expected to appear more nearly normal? Would the range of the distribution of sample means be expected to increase?
   (h) If, instead of finding the mean for two numbers, you determined the mean of eight random numbers, and repeated the process 25 times, would the value of μ be altered?
   (i) In part h, would the value of $\sigma_{\bar{X}}$ decrease?
   (j) In part h, would the sampling distribution be more nearly normal?

(k) What is the shape of the frequency distribution of the individual random digits comprising the random number table?

(l) What mathematical theorem accounts for the normality of the sampling distribution of $\bar{X}$ as n becomes larger?

3. A sample of size n is to be drawn randomly from a population with mean μ and standard deviation σ. The sample size is sufficiently large so that $\bar{X}$ can be assumed to have a normal distribution. Determine the probabilities with which the sample mean will be between the following pairs of points:

(a) $[(\mu - \sigma_{\bar{X}})$ to $(\mu + \sigma_{\bar{X}})]$

(b) $[(\mu - 1.96\sigma_{\bar{X}})$ to $(\mu + 1.96\sigma_{\bar{X}})]$

(c) $[(\mu - 2.58\sigma_{\bar{X}})$ to $(\mu + 2.58\sigma_{\bar{X}})]$

(d) $[(\mu - .675\sigma_{\bar{X}})$ to $(\mu + .675\sigma_{\bar{X}})]$

4. A sample of size n is to be drawn from a population of normally distributed T-scores with mean 50 and variance $\sigma^2 = 100$. Complete the following table by calculating the variance error (σ^2/n) and the standard error $(\sigma/\sqrt{n})$ of $\bar{X}$ for various sample sizes.

	n	$\sigma_{\bar{X}}^2$	$\sigma_{\bar{X}}$
(a)	1	———	———
(b)	2	———	———
(c)	4	———	———
(d)	8	———	———
(e)	16	———	———
(f)	100	———	———
(g)	200	———	———
(h)	400	———	———
(i)	1,000	———	———

(j) As n is doubled, how is the variance error of the mean affected?

(k) As n is quadrupled, how is the standard error of the mean affected?

(l) If $n = 1$, is the sampling distribution of the mean identical to the frequency distribution, and does the standard deviation of the scores equal the standard error of the mean?

5. One survey reported the mean weight of seventeen-year-old females in the United States to be 118 pounds, with $s = 11$ pounds. If the sample of $n = 625$ was chosen randomly from the population, determine the .95 confidence interval for the average weight of seventeen-year-old females in the United States. (Since $v = 624$ is not listed in Appendix Table C, you may use the preceding tabular listing (that is, $v = 500$, for an acceptable and slightly conservative t-value.)

6. The mean height of women in the United States was found to be $\bar{X} = 63.5''$ with a standard deviation of $s = 2.5''$.

(a) Estimate the standard deviation of the sampling distribution of $\bar{X}$ if $n = 100$.

(b) If $n = 100$, find the .95 CI for μ (use Table 9.1).

(c) In the above study, what is the .99 CI for μ?

7. Suppose a random sample of 64 of the 1,500 seniors at Lincoln High School were given a standardized writing test. In grade-equivalent scores, the results were $\bar{X} = 10$ and $s = 2$.

(a) What is the estimate of the standard error of the mean?

(b) What are the limits of the .95 confidence interval for μ?

(c) What are the limits of the .90 confidence interval for μ?

(d) What are the limits of the .99 confidence interval for μ?

(e) If all the seniors had been tested, is it likely that their mean would have been as high as 11?

(f) Other things being equal, compare the values of the standard error of the mean with n's of 16, 64, and 256. What trend is evident?

(g) Other things being equal, would the width of the .95 confidence interval for $n = 16$ be precisely twice that of the .95 CI for $n = 64$?

(h) What is the sampling fraction if $n = 64$?

8. The weather bureau reported that the average maximum temperature on March 15 in Boulder, Colorado is 50°F. Suppose this mean is based on temperature readings for the past 100 years, which have a standard deviation of 15°F. Assuming no warming or cooling trends over time, how accurately does the sample mean of 50°F estimate μ? (Hint: Determine the .95 CI for μ.)

9. In Section 9.7, you selected a random sample of $n = 10$ students from the HSB data set. The math scores of these 10 students are as follows:

$$52 \quad 55 \quad 41 \quad 39 \quad 53 \quad 50 \quad 53 \quad 58 \quad 58 \quad 49$$

For this random sample of $n = 10$ math scores, find the following:

(a) the sum of scores, ΣX

(b) the sample mean, $\overline{X}$

(c) the sum of squares, $SS = \Sigma X^2 - n(\overline{X})^2$

(d) the sample variance, $s^2 = SS/v$

(e) the sample standard deviation, s

(f) the standard error of the mean, $s_{\overline{X}}$

(g) the .90 CI for μ

(h) Express verbally specifically what this confidence interval means.

(i) The percentile equivalent of the lower limit of the .90 CI is P_5. What is the percentile equivalent of the upper limit of the .90 CI?

(j) What is the width of the .90 CI?

(k) Using Table C in Appendix B, find the appropriate t-value for the .95 CI (i.e., $_{.975}t$), and write the .95 CI for μ_{math} based on the random sample of $n = 10$ math scores.

(l) Using Table C in the Appendix, find the appropriate t-value for the .99 CI (i.e., $_{.995}t$), and write the .99 CI for μ_{math} based on the random sample of $n = 10$ math scores.

(m) Compare the widths of the three CI's: .90 CI vs. .95 CI vs. .99 CI. How is the confidence coefficient related to the width of the confidence interval?

10. In Section 9.7, a systematic sample of $n = 10$ students of the HSB population was selected. The science T-scores of the 10 students are as follows:

$$26 \quad 50 \quad 44 \quad 53 \quad 61 \quad 50 \quad 54 \quad 39 \quad 50 \quad 58$$

For this random sample of $n = 10$ science scores, find the following:

(a) the sum of scores, ΣX

(b) the sample mean, $\overline{X}$

(c) the sum of squares, $SS = \Sigma X^2 - n(\overline{X})^2$

(d) the sample variance, $s^2 = SS/v$

(e) the sample standard deviation, s

(f) the standard error of the mean, $s_{\overline{X}}$

(g) Using Table C in the Appendix B, what is the appropriate t-value for the .95 CI (i.e., $_{.975}t$)? Write the .95 CI for $\mu_{science}$ based on the systematic sample of $n = 10$ science scores.

ANSWERS TO PROBLEMS AND EXERCISES

2. (a)
It should begin to suggest a somewhat normal shape.

(b) μ, the mean of all single random digits

(c) $s_{\overline{X}}$

(d) $\sigma_{\overline{X}}$

(e) Yes, all digits appear with the same frequency so that $\mu = (0 + 1 + 2 + 3 + 4 + 5 + 6 + 7 + 8 + 9)/10 = 4.5$.

(g) yes, yes, yes (see Table 4.1)

(h) no

(i) Yes: $\sigma_{\bar{x}} = \sigma / \sqrt{n}$; if $n = 8$, $\sigma_{\bar{x}}$ is only one-half as large as for $n = 2$.

(j) yes

(k) rectangular

(l) the central limit theorem

3. (a) .68 (b) .95 (c) .99 (d) .50

4. (a) 100, 10

(b) 50, 7.07

(c) 25, 5

(d) 12.5, 3.54

(e) 6.25, 2.5

(f) 1, 1

(g) .5, .707

(h) .25, .5

(i) .1, .316

(j) When n is multiplied by 2, $\sigma_{\bar{X}}^2$ is divided by 2.

(k) When n is multiplied by 4, $\sigma_{\bar{X}}$ is divided by $\sqrt{4}$ or 2.

(l) yes, yes

5. $s_{\bar{x}} = s / \sqrt{n} = 11 / \sqrt{625} = .44$;
.95 CI = $[\bar{X} \pm 1.97(.44)] = [118 \pm .87]$
= [117.13, 118.87]

6. (a) $s_{\bar{x}} = 2.5 / \sqrt{100} = .25''$

(b) $[\bar{X} \pm 1.98s_{\bar{x}}] = [63.5'' \pm 1.98(.25'')]$
= $[63.5 \pm .5''] = [63'', 64'']$

(c) $[63.5'' \pm 2.59(.25'')] = [62.83'', 64.17'']$

7. (a) $s_{\bar{x}} = 2.0 / \sqrt{64} = .25$

(b) $[10 \pm 2(.25)] = [9.5, 10.5]$

(c) $[10 \pm 1.67(.25)] = [9.58, 10.42]$

(d) $[10 \pm 2.66(.25)] = [9.33, 10.67]$

(e) No, the upper limit of the .99 CI is 10.67.

(f) $s_{\bar{x}}$ = .5, .25, .125 for n = 16, 64, 256, respectively. A fourfold increase in n reduces the value of the standard error of the mean by one-half.

(g) No, .95 CI for $n = 16$ would be $[\bar{X} \pm 2.13s_{\bar{x}}]$ or $[\bar{X} \pm 2.13(.5)]$ or $[\bar{X} \pm 1.065]$ (a span of 2.13 units). The .95 CI for $n = 64$ would have a span of

2(.5) = 1.0 unit. The CI for $n = 16$ is therefore 2.13/1.0 or 2.13 times wider than the .95 CI for $n = 64$. (The answer would be yes if $\sigma_{\bar{x}}$ were known since the z-multiplier remains 1.96 for all sample sizes.)

(h) $n/N = 64/1,500 = .0427$ or about .043

8. $s_{\bar{x}} = 15 / \sqrt{100} = 1.5$; the .95 CI is $[50° \pm 3°] = [47°, 53°]$. The estimate of μ seems quite accurate.

9. (a) $\Sigma X = 508$

(b) $\bar{X} = 50.8$

(c) $SS = 371.6$

(d) $s^2 = 41.29$

(e) $s = 6.53$

(f) $s_{\bar{x}} = 2.03$

(g) .90 CI for $\mu_{math} = [47.1, 54.5]$

(h) With 90 percent confidence, we conclude that μ_{math} of the HSB data set ($N = 200$) lies in the interval [47.1, 54.5].

(i) P_{95}, the .90 CI for μ_{math} ranges from P_5 to P_{95}.

(j) width = 54.5 − 47.1 = 7.4

(k) At the 97.5th percentile with $V = 9$, $_{.975}t$ = 2.262; .95 CI for $\mu_{math} = [46.2, 55.4]$.

(l) With $V = 9$, $_{.995}t = 3.25$; .99 CI for μ_{math} = [44.2, 57.4].

(m) For the .90 CI, width = 7.4 units; for the .95 CI, width = 9.2 units; for the .99 CI, width = 13.2 units. As the level of confidence increases, the width of the corresponding CI increases.

10. (a) $\Sigma X = 485$

(b) $\bar{X} = 48.5$

(c) $SS = 920.05$

(d) $s^2 = 102.25$

(e) $s = 10.11$

(f) $s_{\bar{x}} = 3.2$

(g) At the 97.5th percentile, $_{.975}t$ = 2.262 with $V = 9$; .95 CI for $\mu_{science}$ = [41.3, 55.7].

 SUGGESTED COMPUTER EXERCISE

1. Using spreadsheet or statistical software and the HSB data set, find the .90, .95, and .99 confidence intervals for the population mean for (a) reading, (b) writing, (c) math, (d) science, and (e) civics.

2. Using the table of random numbers, select a random sample of ten students from the HSB data set. Find the .90, .95, and .99 confidence intervals for the five population means (reading, writing, math, science, and civics) from this random sample of 10 students.

Hypothesis Testing:
Inferences Regarding the Population Mean

❖ 10.1 INTRODUCTION TO HYPOTHESIS TESTING

In Chapter 9, one of the most useful techniques of statistical inference, interval estimation, was developed and illustrated. In this chapter, we shall learn about hypothesis testing—the most common type of statistical inference. Hypothesis testing has become a ubiquitous feature of research in education and the behavioral and social sciences. Articles in research journals can be only partially comprehended if one does not understand the theory and techniques of hypothesis testing. The authors believe that, whereas the use of confidence intervals is underused, the degree of reliance on hypothesis testing in educational and behavioral research is excessive.

Hypothesis testing employs the same concepts that are used in interval estimation. Random sampling, sampling distributions, and probability values associated with confidence intervals will now be viewed in the context of hypothesis testing.

In Chapter 9, a confidence interval was placed about a sample mean, $\overline{X}$, which gave the precision with which the sample mean estimates the mean of the population, μ. We saw that if we randomly select a sample of n observations from a population for which σ is known, compute the mean ($\overline{X}$), and establish the .68 confidence interval [$\overline{X} \pm \sigma_{\overline{X}}$], and if this procedure were repeated many times, 68% of the confidence intervals would, indeed, capture the value of the parameter, μ. The .95 confidence interval is more widely used than the .68 confidence interval because it allows one to be much more confident that the interval contains the mean of the population—the parameter μ lies within 95% of the confidence intervals [$\overline{X} \pm 1.96\sigma_{\overline{X}}$]. The .95 confidence interval is almost twice (1.96 times) as wide as the corresponding .68 CI.

Hypothesis testing and interval estimation are carried out with different terminology, but we shall see that they produce comparable conclusions and results that are easily converted from one to the other. The basic question addressed by both procedures pertains to what can be stipulated about population parameters and at what level of confidence.

❖ **TABLE 10.1** Illustrative statistical hypotheses.

USING SYMBOLS	IN WORDS
A. H_0: $\mu = 100$	The population mean is 100.
B. H_0: $\mu = 0$	The population mean is 0.
C. H_0: $\sigma^2 = 15$	The population variance is 15.
D. H_0: $\mu_1 - \mu_2 = 0$	The difference between two population means is 0.
E. H_0: $\pi = .75$	The population proportion is .75.
F. H_0: $\rho = 0$	The population correlation coefficient is 0.
G. H_0: $\rho_1 - \rho_2 = 0$	The difference between two population correlation coefficients is 0.

❖ 10.2 STATISTICAL HYPOTHESES

The strategy of hypothesis testing is closely related to that used in interval estimation, but hypothesis testing leads to a *decision* regarding a specific statistical hypothesis (H_0). The decision is based on whether or not there is sufficient evidence to conclude that the hypothesis (H_0) is false. A *statistical hypothesis* is a statement specifying a numerical value for an unknown parameter. In Table 10.1, illustrative statistical hypotheses are given. Note that each of the seven hypotheses in Table 10.1 is a statement about a population parameter. Each H_0 specifies a numerical value for some parameter. (Note that a difference between two parameters—see hypotheses D and G—is also a parameter.)

Hypothesis A (H_0: $\mu = 100$) is a statistical hypothesis; it states that the numerical value of the mean of the population is 100. Hypothesis B indicates that, if all observations in the population were included (i.e., if $n = N$), the value of the population mean would be 0. In this chapter, we will be concerned with testing statistical hypotheses like A and B. Hypothesis C in Table 10.1 specifies that the population standard deviation is 15. Hypothesis D states that the difference between two population means is zero. Procedures for testing hypotheses like D are treated in Chapter 11. Hypothesis E asserts that the value of the population proportion parameter π ("pi") in a population is .75; procedures for testing hypotheses like this are treated in Chapter 12. Hypotheses about parameters for correlation coefficients (hypotheses F and G) are treated in Chapter 13.

> **Quiz:** A statistical hypothesis is a statement that specifies the numerical value of a __(1)__ . (2) Which of the following statements are statistical hypotheses? (a) $\mu = \overline{X}$, (b) $\overline{X} = 100$, (c) $\mu = 0$, (d) $\mu - \overline{X} = 0$, (e) $\mu_1 - \mu_2 = 50$, (f) $\mu_1 + \mu_2 - 2\mu_3 = 0$
>
> **Answers:** (1) parameter, (2) c, e, and f are statistical hypotheses; they specify numerical values for parameters.

Once you have mastered the procedures and underlying concepts for testing hypotheses regarding the mean, it is a relatively straightforward matter to apply these concepts to the testing of other even more interesting statistical hypotheses (like hypotheses C–G in Table 10.1).

❖ 10.3 TESTING HYPOTHESES ABOUT A POPULATION MEAN

A statistical hypothesis is either true or false; the numerical value hypothesized for the parameter is either correct or incorrect. Researchers, however, do not conclude that H_0 is true; but when the data strongly contradict H_0, they do conclude that H_0 is false. The stront

❖ **TABLE 10.2** The four steps in testing statistical hypotheses.

Step 1. State the statistical hypothesis: Specify the numerical value for the parameter to be tested (e.g., $H_0: \mu = 100$).

Step 2. Set the level of risk (α) you are willing to take of concluding that H_0 is false when it is true; this is termed a type-I error.

Step 3. Using the appropriate statistic (e.g., z or t) and the associated sampling distribution (e.g., a normal or t-distribution), determine the probability (p) of obtaining a sample statistic that differs from the hypothesized parameter by this much or more, if H_0 is true.

Step 4. Conclude that H_0 is false if $p \leq \alpha$; if $p > \alpha$, conclude that H_0 is tenable (but not proven as true).

egy is similar to that of scientific inquiry generally—a theory is never proven with absolute certainty, but can be disproven. When the prediction from theory is consistent with the findings, the theory may be said to be supported, but not proven. However, if the data are inconsistent with the theory, the theory is said to be false. Likewise, the underlying rationale in hypothesis testing is to accept H_0 as tenable or conceivably true unless strong evidence to the contrary is presented. Statistical hypotheses are assumed to be tenable unless the statistical evidence convincingly demonstrates an implausibility between the sample statistics and the values specified for the parameters by H_0. Hypothesis testing can be viewed as an integral part of a "search and destroy mission," that is, to detect and reject false statistical hypotheses. To reject H_0 is to reject the statement that $\mu = 100$, which is to conclude that $\mu \neq 100$. In this way, erroneous statistical hypotheses can be shown to be false, and correct H_0's can be shown to be plausible.

Quiz: When H_0 is rejected, the evidence is convincing that H_0 is ___(1)___. When H_0 is accepted, it has been demonstrated that H_0 is plausible, but not that H_0 is ___(2)___. If you work through a hypothesis testing problem and conclude that H_0 is true because H_0 was not rejected, you would know that you ___(3)___.

Answers: (1) false, (2) true, (3) need to read the above paragraph again

The procedures of hypotheses testing can be summarized as outlined in the four steps listed in Table 10.2. The details for the steps will be developed throughout the chapter, but a bird's-eye view of the process is useful.

The four step procedure for testing statistical hypotheses is depicted in Figure 10.1 as a flowchart.

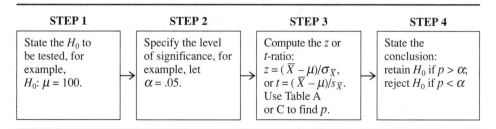

STEP 1	**STEP 2**	**STEP 3**	**STEP 4**
State the H_0 to be tested, for example, $H_0: \mu = 100$.	Specify the level of significance, for example, let $\alpha = .05$.	Compute the z or t-ratio: $z = (\overline{X} - \mu)/\sigma_{\overline{X}}$, or $t = (\overline{X} - \mu)/s_{\overline{X}}$. Use Table A or C to find p.	State the conclusion: retain H_0 if $p > \alpha$; reject H_0 if $p < \alpha$

❖ **FIGURE 10.1** Flowchart of the four-step hypothesis testing procedure.

The purpose of hypothesis testing is to detect and reject false statistical hypotheses. Whenever the sample data are highly unlikely ($p < \alpha$) if H_0 were true, we reject H_0 at the α-level of significance and conclude H_0 is false.

As an illustration, suppose that you are addicted to gambling and that you are observing a game of craps in which a sinister-looking stranger wins consistently. The thought crosses your mind that the dice may not be fair, but to be consistent with the American ideal, "a person is presumed innocent until proven guilty," your instinctual response is to hypothesize that the dice are fair (Step 1). Still you wonder, and decide to observe a bit longer to see if the laws of chance appear to be operating (Step 2). You observe the stranger roll the dice ten times and note that 7 appeared in eight of the ten tosses. Remembering the probability theory you learned in Algebra II, you quickly calculate the probability of this occurrence assuming that the dice are fair, and find that such an amazing occurrence is extremely rare, $p < .00002$ (Step 3). As a budding statistician, you make a mental note to avoid the stranger (Step 4). Your behavior has demonstrated that you are a clever soul and a statistical hypothesis tester of sorts.

> **Quiz:** There are thirty-six possible outcomes when a pair of dice are tossed; six of these outcomes are 7's. The statistical hypothesis that you used in the above illustration is that the expected proportion of 7's, (assuming fair dice) is ___(1)___. Suppose you will give the stranger the benefit of the doubt unless the probability of your findings (eight wins in ten tosses) with fair dice was small, for example, ___(2)___ = .05 or less. You, however, computed the probability of your findings to be ___(3)___ < .00002. Therefore, H_0 is ___(4)___ because ___(5)___ < ___(6)___.
>
> **Answers:** (1) $6/36 = 1/6$, (2) α, (3) p, (4) rejected, (5) p, (6) α

❖ 10.4 TESTING H_0: $\mu = K$: THE ONE-SAMPLE z-TEST

To illustrate the four steps in testing hypotheses, suppose we want to determine whether the mean IQ of adopted children differs from the mean for the general population of children ($\mu = 100$, $\sigma = 15$).

Step 1. Our statistical hypothesis is H_0: $\mu = 100$.

Step 2. We set $\alpha = .05$ (the most commonly used α-level).

Step 3. Using IQ scores from a random sample of $n = 25$ adopted children, we compute the sample mean (suppose for the sample we find that $\overline{X} = 96.0$). From the sampling distribution of the mean (Section 9.11), we determine the probability, p, of obtaining a $|\overline{X} - \mu|$ difference of 4 or more points when $n = 25$ and if, indeed, for this population μ is 100.

If $\mu = 100$, $\sigma = 15$, and $n = 25$, the sampling distribution of $\overline{X}$ is normally distributed with $\mu = 100$ and $\sigma_{\overline{X}} = \sigma/\sqrt{n} = 15/\sqrt{25} = 3$. To find the probability of a sample mean differing by 4 or more points (either above or below μ) from the population mean, we need to find the tail area under this normal curve below 96, and double it. To find this tail area, we transform 96 to a z-score and access Table A in Appendix B.

The z-score formula (Eq. 5.1a) expressed in terms of a sampling distribution, is presented as Equation 10.1. Since it is used to test a hypothesis, it is termed a z-ratio or a z-test:

$$z = \frac{\overline{X} - \mu}{\sigma_{\overline{X}}} \qquad \textbf{(10.1)}$$

In our example, the z-ratio is: $z = (96 - 100)/3 = -1.33$, and from Table A, the tail area below $z = -1.33$ is .0918 (area A in Figure 10.2). The probability of a sample mean of 96 or less is .0918; due to the symmetry of the normal curve, the probability of a sample mean of 4 or more points above the mean is also .0918 (area B in Figure 10.2). Therefore, the probability of a sample mean that differs from 100 by $|4|$ or more points is $2(.0918) = .1836$; in other words, the probability of a sampling error $|\overline{X} - \mu| \geq 4$ is $p = .18$ (area A + area B in Figure 10.2).

Step 4.   Since the probability of these data ($p = .18$) is greater than $\alpha = .05$ ($p = .18 > \alpha = .05$), the statistical hypothesis (H_0: $\mu = 100$) remains tenable. The statistical evidence to the contrary was not sufficiently strong to allow a rejection of the statistical hypothesis that states that the population mean of adopted children is 100. The data did not give conclusive evidence that H_0 is false. Unconvinced that H_0 is false, we cannot justify a "guilty" verdict. Note that we have not proved that $\mu = 100$, only that it remains a plausible possibility.

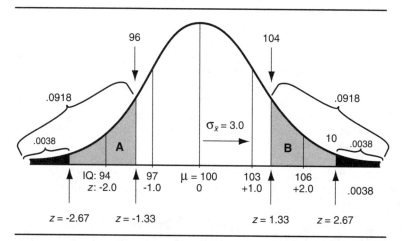

❖ **FIGURE 10.2** The sampling distribution for $\overline{X}$'s when $\mu = 100$, $\sigma = 15$, and $n = 25$. The probability of obtaining a sample mean that deviates by 4 or more points from μ is represented by areas A and B. (The black "tails" of areas A and B reflect the probability of obtaining a sample mean that deviates by 8 or more points from $\mu = 100$.)

Quiz: Find the probability (i.e., the sum of the two corresponding tail areas) of each of the following z-ratios yielded by Equation 10.1. (1) $z_1 = 2.054$ (2) $z_2 = -1.881$ (3) $z_3 = .85$ (4) For which of the above z-ratios would H_0 be rejected if $\alpha = .05$?

Answers: (1) $p = 2(.02) = .04$, (2) $p = 2(.03) = .06$, (3) $p = 2(.1977) = .3954$, (4) For z_1, since only for z_1 is $p < \alpha = .05$.

If, due to a sampling fluke, the data analysis leads us to *reject H_0* when, in fact, it is *true*, we have made an error in inference, termed a *"type-I error."* If 100 students in a statistics class each replicated this study, assuming H_0 is true with α set at the .05 level, five students would be expected to obtain z-ratios of $|1.96|$ or greater, and consequently commit type-I errors. If $\alpha = .05$, then in the long run H_0 will be rejected in five percent of the studies in which it is true—it is the risk of a type-I error. On the other hand, 95 of the 100 of the replicated studies will not reject the true H_0; 95 correct conclusions out of 100 is not too bad. In the real world, there is just a single study, but the probability, p, of the observed findings can be calculated, assuming H_0 is true. When $p < \alpha$, the empirical evidence is sufficient to convince us that H_0 is implausible and we reject it, and conclude that H_0 is false. This does not constitute a metaphysical certitude that H_0 is false, rather it is merely proof beyond a reasonable doubt and makes it rational for us to proceed on the basis that H_0 is false. We know that in the long run, when H_0 is true, it will be incorrectly rejected only 100α percent of the time.

The statistical hypothesis is also called the null hypothesis; it continues to be tenable if p is greater than α. In our example, H_0 is not to be rejected, because $p = .18$ is greater than $\alpha = .05$. Notice, however, that we have not concluded that H_0 is true; we have only decided that H_0 remains tenable; the negative evidence against H_0 was inadequate to warrant a conclusion that H_0 is false. The probability is only .18 that a sampling error $|\overline{X} - \mu| \geq 4$ would be observed if $\mu = 100$ and $n = 25$, but this evidence is not strong enough to convince us that H_0 is false. The probability we observed ($p = .18$) exceeds the maximum risk of a type-I error that we chose to tolerate ($\alpha = .05$);[1] hence, we accept the hypothesis as tenable. To "accept" H_0 simply means that we have failed to adequately demonstrate that H_0 was false; consequently, it remains a plausible possibility that H_0 is true. When H_0 is false, but is not rejected, another kind of error in inference is made; failing to reject a false null hypothesis is termed a "type-II error."

After a decision to reject or to accept H_0, our conclusions may be correct, but not always. We can reject H_0 when it is true (and make a type-I error), or we can accept H_0 when it is false (and make a type-II error). Whenever we reject H_0, we are aware of the risk (p) that we are making a type-I or α-error. However, if we accept H_0, we ordinarily do not know the risk that we have made a type-II or β-error. Historically, the type-II error has been given scant attention in designing and interpreting research studies. The estimation of the probability of a type-II error is illustrated in Chapter 11.

Quiz: Completion quiz items: (Use extra care here, the semantic difficulty caused by double and triple negatives can be mind-boggling.) If a true H_0 is rejected, then ___(1)___

---

[1] For reasons of convenience and simplicity, a 5% risk of a type-I error ($\alpha = .05$) has become conventional. As you progress in your understanding of statistical analysis, you will learn how to make intelligent decisions in establishing the risk of a type-I error that is appropriate in a given situation. Unfortunately, many "researchers" often adhere sheepishly to $\alpha = .05$ without considering the pros and cons of differing significance levels. In certain situations, it may be appropriate to set α at .10 or higher; in other instances, a should be set at .01 or even .001. Unless otherwise specified, we will temporarily employ the conventional $\alpha = .05$ level of significance.

error is committed. If a false H_0 is rejected, then ___(2)___ error is committed. If a true H_0 is retained, then ___(3)___ error is committed. If a false H_0 is retained, then ___(4)___ error is committed.

Answers: (1) a type-I, (2) no, (3) no, (4) a type-II

❖ 10.5 CERTAINTY AND STATISTICAL INFERENCE

As we have seen, a statistical conclusion does not establish the falsity of a hypothesis with absolute certainty—no statistical hypothesis is rejected with 100% confidence. To achieve absolute certainty, one would have to compute the mean based on all N units in the population. When H_0 is rejected, there is always some degree of risk of a type-I error, α. When H_0 is true, it will be rejected and a type-I error will be made in five out of every 100 studies when $\alpha = .05$. Conversely, when we accept H_0, we do not prove that H_0 is true—just that the evidence against H_0 is not sufficiently strong to support a conclusion that the H_0 is false. Failure to reject H_0 when it is *false* is termed a *type-II error*.

> **Quiz:** (1) If the probability of a type-I error is symbolized by α, guess what symbol denotes the probability of a type-II error? (2) Theoretically, how could a H_0 be proven to be true? If H_0 is true and $\alpha = .05$, a type-I error would be expected in about one study in ___(3)___.
>
> **Answers:** (1) β is the best guess. (2) when $n = N$, (3) twenty

❖ 10.6 AN EXAMPLE IN WHICH H_0 IS REJECTED

In the hypothetical study of the mean IQ of adopted children based on a random sample of $n = 25$ adopted children in Section 10.4, suppose we found that a data entry error had been made, and that, instead of $\bar{X} = 96$, the $n = 25$ adopted children actually had a mean IQ of 108. We need to test H_0: $\mu = 100$ using the corrected data.

Step 1. H_0: $\mu = 100$.

Step 2.   Not wanting to buck tradition, we set $\alpha = .05$.

Step 3.   Assuming $\sigma = 15$, then $\sigma_{\bar{X}} = 15/\sqrt{25} = 3$. The z-ratio, then, is $z = (108 - 100)/3 = 2.67$. From the normal curve table in Table A Appendix B, we find that only .0038 of the area in a normal curve falls above a point 2.67 standard deviations above the mean. Note the black portion of area B in Figure 10.2. Of course, there is an equal area below the point $z = -2.67$. Hence, when $\mu = 100$ the probability of observing a sample mean that differs from 100 by eight or more points is only $p = 2(.0038) = .0076$ (only 76 chances in 10,000). In other words, there is less than 1 chance in 100 that we would observe a difference (sampling error) as large as $|8|$ points between $\bar{X}$ and μ if H_0: $\mu = 100$ were true. The evidence against the null hypothesis is strong.

Step 4.   We reject H_0 at the .05 level (and indeed, also at the .01 level) of statistical significance; there is a statistically significant difference between $\overline{X} = 108$ and $\mu = 100$. The probability of having made a type-I error, given a z-ratio of $|2.67|$ is less than .01. Although we were willing to tolerate a five percent ($\alpha = .05$) risk of a type-I error, the risk we actually take (.0076) is less than one percent. A rejection of H_0 at the .01 level of significance ($p < .01$), as compared to the .05 level ($p < .05$), gives us greater confidence that H_0 is false.[2]

Quiz: If H_0 is rejected at the .05 level of significance, the probability of a type-I error is __(1)__ and the probability of a type-II error is (careful) __(2)__. If H_0 is tenable with $p = .12$, the probability of a type-I error is __(3)__.

Answers: (1) $< .05$, (2) $p = 0$; a type-II error can occur only when H_0 is retained, (3) $p = 0$; a type-I can occur only when H_0 is rejected

❖ 10.7 HYPOTHESIS TESTING AND CONFIDENCE INTERVALS

If a confidence interval is set about $\overline{X}$, we can see the "two sides of the same coin" correspondence between hypothesis testing and interval estimation. If $\overline{X} = 108$, $\sigma = 15$, and $n = 25$, the .99 confidence interval for μ is $[\overline{X} \pm 2.58\sigma_{\overline{X}}] = [108 \pm 2.58(3)] = [108 \pm 7.74] = [100.26, 115.74]$. Notice that the .99 confidence interval does not contain the hypothesized value of $\mu = 100$. When the .99 *confidence interval does not include the value of the parameter* specified by the statistical hypothesis, this is tantamount to stating that *the statistical hypothesis is rejected* at the .01 level of significance. Likewise, if $H_0: \mu = K$ is rejected at the .05 level, the .95 confidence interval will not include the hypothesized value, K, for the parameter, μ.

On the other hand, in our previous example with $\overline{X} = 96$, if H_0 is not rejected at the .05 level, we therefore know that the value for the parameter specified by H_0 falls within the .95 confidence interval. With $\overline{X} = 96$, the .95 confidence interval is $[\overline{X} \pm 1.96\sigma_{\overline{X}}] = [96 \pm 1.96(3.0)] = [96 \pm 5.88] = [90.12, 101.88]$. Note that the value of 100 specified in the statistical hypothesis for μ lies within the .95 confidence interval; hence, H_0 will not be rejected at the .05 level.

Quiz: Suppose that, for a random sample of $n = 25$ school principals, the mean GRE quantitative score was 480. Assuming that school principals are as heterogeneous as the test norm ($\sigma = 100$): (1) What is the value of the standard error of the mean, $\sigma_{\overline{X}}$? (2) For the interval $[\overline{X} \pm z\sigma_{\overline{X}}]$, what z-value is used for the .95 CI? (3) Construct the .95 CI for μ. (4) Would $H_0 = 500$ be rejected? Why? (5) Would $H_0 = 520$ be rejected? Why?

Answers: (1) $100/5 = 20$, (2) $z = 1.96$, (3) $[480 \pm 1.96(20)] = [480 \pm 39.2] = [440.8, 519.2]$, (4) No, all K-values between 440.8 and 519.2 would result in retaining H_0 for $\alpha = .05$. (5) Yes, any value less than 440.8 or greater than 519.2 would result in a rejection of H_0 since they are outside the .95 CI for μ.

---

[2]The probability of a type-I error is generally not reported as .0076. The high degree of precision implicit in .0076 is accurate only if all statistical assumptions are perfectly met, which is rarely the case. Researchers usually report probability statements to two or three places, rather than at a value that appears to be extremely precise, such as .13901, .0076, or .0122.

These examples serve to illustrate how the inferential techniques of interval estimation and hypothesis testing are closely related. From a *.95 confidence interval*, one can easily determine the outcome of testing any statistical hypothesis about μ with $\alpha = .05$.

❖ 10.8 THE *z*-RATIO VERSUS THE *t*-RATIO

For simplicity, we have illustrated the concepts and procedures of hypothesis testing with the *z*-test—the ratio obtained by dividing an observed deviation, $(\overline{X} - \mu)$ by $\sigma_{\overline{X}}$, that is, $z = (\overline{X} - \mu)/\sigma_{\overline{X}}$. The advantage of this hypothesis testing procedure for $H_0: \mu = K$ is that the computed *z*-ratio can be used in conjunction with the normal curve table, and specific probability estimates for the statistical results can be readily obtained. The chief drawback to this hypothesis testing procedure for testing $H_0: \mu = K$ is that it requires that the numerical value of σ be known. That is, it is difficult to find a practical application for this splendid *z*-test procedure.

When σ is not known, $\sigma_{\overline{X}}$ cannot be computed; hence, the *z*-ratio of Equation 10.1 cannot be applied. In this case, s, an estimate of σ, must be used to compute $s_{\overline{X}}$, an estimate of $\sigma_{\overline{X}}$, and the ratio of the estimated sampling error $(\overline{X} - \mu)$ to the estimated standard error $(s_{\overline{X}})$ is not a true *z*-ratio—it is termed a *t*-ratio. Thus, a *t*-ratio can be thought of as a *z*-ratio with compensation for the sampling error in the denominator—the sampling error that results from the use of s rather than σ.

$$t = \frac{\overline{X} - \mu}{s_{\overline{X}}} \qquad\qquad \textbf{(10.2)}$$

When n is large, s and $s_{\overline{X}}$ become very accurate approximations of σ and $\sigma_{\overline{X}}$, respectively. Hence, z and t differ negligibly for large n's. However, when n is small, z and t can differ considerably.

Quiz: (1) Is the sampling distribution of $\overline{X}$ normally distributed even if the frequency distribution of *X*'s is not? (2) Is the sampling distribution of $(\overline{X} - \mu)$ normally distributed? (3) Is the sampling distribution of $(\overline{X} - \mu)/\sigma_{\overline{X}}$ normally distributed? (4) When the frequency distribution is perfectly normally distributed, is the sampling distribution of $(\overline{X} - \mu)/s_{\overline{X}}$ normally distributed?

Answers: (1) Yes, as per the central limit theorem. (2) Yes, subtracting a constant (μ) is a linear transformation and therefore does not alter the shape of the distribution. (3) Yes, dividing by a constant $(\sigma_{\overline{X}})$ is a linear transformation, and therefore does not alter the shape of the distribution. (4) No, dividing by a variable is a nonlinear transformation, and therefore does alter the shape of the distribution.

The use of $s_{\overline{X}}$ (rather than $\sigma_{\overline{X}}$) results in a sampling distribution that is not perfectly normal. These distributions are known as Student's *t*-distributions. (Student is the pseudonym used by Gossett, the originator of the *t*-test.) About half the time, $s_{\overline{X}}$ is an underestimate of $\sigma_{\overline{X}}$, and hence the |*t*-ratio| would be "too large" resulting in a sampling distribution with fatter tails than the normal distribution. About half the time, $s_{\overline{X}}$ is an overestimate of $\sigma_{\overline{X}}$ and hence the *t*-ratio would be "too small" resulting in a sampling distribution with a more pronounced, steeper central peak. Consequently, although *t*-distributions are symmetrical, they have fatter tails and skinnier peaks than does the corresponding normal z-distribution and are termed *leptokurtic* distributions.

You may recall, from Chapter 9 and Table 9.1, that the values of t needed to construct confidence intervals vary with the degrees of freedom, $v = n - 1$. For example, Table 9.1 (Section 9.15) showed that, when n is 10, the .95 confidence interval for μ is $[\bar{X} \pm 2.26s_{\bar{X}}]$. If n is 60, the .95 confidence interval for μ is $[\bar{X} \pm 2.00s_{\bar{X}}]$. Likewise, in hypothesis testing, the critical value of t (the minimum t-value at which H_0 will be rejected) is 2.26 when $n = 10$; if $n = 60$, however, the critical value for t is 2.00. A more complete t-table is found in Table C in Appendix B. Table C gives t-values corresponding to various percentiles in t-distributions with various degrees of freedom.[3] Note that the critical values for t for infinitely large samples are identical to the z-values in Table A Appendix B for the same percentile points. For example, if n is infinite for $\alpha = .05$, the critical z-ratio is 1.960 and the critical t-ratio is also 1.960. This shows that, for large sample sizes, z-tests and t-tests are virtually identical for testing hypotheses of the type H_0: $\mu = K$.

> **Quiz:** For the following z and t values, use Tables A and C to determine p, the approximate probability of these z and t values when H_0 is true. For $n = 7$ and $z = 2.447$, $p =$ __(1)__. For $n = 7$ and $t = 2.447$, $p =$ __(2)__. For $n = 28$ and $z = 2.052$, $p =$ __(3)__. For $n = 28$ and $t = 2.052$, $p =$ __(4)__. For $n = 121$ and $z = 1.98$, $p =$ __(5)__. For $n = 121$ and $t = 1.98$, $p =$ __(6)__.
>
> **Answers:** (1) 2(.0071) = .0142 (using Table A) (2) 2(.025) = .05 (using Table C) (3) 2(.0201) = .0402, (4) 2(.025) = .05, (5) 2(.0239) = .0478, (6) 2(.025) = .05

❖ 10.9 THE ONE-SAMPLE *t*-TEST: AN EXAMPLE

Suppose we want to determine whether adults who go on the Lean-N-Mean special diet for a six-week period will maintain a weight loss one year later. A random sample of $n = 20$ adults was selected for the study, and their weights were taken one year after completing the program. The dependent measure is the *difference* in the dieters' weights at the beginning of the diet and their weights one year later (post–pre). The null hypothesis is H_0: $\mu_{diff} = 0$, and α is set as .05. For the sample of 20, suppose we find a mean loss of $\bar{X} = -3.4$ lbs., with a standard deviation $s = 5.80$ lbs.; hence, $s_{\bar{X}} = s / \sqrt{n} = 5.8 / \sqrt{20} = 1.297$. Using Equation 10.2, we find the value of t:

$$t = \frac{\bar{X} - \mu}{s_{\bar{X}}} = \frac{-3.4 - 0}{1.297} = -2.62$$

Is the difference between the sample mean ($\bar{X} = -3.4$) and the hypothesized value of the parameter ($\mu = 0$) large enough to allow us to reject the statistical hypothesis; that is, is the mean loss of 3.4 pounds large enough to eliminate sampling error as a reasonable explanation for the difference? We enter Table C Appendix B at $v = n - 1 = 19$ and $\alpha = .05$, and find the critical values of t to be $|2.093|$. Notice that a computed t with an absolute value greater than 2.093 corresponds to $p < .05$. Thus, an observed t-value greater than +2.093 or less than –2.093 is required to reject H_0 with $\alpha = .05$. Can the null hypothesis be rejected at

---

[3]Notice in Table C that the first row of α-values is for directional (Section 10.10) one-tail hypotheses, α_1, and the second row is for two-tail hypotheses, α_2. At the present time, we will concern ourselves exclusively with two-tail hypotheses and use the α_2 row. If no subscript is given for α, it is assumed that it is α_2.

a more stringent level that .05? The critical value of t for $\alpha = .02$ is $|2.539|$; thus, H_0 is also rejected at the .02 level ($p < .02$). Note, however, that a computed $|t|$ greater than 2.861 is required to reject H_0 with $\alpha = .01$ ($\nu = 19$). Therefore, $.02 > p > .01$, and thus H_0 can be rejected with $\alpha = .02$ but not with $\alpha = .01$. Consequently, we reject the hypothesis that the mean weight loss is zero at the .02 level. In actual practice, t-tests are usually done by computers that print out the actual probability; this should be reported in precise terms (e.g., $p = .018$) rather than in approximate terms, such as $.02 > p > .01$.

Quiz: If $n = 12$, $s_{\overline{X}} = 10$, and $(\overline{X} - \mu) = 24$, using Equation 10.2, $t = $ __(1)__ ; $\nu = $ __(2)__ . With $\alpha = .10$, the critical-t value is __(3)__ , and H_0 is __(4)__ at the .10 level of significance. With $\alpha = .05$, the critical-t value is __(5)__ , and H_0 is __(6)__ at the .05 level of significance. With $\alpha = .01$, the critical-t value is __(7)__ , and H_0 is __(8)__ at the .01 level of significance.

Answers: (1) $24/10 = 2.4$, (2) $n - 1 = 11$, (3) $_{.95}t = |1.796|$, (4) rejected, (5) $_{.975}t = |2.201|$, (6) rejected, (7) $_{.995}t = |3.106|$, (8) tenable

❖ 10.10 ONE-TAIL VERSUS TWO-TAIL TESTS

Up to this point, in testing hypotheses, we have used the absolute value of the critical z or t ratios; in effect, we have been using two critical values, one positive value (for the right-hand tail of the sampling distribution), and one negative value (for the left-hand tail of the sampling distribution). In these two-tail tests, H_0 can be rejected in one of two ways, that is, if $\overline{X} > \mu$, and if $\overline{X} < \mu$. In using the two-tail (nondirectional) t-test to evaluate the null hypothesis, H_0, when entering Table C, we used α_2 (not α_1) to find the critical value of t. Two-tail statistical tests enable us not only to accept or reject H_0, but, when H_0 is rejected, to indicate the direction of the difference, that is, to specify either $\mu > K$ or $\mu < K$. In the preceding Lean-N-Mean weight loss study (Section 10.9), with $\alpha = .05$ and $\nu = 19$, t was computed to be -2.62, the absolute value of which exceeded 2.093, and we concluded that there was a significant weight loss one year later. Instead of a mean loss of 3.4 pounds, suppose there had been a mean weight gain of 3.4 pounds; the obtained t-ratio would have been 2.62; we would also have rejected H_0, and would have concluded that there had been a significant increase in weight between the two testings. In other words, we reject H_0 when $|t|$ is greater than 2.093, and we identify the direction of the difference.

Two-tail statistical tests are more common than one-tail tests, and should ordinarily be used whenever both $\mu > K$ and $\mu < K$ are logical possibilities. However, when it is *implausible* that μ could be less (or greater) than K, one-tail (directional) tests are *preferable* because they are more *powerful* (i.e., more likely to detect a nonchance difference) than two-tail tests in these situations.

We use the symbol α_1 to denote one-tail tests; we use α_2 or simply α to denote two-tail tests. If no subscript is given, α_2 is assumed. A two-tail t-test with $\nu = 19$ and $\alpha = .01$ has critical t-values of ± 2.861. However, with a one-tail test ($\alpha_1 = .01$), H_0 will be rejected if t is greater than 2.539. The critical t-values for directional tests are found using the appropriate α_1 (one-tail) column entry in Table C of Appendix B; critical t-values for testing nondirectional hypotheses are associated with α_2 (two-tail) column entries. In the example (Section 10.9), H_0 could also have been rejected at the .01 level if a one-tail test had been employed ($t = 2.62 > 2.539 = _{.99}t_{19}$), but not with a two-tail test ($t = 2.62 < 2.861 = _{.995}t_{19}$). However, the use of a one-tail test in this situation would have been highly suspect since weight gains, as well as weight losses, are clearly possible outcomes.

If we can specify a priori that if μ differs from K, it must be in the predicted direction, a one-tail test of the null hypothesis is in order. For example, if we wish to test whether there is any increase in height between ages 18 and 20, it would be inefficient to employ a two-tail test. We may not be certain whether or not $\mu_{20} = \mu_{18}$, but we can be certain that μ_{20} will not be less than μ_{18}. In such situations where we can rationally exclude the possibility of $\mu > K$ (or $\mu < K$), all of the critical area (α_1) can be placed in one tail of the sampling distribution, that is, the upper (or positive) tail area. The null hypothesis, therefore, must be phrased so that the region of rejection lies in the upper tail of the sampling distribution.

Note that with $\alpha_1 = .01$, the probability of a type-I error is still .01; we will incorrectly reject H_0 in only one percent of the t-tests we make, even though our critical value for t changed from $|2.861|$ to 2.539. When directional tests are appropriate, their use will be associated with fewer type-II errors, with no change in the proportion of type-I errors; more false null hypotheses will be rejected, but the same percent of true null hypotheses will be rejected.

It is *imperative* that the researcher specify a directional alternative hypothesis *before* conducting the study if a one-tail test is to be used. A decision to employ a one-tail test must be made prior to the collection of any data, or before the researcher has obtained any empirical feedback or clue as to how the results are turning out. If a researcher claims to have made a one-tail test with $\alpha = .05$ after seeing the data; that is, if $\mu > K$ is hypothesized because $\bar{X}$ is larger than K, the actual probability of a type-I error is greater than .05. If one has not definitely committed to a one-tail test before inspecting the data, the temptation to make a one-tail test must be resisted, otherwise guilt will (and should) be the consequence. Also, once committed to a specific one-tail test, a researcher should not fall back on a nondirectional test, even when the data would be significant in the opposite direction. Given below are some illustrations in which a one-tail test could ordinarily be justified:

1. Does early cognitive enrichment increase IQ scores?
2. Do ten-year-olds make greater progress in learning to play the piano than eight-year-olds?
3. Do kindergarten pupils score higher on a reading readiness test at the end of the year than they did at the beginning of the year?
4. Do scores on IQ tests continue to increase between ages sixteen and twenty?
5. Are students who have not had a statistics course able to obtain higher-than-chance scores on a statistics examination?
6. Is life expectancy increased when smokers stop smoking?
7. Do persons claiming to have ESP score higher than chance on a mental telepathy task?
8. Do persons having had a course in statistics score higher on a critical scientific literacy test than comparable students who have not taken statistics?

Even with the questions above, there are certain situations in which a directional test of H_0 would not be advisable. For example, in question 4, a directional test would be in order if IQs at age 16 were compared with IQs at age 20 (unless the drug problem becomes epidemic), but not when comparing IQs at ages 16 and 60. It is not inconceivable to expect a decline in cognitive performance between ages 16 and 60. Two-tail tests are far more common than one-tail tests because both outcomes are usually logically plausible.

With directional hypotheses, the computation of the t-ratio is unchanged. The only procedural difference between a directional and a nondirectional t-test is that there is only one critical t-value for the one-tail test, and it is positive and always smaller than the absolute value of the critical t for two-tail tests.

Quiz: Given two-tail tests for $n = 27$ and $\alpha = .05$, the critical z-ratios are ___(1)___ , and the critical t-ratios are ___(2)___ . Given a directional one-tail test for $n = 27$ and $\alpha_1 = .05$, the critical z-ratio is ___(3)___ , and the critical t-ratio is ___(4)___ .

Answers: (1) 1.96 and -1.96, (2) 2.056 and -2.056, (3) 1.645, (4) 1.706

❖ CHAPTER SUMMARY

Hypothesis testing is the most widely employed technique of statistical inference in educational and behavioral research. In this chapter, we have illustrated the hypothesis testing procedure using statistical hypotheses of the type H_0: $\mu = K$; that is, testing whether μ is equal to some specified number. In hypothesis testing, we proceed computationally as if H_0 were true, and determine the probability, p, of observing a difference as large or larger than that obtained if H_0 were true. If p is smaller than the pre-specified allowable risk of a type-I error, α (usually $\alpha = .05$), H_0 is rejected at the α-level of statistical significance. If H_0 is rejected at the .05 level, in the long run, we will make a type-I error (rejecting H_0 when it is true) in less than one such decision in twenty (5%). If H_0 is rejected at the .01 level of significance, a type-I error will be made in less than one decision in 100 when H_0 is true. If we fail to reject H_0, we cannot make a type-I error, but we can make a type-II error, B. A type-II error is the failure to reject H_0 when it is false.

When σ (but not μ) is known, $\sigma_{\bar{X}} = \sigma / \sqrt{n}$ can be determined, and the z-ratio $[z = (\bar{X} - \mu)/\sigma_{\bar{X}}]$ is the proper test statistic. The critical values of z are fixed based on the normal curve, and do not vary with n. Unfortunately, usually when μ is unknown, so is σ, and we must resort to the t-ratio $[t = (\bar{X} - \mu)/s_{\bar{X}}]$ for the hypothesis testing procedure. The critical values of t depend on the number of degrees of freedom ($\nu = n - 1$) for testing H_0: $\mu = K$. The critical values of t approach the corresponding critical values for z as n increases; t and z differ negligibly when $n > 100$.

If either $\mu > K$ or $\mu < K$ is clearly impossible or implausible, a one-tail test should be employed because one-tail tests are more powerful than two-tail tests; that is, they more efficiently detect and reject false statistical hypotheses for the same α-level. A one-tail test is indicated by α_1; a two-tail test by α_2 or simply α.

Hypothesis testing and interval estimation lead to the same conclusion regarding the null hypothesis. To say that H_0 is rejected at $\alpha = .05$ is equivalent to saying that the .95 confidence interval around $\bar{X}$ does not contain the hypothesized value of μ. If a .99 confidence interval ranges from 60 to 66, we know that any statistical hypothesis for μ having a value less than 60 or greater than 66 would be rejected at the .01 level of significance.

MASTERY TEST

1. z is to $\sigma_{\bar{X}}$, as t is to ____.
   (a) σ (b) σ^2 (c) s (d) $s_{\bar{X}}$

2. Which of these can be properly regarded as statistical hypotheses?
   (a) $\bar{X} = 100$ (b) $\mu = 1.2$ (c) $\sigma = 10$ (d) $\rho = .5$ (e) $s = 10$ (f) $r = 0$

3. Do statistical hypotheses always pertain to parameters?

4. When will $\sigma_{\bar{X}}$ and σ be equal (Hint: $\sigma_{\bar{X}} = \sigma / \sqrt{n}$)?

5. How large must n be for the standard deviation of the sampling distribution of the mean to be only 10% as large as the standard deviation of the frequency distribution, that is, $\sigma_{\bar{X}}/\sigma = .10$?

6. If $z = (\overline{X} - \mu)/\sigma_{\overline{X}} = 2$, we can reject H_0
   (a) at the .01 level of significance.
   (b) at the .05 level, but not at the .01 level of significance.
   (c) at neither the .01 nor the .05 levels of significance.

7. Which one of the following is *least* likely to have occurred by chance, that is, has resulted from sampling error?
   (a) $z = -3.1$ (b) $z = 0$ (c) $z = 2$ (d) $z = 2.58$

8. When H_0 is true, is the probability of observing a z-value greater than 1.31 the same as the probability of observing a z-value less than -1.31?

9. What is the symbol that denotes the risk of a type-I error that one is willing to tolerate?

10. Assuming H_0 is true, the probability of observing a sample mean which deviates from μ by this much or more is denoted by what letter?

11. If $p < \alpha$, will H_0 be rejected?

12. If $p > \alpha$, does H_0 continue to be tenable?

13. If one particular .95 CI for μ is [47.2, 63.4], which of the following statistical hypotheses will be rejected at the .05 level?
    (a) $\mu = 45$ (b) $\mu = 50$ (c) $\mu = 55$ (d) $\mu = 60$ (e) $\mu = 65$

14. Assume H_0: $\mu = 100$ is rejected at the .01 level of significance.
    (a) Does the value of 100 fall within the .99 CI?
    (b) Does the value of 100 fall within the .95 CI?

15. To reject H_0, which one of the following significance levels requires the largest difference between $\overline{X}$ and μ?
    (a) .01 level   (b) .05 level   (c) .10 level

16. The t-statistic is used to test H_0: $\mu = K$ when __?__ is not known.
    (a) n (b) $\overline{X}$ (c) σ (d) α

17. When $n = 20$, are the critical values slightly larger for t than for z ?

18. In which one of the following cases do the critical values of t and z differ most?
    (a) $n = 5$ (b) $n = 100$ (c) $n = 12,000,000$

19. In testing H_0: $\mu = K$, where K is some numerical constant, which is more commonly employed as a test statistic, t or z? Why?

20. How do the z-ratio sampling distributions differ from the t-ratio sampling distributions?

21. For the following values of n, what are the degrees of freedom in testing H_0: $\mu = K$?
    (a) 11   (b) 60   (c) 101

22. If H_0 is true but is rejected, what type of error is made?
    (a) a type-I error   (b) a type-II error   (c) no error

23. If H_0 is true and is rejected, is a type-II error made?

24. When H_0 is true, what is the probability H_0 will be rejected at the .05 level?

25. If $\alpha = .05$ and H_0 is not rejected, do we know the probability of a type-II error?

26. If we set $\alpha = .05$ and find that $p < .01$, can we reject H_0 at the .01 level?

27. If the critical t-values are 2.1 and -2.1, we know that
    (a) a one-tail test is being run.
    (b) a two-tail test is being run.

28. For the .05 level with $v = 20$, what are the critical t-value(s) for making
    (a) a two-tail t-test?
    (b) a one-tail t-test?

29. In question 28, what is the probability of a type-I error for
(a) a one-tail test?
(b) a two-tail test?

30. If a one-tail test is legitimate, which will have greater power?
(a) a one-tail test
(b) a two-tail test

31. Another name for the "statistical hypothesis" is the "___?___ hypothesis".

32. For which of the questions below, does a one-tail test appear to be justified?
(a) Does going to college result in a change in measured intelligence (IQ)?
(b) Do bright college students (high scores on college board exams) study more or less than not-so-bright college students?
(c) Do math majors score higher than English majors on the Quantitative Aptitude Test of the Graduate Record Examination?
(d) Does the reaction time at age 70 differ from reaction time at age 40?

ANSWERS TO MASTERY TEST

1. (d)
2. (b), (c), and (d)
3. yes
4. when $n = 1$, since $\sigma_{\bar{x}} = \sigma / \sqrt{n}$
5. $n = 100$; hence, $\sigma_{\bar{x}} = \sigma / \sqrt{100} = .1\sigma$.
6. (b)
7. (a)
8. yes
9. α
10. p
11. yes
12. yes
13. (a) and (e)
14. (a) no, (b) no
15. (a)
16. (c)
17. Yes, with $\alpha_2 = .05$, the critical value of 1.960 is required for z, but 2.093 is required for t with 19 degrees of freedom.
18. (a)
19. the t-test, because σ is rarely known
20. The z-ratio sampling distributions are perfectly normal distributions, but the t-ratio sampling distributions, especially for small n's, have fat tails and skinny peaks. However, as n increases, the corresponding z and t sampling distributions converge, so that, when n is large, they differ inconsequentially.
21. (a) $v = 10$, (b) $v = 59$, (c) $v = 100$
22. (a)
23. No; a type-II error results when H_0 is false and yet has not been rejected.
24. .05
25. no
26. Yes; α represents the maximum risk that we are willing to take, whereas p indicates the actual risk of a type-I error.
27. (b)
28. (a) $_{.975}t_{20} = \pm2.086$ (b) $_{.95}t_{20} = 1.725$
29. .05 in both (if the one-tail test is defensible)
30. (a)
31. null
32. (a), (c), (d)

PROBLEMS AND EXERCISES

1. Given that the mean height, μ, of the population of adult males in the United States is about 69.7″, suppose the mean height, $\bar{X}$, of a sample of twenty-five mentally retarded adult males was found to be 67″ with $s = 3″$. Does $\bar{X}$ differ significantly from the hypothesized value $\mu = 69.7″$?

(a) Express H_0 using the appropriate symbols.
(b) From the data provided, would you employ z or t as the test statistic?
(c) What is the value of $s_{\bar{X}}$?
(d) What is the value of t?
(e) What is the value of V?
(f) What are the critical values of t for $\alpha = .01$?
(g) Will H_0 be rejected with $\alpha = .01$? at $\alpha = .001$?
(h) Would the critical values for t remain the same if n were increased to 100?
(i) Would the value of $s_{\bar{X}}$ remain the same if n were increased to 100?

2. Suppose a standardized reading test was given to a *sample* of sixteen sixth-grade students enrolled in a special reading enrichment program. In the eighth month of the school year, their mean grade-equivalent score was 8.0. Suppose that the value of σ is unknown, but s for the sixteen pupils was 1.8. The investigator is curious about whether he can conclude that the *population* of pupils in the enrichment program has a mean that differs from 6.8, which represents the mean of all pupils in the nation in the eighth month of the sixth grade.
(a) What is H_0?
(b) Would z or t be used?
(c) What is the value for the denominator of the t-ratio?
(d) Calculate t.
(e) What are the critical values for t at $\alpha = .05$ and $\alpha = .01$?
(f) Can H_0 be rejected at the .05 level? Can H_0 be rejected at the .01 level?
(g) Construct the .95 and .99 CIs; are the results consistent with those in part f?
(h) Can we be certain that the significantly higher mean is the result of the special enrichment program?
(i) If enough information had been available to warrant a one-tail test, would the computed t-value change? Would the critical t-values change?
(j) Can H_0 be rejected with $\alpha_1 = .01$?

3. In Section 9.7, you selected a random sample of $n = 10$ students from the HSB data set whose math scores are as follows:

$$52 \quad 55 \quad 41 \quad 39 \quad 53 \quad 50 \quad 53 \quad 58 \quad 58 \quad 49$$

For this sample $n = 10$, $\bar{X} = 50.8$, and $s = 6.53$. For the general population $\mu = 50$. The statistical hypothesis is that $\mu_{math} = 50$ for the HSB data set.
(a) Should the z-test or the t-test be used? Why?
(b) Compute the t-ratio.
(c) The degrees of freedom = __?__ .
(d) For $\alpha = .05$, the critical t-ratios are __?__ .
(e) Can H_0: $\mu = 50$ be rejected with $\alpha = .05$?
(f) Can H_0: $\mu = 50$ be rejected with $\alpha = .10$?
(g) Can H_0: $\mu = 50$ be rejected with $\alpha = .20$?
(h) Write a summary statement of the results of this hypothesis test.

4. A random sample of $n = 12$ students from the HSB data set yielded the following science T-scores:

$$55 \quad 58 \quad 49 \quad 39 \quad 47 \quad 66 \quad 58 \quad 55 \quad 61 \quad 55 \quad 44 \quad 55$$

How does the evidence of these data impact upon the statistical hypothesis that $\mu = 50$ for the science T-scores of the HSB data set?
(a) Compute ΣX and $\bar{X}$.
(b) Compute SS, s^2, s, and $s_{\bar{X}}$.
(c) Compute the Student t-ratio.
(d) Can H_0: $\mu = 50$ be rejected with $\alpha = .05$?

(e) Can H_0: $\mu = 50$ be rejected with $\alpha = .10$?
(f) Can H_0: $\mu = 50$ be rejected with $\alpha = .20$?
(g) Write a general summary statement of the results of this hypothesis test.

ANSWERS TO PROBLEMS AND EXERCISES

1. (a) H_0: $\mu = 69.7$
   (b) The t is the better choice, since assuming that σ is known is unwarranted.
   (c) $s_{\bar{X}} = s/\sqrt{n} = 3/\sqrt{25} = .6$
   (d) $t = (\bar{X} - \mu)/s_{\bar{X}} = (67 - 69.7)/.6 = -4.5$
   (e) $\nu = 24$
   (f) ± 2.797
   (g) Yes, $t = |-4.5| > 2.797$; yes, $t = |-4.5| > 3.467$.
   (h) No, the critical t-value decreases as n increases.
   (i) No, if n were 100, $s_{\bar{X}}$ would be much smaller.

2. (a) H_0: $\mu = 6.8$
   (b) t, since σ is not known
   (c) $s_{\bar{X}} = s/\sqrt{n} = 1.8/\sqrt{16} = .45$
   (d) $t = (\bar{X} - \mu)/s_{\bar{X}} = (8 - 6.8)/.45 = 2.67$
   (e) Since $\nu = n - 1 = 15$, the critical t-values are 2.131 and 2.947 for $\alpha = .05$ and .01, respectively.
   (f) yes at $\alpha = .05$, no at $\alpha = .01$
   (g) Yes, the .95 CI = $[\bar{X} \pm 2.131 s_{\bar{X}}] = [8 \pm 2.131(.45)] = [8 \pm .96]$, or [7.04, 8.96]; .99 CI = $[8 \pm 2.947(.45)] = [8 \pm 1.33]$, or [6.67, 9.33]. The value of 6.8 falls within the .99 CI, so H_0 would not be rejected for $\alpha = .01$. The value of 6.8 is not included in the .95 CI, so H_0 is rejected at $\alpha = .05$. Yes, the conclusions from the confidence intervals are equivalent to those from the hypothesis testing procedures.
   (h) No, perhaps they were bright students who performed excellently in spite of a poor enrichment program. Causal statements like this require the use of control groups.
   (i) No, the computed t-ratio is identical for both the one-tail and the two-tail test. Indeed, the critical t-ratio will change and will become smaller. For $\alpha_1 = .05$,

   $_{.95}t_{15} = 1.753$, and for $\alpha_1 = .01$, $_{.99}t_{15} = 2.602$.
   (j) H_0 is rejected at $\alpha_1 = .01$ since $t = 2.67 > 2.602 = {}_{.99}t_{15}$.

3. (a) The t-test should be used since σ for the HSB data set is unknown. There is no evidence that the standard deviation of the HSB data set is equal to that of the general population.
   (b) $s_{\bar{X}} = 6.53/\sqrt{10} = 2.065$;
   $t = (50.8 - 50)/2.065 = .39$
   (c) $\nu = n - 1 = 9$
   (d) For $\alpha = .05$, the critical t-values are ± 2.262.
   (e) No, $t = .39 < 2.262 = {}_{.975}t_9$.
   (f) No, $t = .39 < 1.833 = {}_{.95}t_9$.
   (g) No, $t = .39 < 1.383 = {}_{.90}t_9$.
   (h) These data are consistent with H_0; there is no evidence to suggest that H_0 is false. The hypothesis that the math T-score mean of the HSB data set is 50 remains tenable at the .20 level of significance.

4. (a) $\Sigma X = 642$; $\bar{X} = 53.5$
   (b) $SS = 34{,}972 - 34{,}347 = 625$; $s^2 = 625/11 = 56.818$; $s = 7.538$; $s_{\bar{X}} = 2.176$
   (c) $t = (53.5 - 50)/2.176 = 1.608$
   (d) No, $t = 1.608 < 2.262 = {}_{.975}t_{11}$.
   (e) No, $t = 1.608 < 1.796 = {}_{.95}t_{11}$.
   (f) Yes, $t = 1.608 > 1.363 = {}_{.90}t_{11}$.
   (g) These data are quite consistent with H_0; there is little evidence to suggest that H_0 is false. If H_0 were true a computed t-ratio = 1.608 would occur between 10 and 20% of the time due to chance alone. The hypothesis that the science T-score mean of the HSB data set is 50 remains tenable at the .10 level of significance.

SUGGESTED COMPUTER EXERCISE

1. Test the null hypothesis that the HSB civics scores were selected from a population with $\mu = 50$.
2. Test the null hypotheses that the following variables were selected from a population with $\mu = 50$:
   (a) Reading
   (b) Writing
   (c) Math
   (d) Science
3. From the random sample of ten students from the HSB data set (see Suggested Computer Activity 2 for Chapter 9), determine if any of the five subject matter means differ from $\mu = 50$ with $\alpha = .05$.

❖ 11

Testing Hypotheses about the Difference between Two Means

❖ 11.1 INTRODUCTION

If the means for two groups are obtained, how does one determine whether the difference between them is a real difference, or simply the result of sampling error—how does one find out if the difference is statistically significant? The concepts of a sampling distribution, the standard error, and statistical hypotheses developed in Chapters 9 and 10 are foundational for this and subsequent chapters. The present chapter treats the concepts and procedures for testing a hypothesis involving two means (e.g., H_0: $\mu_1 - \mu_2 = 0$), which is the most common type of hypothesis in the behavioral sciences.

❖ 11.2 TESTING STATISTICAL HYPOTHESES INVOLVING TWO MEANS

In Chapter 10, procedures for testing hypotheses involving only a single group mean (H_0: $\mu = K$) were considered. We evaluated whether the mean of the random sample ($\overline{X}$) differed significantly from the numerical value (K) for the hypothesized mean of the population, μ. It is much more common, however, for research questions to pertain to differences in means—is there a difference between the means of populations 1 and 2; does the parameter μ_1 equal the parameter μ_2? For example, in each of the following questions, the statistical hypothesis can be expressed as H_0: $\mu_1 - \mu_2 = 0$: Is the new treatment more effective than the old? Do girls read better than boys? Does drug A lower reaction time when compared to a placebo? Does anxiety lower test performance? Is there a difference in the math proficiency of today's graduating seniors and those of a decade ago? Is there a difference between the number of educational dollars per student spent for children of middle versus children of lower SES?

❖ 11.3 THE NULL HYPOTHESIS

In each of the above questions, the statistical hypothesis is H_0: $\mu_1 = \mu_2$ (or equivalently, H_0: $\mu_1 - \mu_2 = 0$); that is, the means of populations 1 and 2 are equal—there is no difference in the parameters μ_1 and μ_2. Statistical hypotheses are commonly known as *null hypotheses*. The null hypothesis is a claim specifying the numerical value of one or more population parameters; it is the hypothesis that the researcher typically hopes to "nullify." The hypotheses, H_0: $\mu = 0$, H_0: $\rho = 0$, and H_0: $\mu_1 - \mu_2 = 0$, are all examples of null hypotheses; in each instance, a numerical value (here, 0) for a parameter is specified.

When we are comparing the mean of an experimental group ($\overline{X}_E$) with the mean of a control group ($\overline{X}_C$), we are interested in whether the treatment had an impact on the outcome (dependent) variable, that is, whether H_0: $\mu_E = \mu_C$ is plausible. It is interesting to note that the hypothesis that is to be tested, the null hypothesis, is usually opposite to the finding hoped for by the researcher. The researcher ordinarily wants to find a significant difference between the two means, but must continue to entertain the "no-difference" hypothesis unless the evidence to the contrary is convincing. If there is no treatment effect, the measured difference in the two sample means ($\overline{X}_E - \overline{X}_C$) results solely from chance (sampling error). When comparing two means, the value hypothesized for the difference between μ_1 and μ_2 is usually zero,[1] that is, the null hypothesis is H_0: $\mu_1 - \mu_2 = 0$ (or equivalently, H_0: $\mu_1 = \mu_2$).

❖ 11.4 THE z-TEST FOR DIFFERENCES BETWEEN INDEPENDENT MEANS

If one random sample of persons receives a special treatment and a second random sample does not, the two resulting sample means, $\overline{X}_1$ and $\overline{X}_2$, are said to be *independent*. However, if a group is pretested, receives the treatment, and then is posttested, pretest scores ($\overline{X}_1$'s) and posttest scores ($\overline{X}_2$'s) will be correlated; the means will not be independent. Procedures for testing the difference between paired or correlated means such as these are treated later in the chapter (Section 11.17) We will first consider the more common situation, where there are two different independent groups.

We first encountered the z-ratio ($z = (X - \mu)/\sigma$) in Chapter 5 where z was used in determining areas under the normal curve. When the z-ratio is used to test a statistical hypothesis, it is said to be a z-test. All z-tests are particular instances of the following general expression:

$$z = \frac{(\text{observed statistic} - \text{hypothesized parameter})}{\text{standard error of the difference}} \qquad (11.1)$$

In Chapter 10, the z-test (Section 10.4) for testing H_0: $\mu = K$ was $z = (\overline{X} - \mu)/\sigma_{\overline{X}}$. Similarly, the z-test for testing H_0: $\mu_1 - \mu_2 = K$ is given in Equation 11.2a. The hypothesized value for K is almost always 0; thus, the z-test for testing H_0: $\mu_1 - \mu_2 = 0$ is given in Equation 11.2b.

For H_0: $\mu_1 - \mu_2 = K$:

$$z = \frac{(\overline{X}_1 - \overline{X}_2) - (\mu_1 - \mu_2)}{\sigma_{\overline{X}_1 - \overline{X}_2}} \qquad (11.2a)$$

---

[1]Although any numerical value for the $(\mu_1 - \mu_2)$ difference can be specified by the statistical hypothesis, it is rare that any value other than zero is hypothesized.

For H_0: $\mu_1 - \mu_2 = 0$:

$$z = \frac{(\overline{X}_1 - \overline{X}_2)}{\sigma_{\overline{X}_1 - \overline{X}_2}} \qquad \text{(11.2b)}$$

The standard errors in the denominators of the z-tests (such as Eqs. 10.1 and 11.2) are always parameters (not estimates of the parameters, as is the case with the t-test).

Quiz: The z-test differs from the t-test in that the standard error in the denominator of the z-test is a ___(1)___, whereas that of the t-test is a ___(2)___. (3) Surmise whether the following sample descriptions would probably be independent or dependent (correlated) samples: (a) The same group of subjects were tested twice, once prior to viewing the film and then again after viewing the film. (b) A sample of Whites were compared to a sample of Blacks with respect to how high they can jump. (c) Science and civics T-scores were compared for students of the HSB data set.

Answers: (1) parameter, (2) statistic (or estimate of the parameter), (3)(a) dependent, (3)(b) independent, (3)(c) dependent

❖ 11.5 THE STANDARD ERROR OF THE DIFFERENCE BETWEEN MEANS, $\sigma_{\overline{X}_1 - \overline{X}_2}$

The parameter $\sigma_{\overline{X}_1 - \overline{X}_2}$ is the standard error of the difference between means; it is the *standard deviation of the sampling distribution of mean differences* ($\overline{X}_1 - \overline{X}_2$). Despite its fearsome subscript, it is merely a standard deviation; the subscript is just a name tag that tells the viewer that it is the standard deviation of the *difference* between two means.

Let us think through a hypothetical experiment, using what we have learned about the normal curve and sampling distributions. Suppose that the null hypothesis is true, that is, $\mu_1 = \mu_2 = 100$, that the frequency distributions are normal, and $\sigma_1 = \sigma_2 = 15$. Suppose you (and every other student in class) randomly draw a sample of $n_1 = 25$ observations from population 1 and compute $\overline{X}_1$. Next you randomly draw a second random sample of $n_2 = 25$ observations from population 2 and compute $\overline{X}_2$. Then you (and every other student in class) find the difference between the two sample means, ($\overline{X}_1 - \overline{X}_2$). Since each student will have found a difference, we will make a distribution of these differences. The frequency distribution of these differences ($\overline{X}_1 - \overline{X}_2$) approximates a sampling distribution of ($\overline{X}_1 - \overline{X}_2$). If the class was very, very large (actually infinitely large) and each student has found a difference based on his or her independent samples, this sampling distribution would be normally distributed, and its mean would be zero since ($\mu_1 - \mu_2$) = 0. Its standard deviation (termed the standard error of the differences between means) is indicated by the dreaded symbol $\sigma_{\overline{X}_1 - \overline{X}_2}$ and is readily found using Equation 11.3:

$$\sigma_{\overline{X}_1 - \overline{X}_2} = \sqrt{\sigma_{\overline{X}_1}^2 + \sigma_{\overline{X}_2}^2} \qquad \text{(11.3)}$$

where $\sigma_{\overline{X}_1}^2 = \sigma_1^2/n_1$, and $\sigma_{\overline{X}_2}^2 = \sigma_2^2/n_2$.

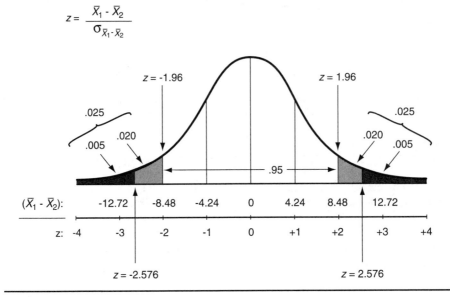

$$z = \frac{\bar{X}_1 - \bar{X}_2}{\sigma_{\bar{X}_1 - \bar{X}_2}}$$

❖ **FIGURE 11.1** Sampling distribution of the difference in means ($\bar{X}_1 - \bar{X}_2$), and associated z-ratios, when H_0: $\mu_1 - \mu_2 = 0$ is true, $\sigma_1 = \sigma_2 = 15$, and $n_1 = n_2 = 25$. Percentile points of z at .005, .025, .975, and .995 are given.

The findings for our thought experiment are shown in Figure 11.1. Note that $\sigma_{\bar{X}_1}^2 = (15)^2/25 = 225/25 = 9$, and $\sigma_{\bar{X}_2}^2 = (15)^2/25 = 9$; hence, $\sigma_{\bar{X}_1 - \bar{X}_2} = \sqrt{9+9} = \sqrt{18} = 4.24$.

In summary, Figure 11.1 gives the sampling distribution of ($\bar{X}_1 - \bar{X}_2$) values when (a) H_0: $\mu_1 - \mu_2 = 0$ is true, (b) both populations have X's that are normally distributed with $\sigma_1 = \sigma_2 = 15$, and (c) $n_1 = n_2 = 25$. In Figure 11.1, the mean of the sampling distribution of ($\bar{X}_1 - \bar{X}_2$) is zero, and the standard deviation is 4.24.

Notice that the sampling distribution in Figure 11.1 is a normal distribution with known parameters—the mean is 0 and the standard deviation is 4.24. Since we now have a rough and ready normal curve etched in our brains, we know that about 68 percent of the absolute differences in two sample means, $|\bar{X}_1 - \bar{X}_2|$, are less than 4.24; about 5 percent of the $|\bar{X}_1 - \bar{X}_2|$ differences are greater than 1.96(4.24) = 8.31. When H_0 is true, 2.5 percent or the phantom students who are replicating the study will find that the mean of their sample 1 ($\bar{X}_1$) will exceed the mean of their sample 2 ($\bar{X}_2$) by 8.31 or more points; similarly, $\bar{X}_2$ will exceed $\bar{X}_1$ by 8.31 or more points in 2.5 percent of the replications of the experiments. Stated differently, a difference between the means of at least 8.31 points is necessary to reject the null hypothesis at $\alpha = .05$; a difference of $|8.31|$ or more will occur by chance only in 5 percent of the replications.

As indicated in Figure 11.1, 2.5 percent of the ($\bar{X}_1 - \bar{X}_2$) differences have associated z-ratios $\geq 1.96 = 8.31/4.24$, and another 2.5 percent fall at or below $z = -1.96$; hence, the two critical z-values at $\alpha = .05$ are ± 1.96. To perform a one-tail test of this hypothesis, the mean of the group assumed to have the smaller mean (if indeed the means differ) is to be subtracted from the other group mean. This procedure allows all of the critical region to be placed in one (the upper) tail of the distribution; hence for $\alpha_1 = .05$, there is only one critical value, $_{.95}z = 1.645$.

The associated z-values for certain mean differences are shown in Figure 11.1. The shaded tail areas indicate the critical regions, the regions in which the null hypothesis will be rejected for specified α-levels. For $\alpha_2 = .05$, the critical region is the extreme 2.5 percent in each tail of the sampling distribution. The smaller black areas (look closely) begin where the associated z-ratios are ± 2.576; when the observed z-ratio falls here, the null hypothesis will be rejected at the .01 level. For two-tail tests, the critical α-region is split between the two tail areas with one-half α in each tail—for one-tail tests, the entire critical α-region is placed in the upper tail.

Quiz: The following questions are based on Figure 11.1, given that the sampling distribution of the difference between two sample means is normally distributed with mean of 0 and standard deviation of 4.24. (Use Table A.)

The middlemost 50 percent of the $(\overline{X}_1 - \overline{X}_2)$ differences have z-scores between $\pm$ __(1)__ . The middlemost 80 percent of the $(\overline{X}_1 - \overline{X}_2)$ differences have z-scores between $\pm$ __(2)__ . The middlemost 90 percent of the $(\overline{X}_1 - \overline{X}_2)$ differences have z-scores between $\pm$ __(3)__ . For $\alpha_2 = .10$, the $|z|$-score at which the null hypothesis will be rejected is __(4)__ . For $\alpha_1 = .10$, the z-score at which the critical region begins is __(5)__ . If you obtained $(\overline{X}_1 - \overline{X}_2) = 6.27$, $z =$ __(6)__ . (7) For $z = 1.479$, would H_0 be rejected at $\alpha_2 = .10$? (8) Suppose that, instead of $\alpha_2 = .10$, $\alpha_1 = .10$; for $z = 1.479$, would H_0 be rejected? (9) For $(\overline{X}_1 - \overline{X}_2) = 11.13$, what is the p-value (i.e., probability of occurrence under a true nondirectional H_0)? (10) With $p = .0088$, would H_0 be rejected at $\alpha_2 = .01$? (11) Could H_0 be rejected at $\alpha_1 = .001$?

Answers: (1) .674, (2) 1.282, (3) 1.645, (4) $|1.645|$, (5) 1.282, (6) $6.27/4.24 = 1.479$, (7) H_0 would not be rejected at $\alpha_2 = .10$. (8) Yes, H_0 would be rejected with $\alpha_1 = .10$. (9) $z = 11.13/4.24 = 2.625$; $p = 2(.0044) = .0088$. (10) Yes, $p < \alpha$ so reject H_0. (11) For a one-tail test, $z = 2.625$, $p = .0044 > .001$, so H_0 is not rejected, and remains tenable at $\alpha_1 = .001$.

❖ 11.6 THE *t*-DISTRIBUTION AND THE *t*-TEST

Recall from Chapter 10 that, when σ is unknown and s must be used as an estimate of σ, the ratio of the mean difference to the *estimated* standard error is termed a t-ratio instead of a z-ratio—t is a rough approximation of z. Whereas $z = (\overline{X} - \mu)/\sigma_{\overline{X}}$, $t = (\overline{X} - \mu)/s_{\overline{X}}$. Likewise, when the mean difference $(\overline{X}_1 - \overline{X}_2)$ is divided by $s_{\overline{X}_1 - \overline{X}_2}$ instead of $\sigma_{\overline{X}_1 - \overline{X}_2}$, the resulting value is a t-ratio rather than a z-ratio.

Usually the standard deviation parameters (σ_1 and σ_2) for the two groups being compared are not known; hence, the t-test (rather than the z-test) is used for testing $H_0: \mu_1 - \mu_2 = 0$. A general statement of the t-test is:

$$t = \frac{\text{observed } (\overline{X}_1 - \overline{X}_2) \text{ difference} - \text{hypothesized } (\mu_1 - \mu_2) \text{ difference}}{\text{estimate of the standard error of the } (\overline{X}_1 - \overline{X}_2) \text{ difference}} \quad \textbf{(11.4)}$$

Equation 11.4 expressed in statistical terms is presented in Equation 11.5a, which is appropriate to test $H_0: \mu_1 - \mu_2 = K$. Ordinarily, however, the null hypothesis being tested is that the population means for the two groups are equal, that is, $H_0: \mu_1 - \mu_2 = 0$, and for testing $H_0: \mu_1 - \mu_2 = 0$, the t-test is simplified to Equation 11.5b:

For testing H_0: $\mu_1 - \mu_2 = K$:

$$t = \frac{(\overline{X}_1 - \overline{X}_2) - (\mu_1 - \mu_2)}{s_{\overline{X}_1 - \overline{X}_2}} \qquad \textbf{(11.5a)}$$

For H_0: $\mu_1 - \mu_2 = 0$:

$$t = \frac{(\overline{X}_1 - \overline{X}_2)}{s_{\overline{X}_1 - \overline{X}_2}} \qquad \textbf{(11.5b)}$$

Note that the denominator of the t-test is not a parameter, but is a statistic and therefore subject to sampling error. The sampling error (the difference between $s_{\overline{X}_1 - \overline{X}_2}$ and $\sigma_{\overline{X}_1 - \overline{X}_2}$) in the denominator causes the distribution of t-ratios to deviate somewhat from a perfectly normal distribution, even if the original observations (the X's) are normally distributed (as assumed in the mathematical derivation).

As you know, when samples are small, the sampling error tends to be greater than with large n's. Although there is only one curve that is a perfect normal z-distribution, there is a *whole family* of t-distributions; there is a t-distribution for each degree of freedom. Figure 11.2 depicts the central[2] t-distributions with 1, 5, 25, and ∞ (infinite) degrees of freedom. Notice that, as n (or v) becomes smaller, the tail areas in the curves become fatter than in the normal distribution, that is, characterized by *leptokurtosis*. The t-distributions quickly become less leptokurtic and more nearly normal as n increases. Note that, with 25 degrees of freedom, the t-distribution differs little from a normal distribution. From Table C of Appendix B, we can determine the t-values at various percentiles in the t-distribution for 1, 2, …, 30, 40, …,1000, and ∞ degrees of freedom. The 95th percentile, P_{95}, with 1 degree of freedom is denoted as $_{.95}t_1$ and equals 6.314; likewise, one can determine the following percentiles: $_{.95}t_5 = 2.015$, $_{.95}t_{25} = 1.708$, and $_{.95}t_\infty = 1.645$. When $n = \infty$, the t-distribution is identical to the normal z-distribution. This is why the entries in Table C for $v = \infty$ (t_∞) are identical to corresponding z-values in Appendix B Table A. For example, the 95th percentile in the t-distribution with infinite degrees of freedom ($_{.95}t_\infty = 1.645$) is identical to the 95th percentile in the z-distribution ($_{.95}z = 1.645$).

Note in Equations 11.4 and 11.5 that the standard error of the difference in means ($s_{\overline{X}_1 - \overline{X}_2}$) is an *estimate* of the parameter, $\sigma_{\overline{X}_1 - \overline{X}_2}$. Recall from Chapter 4 that $E(s^2) = \sigma^2$; likewise, $E(s^2_{\overline{X}_1 - \overline{X}_2}) = \sigma^2_{\overline{X}_1 - \overline{X}_2}$. (Remember that the subscripts are merely name tags to indicate that the variance is of differences between means 1 and 2.) The value of $s^2_{\overline{X}_1 - \overline{X}_2}$ is an unbiased estimate of the variance of this sampling distribution, and $s_{\overline{X}_1 - \overline{X}_2}$ is an estimate of the standard deviation (standard error) of this sampling distribution.[3]

---

[2]The term "central" means "when the null hypothesis is true"; hence, central t-distributions are distributions of the values of t that would result when the null hypothesis is true.

[3]$s_{\overline{X}_1 - \overline{X}_2}$ bears the same relationship to $\sigma_{\overline{X}_1 - \overline{X}_2}$ as s does to σ. $s_{\overline{X}_1 - \overline{X}_2}$ tends to be a slightly biased estimate of $\sigma_{\overline{X}_1 - \overline{X}_2}$, that is, $E(s_{\overline{X}_1 - \overline{X}_2}) < \sigma_{\overline{X}_1 - \overline{X}_2}$. Note in Figure 4.2 that when $n = 2$, $E(s) = .8\sigma$, but if $n = 20$, the bias is negligible: $E(s) \cong .99\sigma$.

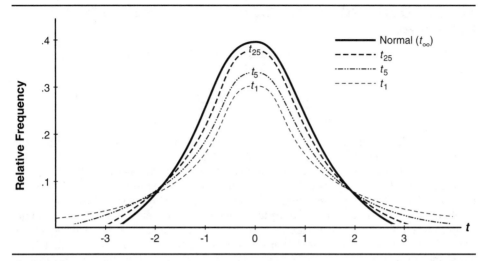

❖ **FIGURE 11.2** The *t*-distributions with 1, 5, and 25 degrees of freedom with the normal distribution of *z*-values.

Quiz: Fill in the blanks with the words which make good sense. As the sample sizes, *n*'s, on which means are based are made larger:

(1) the sampling distribution of ($\overline{X}_1 - \overline{X}_2$) becomes more nearly __?__ and less __?__.
(2) $s_{\overline{X}_1 - \overline{X}_2}$ becomes __?__ in magnitude and a better estimate of __?__. (3) the critical *t*-value becomes __?__ and closer to the critical value for __?__.

Answers: (1) normal, leptokurtic ("fat-tailed"), (2) smaller, $\sigma_{\overline{X}_1 - \overline{X}_2}$, (3) smaller, the corresponding *z*-value

How can we obtain an estimate of the numerical value of the standard deviation of the sampling distribution $s_{\overline{X}_1 - \overline{X}_2}$ when, in any study, we will have only a single value ($\overline{X}_1 - \overline{X}_2$)? Before we proceed to answer this question, we need to become familiar with the underlying assumptions of the *t*-test.

❖ 11.7 ASSUMPTIONS OF THE *t*-TEST

Three statistical assumptions undergird the mathematical derivation of the *t*-test for testing differences in independent means:

1. *Normality of X's:* The distributions of observations (*X*'s), both in population 1 and in population 2, are normal.
2. *Homogeneity of variances:* The variances of the observations in population 1 and in population 2 are equal, that is, $\sigma_1^2 = \sigma_2^2$.
3. *Independence of X's:* The random sample of observations from population 1 is independent of the random sample of observations from population 2.

The practical consequences of violating these assumptions will be considered in Sections 11.12 to 11.15.

❖ 11.8 COMPUTING THE STANDARD ERROR OF THE DIFFERENCE BETWEEN MEANS, $s_{\bar{X}_1 - \bar{X}_2}$

Recall from Equation 4.6 that the variance estimate, s^2, is the ratio of sum of squares, SS, to degrees of freedom, v:

$$s^2 = \frac{\Sigma(X - \bar{X})^2}{n-1} = \frac{\Sigma x^2}{v} = \frac{\text{sum of squares}}{v} = \frac{SS}{v}$$

Notice that, when we have two samples, we have two separate estimates of σ^2; both s_1^2 and s_2^2 are estimates of σ^2: $s_1^2 = \Sigma x_1^2/(n_1 - 1)$, and $s_2^2 = \Sigma x_2^2/(n_2 - 1)$.

Regardless of the value of n, both s_1^2 and s_2^2 are unbiased estimates of their corresponding parameters. If $\sigma_1^2 = \sigma_2^2$, as indicated in assumption 2 of the t-test (Section 11.7), then both s_1^2 and s_2^2 are independent estimates of the same parameter, that is, $\sigma_1^2 = \sigma_2^2 = \sigma^2$. It would be inefficient to use only s_1^2 or s_2^2 to estimate σ^2. Hence, the information from both samples is combined (weighted according to sample size) to obtain the "pooled" or "within groups" estimate (s_W^2) of the population variance (σ^2). (Recall from Chapter 4 that "variance" and "mean square" are synonomous terms; consequently the within groups variance, s_W^2, is also referred to as the mean square within, MS_W. This terminology will be used extensively in Chapters 14–16.)

When $n_1 = n_2$, it is an easy task to find s_W^2 since you only need to average the two sample variances, that is, $s_W^2 = (s_1^2 + s_2^2)/2$. If the n's differ, and computations are done by hand, more steps are required to determine s_W^2. The steps to find s_W^2 (or MS_W) when $n_1 \neq n_2$ are as follows:

Step 1.	Combine the sum of squares within each group to obtain the sum of squares within groups: ($SS_W = SS_1 + SS_2$)
Step 2.	Combine the degrees of freedom within each group to obtain the degrees of freedom within: $v_W = v_1 + v_2$
Step 3.	Divide SS_W by v_W to obtain the within groups variance estimate: $s_W^2 = SS_W/v_W$

These three steps are evident in Equation 11.6:

$$s_W^2 = \frac{SS_1 + SS_2}{v_1 + v_2} = \frac{SS_W}{v_W} = MS_W \tag{11.6}$$

Since s_W^2 is based on a greater number of degrees of freedom than either s_1^2 or s_2^2 alone, s_W^2 will tend to be a better estimate of σ^2. That is, the sampling error $|s_W^2 - \sigma^2|$ is probably less that either $|s_1^2 - \sigma^2|$ or $|s_2^2 - \sigma^2|$. As you might guess, s_W^2 always has a value between s_1^2 and s_2^2; naturally s_W^2 is influenced more by the larger sample than by the smaller. Note that s_W^2 is the weighted average of the two sample variances: If v_1 is twice v_2, $|s_W^2 - s_1^2|$ will be half of $|s_W^2 - s_2^2|$. Being aware of this relationship, you can easily see if your computation of s_W^2 yields a reasonable value.

Quiz: (1) If $n_1 = n_2$, $s_1^2 = 100$, and $s_2^2 = 200$, $s_W^2 = $ _____?_____.

(2) If $n_1 \neq n_2$, but $s_1^2 = s_2^2 = 225$, $s_W^2 = $ _____?_____.

(3) If $v_1 = 2v_2$, $s_1^2 = 10$, and $s_2^2 = 100$, $s_W^2 = $ _____?_____. (Obtain the answer using reasoning, not a formula.)

(4) If for sample I, $v_1 = 10$ and $s_1^2 = 100$, and for sample II, $v_2 = 40$ and $s_2^2 = 200$, $s_W^2 = $ _____?_____. (Use Eq. 11.6.)

Answers: (1) $(100 + 200)/2 = 150$, (2) 225 (Too easy! s_W^2 is always between s_1^2 and s_2^2, so s_W^2 has to be 225.) (3) 40 ($|s_2^2 - s_W^2| = 2 |s_1^2 - s_W^2|$, thus $s_W^2 = 40$.) (4) $SS_1 = (10)(100) = 1,000$; $SS_2 = (40)(200) = 8,000$; so $s_W^2 = (1,000 + 8,000)/(10 + 40) = 180$.)

Once we have computed s_W^2, the unbiased estimate of the population variance, it is a simple matter to estimate the variance in the sampling distribution of differences between two sample means, $s_{\bar{X}_1 - \bar{X}_2}^2$, and the standard error of the differences in means, $s_{\bar{X}_1 - \bar{X}_2}$, by using Equations 11.7a and 11.7b: (See Math Note 12 to review square root operations.)

$$s_{\bar{X}_1 - \bar{X}_2}^2 = s_W^2 \left(\frac{1}{n_1} + \frac{1}{n_2} \right) \tag{11.7a}$$

$$s_{\bar{X}_1 - \bar{X}_2} = s_W \sqrt{\frac{1}{n_1} + \frac{1}{n_2}} \tag{11.7b}$$

$$t = \frac{\bar{X}_1 - \bar{X}_2}{s_{\bar{X}_1 - \bar{X}_2}} = \frac{\bar{X}_1 - \bar{X}_2}{s_W \sqrt{\dfrac{1}{n_1} + \dfrac{1}{n_2}}} \tag{11.8}$$

We now have the background necessary for applying the t-test for testing the difference between two independent means for statistical significance.

❖ 11.9 TESTING THE NULL HYPOTHESIS H_0: $\mu_1 - \mu_2 = 0$ USING THE t-TEST

The four steps in hypothesis testing were defined in Chapter 10. These four steps applied to the t-test for differences in two population means are outlined below:

Step 1. State the statistical hypothesis: H_0: $\mu_1 - \mu_2 = 0$.

Step 2. Specify the maximum allowable risk of a type-I error ($\alpha_2 = .05$ is conventional).

Step 3. Compute the observed t-ratio (Equations 11.6, 11.7, and 11.8).

> **Step 4.**   Make a decision regarding H_0: Compare p with α. If $p > \alpha$, H_0 is tenable; if $p < \alpha$, H_0 is rejected. If computation is done by hand rather than by computer, an equivalent procedure is used: If the observed $|t| \geq$ critical $|t|$-value, then $p < \alpha$ and H_0 is rejected; if the obtained $|t| <$ critical $|t|$-value, then $p > \alpha$ and H_0 is retained as tenable.

This four step hypothesis testing procedure is also outlined in the flowchart given in Figure 11.3.

❖ 11.10 THE *t*-TEST: AN ILLUSTRATION

Suppose we want to ascertain whether an intensive treatment of environmental stimulation increases the measured intelligence of infants. From the thirty-six infants that are available, eighteen are randomly assigned to the experimental (E) group; the remaining eighteen infants serve as the control (C) group. After two years of the treatment, an individual intelligence test was administered to all thirty-six children in random order by an examiner unaware of which were E and which were C infants. Hypothetical results for each group are given in Table 11.1. Since it is inconceivable that the environmental enrichment will have a detrimental effect on IQ scores, a one-tail test is appropriate. Recall (Section 10.10) that when the use of a one-tail test can be justified, it should be used because it is more powerful than the conventional two-tail test; that is, with the same risk of making a type-I error (α, or "alpha error"), there is less chance of making a type-II (β, or "beta error").

Note that in the Table 11.1 example H_0 can be rejected. From Appendix B Table C, we find that for $\alpha_1 = .05$ the critical value for t with 30 degrees of freedom is 1.697.[4] The obtained t (1.87) is greater than the critical t (1.697) which means that $p < \alpha_1$, therefore we reject H_0 at $\alpha_1 = .05$. The evidence against the null hypothesis is strong—it is unlikely that the difference between $\overline{X}_1$ and $\overline{X}_2$ is the result of chance (sampling error). Fortunately, we were clever enough to recognize that a one-tail test was appropriate during the planning stage of this experiment. If we had been guided solely by convention and used $\alpha_2 = .05$, the critical t-value would have been 2.042 ($_{.975}t_{30}$), and we would not have been able to reject the null hypothesis. However, having a lock on the concepts of Chapter 10 and recalling that a one-tail test can never be justified as an afterthought, we made the decision to use a one-tail directional test before the data were collected.

Note that the value of the denominator of the t-test ($s_{\overline{X}_1 - \overline{X}_2}$) is influenced greatly by sample size. Other things being equal, larger values of n result in smaller values of $s_{\overline{X}_1 - \overline{X}_2}$. Obviously, a smaller denominator will result in a larger t-ratio for a given mean difference. This illustrates why we are less likely to make type-II errors with large sample sizes—even small differences in the two sample means can result in large t-ratios if the n's are large.

The central t-distribution with 30 degrees of freedom is shown graphically in Figure 11.4. The associated t-values at percentiles .005, .025, .05, .95, .975, and .995 are indicated. For example, when H_0 is true and $v = 30$, we would observe a t-ratio of -1.697 or less in 5 percent of the t-tests; we would observe t-values of $+1.697$ or greater 5 percent of the time; or, in other words, when $\alpha_2 = .10$, the critical values for t are ± 1.697—if $|t| \geq 1.697$, H_0 is

---

[4]Since $v = 34$ is not reported, we use 30, the next smaller v-value, to be conservative; the difference in $_{.95}t_{30} = 1.697$ and $_{.95}t_{34} = 1.691$ is negligible. Exact critical values and p-values are available in EXCEL and other spreadsheets. When the analysis is done via computer, critical values are not needed because exact probabilities are available.

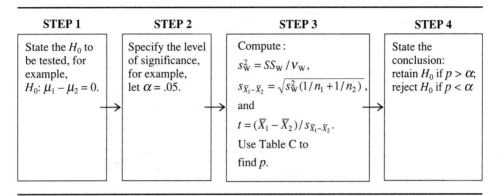

STEP 1	STEP 2	STEP 3	STEP 4
State the H_0 to be tested, for example, H_0: $\mu_1 - \mu_2 = 0$.	Specify the level of significance, for example, let $\alpha = .05$.	Compute: $s_W^2 = SS_W / V_W$, $s_{\bar{X}_1 - \bar{X}_2} = \sqrt{s_W^2(1/n_1 + 1/n_2)}$, and $t = (\bar{X}_1 - \bar{X}_2) / s_{\bar{X}_1 - \bar{X}_2}$. Use Table C to find p.	State the conclusion: retain H_0 if $p > \alpha$; reject H_0 if $p < \alpha$

❖ **FIGURE 11.3** Flowchart of the four-step hypothesis testing procedure for H_0: $\mu_1 - \mu_2 = 0$ when σ is unknown.

rejected at $\alpha = .10$. Five percent of the area under the curve in Figure 11.4 falls to the left of the point $t = -1.697$; another 5 percent falls to the right of $t = 1.697$. In our example, α_1 was set at .05; hence, H_0 is rejected only if the observed t is *greater* than 1.697. When H_0 is true, 95 percent of the obtained t's would fall below 1.697.

   When H_0 is not true (i.e., $\mu_1 - \mu_2 \neq 0$), the observed $|t|$-values will tend to be larger than when the expected value of $(\bar{X}_1 - \bar{X}_2)$ is 0. $E(\bar{X}_1 - \bar{X}_2) = 0$ only when $\mu_1 = \mu_2$. Consequently, when $\alpha = .05$, a false H_0 will be rejected in more than 5 percent (hopefully much more than 5 percent) of the t-tests. For two-tail tests when $\mu_1 \neq \mu_2$, if the observed $|t|$ ex-

❖ **TABLE 11.1** A computational illustration of the *t*-test for the difference between means of independent groups.

	Experimental		Control
	$\bar{X}_1 =$ 108.1		$\bar{X}_2 =$ 98.4
	$n_1 =$ 18		$n_2 =$ 18
	$s_1^2 =$ 289.0		$s_2^2 =$ 196.0
	$\Sigma x_1^2 = SS_1 = 4{,}913$		$SS_2 = 3{,}332^*$

Step 1. H_0: $\mu_1 = \mu_2$. (This is often implicitly stated.)

Step 2. $\alpha_1 = .05$.

Step 3a. $s_W^2 = \dfrac{SS_1 + SS_2}{V_1 + V_2} = \dfrac{4{,}913 + 3{,}332}{17 + 17} = \dfrac{8{,}245}{34} = 242.5$, $s_W = \sqrt{242.5} = 15.57$

Step 3b. $s_{\bar{X}_1 - \bar{X}_2} = s_W \sqrt{\dfrac{1}{n_1} + \dfrac{1}{n_2}} = 15.57 \sqrt{\left(\dfrac{1}{18}\right) + \left(\dfrac{1}{18}\right)} = 15.57\sqrt{.11111} = 5.18$

Step 3c. $t = \dfrac{\bar{X}_1 - \bar{X}_2}{s_{\bar{X}_1 - \bar{X}_2}} = \dfrac{108.1 - 98.4}{5.18} = \dfrac{9.7}{5.18} = 1.87$.

Step 4.   Critical $t = {}_{.95}t_{34} \approx 1.697$; $t = 1.87 > 1.697$, therefore H_0 is rejected; $p < .05$.

(*If necessary, the sum of squares can easily be determined from n and s^2. Since $s^2 = \Sigma x^2/(n-1)$, then $\Sigma x^2 = s^2(n-1)$. Σx^2 can also be determined from the equation, $\Sigma x^2 = \Sigma X^2 - n\bar{X}^2$.)

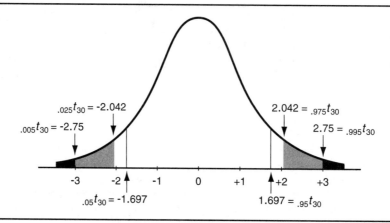

❖ **FIGURE 11.4** A central t-distribution with 30 degrees of freedom. Critical areas are shown for $\alpha_2 = .10$, $\alpha_2 = .05$, and $\alpha_2 = .01$.

ceeds the critical $|t|$, then $p < \alpha$, H_0 is rejected, and no error has been made. However, if $\mu_1 \neq \mu_2$ and $|t| <$ critical $|t|$, $p > \alpha$ and H_0 is retained as tenable—we will make a type-II error. Observe in Figure 11.4 that the smaller the probability of a type-I error (α), the larger is the associated critical value for t. In other words, there is a greater risk of a type-II error (β) at $\alpha = .01$ than at $\alpha = .05$. The probability of *not* making a type-II error is termed *statistical power*. Notice the tradeoff—the greater the risk (α) we take of making a type-I error (rejecting a true H_0), the smaller is the risk (β) we take of making a type-II error (failing to reject a false H_0); that is, statistical power is increased as α is increased from .01 to .05, or from .05 to .10, et cetera.

It is good practice to report probability values as accurately as possible. For example, rather than report $p > .05$, it is more informative to report $.10 > p > .05$. Better yet, have the computer perform the t-test, and report the actual p. Always reject H_0 at the most stringent level allowed by p. Even if you set $\alpha = .05$, you can reject H_0 at the .01 level if the obtained t-ratio exceeds the critical t for $\alpha = .01$. Also, as a reader of research reports, you are not obligated to operate at the same value for α used by the researcher. You may decide the 10 percent risk of a type-I error is more than offset by increased statistical power, and this could turn a reported "no significant difference" finding into a statistically significant difference at a lesser (and more reasonable) alpha level.

Quiz: Please answer True or False:

(1) When H_0: $\mu_1 - \mu_2 = 0$ is rejected, it should be concluded that $\mu_1 \neq \mu_2$.

(2) When H_0: $\mu_1 - \mu_2 = 0$ is tenable, the researcher is convinced that $\mu_1 = \mu_2$.

(3) Responsible researchers always use $\alpha = .05$ or $\alpha_1 = .05$.

(4) Operating at the .05 α-level rather than the .01 α-level will result in a greater risk of a type-I error.

(5) Increasing the risk of a type-I error, decreases the risk of a type-II error.

To increase the statistical power of a study, a researcher might consider (True or False): (6) increasing n, (7) relaxing α (e.g., from .01 to .05), or (8) always employing a one-tail test.

Answers: (1) True, (2) False, H_0: $\mu_1 - \mu_2 = 0$ is a plausible possibility. (3) False, not always, (4) True, (5) True, especially for small sample sizes, (6) True, (7) True, (8) False, only when a one-tail test can be justified logically

❖ 11.11 ONE-TAIL AND TWO-TAIL TESTS REVISITED

If it is conceivable that μ_1 may be either greater than μ_2 or less than μ_2, a two-tail test (i.e., a non-directional hypothesis) is necessary. However, if you are supported by cogent logic, you may declare that if the means do differ, the difference must be in the specified direction. You then use a one-tail test which has more statistical power (if your logic is sound), while holding the risk of a type-I error constant. Recall that the subscript for α_1 distinguishes a one-tail test from the more common two-tail test, α_2 (if no subscript is used, a two-tail test is assumed). In situations where we can exclude either the possibility of $\mu_1 > \mu_2$ or $\mu_2 > \mu_1$, we put all of the critical area of the sampling distribution in the upper tail and become less likely to commit a type-II error.

When a one-tail test is made, the mean of the group predicted to have the smaller mean is subtracted from the mean of the group expected to have the larger mean. This simplifies the procedures by allowing the critical value for t to always be a positive value. For example, if it is predicted that $\mu_2 > \mu_1$, the numerator of the t-ratio is $(\overline{X}_2 - \overline{X}_1)$ and not $(\overline{X}_1 - \overline{X}_2)$, even if the observed sample mean of group 1, $\overline{X}_1$, is greater than the observed sample mean of group 2, $\overline{X}_2$. Note that with one-tail tests, the observed $|t$-ratio$|$ is unchanged, only the critical t-value will differ. In the example in Table 11.1, we saw that a one-tail t-test with $\nu = 30$ and $\alpha_1 = .05$ has a critical t-value of 1.697. However, with a two-tail test ($\alpha_2 = .05$), the critical t-ratio increases to ± 2.042.

Note that the probability of a type-I error for a one-tail test is still .05—we will incorrectly reject H_0 in only 5% of the t-tests we make when H_0 is true, even though the absolute value of the critical value is smaller. When one-tail tests are appropriate, their use will be associated with fewer type-II errors; that is, more false null hypotheses will be correctly rejected. If one has not definitely committed oneself to a one-tail test before inspecting the data, one must resist the temptation to opt for a one-tail test later on. Otherwise, the reported α-level and the probability of a type-I error are spurious. Also, once you proceed on the basis of a one-tail test, you must resist the temptation to fall back to a two-tail test if the data show a huge difference in the means contrary to the predicted direction. The lesson is obvious, when in doubt, use a two-tail test.

Quiz: For which of the following situations could a one-tail test be appropriate? (1) Do children receiving balanced diets have better school attendance than children whose diet is nutritionally inadequate? (2) Does the study of geometry increase logical reasoning ability? (3) Does participation in group counseling enhance self-esteem? (4) If you notice that an observed difference in means would be statistically significant if you changed from $\alpha_2 = .05$ to $\alpha_1 = .05$.

Answers: (1) yes, (2) yes, (3) No, it is not impossible that peer feedback could reduce self-esteem—do you know people who think they are something special, but who are not? (4) Do not even think about it!

Two-tail tests are far more common than one-tail tests because both $\mu_1 > \mu_2$ and $\mu_2 > \mu_1$ are usually reasonable possibilities. For example, a new procedure, method, treatment, et cetera may be either better or worse than the conventional alternative. Girls may have higher or lower scores than boys on an achievement motivation inventory, but if a one-tail test were made (e.g., if it were predicted that $\mu_G > \mu_B$), the null hypothesis could not be rejected even if the computed t were -44.98, or any negative value. The result of an inappropriately applied one-tail test can be a red face, humiliation, ridicule, and a tarnished self-concept. When in doubt, never use a one-tail test.

❖ 11.12 *t*-TEST ASSUMPTIONS AND ROBUSTNESS

As listed in Section 11.7, there are three statistical assumptions that undergird the mathematical derivation of the t-test for testing differences in independent means:

1. *Normality of X's:* The observations (X's), both in population 1 and in population 2, are normally distributed.
2. *Homogeneity of variances:* The variance of the observations in population 1 and variance of the observations in population 2 are equal, that is, $\sigma_1^2 = \sigma_2^2$.
3. *Independence of X's:* The random sample of observations from population 1 is independent of the random sample of observations from population 2.

What are the consequences (if any) of using the t-test procedures when the data fail to meet one or more of these assumptions? When the t-test assumptions are violated, how closely do the actual risks of type-I errors match the nominal (named, stated or tabled) α-levels? The practical importance of these assumptions will now be considered.

❖ 11.13 NORMALITY

The assumption of normality is made, not because the distributions of many variables approximately follow the normal curve, but because of an important mathematical property of normal distributions. The mean and variance of samples from a normal distribution are statistically independent (the values of $\overline{X}$ and s^2 over repeated samples from the same normal population would be uncorrelated). However, since no empirical distribution would precisely satisfy the stated assumptions, we need to know the extent to which the actual and nominal α-values differ when one or more of the assumptions of the statistical test are violated. Naturally, since normality was assumed in the mathematical derivation of the t-test, researchers also assumed that unless the observations were normally distributed the t-test would not be a legitimate statistical option. Fortunately, in recent decades subsequent research has revealed that the violation of the assumption of normality does not nullify the validity of the t-test.

Figure 11.5 is based on research on the t-tests when H_0 is true (Boneau, 1960; Glass, Peckham, & Sanders, 1972; Hsu & Feldt, 1969; Shlomo & Blair, 1992); it gives the proportion of type-I errors (i.e., the actual α) when the nominal or stated α-level was set at .01 and .05. The dark areas denote the proportion of type-I errors when $\alpha = .01$; the grey areas apply for $\alpha = .05$. The various shapes of the population distributions are abbreviated along the baseline; for example, the "R/R" in the left-hand portion of the horizontal axis indicates that the two populations were rectangular in shape (platykurtic). The number in the upper portion of the bars gives the sample size, n (if only one value is given, then $n_1 = n_2$). Note that in the first two bars the actual proportions of type-I errors differed little from the nominal values of .01 and .05. The third bar of Figure 11.5 shows that when $n_1 = 5$, $n_2 = 5$, and both population distributions are skewed, H_0 will be rejected in ap

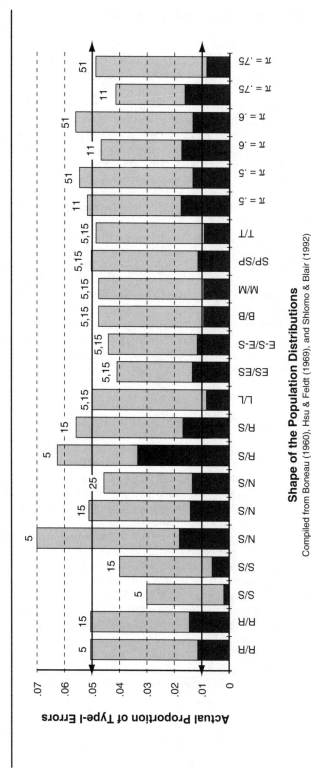

Shape of the Population Distributions

Compiled from Boneau (1960), Hsu & Feldt (1969), and Shlomo & Blair (1992)

❖ **FIGURE 11.5** Actual proportion of type-I errors when nominal alpha = .01 and .05. (R = Rectangular, S = Skewed, N = Normal, L = Leptokurtic, ES = Extreme Skewness, E-S = Extreme Negative Skewness, B = Bimodal, M = Multimodal, SP = Spiked, T = Triangular, π = Dichotomous)

proximately 3% of the tests with the nominal α-value = .05; the fourth bar reveals that H_0 will be rejected at α = .05 in about four percent of the tests when the sample size is increased to $n_1 = n_2 = 15$.

The bars for "N/S" (one population is normal and the other is skewed) reveal that with sample sizes of 5 somewhat more type-I errors than α stipulates occur (.07 vs. .05, and .018 vs. .01); yet when the n's are increased to 15, there is no practical difference between the nominal and actual alphas. For larger sample sizes the probability statements are even more accurate. Beginning with the bar "L/L" (both distributions are leptokurtic), the two sample sizes are different, $n_1 = 5$ and $n_2 = 15$; yet the actual and nominal proportions of type-I errors differ little. Note that, when the n's were 15 or more, the actual proportion of type-I errors was within 1 percent of the nominal value for alpha for both the .05 and .01 levels, a negligible discrepancy for practical purposes.

Observe that even when the dependent variable was a dichotomy (i.e., π = .5, .6, and .75) the nominal p was negligibly different from the actual π. Of course it is the central limit theorem working behind the scene that is producing sampling distributions that are approximately normal, and that accounts for the robustness of the t-test to non-normality—it is from sampling distributions that probability statements are derived.

The probability of a type-II error (power) is virtually unaffected by marked non-normality (Boneau, 1960; Schlomo & Blair, 1992). Consequently, the condition of normality can be largely disregarded as a prerequisite for using the two-tail t-test. The t-test is robust with respect to failure to meet the normality assumption. For one-tail tests, accurate probability statements require a sample size of at least 20 in the smaller group (Schlomo & Blair, 1992).

❖ 11.14 HOMOGENEITY OF VARIANCE

The assumption of homogeneity of variance legitimizes the pooling of the sum of squares and the associated degrees of freedom within both groups to obtain the best estimate of a common population variance parameter. If $\sigma_1^2 = \sigma_2^2$, then the expected value of both s_1^2 and s_2^2 is the parameter σ^2, that is, $E(s_1^2) = E(s_2^2) = \sigma^2$. If both s_1^2 and s_2^2 are unbiased estimates of a common parameter σ^2, it would be inefficient not to combine (pool) the information from both to achieve a better, more accurate estimate, s_w^2.

What are the consequences of using the t-test when this assumption of equal variances is not met? Is the t-test robust with respect to unequal variances; that is, will the obtained t-ratio give an accurate estimate of the probability of the sample data if H_0 is true? Several researchers have studied the empirical consequences of violating the homogeneity of variance assumption. It has been shown (Glass, Peckham, & Sanders, 1972) that the t-test is robust with respect to the violation of the homogeneity of variance assumption when $n_1 = n_2$. Indeed, for practical purposes we do not even need to test the assumption of homogeneity of variance when the n's are equal.

Figure 11.6 illustrates the effects of heterogeneous variance when the n's are equal and when they are not. The relative size (ratio) of σ_1^2 and σ_2^2 is given along the baseline; for example, for baseline 2, $\sigma_1^2/\sigma_2^2 = 2$; for baseline 4, $\sigma_1^2/\sigma_2^2 = 4$. The relative size (ratio) of the n's is given to the right of each curve.

Thoughtfully peruse Figure 11.6 and confirm the following conclusions:

1. When the n's are equal, the specified or nominal α-level is equal to the actual α-level. That is, the p-values of the computed t-statistic are quite accurate.
2. When the larger of the two samples is from the population with the larger variance, the

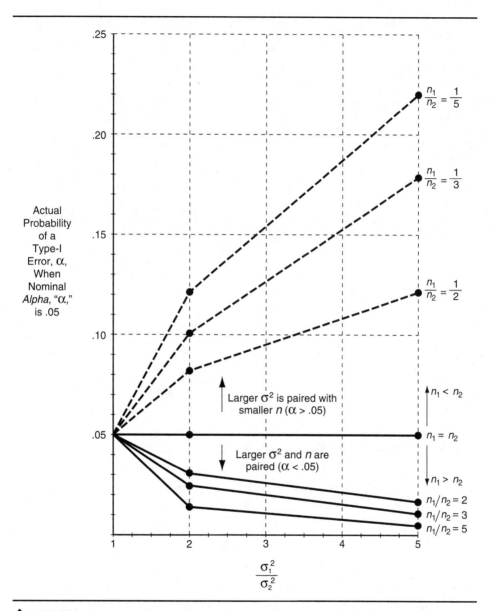

Actual Probability of a Type-I Error, α, When Nominal *Alpha,* "α," is .05

$$\frac{\sigma_1^2}{\sigma_2^2}$$

❖ **FIGURE 11.6** The effect of heterogeneity of variance on alpha (α), the probability of a type-I error, for various ratios of σ_1^2/σ_2^2 and n_1/n_2 using the two-tail t-test when the nominal significance "α_2" is .05. [data from Scheffé (1959) and Hsu (1938)]

nominal α-level > actual α-level. That is, when $n_1 > n_2$ and $\sigma_1^2 > \sigma_2^2$, the p-values based on the observed t-ratio are conservative. Again, if sample 1 has the larger n and the larger σ^2, the actual p-value < nominal p-value, and the probability of a type-I error is less than that indicated by α.

3. When the larger of the two samples is from the population with the smaller variance, the nominal α-level < actual α-level. That is, when $n_1 > n_2$ and $\sigma_1^2 < \sigma_2^2$, the p-values based on the observed t-ratio are liberal. Stated differently, if sample 1 has the larger n but the smaller σ^2, the actual p-value > nominal p-value, and the probability of a type-I error is greater than that indicated by the stated α-level.

The three lower curves of Figure 11.6 indicate that, when the critical t-values from Appendix B Table C are used and "α" is set at .05, the probability of rejecting a true null hypothesis is actually less than .05. For example, if n_1 is twice as large as n_2 ($n_1/n_2 = 2$) and σ_1^2 is five times larger than σ_2^2 ($\sigma_1^2/\sigma_2^2 = 5$), then a true null hypothesis will be rejected in less than two percent of such situations. Again, if n_1 is three times as large as n_2 ($n_1/n_2 = 3$) and σ_1^2 is three times larger than σ_2^2 ($\sigma_1^2/\sigma_2^2 = 3$), then a true null hypothesis will be rejected in about two percent of such situations. Hence, when $n_1 > n_2$ and $\sigma_1^2 > \sigma_2^2$, we are taking an even smaller risk of a type-I error than we claim when we reject H_0.[5] If we reject H_0 at the nominal ".05" level under these conditions, we need have no concern about violating the homogeneity of variance assumption.

The three upper curves in Figure 11.6 give the actual α when $n_1 < n_2$ and $\sigma_1^2 > \sigma_2^2$. When the larger sample has the smaller variance, the actual α is greater than the nominal (stated) probability of a type-I error. How much greater? In Figure 11.6, we see that if $\sigma_1^2/\sigma_2^2 = 5$ and $n_1/n_2 = 1/5$ the probability of a type-I error is not the nominal $\alpha = .05$, but .22! If $n_1/n_2 = 1/10$ or less, the true α would be even higher. Of course, $\sigma_1^2/\sigma_2^2 = 5$ are extremely heterogeneous variances that would be rarely encountered with actual data. However, situations in which $n_1/n_2 = 1/10$ or less are not rare. When a larger sample has the smaller variance, the true α will exceed the stated α (the stated probability of a type-I error). If $\sigma_1^2 > \sigma_2^2$ and $n_2 > n_1$, and we fail to reject H_0, do we need to be concerned about violating the homogeneity of variance assumption? Clearly not, since if we fail to reject H_0 when the true α is greater than .05, we obviously would not reject H_0 if the actual α were .05. For example, if $p > .06$ or $p > .10$, it is superfluous to inquire whether $p < .05$.

❖ 11.15 TESTING FOR HOMOGENEITY OF VARIANCE

The null hypothesis for homogeneity of variance is H_0: $\sigma_1^2 = \sigma_2^2$. If this hypothesis is true, sampling error is the only reason s_1^2 and s_2^2 differ. The ratio of the two sample variances is used to test H_0: $\sigma_1^2 = \sigma_2^2$; this ratio is the F-ratio, as shown in Equation 11.9:

$$F = \frac{s_{\text{larger}}^2}{s_{\text{smaller}}^2} \tag{11.9}$$

For simplicity, the ratio of the larger variance to the smaller is used. Critical values for the F-ratio are given in Appendix B Table F; the critical values are found by using the degrees of freedom of the two sample variances. Note that v for the numerator (the larger sample variance) identifies the correct column, and v for the denominator (the smaller variance) identifies the appropriate row. For example, suppose $s_1^2 = 100$ and $s_2^2 = 200$,

---

[5]We would rest easier with this added protection from making a type-I error if it were not for the fact that it also represents a greater probability of making a type-II error.

with $v_1 = 20$ and $v_2 = 10$; the ratio of the larger variance (200) to the smaller (100) is 2.00. The numerator and denominator have 10 and 20 degrees of freedom, respectively. In Table F, the intersection of these v's gives the critical values, but there is one complexity: *Table F is set up for one-tail tests* (Table F has other uses). Consequently, for testing H_0: $\sigma_1^2 = \sigma_2^2$, the α-values must be doubled, for example, .025 becomes .05. (We suggest that in the first row of Table F, you add a column "α_2," and double the values listed for α.) Now find that the critical value for the F-ratio at $\alpha_2 = .05$ is 2.77; since the observed F-ratio is less that the critical F of 2.77, H_0 is not rejected—the homogeneity of variance assumption is tenable. Table F does not contain values for all v's; if the desired value is missing, use the closest v available (note that the critical values for adjacent columns or rows differ little). In practice, F-tests (as well as all other statistical tests) are typically done using the computer, which will print out the actual p associated with H_0: $\sigma_1^2 = \sigma_2^2$. If $p < \alpha$, H_0 is rejected; if $p > \alpha$, H_0 remains tenable.[6]

❖ 11.16 INDEPENDENCE OF OBSERVATIONS

Independence simply means that the observations within or between the two groups are not paired, correlated, matched, or interdependent in any way. If observations in the two samples are paired, the t-test for dependent (correlated) observations should be used (Section 11.17). If variable 1 is a pretest and variable 2 is a posttest, the observations are not independent; if we correlate the two sets of scores, the correlation coefficient will rarely equal zero.

The condition of independence of observations is important; without it, probability statements pertaining to type-I or type-II errors can be seriously affected. For example, if in the data collection phase of the study, students are allowed to exchange answers or work together as a team, the data would not be independent and any statistical analysis of these data would yield spurious p-values (probability statements). With proper experimental control, dependency among the observations can usually be prevented or taken into account in the analysis (Hopkins, 1982).

Quiz: Please refer to Figures 11.5 and 11.6 when necessary to answer the following questions pertaining to the t-test. Given that $\alpha = .05$, estimate the actual risk of a type-I error under the following conditions, and indicate if a discrepancy is practically consequential or inconsequential: (1) $p = .02$ and all assumptions are met. (2) $p = .05$, n_1 is three times as large as n_2 ($n_1/n_2 = 3$), and σ_1^2 is two times larger than σ_2^2 ($\sigma_1^2/\sigma_2^2 = 2$). (3) $p = .05$, n_2 is three times as large as n_1 ($n_1/n_2 = 1/3$), and σ_1^2 is two times larger than σ_2^2 ($\sigma_1^2/\sigma_2^2 = 2$). (4) $p = .05$, data for sample 1, $n_1 = 5$, are from a rectangular distribution; and data for sample 2, $n_2 = 5$, are from a skewed distribution.

Answers: (1) Risk of a type-I error = .02 (2) Risk of a type-I error is approximately .02 and inconsequential. (3) Risk of a type-I error is approximately .10 and consequential. (4) Risk of a type-I error is approximately six percent and inconsequential.

The special case of nonindependence in which two sets of scores are paired will now be considered.

---

[6]There is now a test, the t-test (Glass & Hopkins, 1996), that does not assume homogeneity of variance. It has been rarely used in the past, probably because it is computationally onerous. Now it is incorporated into most computer programs for testing the difference between two means, and should be considered the "test of choice" when the n's differ.

❖ 11.17 TESTING THE NULL HYPOTHESIS $H_0: \mu_1 = \mu_2$ WITH PAIRED OBSERVATIONS

When each observation in group 1 can be linked to an observation in group 2, the two sets of observations are paired, dependent, and correlated. For example, when posttest scores are compared with pretest scores, the observations are associated (related, dependent, correlated) since pretest scores are almost always correlated with posttest scores; if correlated, they are not independent. A study was made to estimate the "practice effect" on the Wechsler Preschool and Primary Scale of Intelligence (WPPSI). Fifty children at age five were tested, and then retested two to four months later. Obviously there would be some correlation (ρ) between the two sets of scores. When observations are paired, Equation 11.10 can be used to compute $s_{\overline{X}_1 - \overline{X}_2}$, which is the denominator of the t-test.[7] The degrees of freedom for the t-test for correlated or dependent groups are $n - 1$, where n is the *number of pairs*.

$$s^2_{\overline{X}_1 - \overline{X}_2} = s^2_{\overline{X}_1} + s^2_{\overline{X}_2} - 2rs_{\overline{X}_1}s_{\overline{X}_2} \qquad \text{(11.10)}$$

where $s^2_{\overline{X}_1} = s^2_1/n$ and $s^2_{\overline{X}_1} = s^2_2/n$.

If there is no correlation between variables 1 and 2, Equation 11.10 for the variance error of the difference between means is mathematically equivalent to Equation 11.7a, which gives $s^2_{\overline{X}_1 - \overline{X}_2}$ for independent observations. Notice in Equation 11.10 that, as r in-

❖ **TABLE 11.2** An illustration of the t-test for paired observations ($n = 50$).

	Retest	1st Test
	$\overline{X}_1 = 109.2$	$\overline{X}_2 = 105.6$
	$s_1 = 13.3$	$s_2 = 14.8$
	$r = .91$	

$$s^2_{\overline{X}_1 - \overline{X}_2} = s^2_{\overline{X}_1} + s^2_{\overline{X}_2} - 2rs_{\overline{X}_1}s_{\overline{X}_2}$$

$$= (1.88)^2 + (2.09)^2 - 2(.91)(1.88)(2.09)$$

$$s^2_{\overline{X}_1 - \overline{X}_2} = 7.90 - 7.15 = .75$$

$$s_{\overline{X}_1 - \overline{X}_2} = .866$$

$$t = \frac{\overline{X}_1 - \overline{X}_2}{s_{\overline{X}_1 - \overline{X}_2}} = \frac{109.2 - 105.6}{.866} = \frac{3.6}{.866} = 4.16; \; p < .001, \; _{.9995}t_{49} \approx 3.50$$

$$s_{\overline{X}_1} = \frac{s_1}{\sqrt{n_1}} = \frac{(13.3)}{\sqrt{50}} = 1.88$$

$$s_{\overline{X}_2} = \frac{s_2}{\sqrt{n_2}} = \frac{(14.8)}{\sqrt{50}} = 2.09$$

---

[7]If the parameters $\sigma_{\overline{X}_1}$, $\sigma_{\overline{X}_2}$, and ρ are inserted in Equation 11.10 for the corresponding statistics $s_{\overline{X}_1}$, $s_{\overline{X}_2}$, and r, the formula yields the parameter $\sigma^2_{\overline{X}_1 - \overline{X}_2}$.

creases the value of the standard error of the difference between means $(s^2_{\bar{X}_1 - \bar{X}_2})$ decreases. Except for two differences (degrees of freedom and the equation for $s^2_{\bar{X}_1 - \bar{X}_2}$), the procedures for making a dependent t-test are the same as those for the independent t-test. The t-test for dependent observations is illustrated in Table 11.2 using Wechsler's IQ scores on fifty children who were retested two to four months following the initial test.

Note that the mean practice effect is highly significant—H_0 is rejected at the .001 level.[8] We have found that, if H_0 were true, there is less than one chance in 1,000 of obtaining a mean difference as large or larger than that which we observed (3.6 points) for $n = 50$; it is extremely improbable that the practice effect is zero. We confidently conclude that there is a practice effect. How large is the practice effect? Note that a highly statistically significant difference (e.g., $p < .001$) does not necessarily indicate a large or important difference in means; *we should not confuse statistical significance with practical significance*. If the n's are very large or if two variables correlate highly, even small, trivial differences in means can result in large t-ratios, and hence highly significant mean differences. Statistical significance makes us confident that there is some difference between the parameters, but we need to examine the size of the difference. To assess the magnitude of a difference in means, we need to construct the confidence interval for the difference in the two population means.[9]

Quiz: In a diet experiment (such as the weight-loss example in Section 10.9): (1) Explain why these data are not independent samples. Other things being equal, as the value of r increases, the value of the t-ratio __(2)__. To illustrate the effect from the pairing, analyze the data in Table 11.2, pretending that the two sets of scores were independent: $s^2_{\bar{X}_1 - \bar{X}_2} = $ __(3)__ , and $s_{\bar{X}_1 - \bar{X}_2} = $ __(4)__ . Therefore, the computed t would not have been 4.16, but __(5)__ , and the difference between means __(6)__ (would or would not) have been statistically significant.

Answers: (1) Since the same persons will be weighed both prior to and subsequent to the dieting program, the data will be correlated. (2) increases, (3) 7.90, (4) 2.81, (5) 1.28, (6) would not

❖ 11.18 CONFIDENCE INTERVALS FOR THE MEAN DIFFERENCE

Confidence intervals not only give some indication of the precision of the statistical estimates of population parameters, they also help address the issue of statistical significance versus practical significance. In Chapter 10, .95 confidence intervals were established for the population mean: .95 CI = $[\bar{X} \pm (_{.975}t_v)s_{\bar{X}}]$. Similarly, we can set confidence intervals for the difference in the two population means ($\mu_1 - \mu_2$). Confidence intervals are useful, irrespective of whether or not H_0: $\mu_1 - \mu_2 = 0 = $ is rejected. Equation 11.11 gives the .95

---

[8]Actually, a directional hypothesis or one-tail test could have been justified in this situation, since the likelihood that the parameter for the retest mean could be less than the parameter for the pretest mean seems nil.

[9]An alternate computational route yielding identical results is the "direct-difference t-test" for paired observations. This approach converts the two sets of data (e.g., the pretest set and the posttest set) to a single set of data (the set of difference scores), and from that point forward, this direct-difference method is identical to the one-sample t-test in Chapter 10 (refer to the pretest-postest weight loss example in Section 10.9). The steps in performing the direct-difference t-test are to determine: (1) the difference (X_d) between the paired observations for each of the n pairs, (2) the mean difference ($\bar{X}_d$), (3) SS_d, s_d^2, s_d and $s_{\bar{X}_d}$ of the difference scores (Note: $s_{\bar{X}_d}$ is another symbol for $s_{\bar{X}_1 - \bar{X}_2}$), and (4) the t-value, $t = \bar{X}_d / s_{\bar{X}_d}$ and then compare the computed t-value with the critical t-value. Reject H_0 only if the computed t exceeds the critical t.

confidence interval of the mean difference, $(\mu_1 - \mu_2)$. *Caution:* Note that the *t*-value used in Equation 11.11, $(_{.975}t_\nu)$, is the *critical t* for $\alpha = .05$ (not the computed *t*).

$$.95 \text{ CI for } (\mu_1 - \mu_2) = \left[(\overline{X}_1 - \overline{X}_2) \pm (_{.975}t_\nu) s_{\overline{X}_1 - \overline{X}_2}\right] \qquad \textbf{(11.11)}$$

Equation 11.11 is applicable to both independent and paired means (although the equations used to compute $s_{\overline{X}_1 - \overline{X}_2}$ differ). If a confidence coefficient other than .95 is desired, the critical *t*-ratio in Equation 11.11 is replaced accordingly. For the data given in Table 11.2, the observed mean difference $(\overline{X}_1 - \overline{X}_2)$ was 3.60 IQ points, with $s_{\overline{X}_1 - \overline{X}_2} = .866$ and $\nu = 49$ (the value for $\nu = 49$ is not tabled, but it differs conservatively from the *t*-value for $\nu = 40$; if you are a perfectionist, you can get the exact value from spreadsheet or other statistical software, or you can interpolate). Suppose we want to be very confident that we capture the parameter within our span. Let us adapt Equation 11.11 to obtain the .99 CI for $(\mu_1 - \mu_2)$:

$$\begin{aligned}
.99 \text{ CI for } (\mu_1 - \mu_2) &= [(\overline{X}_1 - \overline{X}_2) \pm (_{.995}t_{40}) s_{\overline{X}_1 - \overline{X}_2}] \\
&= [3.60 \pm 2.704(.866)] \\
&= [3.60 \pm 2.34] = [1.26, 5.94]
\end{aligned}$$

It is highly probable that the parameter for the true practice effect $(\mu_1 - \mu_2)$ lies between 1.26 and 5.94 IQ points. More simply, the retest mean IQ (μ_2) probably exceeds the population mean of the initial test (μ_1) by at least 1.26 points, and perhaps as much as 5.94 points. If the entire population of five-year-olds had been tested and retested, the retest mean would be expected to exceed the mean of the initial test by 1.26 to 5.94 IQ points.

Quiz: In the weight-loss example given in Section 10.9, it was found that $s_{\overline{X}_1 - \overline{X}_2} = 1.297$, $(\overline{X}_1 - \overline{X}_2) = 3.4$, and $\nu = 19$. Find: (1) the .95 CI for $(\mu_1 - \mu_2)$ and (2) the .99 CI for $(\mu_1 - \mu_2)$. (3) Given your result for the .95 CI, can H_0 be rejected at $\alpha_2 = .05$? (4) Given your result for the .99 CI, can H_0 be rejected at $\alpha_2 = .01$?

Answers: (1) $[3.4 \pm 1.297(2.093)] = [3.4 \pm 2.715] = [.685, 6.115]$, (2) $[3.4 \pm 1.297(2.861)] = [3.4 \pm 3.711] = [-0.311, 7.111]$, (3) Yes, H_0 is rejected since the .95 CI does not include the hypothesized value of 0. (4) No, H_0 is not rejected at $\alpha_2 = .01$ since the .99 CI includes the hypothesized value of 0.

❖ 11.19 EFFECT SIZE

When the dependent variable is expressed in a metric that is well understood (e.g., dollars, distance, time, temperature), the difference in means is expressed in numbers that are interpretable and meaningful. Even measures of IQ, GPA, and grade equivalents allow one to attach psychological meaning to the magnitude of a difference. However, when mean differences are expressed in raw-score units on tests of arbitrary length, it is no simple task to evaluate the magnitude of a difference. A five-point difference in means on a twenty-five-item test would become a difference of approximately twenty points if a 100-item test were used. The use of percent-correct scores (a linear transformation, one that does not alter the shape of the distribution) on cognitive and psychomotor tests is a step in the right direction, but percentage scores are not very useful on attitude and other affective measures where right-wrong scoring makes no sense.

In situations in which the metric of the dependent measure is arbitrary, the use of the *effect size*, a standardized unit to convey the magnitude of a difference in two means, can be helpful (Glass, McGaw & Smith, 1981). As in the famous *z*-score formula, the effect size expresses the obtained difference in means in standard deviation units:

$$\Delta = \frac{\mu_1 - \mu_2}{\sigma} \tag{11.12}$$

An estimate of the parameter Δ in Equation 11.12 is the statistic $\hat{\Delta}$ in Equation 11.13:

$$\hat{\Delta} = \frac{\overline{X}_1 - \overline{X}_2}{s} \tag{11.13}$$

where s is the standard deviation of the reference (control) group (or s_w).[10]

When one group can be considered to be a meaningful reference group—a standard for comparison—like a control group, its standard deviation should be used in the denominator of Equation 11.12. If neither group can be viewed as a control group, s_w should be used. For the data in Table 11.2, the effect size, $\hat{\Delta}$, is $(109.2 - 105.6)/14.8 = .24$; the point estimate of the practice effect is .24 standard deviations. To establish a confidence interval for Δ, the lower and upper limits of the CI for $(\mu_1 - \mu_2)$ can be expressed in the effect size metric by dividing each limit by s.

Quiz: Please refer to Table 11.1 in reference to the following inspirational questions: (1) The standard deviation of the control group was __?__. (2) The difference in the group means was __?__. (3) The estimated effect size, $\hat{\Delta}$, is __?__. (4) Comment upon your previous answer with respect to the significance of this effect size.
Answers: (1) 14, (2) 9.7, (3) $\hat{\Delta} = 9.7/14 = .693$ standard deviation units. (4) A difference of about .7 standard deviations is a large difference; differences of this magnitude have practical significance if the outcome variable is of any importance at all.

❖ 11.20 CAUTIONS REGARDING MATCHED-PAIR RESEARCH DESIGNS

When properly used, a paired *t*-test research design can be more powerful than a design in which the subjects are randomly assigned to treatment groups. If subjects are grouped into homogeneous pairs on a variable (such as IQ) that correlates with the criterion (such as reading performance), and then one member of each pair is randomly assigned to each of the two treatment groups, the resulting *t*-test for paired observations will have greater power than a design in which the same subjects are simply randomly assigned to treatment groups without pairing. This type of research design should not be confused with the conventional matched-pair design in which there is after-the-fact pairing.

Matched-pair designs have been widely used and misused in behavioral research. Their purpose is to match (pair) each person in group A (e.g., delinquents) with a person in group

---

[10]The estimator in Equation 11.13 is somewhat biased relative to the parameter in Equation 11.12. For *n*'s above 10, the bias is less than ten percent (Hedges & Olkin, 1985).

B (e.g., nondelinquents) on some variable (e.g., IQ), and then to compare the two groups on a dependent variable (e.g., reading ability). However, researchers are mistaken if they believe that the two groups have been fully equated on the matching variable. A researcher may conclude erroneously that a significant difference on some dependent variable such as reading proficiency is due, not to intelligence differences, but to the delinquency factor. The fallacies of the matched-pair design are the assumptions that matching equates the groups on a continuous variable (the matching variable) and that the groups do not differ with respect to other relevant variables. If the groups have substantially different means on the matching variable (and if not, why match?), the matching does not fully equate the groups even on that one differentiating variable, to say nothing of all the other unmatched variables. The pair members will each regress toward their respective group means when they are retested. In other words, if we immediately retest our delinquents and nondelinquents on another intelligence test, the nondelinquents would regress toward their mean (100) and the delinquents would regress toward their mean (90). It is beyond the scope of this book to develop fully the underlying rationale for this subtlety; the matching fallacy results primarily from measurement error and the regression effect. The practical consequences of the use of matched pair designs are the following:

1. The groups are rarely fully equated on the variable on which they are paired; hence, the matching variable is partially confounded with the independent variable.
2. The sample of pair members from at least one of the groups is rarely representative of its respective population.
3. It is likely that the groups differ on a host of other variables, such as social, psychological, physical, et cetera.

❖ CHAPTER SUMMARY

A hypothesis that specifies a numerical value for a parameter is termed a statistical or null hypothesis. The null hypothesis implies that any difference in the two sample means is attributable to chance (sampling error). If, assuming H_0: $\mu_1 - \mu_2 = 0$ is true, the probability of obtaining a difference in means as large or larger than that which was observed is very small—that is, if $p < \alpha$—we reject H_0 and conclude that $\mu_1 \neq \mu_2$. The smaller our risk of a type-I error (rejecting a true H_0), α, the greater our risk of a type-II error (failing to reject a false H_0), β. Conversely, we have greater power (i.e., we are less likely to make a type-II error) when $\alpha = .10$ than when $\alpha = .05$ or $\alpha = .01$.

When either $\mu_1 > \mu_2$ or $\mu_2 > \mu_1$ is logically implausible, a one-tail t-test (i.e., a directional hypothesis) should be considered. When used appropriately, the one-tail t-test gives greater power than the two-tail test, without an increase in the probability of a type-I error.

If σ_1^2 and σ_2^2 are known, the z-test is more powerful than the t-test and should be used to test the statistical hypothesis H_0: $\mu_1 - \mu_2 = 0$. Since the population variances are rarely known, the parameter $\sigma_{\bar{X}_1 - \bar{X}_2}$ is usually unavailable to the researcher and the estimate $s_{\bar{X}_1 - \bar{X}_2}$ must be used. The difference in a z-test and a t-test is in the denominator of the ratio: $z = (\bar{X}_1 - \bar{X}_2)/\sigma_{\bar{X}_1 - \bar{X}_2}$, but $t = (\bar{X}_1 - \bar{X}_2)/s_{\bar{X}_1 - \bar{X}_2}$. Sampling error appears in both the numerator and denominator of the t-test, which causes the critical values of t to be higher than the critical values of z (although the difference becomes small as the sample sizes increase).

Whereas there is one normal z-distribution, there is an infinite number of central t-distributions, one for each "degree of freedom" associated with the estimate of the common variance of the two populations involved (s_w^2). With few degrees of freedom, the t-distribution is highly leptokurtic (fat tails and peaked middles), but it quickly approaches a normal distribution as the number of degrees of freedom increases. In the limit ($V = \infty$), the t-distribution is a normal distribution.

The t-test is robust to a violation of the assumption of normality—the actual proportion of type-I errors approximates the nominal α-level. It is also robust to a violation of the assumption of homogeneity of variance when the n's are equal. If $n_1 > n_2$ and $\sigma_1^2 > \sigma_2^2$, the actual $\alpha <$ the nominal alpha. However, if $n_1 < n_2$ and $\sigma_2^2 > \sigma_1^2$, the actual $\alpha >$ the nominal α. The homogeneity of variance assumption can be tested using the F-test.

If the observations are matched or paired in some manner, the t-test for dependent observations should be used. Any positive correlation between the pairs of observations reduces the value of $s_{\overline{X}_1 - \overline{X}_2}$. Caution must be exercised in the interpretation of matched-pair studies since rarely are the groups truly equated on the matching variable or other relevant variables.

MASTERY TEST

1. Which of these are valid null hypotheses? Which two are identical in meaning?
   (a) $\mu_1 - \mu_2 = 0$ (b) $(\overline{X}_1 - \overline{X}_2) = 0$ (c) $\mu_1 = \mu_2$

2. Can H_0: $\mu_1 = \mu_2$ be appropriately termed a null hypothesis?

3. If the pretest weights of adults in a weight-loss program were compared to their posttest weights, would the two sets of observations be independent?

4. Which of these is not assumed for purposes of performing the t-test of differences between two independent means?
   (a) X's are normally distributed within both populations
   (b) $\sigma_1 = \sigma_2$
   (c) n is very large

5. Which options in question 4 are assumed in the z-test for differences in means?

6. When would the z-test rather than the t-test be used for testing a null hypothesis pertaining to the differences between two means?

7. When n_1 and n_2 are very small, the shape of the t-distribution is
   (a) normal.   (b) rectangular.   (c) bimodal.   (d) leptokurtic.

8. If *all* assumptions are met, in which of these situations will the central t-distribution differ *least* from a normal distribution?
   (a) $n_1 = 10$, $n_2 = 10$
   (b) $n_1 = 50$, $n_2 = 50$
   (c) $n_1 = 20$, $n_2 = 20$

9. The mean of the central t-distribution for any degrees of freedom is _____.

10. Which of these denotes an *estimate* of the standard error of the difference in means?
    (a) $s_{\overline{X}}$ (b) $s_{\overline{X}_1 - \overline{X}_2}$ (c) $\sigma_{\overline{X}_1 - \overline{X}_2}$ (d) $s_{\overline{X}_1 - \overline{X}_2}^2$

11. Does $_{.10}t_{60} = -_{.90}t_{60}$?

12. If $V = 60$, what are the critical values for t with $\alpha = .10$, $\alpha = .05$, and $\alpha = .01$?

13. The probability of a type-I error is *least* for which one of the following levels of significance?
    (a) .10   (b) .05   (c) .01   (d) .001

14. Other things being equal, the probability of a type-II error is *least* for which one of the following levels of significance?
    (a) .10   (b) .05   (c) .01   (d) .001

15. With $\alpha = .05$, will the critical t-value decrease in absolute value as n increases?

16. With $v = 60$, $\alpha = .01$, and $s_{\bar{X}_1 - \bar{X}_2} = 2.0$, how large must $(\bar{X}_1 - \bar{X}_2)$ be to require that H_0 be rejected? How large for $\alpha_1 = .05$?

17. If $s_1^2 = 50$ and $s_2^2 = 100$, when will the pooled variance estimate s_w^2 equal 75?

18. What is the square of $s_w \sqrt{(1/n_1 + 1/n_2)}$?

19. If with $n_1 = 11$ and $n_2 = 11$, the observed t-ratio is 2.0, which of these are correct if α is set at the .05 level?
    (a) $v_w = 20$
    (b) $p > .05$
    (c) $p < .05$
    (d) $p < .10$
    (e) critical t-value = 2.09
    (f) $.10 > p > .05$

20. Does an increase in sample size decrease the probability of a type-I error?

21. For a fixed value of α, does an increase in sample size decrease the probability of a type-II error?

22. Which of these are correct?
    (a) $E(s) < \sigma$ (b) $E(s^2) = \sigma^2$ (c) $E(s_{\bar{X}_1 - \bar{X}_2}^2) = \sigma_{\bar{X}_1 - \bar{X}_2}^2$

23. Based on the same data, the appropriate use of a one-tail test, as compared to a two-tail test will: [T or F]
    (a) have fewer degrees of freedom.
    (b) have a greater probability of detecting a false H_0.
    (c) have less statistical power.
    (d) have smaller critical t-values.
    (e) result in a smaller standard error of the difference between means.
    (f) result in larger computed t-values.
    (g) result in fewer type-I errors.
    (h) result in fewer type-II errors.

24. Suppose population variances are heterogeneous: $\sigma_1^2 = 300$, $\sigma_2^2 = 100$. In which of the following situations must the investigator be concerned about the assumption that the two population variances are equal when using the t-test for independent samples? (H_0: $\mu_1 - \mu_2 = 0$)
    (a) $n_1 = n_2$, and H_0 is rejected
    (b) $n_1 = n_2$, and H_0 is tenable
    (c) $n_1 = 50$, $n_2 = 20$, and H_0 is rejected
    (d) $n_1 = 50$, $n_2 = 20$, and H_0 is tenable
    (e) $n_1 = 20$, $n_2 = 50$, and H_0 is rejected
    (f) $n_1 = 20$, $n_2 = 50$, and H_0 is tenable

25. The assumption of normality must be tested before interpreting the t-test when
    (a) $n_1 = 5$, $n_2 = 5$ (b) $n_1 = 10$, $n_2 = 50$ (c) neither a nor b

26. For testing H_0: $\mu_1 - \mu_2 = 0$, in which of these situations can the assumption of homogeneity of variance be safely ignored?
    (a) $n_1 = n_2 = 10$
    (b) $n_1 = 100$, $n_2 = 200$
    (c) $n_1 = 5$, $n_2 = 15$
    (d) $n_1 = 50$, $n_2 = 50$

27. Which of these statements have been demonstrated empirically for the t-test? The t-test is robust with respect to the
    (a) normality assumption.
    (b) homogeneity of variance assumption when the n's are equal.
    (c) homogeneity of variance assumption when the n's are not equal.

28. In Figure 11.5 bar "L/L" with $n_1 = 5$ and $n_2 = 15$, both populations I and II were leptokurtic. What were the actual probabilities of a type-I error when nominal $\alpha = .05$ and nominal $\alpha = .01$?

29. Using Figure 11.6, if $\sigma_1^2 = 10$, $\sigma_2^2 = 5$, $n_1 = 10$, and $n_2 = 50$, estimate the actual probability of a type-I error when the nominal $\alpha = .05$.

30. In which of these situations are the observations correlated?
    (a) At age 5, the reading scores of 50 boys and 50 girls are compared.
    (b) Pretest and posttest IQ scores are compared for the treated group.
    (c) Forty students taking psychology are randomly assigned to either treatment A or B and $H_0: \mu_A = \mu_B$ is tested.
    (d) Delayed posttest achievement scores were compared with immediate posttest scores for all participants.
    (e) Grade-equivalent scores in reading were compared with those in math for 100 bilingual students.
    (f) Strength is measured at ages 10 and 12 for the same 21 pupils.

31. Suppose a researcher fails to recognize that the observations in item 30 (f) above are positively correlated, and the t-test for independent observations is used. How would these results differ from those from the appropriate t-test for paired observations? (T or F)
    (a) The value of $(\overline{X}_1 - \overline{X}_2)$ will differ.
    (b) The researcher's value for $s_{\overline{X}_1-\overline{X}_2}$ will be too large.
    (c) The researcher's value for the t-ratio will be too small.

32. For $\alpha_2 = .05$, the researcher in question 31 probably uses a critical t-value of ___?___, whereas the correct critical t-value is ___?___.

33. Even though the correct analysis has a larger critical t-value, will the correct analysis have more power for rejecting $H_0: \mu_1 - \mu_2 = 0$?

34. For each of the questions below, does a one-tail test seem to be appropriate?
    (a) Does going to college result in a change in measured IQ?
    (b) Does time spent in study differ for bright college students (high scores on college board exams) versus not-so-bright college students?
    (c) Do math majors score higher than English majors on the GRE quantitative aptitude test?
    (d) Does the reaction time at age 70 differ from the reaction time at age 40?

ANSWERS TO MASTERY TEST

1. (a) and (c), (a) and (c)
2. yes
3. no
4. (c)
5. (a)
6. when σ_1^2 and σ_2^2 are known
7. (d)
8. (b)
9. 0
10. (b)
11. yes
12. 1.671, 2.00, 2.66
13. (d)
14. (a)
15. yes

16. Since $(\overline{X}_1 - \overline{X}_2)/s_{\overline{X}_1-\overline{X}_2} = {}_{.995}t_{60} = 2.66$, algebraically $|(\overline{X}_1 - \overline{X}_2)|$ must be $\geq 2.66 s_{\overline{X}_1-\overline{X}_2} = 2.66(2) = 5.32$ to be rejected at $\alpha = .01$. For $\alpha_1 = .05$ where the μ_1 was predicted to $\geq \mu_2$, $(\overline{X}_1 - \overline{X}_2)$ must be $\geq 1.671(2) = 3.342$.
17. when $n_1 = n_2$
18. $s_w^2(1/n_1+1/n_2)$
19. (a), (b), (d), (e), (f)
20. No, but it decreases the probability of a type-II (β-error).
21. yes
22. All are correct.
23. (a) F, (b) T, (c) F, (d) T, (e) F, (f) F, (g) F, (h) T

24. (d); decreased α means an increased β and (e); increased α means a higher risk of a type-I error

25. (c)

26. (a) and (d)

27. (a) and (b)

28. Actual $\alpha = .05 =$ nominal α; actual $\alpha = .008$ for nominal $\alpha = .01$.

29. Actual $\alpha \approx .12$.

30. (b), (d), (e), and (f)

31. (a) F, (b) T, (c) T

32. $_{.975}t_{40} = 2.021$, $_{.975}t_{20} = 2.086$

33. Yes, some positive correlation between the measurements at ages ten and twelve will reduce the value of $s_{\bar{X}_1 - \bar{X}_2}$, and hence will yield a larger t-ratio for the same difference in means.

34. (a) yes, (b) no, (c) yes, (d) yes

PROBLEMS AND EXERCISES

1. An experiment was performed on the effects of "advance organizers" (introductory material that mentally organizes the material to be learned) on achievement in abstract mathematics. Fifty college students were randomly assigned to two groups: 25 subjects in group E studied a 1,000-word essay on topology after having been exposed to an advance organizer on the subject; 25 subjects in group C read the same essay on topology after having read a 1,000-word historical sketch of Euler and Riemann, two famous mathematicians. At the end of the experimental period, each group was given an objective test on the topological concepts. The dependent variable was "number of correct answers."

The following results were obtained:

Advance Organizer (E)	Historical Sketch (C)
$n_1 = 25$	$n_2 = 25$
$\bar{X}_1 = 7.65$	$\bar{X}_2 = 6.00$
$s_1^2 = 6.5$	$s_2^2 = 5.9$

(a) State H_0.

(b) What is the value of the pooled variance estimate, s_w^2? Compute s_w.

(c) Compute $s_{\bar{X}_1 - \bar{X}_2}$

(d) Compute t.

(e) What is the critical t-value if $\alpha = .05$?

(f) Is H_0 rejected?

(g) Determine the .95 CI for the difference in population means.

(h) Give a summary conclusion and estimate the effect size.

2. One investigator reported Minnesota Teacher Attitude Inventory scores for a sample of 14 athletes and 28 nonathletes; the findings are summarized below:

Athletes	Nonathletes
$\bar{X}_1 = 116$	$\bar{X}_2 = 119.5$
$s_1^2 = 968$	$s_2^2 = 1,050$
$n_1 = 14$	$n_2 = 28$

Test the null hypothesis at the .05 level that, in the population of athletes and nonathletes sampled, the two population means are equal.

3. A researcher performed an experiment to determine if the presence of pictures (the usual method) facilitated or interfered with young children's learning of words. Twenty pre-first-grade children were randomly assigned either to learn words which were illustrated with simple pictures (C) or to learn the same words without pictures (E). After several learning trials, each child was tested on his knowledge of the words taught. The means and standard deviations of the number of correct responses on the test trials for each group is given below:

Nonpicture	Picture
$\overline{X}_1 = 19.20$	$\overline{X}_2 = 11.3$
$s_1 = 7.93$	$s_2 = 5.79$
$n_1 = 10$	$n_2 = 10$

Test the null hypothesis at the .05 level of significance that the two groups can be considered to be random samples from two populations with the same mean. Give the .95 confidence interval for the difference in population means. Estimate the effect size. Is the effect size a precise estimate? Why?

4. A study of 215 Hispanic boys reported the following results for IQ scores on verbal and performance subtests of the Wechsler Intelligence Scale for Children. Test $H_0: \mu_p = \mu_v$ at $\alpha = .01$.

Performance	Verbal
$\overline{X}_1 = 91.1$	$\overline{X}_2 = 83.4$
$s_1 = 12$	$s_2 = 11.5$
$r = .65$	

(a) $s_{\overline{X}_1 - \overline{X}_2} = ?$
(b) $t = ?$
(c) Is H_0 rejected?
(d) Set the .95 confidence interval about ($\overline{X}_1 - \overline{X}_2$).

5. A sample of 36 first-grade boys were rated by their first-grade teachers on an "aggressiveness" scale of 30 items. The same 36 students were rated one year later on the same scale by their second-grade teachers. The 36 pairs of scores are summarized below. Was there a significant change in means with $\alpha = .10$?

First Grade	Second Grade
$\overline{X}_1 = 53.08$	$\overline{X}_2 = 51.33$
$s_1^2 = 156.8$	$s_2^2 = 108.1$
$r = .71$	

6. In a remedial reading study, 125 students who scored more than 2.0 grade equivalents below their current grade level participated in a remedial reading program. The pupils were retested after eight months in the program. The results are given below:

Pretest	Posttest
$\overline{X}_1 = 4.5$	$\overline{X}_2 = 5.9$
$s_1 = 1.8$	$s_2 = 1.9$
$s_{\overline{X}_1} = .16$	$s_{\overline{X}_2} = .17$
$r = .8$	

(a) Is a one-tail test justified? What is the critical t for $\alpha_1 = .01$?
(b) Did the mean increase significantly?
(c) Would $H_0: \mu_1 = \mu_2$ be rejected with $\alpha = .001$?

(d) Was the gain in means significantly greater than .8 grade equivalents? That is, can
$H_0: \mu_2 - \mu_1 - .8 = 0$ be rejected at $\alpha = .001$?
[Hint: $t = (\overline{X}_2 - \overline{X}_1 - .8)/s_{\overline{X}_1 - \overline{X}_2}$]

(e) Does this prove that the remedial reading program was resoundingly effective?

7. The effectiveness of a marital enrichment program was being researched using an experimental (E) group and a control (C) group randomly selected from the same large pool of couples who had indicated an interest in such a program. An appropriate length of time after the conclusion of the program, a measure of "unconditional regard" was obtained from both the E and C group couples. (The lowest scoring participant had the following bumper sticker, "If you love him, let him go. If he doesn't come back, track him down and kill him.") Do the experimental and control group means differ with $\alpha = .10$?

Experimental group scores: 80,   72,   51,   65,   50,   56,   60,   78

Control group scores: 47,   55,   62,   44,   60,   44,   50,   38

(a) State H_0.

(b) What is the critical t-value?

(c) Determine: SS_E, SS_C, s_W^2, s_W, and $s_{\overline{X}_1 - \overline{X}_2}$.

(d) Compute t and find p. Can H_0 be rejected for $\alpha = .10$, $\alpha = .05$, or $\alpha = .01$?

(e) Write the .90, .95, and .99 CI's for $(\overline{X}_1 - \overline{X}_2)$.

(f) Determine the estimated effect size, $\hat{\Delta}$.

(g) Make a summary statement about these data.

8. The reaction time for a random group of $n = 10$ totally sober, beer-loving college students was measured one-half hour prior to consuming three cans of beer and one-half hour afterwards. The reaction times, measured in hundreds of seconds, are as follows:

Student:	1	2	3	4	5	6	7	8	9	10
Before:	15	9	10	7	12	15	9	10	13	11
After:	20	25	15	10	16	26	15	16	20	18

(a) Does a one-tail test seem appropriate?

(b) Does an independent t-test seem appropriate? The correlation between the paired scores is .616.

(c) Compute $s_{\overline{X}_1 - \overline{X}_2}$ using Equation 11.10.

(d) Compute the t-ratio and use Table C to determine the associated p-value, $p <$ _?_ .

(e) What is the most stringent α-level at which H_0 can be rejected?

ANSWERS TO PROBLEMS AND EXERCISES

1. (a) $H_0: \mu_1 - \mu_2 = 0$

(b) $s_W^2 = 6.20$, $s_W = 2.49$

(c) $s_{\overline{X}_1 - \overline{X}_2} = 2.49\sqrt{(1/25) + (1/25)}$

$= 2.49(.283) = .704$

(d) $t = (7.65 - 6.00)/.704 = 2.34$

(e) $v = n_1 + n_2 - 2 = 48$; $_{.975}t_{40} = 2.021$. The precise critical t-value would fall between 2.021 and 2.008, the t-values corresponding to 40 and 50 degrees of freedom. We use the next smaller v-value listed in the table (i.e., $v = 40$).

(f) yes

(g) .95 CI = $[1.65 \pm (2.021)(.704)]$

$= [.22, 3.07]$

(h) $\mu_1 > \mu_2$; the observed means differ more than expected by chance alone: Estimated effect size = $(7.65 - 6.00)/5.9 = .28$. The advance organizer appears to facilitate achievement.

2. Since $SS = vs^2$, $SS_1 = 968(13) = 12{,}584$; similarly $SS_2 = 28{,}350$; $s_W^2 = (12{,}584 + 28{,}350)/(14 + 28 - 2) = 1{,}023.35$; $s_W = 31.99$ or 32.0; $s_{\bar{X}_1 - \bar{X}_2} = 32\sqrt{.1071} = 10.47$. $t = -3.50/10.47 = -.334$, which is not significant at the .05 level since $_{.975}t_{40} = 2.021$; $p > \alpha$ (also $p > .50$).

3. $t = 7.9/3.105 = 2.544$. Since $_{.975}t_{18} = 2.101$, the value of t is significant at the .05 level; $.02 < p < .05$. It is not plausible to view the two groups as random samples from populations with equal means. .95 CI $= [7.9 \pm 2.101(3.105)] = [1.38, 14.4]$. Effect size $= 1.36$. No, because the sample sizes are so small.

4. (a) $s_{\bar{X}_1 - \bar{X}_2}^2 = .670 + .615 - .835 = .450$, $s_{\bar{X}_1 - \bar{X}_2} = .671$
(b) $t = (91.1 - 83.4)/.671 = 11.48$
(c) Yes, $p < .001$.
(d) .95 CI for $(\mu_1 - \mu_2) = [7.7 \pm 1.972(.671)] = [6.38, 9.02]$

5. For first grade, $s_{\bar{X}_1}^2 = 156.8/36 = 4.3556$, $s_{\bar{X}_1} = 2.09$.
For second grade, $s_{\bar{X}_2}^2 = 108.1/36 = 3.0028$, $s_{\bar{X}_2} = 1.73$.
$s_{\bar{X}_1 - \bar{X}_2}^2 = 4.3556 + 3.0028 - 2(.71)(2.09)(1.73) = 2.2241$, $s_{\bar{X}_1 - \bar{X}_2} = 1.49$.
$t = 1.75/1.49 = 1.17$; critical $t = 1.69$; $p > .10$, or more explicitly, $.40 > p > .20$.
There is not a significant difference between the mean aggressiveness score at first grade as compared to that of second grade.

6. (a) Yes, $_{.99}t_{124} \approx _{.99}t_{120} = 2.358$.
(b) Yes, $s_{\bar{X}_1 - \bar{X}_2}^2 = (.16)^2 + (.17)^2 - 2(.8)(.16)(.17) = .0110$, $s_{\bar{X}_1 - \bar{X}_2} = .105$; $t = (5.9 - 4.5)/.105 = 13.3$, $t >$ critical t, $p < .0005$.
(c) Yes, $p < \alpha = .001$.
(d) Yes, $t = .6/.105 = 5.71 > _{.99}t_{120} = 2.358$; so, yes, H_0 can be rejected at the .0005 level; the increase in scores is significantly greater than .8 grade equivalents.
(e) No, the posttest scores are influenced by the regression effect. The fact that H_0 can be confidently rejected only indicates that something more than chance is influencing the scores. In other words, a significance test never explicates the cause for the difference, but only indicates that the difference is greater than can be reasonably attributed to chance (sampling error). It is the design of the study that allows the researcher to specify causes. (This same example was used in problems 33–36 of Chapter 8, in which the significant increase in posttest scores was totally attributable to regression.)

7. (a) H_0: $\mu_1 - \mu_2 = 0$
(b) For $\alpha = .10$, the critical $t = _{.95}t_{14} = 1.761$.
(c) $SS_E = 962$, $SS_C = 494$, $s_W^2 = (962 + 494)/14 = 104.00$, $s_W = 10.20$, $s_{\bar{X}_1 - \bar{X}_2} = 5.10$.
(d) $t = (64 - 50)/5.1 = 2.75$, $.02 > p > .01$. H_0 is rejected for $\alpha = .10$ and .05, but not for $\alpha = .01$.
(e) .90 CI for $(\mu_1 - \mu_2)$: $[14 \pm 1.761(5.1)] = [14 \pm 8.98] = [5.02, 22.98]$.
.95 CI for $(\mu_1 - \mu_2)$: $[14 \pm 2.145(5.1)] = [14 \pm 10.94] = [3.06, 24.94]$.
.99 CI for $(\mu_1 - \mu_2)$: $[14 \pm 2.977(5.1)] = [14 \pm 15.18] = [-1.18, 29.18]$.
(f) $\hat{\Delta} = 14/8.4 = 1.67$
(g) There is strong evidence against H_0; it is rejected beyond the .05 level of significance. We are convinced that the mean of the experimental group exceeded that of the control group by some amount between 3.06 and 24.94 points. The estimated effect size was 1.67—the mean of the experimental group exceeded the mean of the control group by more than 1.5 s (control group standard deviation).

8. (a) Yes, the one-tail test seems appropriate from common knowledge of the effects of beer.
(b) No, it makes sense to pair the two scores for each person; a t-test for paired data seems most appropriate.
(c) $s_{\bar{X}_1 - \bar{X}_2}^2 = s_{\bar{X}_1}^2 + s_{\bar{X}_2}^2 - 2rs_{\bar{X}_1}s_{\bar{X}_2}$; $s_{\bar{X}_1 - \bar{X}_2}^2 = 6.989/10 + 23.433/10 - 2(.616)(.836)(1.531) = 1.4660$; $s_{\bar{X}_1 - \bar{X}_2} = 1.211$.
(d) $t = 7/1.211 = 5.78$, $.001$
(e) Reject H_0 at the .001 α-level.

SUGGESTED COMPUTER EXERCISE

1. The first variable of the HSB data set is sex, where $1 =$ male and $2 =$ female. Determine if the genders have significantly different means in reading if $\alpha_2 = .05$.

2. For writing, math, science, and civics, do the genders have significantly different means with $\alpha = .05$?

3. Does the HSB sample have a significantly higher mean in reading than in writing with $\alpha = .05$?

❖ 12

Inferences about Proportions

❖ 12.1 STATISTICS FOR CATEGORICAL VARIABLES

Many research questions deal with proportions or percentages. For example, what percent of births are to unmarried mothers? Do the percentages differ by ethnic group or region of the country. Does the proportion of professors who are male (overweight, Hispanic, senile, sadistic, etc.) differ among university departments? Do certain groups differ with respect to the proportions of suicides, peptic ulcers, illiterates, unemployed, and so on? We now turn our attention to methods of inference for setting confidence intervals and testing hypotheses pertaining to proportions.

Unlike the dependent variables illustrated in Chapters 10 and 11, where the outcome measures indicated a level or degree of performance, the dependent variable in this context is *categorical* or nominal, such as gender, political affiliation, religion, occupation, marital status, whether a person smokes, has AIDS, or owns a handgun, et cetera (See Section 3.2 for a review of nominal measurement scales.) For example, in each of the following questions, there is an implicit hypothesis regarding a classificatory variable: Does the school dropout rate differ for males versus females? Do the reasons given for dropping out differ among ethnic groups? Has the relative frequency of anorexia changed in the past twenty-five years? Did the proportion of subjects who returned a mailed questionnaire differ among geographic regions sampled? Do adults from various religious or denominational groups differ with respect to the proportions who voted in the last national election?

❖ 12.2 THE SAMPLING DISTRIBUTION OF A PROPORTION

Suppose we wish to know: (1) the proportion of adults in the United States who carry a certain defective gene, (2) the proportion of children in Los Angeles County from single-parent homes, (3) the proportion of parents of children in the public schools of Colorado who think the public schools are doing a good job, or some other question of interest. For example, to answer question 1, a random sample of the target population is surveyed to find the proportion p in the sample with the gene. (Note: p, in this context, represents sample "proportion," not the p-value associated with a hypothesis test.) We wonder, how does the p-statistic differ from the population parameter π—how large is the sampling error $(p - \pi)$? Interesting questions begin to arise in your mind: What is known about the sampling distribution of p? How can confidence intervals for the population parameters be constructed from sample p estimates?

A sampling distribution of p is simply a frequency distribution of the proportions (p) from many samples, where each sample p is based on a random sample of n observations. To illustrate the theory, let us assume that the proportion in the population who carry the defective gene is $\pi = .50$, that is, one-half of the units (individuals) in the population possess the characteristic in question. Let us take a random sample of $n = 100$ persons, and find f, the number of carriers. Naturally, the sample proportion, p, is the ratio of f to n, that is, $p = f/n$. This p-statistic is an unbiased estimate of the parameter π. Let us do a thought experiment to illustrate the theory. We have an army of researchers who each replicate the study, and we collect the value of p from each researcher. If we make a frequency distribution of these many, many values of p, we will have a good approximation of the sampling distribution of p based on n observations.

For a dichotomous variable, the outcome variable X is coded 1 for an individual when the characteristic of interest is present, and 0 when it is not present. The proportion in category 1 is: $p = \Sigma X/n = \overline{X}$; thus, the proportion is a mean—a mean of a dichotomous frequency distribution comprised of units coded either as 1 or 0. The central limit theorem (Section 9.17) assures us that, regardless of the shape of the distribution in the population (even if it is bimodal, dichotomous, or any bizarre configuration), the sampling distribution of the mean (and therefore of p) will approach normality as n increases.

> **Quiz:** Proportions are used with categorical (nominal), not continuous, variables. Which of the following variables represent categorical variables? gender, age, math scores, ethnicity, weight, marital status, reaction time, pulse rate, years of experience, handedness, enrollment status, favorite statistic, family income, and poverty status measured as having income above or below the poverty line
>
> **Answers:** gender, ethnicity, marital status, handedness, enrollment status, favorite statistic, and poverty status

❖ 12.3 THE STANDARD ERROR OF THE PROPORTION

We now know that the sampling distribution of p is normally distributed when the sample size is large, but we also wish to know the variability of the distribution. If the standard deviation (the standard error of p) of this normal distribution can be computed, we will be able to construct confidence intervals for the parameter π, the proportion in the population.

Mathematical statisticians have proved that this sampling distribution of p when n is large has three important characteristics:

1. The sampling distribution of p is normally distributed.
2. Its mean is equal to π.
3. Its variance (the variance error of the proportion) and its standard deviation (the standard error of the proportion) are given by Equations 12.1a and 12.1b, respectively:

$$\sigma_p^2 = \frac{\pi(1-\pi)}{n} \qquad \text{(12.1a)}$$

$$\sigma_p = \sqrt{\sigma_p^2} \qquad \text{(12.1b)}$$

For example, suppose 50 percent ($\pi = .5$) of the individuals of the population carry a defective gene. If an infinite number of random samples with 100 observations are selected, $\sigma_p^2 = (.5)(1 - .5)/100$ or $\sigma_p^2 = .0025$, and the standard error of the proportion $\sigma_p = \sqrt{.0025} = .05$. This sampling distribution is normally distributed, and has a mean of .5 and a standard deviation of .05. You will be pleased to learn that concepts that you learned previously pertaining to areas under the normal curve can now be applied to sampling distributions of p. In fact, many questions pertaining to sampling distributions are remarkably similar to questions you encountered in Chapters 5, 9, 10, and 11.

Quiz: Given $\pi = .5$ and $n = 100$, answer the questions below that pertain to the sampling distribution of p. (1) In what percent of the samples will the proportion with the gene be greater than .55 ($p > .55$)? (2) In what percent of the samples will the proportion exceed .58 ($p = .58$)? (3) What percent of the samples will obtain a proportion (p) greater than .40? (4) What percent of the samples will yield a proportion of less than .45?

Answers: (1) $z = (.55 - .5)/.05 = 1$; so the area above $z = 1$ is about 16%. (2) $z = (.58 - .5)/.05 = 1.61$; so the area above $z = 1$ is about 5.48%. (3) $z = -2$; so the area above is about 97.86%. (4) The area below $z = -1$ is about 16%.

The approximate sampling distribution of p when $\pi = .5$ and $n = 100$ is shown in Figure 12.1.

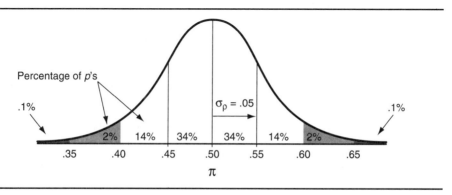

❖ **FIGURE 12.1** The sampling distribution of p when $\pi = .5$ and $n = 100$ ($\sigma_p = .05$).

❖ 12.4 THE INFLUENCE OF THE SAMPLING FRACTION ON σ_p

Contrary to our intuitive sense, *the accuracy with which the* p-*value from a sample estimates the parameter,* π, *depends almost entirely on the size of the sample,* and not on the proportion of the population that is sampled. A random sample of 400 estimates a parameter for a population of 100,000,000,000 almost as accurately as a sample of 400 drawn randomly from a population of 10,000. Common sense says that, if the number of cases in the population is large, one will need a larger sample for the same degree of accuracy. However, the value of N for the population rarely has any influence on how much sampling error is associated with an inferential statistic like p. Survey researchers often make precise inferences by drawing a random sample of .001 percent (or less) of the population.

There are some situations, however, in which the sampling fraction is large enough (e.g., $n/N > 5$ percent) to give a slightly more accurate estimate of the standard error, p, and therefore yield a slightly more precise confidence interval and a slightly more powerful hypothesis test. For example, if a random sample of 25 percent of the school superintendents in a given state is interviewed, and asked if they favor some proposal (e.g., the voucher plan, merit pay, etc.), the confidence interval using σ_p, assuming there are an infinite number of superintendents in the population, will be conservative and slightly wider than it needs to be. When sampling from finite populations, and the sampling fraction n/N exceeds 5 percent, Equation 12.2 (which includes the sampling fraction) gives the value of σ_{pf}, the standard error of the proportion for finite populations:

$$\sigma_{p_f} = \sigma_p \sqrt{1-(n/N)} \tag{12.2}$$

where σ_p for infinite populations is given by Equation 12.1b. When the sampling fraction is included in the computation, the magnitude of the standard error of a proportion decreases by the factor $\sqrt{1-(n/N)}$.

> **Quiz:** Given a population consisting of $N = 500$ persons with $\pi = .50$, and a random sample of $n = 100$ persons: (1) What is the sampling fraction? If N were assumed to be infinite, the value of the standard error of p (σ_p) would equal __(2)__; whereas, the standard error of p that considers the sampling fraction (σ_{p_f}) is __(3)__. In other words, when the sampling fraction was included in the calculation of the standard error of p, its value decreased by __(4)__.
> **Answers:** (1) $100/500 = .20$, (2) .05, (3) $\sigma_p \sqrt{.80} = .0447$, (4) 10.6 percent ($[1 - (.0447/.05)]100$)

As the sampling fraction (n/N) decreases, the disparity between σ_p and σ_{p_f} decreases. Figure 12.2 presents a visual display of the effect of taking the sampling fraction into account on the standard error of a proportion. Notice in Figure 12.2 that effects of the sampling fraction are trivial unless the sampling fraction (n/N) is about .05 or more.

> **Quiz:** Other things being equal, as the sampling fraction n/N becomes larger, the ($\sigma_p - \sigma_{p_f}$) difference becomes __(1)__. (2) Under what conditions will σ_p and σ_{p_f} differ negligibly?
> **Answers:** (1) greater, (2) when the sampling fraction, n/N, is very small, for example, $< .05$

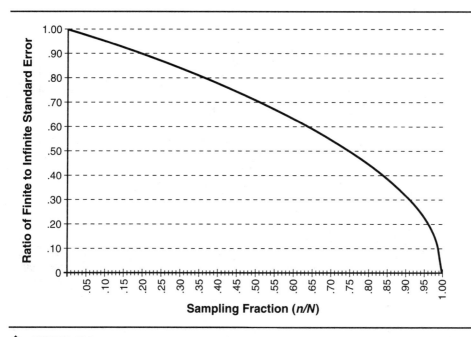

❖ **FIGURE 12.2** Relative magnitude of the standard error of a proportion for sampling fractions from 0 to 1.0 versus the assumption of an infinite population.

❖ 12.5 THE EFFECT OF SAMPLE SIZE ON σ_p

Sampling error is the difference in the sample statistic and the related parameter. The sampling error pertaining to a sample mean is the difference $(\overline{X} - \mu)$; in like manner, the sampling error pertaining to a sample proportion is $(p - \pi)$. Please observe that in Equation 12.1b, when n is small, σ_p is large and, consequently, the sampling error is large. When n is large, σ_p is small and, consequently, the sampling error is small. As the sample size *increases*, the magnitude of the sampling errors *decreases*—this relationship between the sample size and the magnitude of the sampling error is extremely important, and is true for all inferential statistics. Figure 12.3 gives the sampling distributions of p with $n = 25$, 100, and 400 when $\pi = .5$; the standard errors (σ_p) of these three sampling distributions are .10, .05, and .025, respectively. When the sampling distribution of p is approximately normal (as in Figure 12.1) and when σ_p is .05, about 68 percent of the sampling errors for p are less than $|.05|$; about 95 percent of them are less than $|.10|$. In Figure 12.3, note that when n is 25 about 16 percent of the samples will result in $p < .40$, but when n is 100, only about 2 percent of the random samples will yield $p < .40$. When n is 400, an outcome of $p = .40$ would be 4 standard errors below the mean $(z = -4.0)$ and would be expected only about 32 times in a million samples!

Quiz: Given: For n_1, $\sigma_p = .04$. Find the value of the standard error of p if: (1) $n_2 = 4n_1$, (2) $n_3 = 4n_2$, and (3) $n_4 = 4n_3$. Notice that when n is quadrupled σ_p is ___(4)___. When n is multiplied by 16, σ_p is divided by ___(5)___.

Answers: (1) $\sigma_p = .04/2 = .02$., (2) $\sigma_p = .01$., (3) $\sigma_p = .005$., (4) halved, (5) 4

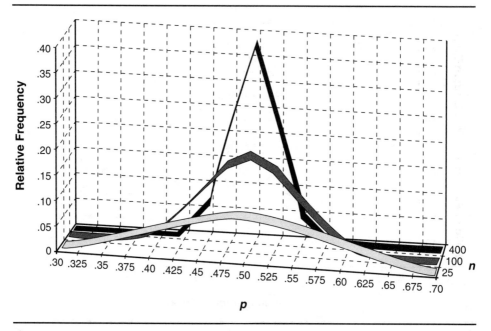

❖ **FIGURE 12.3** Sampling distributions of *p* for sample sizes of 25, 100, and 400 when the population proportion (π) is .50.

❖ 12.6 CONFIDENCE INTERVALS FOR *p* FOR NORMAL SAMPLING DISTRIBUTIONS

In an actual study, we will observe only a single value of *p*. Suppose π is .50 and *n* includes 100 observations, what is the probability that the value of the *p*-statistic for the random sample of 100 observations will deviate from the parameter π by .10 or more? Notice in Figure 12.1 that less than 5 percent of the *p*'s differ from π (.5) by as much as .10. In other words, if a interval of width $\pm 1.96\sigma_p$ could be placed about each *p* in the sampling distribution, 95 percent of such intervals would include the parameter π (which, in our example, is .5). Stated differently, 95 percent of the .95 confidence intervals [$p \pm 1.96(.05)$] will capture the parameter π.

What if we had used a sample of *n* = 2,500 in Figure 12.1? The variance of the sample proportions would then be $\sigma_p^2 = (.5)(.5)/2,500 = .0001$, and $\sigma_p = .01$. In other words, 95 percent of the sample proportions would be within 1.96(.01), or about .02, of the parameter π. A sample proportion based on 2,500 observations is rarely in error by more than |.02| from the population parameter. This illustrates the precision of modern methods of opinion polling and survey research if the *n* observations are a random sample. Television ratings and voting preferences at a point in time can be estimated quite accurately for the nation from a random sample of 2,500 viewers or voters. Of course, obtaining a truly random sample is easier said than done.

❖ 12.7 THE SAMPLING DISTRIBUTION OF p: AN EXAMPLE

Suppose Thor parlays his limited intelligence and a "cool" indifference to studying into a state of perfect ignorance. On any true-false question with which he is confronted, he stands a 50–50 chance of answering it correctly. Since the student is expected to guess the correct answer on one-half of the questions, the parameter π is .50. If the instructor gives a 25-item true-false exam, what is the probability that Thor will answer 60 percent ($p = .60$) of the 25 items correctly by chance alone?

The standard error of a sample proportion based on $n = 25$ observations when $\pi = .5$ is given by Equation 12.1a:

$$\sigma_p^2 = .5(.5)/25 = .01, \text{ and } \sigma_p = \sqrt{.01} = .10$$

The sampling distribution of p will be normally distributed with mean $\pi = .50$ and $\sigma_p = .10$. What is the probability that p in a single random sample of 25 items will lie more than one standard error above the mean of the sampling distribution? The probability of an observation, selected from any normally distributed variable, falling more than one standard deviation above the mean is .16. Thus, Thor has a probability of .16 (or about 1 chance in 6) of guessing his way to a score of 60 percent or more on the final exam.

Suppose a score of 70 percent is required for a passing grade. What are the odds that our knowledgeless Thor will earn a passing score. (Equivalently, what proportion of naive examinees who flip a coin to determine their answers will score 70 percent or more on the test?) A score of 70 percent is $2\sigma_p$ above the mean (50%); hence, the odds are only about 1 in 50 (2%) of achieving a passing score on the "guessing game." Do the low odds surprise you? Our intuitive notions about chance probabilities often are not very good.

If there were 100 rather than 25 items on a true-false (or two-choice) test, the standard error of the proportion, σ_p, would equal: $\sigma_p = \sqrt{.5(.5)/100} = .05$. The probability is only about .02 that our perfectly ignorant examinee would answer 60 percent ($\pi + 2\sigma_p$) or more of the items correctly. His chances of guessing his way to a passing score on the true-false test are infinitesimal ($z = 4$, from Table A: $p = .0000317$ or about 3 chances in 100,000!).

Notice that the sampling distribution of p on the 100-item two-option test is identical to that given for $n = 100$ in Figure 12.1. Of course, the same can be said for any other application in which $\pi = .5$ and $n = 100$. For example, if you tossed an unbiased coin 100 times, the probability of more than 55 heads is about .16 ($\pi + \sigma_p$), while the probability of more than 60 ($\pi + 2\sigma_p$) heads is only about .02. Since the distribution of p in the sampling distribution is approximately normal, we can determine from Appendix B Table A that the probability of 65 or more heads is extremely small ($z = 3.0$)—only about 1 in 1,000 (.0013). Offer your friends odds of 100 to 1 that they cannot toss 65 heads in throwing 100 coins (or tossing one coin 100 times), and you will soon become a millionaire if you have enough takers. You will have to pay off only about 13 times in 10,000. In 10,000 one-dollar bets, you will lose and have to pay $100 about 13 times ($1,300), but you will win about 9,987 times, and fleece your friends and relatives to the tune of $8,700! All gaming devices operate on the same principle, but with less unfair odds (often the "house" pays out $9 or thereabouts for each $10 it takes in).

Quiz: Suppose that your exam has 100 multiple-choice items, each with five options, and that you roll a die to respond to each of the 100 items. (1) What is π? (2) Compute σ_p (Eq. 12.1b). (3) Estimate the probability that you will answer at least 25 of the 100 questions correctly? (4) How likely is it that you will answer 30 percent of the items correctly?

Answers: (1) $\pi = .2$, (2) .04, (3) .1056, (4) .0062

You probably noticed in Equation 12.1a that the parameter π is called for, not the sample value p. Fortunately, if n is very large, little error results in using p instead of π in Equation 12.1a. For example, if $n = 100$ and $\pi = .5$, the correct value of σ_p is .05. Even if the sample proportion were .6 (or .4), the estimated value of σ_p would be .049, a negligible degree of error for research purposes. In other words, the error in using p in place of π in Equation 12.1a is not serious if n is large enough. How large is large enough? This very good question is addressed in Section 12.9 after some discussion of how π affects the sampling distribution of p in Section 12.8.

❖ 12.8 THE INFLUENCE OF π ON THE SAMPLING DISTRIBUTION OF p

From Eq. 12.1a, notice that σ_p is a function, not just of n, but also of $\pi(1 - \pi)$. Notice that $\pi(1 - \pi)$ decreases as π deviates from .50. When π takes values of .5, .6, .7, .8 and .9, $\pi(1 - \pi)$ becomes .25, .24, .21, .16, and .09, respectively. Thus, $\pi(1 - \pi)$ is a maximum when $\pi = .5$, and therefore for any value of n, σ_p is a maximum when $\pi = .5$, and for any value of π, $\sigma_p \leq \sqrt{.5(.5)/n}$.

The parameter, π, also influences the *shape* of the sampling distribution of p, especially when n is small. The sampling distribution of p is perfectly symmetrical only when $\pi = .5$; as π deviates more and more from .5, the sampling distribution becomes more and more skewed unless n is very large. Notice that when π is .90 p can exceed π by at most .10, but it can underestimate π by as much as .90. If π differs greatly from .50 and n is small, the sampling distribution is severely skewed; the skewness is positive if $\pi < .5$, and negative if $\pi > .5$. Figure 12.4 illustrates the degree of skewness in sampling distributions of p for π-values from .10 to .90 when the sample size is very small ($n = 10$).

> **Quiz:** When $n = 25$, as p deviates more and more from .50, the magnitude of σ_p __(1)__ , and the sampling distribution of p becomes increasingly __(2)__ . Even if π deviates greatly from .50 (e.g., $\pi = .90$), as the value of n increases, the magnitude of σ_p __(3)__ , and the shape of the sampling distribution becomes more nearly __(4)__ .
>
> **Answers:** (1) decreases, (2) skewed, (3) decreases, (4) normal

❖ 12.9 CONFIDENCE INTERVALS FOR π

The central limit theorem holds that the shape of the sampling distribution of the mean will approach a normal distribution as n increases. From Section 12.2, it is evident that p can be viewed as a mean of a distribution comprised of the codes 1 and 0. Consequently, the sampling distribution of a proportion will approach normality if n is "large enough."

How large is "large enough?" Some sources have offered guidelines regarding the required sample size, such as, $n > 100$ (Hays, 1988), or that both $n\pi$ and $n(1 - \pi)$ should exceed 10 (Moore & McCabe, 1989). However, such guidelines are overly crude and fail to give the necessary precision (Jaeger, 1984, p. 58).

As you may surmise from Figure 12.5, the sample size required for accurate .95 confidence intervals for π, using σ_p and the z-normal curve, depends upon the parameter π. Figure 12.5 gives the sample size needed for fairly accurate ($\pm1\%$) .95 confidence intervals

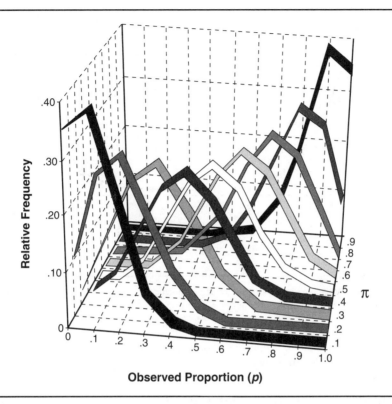

❖ **FIGURE 12.4** Sampling distributions of p for population proportions (π) of .9, .8, . . . ,.1, with $n = 10$.

for π in relation to the sample proportion, p (Cochran, 1977, p. 58). As you peruse Figure 12.5 you will discern that there are many applications for which the normal approximation is inadequate and for which derived confidence intervals are inaccurate. As indicated in Figure 12.5, for p-values in the .4 to .6 range, a sample size of 50 will have a sampling distribution that approximates a normal distribution, and will give accurate .95 confidence intervals, but p-values of .1 and .9 will require sample sizes in the neighborhood of $n = 600$.

Quiz: For the following p-values, use Figure 12.5 to estimate the sample size required to give a sampling distribution which is essentially normal: (1) $p = .05$, (2) $p = .10$, (3) $p = .20$, (4) $p = .45$.

Answers: (1) $n = 1,400$, (2) $n = 600$, (3) $n = 200$, (4) $n = 40$

Several procedures have been proposed for setting confidence intervals for π based on the binomial distribution (Hald, 1952; Burstein, 1971; Sachs, 1982; Hays, 1988, including the widely reproduced graphs from Pearson & Hartley, 1966). It has recently been demonstrated that all these methods yield confidence intervals that are too wide. Although beyond the scope of this text, the method proposed by Ghosh (1979) is very accurate, and is therefore the method of choice to determine confidence intervals for π for all values of p and n.

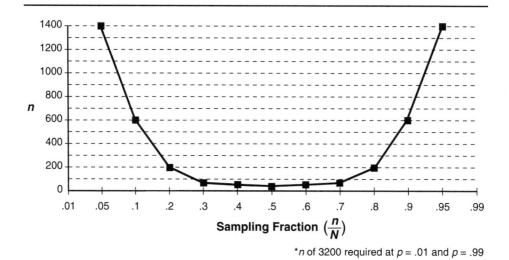

*n of 3200 required at p = .01 and p = .99

❖ **FIGURE 12.5** Minimum sample size (*n*) needed for a sample proportion (*p*) to warrant the use of the normal approximation when finding confidence limits on a population proportion, π.

(See Glass & Hopkins, 1996, Section 13.8 for additional details, formulas, and examples of the Ghosh method of determining confidence intervals for π.)

❖ 12.10 CONFIDENCE INTERVALS FOR π USING GRAPHS

The simplest method for obtaining reasonably accurate confidence intervals for π is to use charts. Figure 12.6 (for .95 CI) and Figure 12.7 (for .99 CI) are based on the recommended Ghosh method of determining confidence intervals, and if used carefully, the confidence intervals obtained using the figures can be quite accurate. Figures 12.6 and 12.7 do not assume that the sampling distribution of π is normal (or even symmetrical) and are appropriate for all values of *p* and *n*.

Suppose we asked a random sample of *n* = 100 registered voters a question (e.g., "Do you favor a line-item veto for the president?") and found that 80 percent (*p* = .80) favored the proposition. From either Figure 12.6 (.95 CI) or Figure 12.7 (.99 CI), we find the upper and lower limits for the confidence interval that corresponds to the particular *p* and *n* in question. Notice that the vertical lines represent *p*-values and the curved lines represent *n*-values. The lower limit of the confidence interval is the intersection of the *p*-vertical line with the lower curved line representing *n*, and the upper limit is the intersection of the *p*-vertical line and the upper curved line representing *n*. From each of these two points, one reads across to the left margin to find the upper and lower limits of the confidence interval.

As an example, let us find the .95 confidence interval for the line-item veto survey described above. First locate *p* = 0.8 along the baseline of Figure 12.6, then move up to where this line intersects the lower *n* = 100 curved line, and then to the upper *n* = 100 curve, and finally read across to the left margin to determine the confidence interval limits. Confirm that for *p* = .8 and *n* = 100, the .95 confidence interval is [.70, .87]. In other words, we

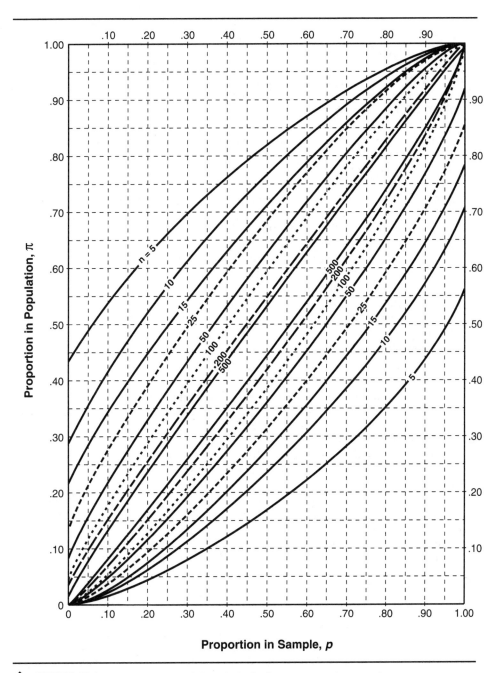

❖ **FIGURE 12.6** Graph giving .95 confidence limits for the parameter π from p and n.

can be 95 percent confident that, had we queried the entire population, between 70 percent and 87 percent would have favored a presidential line-item veto.

Notice that the CI is not symmetrical around $p = .8$, but a negatively skewed sampling distribution is indicated. The lower limit of .70 differs from the observed sample value of p (.80) by .10, whereas the upper limit of .87 differs from the observed p by .07. A confidence interval for π will be symmetrical around p only when p is .50 or when n is very large. When $p > .50$, the sampling distribution is skewed negatively; but when $p < .50$, the sampling distribution is skewed positively, that is, the skewing is always toward .50.

Suppose 25 percent ($p = .25$) of a random sample of fifty persons with anorexia are male. Using Figure 12.6, confirm that the .95 confidence interval for the proportion (π) of persons who have anorexia who are males is [.15, .38].

> **Quiz:** For the anorexia survey above: The absolute value of the difference between p and the lower limit of the .95 CI is __(1)__ . The absolute value of the difference between p and the upper limit of the .95 CI is __(2)__ . A comparison of these two differences suggests that the shape of the sampling distribution of p is __(3)__ . (4) With 95 percent confidence, we can conclude that if the entire population were included the percent who are males is somewhere between __?__ and __?__ percent. (5) If n had been greater than 200, the sampling distribution of p would have been approximately __?__ . [Figure 12.5.] (6) If p had been .50, rather than .25, even with a small n, the sampling distribution of p would have been approximately __?__ . (7) The sampling distribution of p is severely negatively skewed if __?__ and __?__ .
>
> **Answers:** (1) $|.15 - .25| = .10$ (2) $|.25 - .38| = .13$, (3) skewed positively, (4) 15, 38, (5) normal, (6) normal, (7) p is much greater than .50, n is very small

Figure 12.7 has the same format as Figure 12.6 except that the chart yields .99 confidence intervals. If $p = .6$ and $n = 25$, the .99 confidence interval for π extends from .36 to .81. The careful use of Figure 12.6 or Figure 12.7 yields confidence intervals that are sufficiently precise for most applications.

Suppose from a survey of a random sample of 500 registered voters in a school district, it was found that only 200 favored a bond issue.[1] Using Figure 12.7, we can determine the likelihood that the bond issue will pass if all of the registered voters turn out (assuming that the respondents answered truthfully and that voter attitudes remain unchanged between the survey and the vote). From Figure 12.7, we find that the .99 confidence interval about p ($p = 200/500 = .40$) extends from .35 to .46. Hence, it is very improbable that $\pi > .5$. (In the long run, 99% of .99 CI's contain the parameter, π). Suppose, however, that we found that only 100 of the 500 respondents indicated that they planned to vote on the issue, and 40 ($p = 40/100 = .40$) of those planning to vote favored the bond issue. The prospects for approval are not hopeless; the .99 confidence interval for π extends from about .28 to .53.

> **Quiz:** (1) Using Figure 12.5, does it appear that the sampling distribution of p would be approximately normal for the above school bond example where $p = .4$ and $n = 100$? (2) Estimate σ_p for this example. (3) Find $_{.995}z$ from Table A in Appendix B. (4) Write

---

[1]Notice in this example that we have assumed that all 500 voters in the random sample responded to the survey. In practice, this will rarely be the case, although the use of structured interviews or telephone surveys often yields data on 90 percent or more of those sampled. Mail surveys often have much lower response rates.

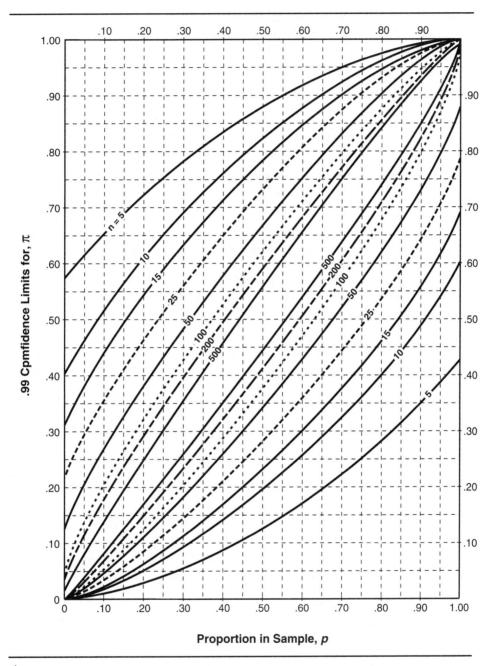

❖ **FIGURE 12.7** Graph giving .99 confidence limits for the parameter π from p and n.

the .99 confidence interval for π. (5) How does this .99 confidence interval compare to the one obtained by using Figure 12.7?

Answers: (1) Yes, according to Figure 12.5, if $n > 50$, the sampling distribution of p would be approximately normally distributed. (2) $\sigma_p = \sqrt{.4(.6)/100} = .049$. (3) $z = 2.576$. (4) $[.40 \pm 2.576(.049)] = [.40 \pm .126] = [27.4, 52.6]$. (5) From Figure 12.7, .99 CI $= [.28, .53]$; Both methods give comparable results.

❖ 12.11 THE *CHI*-SQUARE GOODNESS-OF-FIT TEST

Research questions concerning frequencies and proportions involving categorical variables are very common in the behavioral, social, and biological sciences. A statistical procedure which is particularly useful for categorical variables is the *chi*-square (χ^2) statistic; this statistic is applicable when the nominal variable is comprised of two or more categories.

The *chi*-square (χ^2) test has two principal applications: (1) the *chi*-square goodness-of-fit test, and (2) the *chi*-square test of association (Section 12.14). Both *chi*-square tests are used to determine whether the observed frequencies (O) in the categories differ significantly from the expected frequencies (ε). For the goodness-of-fit test, the expected frequencies are hypothesized on the basis of some a priori theory; this χ^2 statistical test assesses whether the distribution of observed frequencies differs from the a priori theoretical distribution of frequencies by more than expected by chance. For example, when examinees do not know the correct answer on true-false items, do they tend to guess "true" and "false" with equal frequency, or is there a response bias favoring one of the options? If chance alone is operating, 50 percent of the population should choose "true" and 50 percent should select "false." The *chi*-square goodness-of-fit test can assess whether the observed distribution of choices differs significantly from the hypothesized distribution, or whether sampling error remains a tenable explanation for any obtained differences.

The four-step procedure to test null hypotheses using the *chi*-square goodness-of-fit test is given below.

Step 1.	State the null hypothesis to be tested, for example, H_0: $\pi_1 = \pi_2 = .50$.
Step 2.	Specify the level of risk you are willing to take (α) of concluding that H_0 is false when it is true, that is, the risk of a type-I error. (If unstated, the convention $\alpha = .05$ is implicit.)
Step 3.	Compute the χ^2 (Eq. 12.3) statistic: For each of the J categories (or cells) find the difference between the observed frequency (O_j) and expected frequency (ε_j—the frequency prophesied by the a priori statistical hypothesis). Square this difference and divide it by the expected frequency. Compare the computed χ^2 with the critical *chi*-square value (Table D) to see if p is less than α. When the analysis is done by computer, the probability of obtaining a *chi*-square value as large as that which was observed is printed on the output. In the typical *chi*-square goodness-of-fit test, the critical value is based on the degrees of freedom—the number of cells minus one.

$$\chi^2 = \Sigma \frac{(O_j - \varepsilon_j)^2}{\varepsilon_j} \qquad \textbf{(12.3)}$$

The summation sign indicates that the value of $(O\text{-}\varepsilon)^2/\varepsilon$ is computed for each cell and summed over all J cells.

Step 4. Conclude that H_0 is false if $p \leq \alpha$, (i.e., $\chi^2 > {}_{.95}\chi_{J-1}{}^2$); if $p > \alpha$, conclude that H_0 is accepted as tenable.

A flowchart of this hypothesis testing procedure for the χ^2 goodness-of-fit test is depicted in Figure 12.8.

In one study of 200 college students, it was observed that 124 ($O_1 = 124$) of the 200 examinees guessed "true" to an unfamiliar question, and $O_2 = 76$ guessed "false." Do the observed frequencies of $O_1 = 124$ and $O_2 = 76$ differ significantly from chance ($\varepsilon_1 = \varepsilon_2 = 100$).

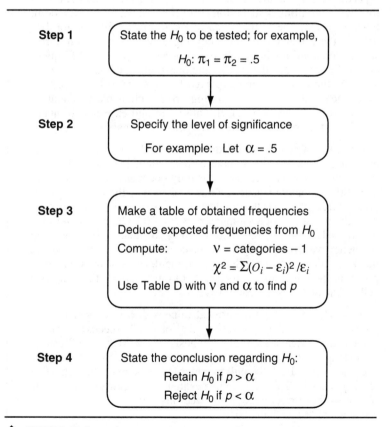

Step 1 — State the H_0 to be tested; for example,
H_0: $\pi_1 = \pi_2 = .5$

Step 2 — Specify the level of significance
For example: Let $\alpha = .5$

Step 3 — Make a table of obtained frequencies
Deduce expected frequencies from H_0
Compute: ν = categories − 1
$\chi^2 = \Sigma(O_i - \varepsilon_i)^2 / \varepsilon_i$
Use Table D with ν and α to find p

Step 4 — State the conclusion regarding H_0:
Retain H_0 if $p > \alpha$
Reject H_0 if $p < \alpha$

❖ **FIGURE 12.8** Flowchart of the four-step hypothesis-testing procedure using the *chi*-square goodness-of-fit test.

Step 1: H_0: $\pi_1 = \pi_2 = .50$

Step 2:   Let us set $\alpha = .05$.

Step 3:   Under the H_0, since the hypothesized (expected) proportion for both "true" and "false" is .50, the expected frequency (e) of both "true" and "false" is $200(.50) = 100$.

Category	O	ε	$(O\text{-}\varepsilon)$	$(O\text{-}\varepsilon)^2/\varepsilon$
True	124	100	24	5.76
False	76	100	−24	5.76
	200	200	0	11.52

Is the observed $\chi^2 = 11.52$ significant? Do the observed frequencies differ from the expected frequencies more than would be expected by chance alone? Do the discrepancies between the observed and hypothesized frequencies give strong evidence that H_0 is false? Table D in Appendix B gives selected percentile points for the χ^2 sampling distributions for differing degrees of freedom. For the χ^2 test, the critical area of the sampling distribution lies only in the upper tail of the sampling distribution, which corresponds to situations in which the observed and expected frequencies differ most. For the χ^2 test, the questions under consideration are, "Do the observed and expected frequencies differ more than by chance amounts?" "Is sampling error a plausible explanation for any differences between the observed and expected frequencies?" in other words, "Is the null hypothesis tenable?"[2]

The number of degrees of freedom in χ^2 goodness-of-fit tests is the number of cells less the number of restrictions placed on the data. For the present example, there was only one restriction, which was $n = 200$. In this *chi*-square goodness-of-fit test, the number of degrees of freedom (v) is the number of cell frequencies that are free to vary given that the total sample size is $n = 200$. Once we determine that $O_1 = 124$, O_2 is fixed ($200 - 124 = 76$); that is, only one cell frequency was free to vary in this instance. In most instances where the χ^2 goodness-of-fit test is applied, the degrees of freedom, v, is given by the number of cells less 1. In our example, there are two cells (True and False); hence, $v = 2 - 1 = 1$.

Step 4:   In Table D, we find that the critical value with $\alpha = .05$ and $v = 1$ is 3.84 (i.e., $_{.95}\chi^2_1 = 3.84$). The observed χ^2 of 11.52 exceeds the critical value of 3.84, hence the null hypothesis (H_0: $\pi_1 = \pi_2 = .50$) can be rejected at the .05 level. Indeed, since the observed *chi*-square value exceeds $_{.999}\chi^2_1 = 10.8$, the null hypothesis can be rejected at the .001 level ($p < .001$). The study indicates that, when college students do not know the correct answer to a true-false question, they are more apt to guess "true" than "false."

---

[2]Almost never is a researcher interested in whether the expected and observed frequencies differ by less than is expected by chance; that is, he or she is almost never interested in the lower tail of the central χ^2-distribution.

Quiz: Three candidates are running for the same office. The question of interest to the researcher is whether he or she could conclude with 99 percent confidence that there is a front-runner or are the three candidates equally preferred among the electorate? The researcher had enough cash to pay some starving graduate students to query a random sample of $n = 90$ registered voters. Apply the χ^2 goodness-of-fit test. For step 1, H_0: ___(1)___. For step 2, $\alpha =$ ___(2)___. (3) For step 3, given $J = 3$, $V =$ ___(a)___. The expected cell frequency for each cell if H_0 is true is ___(b)___. After the data were collected, sorted, and counted, $O_1 = 22$, $O_2 = 26$, and $O_3 =$ ___(c)___. The χ^2 component for candidate 1 (cell 1) is ___(d)___; for cell 2, ___(e)___; and for cell 3, ___(f)___; the sum of the three components is $\chi^2 =$ ___(g)___. (h) Accessing Table D with $V = 2$, the probability of the computed χ^2 falls between what two values? (4) For step 4, is H_0 rejected or retained? (5) If α had been set at .05 instead of .01, would H_0 have been rejected?

Answers: (1) $\pi_1 = \pi_2 = \pi_3 = .333$, (2) .01, (3) (a) 2 since the third cell frequency would be $(90 - O_1 - O_2)$, (b) $\varepsilon_1 = \varepsilon_2 = \varepsilon_3 = 30$, (c) 42, (d) $(22 - 30)^2/30 = 64/30 = 2.13$, (e) $(26 - 30)^2/30 = 16/30 = .53$, (f) $(42 - 30)^2/30 = 4.80$, (g) $\chi^2 = 7.46$, (h) $.025 > p > .01$ (4) H_0 cannot be rejected with $\alpha = .01$; we are not 99 percent convinced that H_0 is false, and therefore retain H_0 as tenable at this time and await further evidence. (5) Yes, but to play the game fair, you cannot modify α after the fact.

❖ 12.12 AN EXAMPLE OF A *CHI*-SQUARE GOODNESS-OF-FIT TEST

We well remember a winsome twelve-year-old lad who claimed to have a system for throwing 6 when tossing a die. It was not clear whether he believed in psychokinesis or that his method of holding or tossing the die caused the "effect." He was asked to toss the die 200 times. The results are given in Table 12.1.

These data could have been analyzed as a dichotomous variable with "6" and "not 6" as the outcome measures. However, since his theory was not thoroughly thought out, we used all six categories since perhaps his method might, unbeknownst to him, yield a more exotic or irregular pattern of chance-defying results. To the lad's father, the .10 level of significance seemed acceptable for this investigation.

For step 1, $H_0 = \pi_1 = \pi_2 = \pi_3 = \pi_4 = \pi_5 = \pi_6 = 1/6$ or .167.

For step 2, α is set at .10 to give more statistical power to detect and reject false null hypotheses.

For step 3, as indicated in Table 12.1, $\chi^2 = 2.62$. The degrees of freedom in this application are $V = 6 - 1 = 5$. From Table D, the computed $\chi^2 = 2.62$ is off the table to the left of

❖ **TABLE 12.1** A computational illustration of a χ^2 goodness-of-fit test using $n = 200$ tosses of a die.

RESULT	O	ε	$(O-\varepsilon)$	$(O-\varepsilon)^2/\varepsilon$
1	34	33.33	.67	.013
2	36	33.33	2.67	.214
3	26	33.33	−7.33	1.612
4	36	33.33	2.67	.214
5	31	33.33	−2.33	.163
6	37	33.33	3.67	.404
	200	199.98		2.620

P_{50}, hence $p > .50$. Sadly, the null hypothesis must be retained as tenable at the .10 level of significance, indeed a computed $\chi^2 = 2.62$ would occur more than 50 percent of the time by chance alone. However, the esoteric statistical test failed to convince the determined lad ("I just had an unlucky streak!"). Alas, another failure of behavioral research and another promising prospect for Las Vegas!

❖ 12.13 *CHI*-SQUARE GOODNESS-OF-FIT TEST OF NORMALITY

The *chi*-square goodness-of-fit test compares any set of observed frequencies (or proportions) with any theoretical distribution to detect if the discrepancies between theoretical and observed frequencies exceed those expected due to randomness (sampling error) alone. This test can be used to test whether an empirical distribution departs significantly from a normal curve. For example, consider the reading scores of the HSB data set as listed in the Table I of Appendix B. Let us examine whether it is defensible to consider these $n = 200$ reading T-scores as randomly selected from a normal population with $\mu = 50$ and $\sigma = 10$.[3]

To determine the expected frequencies, the normal curve is partitioned into a number (the actual number is arbitrary, but should be at least five) of score segments or "slices." Suppose we take T-score segments of five units in width as indicated in Table 12.2. The T-score ranges are converted to their corresponding z-score ranges $[z = (T - 50)/10]$ to expedite finding the areas for each T-range. The areas of the normal curve below a z-score (Section 5.11) and the area between two z-scores (Section 5.13) can be obtained by referring to Table A. For example, the area below $z = -1.75$ is .0401, so the expected frequency of this category is $200(.0401) = 8.0$. The proportional area of the T-range from 32.5 to 37.5 would be $(.1056 - .0401) = .0655$, so the expected frequency in segment 2 = $200(.0655) = 13.1$, and so forth.

❖ **TABLE 12.2** The χ^2 goodness-of-fit test to test the hypothesis that the HSB data Reading scores were selected from a normal distribution with $\mu = 50$ and $\sigma = 10$.

Segment	T-range	z-range	ε	o	$(o-\varepsilon)^2/\varepsilon$
1	$T < 32.5$	$z < -1.75$	8.0	2	4.5
2	32.5–37.5	−1.25–(−1.75)	13.1	12	0.1
3	37.5–42.5	−0.75–(−1.25)	24.2	23	0.1
4	42.5–47.5	−0.25–(−0.75)	34.9	45	2.9
5	47.5–52.5	0.25–(−0.25)	39.5	33	1.1
6	52.5–57.5	0.75–0.25	34.9	29	1.0
7	57.5–62.5	1.25–0.75	24.2	10	8.3
8	62.5–67.5	1.75–1.25	13.1	26	12.7
9	$T > 67.5$	$z > 1.75$	8.0	20	18.0
			200	200	48.7

---

[3]This is not the same as testing whether the observations are normally distributed about their own mean. To respond to that question, we would compute the sample mean and sample standard deviation from the obtained observations, and use these statistics to partition the data into "segments." The computation of the sample mean and sample standard deviation uses two degrees of freedom and imposes two additional restrictions on the data; thus, the degrees of freedom would be the number of categories or "segments" minus three.

The observed frequencies of the HSB data reading scores falling in the nine *T*-range categories are listed in Table 12.2.

For step 1, H_0: $\pi_1 = \pi_9 = .0401$, $\pi_2 = \pi_8 = .0655$, $\pi_3 = \pi_7 = .1210$, $\pi_4 = \pi_6 = .1747$, $\pi_5 = .1974$. For step 2, set $\alpha = .01$.

For step 3, as indicated in Table 12.2, the χ^2 components add up to $\chi^2 = 48.7$. The number of degrees of freedom is 8 ($n_{cells} - 1$). The probability of a computed $\chi^2 = 48.7$ with $v = 8$, according to Table D, is $p < .001$.

For step 4, since $p < .001$, H_0 is rejected at the .001 level. It is concluded that these reading scores do not represent a normally distributed population with $\mu = 50$ and $\sigma = 10$. By perusing the χ^2 components in Table 12.2, it is rather obvious that the discrepancies between expected and observed frequencies in the tail areas are responsible for the huge χ^2 statistic—there are higher observed frequencies than expected in the upper tail region, but vice versa in the lower tail region.

❖ 12.14 THE *CHI*-SQUARE TEST OF ASSOCIATION[4]

Suppose you are interested in the issue of merit pay for teachers. To determine whether the proportions for and against merit pay are equal among teachers, you could use the χ^2 good-ness-of-fit test. To respond to the same question among parents, or among principals, or among any other defined group, you could use the χ^2 goodness-of-fit test for each target group. However, to respond to the question of whether attitude toward merit pay is related to, or is independent of, the role of the educator, you would apply the χ^2 test of association. As another example, in the HSB data set, you could apply the χ^2 test of association to the question, "Is gender related to the type of school program (general, academic, or vocational)?" In other words, when you wish to determine whether two categorical variables are related or whether they are independent, the χ^2 test of association is the statistical method of choice. Other illustrative questions that call for the *chi*-square test of association: Is left-handedness more common in boys than in girls? Is the drop-out rate greater among certain ethnic groups than others? Is there a home field advantage in sports—is the proportion of wins independent of the site of the game? Is cognitive style related to gender? Is infant mortality related to SES? Is the proportion of males who are HIV positive related to the region of the country.

The four-step procedure to test null hypotheses using the *chi*-square test of association with J rows (categories of variable 1) and K columns (categories of variable 2) is given below. Due to the unfamiliar symbols herein, you will probably need to work through a couple of examples before you feel comfortable.

> **Step 1.** State the statistical hypothesis to be tested in a narrative format (e.g., political affiliation is unrelated to race). (Although H_0 could be expressed in symbols using π_{11}, π_{12}, π_{13}, et cetera, it is awkward and confusing when there are more than two categories comprising the variables.)

---

[4]A distinction is sometimes made between a χ^2 test of independence and a χ^2 test of homogeneity. The latter fixes the number of observations sampled within each category; the former classifies observations into cells after a sample has been drawn. The computation and practical interpretation of each procedure are identical. We use the "test of association" to subsume both types, and we will not make the subtle distinction between them.

Step 2.   Specify the level of risk you are willing to take (α) of incorrectly concluding that H_0 is false when it is true, that is, a type-I error. If the level of risk is unstated, a .05 risk is conventional.

Step 3.   a) Construct a contingency table of cell frequencies; find the number of observations falling in each cell (O_{jk}), each row ($O_{j.}$), and each column ($O_{.k}$).

b) Compute the degrees of freedom, that is, the number of cell frequencies free to vary given the row and column marginal totals. This can be computed by Equation 12.4—the number of rows less one ($J - 1$) multiplied by the number of columns less one ($K - 1$). For the degrees of freedom for the χ^2 test of association:

$$v = (J - 1)(K - 1) \qquad \textbf{(12.4)}$$

c) Compute the expected cell frequencies. When H_0 is true, the cell frequencies of each column are expected to be distributed in the same proportions as the row frequency totals. These expected frequencies for the χ^2 test of association can be computed by Equation 12.5:

$$\varepsilon_{jk} = \frac{(n_{j.})(n_{.k})}{n_{..}} \qquad \textbf{(12.5)}$$

This equation is mathematically equivalent to saying that the cell expected frequency (ε_{jk}) is to the column sum ($n_{.j}$) as its row sum ($n_{j.}$) is to the grand total ($n_{..}$).

d) Compute the χ^2 statistic (Eq. 12.6).

$$\chi^2 = \sum_j \sum_k \frac{(O_{jk} - \varepsilon_{jk})^2}{\varepsilon_{jk}} \qquad \textbf{(12.6)}$$

The summation signs indicate that the value of $(O-\varepsilon)^2/\varepsilon$ is computed for each cell, and then summed over all JK cells.

e) Then, knowing α and v, you can access the χ^2 sampling distribution in Table D to determine the probability (p) of the computed χ^2 statistic if H_0 were true.

Step 4.   Conclude that H_0 is false if $p \leq \alpha$; if $p > \alpha$, conclude that H_0 is tenable.

This procedure is summarized by the flowchart of Figure 12.9. Notice the many similarities between this flowchart for the χ^2 test of association and Figure 12.8, the flowchart for the χ^2 goodness-of-fit test.

Let us work through an example to clarify the above four-step procedure. Among the data included in the HSB data set, there are several categorical or classificatory variables such as gender, SES (socio-economic status), race, type of school program (general, academic, or vocational), and type of school (private or public). Suppose we are curious as to whether gender is related to type of school program (general, academic, or vocational) among high school students. The χ^2 test of association would be applicable to determine if the two categorical variables (sex and type of school program) are independent or unrelated to each other. To test the null hypothesis that gender is unrelated to type of school program using the χ^2 test of association, we can follow the four-step procedure presented above. Although in practice the analyses are usually done using the computer, the process can best be understood if we follow through an example by hand.

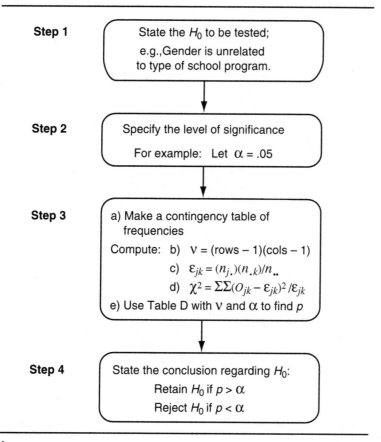

Step 1

State the H_0 to be tested;

e.g., Gender is unrelated to type of school program.

Step 2

Specify the level of significance

For example: Let $\alpha = .05$

Step 3

a) Make a contingency table of frequencies

Compute: b) $\nu = (\text{rows} - 1)(\text{cols} - 1)$

c) $\varepsilon_{jk} = (n_{j.})(n_{.k})/n_{..}$

d) $\chi^2 = \Sigma\Sigma(O_{jk} - \varepsilon_{jk})^2/\varepsilon_{jk}$

e) Use Table D with ν and α to find p

Step 4

State the conclusion regarding H_0:

Retain H_0 if $p > \alpha$

Reject H_0 if $p < \alpha$

❖ **FIGURE 12.9** Flowchart of the four-step hypothesis-testing procedure using the *chi*-square test of association.

Step 1. The null hypothesis for this χ^2 statistical test expressed in a narrative form is that gender and type of school program are unrelated. Stated differently: There is no relationship between gender and type of school program. Alternately, the null hypothesis could be expressed in symbols, H_0: $\pi_{11} = \pi_{12} = \pi_{13}$. That is, the proportions of males (or of females) in the general, academic, and vocational programs are equal. The use of symbols, however, becomes unwieldy when there are three are more rows and columns.

Step 2. Let us opt for $\alpha = .05$.

Step 3. a) The computer was used to obtain the observed cell frequencies by specifying how many males were in each of the three programs and how many females were in each of the three programs. The obtained frequencies are displayed in Table 12.3.

b) $v = (J - 1)(K - 1) = (2 - 1)(3 - 1) = 2$.

c) The expected cell frequencies for row 1 (males) are:

$\varepsilon_{11} = (n_{1.})(n_{.1})/n_{..} = (91)(45)/200 = 20.5$

$\varepsilon_{12} = (n_{1.})(n_{.2})/n_{..} = (91)(105)/200 = 47.8$

$\varepsilon_{13} = (n_{1.})(n_{.3})/n_{..} = (91)(50)/200 = 22.8$

The expected cell frequencies for row 2 (females) are:

$\varepsilon_{21} = (n_{2.})(n_{.1})/n_{..} = (109)(45)/200 = 24.5$

$\varepsilon_{22} = (n_{2.})(n_{.2})/n_{..} = (109)(105)/200 = 57.2$

$\varepsilon_{23} = (n_{2.})(n_{.3})/n_{..} = (109)(50)/200 = 27.3$

For the expected cell frequencies, notice in Table 12.3 that the male-to-female ratios of the expected frequencies for all three columns are equal to the male-to-female ratio of the total sample, that is, 91/109 = 20.48/24.52 = 47.77/57.23 = 22.75/27.25 = .835.

d) $\chi^2 = (21 - 20.48)^2/20.48 + (47 - 47.77)^2/47.77 + (23 - 22.75)^2/22.75 + (24 - 24.52)^2/24.52 + (58 - 57.23)^2/57.23 + (27 - 27.25)^2/27.25 = .051$.

e) From Appendix B Table D: $_{.50}\chi_2^2 = 1.39$, thus $p > .50$.

Step 4. The computed χ^2 of .051 falls below P_{50}, that is, $p > .50$. Since $p > \alpha$, H_0 is retained as tenable. The hypothesis that gender is not related to the type of school program survives the challenge and remains credible. These data fail to give any basis for concluding that gender is associated with the type of school program.[5]

[5]At one time it was thought that a chi-square test should not be used unless the minimum expected frequency exceeded 5 in each cell. Several studies (Roscoe & Byars, 1971; Conover, 1974; Camilli & Hopkins, 1978, 1979) have shown that the chi-square test works well even when the average expected frequency is as low as 2. (Note that average frequency is less restrictive than minimum expected frequency.) In addition it has been found (Camilli & Hopkins, 1978) that the "Yates' correction for continuity" that is usually recommended for 2 × 2 chi-square tests is not only unnecessary, but causes the already conservative probabilities for alpha to be even more conservative.

❖ **TABLE 12.3** A contingency table of the HSB data set of $n = 200$ high school students classified by gender and type of school program with related statistics pertaining to a χ^2 **test**.

	Type of School Program			
Gender	General	Academic	Vocational	
Male	$O_{11} = 21\ (23\%)$	$O_{12} = 47\ (52\%)$	$O_{13} = 23\ (25\%)$	$n_{1\cdot} = 91$
	$\varepsilon_{11} = 20.5$	$\varepsilon_{12} = 47.8$	$\varepsilon_{13} = 22.8$	
	$(O-\varepsilon)^2/\varepsilon = .013$	$(O-\varepsilon)^2/\varepsilon = .012$	$(O-\varepsilon)^2\varepsilon = .003$	
Female	$O_{21} = 24\ (22\%)$	$O_{22} = 58\ (53.2\%)$	$O_{23} = 27\ (24.8\%)$	$n_{2\cdot} = 109$
	$\varepsilon_{21} = 24.5$	$\varepsilon_{22} = 57.2$	$\varepsilon_{23} = 27.3$	
	$(O-\varepsilon)^2/\varepsilon = .011$	$(O-\varepsilon)^2/\varepsilon = .010$	$(O-\varepsilon)^2\varepsilon = .002$	
	$n_{\cdot 1} = 45$	$n_{\cdot 2} = 105$	$n_{\cdot 3} = 50$	$n_{\cdot\cdot} = 200$

$$\chi^2 = \sum_j \sum_k \frac{(O_{jk} - \varepsilon_{jk})^2}{\varepsilon_{jk}} = .013 + .012 + .003 + .011 + .010 + .002 = 0.051$$

❖ 12.15 INDEPENDENCE OF OBSERVATIONS

The *chi*-square test can be used with any contingency table in which each observation is statistically independent from all other observations. "Independence" in this context means that no more than one observation comes from each observational unit. The most common observational unit in educational and psychological research is a person. If there are ninety-six persons being studied, the total number of observations in the contingency table should be 96. If the same person contributes more than one entry in a table, the *chi*-square test is not appropriate.

❖ CHAPTER SUMMARY

The sampling distribution of proportions (p) from random samples is normal only when π is .50, unless the sample size is very large. The standard error of the proportion in a sample (σ_p) can be used to establish approximate confidence intervals for the parameter π only when the sampling distribution is approximately normal. Confidence intervals can be more accurately set using Figures 12.6 and 12.7. The confidence intervals will not be symmetrical if n is small and p differs substantially from .50.

The *chi*-square test is used to determine whether observed proportions (or frequencies) differ from expected proportions (or frequencies). When the expected proportions are determined on the basis of theory, the χ^2 test is a goodness-of-fit test. The goodness-of-fit test assesses how well the observed proportions fit the expected theoretical proportions. When the expected proportions are estimated from the data in the sample, the χ^2 test of association is used. It answers the question, "Is the row variable related to the column variable; that is, is there some degree of association or relationship between the two categorical variables?"

MASTERY TEST

1. The largest value for σ_p occurs when π equals _____.
2. If n is 100, and $p = .5$, estimate the values of σ_p^2 and σ_p.

3. If you repeatedly draw random samples with $n = 100$ from a population in which 50% ($\pi = .50$) favor candidate A, how often will you obtain a sample in which at least 60% favor candidate A?

4. In question 3, what percentage of repeated samples would show between 45% and 55% of the respondents favoring candidate A?

5. If 80% of the voters favor a bond issue, estimate σ_p for the following values of n.
   (a) $n = 100$ (b) $n = 400$ (c) $n = 1600$

6. What generalization regarding the precise relationship between sample size and σ_p is suggested in question 5?

7. If $\sigma_p = .05$ with $n = 100$, what is its value when $n = 25$?

8. In a random sample of $n = 100$ teachers, 50 preferred merit pay. Set a .95 CI around the sample proportion of .50.

9. Use Figure 12.6 to determine the .95 confidence interval in question 8. Compare the result with that for question 8.

10. Use Figure 12.6 to establish the .95 CI for π if:
    (a) $p = .2$, $n = 50$ (c) $p = .6$, $n = 50$
    (b) $p = .4$, $n = 50$ (d) $p = .6$, $n = 100$

11. Other things being equal, which of the following confidence intervals will have the greatest width?
    (a) .90   (b) .95   (c) .99

12. Which one of these symbols denotes the critical value for *chi*-square when $\alpha = .05$ with 2 degrees of freedom?
    (a) $_{.90}\chi_2^2$ (b) $_{.95}\chi_2^2$ (c) $_2\chi_{.95}^2$ (d) $_{.95}\chi^2$

13. Which of the following is largest?
    (a) $_{.90}\chi_1^2$ (b) $_{.95}\chi_1^2$ (c) $_{.99}\chi_1^2$

14. Which of the following is largest?
    (a) $_{.95}\chi_1^2$ (b) $_{.95}\chi_2^2$ (c) $_{.95}\chi_3^2$

15. In the χ^2 goodness-of-fit test, are the expected proportions known prior to the collection of the data?

16. In a 2×5 χ^2 test of association, what is the critical value of χ^2 with $\alpha = .01$?
    (a) $_{.99}\chi_1^2$ (b) $_{.99}\chi_4^2$ (c) $_{.99}\chi_5^2$ (d) $_{.01}\chi_4^2$

17. In Appendix B Table D, study the pattern of $_{.50}\chi^2$-values for various v values. What relationship did you observe?

18. Does $_{.50}\chi_{40}^2$ approximately equal 40?

19. If $v = 10$ and the computed value of χ^2 is 10 or less, is it necessary to look in Appendix B Table D to see if H_0 can be rejected with $\alpha = .05$?

20. Suppose the 120 students who want to take Algebra I during period 3 have a choice of instructors and four different instructors are available. A χ^2 test is used to determine whether the proportion desiring (or avoiding) certain teachers differs significantly from chance. (H_0: $\pi_1 = \pi_2 = \pi_3 = \pi_4$)
    (a) What is the expected proportion for each instructor?
    (b) What is the expected frequency for each instructor?
    (c) What is the critical value for χ^2 with $\alpha = .05$?
    (d) If the computed χ^2 value is 15.4, could H_0 be rejected at the .05 level? .01 level? .001 level?

21. Could χ^2 be used to determine if the proportion of left-handedness in 116 boys was significantly different from that for 78 girls?

22. In question 21, is the χ^2 application a goodness-of-fit test?

23. Can the χ^2 statistic be used:

(a) to compare proportions, H_0: $\pi_1 = \pi_2$?

(b) to determine if two categorical variables are associated?

24. In a 3×3 contingency table, if H_0 was rejected using χ^2, is it possible that the observed and expected values of some cells were equal?

25. If the χ^2 computation involves only one variable or factor (i.e., does not involve a contingency table), we know that it is a *chi*-square

(a) goodness-of-fit test.   (b) test of association.

26. Problem 5 in the Problems and Exercises section of this chapter, involves a $J = 3 \times 4 = K$ contingency table. To determine the critical value for χ^2, the number of degrees of freedom is needed. In that instance, what is v?

27. In the HSB data set, the variable of race has four levels and SES has three levels. The following items pertain to the test to determine if SES is unrelated to race.

(a) Which statistical test do you recommend?

(b) The degrees of freedom is equal to ___?___.

(c) For $\alpha = .01$, the critical χ^2 value is ___?___.

(d) Given that χ^2 was computed and found to be 14.56, can H_0 be rejected at $\alpha = .01$?

(e) How would you interpret your decision in option (d) above?

28. Recall that in step 3 of the four-step hypothesis testing procedure, that the probability (p) of the computed statistic is determined assuming that H_0 is true. *Using the appropriate tables in Appendix B* (which will require some review of procedures used in previous chapters), estimate p for the following statistical outcomes.

(a) $\chi^2 = 4.44$ when $v = 2$.

(b) $t = 2.25$ when $v = 60$.

(c) For a 3×4 contingency table, $\chi^2 = 20.55$.

(d) For the z-test, $z = -1.21$.

(e) For a χ^2 goodness-of-fit test with 7 cells, $\chi^2 = 28.8$.

(f) For a sample of $n = 18$ students, the gain scores (posttest–pretest) yielded a t-ratio of -1.82.

(g) For a 6×7 contingency table, $\chi^2 = 44.6$.

(h) For $n = 12$ experimental students and $n = 18$ control students, $t = 3.41$.

(i) For a sample of $n = 600$ self-concept scores, $\bar{X} = 48$ and $s = 8$. To determine if the distribution deviated from the parent population having $\mu = 50$ and $\sigma = 10$, the data were partitioned into 12 categories and χ^2 was computed to be 14.96.

29. In questions a–j, when other things are assumed to be equal:

(a) how are α and β related?

(b) how are n and σ_p related?

(c) how is n related to how well the sampling distribution of p approximates normality?

(d) is the sample size n related to the expected value of test statistics t, z, or χ^2 when H_0 is false?

(e) is the sample size n related to the expected value of test statistics t, z, or χ^2 when H_0 is true?

(f) how is degrees of freedom related to the critical values of t and χ^2?

(g) how is π related to the shape of the sampling distribution of p when n is not large?

(h) how is α related to the critical values of z, t, and χ^2?

(i) how is n related to the widths of the confidence intervals?

(j) is n related to the degrees of freedom for either the t-test or the χ^2-test?

30. Based on your understanding of this and previous chapters, specify what statistical test you would recommend for the following questions pertaining to the HSB data set.

(a) Does the civics mean for males differ from that of females?

(b) Is SES level related to race?

(c) Do students who participate in the special tutorial program show a significantly improved (posttest–pretest) math mean score?

(d) Are there equal proportions of students enrolled in each of the three types of high school programs (vocational, academic, and general)?

(e) Is type of school (public or private) program related to SES level (low, middle, and high)?

(f) Are the science scores normally distributed with $\mu = 50$ and $\sigma = 10$?

(g) When retested, do students have a significantly higher mean writing score on the retest than on the pretest?

(h) If the math scores were partitioned as "above" or "below" the median, would the level of math achievement be related to gender?

ANSWERS TO MASTERY TEST

1. For any value of n, the largest value of σ_p occurs at $\pi = .5$.

2. $\sigma_p^2 = (.5)(.5)/100 = .0025$,
$\sigma_p = \sqrt{.0025} = .05$

3. $z = (.60 - .50)/.05 = 2.0$. Therefore in approximately 2% of the samples, the observed p would equal or exceed .60.

4. approximately 68%

5. (a) .04, (b) .02, (c) .01

6. If n is quadrupled, σ_p is reduced by half.

7. $\sigma_p = .10$

8. .95 CI $= [.5 \pm 1.96(.05)] = [.402, .598]$

9. .95 CI $= [.39, .59]$; the two methods gave comparable results.

10. (a) [.12, .33], (b) [.27, .53], (c) [.45, .72], (d) [.48, .69]

11. (c)

12. (b)

13. (c)

14. (c)

15. yes

16. (b)

17. The value of $_{.50}\chi^2$ (the median in the χ^2-distribution) is about equal to the corresponding v-value, especially as v increases.

18. yes

19. no (see questions 17 and 18)

20. (a) The expected proportion is 30/120 or .25.

(b) 25% of $120 = 30$ the expected frequency if H_0 were true.

(c) The critical value of chi-square for $v = 3$ at the .05 level of significance is 7.81.

(d) Yes, $15.4 > 7.81$; yes, $15.4 > 11.3$; no, $15.4 < 16.3$; $.01 > p > .001$.

21. yes

22. No, it is the chi-square test of association.

23. (a) yes, (b) yes

24. yes

25. (a)

26. $(J - 1)(K - 1) = (3)(2) = 6$

27. (a) χ^2 test of association

(b) $v = (4 - 1)(3 - 1) = 6$

(c) $_{.99}\chi_6^2 = 16.8$

(d) No, $\chi^2 = 14.56 < {}_{.99}\chi_6^2 = 16.8$.

(e) H_0 was not shown to be false, but that is very different from concluding or believing H_0 is true; H_0 remains tenable because α was set equal to only .01. Probably our conclusion is a type-II error. This illustrates the trade-off between type-I and type-II errors, and why the conventional value for a is .05 and not .01.

28. (a) $.25 > p > .10$

(b) $.05 > p > .02$

(c) for $v = 6$, $.01 > p > .001$

(d) $p = 2(11.51) = .23$

(e) for $v = 6$, $p < .001$

(f) for $v = 17$, $.10 > p > .05$

(g) for $v = 30$, $.05 > p > .025$

(h) for $v = 28$, $.002 > p > .001$

(i) $v = (12 - 1) = 11$, $.25 > p > .10$

29. Other things being equal:

(a) As α is increased from .01 to .05, β decreases; that is, if the level of significance is raised, the probability of a type-II error is lowered.

(b) Inversely, that is, as n is increased, σ_p is decreased.

(c) As n increases, the sampling distribution of p becomes closer to a normal distribution.

(d) Yes, when H_0 is false, the expected values of all test statistics increase.

(e) No, when H_0 is true, the expected value of a test statistic is the mean of its sampling distribution (e.g., 0 for t and z).

(f) As v increases, the critical t decreases, but the critical value of χ^2 increases.

(g) As π approaches .50, the sampling distribution of p becomes more nearly symmetrical and more nearly approximates a normal distribution.

(h) As α gets smaller and smaller (e.g., from .05 to .01 to .001), the critical values of z, t, and χ^2 increase.

(i) As n increases, the widths of the confidence intervals decrease.

(j) Yes, but only for the t-test—as n increases, v increases; for the χ^2-test, v is not determined by n, but by the number of levels in the categorical variables.

30. (a) t-test for independent observations
(b) χ^2 test of association
(c) t-test for paired observations
(d) χ^2 goodness-of-fit test
(e) χ^2 test of association
(f) χ^2 goodness of fit test
(g) paired (related, dependent, correlated) t-test
(h) χ^2 test of association

PROBLEMS AND EXERCISES

1. On true-false exams, is "true" as likely to be the correct answer as "false"? In one investigation, examinations developed by several instructors were studied. The following result was typical:

Correct Answer

"True"	"False"
61	39

(a) Based on H_0, what is the expected proportion for each cell?
(b) H_0: ____ = ____ = .5?
(c) Compute the value of the *chi*-square statistic?
(d) $v =$ ____, and the critical value of *chi*-square for $\alpha = .05$ is ____.
(e) If $\alpha = .05$, act on H_0.
(f) Can H_0 be rejected at the .01 level?
(g) Use Figure 12.6 to determine the .95 CI for π_{true} and for π_{false}.

2. Is the correct answer on a multiple-choice exam more likely to be in one response position than in another—is there a bias in the key position? The table below gives the position for the correct answer for 100 items on the verbal section of the adult level for the Lorge-Thorndike Intelligence Test.

	Option					
	1	*2*	*3*	*4*	*5*	*Total*
Frequency	16	24	25	21	14	100

(a) To answer the question about keying bias, which *chi*-square test should be used?
(b) What are the expected proportions for all five cells? Use this result in the null hypothesis.
(c) Compute the *chi*-square statistic.
(d) Degrees of freedom, v, = ____.
(e) What is the critical value for *chi*-square at the .05 level?
(f) Is H_0 tenable?

3. A classic study by Hartshorn and May investigated the relationship between socioeconomic status (SES) and cheating in school. The results are given below for a sample of 400 children.

	Socioeconomic Status			
Cheated?	Lower	Middle	Higher	Row Totals
Yes	28	72	37	137
No	16	71	176	263
Column Totals	44	143	213	400

(a) Can H_0 be stated as H_0: $\pi_{11}/\pi_{.1} = \pi_{12}/\pi_{.2} = \pi_{13}/\pi_{.3}$ (or H_0: $\pi_{21} = \pi_{22} = \pi_{23}$)?
(b) Is this a *chi*-square goodness-of-fit test?
(c) What is the value of the *chi*-square statistic?
(d) Can H_0 be rejected at the .001 level of significance?
(e) Using Figure 12.6, determine the approximate .95 CI's for the proportion cheating in a) the lower SES population, b) the middle SES population, and c) the higher SES population.
(f) Conclusion? Since the data were obtained several decades ago, can the findings be safely generalized to the present?

4. One study reported the incidence of child abuse in families of various sizes in the United States and England. Fifty English families and forty-five U.S. families in which there were known child abusers were classified by size of family and nationality. A 4×2 contingency table is given below. (Data have been rounded to the nearest percent.)

Number of Children in Family	United States	England	Row Totals
1	8 (18%)	12 (24%)	20 [21%]
2	10 (22%)	22 (44%)	32 [34%]
3	9 (20%)	10 (20%)	19 [20%]
4+	18 (40%)	6 (12%)	24 [25%]
Column Totals	45	50	95

(a) Can the differences in the observed frequencies in the above table be plausibly viewed as chance fluctuations with $\alpha = .05$ (i.e., is H_0 tenable)?
(b) Study the contingency table and interpret the findings.

5. In a study of 1,405 high school and college students, an investigator found the following relationships between religious participation and the response to the question, "How happy has your home life been?" Observed frequencies are given for each cell.

	Participation in Religious Activities				
Student Response	Not At All	Very Little	Some- what	Very Much	Row Totals
Very Happy	105	257	368	151	881
Fairly Happy	78	149	153	52	432
Unhappy	25	30	24	13	92
Column Totals	208	436	545	216	1,405

(a) What is the critical value of *chi*-square at the .001 level?
(b) Can H_0 be rejected at the .001 level?
(c) Conclusion?

❖ **TABLE 12.PE** A contingency table of the HSB data set of $n = 600$ high school students classified by type of school (public or private) and type of school program (general, academic, and vocational).

		Type of School Program			
		General	*Academic*	*Vocational*	
S	*Public*	$O_{11} = 134$	$O_{12} = 233$	$O_{13} = 139$	$n_{1.} =$ ___
C		$\varepsilon_{11} =$ ___	$\varepsilon_{12} =$ ___	$\varepsilon_{13} =$ ___	
H		$(O\text{-}\varepsilon)^2/\varepsilon =$ ___	$(O\text{-}\varepsilon)^2/\varepsilon =$ ___	$(O\text{-}\varepsilon)^2/\varepsilon =$ ___	
O					
O	*Private*	$O_{21} = 11$	$O_{22} = 75$	$O_{23} = 8$	$n_{2.} =$ ___
L		$\varepsilon_{21} =$ ___	$\varepsilon_{22} =$ ___	$\varepsilon_{23} =$ ___	
		$(O\text{-}\varepsilon)^2/\varepsilon =$ ___	$(O\text{-}\varepsilon)^2/\varepsilon =$ ___	$(O\text{-}\varepsilon)^2/\varepsilon =$ ___	
		$n_{.1} =$ ___	$n_{.2} =$ ___	$n_{.3} =$ ___	$n_{..} = 600$

$$\chi^2 = \sum_j \sum_k \frac{(O_{jk} - \varepsilon_{jk})^2}{\varepsilon_{jk}} = \underline{\quad} + \underline{\quad} + \underline{\quad} + \underline{\quad} + \underline{\quad} + \underline{\quad} = \underline{\quad}$$

6. This problem is based on the data in Table 12.PE above. Two categorical variables included in the HSB data set are type of school (public or private) and type of school program (general, academic, or vocational). The following questions pertain to whether there is a relationship between type of school and type of school program by using the larger original high school sample of $n = 600$ student. A 2×3 contingency table of these variables is given in the above table.
   (a) In words, state the null hypothesis.
   (b) Select an α-level such that the probability of a type-I error is less than the conventional risk.
   (c) Compute the row and column marginal frequencies: $n_{1.} = \underline{\ ?\ }$; $n_{2.} = \underline{\ ?\ }$; $n_{.1} = \underline{\ ?\ }$; $n_{.2} = \underline{\ ?\ }$; and $n_{.3} = \underline{\ ?\ }$.
   (d) Public school students comprised what proportion of the total sample?
   (e) Determine the expected frequencies of row 1: $\varepsilon_{11} = \underline{\ ?\ }$, $\varepsilon_{12} = \underline{\ ?\ }$, $\varepsilon_{13} = \underline{\ ?\ }$.
   (f) Determine the expected frequencies of row 2: $\varepsilon_{21} = \underline{\ ?\ }$, $\varepsilon_{22} = \underline{\ ?\ }$, $\varepsilon_{23} = \underline{\ ?\ }$.
   (g) Compute the χ^2 components for all cells and sum them to obtain the value of the χ^2 statistic.
   (h) Access Table D to determine the probability of observing a χ^2 this large or larger when H_0 is true.
   (i) Make a conclusion regarding H_0.
   (j) Verbalize what the nature of the relationship is between type of school and type of school program.

7. We wonder if the HSB data reading scores are normally distributed about their own mean. To check this out, we use the $n = 200$ reading scores to compute their mean and standard deviation; thus, placing two additional restraints upon the data, and reducing the degrees of freedom to $V = 6$. The mean = 52.23 and the standard deviation is 10.1.
   (a) Step 1: Would H_0 be identical to that for Table 12.2?
   (b) Step 2: If we wanted to be very careful not to make a type-I error, we would set $\alpha = \underline{\ ?\ }$.
   (c) Step 3: If we used the same nine partitions, (see Table 12.2) there will be __(1)__ categories and __(2)__ degrees of freedom, and the expected frequencies would be identical to those in __(3)__. The observed frequencies for the nine categories 1 through 9 are: 8, 14, 30, 31, 34, 27, 26, 21, 9, respectively; $\chi^2 = \underline{(4)} + \underline{(5)} + \underline{(6)} + \underline{(7)} + \underline{(8)} + \underline{(9)} + \underline{(10)} + \underline{(11)} + \underline{(12)} = \underline{(13)}$.
   (d) Step 4: Can the null hypothesis that the HSB data reading scores are normally distributed be rejected at $\alpha = .01$?

ANSWERS TO PROBLEMS AND EXERCISES

1. (a) The expected proportion for each cell is .50 (50%).
   (b) H_0: $\pi_{\text{true}} = \pi_{\text{false}} = .5$
   (c) $\chi^2 = (61 - 50)^2/50 + (61 - 50)^2/50 = 121/50 + 121/50 = 4.84$
   (d) 1, 3.84
   (e) Since 4.84 > 3.84, H_0 is rejected; $p < .05$.
   (f) No: $_{.99}\chi_1^2 = 6.63$; $.05 > p > .01$.
   (g) For π_{true}, the .95 CI = [.48, .70]; For π_{false}, the .95 CI = [.30, .50].

2. (a) *chi*-square goodness-of-fit test
   (b) The expected proportion for each of the five cells is 1/5 or 20% or .20. H_0: $\pi_1 = \pi_2 = \pi_3 = \pi_4 = \pi_5 = .20$; the expected frequencies are 100(.20) = 20.
   (c) $\chi^2 = (-4)^2/20 + 4^2/20 + 5^2/20 + 1^2/20 + (-6)^2/20 = 94/20 = 4.70$
   (d) $v = (J - 1) = (5 - 1) = 4$
   (e) The critical value of χ^2 for $v = 4$ with $\alpha = .05$ is 9.49.
   (f) Yes, $.50 > p > .25$; H_0 is tenable even at the .25 level.

3. (a) Yes, but the narrative format seems preferable. For example, in the three SES populations, there is no difference in the proportions who would cheat. (Alternatively, among the three SES levels, there are equal proportions who would not cheat. Stated differently, SES level is unrelated to cheating behavior.)
   (b) No, this is the *chi*-square test of association.
   (c) $\chi^2 = (28 - 15.07)^2/15.07 + (16 - 28.93)^2/28.93 + (72 - 48.98)^2/48.98 + (71 - 94.02)^2/94.02 + (37 - 72.95)^2/72.95 + (176 - 140.05)^2/140.05 = 11.09 + 5.78 + 10.82 + 5.64 + 17.72 + 9.23 = 60.3$
   (d) Yes, 60.3 > 13.8 ; $p < .001$.
   (e) a) For the lower, middle, and higher SES populations, the approximate .95 CI's are [.50, .77], [.42, 58], and [.12, .22], respectively.
   (f) Several decades ago there was a significant relationship between SES and cheating, that is, the proportion of children who cheat is least for the higher SES population. Since the .95 confidence intervals overlap for the lower and middle SES groups, no safe conclusion regarding differences between these two populations in cheating proportions can be drawn. However, there may have been substantial social and cultural changes in the decades since the data were collected so that the findings cannot legitimately be generalized to the present time.

4. (a) No, since $\chi^2 = (1.47)^2/9.47 + (1.47)^2/10.53 + (5.16)^2/15.16 + (5.16)^2/16.84 + 0 + 0 + (6.63)^2/11.37 + (6.63)^2/12.63 = 11.1$; $p < .025$.
   (b) An abused child is more likely to be from a large (4 or more) family in the United States than in England. (Note that these data do not say that the proportion of children from large families that are abused is greater in the United States than in England. Before this conclusion could be made, one would need to consult census data regarding family size. If the proportion of families in the United States that have 4 or more children is three times greater than in England, the proportion of large families who abuse their children could be the same.)

5. (a) $_{.999}\chi_6^2 = 22.5$
   (b) Yes, the computed value of *chi*-square is approximately 32.4; 32.4 > 22.5; $p < .001$.
   (c) There was a positive relationship between the amount of participation in religious activities and the self-rated level of happiness of home life. Among the "very happy" home life group, about 59 percent reported higher levels of participation ("somewhat" and "very much") in religious activities, whereas about 41 percent reported little or no participation. Among the "unhappy" home life group, about 40 percent reported higher levels of participation ("somewhat" and "very much") in religious activities, whereas about 60 percent reported little or no participation.

Of course, all self-report data in the affective domain are flagrantly fragile and subject to a variety of interpretations to suit the bias of the interpreter.

6. (a) High school program enrollment is unrelated to (independent of) the type of school attended.

(b) Set $\alpha = .01$ (or some other value less than .05) to reduce the probability of rejecting a true H_0 to 1 chance in 100.

(c) $n_{1.} = 506$; $n_{2.} = 94$; $n_{.1} = 145$; $n_{.2} = 308$; $n_{.3} = 147$.

(d) $506/600 = .843$

(e) $\varepsilon_{11} = .843(145) = 122.3$,
$\varepsilon_{12} = .843(308) = 259.7$,
$\varepsilon_{13} = .843(147) = 124$

(f) $\varepsilon_{21} = .157(145) = 22.7$, $\varepsilon_{22} = 48.3$, $\varepsilon_{23} = 23$

(g) $1.12 + 2.75 + 1.82 + 6.03 + 14.76 + 9.78 = 36.3$

(h) $\chi^2 = 36.3 > {}_{.999}\chi^2_2$, so $p < .001$

(i) The null hypothesis is rejected beyond the .001 level. These data give convincing evidence that H_0 is false. Type of school and type of school program are related—the proportions of students within the program types differ for public versus private schools.

(j) A greater percentage of private school students are in the academic program (80% vs. 46%), whereas a greater percentage of the public school students are in the nonacademic school programs.

7. (a) yes, (b) .01 or .001, (c) (1) 9, (2) $9 - 3 = 6$, (3) Table 12.2, (4) 0.00, (5) 0.06, (6) 1.39, (7) 0.44, (8) 0.78, (9) 1.79, (10) 0.13, (11) 4.76, (12) 0.13, (13) 9.48, (d) No, $\chi^2 = 9.48$ with $v = 5$, $.10 > p > .05$, is not significant at the .05 level of significance. There is no strong evidence to suggest that these HSB data reading scores deviate significantly from normality.

 SUGGESTED COMPUTER EXERCISE

Based on the HSB data set:

1. Is gender related ($\alpha = .05$) to (a) race, (b) SES, (c) school program, or (d) type of school attended?

2. Is race related ($\alpha = .05$) to (a) SES, (b) school program, or (c) type of school attended?

3. Is SES is related ($\alpha = .05$) to (a) school program, or (b) type of school attended?

4. Is type of school program associated ($\alpha = .05$) with type of school attended?

❖ 13

Inferences Regarding Correlations

❖ 13.1 INTRODUCTION

One of the most frequent objectives in behavioral research is to determine the degree to which two variables are intercorrelated. In Chapter 6, we introduced the correlation coefficient, r, the statistical measure that quantifies the direction and strength of the linear relationship between two variables. How does one know whether the value of r is significantly greater than 0? How does one test that pessimist, the null hypothesis, that states that the correlation coefficient in the population (ρ, pronounced "rho") is 0? In this chapter we will answer these and related questions, and learn about sampling distributions and confidence intervals for r.

❖ 13.2 THE BIVARIATE NORMAL DISTRIBUTION

A large number of two-dimensional frequency distributions (scatterplots) produced from variables in the social and behavioral sciences show the characteristic elliptical shape as depicted in Figures 8.1 and 8.2. In Chapter 6, frequency was represented by the density of the points in the two-dimensional plane. Now if we depict the density of the population of cases as a third dimension, frequency (see Figure 13.1), we can visualize the three dimensions of the bivariate normal distribution: (1) variable X, (2) variable Y, and (3) frequency. Notice that the bivariate normal distribution in Figure 13.1 is shaped something like a bell or hat. If the population parameter ρ is zero, the base or surface on the XY-plane will be a circle; but as the correlation ρ increases, the base becomes increasingly elliptical, as we saw in Chapter 6.

All bivariate normal distributions have the following characteristics:

1. For each value of X, the distribution of the associated Y-values is a normal distribution; likewise, for each value of Y, the distribution of the associated X-values is a normal distribution.

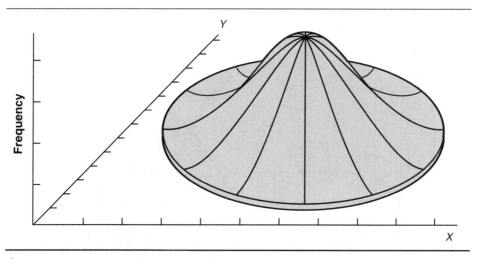

❖ **FIGURE 13.1** A bivariate normal distribution.

2. The Y-means for each value of X fall on a straight line (i.e., the relationship is linear).
3. The scatterplot possesses homoscedasticity (i.e., the standard deviation of the Y-values is constant for all values of X, and vice versa). Homoscedasticity means that the variance in residuals about the regression line is uniform.

Interestingly, this smooth, continuous, bell-shaped (bivariate) distribution is approximated by many empirical frequency distributions when the number of observations is very large. The bivariate normal distribution has important mathematical properties that enables one to estimate the sampling error when the statistic r is used to estimate the parameter ρ; this bivariate distribution is also used when testing the null hypothesis, H_0: $\rho = 0$.

❖ 13.3 SAMPLING DISTRIBUTIONS OF PEARSON r

Suppose each member of an army of a zillion researchers takes a random sample of n subjects, obtains measures of variables X and Y from each of the n cases, and computes r. If we make a frequency distribution of these zillion values of r, we have constructed a very good approximation of the sampling distribution of r for $v = n - 2$ degrees of freedom. The characteristics of the sampling distribution of r are summarized below.

1. The sampling distribution of r is normally distributed, has a mean of 0, and a standard deviation (standard error) of $\sigma_r = 1/\sqrt{(n-1)}$ when, and only when, $\rho = 0$.
2. When $\rho \neq 0$, the sampling distribution is skewed: (a) When $\rho > 0$, the sampling distribution is skewed to the left (negatively); (b) when $\rho < 0$, the sampling distribution is skewed to the right (positively); (c) the severity of the skewness decreases as ρ approaches zero and as n increases. The skewness is greatest when $|r|$ is very large and n is very small. Panel A of Figure 13.2 shows the effect of ρ on the sampling distribution of r, and Panel B shows the effect of sample size when $\rho = .75$.

When ρ is not zero, the sampling distribution is skewed, and therefore the confidence interval for ρ is not symmetrical about the sample value r. Figure 13.2 depicts the pattern of the skewness of the sampling distributions of r in relation to the value of ρ.

Panel A: Sampling distribution of *r* based on small samples for selected values of *r* from ρ = 0 to ρ = .9.

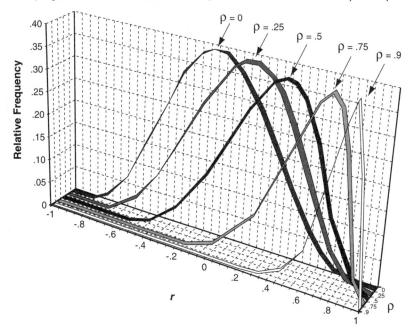

Panel B: Sampling distribution of *r* for selected sample sizes from *n* = 10 to *n* = 160 when ρ = .75.

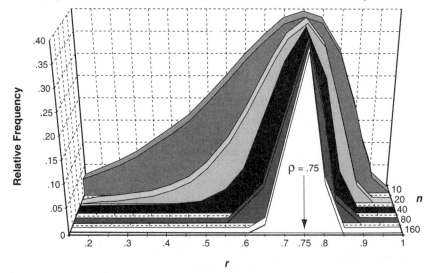

❖ **FIGURE 13.2** Sampling distributions of *r* for various values of ρ when *n* is small (Panel A) and for various sample sizes when *n* is set at ρ = .75 (Panel B).

You may have cleverly noticed the similarities between the set of sampling distributions of r in Figure 13.2 to the set of sampling distributions of p in Figure 12.3; that is, as the parameter approaches the midpoint of the range of possible values, the sampling distribution approaches normality, but as the parameters take values near the extremes, the sampling distributions become severely skewed. In Section 13.7 and following, we will discuss the special procedures needed to construct accurate confidence intervals for ρ.

Quiz: The sampling distribution of r will be normally distributed only when $\rho =$ __(1)__ , or when __(2)__ is very large. If $\rho = 0$ and $n = 101$, the sampling distribution of r is __(3)__ distributed with a mean of __(4)__ and a standard deviation, σ_r, of __(5)__ . For this distribution, the middlemost 95 percent of this sampling distribution ranges from a lower limit of __(6)__ to an upper limit of __(7)__ . (8) If n is held constant, which of the following sampling distributions would be least skewed? (a) the sampling distribution of r when $\rho = .30$, or (b) the sampling distribution of r when $\rho = .60$. (9) If $\rho = .80$, which of the following sampling distributions would be least skewed? (a) the sampling distribution of r when $n = 100$, or (b) the sampling distribution of r when $n = 600$.

Answers: (1) 0, (2) n, (3) normally, (4) 0, (5) .10, (6) $(-1.96)(.10) = -.196$, (7) $(1.96)(.10) = .196$, (8) $\rho = .30$, since it is closer to $\rho = 0$. (9) $n = 600$, since as n increases, the skewness decreases.

❖ 13.4 TESTING THE NULL HYPOTHESIS, H_0: $\rho = 0$

When two variables are uncorrelated ($\rho = 0$), the resulting sampling distribution is normally distributed with a known mean and standard deviation. This allows a simple z-test of the H_0: $\rho = 0$. The Pearson r, like all other statistics, is subject to sampling error—the difference between the statistic r and the parameter ρ (i.e., $r - \rho$). As with other statistics, the sampling error of r can be substantial, especially when n is small. How does one decide whether a computed correlation coefficient is significantly different from zero; how is H_0: $\rho = 0$ tested? You will be pleased to learn that the general four-step hypothesis testing procedures that are used to test hypotheses involving means (Chapters 10 and 11) and hypotheses involving proportions (Chapter 12) are also applicable to test the null hypothesis, H_0: $\rho = 0$. The statistical concepts of sampling distributions, null hypotheses, confidence intervals, and type-I and type-II errors may seem pleasantly repetitive (but never boring).

The four-step hypothesis-testing procedure, tailored to testing H_0: $\rho = 0$ is given below.

Step 1.	State the statistical hypothesis to be tested (e.g., H_0: $\rho = 0$).
Step 2.	Specify the level of risk of making a type-I error (α) you are willing to take (i.e., of concluding that H_0 is false when it is true). The conventional value for α is .05.
Step 3.[1]	Compute the z-ratio (Eq. 13.1) and access the normal distribution in Table A of Appendix B to determine the probability (p) of the computed z-statistic if H_0 were true:

[1]Step 3 can also be accomplished by accessing Table E with the computed r to determine p and/or the critical r-value.

$$z = \frac{r}{\sigma_r} = \frac{r}{\frac{1}{\sqrt{n-1}}} = r\sqrt{n-1}$$

$$(13.1)$$

Step 4. Conclude that H_0 is false if $p \leq \alpha$; if $p > \alpha$, conclude that H_0 is tenable.

The four-step procedure tailored to test the null hypothesis $\rho = 0$ is depicted as a flow-chart in Figure 13.3.

An Illustration. Suppose we are curious about a possible relationship between the two variables anxiety and creativity. We select a random sample of 101 persons, obtain measures of these variables for each of the 101 persons in the sample, and compute the correlation coefficient; we find that $r = .30$. Do these data provide statistical evidence that is sufficient to contradict the null hypothesis—is $|\rho| > 0$?

Step 1: H_0: $\rho = 0$.

Step 2: Assume that "beyond a reasonable doubt" to us means $\alpha = .001$!

Step 3: We compute z, $z = r\sqrt{100} = .3(10) = 3.0$ According to Table A for a computed z-ratio = 3.0, $p = 2(.0013) = .0026$.

Step 4. H_0 cannot be rejected with $\alpha = .001$ since $p = .0026 > .001$. Due to our fear of a type-I error (and our flagrant disregard of the risk of a type-II error), we must conclude that H_0 is tenable with $\alpha = .001$.

A reader of research is not obligated to use the same value for α as that set by the investigator. Perhaps you, as a knowledgeable reader of research reports, wish to use a more reasonable balance between the risks of type-I and type-II errors, and adopt an allowable type-I error risk of .01, .05, or .10. In that case, you reject the researcher's conclusions based on his or her skewed approach; and you conclude that the data are actually sufficiently conclusive that H_0 is false, and that there is a slightly positive relationship between anxiety and creativity.

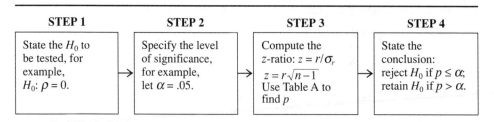

STEP 1	STEP 2	STEP 3	STEP 4
State the H_0 to be tested, for example, H_0: $\rho = 0$.	Specify the level of significance, for example, let $\alpha = .05$.	Compute the z-ratio: $z = r/\sigma_r$ $z = r\sqrt{n-1}$ Use Table A to find p	State the conclusion: reject H_0 if $p \leq \alpha$; retain H_0 if $p > \alpha$.

❖ **FIGURE 13.3** Flowchart of the four-step procedure for testing the null hypothesis, H_0: $\rho = 0$.

Quiz: One study (White & Hopkins, 1975) found that, for $n = 511$ elementary school pupils, the correlation between socioeconomic status and standardized achievement scores was $r = .154$. (1) For step 1, $H_0 = $ __?__. (2) For step 2, if the maximum risk of a type-I error is to be 2 percent, $\alpha = $ __?__. (3) For step 3, $z = $ __(a)__, and for this computed z, $p = $ __(b)__. (4) For step 4, the conclusion is that H_0 is __?__. (5) What is your interpretation of this conclusion?

Answers: (1) $H_0: \rho = 0$, (2) $\alpha = .02$, but this level of significance is rarely used, (3)(a) $.154(22.583) = 3.48$, (3)(b) $2(.00034) = .00068$, $p < .001$, (4) rejected at the .001 level of significance, (5) There is a statistically significant, but very weak, positive correlation between SES level and standardized achievement scores in the population of elementary school children that was sampled.

❖ 13.5 TESTING THE SIGNIFICANCE OF *r* USING THE *t*-TEST

The use of the *z*-test for testing $H_0: \rho = 0$ is completely valid and is best for a conceptual understanding of the process and rationale for testing the null hypothesis. The *t*-test is slightly more powerful, hence it is the method-of-choice in actual application. It gains its power by using the sample estimate *r* (not just *n*) to estimate the standard error, as evident in Equation 13.2:

$$t = \frac{r}{s_r} = \frac{r}{\sqrt{\dfrac{1 - r^2}{v}}} \tag{13.2}$$

Let us use the data from the previous quiz to illustrate the use of the *t*-test to test $H_0: \rho = 0$. The steps are identical except that *t*, not *z* is used in step 3. From Equation 13.2:

$$t = \frac{r}{s_r} = \frac{.154}{\sqrt{\dfrac{1 - (.154)^2}{511 - 2}}} = \frac{.154}{\sqrt{\dfrac{.9763}{509}}} = 3.52$$

The critical *t*-value, $3.310 = {}_{.9995}t_{500}$, is found from Appendix B Table C. Since the observed *t*-ratio is greater than 3.310, the null hypothesis is rejected at the .001 level. (The actual *p* value obtained from a computer analysis is $p = .00047$, trivially less than the $p = .00068$ value found using the *z*-test—this will always be the case.)

Equation 13.2 can be rearranged to yield the *minimum value* for which $H_0: \rho = 0$ can be rejected (i.e., the critical value of *r*) by supplying degrees of freedom ($v = n - 2$) and the critical value of *t*. The minimum value for *r* at which the null hypothesis can be rejected is:

$$\text{Critical } r = \frac{\text{Critical } t}{\sqrt{(\text{Critical } t)^2 + v}} \tag{13.3}$$

where $v = n - 2$.

Equation 13.3 shows that, if the values of v and critical t for $v = n - 2$ degrees of freedom are substituted into Equation 13.3, the minimum r necessary to reject H_0: $\rho = 0$ can be found. For example, how large must r be in order to reject the null hypothesis at $\alpha = .05$, if $n = 25$ ($v = 23$)? From Appendix B Table C, we find $_{.975}t_{23} = 2.069$; hence:[2]

$$\text{Critical } r = \frac{2.069}{\sqrt{(2.069)^2 + 23}} = \frac{2.069}{\sqrt{27.28}} = .396$$

In other words, if $n = 25$, we need not compute t since the critical value for r is .396. If $|r| <$ .396, H_0 is tenable; if $|r| > .396$, H_0 is rejected at $\alpha_2 = .05$.

The critical values of r have been graphically displayed in Figure 13.4 for selected n's and α-values. For example, if $r = .35$ and $n = 40$, would H_0: $\rho = 0$ be rejected at $\alpha_2 = .05$? At $\alpha_2 = .01$? H_0 could be rejected at $\alpha_2 = .05$ since .35 is greater than the critical r of .31 at $\alpha_2 = .05$; H_0 could not be rejected at $\alpha_2 = .01$ because $r = .35$ is less than .40, the critical r at $\alpha_2 = .01$. Note that the critical values for a two-tail test at $\alpha_2 = .10$ are identical with those for a one-tail test with $\alpha_1 = .05$.

Notice in Figure 13.4 how the critical value of r decreases as n increases. This relationship explains how the correlation of .154 between SES and academic achievement, although very slight, was significant at the .001 level—the sample size was large ($n = 511$). If n is large, very small values of r allow a rejection of H_0: $\rho = 0$.

Figure 13.4 can also be used to determine the sample size, n, associated with a particular critical value for r. For example, how large a sample is required to allow rejection of H_0: $\rho = 0$ if the observed value of r is .4? The null hypothesis is rejected at $\alpha_2 = .10$, $\alpha_2 = .05$, $\alpha_2 = .01$, and $\alpha_2 = .001$ if n's are 18, 25, 40, and 65, respectively.

Quiz: Based on Figure 13.4: if $n = 20$ and $\alpha = .05$, the critical value of $r = $ __(1)__ ; but if n is quadrupled while holding the alpha level at .05, the critical value of r is __(2)__. For $n = 30$ and $\alpha = .001$, the critical value of r is __(3)__ ; but if n is quadrupled while holding α at .001, the critical value of r is __(4)__. (5) Based on these findings, is it precisely true that if the sample size is quadrupled the critical value of r is cut in half?

Answers: (1) $\approx .44$, (2) $\approx .22$, (3) $\approx .57$, (4) $\approx .30$, (5) No, not precisely true, but approximately so.

❖ 13.6 DIRECTIONAL ALTERNATIVES: TWO-TAIL VERSUS ONE-TAIL TESTS

As is the case with statistical tests of sample means (Chapters 10 and 11), a statistical test for H_0: $\rho = 0$ can be designated as either a two-tail (nondirectional) or a one-tail (directional) test. A two-tail test of H_0: $\rho = 0$ seeks to detect significant correlations in either the positive or negative direction, and the conclusion of the statistical test allows us to conclude either that $\rho > 0$ or that $\rho < 0$ when H_0: $\rho = 0$ is rejected. If the investigator can build a strong case using empirical and/or logical arguments, that the case can be made that if ρ is not zero it will be positive (or negative, as the situation at hand may dictate) and that it is

---

[2]See Math Note 16 in Appendix A to review the procedures to follow in algebraically rearranging mathematical equations.

inconceivable that ρ could be otherwise, then a one-tail test is in order. To opt for the directional hypothesis means that the investigator is totally convinced that ρ could not be contrary to the predicted direction.

One should not employ one-tail tests carelessly. Once committed to a one-tail test, we cannot later turn around and perform a two-tail test after being surprised by the results. However, when properly guided by sound theory and/or empirical research, one-tail tests are appropriate and have greater power to detect false null hypotheses than do their nondirectional counterparts. The increased power of the one-tail test results from the fact that all of the critical region for rejecting H_0: $\rho = 0$ is placed in one tail of the sampling distribution of r, hence the critical value of r is smaller than for a two-tail test with the same α-level. For example, Table E specifies that the critical value of r with $n = 50$ and $\alpha_2 = .05$ is .276, but for $\alpha_1 = .05$, the critical value of r is .235. Figure 13.4 visually portrays the differences between the critical values for directional and nondirectional tests of r for a variety of samples sizes.

Directional hypotheses might be justified in testing the correlations for the following pairs of variables, where our expectations are strong that each pair of variables is positively correlated.

1. Reading vocabulary and speaking vocabulary
2. Age and strength for pupils in the elementary grades
3. Spelling ability and IQ
4. Height and weight
5. Socioeconomic status and GPA

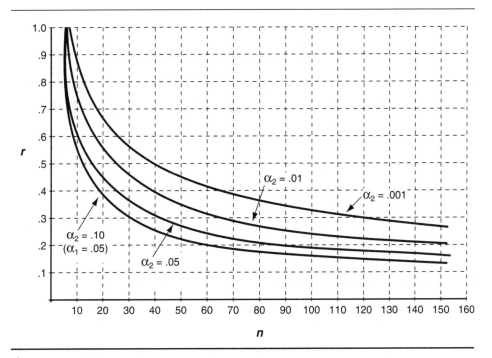

❖ **FIGURE 13.4** Critical values of Pearson's r for rejecting H_0: $\rho = 0$ for selected values of α and n.

6. Musical ability and cognitive ability
7. GPA's of siblings

One-tail tests are usually inappropriate for novel, innovative, or pioneering areas of original research. Unless otherwise specified, it is conventional to assume that statistical tests are nondirectional.

Quiz: (1) For $n = 15$, how large must r be in order to be statistically significant (i.e., what is the critical r) with $\alpha_2 = .05$, and $\alpha_1 = .05$? (2) For $n = 100$, find the critical r for $\alpha_2 = .01$, and $\alpha_1 = .01$. (3) For $n = 500$, find the critical r for $\alpha_2 = .001$, and $\alpha_1 = .001$.
Answers: (1) .514, .441, (2) .256, 232, (3) .147, .115

❖ 13.7 CONFIDENCE INTERVALS FOR ρ USING FISHER'S Z-TRANSFORMATION

Recall that the sampling distribution of r is skewed for all values of ρ except when $\rho = 0$. Therefore, special procedures must be employed to accurately determine confidence intervals.

Several decades ago, the father of experimental statistics, the Englishman Sir Ronald Fisher, devised the Z_r-transformation, a mathematical transformation of r that has a sampling distribution that is essentially normal irrespective of ρ or n. This transformation statistic, known as *Fisher's Z_r*, is defined in the following formula:[3]

$$|Z_r| = .5 \ \ln\left(\frac{1+|r|}{1-|r|}\right) \tag{13.4}$$

If your knowledge of logarithms is rusty—no problem! The calculations have been performed and tabulated for us in Table G of Appendix B, which gives the value of the Fisher Z_r from $r = .000$ to $r = .995$. Notice that Table G has five double columns pairing positive r to positive Z_r. (Fisher's Z_r-transformation has symmetry, so if r is negative, Z_r is also negative.) Verify from Table G that for an r of .39, the corresponding Z_r is .412.

Quiz: (1) For the following r-values, find their corresponding Z_r values in Table G (or from your calculator or spreadsheet): (a) $r = .15$, (b) $r = .35$, (c) $r = -.55$, (d) $r = .75$, (e) $r = -.95$. (2) For the following Z_r-values, use Table G "in reverse" (or your calculator or spreadsheet) to retrieve their corresponding r-values:
(a) $Z_r = .090$, (b) $Z_r = -.332$, (c) $Z_r = .670$, (d) $Z_r = -.950$, (e) $Z_r = 1.738$.
Answers: (1) (a) $Z_r = .151$, (b) $Z_r = .365$, (c) $Z_r = -.618$, (d) $Z_r = .973$, (e) $Z_r = -1.422$, (2) (a) $r = .09$, (b) $r = -.32$, (c) $r = .585$, (d) $r = -.74$, (e) $r = .89$

❖ 13.8 THE SAMPLING DISTRIBUTION OF FISHER'S Z_r

Suppose the army of researchers in our thought experiment sets out to build a sampling distribution; each researcher takes a random sample of size n from a bivariate normal popu-

---

[3]Not to be confused with the z-ratio or z-test. We will use the capital letter Z when referring to Fisher's Z; we will continue to use the lowercase z for the z-test or z-score.

lation and computes r for our sample, and converts it to Z_r. We construct a frequency distribution of the Z_r's. The characteristics of the sampling distribution of Z_r are given below.

1. The sampling distribution of Z_r is approximately normally distributed, as depicted in Figure 13.5.
2. The mean of the sampling distribution equals the Fisher Z_r parameter, Z_ρ, corresponding to ρ.
3. The variance and standard deviation (standard error) of the sampling distribution are:

$$\sigma_{\bar{Z}}^2 = \frac{1}{n-3} \qquad \textbf{(13.5)}$$

$$\sigma_Z = \frac{1}{\sqrt{n-3}} \qquad \textbf{(13.6)}$$

Unlike the sampling distribution of r, the Fisher Z_r's are normally distributed; the Fisher Z_r-transformation is just what the doctor ordered to set confidence intervals around r. The strategy is to take the computed Pearson r-value, enter the wonderful world of the Fisher Z_r-transformation (using Table G, or your calculator or spreadsheet), then, while there, form a confidence interval around Z_r, and finally exit to the Pearson world by converting the lower and upper limits of the confidence interval into the r metric.

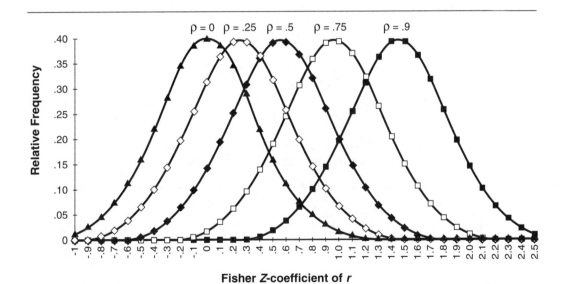

❖ **FIGURE 13.5** Sampling distributions of Fisher's Z-coefficients transformed from sampling distributions for $\rho = 0$, .25, .5, .75, and .9.

Using the Fisher Z_r-transformation, the procedure to establish .95 confidence intervals for ρ is outlined below.

Step 1.   Convert r to Fisher Z_r (Table G, or your calculator or spreadsheet).

Step 2.   Compute the standard error of Z_r using Equation 13.6.

Step 3.   Compute the .95 CI around Z_r: .95 CI for $Z_\rho = Z_r \pm 1.96\sigma_Z$.

Step 4.   Convert the lower and upper limits of the Z_r-CI to the lower and upper limits of the .95 CI for ρ using Table G or your calculator or spreadsheet.

This four-step procedure to set a .95 confidence interval for ρ is depicted as a flowchart in Figure 13.6.

To illustrate the four steps, an r of .83 was observed between the IQ's of 30 pairs of identical twins reared apart. With $n = 30$, how precisely does r estimate ρ? Suppose a confidence interval with confidence coefficient .95 is desired.

For step 1, enter Table G with $r = .83$, and retrieve the corresponding $Z_r = 1.188$.
For step 2, compute $\sigma_Z = 1/\sqrt{27} = .1925$.
For step 3, the .95 CI around $Z_r = [1.188 \pm 1.96(.1925)] = [1.188 \pm .377] = [.811, 1.565]$.
For step 4, read Table G "in reverse" to retrieve the r's corresponding to the lower and upper limits of the CI for Z_ρ. The lower Z_r-limit of .811 corresponds to an r of .670, and the upper Z_r-limit of 1.565 corresponds to an r of .916; therefore, the .95 CI for ρ is [.670, .916].

Quiz: A second correlation of $r = .93$ was observed between IQ scores of 83 pairs of identical twins reared together. (1) Perform the four steps required to establish the .95 CI for ρ: (a) $Z_r = \underline{\ ?\ }$, (b) $\sigma_Z = \underline{\ ?\ }$, (c) .95 CI around $Z_r = \underline{\ ?\ }$, (d) .95 CI for $\rho = \underline{\ ?\ }$.

(2) In exercise c above, replace 1.96 (the z required for the .95 CI) with the z-value for the .99 CI, find the .99 CI around Z_r, and then convert to the .99 CI for ρ.

Answers: (1) (a) 1.658, (b) .112, (c) [1.438, 1.878], (d) [.893, .954], (2) [1.658 ± 2.58(.112)] = .99 CI around $Z_r = [1.369, 1.947]$; .99 CI for $\rho = [.878, .96]$.

The procedure for determining the .68, .90, .95, .99, and .999 confidence intervals for ρ are all identical except that the z-multiplier in step 3 is modified accordingly. According to

---

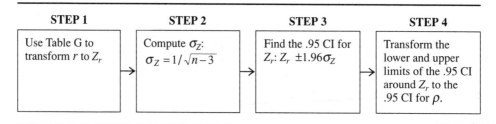

STEP 1	STEP 2	STEP 3	STEP 4
Use Table G to transform r to Z_r	Compute σ_Z: $\sigma_Z = 1/\sqrt{n-3}$	Find the .95 CI for Z_r: $Z_r \pm 1.96\sigma_Z$	Transform the lower and upper limits of the .95 CI around Z_r to the .95 CI for ρ.

❖ **FIGURE 13.6** Flowchart for setting a .95 confidence interval for ρ.

Table A, the z-multipliers for these five confidence intervals are 1.0, 1.645, 1.96, 2.576, and 3.29, respectively.

❖ 13.9 DETERMINING CONFIDENCE INTERVALS GRAPHICALLY

If extreme precision is not required, the approximate limits of the .95 confidence interval for ρ can be estimated directly from Figure 13.7. From the figure, we find the upper and lower limits for the confidence interval that corresponds to the particular r and n in question. Notice that the vertical lines represent r-values, and that there are a *pair* of curved lines

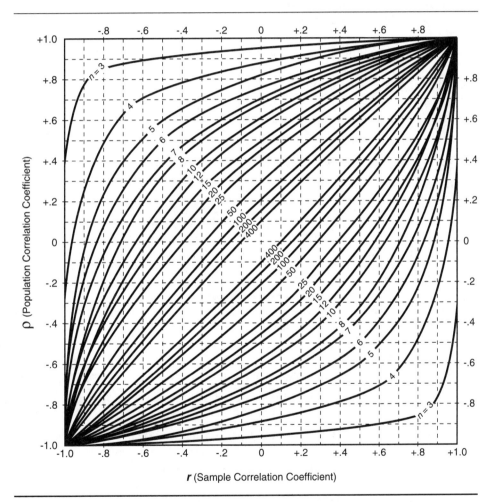

❖ **FIGURE 13.7** Nomograph for constructing .95 confidence intervals for ρ. Enter r on base axis and read ρ's where the values of r and n intersect. For example, the .95 confidence interval for ρ if $r = +.6$ and $n = 50$ is .4 to .76. [Reprinted from E.S. Pearson & H.O. Hartley, (Eds.), *Biometrika Tables for Statisticians*, 2nd ed. (Cambridge: Cambridge University Press, 1966), by permission of the *Biometrika* Trustees and Cambridge University Press].

that represent each n-value. The lower limit of the confidence interval is the intersection of the vertical line representing r with the lower curved line representing n, and the upper limit is the intersection of the same vertical line and the upper curved line representing n. From each of these two points of intersection, one reads across to the left vertical margin to find the lower and upper limits of the .95 confidence interval for ρ.

For example, if $r = .20$ with $n = 25$, the vertical line representing $r = .20$ intersects the two curved lines representing $n = 25$. The numerical value of these intersections points are read from the left margin. These points of intersection represent the lower and upper limits of the .95 confidence interval for ρ [–.20, .55]. Recall that when the .95 CI does not include the numerical value specified by H_0, the null hypothesis will be rejected at $\alpha_2 = .05$; consequently, since this .95 confidence interval includes zero, the null hypothesis is retained, and the r of .20 would not be statistically significant with $\alpha_2 = .05$.

Quiz: For the following n and r values, use Figure 13.7 to determine the .95 CI's: (1) $n = 10$, $r = .40$, (2) $n = 25$, $r = .9$, (3) $n = 15$, $r = .20$, (4) $n = 200$, $r = 0.0$. (5) For which of the preceding confidence intervals would H_0: $\rho = 0$ be rejected with $\alpha_2 = .05$?
Answers: (1) [–.30, .81], (2) [.70, 95], (3) [–.34, .63], (4) [–.15, .15], (5) In question 2 the CI does not include zero indicating that the null hypothesis is rejected.

❖ 13.10 TESTING INDEPENDENT CORRELATION COEFFICIENTS: H_0: $\rho_1 = \rho_2$

In Section 13.8, we determined the .95 confidence interval for r both for identical twins reared apart and reared together. Do the two r's differ significantly; can the null hypothesis H_0: $\rho_1 = \rho_2$ be rejected? At times, we are interested in hypotheses regarding *differences* in ρ's. Are the IQ's of identical twins reared together correlated more highly than the IQ's of identical twins reared apart? If intellectual performance is determined solely by hereditary factors, we would expect the ρ's to be equal. To answer the question, we will make another application of the z-test with which we have become familiar.

The four-step procedure tailored to test null hypotheses involving differences between correlation coefficients is given below.

Step 1.   State the statistical hypothesis to be tested (e.g., H_0: $\rho_1 = \rho_2$).

Step 2.   Specify the level of risk you are willing to take (α) of concluding that H_0 is false when it is true, that is, a type-I error.

Step 3.   Compute the $\sigma_{Z_{r_1}-Z_{r_2}}$ (Eq. 13.8) and the z-ratio (Eq. 13.7) and access the normal distribution in Appendix B Table A to determine the probability (p) of the computed z-statistic if H_0 were true:

$$z = \frac{Z_{r_1} - Z_{r_2}}{\sigma_{Z_{r_1}-Z_{r_2}}}$$ **(13.7)**

$$\sigma_{Z_{r_1}-Z_{r_2}} = \sqrt{\sigma_{Z_{r_1}} + \sigma_{Z_{r_2}}} = \sqrt{\frac{1}{n_1 - 3} + \frac{1}{n_2 - 3}} \quad \textbf{(13.8)}$$

Step 4.   Conclude that H_0 is false if $p \leq \alpha$; if $p > \alpha$, conclude that H_0 is accepted as tenable (but never as true).

As an example, let us work through the steps for testing H_0: $\rho_1 = \rho_2$ for the independent correlation coefficients between (1) the IQ scores of identical twins reared together, and (2) the IQ scores of identical twins reared apart. The data were reported as follows:

Twins Reared Together: $n_1 = 83$, $r_1 = .93$
Twins Reared Apart: $n_2 = 30$, $r_2 = .83$

For step 1, H_0: $\rho_1 = \rho_2$.
For step 2, let $\alpha = .05$.
For step 3, first compute the standard error using Equation 13.8:

(a) $\sigma_{Z_{r_1}-Z_{r_2}} = \sqrt{1/(n_1 - 3) + 1/(n_2 - 3)} = \sqrt{1/80 + 1/27} = \sqrt{.0425} = .2225.$

(b) Next compute the z-ratio using Eq. 13.7:

$$r_1 = .93 \rightarrow Z_{r_1} = 1.658; r_2 = .83 \rightarrow Z_{r_2} = 1.188;$$

$$z = (Z_{r_1} - Z_{r_2})/\sigma_{Z_{r_1}-Z_{r_2}} = (1.658 - 1.188)/.2225 = 2.11.$$

For step 4, $p = 2(.0174) = .0348$. Since $p < \alpha$, reject H_0 at the .05 level of significance. The mean IQ score of identical twins reared together is significantly greater than that of identical twins reared apart.

Notice that the procedures for testing H_0: $\rho_1 = \rho_2$ are for *independent* r's, that is, the two r's were obtained on two different samples of persons. When the same sample is used for both correlation coefficients, the r's would not be independent. In such cases, a more sophisticated analysis is necessary. Procedures for testing the null hypothesis when the r's are dependent are treated elsewhere (see Glass & Hopkins, 1996).

Quiz: (1) If for sample 1, $n_1 = 53$, and if for sample 2, $n_2 = 103$, compute $\sigma_{Z_{r_1}-Z_{r_2}}$. (2) If for sample 1, $r_1 = .40$, $Z_{r_1} = \underline{\quad ? \quad}$. (3) If for sample 2, $r_2 = .60$, $Z_{r_2} = \underline{\quad ? \quad}$. (4) To test H_0: $\rho_1 = \rho_2$, the z-ratio $= \underline{\quad ? \quad}$ and $p = \underline{\quad ? \quad}$. (5) If $\alpha = .05$, would H_0 be rejected?

Answers: (1) $\sigma_{Z_{r_1}-Z_{r_2}} = .1732$, (2) .424, (3) .693, (4) $(.693 - .424)/.1732 = 1.55$, $2(.0606) = .121$, (5) No, $p > .05$.

❖ CHAPTER SUMMARY

We can test the statistical hypothesis H_0: $\rho = 0$ by using the z-test or the t-test (or, equivalently, using Appendix B Table E). The critical value of r decreases as n increases and as α increases (e.g., from .01 to .05). A one-tail directional test is more powerful (more capable of detecting a false H_0) than the typical nondirectional test, when its use can be justified.

The sampling distribution of r is normal only when $\rho = 0$; it is skewed to the extent that ρ deviates from zero. The skewness becomes progressively less and the sampling distribution moves toward normality as n increases.

The Fisher Z_r-transformation approximates a normal distribution irrespective of the values of n or ρ. It can be used to set confidence intervals for ρ. Figure 13.7 can also be used to set .95 confidence intervals for ρ if high precision is not needed. Fisher Z_r-transformations are also used in the z-test for independent r's. If the r's are obtained on different subjects, they are independent r's; two r's obtained on the same group of persons are not independent.

MASTERY TEST

1. Under what conditions can the precise value of ρ be known?

2. In each of the following instances, indicate whether a type-I error, a type-II error, or no error was committed by the researcher:

H_0	True Value of ρ	Decision Based on r
(a) $\rho = 0$	0	H_0 rejected
(b) $\rho = 0$	.40	H_0 rejected
(c) $\rho = 0$	0	H_0 retained
(d) $\rho = 0$	−.50	H_0 retained

3. The hypothesis H_0: $\rho = 0$ is true, and was tested with a sample of $n = 50$ subjects with $\alpha_2 = .05$. What is the probability that a type-I error will be made? What if a one-tail test had been performed with $\alpha_1 = .05$; what is the probability of a type-I error? In this situation, what is the probability of a type-II error (careful)?

4. Jackson drew a sample of $n = 200$ paired observations from a bivariate normal distribution and found $r = .10$. Jackson reasoned correctly that, if ρ is zero, then the sampling distribution of r is distributed normally with a mean of zero and a standard deviation of .071. Jackson rejected the null hypothesis; what is the probability that Jackson made a type-I error if in fact $\rho = 0$? (Hint: What percentage of the area under a normal curve lies in the tails of the sampling distribution beyond $|.10|$?)

5. In each of the following instances, indicate whether the critical region for the rejection of H_0 lies in the upper tail, or is divided between both tails of the sampling distribution of r.
   (a) $\alpha = .05$ (b) $\alpha_1 = .05$ (c) $\alpha_2 = .05$

6. Researcher Matthew is testing H_0: $\rho = 0$ at the .05 level with $n = 100$; researcher Elizabeth is testing H_0: $\rho = 0$ at the .05 level with $n = 25$.
   (a) Who has the higher risk of a type-I error if $\rho = 0$?
   (b) If $\rho = .10$, who has the higher risk of a type-II error?
   (c) Which researcher is performing a significance test that has greater power to reject H_0 if $\rho = .10$?

7. Other things being equal, when ρ is not equal to zero, is the probability of a type-II error greater with $\alpha = .01$ or .05?

8. With $n = 200$ and $\rho = 0$, $\sigma_r = .071$; what percentage of the sampling distribution of r-values falls within the following intervals?
(a) between 0 and .071
(b) between 0 and −.071
(c) above .071
(d) below −.071
(e) above $(1.96)(.071)$
(f) below $(−1.96)(.071)$
(g) either above $(2.576)(.071) = .183$ or below −.183

9. When $n = 101$ and $\rho = 0$, what is the standard deviation of the sampling distribution of r? $(\sigma_r = 1/\sqrt{n-1})$

10. Given $\rho = .196$, $n = 101$, and $\sigma_r = .1$:
(a) What is the probability that H_0: $\rho = 0$ will be rejected at $\alpha = .05$?
(b) What is β, the probability of a type-II error, with $\alpha = .05$?
(c) What is the term applied to the probability that a H_0 will be rejected?

11. Using Figure 13.4, determine how large a sample is needed to reject H_0: $\rho = 0$ with an r-value of .3 under the following circumstances.
(a) $\alpha = .001$ (b) $\alpha = .01$ (c) $\alpha = .05$ (d) $\alpha_1 = .05$ (e) $\alpha = .10$

12. Assume H_0: $\rho = 0$ is true.
(a) Does the probability of rejecting H_0 increase as n increases?
(b) Will the critical value of r decrease as n increases?
(c) Will the critical value of r be larger at $\alpha = .05$ than at $\alpha = .01$?

13. Which of these statements *best* describes why the Fisher Z-transformation is needed?
(a) The sampling distribution of r is skewed when ρ is not 0.
(b) The t-test and z-test for H_0: $\rho = 0$ are not powerful for small n's.
(c) The sampling distribution of r is not normal when $\rho = 0$.

14. If $r = .50$, are the .90 CI's for ρ given below plausible?
(a) −.1 to .51   (b) −.2 to .84   (c) .42 to .57   (d) .48 to .55

15. Knowledge of which concepts were required in answering question 14?
(a) The sampling distribution of r is approximately normal with large n's.
(b) The sampling distribution of r is positively skewed when $\rho > 0$.
(c) The sampling distribution of r is negatively skewed when $\rho > 0$, unless n is large.

16. Other things being equal, which of these CI's spans the greatest range of values?
(a) .68 CI   (b) .95 CI   (c) .99 CI

17. The authors compared the predictive validity of an IQ test and of a reading readiness test, given at the beginning of first grade, for predicting reading success in grade 1 (teachers' marks at the end of grade 1). The correlations were .513 and .595 for the IQ and the reading readiness tests, respectively, each obtained on the same 157 pupils.
(a) Could Equation 13.7 be used to test H_0: $\rho_{12} = \rho_{13}$?
(b) Could Equation 13.7 be used to test whether the predictive validity of the IQ scores was different for boys than for girls?
(c) Could Equation 13.7 be used to test whether the predictive validity of the IQ scores for boys was different from the predictive validity of the reading readiness scores for girls?

18. Which of these determine the value of σ_Z? $(\sigma_r = 1/\sqrt{n-1})$
(a) r (b) n (c) ρ

19. Using Figure 13.7, determine the .95 CI if $r = .20$ and $n = 50$.

20. In the preceding item, would H_0: $\rho = 0$ be rejected with $\alpha = .05$?

21. Using Table E of Appendix B, find p for the following examples when a one-tail directional hypothesis is justified.
    (a) $n = 15$, $r = .46$
    (b) $n = 30$, $r = .46$
    (c) $n = 150$, $r = .12$
    (d) $n = 1,000$, $r = .12$

22. Using Table E, find p for the following examples when a nondirectional hypothesis is used.
    (a) $n = 15$, $r = .46$
    (b) $n = 30$, $r = .46$
    (c) $n = 150$, $r = .12$
    (d) $n = 1,000$, $r = .12$

ANSWERS TO MASTERY TEST

1. when based on the total population.
2. (a) type-I error (b) no error (c) no error (d) type-II error
3. .05, .05. A type-II error cannot be committed when the null hypothesis is true since the definition of a type-II error is that it is the failure to reject a false H_0.
4. The probability of a type-I error is approximately .16, since $z = .10/.071 = 1.41$; and from Appendix B Table A, the percentage equals $2(.0793) = .1596$ or about 16%.
5. (a) divided between both tails, (b) upper tail, (c) divided between both tails
6. (a) The probability of a type-I error is the same for both; $\alpha = .05$.
   (b) Elizabeth has a greater probability of making a type-II error since she has the smaller sample.
   (c) Matthew, since power increases with n
7. β is greater with $\alpha = .01$. Other things being equal, as α is increased, β is decreased, and vice versa.
8. (a) 34% (b) 34% (c) 16% (d) 16% (e) 2.5% (f) 2.5% (g) 1%
9. $\sigma_r = 1/\sqrt{100} = .1$
10. (a) .50 (b) $(1 - .50) = .50$ (c) power
11. (a) 120 (b) 72 (c) 45 (d) 31 (e) 31
12. (a) No; but if $\rho \neq 0$ zero, the probability of rejecting H_0 increases.
    (b) Yes, and importantly so when n is small.

(c) No, critical values of r decrease as the level of significance increases; the critical values of r are greater at the $\alpha = .01$ level than at $\alpha = .05$.
13. (a)
14. (a) no, (b) yes, if n is small, (c) yes, if n is large, (d) no
15. (a) and (c)
16. (c)
17. (a) No, because the r's would not be independent.
    (b) Yes, these r's are independent.
    (c) Yes; although the test may answer an uninteresting question, the z-test would be statistically valid. Any two independent r's can validly be tested even if r_1 is between variables A and B and r_2 is between variables C and D.
18. (b), $\sigma_Z = 1/\sqrt{n-3}$
19. approximately $-.08$ to $+.46$
20. H_0 would be retained with $\alpha = .05$ since zero is included in the .95 confidence interval.
21. (a) $.05 > p > .025$
    (b) $.01 > p > .005$
    (c) $p > .05$
    (d) $p < .0005$
22. (a) $.10 > p > .05$
    (b) $.02 > p > .01$
    (c) $p > .1$
    (d) $p < .001$

PROBLEMS AND EXERCISES

1. If it is implausible that ρ could be negative (e.g., the correlation between reading and spelling), what is the critical value of r for $\alpha_1 = .05$ and $\alpha_1 = .01$ if $n = 25$? (Use Table E.)

2. If $n = 1,000$, how large must the value of r be in order to be statistically significant with $\alpha_1 = .01$? With $\alpha_2 = .01$? With $\alpha_2 = .001$?

3. Given that $r = .80$, determine the .68 CI for ρ if n is:
   (a) 12   (b) 28   (c) 103   (d) 403

4. Study the results of the preceding problem and describe the effects of n on the shape and variability of the sampling distribution of r.

5. A correlation of $r = .50$ was observed on 236 students between the group's verbal IQ scores at grade one and IQ scores 10 years later. The correlation between nonverbal IQ scores over this time interval was $r = .29$ for these same students.
   (a) Can both null hypotheses, $H_0: \rho = 0$, be rejected with $\alpha_1 = .01$?
   (b) Use Figure 13.7 to determine .95 CI's for the two corresponding parameters.
   (c) Are these two r's independent and could Equation 13.7 be used to test $H_0: \rho_1 = \rho_2$?

6. On a group intelligence test, IQ scores of 150 girls at grade 3 correlated .75 with their IQ scores four years later. The corresponding r for 154 boys was .71. Is $H_0: \rho_1 = \rho_2$ tenable at the .05 level?

7. The correlation between numerical ability test scores and course grades in Spanish I was found to be .56 for a sample of 204 students. A correlation of .40 was reported between verbal reasoning test scores and grades in Spanish I for a different sample of 186 students.
   (a) Set .68 CI's about each r using Fisher's Z-transformation.
   (b) Do grades in Spanish I correlate significantly more highly with numerical than with verbal ability scores at $\alpha = .05$?

8. Earlier in this chapter, we found that the correlation of the IQ's of identical twins reared apart was significantly lower than the correlation for identical twins reared together. Now compare the r's for identical twins reared apart with those of fraternal twins reared together ($H_0: \rho_1 = \rho_2$) with $\alpha = .01$.

   Identical Twins Reared Apart: $r = .83$, $n = 30$
   Fraternal Twins Reared Together: $r = .54$, $n = 172$

9. A correlation of .73 was observed between an instructor's interest and enthusiasm and the general excellence of the instructor with $n = 247$. Establish the .95 CI using Figure 13.7 and compare with the .95 CI obtained using Fisher's Z-transformations. Is there a practical difference between the two intervals?

10. A study was conducted to assess the relationship between a new measure of SES and scores on standardized achievement tests.
    (a) Is a one-tail test justified in this instance? The study (White & Hopkins, 1975) found that, for $n = 511$ elementary school pupils, the Pearson r between socioeconomic status and standardized achievement scores was $r = .154$.
    (b) Using Table E, can $H_0: \rho = 0$ be rejected with $\alpha_1 = .01$? At $\alpha_1 = .001$?
    (c) Alternatively, if the z-test, $z = r\sqrt{n-1}$ is used, can $H_0: \rho = 0$ be rejected at the .001 level?
    (d) Table E is just a shortcut for testing $H_0: \rho = 0$ using the t-test, $t = r / \sqrt{(1-r^2)(n-2)}$ Use the t-test to act on the null hypothesis. (If you have access to a spreadsheet, compare the actual p's for the z and t-tests.)

ANSWERS TO PROBLEMS AND EXERCISES

1. For $\alpha_1 = .05$, $_{.95}r = .337$; for $\alpha_1 = .01$, $_{.99}r = .462$.

2. .074, .081, .104

3. (a) for Z_ρ, [1.099 ± .333], for ρ, [.64, .89]

   (b) for Z_ρ, [1.099 ± .200], for ρ, [.72, .86]
   (c) for Z_ρ, [1.099 ± .100], for ρ, [.76 to .83]
   (d) for Z_ρ, [1.099 ± .050], for ρ, [.78 to .82]

4. As n increases, the variability of the sam-

pling distribution decreases and the sampling distribution becomes less skewed and more nearly normal.

5. (a) Yes, both r's exceed the critical value of r (.164) for $n = 200$ with $\alpha = .01$; indeed $p < .0005$.

   (b) .95 CI with $r = .50$: [.40, .60]; .95 CI with $r = .29$: [.16, .42].

   (c) No, the r's are dependent since they were both obtained on the same 236 persons.

6. Yes, $z = (.973 - .887)/.116 = .741 < 1.96$; therefore, H_0 is tenable.

7. (a) For $r = .56$, the .95 CI for ρ is [.51, .61], since the .95 CI for Z_ρ is [.633 ± .071]. For $r = .40$, the .95 CI for ρ is [.34, .46], since the .95 CI for Z_ρ is [.424 ± .074].

   (b) Yes:
   $$z = \frac{.633 - .424}{\sqrt{(.071)^2 + (.071)^2}} = 2.04, \quad p < .05.$$

8. $Z_{r_1} = 1.188$, $Z_{r_1} = .604$, $\sigma_{Z_{r_1}}^2 = .0370$, $\sigma_{Z_{r_2}}^2 = .0059$; $z = (1.188 - .604)/.207 = 2.82$; $p < .01$, reject H_0 at $\alpha = .01$.

9. .95 CI = [.66, .77]; $\sigma_Z = .064$, $Z \pm 1.96(\sigma_Z)$ = [.929 ± .125] for Z_ρ; [.67, .78] for ρ. No, the difference is inconsequential.

10. (a) Yes.

    (b) Yes; Yes; $p < .001$ and H_0 is rejected at the .001 level of significance. (If H_0 is rejected at the .001, it is also rejected at the .01 level.)

    (c) Yes, $z = .154(22.583) = 3.48$, $p < .001$, and H_0 can be rejected at the .001 level of significance.

    (d) Yes ($t = .154/.0438 = 3.516$, and from Table C, $t > {}_{.9995}t_{500}$, so $p < .001$) H_0 can be rejected at the .001 level of significance. ($p = .00025$ and $p = .00024$ for z and t, respectively.)

SUGGESTED COMPUTER EXERCISE

Using the HSB data set, answer the following questions.

1. Is reading significantly ($\alpha_1 = .01$) related to (a) writing, (b) math, or (c) SES.

2. In the suggested computer activity for Chapter 6, we pointed out that, if one of the two variables being correlated is a dichotomy (e.g., sex) and the other variable is continuous (e.g., reading scores), the Pearson formula for r results in the point-biserial correlation coefficient (see Glass & Hopkins, Section 7.19, 1996). Point-biserial correlations are tested for significance like other r's. Use point-biserial r's to assess gender differences in (a) reading, (b) math, (c) science, (d) writing, and (e) civics.

3. Use point-biserial r's to assess whether the difference between public and private school students is significant at $\alpha_2 = .05$ for (a) reading, (b) math, (c) science, (d) writing, and (e) civics.

❖ 14

The One-Factor Analysis of Variance
Comparisons among Means

❖ 14.1 INTRODUCTION

In Chapter 11, the t-test was used to find whether the means of two groups differed significantly. What if there are three or more groups to be compared? The statistical technique known as the analysis of variance[1] or ANOVA is used to determine whether the differences among several sample means are greater than would be expected by chance alone if the null hypothesis were true.

In this chapter, we will consider the one-factor (one-way) analysis of variance (ANOVA) procedures. By "one-factor ANOVA," we mean that there is just one independent variable (such as treatment, gender, race, age-level, geographical region, or marital status) and one dependent variable (such as IQ, achievement, attitude, income, or GPA) in the statistical analysis. Two-factor ANOVA, which allows the effects of two independent variables to be examined simultaneously, is examined in Chapter 16.

❖ 14.2 WHY ANOVA RATHER THAN MULTIPLE t-TESTS?

If the means of three groups are to be compared, why not just make three t-tests; that is, why not just compute the t-ratio for the three null hypotheses separately: $H_0: \mu_1 - \mu_2 = 0$, $H_0: \mu_1 - \mu_3 = 0$, and $H_0: \mu_2 - \mu_3 = 0$? Suppose that five groups (parents, students, teachers, principals, and superintendents) are to be compared in attitude toward a voucher proposal, why not just use the t-test for all ten combinations of two group means? [If there are J groups, the number of separate t-tests will be $J(J - 1)/2$; in this example where J is 5, the number of different comparisons is $5(4)/2$ or 10.]

---

[1]For an interesting historical account of the analysis of variance, see Kruskal (1980).

Quiz: (1) If $J = 4$ groups, how many t-tests (or pairwise comparisons) are there? (2) List all pairwise comparisons.

Answers: (1) $4(3)/2 = 6$, (2) Groups 1 and 2, groups 1 and 3, groups 1 and 4, groups 2 and 3, groups 2 and 4, and groups 3 and 4.

The major problem with using multiple t-tests is that the probability of a type-I error (α) is dramatically increased. When more than one t-test is performed, the probability of one or more type-I errors is greater than the stated α-level. Since ten t-tests would be required to make all possible pairwise comparisons when there are $J = 5$ groups, then there would be ten chances of making a type-I error when H_0 is true. The probability of incorrectly rejecting at least one of the ten null hypotheses is far greater than the specified alpha level. Indeed, for $\alpha = .05$, if all ten t-tests were independent, the probability of at least one type-I error would be .40! Table 14.1 contains estimates of the actual probability of at least one type-I error when $J = 2, 3, 5,$ and 10. Within a given study, some of the t-tests are independent, and others are not. Even though we cannot precisely estimate when the t-tests are independent, the estimates in Table 14.1 serve to illuminate a major problem with multiple t-tests: The probability of a type-I error becomes unacceptably excessive.

The statistical technique known as the analysis of variance (ANOVA), developed by the English statistician Sir Ronald Fisher in the 1920s, permits the control of α at a predetermined level when testing the equality of J group means, where $J \geq 2$. In ANOVA, the means are examined simultaneously to assess the probability that all J sample means came from the same population (i.e., populations with identical parameters). In other words, the ANOVA procedures can be used to determine whether it is reasonable to conclude that not all of the J sample means are from the same population.

For ANOVA, the null hypothesis is a single but omnibus, all-inclusive hypothesis:

$$H_0: \mu_1 = \mu_2 = \ldots = \mu_J$$

The null hypothesis in ANOVA is conceptually similar to that encountered with the χ^2 test of association. For the χ^2 test of association, the single null hypothesis specifies that all J group proportions are identical. Likewise in ANOVA, although several groups may be involved, a single overall null hypothesis is tested—there is not a separate null hypothesis for each pair of group means.

Quiz: What statistical technique would you recommend to determine if there is a significant difference: (1) between two group means, (2) between four group means, (3)

❖ **TABLE 14.1** Estimated probability of at least one type-I error if t-tests between all pairs of means were made and all t-tests were independent.

Number of Groups (J)	Number of Pairwise Comparisons (C)	Probability* of at Least One Type-I Error with $\alpha = .05$
2	1	.05
3	3	.14
5	10	.40
10	45	.90

*$p = 1 - (1 - \alpha)^c$ if the C comparisons are independent; for $\alpha = .05$: $p = 1 - (.95)^c$.

between ethnic groups with respect to the proportions who voted in the last national presidential election?

Answers: (1) *t*-test or ANOVA, (2) ANOVA, (3) χ^2 test of association

ANOVA is an efficient and powerful statistical technique; if the omnibus null hypothesis is tenable (i.e., if no strong evidence is found to reject it), one ordinarily does not proceed with further statistical comparisons among means.[2] The analysis of variance is a method of statistical inference that analyzes empirical data to determine whether there are significant differences among the set of *J* means—differences greater than can be accounted for by sampling error. When *J* = 2 groups, ANOVA and the independent *t*-test are equivalent statistical procedures; the *p*-values will always be identical—they are mathematically equivalent. When *J* > 2, ANOVA has distinct advantages over multiple *t*-tests: (1) It gives an umbrella of protection against type-I errors, whereas the actual α for the set of several separate *t*-tests is uncontrolled; (2) it is powerful and efficient, and it lends itself to more advanced analyses such as factorial ANOVA and the analysis of covariance; and (3) it will impress others with your statistical savoir faire!

❖ 14.3 THE ANOVA *F*-RATIO

If you suspect that the *analysis of variance* pertains to a *comparison of variances,* you are right. Do you recall that a variance is the ratio of the sum of squares (*SS*) to its degrees of freedom (*V*): $s^2 = SS/V$ (see Eq. 4.6 in Section 4.9)? In one-factor ANOVA we estimate the population variance in two distinct and independent ways, then compare the two estimates.

> **Quiz:** If $SS = \Sigma x^2 = 12$ and $V = 3$, $s^2 =$ ___(1)___ and $s =$ ___(2)___ . If $s = 5$ and $V = 10$, s^2 (or *MS*) = ___(2)___ and $SS =$ ___(4)___ .
>
> **Answers:** (1) 12/3 = 4, (2) 2, (3) 25, (4) 10(25) = 250

In the ANOVA context, the term "variance" is replaced by an alias, mean square (*MS*). In using the ANOVA procedures, two independent estimates of the population variance (σ^2) are compared, both of which have been touched upon in preceding chapters. These two estimates of σ^2 are symbolized as MS_W and MS_B. The first of these, $s^2 = MS_W = (SS_1 + SS_2)/(V_1 + V_2)$, was used in Section 11.8, but was limited to two groups; the procedures in ANOVA are expanded to include *J* groups. MS_W is the weighted average of the variances of the observations about the group mean in each of the *J* groups—it is not affected by differences among the group means. The meaning of MS_W is easiest to understand when the design is balanced, where MS_W is simply the average of the *J* sample variances.

The second of the two estimates of σ^2, MS_B, was introduced in Chapter 9 (see Section 9.15) when you studied $s_{\bar{X}}$, the standard error of the mean, $s_{\bar{X}} = s/\sqrt{n}$. The square of this equation, when rearranged, specifies that s^2 (or MS_B) = $ns_{\bar{X}}^2$. MS_B, the mean square between groups, is an estimate of σ^2 which reflects only the variability among group means and is not affected by the variability of the observations within groups. The keyword here is "between," and the estimate stems only from the differences *between* the group means.

We now have two separate and independent estimates of σ^2, MS_W and MS_B, one that

---

[2]There are exceptions to this generalization, namely when certain select hypotheses are specified in advance, such as planned orthogonal contrasts. These techniques are beyond the scope of the present coverage, but are treated elsewhere (Glass & Hopkins, 1996).

reflects variability among observations within groups, and the other that reflects variability between group means. When sampling from the same population (i.e., H_0 is true), both MS_B and MS_W estimate the same parameter, and their ratio (the F-ratio, named in honor of Sir Ronald Fisher), $F = MS_B/MS_W$, has the expected value of 1.0. When H_0 is false, and the differences among the J means are greater than expected by chance (sampling error), MS_B is expected to exceed MS_W, and their F-ratio is expected to be greater than 1.0. The test statistic for ANOVA is the F-ratio:

$$F = \frac{MS_B}{MS_W} \qquad\qquad (14.1)$$

Quiz: (1) Which mean square is influenced by differences among the J group means? (2) Which mean square reflects the variability of the observations within the J groups?

Answers: (1) MS_B reflects differences among means. (2) MS_W reflects variability among the scores within groups.

❖ 14.4 THE *F*-DISTRIBUTION

The theory underlying the F-test of ANOVA is based on the same assumptions as the t-test; these assumptions were considered in Chapter 11 (Section 11.12), namely that the observations (X's) in each of the J populations are (1) independent and (2) normally distributed, and (3) have equal variances (i.e., $\sigma_1^2 = \sigma_2^2 = \ldots = \sigma_J^2$). Assume for the moment that all three assumptions are met, $J = 3$, and the null hypothesis of equal means is true. Suppose that each member of an army of researchers draws a random sample of eleven observations from each of the three populations and computes $F = MS_B/MS_W$; the resulting distribution is a sampling distribution of F-ratios, and a distribution of an infinite number of such F-ratios when H_0 is true is called the central F-distribution. The frequency distribution of these F-ratios would resemble the positively skewed mathematical curve in Figure 14.1. From the central F-distribution, the mathematical statistician has calculated critical F-ratios, that is, the F-value that will be exceeded by only 100α percent (e.g., 5% or 1%) of the F-ratios when H_0 is true. Since the F-ratio is the quotient of two nonnegative numbers (variances are never negative), the F-ratio is also nonnegative and theoretically ranges from zero to infinity.

In Table F of Appendix B, the 75th, 90th, 95th, 97.5th, 99th, and 99.9th percentiles in the central F-distribution are given. The critical F-ratio depends on the degrees of freedom for the numerator ($v_B = J - 1$, i.e., the number of groups less one) and the degrees of freedom for the denominator of the F-ratio ($v_W = n. - J$, i.e., the total number of observations minus the number of groups). (Note: For one-factor ANOVA, the total number of observations is symbolized by n..)

To find the 95th percentile in the F curve with $v_B = 2$ and $v_W = 30$ degrees of freedom, find the intersection of column 2 ($v_B = 2$) and row 30 ($v_W = 30$); then read the entry for the 95th percentile. The value of $_{.95}F_{2,30}$ is 3.32.[3]

Quiz: Using Table F, estimate p for the following situations: (1) Estimate p if $v_B = 1$, $v_W = 30$, and $F = 4.00$. (2) Estimate p if $v_B = 2$, $v_W = 30$, and $F = 4.00$. (3) Estimate p

---

[3]When there is no table entry for a given row or column v-value, the closest smaller value is used. For example, for $_{.95}F_{1,29}$, use $_{.95}F_{1,28} = 4.20 \approx _{.95}F_{1,29}$. For $_{.99}F_{4,150}$, use $_{.99}F_{4,120} \approx 3.48$. If greater accuracy is needed, one can interpolate, or better yet, obtain the value from your spreadsheet.

if $v_B = 3$, $v_W = 30$, and $F = 4.00$. (4) Estimate p if $v_B = 4$, $v_W = 30$, and $F = 4.00$. (5) Estimate p if $v_B = 5$, $v_W = 30$, and $F = 4.00$.

Answers: (1) $p < .10$, (2) $p < .05$, (3) $p < .025$, (4) $p < .025$, (5) $p < .01$. (Exact p's via spreadsheet are, respectively, .055, .029, .016, .0102, and .007.)

What if the null hypothesis is not true? When H_0 is false, MS_W is not expected to change, but MS_B is expected to be larger than if the null hypothesis were true. When H_0 is false, the F-ratios (MS_B/MS_W) obtained by the army of researchers independently replicating the study do not have a central F-distribution, but instead have a noncentral F'-distribution; the noncentral F'-distribution has a mean greater than that of the central F-distribution. For false H_0's, the distribution of observed noncentral F ratios will be larger on the average than the distribution of central F-ratios, and is represented by curve F' in Figure 14.1. Notice that the F-ratio shifts to the right (increases) when the null hypothesis is false. Of course, as differences among the population means increase, the F'-distribution shifts further and further to the right; and when differences among the population means are great, there may be very little overlap between the F-distribution and the F'-distribution.

Is a computed F-ratio greater than 3.32 more likely to occur if the null hypothesis is true or if it is false? In Figure 14.1, compare the areas under the two curves to the right of the point 3.32 and see which area is larger (i.e., which shows a greater probability of yielding a value of F greater than 3.32). Only a small proportion (.05) of the area of the central F-distribution falls above the value of 3.32, whereas perhaps a third of the area in the F'-distribution exceeds 3.32. Statistical power (i.e., the probability of rejecting H_0 when it is false) is represented by the shaded area in the noncentral F'-distribution in Figure 14.1.

What if we obtained an F-ratio of 3.51? Since the 95th percentile of the curve $F_{2,30}$ is 3.32, a rare event has occurred if H_0 is true. Other things being equal, fewer than five times in 100 is an F-ratio as large or larger than 3.32 obtained when the null hypothesis is true. If the null hypothesis is false, then large values of F are more likely to be observed.

If the value of the obtained F-ratio would occur less than 5% of the time under a true null hypothesis (i.e., if the F-ratio is greater than the 95th percentile of the corresponding

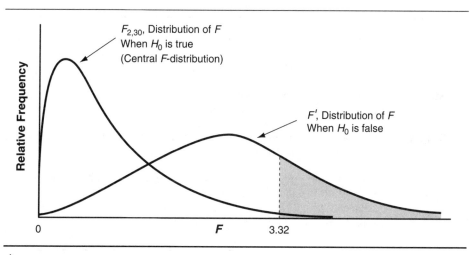

❖ **FIGURE 14.1** Sampling distributions of $F = MS_B/MS_W$ when H_0 is true (curve $F_{2,30}$) and a non-central F-distribution (i.e., a distribution when H_0 is false).

central F-distribution), then we will reject the null hypothesis at the .05 level of significance ($p < .05$). It seems probable that such a value indicates a false null hypothesis since such large F-ratios are more likely if the null hypothesis is false. As in making other statistical tests, choosing the 95th percentile of the curve $F_{2,30}$ as the point on which the decision about H_0 hinges is arbitrary. One could have chosen the 90th, 99th, or 99.9th percentile point. What if the 75th percentile point had been chosen? One would have a probability of $p = .25$ of rejecting H_0 (making a type-I error) when it is true. One-fourth of the army of researchers would make a type-I error and conclude that there are treatment effects when actually the treatments were equally effective. To guard against these type-I errors, we will conclude that the null hypothesis is false only when the computed F-ratio has a sufficiently small probability of occurrence when the null hypothesis is true ("sufficiently small" usually means p-values of .10, .05, or .01).

Some of your predecessors have made the mistake of thinking that whenever the computed F-ratio is statistically significant it means that the null hypothesis is therefore certainly false. Actually, as you well know, such assertions are not possible except when the entire population has been included in the analysis. For sample data, a researcher makes a conclusion of the form "I reject H_0 as a true statement" when there is sufficient empirical evidence to warrant it; or "I do not reject H_0 as a true statement" when such strong evidence to the contrary is lacking. Although we may have a high level of confidence in our conclusion to reject H_0 as untenable, we are never absolutely certain that a rejected H_0 is in fact false. On the other hand, when we retain H_0 as tenable, it is because we lack sufficient cause to conclude it to be false, not that we believe that H_0 is proven to be true.

❖ 14.5 HYPOTHESIS TESTING USING THE ANOVA F-RATIO

The steps to perform a one-factor ANOVA test of a null hypothesis are listed below. Although there are other mathematically equivalent computational algorithms to compute F, we feel that the following approach is best for illuminating the underlying rationale of ANOVA.

Step 1. State the statistical hypothesis to be tested. For example:

$$H_0: \mu_1 = \mu_2 = \ldots = \mu_J$$

Step 2. Specify the level of risk you are willing to take of concluding that H_0 is false when it is true. For example: $\alpha = .05$.

Step 3. Compute the F-ratio and find its p-value. To do this you need to compute: (a) MS_B, (b) MS_W, (c) F, and (d) find p from Table F.

(a) Compute "mean square between" (MS_B), the estimate of the population variance using the differences among the J means. In a balanced design ($n_1 = n_2 = \ldots n_j$), the computations can be accomplished by using Equations 14.2 and 14.3:

$$MS_B = n s_{\bar{X}}^2 \qquad (14.2)$$

$$s_{\bar{X}}^2 = \frac{\Sigma_j(\bar{X}_j - \bar{X}_{\boldsymbol{\cdot}})^2}{J-1} \qquad \textbf{(14.3)}$$

That is, $s_{\bar{X}}^2$ is the variance among the J group means. For unbalanced designs with unequal sample sizes, Equations 14.4, 14.5, and 14.6 can be used to compute MS_B:

$$MS_B = \frac{SS_B}{v_B} \qquad \textbf{(14.4)}$$

$$SS_B = \Sigma n_j(\bar{X}_j - \bar{X}_{\boldsymbol{\cdot}})^2 \qquad \textbf{(14.5)}$$

$$v_B = J - 1 \qquad \textbf{(14.6)}$$

(b) Compute the "mean square within" (MS_W), the estimate of the population variance using the variances of the observations within the J samples. In a balanced design the computation of MS_W is simply the mean of the J variances as shown in Equation 14.7:

$$MS_W = \frac{\Sigma s_j^2}{J} = \frac{s_1^2 + s_2^2 + \ldots + s_J^2}{J} \qquad \textbf{(14.7)}$$

For an unbalanced design, Equations 14.8–14.10 can be used to compute MS_W:

$$MS_W = \frac{SS_W}{v_W} \qquad \textbf{(14.8)}$$

$$SS_W = \sum_j SS_j = \sum_j (\sum_i X_{ij}^2 - n_j \bar{X}_j^2) \qquad \textbf{(14.9)}$$

$$v_W = n_{\boldsymbol{\cdot}} - J \qquad \textbf{(14.10)}$$

(c) Compute the ratio, F, of these two variance estimates:

$$F = \frac{MS_B}{MS_W} \qquad \textbf{(14.11)}$$

(d) Find the probability (p) of a computed F-ratio this large if H_0 were true. (Use either Table F or obtain p from a computer program).

> **Step 4.**   Conclude that H_0 is false if $p \leq \alpha$; if $p > \alpha$, conclude that H_0 is tenable.

A flowchart of this hypothesis testing procedure for one-factor ANOVA is depicted in Figure 14.2.

An illustration of the sequence to test $H_0: \mu_1 = \mu_2 = \mu_3$ using the ANOVA F-test procedures for $J = 3$ groups with equal sample sizes is given in Table 14.2.

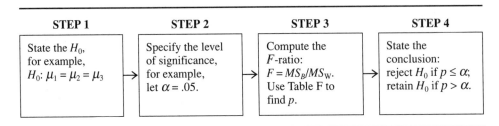

STEP 1	STEP 2	STEP 3	STEP 4
State the H_0, for example, $H_0: \mu_1 = \mu_2 = \mu_3$	Specify the level of significance, for example, let $\alpha = .05$.	Compute the F-ratio: $F = MS_B/MS_W$. Use Table F to find p.	State the conclusion: reject H_0 if $p \leq \alpha$; retain H_0 if $p > \alpha$.

❖ **FIGURE 14.2** Flowchart of the hypothesis testing procedures for the ANOVA F-test.

❖ **TABLE 14.2** An illustration of the sequence to test $H_0: \mu_1 = \mu_2 = \mu_3$ using the ANOVA F-ratio for $J = 3$ treatment groups with hypothetical IQ data and equal sample sizes ($n = 4$).

	Observations	n	$\overline{X}$	s^2
Intensive Treatment:	107, 100, 101, 92	4	100	38.0
Parent Treatment:	91, 95, 90, 88	4	91	8.67
Control Group:	87, 86, 82, 85	4	85	4.67
For the composite sample:		$n_. = 12$	$\overline{X}_. = 92$	

Step 1:   State the null hypothesis: $H_0: \mu_1 = \mu_2 = \mu_3$
Step 2:   Specify the level of significance: $\alpha = .05$
Step 3:   Compute the F-ratio and find its p-value:
  (a)   Compute $MS_B = ns_{\overline{X}}^2$, where $s_{\overline{X}}^2 = \Sigma(\overline{X}_j - \overline{X}_.)^2/(J-1)$.
    $s_{\overline{X}}^2 = [(100 - 92)^2 + (91 - 92)^2 + (85 - 92)^2]/2 = 57$
    $MS_B = ns_{\overline{X}}^2 = 4(57) = 228$
  (b)   Compute $MS_W = \Sigma s_j^2/J$
    $MS_W = (s_1^2 + s_2^2 + s_3^2)/3 = (38.0 + 8.67 + 4.67)/3 = 17.11$
  (c)   Compute $F = MS_B/MS_W = 228/17.11 = 13.32$
  (d)   From Table F, $.01 > p > .001$.

ANOVA Summary Table

SV	v	MS	F	p
Between groups	2	228.0	13.32	<.01[a]
Within groups	9	17.11		

[a]Actual $p = .002$ (from computer).

Step 4:   Reject H_0 and conclude that the three group means are not all equal.

❖ 14.6 ONE-FACTOR ANOVA: AN ILLUSTRATION

We will illustrate this hypothesis testing procedure with some data from the HSB data set (Appendix B Table I). Recall that the students of the HSB data set were classified according to three types of high school programs: general, academic, and vocational. We are curious as to whether the writing ability of the students differs among the three types of high school programs; that is, is there a significant difference between the writing means between the three types of high school programs at the .05 level? (Since our purpose is to illustrate the process, we will simplify the analysis by using only a random sample of six students from each of the three high school programs.) Table 14.3 gives the raw scores as well the computations needed to determine the ANOVA F-ratio and complete the hypothesis test of H_0. The results are conveniently summarized in the ANOVA summary table found in Table 14.3.

Since $p < .01$, we can reject H_0 at the .01 level. We are convinced that the population means for the general, academic, and vocational programs are not all equal. From a cursory view of the group means in Table 14.3, it would appear that the mean of the vocational group is less than the other two group means. However, such informal guesses are often hazardous. We will learn how to use one of the "multiple comparison" procedures following the ANOVA to ferret out which means differ from which other means in Chapter 15.

❖ **TABLE 14.3** An illustration of the ANOVA F-test procedure to test the null hypothesis of equivalent writing score means for the $J = 3$ types of high school programs with $n = 6$ subjects per group.

	Observations	n	$\overline{X}$	s^2
General Program:	65, 54, 54, 59, 47, 65	6	57.33	49.87
Academic Program:	62, 52, 59, 62, 65, 62	6	60.33	20.27
Vocational Program:	57, 54, 49, 39, 46, 43	6	48.00	45.60
For the composite sample:		$n_. = 18$	$\overline{X}_. = 55.22$	

Step 1: State the null hypothesis. H_0: $\mu_1 = \mu_2 = \mu_3$.
Step 2: Specify the level of significance: $\alpha = .05$.
Step 3: Compute the F-ratio and find its p-value:
    (a) Compute $MS_B = ns_{\overline{X}}^2$, where $s_{\overline{X}}^2 = \Sigma(\overline{X}_j - \overline{X}_.)^2/(J-1)$.
        $s_{\overline{X}}^2 = [(57.33 - 55.22)^2 + (60.33 - 55.22)^2 + (48 - 55.22)^2]/2 = 41.35$
        $MS_B = ns_{\overline{X}}^2 = 6(41.35) = 248.1$
    (b) Compute $MS_W = \Sigma s_j^2/J$
        $MS_W = (s_1^2 + s_2^2 + s3^2)/3 = (49.87 + 20.27 + 45.60)/3 = 38.58$
    (c) Compute $F = MS_B/MS_W = 248.1/38.58 = 6.43$
    (d) From Table F, $p < .01$.

ANOVA Summary Table

SV	ν	MS	F	p
Between groups	2	248.1	6.43	<.01[a]
Within groups	15	38.58		

Critical F-value for $\alpha = .05$: $._{95}F_{2,15} = 3.68$

[a]Actual $p = .0096$.

Step 4: Since $p < \alpha$, reject H_0 as untenable; we are convinced that H_0 is false, that the writing score means for the three high school programs are not all identical.

❖ 14.7 THE ANOVA TABLE

The ANOVA summary table is a convenient and common method of reporting ANOVA findings. ANOVA summary tables become even more important with two-factor (Chapter 16) and other more complex ANOVA designs. The ANOVA summary table in Table 14.3 shows that the variance estimate from the differences among the group means was 6.43 times greater than the variances estimate based on observations within the three program types, and that such a large F-ratio would occur by chance less than one time in 100.

❖ 14.8 ANOTHER ANOVA ILLUSTRATION

An extrasensory perception (ESP) experiment was conducted in which twenty persons were randomly assigned to either an experimental or a control group. Both groups viewed the same four geometric shapes. In the experimental group, the researcher served as a "transmitter," concentrating on one of the shapes; the other persons in this group tried to receive the "signal" which was transmitted. In the control group, the persons were instructed to guess randomly before any "signal" was mentally transmitted. The null hypothesis states that both population means are equal—the ESP treatment will have no effect.

Scores and preliminary computations for the ten experimental subjects and ten control subjects are given in Table 14.4. Is the difference in observed means ($\overline{X}_E = 5.0$ vs.

❖ **TABLE 14.4** An Illustration of the ANOVA F-test procedure using ESP data with $J = 2$ groups and $n = 10$ subjects per group.

	Observations	n	$\overline{X}$	s^2
Experimental Group:	2, 3, 3, 3, 4, 5, 6, 6, 8, 10	10	5.0	6.44
Control Group:	3, 3, 4, 4, 4, 4, 5, 5, 6, 7	10	4.5	1.61
For the composite sample:		$n_. = 20$	$\overline{X}_. = 4.75$	

Step 1: State the null hypothesis: $H_0: \mu_1 = \mu_2$.
Step 2: Specify the level of significance: $\alpha = .10$.
Step 3: Compute the F-ratio and find its p-value:
(a) Compute $MS_B = ns_{\overline{X}}^2$, where $s_{\overline{X}}^2 = \Sigma(\overline{X}_j - \overline{X}_.)^2/(J - 1)$
$s_{\overline{X}}^2 = [(5 - 4.75)^2 + (4.5 - 4.75)^2]/1 = .125$
$MS_B = ns_{\overline{X}}^2 = 10(.125) = 1.25$
(b) Compute $MS_W = \Sigma s_j^2/J$
$MS_W = (s_1^2 + s_2^2)/2 = (6.44 + 1.61)/2 = 4.025$
(c) Compute $F = MS_B/MS_W = 1.25/4.025 = .31$
(d) From Table F, $p > .25$.

ANOVA Summary Table

SV	v	MS	F	p
Between groups	1	1.25	.310	>.25[a]
Within groups	18	4.03		

Critical F-value for $\alpha = .10$: $_{.90}F_{1,18} = 3.01$

[a]Actual $p = .58$.

Step 4. Since $p > \alpha$, retain H_0 as tenable; we are not convinced that H_0 is false.

$\overline{X}_C = 4.5$) large enough to allow the null hypothesis (H_0: $\mu_1 = \mu_2$) to be rejected? The four-step hypothesis testing procedure portrayed in Figure 14.2 is illustrated in Table 14.4, using $\alpha = .10$.

The obtained F-ratio of .31 is far below the critical value of 3.01 for $\alpha = .10$ (indeed $p > .25$); hence, this experiment provides no evidence of an ESP phenomenon. When the null hypothesis is true, MS_B and MS_W are independent estimates of the same parameter, σ; thus, the expected value of the F-ratio when H_0 is true is approximately 1. In other words, in the ESP experiment, not only did the means not differ significantly, the difference was even less than one would ordinarily observe when the population means are equal.

❖ 14.9 THE *F*-RATIO VERSUS THE *t*-RATIO

Of course, since $J = 2$ in Table 14.4, we have the option of either using ANOVA or the independent *t*-test. Since "Life is too short not to have a little fun," let us enjoy testing the null hypothesis of Table 14.4 ($H_0 = \mu_1 = \mu_2$) using the independent *t*-test.

The equation for the independent *t*-test (Eq. 11.8) is included and expanded below:

$$t = \frac{(\overline{X}_1 - \overline{X}_2)}{s_{\overline{X}_1 - \overline{X}_2}} = \frac{(\overline{X}_1 - \overline{X}_2)}{s_W \sqrt{(1/n_1 + 1/n_2)}} = \frac{(\overline{X}_1 - \overline{X}_2)}{\sqrt{MS_W(1/n_1 + 1/n_2)}}$$

$$t = (5.0 - 4.5)/\sqrt{4.03(1/10 + 1/10)}$$

$$t = .5/\sqrt{.806} = .5/.898 = .557$$

For these data, the critical *t*-ratio is $_{.95}t_{18} = 1.734$, and since the computed $t <$ the critical t, H_0 is retained as tenable. These data give no support for the view that H_0 is false.

Note that $t^2 = (.557)^2 = .310 = F$. In other words, when there are only two group means, $F = t^2$, and the *t*-test and ANOVA are equivalent ways of testing H_0: $\mu_1 - \mu_2 = 0$. However, if J is ≥ 3, ANOVA should definitely be used to avoid an excessive risk of type-I errors.

Quiz: When $J = 2$, if $t = 2.2$, $F = \underline{\quad(1)\quad}$, and if $F = 9$, $t = \underline{\quad(2)\quad}$.
Answers: (1) $(2.2)^2 = 4.84$, (2) $\sqrt{9} = 3$.

❖ 14.10 TOTAL SUM OF SQUARES

Given J sample groups of data, there will be J sample means, but only one grand mean, $\overline{X}. = \Sigma\Sigma X_{ij}/n.$, the mean of all raw scores from all groups. For one-factor ANOVA, the grand mean is symbolized by $\overline{X}.$; for two-factor ANOVA (Chapter 16), $\overline{X}..$ is the symbol for the grand mean; $\overline{X}...$ for three-factor ANOVA (next statistics course), et cetera.

Quiz: When will the grand mean equal the mean of the J sample means?

Answers: Only when all groups are comprised of the same number of observations, that is, when all of the group n's are equal (or when all group means are identical).

When ANOVA was computed by hand, extensive use was made of sums of squares in testing null hypotheses. SS_{total} is the sum of the squared deviations of all scores from the grand mean:

$$SS_{total} = \Sigma\Sigma(X_{ij} - \overline{X}_{.})^2 \qquad \textbf{(14.12a)}$$

$$SS_{total} = \Sigma\Sigma x_{ij}^2 = \Sigma\Sigma X_{ij}^2 - n.\overline{X}_{.}^2 \qquad \textbf{(14.12b)}$$

$$SS_{total} = \Sigma\Sigma X_{ij}^2 - (\Sigma\Sigma X_{ij})^2 / n. \qquad \textbf{(14.12c)}$$

The total sum of squares in any set of data is a composite that is an aggregate of differences among means and individual differences within the groups. *In one-factor ANOVA, the total sum of squares can be partitioned into just two independent sources of variation, SS_B and SS_W.* SS_B, the sum of squares between groups, is the SS attributable to the differences between the J group means; and SS_W, the sum of squares within groups, is the SS attributable to the variability of group raw scores about their own group mean. Equation 14.13 makes explicit the relationship between these three sums of squares:

$$SS_{total} = SS_B + SS_W \qquad \textbf{(14.13)}$$

If any two of them are known, the third can readily be obtained arithmetically. For example, if SS_{total} and SS_B are known, SS_W can be obtained by taking the difference between SS_{total} and SS_B.

Quiz: (1) If $SS_{total} = 444$ and $SS_B = 124$, $SS_W = \underline{\quad?\quad}$. (2) If $SS_B = 68$ and $SS_W = 255$, $SS_{total} = \underline{\quad?\quad}$.
Answers: (1) 320, (2) 323

❖ 14.11 THE MEAN SQUARE BETWEEN GROUPS, MS_B, REVISITED

In Chapter 9, we saw that when many random samples of size n are drawn from a population, the expected value of the mean of the sample means is μ and the expected value of the variance of the J means will be σ^2/n. If J samples are randomly drawn from a single population (i.e., H_0 is true), as illustrated in Panel B of Figure 14.3, we expect the variance of the sampling distribution of these J sample means (Panel C) to be about σ^2/n. Then, n times the variance of the J sample means will estimate σ^2, that is, $ns_{\overline{X}}^2$ estimates σ^2.

❖ 14.12 MEAN SQUARE WITHIN, MS_W, REVISITED

Let us look back at the J samples (Panel B of Figure 14.3). Each of the J samples gives an unbiased estimate s_j^2 of the common population variance, σ^2. If we averaged all of these variance estimates, we would obtain an even better estimate of σ^2. Hence, as we saw in Equation 14.7, with a balanced design:

$$MS_W = \frac{\Sigma s_j^2}{J} = \frac{s_1^2 + s_2^2 + \ldots + s_J^2}{J}$$

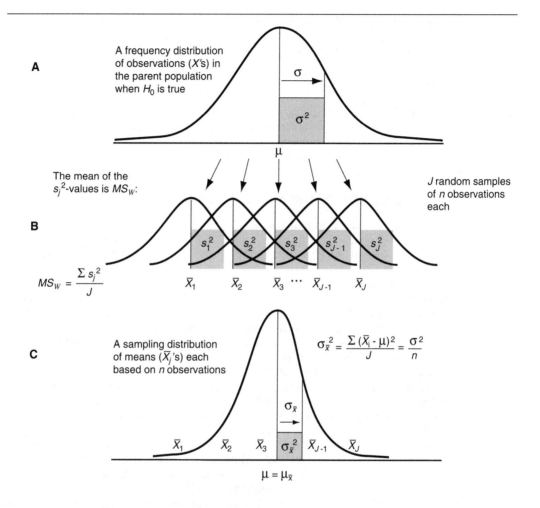

1. Since $s_{\bar{x}}^2 = \frac{s^2}{n}$, $ns_{\bar{x}}^2 = s^2$. Hence, $E(ns_{\bar{x}}^2) = \sigma^2$; $ns_{\bar{x}}^2$ is called the mean square between, or MS_B.

2. $\dfrac{\Sigma s_j^2}{J} = \dfrac{(s_1^2 + \cdots + s_J^2)}{J} = s_W^2$; $E(s_W^2) = \sigma^2$; s_W^2 is called the mean square within, or MS_W

3. Therefore, the expected value $F = \dfrac{MS_B}{MS_W} \approx 1$ when the null hypothesis is true.

❖ **FIGURE 14.3** Theoretical basis of the ANOVA. The variance error of the mean, $s_{\bar{x}}^2$, when multiplied by n, gives an unbiased estimate of the variance among the observations in the frequency distribution of the population when the null hypothesis is true.

When the n's are equal, MS_W is the average of the J group sample variances.

Quiz: If all $J = 3$ groups have the same n, and if $s_1^2 = 15$, $s_2^2 = 24$, and $s_3^2 = 30$, $MS_W = \underline{\quad ? \quad}$.

Answer: $69/3 = 23$

In Panel B of Figure 14.3, MS_W is the average of the shaded boxes. When the ANOVA assumptions have been met, MS_W (like MS_B) estimates σ^2. *An important fact about MS_W is that it unbiasedly estimates σ^2 whether or not the null hypothesis is true, whereas the expected value of MS_B is greater than σ^2 when H_0 is false.*

❖ 14.13 OVERVIEW OF THE ANOVA RATIONALE

In this section, we will attempt to clarify and summarize some of the basic concepts in ANOVA. We will review why the mean square between and the mean square within are defined as they are, why they are compared as a ratio, and why that ratio is relevant to the null hypothesis.

Suppose that the null hypothesis $H_0: \mu_1 = \mu_2 = \ldots = \mu_J$ is true. That is, the J population means about which one wishes to make an inference all have the same value. This hypothesis when combined with the ordinary ANOVA assumptions implies that there are J populations, all of which are normal in shape and have identical means, μ, and variances, σ^2. In effect, if the null hypothesis is true, there are not J different populations; in terms of the statistical parameters, there is only one population. Thus, the J random samples each of size n are actually drawn from a single population.

Note that if the null hypothesis is true, then MS_B and MS_W are both estimates the same parameter, namely, σ^2. Although we cannot prove so here, MS_B and MS_W are independent estimates of σ^2 under these circumstances. If we compare MS_B and MS_W by taking their ratio, $F = MS_B/MS_W$, we can get some idea whether they are estimating the same or different values. If the ratio of MS_B to MS_W is about 1, then it is reasonable to retain the hypothesis that they are both estimating σ^2, that is, that the null hypothesis is tenable. How much greater than a value of 1 can the F-ratio $= MS_B/MS_W$ be and the null hypothesis remain tenable is best determined by finding p, the probability of obtaining an observed F-ratio this large when the null hypothesis is true. The p-value can be estimated by comparing the observed F-ratio to the central F-distribution (Table F). The central F-distribution describes the distribution of the ratio of two independent estimates of the same variance when H_0 is true for many combinations of v_B and v_W. When the computations are performed by computer, the central F-distribution is a part of the computational process, and p is reported precisely.

If the null hypothesis, H_0, is false, then the variance estimate resulting from differences among the J sample means (MS_B) is expected to be larger than when H_0 is true; MS_B estimates a number greater than σ^2 when H_0 is false. However, MS_W is expected to remain the same whether or not the null hypothesis specifying identical means is true, because it is based on variances of scores *within* the J samples and is not affected by differences *among* the J means. Consequently, a false null hypothesis tends to result in a larger ratio of MS_B to MS_W.

Such are the reasons for forming $F = MS_B/MS_W$, obtaining p by comparing it to the central F-distribution. H_0 is regarded as tenable if the ratio $F = MS_B/MS_W$ is not particularly large, but is rejected as false when $F = MS_B/MS_W$ is larger than the α-critical value.

If H_0 is rejected, does it necessarily follow that $\mu_1 \neq \mu_2 \neq \mu_3 \neq \ldots \neq \mu_j$? Certainly not; perhaps $\mu_1 > \mu_2 = \mu_3 = \ldots = \mu_j$, or $\mu_1 = \mu_2 > \mu_3 = \ldots = \mu_j$, or any one of several patterns of results is possible. How, then, does one decide which means differ significantly from which other means? The answer to this excellent question is the topic of multiple comparisons, and is addressed in Chapter 15.

❖ 14.14 CONSEQUENCES OF VIOLATING ANOVA ASSUMPTIONS

The assumptions of ANOVA are identical to those of the t-test: (1) normality, (2) homogeneity of variance, and (3) independence of samples. This is hardly surprising since, when $J = 2$, $t^2 = F$. Study Figure 11.5 (Section 11.13) to confirm that non-normality has benign consequences; ANOVA is robust with respect to violations of the normality assumption.

Study Figure 11.6 (Section 11.14) to review the consequences of heterogeneous variances; note that only when the n's are equal is ANOVA robust with respect to violating the assumption: $\sigma_1^2 = \sigma_2^2 = \ldots = \sigma_j^2$. Note also in Figure 11.6 that, when the larger n is paired with the larger σ^2, we have a conservative test of H_0; that is, the true probability of a type-I error is less than the apparent, nominal, or stated level of significance, α, associated with the tabled critical values. However, if the larger n is paired with the smaller σ^2, we have a liberal test, and erroneously reject true H_0's more often than the α associated with the tabled critical value; that is, the probability of a type-I error will be larger than the nominal α-value. This pattern generalizes to situations in which $J > 2$.

As with the t-test, it is recommended that the n's be equal whenever possible. So that even if the variances are heterogeneous, the consequences can be disregarded.[4]

The independence assumption is more difficult to evaluate (Section 11.16). Independence in the sampling of observations requires that the observations within (or between) groups not be influenced by each other. Whenever the treatment is individually administered, independence is ordinarily no problem. However, where treatments involve interaction among persons in groups, such as "discussion" method, group counseling, and encounter groups, the observations may influence each other. If the observations are analyzed as if the data were independent, the true probability of a type-I error is apt to be larger than the nominal . In other words, nonindependence of observations increases the probability that treatment effects will be claimed for non-efficacious treatments (Hopkins, 1982).

❖ CHAPTER SUMMARY

When two means ($J = 2$) are to be compared, either the independent t-test or ANOVA is appropriate; they are mathematically equivalent ($t^2 = F$) and always yield identical p-values and conclusions regarding H_0. If $J > 2$, running several t-tests among the J means is undesirable because it results in an increased probability of type-I errors. When two or more means are to be compared, the analysis of variance (ANOVA) should be used to test the omnibus null hypothesis, H_0: $\mu_1 = \mu_2 = \ldots = \mu_J$.

ANOVA allocates the total sum of squares (SS_{total}) in a set of observations to two independent sources of variation: (1) differences among means (SS_B) and (2) differences among observations within groups (SS_W). When SS_B and SS_W are divided by their degrees of freedom, two independent variance estimates (MS_B and MS_W) are obtained. When H_0 is true,

---

[4]Procedures for testing the homogeneity of variance assumption are included in most computer programs for ANOVA. In addition to Equation 11.9 of Chapter 11, various other methods are treated in Glass & Hopkins, 1996.

both MS_B and MS_W estimate the same parameter, σ^2, and the expected value of the F-ratio (MS_B/MS_W) is approximately 1. If H_0 is false, the expected value of MS_B is increased, and the expected value of the F-ratio is increased. The distribution of F-ratios when H_0 is true is termed the central F-distribution. The observed F-ratio is referenced to the central F-distribution to find p, the probability of an F-ratio this large when the null hypothesis is true; when $p < \alpha$, H_0 is rejected, when $p > \alpha$, H_0 remains tenable.

ANOVA assumes that the observations in the J populations are (1) normally distributed, (2) have equal variances, and (3) are independent. When the n's are equal, ANOVA is robust to assumptions 1 and 2 (i.e., violations of the statistical assumptions have negligible consequences on p, the probability of a type-I error). When the n's are not equal, however, homogeneity of variance is necessary for accurate results. If larger n's and larger σ^2's are paired, the true α is less than the stated α; if we reject H_0 under these conditions, our claims are credible. However, if we retain H_0 under these conditions, there is a greater risk of a type-II error. If larger n's are paired with smaller σ^2's, the true α is greater than the nominal α. Hence, rejecting H_0 under these conditions is made with greater risk of a type-I error; retaining H_0 under these conditions results in a lesser risk of a type-II error.

The assumption of independence of X's is not violated if the observations within each group do not influence each other. Nonindependence is more apt to be a problem when treatments are group-oriented, such as in group counseling.

MASTERY TEST

1. Suppose pupils in grades 7, 8, 9, 10, 11, and 12 ($J = 6$) were compared with respect to absenteeism (% of days absent). If ANOVA is used rather than multiple t-tests, the probability of a
  (a) type-I error is less.
  (b) type-II error is less.

2. How many different t-tests would be required to make all possible pairwise comparisons of means in question 1 above where $J = 6$? [$C = J(J-1)/2$]

3. Write the null hypothesis for the omnibus F-test in question 1. (Use grade levels for subscripts for the respective means.)

4. If ANOVA is performed and the critical F-value associated with $\alpha = .05$ is used, is the probability of a type-I error equal to .05 when H_0 is true?

5. If H_0 is true, and if multiple t-tests were used, and if the critical t-value with $\alpha = .05$ were used, the probability of rejecting at least one of the 15 H_0's is
  (a) slightly less than .05.   (c) slightly greater than .05.
  (b) .05.   (d) much greater than .05.

6. A synonym for sum of squares (SS) is
  (a) $\overline{X}$.   (b) Σx^2.   (c) ΣX^2.   (d) $(\Sigma X)^2$.

7. In question 6 above, does option c equal option d?

Questions 8–10 refer to the following scores, X: 8, 9, 10.

8. What is the numerical value of ΣX?

9. What is the numerical value of n?

10. What is the numerical value of $SS = \Sigma x^2$?

11. When a sum of squares (SS) is divided by its degrees of freedom (v), the result is a variance estimate. What is another name for a variance estimate?

For questions 12 and 13: In ANOVA, the total sum of squares can be divided into two sources of variation: (1) the SS due to differences between group means and (2) the SS due to differences among the X's within groups.

12. Which of these sources has $v = (J - 1)$ degrees of freedom, SS_B or SS_W?

13. Which of these has $v = (n. - J)$ degrees of freedom, SS_B or SS_W?

14. In ANOVA, which of these is the numerator of the F-test, MS_B or MS_W?

15. If $J = 3$ and $\overline{X}_1 = \overline{X}_2 = \overline{X}_3 = 110$, what is MS_B?

16. In question 15, what is the numerical value of the grand mean, $\overline{X}.$?

17. In question 15, will $SS_{total} = SS_W$?

18. In ANOVA, if H_0 is true, the expected values of both MS_B and $MS_W = $ __?__.

19. If the observed F-ratio is 1.0 or less, will H_0 be rejected even with $\alpha = .25$?

20. The mean of the thirty-one persons in the E group was compared to the mean for the thirty-one persons in the C group using a t-test. The computed t-value was 2.5. If ANOVA is performed on the same data, what numerical value will the F-ratio have?

21. The critical value for t in question 20 with $\alpha = .05$ is 2.00; what is the critical F-value $(_{.95}F_{1,60})$?

In questions 22–24 below, indicate which F-value will be the smallest. (Note trends in Table F.)

22. (a) $_{.90}F_{2,30}$ (b) $_{.95}F_{2,30}$ (c) $_{.99}F_{2,30}$

23. (a) $_{.95}F_{3,1}$ (b) $_{.95}F_{3,30}$ (c) $_{.95}F_{3,60}$

24. (a) $_{.95}F_{1,60}$ (b) $_{.95}F_{2,60}$ (c) $_{.95}F_{3,60}$

Answer questions 25–34 below given that J = 4.

ANOVA Summary Table

SV	SS	v	MS	F	p
Between	30	___	___	___	___
Within	___	60	2.0		

Critical F-value for $\alpha = .05$: ___F___,___ = ___

25. What is the numerical value of v_B?

26. What is the numerical value of MS_B?

27. Compute the F-ratio.

28. If $\alpha = .05$, what is the critical value of F?

29. Will $H_0: \mu_1 = \mu_2 = \mu_3 = \mu_4$ be rejected at $\alpha = .05$?

30. Can H_0 be rejected at $\alpha = .01$?

31. Can H_0 be rejected at $\alpha = .001$?

32. What is $n.$ for this example?

33. What is the numerical value of SS_W?

34. What is the numerical value of SS_{total}?

35. Will non-normality of X's ordinarily lead us to erroneous conclusions regarding H_0 when ANOVA is used?

36. When using ANOVA with equal n's, do we need to be concerned about the homogeneity of variance assumption?

37. When using ANOVA with *unequal n's*, should we be concerned about the assumption of equal group variances?

38. If $n_1 > n_2$ and $\sigma_1 > \sigma_2$ and H_0 is rejected, is the action suspect?

39. If the larger n's are paired with the smaller variances and H_0 is not rejected, is the conclusion suspect?

40. The independence of X's assumption is *least* apt to be satisfied in which of the following circumstances?
(a) The treatment is administered separately to each individual.
(b) The treatment is administered to a group of persons simultaneously.

41. If the n's are equal, will $\bar{X}. = \Sigma \bar{X}_j/J$?

42. Given that the $J = 4$ groups have equal n's in the ANOVA table preceding question 25, what is the average group variance? (See Eq. 14.7.)

43. The *average* standard deviation for the four groups in question 42 would be somewhere in the neighborhood of
(a) 1.   (b) 1.5.   (c) 2.0.   (d) 2.5.

44. If the ranges of scores within groups 1 through 4 are found to be 6, 5, 4, and 5 when $n = 16$, does the value of $MS_W = 2.0$ seem reasonable? (See Table 4.1.)

ANSWERS TO MASTERY TEST

1. (a)

2. 15

3. $H_0: \mu_7 = \mu_8 = \mu_9 = \mu_{10} = \mu_{11} = \mu_{12}$

4. yes

5. (d)

6. (b)

7. no

8. 27

9. 3

10. $SS = 1^2 + 0^2 + (-1)^2 = 2$

11. mean square

12. SS_B

13. SS_W

14. MS_B

15. Zero; if all observed group means are equal, $SS_B = 0$ and $MS_B = 0$.

16. $\bar{X}. = 110$

17. Yes, since $SS_B = 0$.

18. σ^2

19. No; the expected value for F when H_0 is true is 1.

20. $(2.5)^2 = 6.25$ (F = t^2)

21. $_{.95}F_{1,60} = 4.00$ (When $J = 2$, $F = t^2$.)

22. (a)

23. (c)

24. (c)

25. $\nu_B = J - 1 = 3$

26. $MS_B = SS_B/\nu_B = 30/3 = 10$

27. $F = 10/2 = 5.0$

28. $_{.95}F_{3,60} = 2.76$

29. Yes; $F = 5.0 > 2.76 = _{.95}F_{3,60}.$

30. Yes; $F = 5.0 > 4.13 = _{.99}F_{3,60}.$

31. No; $F = 5.0 < 6.17 = _{.999}F_{3,60}.$

32. Since $\nu_{Total} = 63 = n. - 1$, $n. = 64$.

33. $120 = \nu_W(MS_W)$

34. 150 ($SS_{total} = SS_B + SS_W$)

35. no

36. no

37. Yes; ANOVA is robust to a violation of the homogeneity of variance assumption only when the n's are equal.

38. No; when larger n's and larger variances are associated, the probability of a type-I error is even less than the nominal α.

39. No; when the larger n's are paired with the smaller variances, the probability of a type-I error is greater than the nominal α. Hence, if H_0 is not rejected at the nominal α, it certainly would not be rejected at the true α.

40. (b)

41. yes

42. $MS_W = \Sigma s_j^2/J = 2.0$

43. (b) since the average s^2 is 2.0, the average standard deviation within groups would be expected to be about 1.4 or 1.5.

44. Yes; with $n = 16$, the range is expected to span about 3 or 4 standard deviations. (See Table 4.1.)

PROBLEMS AND EXERCISES

1. Given the data in the ANOVA summary table below: First, fill in the blanks, and then test H_0 using ANOVA with $\alpha = .10$.

ANOVA Summary Table

SV	SS	v	MS	F	p
Between	80	4	____	____	____
Within	____	____	____		
Total	480	44			

Critical *F*-value = __*F*__.__ = ____

2. A researcher experimented with the order of meta-cognitive "organizers" designed to provide a structure for the material to expedite learning. A group of thirty persons was randomly split into three groups of ten each. Group I received organizing material before studying the instructional materials on mathematics; group II received the "organizer" after studying the material; group III received the math materials but no organizing materials. On a ten-item test over the mathematics covered, the following scores were obtained. Perform a one-factor ANOVA to test the H_0: $\mu_1 = \mu_2 = \mu_3$ at $\alpha = .01$.

	Observations	n	$\overline{X}$	s_j^2
Preorganizer:	5, 4, 4, 7, 8, 7, 6, 4, 4, 7			
Postorganizer:	4, 5, 3, 6, 6, 3, 3, 4, 4, 2			
No Organizer:	5, 4, 6, 2, 2, 2, 6, 4, 3, 5			

3. A study was designed to determine whether the type of examination anticipated (essay [E], objective [O], or a combination [C] of both) had an effect on test performance on objective or essay tests. On a common assignment, one-third of a class of thirty-three students expected an objective test, one-third expected an essay test, and one-third expected both types of items. The actual examination consisted of both an objective and an essay test over the common material. The ANOVA for the objective test is given below.

(The means for the three groups were: $\overline{X}_E = 27.3$, $\overline{X}_O = 27.2$, $\overline{X}_C = 29.1$.

ANOVA Summary Table

SV	SS	v	MS	F	p
Between	28.12	2	14.06	0.60	>.25[a]
Within	700.5	30	23.35		

[a]Actual $p > .56$ (from computer).

(a) What conclusion can be drawn from these results?

(b) A partial ANOVA summary table for scores on the essay subtest is given below; fill in the missing parts.

ANOVA Summary Table

SV	SS	v	MS	F	p
Between	519.0	2	____	____	____
Within	5406	30	____		

(c) The three observed means on the essay subtest (graded anonymously) were as follows:

$\bar{X}_O = 45.3$, $\bar{X}_E = 43.4$, $\bar{X}_C = 52.6$. $(\bar{X}_. = 47.1)$

Compute the variance of the three means: $s_{\bar{X}}^2 = \Sigma(\bar{X}_j - \bar{X}_.)^2/(J-1)$

(d) Compute a variance estimate: Estimate of $\sigma^2 = ns_{\bar{X}}^2$. Compare the result with MS_B.

4. Calculators were randomly assigned to twenty of the forty students in a statistics class. All students were instructed to work out ten problems involving complex arithmetic operations. The mean test score of the calculator group was 6.40; the mean of the hand-computation group was 5.9; SS_{total} was 149.1. Perform an ANOVA and present the results in an ANOVA summary table. Can H_0 be rejected for $\alpha = .10$?

5. An experiment was performed on the effects of "advance organizers" (introductory material that mentally organizes the material to be learned) on achievement in abstract mathematics. Fifty college students were randomly assigned to two groups: Twenty-five subjects in group 1 studied a 1,000-word essay on topology after having been exposed to an advance organizer on the subject; twenty-five subjects in group 2 read the same essay on topology after having read a 1,000-word historical sketch of Euler and Riemann, two famous mathematicians. At the end of the experimental period, each group was given an objective test on the topological concepts. The dependent variable was "number of correct answers."

The following results were obtained:

Advance Organizer	*Historical Sketch*
$n_1 = 25$	$n_2 = 25$
$\bar{X}_1 = 7.65$	$\bar{X}_2 = 6.00$
$s_1^2 = 6.5$	$s_2^2 = 5.9$

(a) Use ANOVA to test $H_0: \mu_1 - \mu_2 = 0$. Do these means differ significantly at the .05 level? (Use Eq. 14.9 to compute MS_W.)

(b) If these data were analyzed using the independent *t*-test, the *t*-ratio would have what value? Compare your answer with that for problem 1 in the Problems and Exercises of Chapter 11.

6. One investigator reported Minnesota Teacher Attitude Inventory scores for a sample of fourteen athletes and twenty-eight nonathletes. His findings are summarized below: (Note the unequal sample sizes.)

Athletes	*Nonathletes*
$\bar{X}_1 = 116$	$\bar{X}_2 = 119.5$
$s_1^2 = 968$	$s_2^2 = 1,050$
$n_1 = 14$	$n_2 = 28$

(a) Use ANOVA to test $H_0: \mu_1 - \mu_2 = 0$. Do these means differ significantly with $\alpha = .05$?

(b) If these data were analyzed using the independent *t*-test, the *t*-ratio would have what value? Compare your answer with that for problem 2 in the Problems and Exercises of Chapter 11.

ANSWERS TO PROBLEMS AND EXERCISES

1. Step 1: H_0: $\mu_1 = \mu_2 = \mu_3 = \mu_4 = \mu_5$

Step 2: $\alpha = .10$

Step 3:

ANOVA Summary Table

SV	SS	ν	MS	F	p
Between	80	4	20	2.0	<.25
Within	400	40	10		
Total	480	44			

Critical F-value = $_{.90}F_{4,40}$ = 2.09

Step 4: H_0 is tenable at $\alpha = .10$ since $p > \alpha$ (also since $2.0 < 2.09 = _{.90}F_{4,40}$).

2. The F-test of H_0:

	Observations	n	$\overline{X}$	s_j^2
Preorganizer:	5, 4, 4, 7, 8, 7, 6, 4, 4, 7	10	5.6	2.49
Postorganizer:	4, 5, 3, 6, 6, 3, 3, 4, 4, 2	10	4.0	1.78
No Organizer:	5, 4, 6, 2, 2, 2, 6, 4, 3, 5	10	3.9	2.54
For the composite sample:		$n_. = 30$	4.5	

Step 1: H_0: $\mu_1 = \mu_2 = \mu_3$

Step 2: $\alpha = .05$

Step 3(a): $s_{\overline{X}}^2 = [(1.1)^2 + (-.5)^2 + (-.6)^2]/2 = .91$; $MS_B = ns_{\overline{X}}^2 = 10(.91) = 9.1$

Step 3(b): $MS_W = (2.49 + 1.78 + 2.54)/3 = 2.27$

Step 3(c): $F = MS_B/MS_W = 9.10/2.27 = 4.01$

Step 3(d): From Table F, $.05 > p > .025$.

ANOVA Summary Table

SV	SS	ν	MS	F	p
Between	18.2	2	9.10	4.01	<.05
Within	61.3	27	2.27		

Critical F-value = $_{.95}F_{2,26}$ = 3.37

Step 4: Reject H_0; we are convinced that H_0 is false; μ_1, μ_2, and μ_3 are not all equal.

3. (a) The type of exam expected by the student had no discernible effect on test performance on the objective test.

(b)

ANOVA Summary Table

SV	SS	ν	MS	F	p
Between	519.0	2	259.5	1.44	<.25
Within	5406	30	180.2		

(c) $s_{\bar{X}}^2 = [(-1.8)^2 + (-3.7)^2 + (5.5)^2]/2 = 47.18/2 = 23.59$

(d) $s^2 = 11(23.59) = 259.49 = MS_B$; they are the same.

4. Step 1: $H_0: \mu_1 = \mu_2$

  Step 2: $\alpha = .10$

  Step 3(a) $\bar{X}_\bullet = 6.15; s_{\bar{X}}^2 = [(.25)^2 + (-.25)^2]/1 = .125; MS_B = 20(.125) = 2.50$

  Step 3(b) $SS_W = SS_{total} - SS_B = 149.1 - 2.5 = 146.6; MS_w = 146.6/38 = 3.86$

  Step 3(c) $F = 2.5/3.86 = .65$

  Step 3(d)   From Table F, p > .25.

ANOVA Summary Table

SV	SS	v	MS	F	p
Between	2.5	1	2.5	.65	>.25
Within	146.6	38	3.86		

Critical F-value = $_{.95}F_{1,30} = 2.88$

Step 4: Retain H_0; we are not convinced that H_0 is false.

5. (a) Step 1: $H_0: \mu_1 = \mu_2$

  Step 2: $\alpha = .05$

  Step 3(a) $\bar{X}_\bullet = 6.825; s_{\bar{X}}^2 = [(-.825)^2 + (.825)^2]/1 = 1.361; MS_B = 25(1.36) = 34.03$

  Step 3(b) $MS_W = (6.5 + 5.9)/2 = 6.2$

  Step 3(c) $F = 34.03/6.2 = 5.49$

  Step 3(d)   From Table F, $.025 > p > .01$.

ANOVA Summary Table

SV	SS	v	MS	F	p
Between	34.03	1	34.03	5.49	<.025
Within	297.6	48	6.2		

Critical F-value = $_{.95}F_{1,40} = 4.08$

Step 4: Reject H_0; we are convinced that H_0 is false.

(b) $t = \sqrt{5.49} = 2.34$. This is the same answer that was reported for this problem in Chapter 11 using the t-test. (See problem 1 of Problems and Exercises, Chapter 11.)

6. (a) Step 1: $H_0: \mu_1 = \mu_2$

  Step 2: $\alpha = .05$

  Step 3(a) $SS_B = 114.33; v_B = 1; MS_B = 114.33$

  Step 3(b) $SS_W = 13(968) + 27(1050) = 40,934; v_W = 40; MS_W = 40,934/40 = 1,023.35$

  Step 3(c) $F = 114.33/1,023.35 = .112$

  Step 3(d)   From Table F, $p > .25$.

ANOVA Summary Table

SV	SS	v	MS	F	p
Between	114.33	1	114.33	.112	>.25
Within	40,934	40	1,023.33		

Critical F-value = $_{.95}F_{1,40} = 4.08$

Step 4: Retain H_0; we are not convinced that H_0 is false.

(b) $t = \sqrt{.112} = .335$. This is the same answer that was reported for this problem in Chapter 11 using the t-test. (See problem 2 of Problems and Exercises, Chapter 11.)

SUGGESTED COMPUTER EXERCISE

1. For the HSB data set, determine if there is a significant difference among the means of the four ethnic groups with respect to (a) reading scores, (b) writing scores, (c) math scores, (d) science scores, and (e) civics scores. (Codes for race: Hispanic = 1, Asian = 2, Black = 3, White = 4.)

2. For the HSB data set, determine if there is a significant difference among the means of the three SES groups with respect to (a) reading scores, (b) writing scores, (c) math scores, (d) science scores, and (e) civics scores. (Codes for SES: Low SES = 1, Middle SES = 2, High SES = 3.)

3. For the HSB data set, determine if there is a significant difference between the public versus private school means with respect to (a) reading scores, (b) writing scores, (c) math scores, (d) science scores, and (e) civics scores. (Codes for school type: Public = 1, Private = 2.)

4. Verify that $t^2 = F$ when $J = 2$ for the reading data in activity 3 above.

❖ 15

Multiple Comparisons:
The Tukey and the
Newman-Keuls Methods

❖ 15.1 INTRODUCTION

The overall or omnibus F-test in an analysis of variance (ANOVA) is a test of the hypothesis, H_0: $\mu_1 = \mu_2 = \ldots = \mu_J$; but what if H_0 is rejected? Rejecting H_0 is equivalent to concluding that not all J sample means come from populations having the same mean, μ—there are significant differences among the J sample means. When $J = 2$, there is only one difference between means, but when $J > 2$, statistical procedures known as multiple comparisons (MC) are used to find which differences are statistically significant. This chapter presents two of the most useful methods of multiple comparisons, the Tukey and Newman-Keuls, which are designed to determine which pair(s) of sample means differs by more than would be expected from sampling error alone.

> **Quiz:** Is there a need to apply MC methods if: (1) There are only $J = 2$ groups; (2) there are $J = 4$ groups and $p > \alpha$; (3) there are $J = 3$ groups and the F-ratio is statistically significant?
>
> **Answers:** (1) No, MC methods are not needed because there is only one difference between means. (2) No, MC methods are not needed when H_0 is not rejected. (3) Yes, MC methods are needed since we have concluded that the three population means are not all equal.

❖ 15.2 THE TUKEY METHOD

In recent decades, a number of mathematical statisticians have developed statistical methods for comparing pairs of means from a larger set of J means. These methods are known as *multiple comparisons* procedures. Although each of the several multiple comparisons techniques has certain advantages, only the Tukey and the Newman-Keuls methods will be considered and illustrated in this chapter. In addition to being among the most useful and widely used multiple comparisons methods, these procedures are computationally straightforward and are basic to several other common multiple comparison methods. For a comprehensive treatment of the topic, see Chapter 17 in Glass & Hopkins (1996).

❖ 15.3 THE STUDENTIZED RANGE STATISTIC, q

The test statistic used by the Tukey, the Newman-Keuls, and certain other multiple comparison methods is the Studentized range statistic, q. The statistic q is the *ratio* of the difference between a pair of sample means ($\overline{X}_i - \overline{X}_j$) to the standard error of the mean, $s_{\overline{X}}$:

$$q = \frac{\overline{X}_i - \overline{X}_j}{s_{\overline{X}}} = \frac{\overline{X}_i - \overline{X}_j}{\sqrt{MS_w / n}} \tag{15.1}$$

where $\overline{X}_i > \overline{X}_j$, and n is the number of scores per group.[1]

We will do a thought experiment to help illustrate the Studentized range statistic, q. Suppose each of our army of researchers selects from a common population J random samples, each based on n observations, and computes q (see Eq. 15.1) for the difference between the largest and smallest means. If we make of distribution of these many, many values of q, we have constructed the sampling distribution of q for J sample groups with $J(n-1)$ degrees of freedom. The 90th, 95th, and 99th percentile points for the sampling distribution of q for $J = 2$ through $J = 18$ groups are given in Table H of Appendix B. To find the critical value of q in Appendix Table H for J sample means, find the intersection of the J *column* with the v_w row [where $v_w = J(n-1)$ and can be read from the ANOVA table], and read the critical values of q associated with the three α-values of .10, .05, and .01.

To use the Tukey method of multiple comparisons:

Step 1. Rank the J sample means from 1 (largest) to J (smallest), and find the greatest difference between any pair of means: $\overline{X}_1 - \overline{X}_J$.

Step 2. Compute (a) $s_{\overline{X}} = \sqrt{MS_w / n}$, and (b) $q_1 = (\overline{X}_1 - \overline{X}_J)/s_{\overline{X}}$ (Eq. 15.1).

Step 3. If $p \leq \alpha$ (i.e., if $q_1 \geq$ critical q), reject H_0: $\mu_1 = \mu_J$. If $p > \alpha$ (i.e., $q_1 <$ critical q), conclude that all H_0's: $\mu_i = \mu_j$ between pairs of means are tenable.

Step 4. If the preceding step was statistically significant, find q_2 for the next greatest difference between a pair of means and compute q_2. Repeat step 3 until a nonsignificant difference is obtained, at which point conclude that all remaining pairwise comparisons are nonsignificant.

This four-step procedure for the Tukey multiple comparison procedure (H_0: $\mu_i = \mu_j$) is depicted in the flowchart in Figure 15.1.

---

[1]Although in the derivation of the Tukey method all means are assumed to be based on the same number of observations, a modification proposed by Kramer (1956) has been shown to yield accurate results with unequal n's (Smith, 1971). If the n's are unequal, the value of $s_{\overline{X}}^2$ (and hence its square root, $s_{\overline{X}}$) can be obtained using the formula below where n_i and n_j are the number of observations associated with the pair of means being compared:

$$s_{\overline{X}}^2 = MS_w \left(\frac{1}{2n_i} + \frac{1}{2n_j} \right)$$

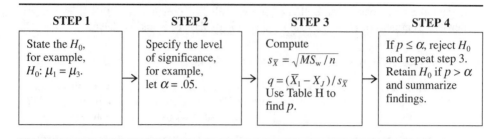

STEP 1	STEP 2	STEP 3	STEP 4
State the H_0, for example, H_0: $\mu_1 = \mu_3$.	Specify the level of significance, for example, let $\alpha = .05$.	Compute $s_{\bar{X}} = \sqrt{MS_w / n}$ $q = (\bar{X}_1 - \bar{X}_J)/s_{\bar{X}}$ Use Table H to find p.	If $p \le \alpha$, reject H_0 and repeat step 3. Retain H_0 if $p > \alpha$ and summarize findings.

❖ **FIGURE 15.1** Flowchart of the four-step procedure for the Tukey multiple comparison method subsequent to a significant ANOVA *F*-ratio to determine which pairs of means differ significantly when $J \ge 3$.

❖ 15.4 AN EXAMPLE USING THE TUKEY METHOD

One research study compared phonic (letter) and look-say (word) methods of beginning reading instruction on a measure of transfer of training. Twenty kindergarten pupils learned a list of eight words by the phonic method and twenty pupils learned the same words by the look-say method. A control group of twenty pupils did not learn the original list of words. All sixty pupils were subsequently taught a new list of eight words, the dependent variable in the experiment was the number of trials required to learn the second list. To simplify computation, the group with the largest mean is designated as group 1, and the group with the smallest mean is designated as group J (3). Table 15.1 presents the data pertaining to this example.

The obtained F-ratio of 14.37 is greater than the critical F-ratio found in Table F; indeed, $p < .001$, and H_0: $\mu_1 = \mu_2 = \mu_3$ is rejected at the .001 level of significance. Does the rejection of H_0: $\mu_1 = \mu_2 = \mu_3$ imply that all differences among pairs of means are statistically significant at $\alpha = .05$? Not at all; the rejection of H_0: $\mu_1 = \mu_2 = \mu_3$ only indicates that some mean(s) differs significantly from some other mean(s). Perhaps the look-say method is no better than the control method, but both of these methods are less effective than the phonic method. A significant omnibus F-test in ANOVA indicates that we should look further to

❖ **TABLE 15.1** Summary table and descriptive statistics pertaining to a study of three methods of teaching reading to kindergarten pupils.

	Control (1)	Look-Say Method (2)	Phonic Method (3)	Composite
$\bar{X}_j$:	29.25	27.20	13.50	$\bar{X}_. = 23.32$
s_j:	9.99	10.37	9.94	
n_j:	20	20	20	$n_. = 60$

ANOVA Summary Table

SV	SS	v	MS	F	p
Between	2,933.08	2	1,466.54	14.37[a]	<.001
Within	5,816.85	57	102.05		

[a]Critical F-value for $\alpha = .05$: $_{.95}F_{2,57} = 3.23$

find which means differ from which other means.[2] On the other hand, if the omnibus F-test does not allow H_0 to be rejected, we ordinarily do not pursue the matter further, but continue to entertain the null hypothesis that all J population means are equal.[3]

Since H_0: $\mu_1 = \mu_2 = \mu_3$ was rejected in our example, we should examine the differences among the pairs of means. We will employ the Tukey method to test the differences between means.

Step 1. Rank the J sample means: (1) = Control group, (2) = Look-Say method, (3) = Phonics method.
Construct a matrix of the differences between the pairs of means.

		Control	Look-Say	Phonics
	Group:	(1)	(2)	(3)
Group:	*Means:*	29.25	27.20	13.50
(1)	29.25	0	2.05	15.75**
(2)	27.20		0	13.70**

As is often the case, "" represents $p < .01$.

Step 2. Compute (a) $s_{\bar{X}}$ and (b) q_1. $s_{\bar{X}} = \sqrt{102.05/20} = 2.259$; $q_1 = (15.75)/2.259 = 6.97$.

Step 3. Since $q_1 = 6.97 >$ critical q for $\alpha = .01$, H_0: $\mu_1 = \mu_3$ is rejected at the .01 level.

Step 4. Test the next-largest difference ($\bar{X}_2 - \bar{X}_3 = 13.70$).

$q_2 = (13.7)/2.259 = 6.06 >$ critical q for $\alpha = .01$; therefore,

H_0: $\mu_2 = \mu_3$ is rejected. Finally, compare $\bar{X}_1$ versus $\bar{X}_2$.

$q_3 = (2.05)/2.259 = .91$. Since $q_3 = .91 < 3.44 \approx$ critical q,

H_0: $\mu_1 = \mu_2$ is tenable.

For a summary statement we can say that both the control and the look-say groups required significantly more trials to learn the word list than did the phonics group, but there was no significant difference between the control and the look-say groups. As indicated in the matrix above, significant differences can be visually represented by appending an asterisk to each significant pairwise difference in the matrix of ranked mean differences.

When all group n's are equal, the entire Tukey procedure can be simplified by finding

---

[2]Although very unlikely, it is mathematically possible for the omnibus F-test to be significant, but to find no statistically significant difference between pairs of means using the Tukey or some other multiple comparisons procedure. When $J > 2$, a significant omnibus F-test indicates that some subset of means differs from some other subset of means; these subsets may be of no interest to the researcher, however. The Scheffé method (Glass & Hopkins, 1996), although not very efficient for comparing pairs of means, is the appropriate procedure if one wishes to test not just pairs of means, but all possible combinations (e.g., H_0: $(\mu_1 + \mu_2)/2 = \mu_3$).

[3]There are exceptions to this strategy, such as planned contrasts (see Glass & Hopkins, 1996), but it is beyond the scope of this book to treat these special techniques.

the minimum difference in two means necessary to reject the null hypothesis. This minimum difference is termed the "honest significant difference," or "*HSD*." By inserting the critical *q*-value (from Table H) into Equation 15.1 and rearranging the formula as displayed in the equation below, we obtain the minimum difference between any two means necessary to reject the null hypothesis at the α-level of significance; in other words, *HSD* is the minimum difference between a pair of means for which the null hypothesis can be rejected at the α-level of significance. When all group *n*'s are equal:

$$HSD = s_{\bar{X}}(\text{critical } q) \qquad \textbf{(15.2)}$$

In our example, with $J = 3$, $v_w = 57$, and $\alpha = .05$, the honest significant difference is: $_{.95}HSD = (2.259)(3.44) = 7.771$. Consequently, any pairwise mean difference greater than 7.77 is sufficient to reject H_0 at the .05 level. Differences greater than $(2.259)(4.28) = 9.669$ are significant at the .01 level. Once the matrix of ordered mean differences is developed, it is apparent at a glance which pair(s) of means differs significantly.

❖ 15.5 THE FAMILY OF NULL HYPOTHESES AS THE BASIS FOR ALPHA

It should be noted that α, the level of significance with the Tukey method, is defined differently from all other tests of significance we have used in this book. For the Tukey MC test, α is the type-I error rate based on the "experiment" or "family" of hypotheses to be tested, and is not based on the probability of a type-I error for each individual hypothesis that is tested. Thus, α pertains to the entire set or family of hypotheses tested in the study.

Suppose that each member of our army of researchers replicated a study in which the null hypothesis was true, and suppose that each researcher used the Tukey MC procedure to test all mean differences for statistical significance. Since the null hypothesis ($\mu_1 = \mu_2 = \ldots = \mu_J$) is true, α gives the proportion of the researchers will make at least one type-I error. In other words, if $\alpha = .05$, 95 percent of the researchers will not make any type-I errors; on the other hand, 5 percent of the researchers will make one or more type-I errors within the set of pairwise contrasts that they will evaluated; that is, the risk of falsely rejecting one or more of the family of $J(J-1)/2$ hypotheses between pairs of means is α. For example, if $J = 5$, there are $5(4)/2 = 10$ pairs of means, and 10 H_0's. If $\alpha = .05$, there is only a 5 percent probability that a type-I error will occur in the set of 10 hypothesis tests; α is the proportion of the "experiments" (or replications) under null conditions which will contain one or more incorrect rejections of H_0: $\mu_i = \mu_j$. The probability of a type-I error anywhere in the set of $J(J-1)/2$ hypotheses tested is α.

❖ 15.6 THE NEWMAN-KEULS METHOD

We will now consider another widely used method of multiple comparisons, the Newman-Keuls (N-K) method. The N-K method is very similar to the Tukey method except that the type-I error rate is per comparison (i.e., per hypothesis tested) rather than for the aggregate set of hypotheses tested. Like other hypotheses that have been tested in this book, each H_0 that is rejected at $\alpha = .05$ is associated with a 5 percent probability of a type-I error.

The N-K and the Tukey methods use the same test statistic, the Studentized range (q) that is obtained using Equation 15.1, but for the N-K method, the critical q-value decreases as the range (r) of the ranked means decreases. That is, for Newman-Keuls, the critical q-

value is based on the inclusive range (r) or number of group means in the subset of means currently under consideration. For example, in comparing means of ranks 1 and 8, $r = 8$; in comparing means ranked 1 and 6, $r = 6$; in comparing means of ranks 2 and 6, $r = 5$; in comparing means ranked 2 and 4, $r = 3$.

Quiz: The inclusive range r is needed to obtain the critical value of q for the N-K method. What is the number of groups in the inclusive range, r, for the N-K MC procedure for comparing means of ranks: (1) 1 and 7, (2) 1 and 6, (3) 2 and 7, (4) 1 and 5, (5) 2 and 6, (6) 3 and 7, (7) 4 and 6, (8) 3 and 4.

Answers: (1) $r = 7$, (2) $r = 6$, (3) $r = 6$, (4) $r = 5$, (5) $r = 5$, (6) $r = 5$, (7) $r = 3$, (8) $r = 2$.

For the initial H_0 tested for both the Tukey and the N-K MC procedures, (1) the difference between the smallest mean ($\overline{X}_J$) and the largest mean ($\overline{X}_1$) where $r = J$ and (2) the critical q-values are identical. However, for subsequent tests, the critical q-value for the N-K method will be smaller than that for the Tukey method. Like the Tukey method, whenever a nonsignificant difference is found, no further comparisons within that subset of means is considered—all pairwise H_0's within this subset are considered tenable.

Quiz: For the following situations, determine the critical q-value for both the Tukey and the N-K MC methods: (1) $J = 5$, $\alpha = .05$, $v_w = 20$, and H_0: $\mu_1 - \mu_4 = 0$; (2) $J = 7$, $\alpha = .01$, $v_w = 40$, and H_0: $\mu_1 - \mu_7 = 0$; (3) $J = 15$, $\alpha = .10$, $v_w = 120$, and H_0: $\mu_4 - \mu_{12} = 0$.
Answers: (1) For Tukey $_{.95}q_{5,20} = 4.23$; for N-K, $r = 4$, $_{.95}q_{4,20} = 3.96$. (2) Since $r = J$, both methods have the same critical q-value, $_{.99}q_{7,40} = 5.27$. (3) For Tukey, $_{.90}q_{15,120} = 4.59$; for N-K, $r = 9$, $_{.90}q_{9,120} = 4.10$.

❖ 15.7 AN EXAMPLE USING THE NEWMAN-KEULS METHOD OF MULTIPLE COMPARISONS

One study examined the effects of "advance organizers" on comprehension of an assigned reading task. There were $n_. = 140$ subjects randomly assigned into $J = 7$ groups of $n = 20$ each. These seven groups differed by whether and how meta-cognitive organizers were used. Table 15.2 gives the ANOVA results and descriptive statistics for this example.

❖ **TABLE 15.2** Summary table and descriptive statistics pertaining to the study of meta-cognitive organizers.

		ANOVA Summary Table			
SV	*SS*	*v*	*MS*	*F*	*p*
Between	3,036	6	506	2.44	<.05
Within	27,531	133	207		

			Group Identification				
	A	*B*	*C*	*D*	*E*	*F*	*G*
$\overline{X}$:	36	35	30	40	43	33	42
n:	20	20	20	20	20	20	20

The only modification of the four-step hypothesis-testing procedure used for the Tukey method when the N-K method is used is in step 4, where the critical value of q is based, not on J, but on r, the number of the means in the subset being compared. The procedure will be illustrated with $\alpha = .10$.

Step 1.

6×7 Matrix of Ordered Group Mean Differences

Group:		E	G	D	A	B	F	C
Order:		1	2	3	4	5	6	7
	$\overline{X}_j$:	43	42	40	36	35	33	30
1	43	0	1	3	7	8	10	13*
2	42		0	2	6	7	9	12*
3	40			0	4	5	7	10
4	36				0	1	3	6
5	35					0	2	5
6	33						0	3

Step 2. (a) Compute $s_{\overline{X}} = \sqrt{207/20} = 3.217$, (b) compute q:
$q_1 = 13/3.217 = 4.04$

Step 3. $_{.90}q_{7,120} = 3.86$; since $4.04 > 3.86$, reject H_0: $\mu_1 - \mu_7 = 0$.

Step 4. Compute q_2: $q_2 = (\mu_2 - \mu_7)/s_{\overline{X}} = 12/3.217 = 3.73$; critical q (with $r = 6$) $= _{.90}q_{6,120} = 3.71$. Since $3.73 > 3.71$, reject H_0: $\mu_2 - \mu_7 = 0$.

Since q_2 is statistically significant, repeat step 4: Compute $q_3 = (\mu_1 - \mu_6)/s_{\overline{X}} = 10/3.217 = 3.108$; with $r = 6$, critical $q = 3.71$; since $q = 3.108 < 3.71$, retain H_0: $\mu_1 = \mu_6$. No further tests need be made.

Groups 1 and 2 (groups E and G) had significantly higher means than did group 7 (group C). Note that the asterisks in the above matrix of ordered pairwise mean differences indicate which pairwise differences attained statistical significance.

❖ 15.8 NEWMAN-KEULS VERSUS TUKEY MULTIPLE COMPARISONS

Some of the similarities and differences between the Newman-Keuls and the Tukey methods are as follows:

1. Both methods use the Studentized range statistic, q, as given by Equation 15.1.
2. For a given study, there is just one critical q-ratio for the Tukey method; for the N-K method, successive tests of pairwise differences have different (and smaller) critical q-values based on the range of ranked means involved.
3. The error rate for the Tukey method is associated with the entire family of hypotheses tested in a given study. The error rate for the N-K method is associated with each individual H_0 that is tested.
4. The use of the N-K method rather than the Tukey method will result in making more type-I errors,

5. The use of the N-K method rather than the Tukey method will result in making fewer type-II errors; that is, the N-K method has greater statistical power than the Tukey method except for the initial comparison for which the two methods are identical.

Which type of error rate is preferable is a matter of opinion and controversy.[4] In the long run, the contrast-based error rate has greater power, but makes more type-I errors. Conversely, the family error rate results in fewer type-I errors, but more type-II errors. The rationale for a family error-rate is weakened by the arbitrariness of the decision as to what constitutes a family, especially when there are two or more factors in the design (Chapter 16). The authors, like Miller (1966, 1977), feel that the contrast based error rate is advantageous for most applications since it is consistent with the rationale that researchers employ for almost all other hypotheses that they test, and does not suffer from the conservativeness (and loss of power) of the family error rate, especially when J is large.

❖ CHAPTER SUMMARY

If the omnibus F-test in an ANOVA results in the rejection of the null hypothesis H_0: $\mu_1 = \mu_2 = \ldots = \mu_J$, when $J > 2$, an additional statistical analysis is needed to find which means differ significantly from which other means. Such procedures are termed multiple comparisons techniques.

Two of the most useful multiple comparisons procedures are the Tukey and the Newman-Keuls (N-K) methods. The means are ordered according to magnitude: $\overline{X}_1$ is the largest mean, $\overline{X}_J$ is the smallest mean. The initial hypothesis tested is H_0: $\mu_1 = \mu_J$; if this difference is not significant, all other differences among pairs of means are not significant. Both methods of multiple comparisons use the Studentized range statistic (q), which is the ratio of the difference between a pair of means to the standard error of the mean ($s_{\overline{X}}$).

The Tukey method uses the entire family or set of hypotheses between pairs of means as the base for the probability of a type-I error (α), whereas for the N-K method, α is associated with each individual hypothesis. When the family is used as the base for α, the probability of a type-I error anywhere among the entire set of hypotheses tested is just α. The N-K method of multiple comparisons has greater power than the Tukey method, but has somewhat less protection from type-I errors.

MASTERY TEST

1. If a t-test is used to compare the largest mean with the smallest mean in a set of five means, the probability of a type-I error is _____ the α associated with the critical t-value.
   (a) greater than   (b) equal to   (c) less than
2. Are multiple t-tests recommended for locating significant mean differences when $J > 2$?
3. If the omnibus F-test in ANOVA is not significant, one ordinarily
   (a) employs the Tukey method of multiple comparisons.

---

[4]For example, in factorial ANOVA (Chapter 16), a per-contrast error rate is ordinarily used to test each main effect and interaction, rather than a family error rate for the entire "package" of main effects and interactions. Indeed, each F-test is a special case of planned orthogonal contrasts (Glass & Hopkins, 1996, Section 17.16). Miller (1966, p. 35) observed, "There are no hard-and-fast rules for where the family lines should be drawn, and the statistician must rely on his own judgment for the problem at hand. Large single experiments cannot be treated as a whole (family) without an unjustifiable loss in sensitivity."

(b) employs the N-K method of multiple comparisons.

(c) does not employ multiple comparison techniques.

The following data apply to questions 4–15:

$$J = 4, MS_W = 99, \quad n = 11, \quad \overline{X}_1 = 137, \quad \overline{X}_2 = 133, \quad \overline{X}_3 = 125, \quad \overline{X}_4 = 120.$$

4. What is the value of v_W? ($v_W = n. - J$)

5. Construct a matrix of the differences between the means.

6. Compute $s_{\overline{X}}$, the standard error of the mean.

7. Determine how large the difference in means must be to reject H_0 using the Tukey *HSD* method with $\alpha = .05$, and $\alpha = .01$?

8. Using the Tukey procedure, which H_0's can be rejected at $\alpha = .01$? (In the matrix of differences in means [item 5], place a double asterisk after the differences that are statistically significant at the .01 level.)

9. Using the Tukey procedure, which H_0's can be rejected at $\alpha = .05$? (Place a single asterisk on the differences that are statistically significant at the .05 level.)

10. (a) How many pairwise comparisons are there when $J = 4$? [$C = J(J - 1)/2$]

    (b) Based on the Tukey procedure, how many H_0's remain tenable at $\alpha = .01$?

11. (a) Compute q_1 to test $H_0: \mu_1 = \mu_4$.

    (b) For the N-K procedure, find the critical q-values for $\alpha = .01$, and $\alpha = .05$.

    (c) When applying the N-K method, is q_1 statistically significant at the .01 and/or the .05 level?

12. (a) The numerical value of the second largest pairwise mean difference is __?__ between the means of groups __?__ and __?__.

    (b) For this difference, compute $q_2 = $ __?__.

    (c) For this comparison, $r = $ __?__; the N-K critical q-value for $\alpha = .05$ is __?__, and the critical q for $\alpha = .01$ is __?__.

    (d) When applying the N-K method, is q_2 statistically significant at the .01 or the .05 level?

13. (a) The third largest difference between pairs of means is __?__ between the means of groups __?__ and __?__.

    (b) For this difference, $q_3 = $ __?__.

    (c) For this comparison, $r = $ __?__ the N-K critical q-value for $\alpha = .05$ is __?__, and the critical q for $\alpha = .01$ is __?__.

    (d) When applying the N-K method, is q_3 statistically significant at the .01 or the .05 level?

14. (a) The fourth largest pairwise mean difference is __?__ between the means of groups __?__ and __?__.

    (b) For this difference, $q_4 = $ __?__.

    (c) For this comparison, $r = $ __?__; the N-K critical q-value for $\alpha = .05$ is __?__, and the critical q for $\alpha = .01$ is __?__.

    (d) When applying the N-K method, is q_4 statistically significant at the .01 and/or the .05 level?

    (e) Do you need to continue this N-K process further?

15. For this example, compare the summary of your findings between the Tukey and the N-K MC methods.

16. Holding α and v_W constant, how is J related to the magnitude of critical q?

17. Holding α and J constant, how is critical q related to v_W?

18. In the Tukey method, the probability of a type-I error is α for

    (a) each H_0 tested.

    (b) the entire set of H_0's tested in a given set of data.

19. In the Newman-Keuls method, the probability of a type-I error is α for
(a) each H_0 tested.
(b) the entire set of H_0's tested in a given set of data.

20. In the long run, with respect to the Tukey and the N-K MC procedures, which MC procedure will
(a) indicate a greater number of statistically significant mean differences?
(b) produce a greater number of type-I errors?
(c) produce a greater number of type-II errors?
(d) fail to detect a greater number of false H_0's?

ANSWERS TO MASTERY TEST

1. (a)
2. no
3. (c)
4. $v_W = n_. - J = 44 - 4 = 40$
5.

	Group:	(1)	(2)	(3)	(4)
Group:	Means:	137	133	125	120
(1)	137	0	4	12*	17**
(2)	133		0	8	13*
(3)	125				5

$$_{.95}q_{4,40} = 3.79; \; _{.99}q_{4,40} = 4.70$$

6. $s_{\bar{X}} = \sqrt{99/11} = 3$
7. $_{.95}HSD = s_{\bar{X}}(_{.95}q_{4,40}) = 3(3.79) = 11.37$ for $\alpha = .05$
$_{.99}HSD = s_{\bar{X}}(_{.99}q_{4,40}) = 3(4.70) = 14.1$ for $\alpha = .01$
8. $H_0: \mu_1 = \mu_4$ is rejected at $\alpha = .01$ since $17 > {_{.99}}HSD = 14.1$.
9. $H_0: \mu_1 = \mu_4$ is also rejected at $\alpha = .05$ since it was rejected at the .01 level.
$H_0: \mu_1 = \mu_3$ is rejected at $\alpha = .05$ since $12 > {_{.95}}HSD = 11.37$.
$H_0: \mu_2 = \mu_4$ is rejected at $\alpha = .05$ since $13 > {_{.95}}HSD = 11.37$.
10. (a) $C = 4(3)/2 = 6$
(b) $6 - 3 = 3$ H_0's remain tenable at $\alpha = .05$.
11. (a) $q_1 = 17/3 = 5.67$
(b) $_{.95}q_{4,40} = 3.79$, $_{.99}q_{4,40} = 4.70$ (These critical values are identical to those for the Tukey procedure.)
(c) Yes, $q = 5.67 > 4.70 = {_{.99}}q_{4,40}$, hence q is statistically significant at both the .01 and the .05 levels.
12. (a) 13, 2, 4
(b) $q_2 = 13/3 = 4.33$
(c) 3, 3.44, 4.37
(d) q_2 is statistically significant at the .05 level, but not at the .01 level.
13. (a) 12, 1, 3
(b) $q_3 = 12/3 = 4.00$
(c) 3, 3.44, 4.37
(d) Using the N-K method, q_3 is statistically significant at the .05 level, but not at the .01 level of significance.

14. (a) 8, 2, 3

(b) $q_4 = 8/3 = 2.67$

(c) 2, 2.86, 3.82

(d) q_4 is not statistically significant at the .01 and/or the .05 level.

(e) No, the remaining comparisons are all nonsignificant.

15. In this instance, the pattern of significant differences is identical for the Tukey and the N-K MC procedures.

16. As J increases, so does the critical q.

17. As v_W increases, critical q decreases.

18. (b)

19. (a)

20. (a) N-K, (b) N-K, (c) Tukey, (d) Tukey

PROBLEMS AND EXERCISES

1. Four methods of teaching percentage (Case method, Formula method, Equation method, and the Unitary analysis method) were compared. Twenty-eight sixth-grade classes were randomly assigned to the four methods; seven classes studied under each method, that is, $n = 7$ and $n_. = 28$. The observational unit was the class mean. At the conclusion of the teaching unit, a 45-item test on computing percentages was administered to each class. The following means were obtained, each based on seven observations.

Method of Teaching Percentage

	(1) Unitary	*(2) Equation*	*(3) Formula*	*(4) Case*
$\overline{X}_j$:	32.52	27.84	21.25	18.68

(a) Fill in the blanks in the ANOVA table below.

ANOVA Summary Table

SV	SS	v	MS	F	p
Between	____	—	276.73	____	____
Within	____	—	17.37		

Critical F-value for $\alpha = .001$: $_{.999}F$____, ____ = ____

(b) Can H_0: $\mu_1 = \mu_2 = \mu_3 = \mu_4$ be rejected at $\alpha = .001$?

(c) Use the Tukey HSD method of multiple comparisons to find the untenable H_0's involving pairs of means for $\alpha = .05$ and $\alpha = .01$. Order the means from the largest (1) to the smallest (4) and prepare a 3×4 matrix of the differences between the pairs of means. Use a single asterisk to indicate significance at the .05 level and a double asterisk to indicate significance at the .01 level.

2. A study of the effects of meta-cognitve organizers (preorganizer, postorganizer, and no organizer) on math achievement involved three treatment groups with ten subjects in each group. The
means of the three treatment groups and an incomplete ANOVA summary table are presented
below.

ANOVA Summary Table

SV	SS	ν	MS	F	p
Between	18.2	—	____	____	____
Within	61.29	—	____		

Critical F-value for $\alpha = .05$: $_{.95}F$____, ____ = ____

$\overline{X}_1 = 5.6$ (Postorganizer); $\overline{X}_2 = 4.0$ (Preorganizer); $\overline{X}_3 = 3.9$ (No organizer)

(a) Complete the ANOVA summary table above.
(b) Use the N-K MC method to test $H_0: \mu_1 = \mu_3$ at $\alpha = .05$.
(c) Use the N-K method to determine if $H_0: \mu_1 = \mu_2$ can be rejected at $\alpha = .05$.
(d) Does $H_0: \mu_1 = \mu_3$ need to be tested?

3. Table 14.3 of the preceding chapter presented an ANOVA table with a significant difference
in writing score means between students enrolled in three types of high school programs.
Use the Tukey MC procedure to evaluate the pattern of mean differences for significance
with $\alpha = .05$.

ANSWERS TO PROBLEMS AND EXERCISES

1. (a) $\nu_W = 24$, $SS_W = 24(17.37) = 416.88$; $\nu_B = 3$, $SS_B = 3(276.73) = 830.19$;
$F = 276.73/17.37 = 15.93$; $p < .001$; critical F for $\alpha = .001$: $_{.999}F_{3,24} = 7.55$.
(b) Yes; $15.93 > 7.55 = _{.999}F_{3,24}$

(c)

		Unitary	Equation	Formula	Case
	Group:	(1)	(2)	(3)	(4)
Group:	Means:	32.52	27.84	21.25	18.68
(1)	32.52	0	4.68	11.27**	13.84**
(2)	27.84		0	6.59*	9.16**
(3)	21.25				2.57

$s_{\overline{X}} = \sqrt{17.37/7} = 1.575$; $_{.99}HSD = 1.575(4.91) = 7.73$; $_{.95}HSD = 1.575(3.90) = 6.14$
$H_0: \mu_1 = \mu_4$ is rejected at $\alpha = .01$ since $13.84 > _{.99}HSD$ (7.73);
$H_0: \mu_1 = \mu_3$ is rejected at $\alpha = .01$ since $11.27 > _{.99}HSD$ (7.73);
$H_0: \mu_2 = \mu_4$ is rejected at $\alpha = .01$ since $9.16 > _{.99}HSD$ (7.73);
$H_0: \mu_2 = \mu_3$ is rejected at $\alpha = .05$ since $6.59 > _{.95}HSD$ (6.14).

2. (a) $\nu_B = 3 - 1 = 2$, $MS_B = 18.2/2 = 9.1$;
$\nu_W = 30 - 3 = 27$, $MS_W = 61.29/27 = 2.27$; $F = 9.1/2.27 = 4.01$; $p < .05$; critical F-value for
$\alpha = .05$: $_{.95}F_{2,27} = 3.37$.

(b) $s_{\bar{x}} = \sqrt{2.27/10} = .476$; for H_0: $\mu_1 = \mu_3$, $q_1 = 1.7/.476 = 3.57$; critical $q = 3.53$;
reject H_0: $\mu_1 = \mu_3$.

(c) For H_0: $\mu_1 = \mu_2$, $q_2 = 1.6/.476 = 3.36$; $_{.95}q_{2,27} = 2.92$; reject H_0: $\mu_1 = \mu_2$.

(d) Yes, since the preceding pairwise mean difference was statistically significant.
For H_0: $\mu_2 = \mu_3$; $q = .1/.476 = .21$; critical $q = 2.92$; retain H_0: $\mu_2 = \mu_3$ as tenable.

3.

		Academic	General	Vocational
	Group:	(1)	(2)	(3)
Group:	Means:	60.33	57.33	48.00
(1)	60.33	0	3.00	12.33*
(2)	57.33		0	9.33

$s_{\bar{x}} = \sqrt{38.58/6} = 2.536$; critical $q = 3.70$, $HSD = 2.536(3.7) = 9.38$; hence, only H_0: $\mu_1 = \mu_3$
is rejected as untenable.

SUGGESTED COMPUTER EXERCISE

1. For the HSB data set, use the Tukey MC procedure to find which pairs of means differ significantly among the four ethnic groups with respect to (a) reading scores, (b) writing scores, (c) math scores, (d) science scores, and (e) civics. (Codes for race: Hispanic = 1, Asian = 2, Black = 3, White = 4.)

2. From the ANOVA results for the previous exercise (and a little work by hand), use the N-K MC procedure to determine which pairs of means differ significantly among the four ethnic groups with respect to the civics scores.

❖ 16

Two-Factor ANOVA:
An Introduction to Factorial Design

❖ 16.1 INTRODUCTION

ANOVA with two independent variables (factors), such as treatment and gender, and a single dependent variable, such as reading achievement, is known as two-factor or two-way ANOVA. The two-factor ANOVA design is the simplest type of *factorial design*, but the concepts and procedures enjoyed in this design are directly applicable to more complex factorial ANOVA designs that investigate three or more independent variables (factors).

Factorial designs have some important advantages over simple one-factor designs since they not only provide some information on the effects of each factor separately (*main effects*), but also they give information on the *interaction* between the factors—the effects for various combinations of the factors.

In two-factor ANOVA designs, three separate null hypotheses are tested via *F*-tests: (1) the H_0 for the *A main effect*, (2) the H_0 for the *B main effect*, and (3) the H_0 for the *interaction* between factors *A* and *B*. That is, three separate and independent null hypotheses are tested, and each is either rejected or retained independently of the other two. Obviously, the H_0's for factor *A* and factor *B* could be tested if two separate one-factor ANOVA's were run. The unique question addressed by the two-factor ANOVA pertains to the interesting question pertaining to interaction; that is, *are there certain combinations of the factors that have effects over and above those that would be evident if the two factors were considered separately, independently, and additively?*

❖ 16.2 THE MEANING OF INTERACTION

The concept of interaction is of central importance in research in education and the behavioral sciences. When an interaction effect is present, the interpretation of any main effects requires qualification. For example, suppose factor *A* is instructional method and factor *B* is ability level; if the new method is more effective only for bright students, this will be evidenced by a significant $A \times B$ interaction. If there is no interaction effect, the effectiveness of the new method can be generalized to all ability levels.

In practice we are interested in whether a treatment (independent) variable has an effect on the outcome (criterion, or dependent) variable, but we are also interested in whether the treatment is equally effective (or ineffective) for certain types of individuals. Is the treatment effect greater at grade six than at grade three? Is the new method equally effective for high and low-ability students? This capability of factorial ANOVA designs to detect differential treatment effects for different types of students is extremely important.

An interaction between two factors is said to exist if the mean differences among the J levels (categories) of factor A are *not constant* across the K levels (categories) of factor B. For example, suppose two different methods of teaching are being compared. If one teaching method is better for boys but the other method is better for girls, there is an interaction between the two factors, teaching method and gender. An interaction is also said to exist if one method is much better than the other for boys, but just a little (or no) better than the other for girls.

❖ 16.3 INTERACTION EXAMPLES

In recent years, behavioral and educational research has become increasingly concerned with assessing interaction effects. The following three examples are studies in which the interaction hypothesis was of primary interest.

Example One. In studies of gender differences, two types of test formats (multiple-choice and essay) have been used. The research question is whether the magnitude of the gender difference is affected by the test format used. Is the difference between the two sexes the same for both item types, that is, is there an interaction between the two factors, gender and type of test? If the mean difference between the two sexes is the same for both test formats, there is no interaction between the two factors. The research has found that the mean difference between the two sexes depends on the format of the measuring instrument. Males do relatively better on multiple-choice items, whereas females do relatively better on essay items; hence, a gender-by-item type interaction is said to exist. The implications of this finding are obvious; for example, a study of gender difference in science achievement will be influenced by the format of the test.

This does not mean that all gender differences are due to test format, but only that the magnitude of the gender difference is affected by the type of test. For example, if males outperform females in science achievement, the difference will be magnified if measured by a multiple-choice test; if females outperform males in history, the difference will be less if multiple-choice tests are used than if it is assessed by essay tests.

Example Two. In a learning experiment, the effects of immediate versus delayed reinforcement on vocabulary acquisition were compared for pupils of low and middle socioeconomic status (SES). The researcher expected to find an interaction between the two factors, factor A (treatment, i.e., timing of reinforcement) and factor B (socioeconomic status). It was hypothesized that delay of gratification is more characteristic of middle-SES families; hence, a substantial difference was expected between immediate and delayed reinforcement for low-SES students, but little difference was anticipated for middle-SES students. A graphic illustration of the researcher's hypothesis is given in Figure 16.1. A two-factor (treatment X SES) analysis of variance will reveal there is a significant treatment-by-SES interaction.

Example 3. A bilingualism-biculturalism study used a two-factor (teacher ethnicity and pupil ethnicity) ANOVA design. "Hispanic" and "Anglo" team teachers each independently

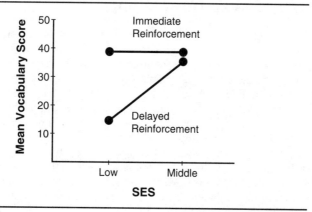

❖ **FIGURE 16.1** A hypothetical illustration of a two-factor (treatment-by-SES) interaction.

rated the same Hispanic and Anglo students for "adaptive behavior" on a behavior rating scale. Cell means are given on the left of Figure 16.2; the interaction that is evident is shown graphically on the right of Figure 16.2. No significant difference was found between the two means on the teacher ethnicity factor or between the two means on the pupil ethnicity factor; that is, both null hypotheses for the two main effects were tenable. However, there was a dramatic, significant interaction between the teacher ethnicity and pupil ethnicity factors, as shown in the figure.

The interaction in Figure 16.2 shows that the two factors are not independent. Hispanic teachers rated the behavior of Hispanic students as more adaptive than the behavior of Anglo students, whereas the pattern was reversed for the Anglo teachers. (The statistical analysis is unable to determine whether the interaction resulted from bias in the ratings, or whether the pupils' behavior is influenced by the teacher's ethnicity.)

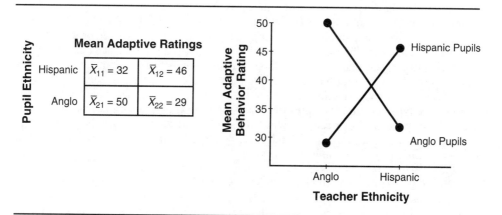

❖ **FIGURE 16.2** An illustration of a significant interaction with neither main effect being significant.

❖ 16.4 INTERACTION AND GENERALIZABILITY

A generalization about the effect of treatment is an inference about the difference between the means in the populations. If there is no interaction between the treatment factor and personological variables of the students, the findings can be generalized with greater simplicity, accuracy, and confidence. However, if interaction is present, the generalization of treatment effects must be qualified. Perhaps bright students find the "new math" more interesting, while low-ability students find it less interesting than the "old math"; average students may be equally interested in both. Notice that this question is not directly concerned with whether ability levels differ in interest, or whether the interest means differ for "old" versus "new math." Questions about overall differences are questions about *main effects*. The null hypothesis that pertains to the interaction is: Does the effect, if any, of factor A differ depending on factor B, or vice versa? More simply, is the student's interest level in the new or old math related to the student's ability level? In other words, is the difference in interest level between the new and old math the same for all ability levels? If the $A \times B$ interaction is not significant, there is no empirical evidence to suggest that the generalizations of the effects of factor A need to be qualified; we can generalize the overall effect of factor A to all levels of factor B without qualification.

Often a second factor is included in a research design not because interaction is expected, but because the absence of an interaction provides an empirical basis for the generalization of the treatment effect to all levels of the second factor. For example, consider a hypothetical study in which two instructional methods (experimental, E, and control, C) are compared for students from an upper-middle socioeconomic status community. If the study contrasted only the means for the experimental and control groups (i.e., used a t-test or a one-factor ANOVA), we would not be sure that the finding generalized to low-ability pupils since they probably made up a relatively small proportion of the sample. However, if a two-factor design were employed using, in addition to the treatment factor, several levels (categories or classifications) of a second factor, ability, the treatment-by-ability interaction would be statistically evaluated, as shown in Figure 16.3. In addition to comparing the means of the E and C groups, this design allows us to determine whether the treatment effect, if any, is constant for all ability levels—whether there is a significant interaction between treatment and ability level. Study Figure 16.3 to confirm that, although there is no interaction, there are significant treatment and ability effects.

Notice that the *difference* in E and C means is about the same for all ability levels—the treatment effect does not interact with ability level. Even though the E and C groups may both be above average in ability, the findings are generalizable to average or even below-average students, since the treatment effect did not depend on the student's ability level.

It should be clear that the examination of interaction between treatment and various subject characteristics contributes information that is critical to the generalizability of research findings. If an interaction is not significant, one can generalize with greater confidence to the types of subjects represented in the design. If an interaction is significant, it should be graphed (as illustrated in Figures 16.1–16.3) and studied so that the proper interpretation can be made. In many research studies, *although an interaction is not expected, factors in addition to the treatment factor are often included* so that the generalizability of the study can be empirically assessed.

What if the ability factor in Figure 16.3 were replaced by a teacher factor—six teachers each tried the E method with a random one-half of their students and the C method with the other half. We could then assess whether the E method (or the C method) is superior for all teachers, or whether the efficacy of the treatment depends on (i.e., interacts with) the par-

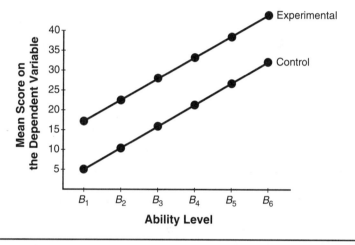

Cell Means for a 2 x 6 Treatment-by-Ability Design

❖ **FIGURE 16.3** Illustration of the absence of interaction between treatment and ability factors, but with two significant main effects (treatment and ability).

ticular teacher involved. If there is no treatment-by-teacher interaction, we can be more confident that the *E* method will result in superior performance with other teachers like those represented in the study. Parallel applications of this example can be made to virtually all fields by replacing teachers with psychotherapists, nurses, and the like.[1]

Another Example. The advantage of a two-factor ANOVA design will be illustrated by using hypothetical data from an ESP experiment. There are two levels of the treatment

---

[1]Indeed, if a three-factor (treatment-by-teacher-by-ability) ANOVA design were employed, we would be able to test the treatment-by-ability and treatment-by-teacher interaction in the same analysis, as well as the three-factor interaction (treatment-by-teacher-by-ability). In this illustration, the absence of a significant three-factor interaction would indicate that the pattern of results between treatment and ability level was the same for all teachers. If the results shown in Figure 16.3 were obtained for all teachers, there would be no treatment-by-teacher-by-ability interaction. It is beyond the scope of this text to examine the meaning of higher-order interactions (interactions involving three or more factors). Designs involving three and more factors are becoming increasingly common in behavioral research and are developed in intermediate and advanced texts on statistics and experimental design, such as Glass & Hopkins (1996), Kirk (1982), and Winer, Brown, & Michels (1991).

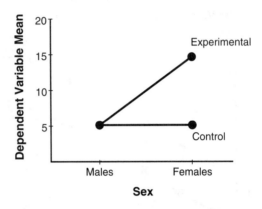

Treatment	Sex		Row Mean
	Males	Females	
Experimental	$\bar{X}_{11} = 5.0$	$\bar{X}_{12} = 15.0$	$\bar{X}_{1\bullet} = 10.0$
Control	$\bar{X}_{21} = 5.0$	$\bar{X}_{22} = 5.0$	$\bar{X}_{2\bullet} = 5.0$
Column Mean	$\bar{X}_{\bullet 1} = 5.0$	$\bar{X}_{\bullet 2} = 10.0$	$\bar{X}_{\bullet\bullet} = 7.5$

❖ **FIGURE 16.4** Hypothetical data for a two-factor ANOVA with a treatment-by-gender interaction. [Note: We will consistently denote the row (j) as the first subscript and the column factor (k) as the second subscript of a mean. For example, the mean of row 1, column 2, is $\bar{X}_{12}$. The symbol $\bar{X}_{1\bullet}$ is the mean of all observations in row 1 (experimental group in the example). The grand mean, $\bar{X}_{\bullet\bullet}$ is based on all observations. Further explanation of notation appears later in this chapter, Section 16.6.]

factor (level 1 is the experimental treatment; level 2 is the control) and two levels of the gender factor (level 1 is male; level 2 is female). The experimental treatment attempts to instruct persons how to send and receive a mentally transmitted message, and level 2 is the control no-treatment group. Suppose in this study that the mean of the experimental group was significantly greater than the mean of the control group. Does it necessarily follow that ESP was evidenced for all persons in the experimental group? Certainly not. It is possible that only certain persons in the E group were sensitive to the treatment. Perhaps ESP is a sex-linked trait and appears only in females. If females were capable of ESP and males were not, the mean of the experimental group taken as a whole would still exceed the control group mean as a consequence of the higher female scores in the experimental group. This fact is illustrated graphically in Figure 16.4; if the mean of the females in the E group ($\bar{X}_{12} = 15.0$) exceeds the mean of the females in the C-group ($\bar{X}_{22} = 5.0$), the mean of the experimental group ($\bar{X} = 10.0$) would exceed the control group mean ($\bar{X}_{2\bullet} = 5.0$) even if the males in both the E and C groups had equal means ($\bar{X}_{11} = 5.0$, $\bar{X}_{21} = 5.0$).

In many research studies, real interactions go undetected because of the failure to employ factorial designs, that is, designs that examine the effects of two or more factors (independent variables) simultaneously. If only a one-factor ANOVA design had been employed for the data represented in Figure 16.4, the null hypothesis for the treatment effect would have been rejected on the basis of $\overline{X}_E = 10.0$ and $\overline{X}_C = 5.0$. Using the factorial design allowed us to discover that the ESP instruction was evidenced only by the females. Thus, the two-factor ANOVA design clarified the nature of the findings. Since the treatment effect is not the same for both sexes, a treatment-by-gender interaction exists, as depicted in the interaction graph in Figure 16.4.

There would be no interaction between the two factors, treatment and gender, in Figure 16.4 if the difference between the E and C means for males were comparable to that for females. Notice in Figure 16.4 that the treatment factor interacts with the gender factor because the treatment effect for males ($\overline{X}_{11} - \overline{X}_{21}$) is 0, but the treatment effect for females ($\overline{X}_{12} - \overline{X}_{22}$) is 10. In more general terms, if the differences between the cells in one column are consistent across all columns, there is no interaction. Equivalently, if the differences between the cells of one row are consistent across all rows, there is no interaction.

The question of the statistical significance of this apparent interaction must be answered by means of an F-test. An ANOVA for the hypothetical data in Figure 16.4, assuming five observations per cell ($n = 5$) and an average within-cell variance (MS_W) of 10, is shown in Table 16.1, along with the corresponding three null hypotheses being tested.

Null hypotheses H_{0_1} and H_{0_2} represent main effects, whereas H_{0_3} represents an interaction hypothesis. The illustrative data represented in Figure 16.4 are evaluated for statistical significance in the ANOVA table of Table 16.1, and demonstrate that, when a significant treatment-by-gender interaction exists, the interaction influences the interpretation of the main effects. It is certainly true that we can conclude that the $\mu_E > \mu_C$, and $\mu_F > \mu_M$, but we can make a more precise and informative conclusion if the treatment-by-gender interaction is considered.

A second advantage of factorial designs is the *increase in power* that often accompanies their use. A two-factor ANOVA design often has greater power than two separate one-factor ANOVA designs; that is, the probability of detecting treatment effects is often increased in factorial designs. The increase in power for factorial designs is accomplished by partitioning the total sum of squares into a greater number of smaller components, only one of which (SS_W) is the basis for MS_W, the divisor of the F-test. For example, in a one-factor ANOVA, the total sum of squares is partitioned into two components: SS_B and SS_W. In a two-factor ANOVA, the total sum of squares is partitioned into four separate components: one for each of the two main effects, a SS for interaction, and the SS_W. When there are main or interaction effects, more of the total sum of squares is attributable to other sources, therefore it leaves a smaller total for SS_W (now within cells, not within groups) and thereby a smaller divisor, MS_W; thus, there is a larger F-ratio, and a greater likelihood of rejecting the null hypotheses. Conceptually, it is as though the within-groups SS_W for the one-factor analysis is further partitioned into three components: SS_B, $SS_{A \times B}$, and within-cells, SS_W. As

❖ **TABLE 16.1** Two-factor ANOVA table corresponding to hypothetical data in Figure 16.4 with corresponding null hypotheses being tested.

Source	SS	v	MS	F	H_0
Treatment (T)	125	1	125	12.5[a]	H_{0_1}: $\mu_{1.} = \mu_{2.}$
Sex (S)	125	1	125	12.5[a]	H_{0_2}: $\mu_{.1} = \mu_{.2}$
$T \times S$	125	1	125	12.5[a]	H_{0_3}: $\mu_{11} - \mu_{12} = \mu_{21} - \mu_{22}$[b]
Error (within)	160	16	10		

[a]$p < .01$, $_{.99}F_{1,16} = 8.53$

[b]Equivalently, $\mu_{11} - \mu_{21} = \mu_{12} - \mu_{22}$, or $(\mu_{11} - \mu_{21}) - (\mu_{12} - \mu_{22}) = 0$.

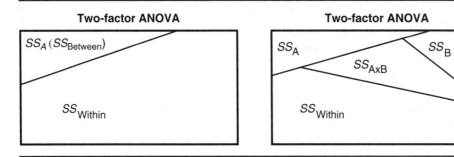

❖ **FIGURE 16.5** Partitioning of the total sum of squares for the one-factor ANOVA and for the two-factor ANOVA. Note that the sum of squares for factor A is the same in both but that the sum of squares within is smaller in the two-factor design.

SS_B and $SS_{A \times B}$ increase, the within cell variance decreases; thus, the F-ratios are increased, and the probability of detecting treatment effects (power) is increased. In Figure 16.5, note that the within groups sum of squares for one-way ANOVA is greater than the within cells sum of squares for two-way ANOVA. Therefore, the basis for the denominator of the F-test (within cells) in the two-factor design is smaller than for the one-factor design (within groups) which results in larger F-ratios. For three-factor and higher-order factorial ANOVA, the total sum of squares is partitioned into even more components which can decrease the SS_w still further and contribute additional statistical power to the analysis.[2]

❖ 16.5 THE RATIONALE OF THE ANOVA *F*-TEST REVISITED

In one-factor ANOVA, the SS_{total} is made up of two independent parts—the sum of squares between-groups (SS_A), which is the variability attributable to the levels of factor A, and the sum of squares within-groups (SS_W), which is the residual SS stemming from individual differences among the subjects within the treatment groups. For one-way ANOVA:

$$SS_{total} = SS_A + SS_W$$

These two SS's, when divided by their respective degrees of freedom, give independent estimates of σ^2; and their ratio, MS_A/MS_W, is the F-ratio (in honor of Sir Ronald Fisher, the father of ANOVA). When H_0 is true, both MS's are unbiased estimates of the same parameter, σ^2, and the F-ratio has an expected value of about 1, that is, $E(F) = 1$. However, when H_0 is false, the numerator, MS_A, is expected to exceed the denominator, MS_W, with the result that the observed F-ratio becomes larger than expected from sampling error alone.

The same rationale holds for two-factor ANOVA. For two-factor ANOVA, SS_{total} is composed of four independent sources: SS_A attributable to factor A, SS_B attributable to factor B, $SS_{A \times B}$ attributable to the interaction between A and B, and SS_W attributable to individual differences among subjects in the same treatment combination. For two-way ANOVA:

$$SS_{total} = SS_A + SS_B + SS_{A \times B} + SS_W \tag{16.1}$$

---

[2]For a more detailed and thorough explanation of how factorial designs increase statistical power, see Glass & Hopkins (1996).

Figure 16.5 is a visual representation of the components of SS_{total} if the same set of data were analyzed by both the one-factor ANOVA design and the two-factor ANOVA design where main and interaction effects are operative.

Each of the four SS's components of the two-factor design, when divided by their respective degrees of freedom, give unbiased estimates of the population σ^2 (i.e., MS's) when there are no treatment or interaction effects. On the contrary, if there are treatment effects for factor A, MS_A will overestimate σ^2; if there are treatment effects for factor B, MS_B will overestimate σ^2; and if there are interaction effects for factors A and B, $MS_{A \times B}$ will overestimate σ^2. However, the within-cell variance, MS_W, is an unbiased estimate of σ^2 whether any of the three H_0's is true, and consequently it forms the basis of comparison for the other three potentially biased mean squares. That is, MS_W is always an unbiased estimate of σ^2, and hence is the denominator for each of the three F-tests of a two-factor ANOVA: F_A, F_B, and $F_{A \times B}$.

When all three H_0's of a two-way ANOVA are true, each of the three F-ratios of the two-way ANOVA is expected to be somewhere in the neighborhood of 1. When an H_0 is false, the corresponding F-ratio is expected to increase.

The decision strategy concerning whether an H_0 is to be rejected or not remains consistent for all statistical tests: If the probability of the computed F-ratio falls below α (the adopted level of significance), H_0 is rejected as false; but if the probability of the obtained F-ratio exceeds α, the corresponding H_0 remains tenable.

❖ 16.6 NOTATION IN TWO-FACTOR ANOVA

Before working through some marginally exciting examples, we will define some catchy symbols and often encountered terms:

A, the row factor displayed as J horizontal rows
B, the column factor displayed as K vertical columns
$A \times B$, the interaction (composite effects) of factors A and B
JK, the number of cells in the design (If $J = 2$ rows and $K = 3$ columns, $JK = 2 \times 3 = 6$ cells.)
n, the number of observations in each cell

Concerning Subscripts:

$\overline{X}_{jk}$, the cell mean of scores in row j and column k (For example, $\overline{X}_{23}$ = the cell mean of row 2 and column 3.)
$\overline{X}_{\cdot k}$ the mean of column k (e.g., $\overline{X}_{\cdot 4}$, mean of column 4)[3]
$\overline{X}_{j \cdot}$ the mean of row j (e.g., $\overline{X}_{4 \cdot}$, mean of row 4)[3]
$\overline{X}_{\cdot \cdot}$ the grand mean for the total sample for a two-factor design

Quiz: What do the following symbols represent?
(1) $\overline{X}_{14}$, (2) $n_{\cdot \cdot}$, (3) $\overline{X}_{\cdot 1}$, (4) $n_{2 \cdot}$, (5) ΣX_{33}

Answers: (1) mean of the scores in the cell of row 1 and column 4, (2) total number of scores in the sample of a two-factor design, (3) mean of the scores in column 1, (4) number of scores in row 2, (5) the sum of the scores in the cell of row 3 and column 3.

---

[3]See Math Note 18 to review dot notation with two subscripts.

❖ 16.7 COMPUTATIONAL STEPS FOR BALANCED TWO-FACTOR ANOVA DESIGNS

The computational steps for a two-factor analysis of variance design[4] with equal numbers of scores (n) per cell[5] are outlined below. The analysis can be achieved with a plethora of computational algorithms, using a delightful array of formulas. We recommend the following five-step computational procedure for hand-computation as a means to further your understanding of the rationale underlying two-factor ANOVA, even though in practice you will have the computer do the chores.

The computational approach suggested here for the balanced two-factor ANOVA is comprised of five steps:

1. Compute MS_W; calculate the variance, s_{jk}^2, within each of the JK cells. Average the cell variances to obtain MS_W.
2. Compute the between-cells sum of squares, $SS_{b/cells}$. (This is an aggregate of SS_A, SS_B, and $SS_{A \times B}$).
3. Compute the F-ratio for factor A: Compute SS_A, MS_A; $F_A = MS_A/MS_W$.
4. Compute the F-ratio for factor B: Compute SS_B, MS_B; $F_B = MS_B/MS_W$.
5. Compute the F-ratio for the $A \times B$ interaction: Compute $SS_{A \times B}$, $MS_{A \times B}$; $F_{A \times B} = MS_{A \times B}/MS_W$.

These steps are described in more detail below.

Step 1. Find s_{jk}^2 for each cell and find their average by using Equation 16.2.

$$MS_W = \Sigma\Sigma s_{jk}^2/JK \qquad \textbf{(16.2)}$$

$$v_W = JK(n-1) \qquad \textbf{(16.3)}$$

Step 2. To compute the between-cells sum of squares ($SS_{b/cells}$), consider each cell as a separate group, and proceed as in one-factor ANOVA. The following equation may be helpful:

$$SS_{b/cells} = n\Sigma(\overline{X}_{jk} - \overline{X}_{..})^2 \qquad \textbf{(16.4)}$$

---

[4]In this chapter, all factors illustrated are considered to be fixed, not random, effects. When a factor is fixed, the results can be generalized only to the specific levels of the factors represented in the design. Factors such as treatment, sex, ability level, and grade level are fixed factors. A factor like teacher is fixed if we wish to generalize the results only to these particular teachers; teacher is a random factor if we wish to generalize to other teachers like these. Even when dealing with random factors, it is sensible to view all factors as fixed in the initial analysis; and then, only if there is significance, to define the factor(s) as random (Hopkins, 1983). Procedures for dealing with random factors in the analysis of variance are beyond the scope of this text. The interested reader is referred to Glass & Hopkins, 1996.

[5]When cell frequencies are unequal in ANOVA designs having two or more factors, the computation becomes much more complex and the analysis and interpretation of the results less unequivocal. There are several methods of analyzing such data, and they do not give exactly the same results in every situation. Consult a statistician if you find yourself in this situation. Better yet, stick to balanced designs whenever possible.

Step 3. To compute MS_A (similar to one-factor ANOVA), the following equations may be helpful:

$$SS_A = nK\Sigma(\overline{X}_{j\bullet} - \overline{X}_{\bullet\bullet})^2 \qquad \textbf{(16.5)}$$

$$\nu_A = J - 1 \qquad \textbf{(16.6)}$$

$$MS_A = SS_A/\nu_A \qquad \textbf{(16.7)}$$

$$F_A = MS_A/MS_W \qquad \textbf{(16.8)}$$

Step 4. To compute MS_B, the following equations may be helpful:

$$SS_B = nJ\Sigma(\overline{X}_{\bullet K} - \overline{X}_{\bullet\bullet})^2 \qquad \textbf{(16.9)}$$

$$\nu_B = K - 1 \qquad \textbf{(16.10)}$$

$$MS_B = SS_B/\nu_B \qquad \textbf{(16.11)}$$

$$F_B = MS_B/MS_W \qquad \textbf{(16.12)}$$

Step 5. To compute $MS_{A\times B}$, the following equations may be useful:

$$SS_{A\times B} = SS_{b/cells} - (SS_A + SS_B) \qquad \textbf{(16.13)}$$

$$\nu_{A\times B} = (J - 1)(K - 1) \qquad \textbf{(16.14)}$$

$$MS_{A\times B} = SS_{A\times B}/\nu_{A\times B} \qquad \textbf{(16.15)}$$

$$F_{A\times B} = MS_{A\times B}/MS_W \qquad \textbf{(16.16)}$$

❖ 16.8 TWO-FACTOR ANOVA EXAMPLE

A demonstration experiment was conducted in a statistics course on the effect of using hand calculators on computational accuracy. Since the effect of the treatment [factor A:

row 1 (with calculator) vs. row 2 (without calculator)] might interact with the math background of the students, the students were categorized into two groups [factor B: column 1 (students with college math) vs. column 2 (students without college math)]. The resulting research design then has two levels of the treatment factor ($J = 2$) and two levels of the math-background factor ($K = 2$), that is, a 2×2 treatment-by-math background ANOVA design. There were twenty students in each of the two math-background categories; within each category, students were randomly assigned to either the calculator or no-calculator group, resulting in ten students in each of the four cells.[6] All subjects were then given ten problems requiring complex arithmetic computations under limited time conditions. The raw scores and means for the study appear in the Math Background section of Table 16.2.

Note in Table 16.2 that the observed mean ($\overline{X}_{1.} = 6.30$) of the calculator group (row 1) is greater than the mean ($\overline{X}_{2.} = 6.00$) of the control group (row 2) who had to do the computations without calculators. The college-math group (column 1) also had a higher mean ($\overline{X}_{.1} = 6.4$) than the group having no college math (column 2, $\overline{X}_{.2} = 5.9$). Did the students with college math benefit more (or less) from the use of a calculator than the students with no college math? Is the pattern of results reliable? Would they be replicated if the study was repeated? Can this pattern be generalized to the population of statistics students like these? A two-factor ANOVA will be used as a basis to respond to these questions.

The F-tests in the ANOVA table in Table 16.2 indicate that neither of the two null hypotheses for the main effects (H_{0_1}: $\mu_{1.} = \mu_{2.}$ or H_{0_2}: $\mu_{.1} = \mu_{.2}$) nor the null hypothesis for the interaction effect (H_{0_3}: $\mu_{11} - \mu_{12} = \mu_{21} - \mu_{22}$) can be rejected even at the .25 level of significance—each of the computed F-ratios (.23, .64, and 1.25) is less than the value of $1.38 = {}_{.75}F_{1,36}$. These data failed to provide any cogent evidence against the validity of the three null hypotheses of this study. We cannot conclude that providing calculators to students like these has an effect upon their ability to do complex arithmetic computations under limited time conditions. In addition, we cannot conclude that students with one or more college courses in mathematics perform differently than those without this math background. Finally, we cannot conclude that the effect of the treatment is related to (interacts with) the math background of the students.

Quiz: Based on the summary table of Table 16.2: (1) Which type of error could have been made—type-I errors or type-II errors? (2) Estimate the average value of the standard deviation of the ten math scores within a cell. (3) If a larger number of students had participated in the study, would the MS_W be expected to increase?

Answers: (1) When H_0's are retained, there is some probability of a type-II error, but not a type-I error. (2) Since $MS_W = s^2 \approx 4$, $s \approx 2$. (3) No, the variance is an unbiased estimate of the population variance; as n increases, MS_W more closely approximates σ^2.

---

[6]Actually, there were forty-three persons in the class; three students were randomly discarded so that there would be an equal number of students in the two levels of the math background. In two-factor ANOVA designs, if the n's are equal, not only is the analysis simpler, but the results are less ambiguous. In addition, recall that the homogeneity-of-variance assumption can be disregarded only when the n's are equal (see Figure 11.6 in Section 11.14). Note that we first stratified the students by math background, then randomly assigned them to treatment group. In this way, we can maintain equal n's in the cells. If we randomly assigned the students to a treatment group and then classified them according to math background, the cell n's would rarely be equal.

❖ **TABLE 16.2** Computational illustration of a 2×2 ANOVA with $n = 10$.

	MATH BACKGROUND		
	College Math	*No College Math*	*Row Totals*
Calculator Group	X: 4 5 6 8 10 3 5 6 8 7 $\overline{X}_{11} = 6.20$ $s_{11}^2 = 4.4$ $n_{11} = 10$	5 5 7 8 9 4 5 6 7 8 $\overline{X}_{12} = 6.40$ $s_{12}^2 = 2.71$ $n_{12} = 10$	$\overline{X}_{1\cdot} = 6.30$ $n_{1\cdot} = 20$
Control Group	X: 7 5 7 8 9 3 4 8 6 9 $\overline{X}_{21} = 6.60$ $s_{21}^2 = 4.27$ $n_{21} = 10$	3 5 6 8 7 4 5 3 4 9 $\overline{X}_{22} = 5.40$ $s_{22}^2 = 4.27$ $n_{22} = 10$	$\overline{X}_{2\cdot} = 6.00$ $n_{2\cdot} = 20$
Column Totals	$\overline{X}_{\cdot 1} = 6.4$ $n_{\cdot 1} = 20$	$\overline{X}_{\cdot 2} = 5.9$ $n_{\cdot 2} = 20$	$\overline{X}_{\cdot\cdot} = 6.15$ $n_{\cdot\cdot} = 40$

Step 1: $MS_W = \Sigma\Sigma s_{jk}^2/JK = (4.4 + 2.71 + 4.27 + 4.27)/4 = 3.91$
$\quad\quad\quad v_W = n_{\cdot\cdot} - JK = 40 - 4 = 36 \; [SS_W = v_W(MS_W) = 36(3.91)) = 140.8]$
Step 2: $SS_{b/cells} = n_{jk}\Sigma(\overline{X}_{jk} - \overline{X}_{\cdot\cdot})^2$
$\quad\quad\quad SS_{b/cells} = 10[(6.2 - 6.15)^2 + (6.4 - 6.15)^2 + (6.6 - 6.15)^2 + (5.4 - 6.15)^2] = 8.30$
Step 3: $SS_A = nK\Sigma(\overline{X}_{j\cdot} - \overline{X}_{\cdot\cdot})^2 = 20(6.3 - 6.15)^2 + 20(6.0 - 6.15)^2 = .45 + .45 = .90$
$\quad\quad\quad v_A = J - 1 = 2 - 1 = 1; \; MS_A = .90/1 = .90; \; F = MS_A/MS_W = .90/3.91 = .23$
Step 4: $SS_B = nJ\Sigma(\overline{X}_{\cdot j} - \overline{X}_{\cdot\cdot})^2 = 20(6.4 - 6.15)^2 + 20(5.9 - 6.15)^2 = 1.25 + 1.25 = 2.5.$
$\quad\quad\quad v_B = K - 1 = 2 - 1 = 1; \; MS_B = SS_B/v_B = 2.5; \; MS_W = 2.5/3.91 = .64$
Step 5: $SS_{A\times B} = SS_{b/cells} - SS_A - SS_B = 8.3 - .9 - 2.5 = 4.9$
$\quad\quad\quad v_{A\times B} = (J - 1)(K - 1) = 1; \; MS_{A\times B} = 4.9/1 = 4.9; \; F_{A\times B} = 4.9/3.91 = 1.25$

ANOVA Summary Table

SV	SS	v	MS	F	p
Treatment (A)	.90	1	.90	.23	>.25
Background (B)	2.50	1	2.50	.64	>.25
A × B	4.90	1	4.90	1.25	>.25
Within Cell	140.8	36	3.91		

Critical *F*-value for $\alpha = .25$: $_{.75}F_{1,36} = 1.38$

❖ 16.9 A SECOND COMPUTATIONAL EXAMPLE OF TWO-FACTOR ANOVA

Do three ethnic groups differ in attitude toward school? Does school attitude change between grades 5 and 11? Is the pattern of change the same for each of the three ethnic groups? To answer these questions, samples of Black, Hispanic, and Anglo students in grades 5 and 11 in Colorado were selected and administered a school attitude inventory. To achieve a balanced design (equal cell sizes), students were randomly discarded from the sample group until 100 students remained in each of the six cells. The results of the 3×2 ethnicity-by-grade $(E \times G)$ ANOVA are given in Table 16.3.

❖ **TABLE 16.3** Illustration of a 3 × 2 ethnicity-by-grade two-factor ANOVA with $n = 100$ per cell.

		GRADE LEVEL		
		Grade 5	Grade 11	Row Totals
	Black	$\overline{X}_{11} = 54.9$ $n_{11} = 100$	$\overline{X}_{12} = 51.8$ $n_{12} = 100$	$\overline{X}_{1.} = 53.35$ $n_{1.} = 200$
ETNICITY	Hispanic	$\overline{X}_{21} = 55.8$ $n_{21} = 100$	$\overline{X}_{22} = 51.7$ $n_{22} = 100$	$\overline{X}_{2.} = 53.75$ $n_{2.} = 200$
	Anglo	$\overline{X}_{31} = 55.6$ $n_{31} = 100$	$\overline{X}_{32} = 50.9$ $n_{32} = 100$	$\overline{X}_{3.} = 53.25$ $n_{3.} = 200$
Column Totals		$\overline{X}_{.1} = 55.43$ $n_{.1} = 300$	$\overline{X}_{.2} = 51.47$ $n_{.2} = 300$	$\overline{X}_{..} = 53.45$ $n_{..} = 600$

(Note: Given $SS_W = 22{,}691$ for the 600 raw scores.)

Step 1: $SS_W = 22{,}691$ (Given); $v_W = 600 - 6 = 594$; $MS_W = 22{,}691/594 = 38.2$

Step 2: $SS_{b/cells} = n_{jk}\Sigma(\overline{X}_{jk} - \overline{X}_{..})^2 = 100[(1.45)^2 + (1.65)^2 + (2.35)^2 + (1.75)^2 + (2.15)^2 + (2.55)^2]$
$= 2{,}453.5.$

Step 3: $SS_A = nK\Sigma(\overline{X}_{j.} - \overline{X}_{..})^2 = 200(-.1)^2 + 200(.3)^2 + 200(-.2)^2 = 2 + 18 + 8 = 28.$
$v_A = J - 1 = 2; MS_A = 28/2 = 14; F = MS_A/MS_W = 14/38.2 = .37$

Step 4: $SS_B = \Sigma nJ(\overline{X}_{.j} - \overline{X}_{..})^2 = 300(1.98)^2 + 300(-1.98)^2 = 2{,}352.24; v_B = K - 1;$
$MS_B = SS_B/v_B = 2{,}352.24/1 = 2{,}352.24; F_B = MS_B/MS_W = 2{,}352.24/38.2 = 61.58$

Step 5: $SS_{A\times B} = SS_{b/cell} - (SS_A + SS_B) = 2{,}453.5 - (28 + 2{,}352.24) = 73.26$
$v_{A\times B} = (J - 1)(K - 1) = 2; MS_{A\times B} = 73.26/2 = 36.63; F_{A\times B} = 36.63/38.2 = .96$

ANOVA Summary Table

SV	SS	v	MS	F	p
Ethnicity (E)	28.00	2	14.00	.37	>.25
Grade (G)	2,352.24	1	2,352.24	61.58	<.001
$A \times B$	73.26	2	36.63	.96	>.25
Within Cell	22,691.00	594	38.2		

Critical F-value for $\alpha = .001$: $_{.999}F_{1,594} \approx 11.00$

Notice in the ANOVA table of Table 16.3 that there were highly significant differences between the means for the two grade levels ($F = 61.58$). (As a mnemonic aid, it is common practice to use the initial letter of the factor name, rather than A and B, to represent the factors.) By studying the means for grades 5 and 11 in the Grade Level section, we see that school attitude was more favorable (high scores represent positive attitudes) at grade 5 than at grade 11.

To better grasp the magnitude of the difference, the effect size ($\hat{\Delta}$) (Section 11.19) expresses the difference between the means in standard deviation units:

$$s = \sqrt{MS_W}, \quad \hat{\Delta} = \frac{\overline{X}_{.1} - \overline{X}_{.2}}{s} = \frac{55.43 - 51.47}{6.18} = .64$$

An effect size of .64 is quite large; it indicates that the average pupil at grade 5 would have had a z score of .64 (P_{74}; Appendix Table A) in the grade 11 distribution. It follows that approximately three-fourths of the grade 11 students fell below the grade 5 average in school attitude. The ANOVA table in Table 16.3 shows that there were no significant differences among the means for the three ethnic groups ($F = .37$). The absence of a significant interaction between the ethnicity and grade factors indicates that the pattern of higher school attitude at grade 5 was consistent (and to a comparable degree) for all three ethnic groups. A significant $E \times G$ interaction would have indicated that the difference between means at grades 5 and 11 was greater for certain ethnic groups than for others. The lack of an interaction makes the findings more generalizable: The attitudes of all three ethnic groups were comparable at both grades 5 and 11, and the higher mean at grade 5 versus grade 11 was consistent for the three ethnic groups. (If an interaction is significant, it should be graphed, as was illustrated in Figures 16.1–16.4.)

❖ 16.10 CONFIDENCE INTERVALS FOR ROW AND COLUMN MEANS

The standard error of the mean for the row factor, A, is:

$$s_{\bar{X}_j} = \sqrt{\frac{MS_W}{nK}} \qquad (16.17)$$

In Table 16.3, $nK = 200$ and $MS_W = 38.20$, thus $s_{\bar{X}_j} = .437$ (Eq. 16.17). MS_W is based on 594 degrees of freedom, hence the .95 confidence interval shows that the population mean of the first row (Blacks) is quite precisely estimated:

$$.95 \text{ CI} = [53.35 \pm {}_{.975}t_{594}s_{\bar{X}_j}] = [53.35 \pm 1.965(.437)] \text{ or } [52.49, 54.21].$$

Likewise, the standard error of the mean for the column factor, B, is:

$$s_{\bar{X}_k} = \sqrt{\frac{MS_W}{nJ}} \qquad (16.18)$$

In addition to their use for setting confidence intervals, these standard errors are also used for Tukey and Newman-Keuls multiple comparisons procedures.

❖ CHAPTER SUMMARY

ANOVA is a very flexible statistical model; the effects of the two or more independent variables (factors) can be assessed separately and simultaneously in the same analysis. In this chapter, a balanced two-factor ANOVA has been considered—the simplest example of a factorial design. In addition to testing main effects, two-factor ANOVA can identify interactions between the two factors. If there are particular combinations of the factors that result in effects above or below those attributable to the two factors separately, the factors are said to interact. The absence of interaction indicates that the effects of factor A are constant across the levels of factor B, and that the results for factor A are generalizable over all categories of factor B. The absence of interaction provides empirical support for enhancing the generalizability of the findings.

The use of a two-factor ANOVA rather than two separate one-factor ANOVAs, in addition to addressing the interaction question, is a more efficient use of data and is often more powerful in testing the main effects for factors A and B.

MASTERY TEST

Questions 1–10: Given that a study was made of attendance of elementary, junior high, and senior high school students for three ethnic groups (I, II, and III):

1. If a two-factor ANOVA is used, what are the two independent variables?
2. What is the dependent variable?
3. How many levels (categories) are there of each factor?
4. The design can be described as a ___?___ design.
   (a) 2×2 (b) 2×3 (c) 3×3 (d) 3×2 (e) 3×4
5. Complete the ANOVA table pertaining to the analysis of the data above.

ANOVA Summary Table

SV	SS	v	MS	F	p
School Level (S)	900	—	___	___	___
Ethnicity (E)	___	2	250	___	___
$S \times E$	1,200	—	___	___	___
Within Cell	45,000	900	___		

6. What are the critical F-values for the two main effects and for the interaction with $\alpha = .05$, $\alpha = .01$, and $\alpha = .001$?
7. Can H_0 for the two main effects be rejected at either the .05, .01, or the .001 level of significance?
8. Does the F-test for the $S \times E$ interaction indicate that the attendance trend did not follow the same pattern for the three ethnic groups; that is, is the $S \times E$ interaction statistically significant? Can H_0 be rejected at $\alpha = .001$?
9. Which of the figures below, (a), (b), or (c), is *consistent* with all the information in the ANOVA table in question 5?

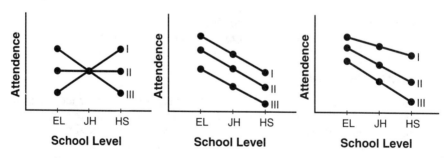

10. If a one-factor ANOVA had been performed comparing the three levels of school, are the following statements true or false?
    (a) The F-ratio for school level would have been less.
    (b) The interaction of school level and ethnicity would not be tested.
11. Which of these are advantages of two-factor ANOVA over one-factor ANOVA?

(a) The denominator of the F-test is increased.
(b) The generalizability of the results is enhanced.
(c) Interaction between factors can be identified.
(d) Power is often increased.

12. Given a 2×4, $A \times B$ ANOVA: $SS_{\text{total}} = 100$, $SS_{\text{b/cells}} = 50$, $SS_A = 25$, $SS_B = 10$.
(a) What is the value of SS_w?
(b) What is the value of $SS_{A \times B}$?
(c) What is the value of $v_{A \times B}$?
(d) What is $MS_{A \times B}$?

13. Which is largest: $n_{1\cdot}$ or $n_{\cdot 1}$ or $n_{\cdot\cdot}$?

14. Graph the interaction of factor B, Traditional Orthography (TO) versus Initial Teaching Alphabet (ITA), and factor A, Sex, from the following cell means expressed in grade-placement units on a standardized reading test. Does the interaction seem to be significant?

	TO	ITA
Boys	$\bar{X}_{11} = 4.6$	$\bar{X}_{12} = 4.5$
Girls	$\bar{X}_{21} = 4.9$	$\bar{X}_{22} = 4.8$ 6

15. The figure below represents cell, row, and column *population* means (μ's) in a two-factor ANOVA design.

		FACTOR B			
		B_1	B_2	B_3	*Row Totals*
FACTOR A	A_1	$\mu_{11} = 15$	$\mu_{12} = 10$	$\mu_{13} = 5$	$\mu_{1\cdot} = 10$
	A_2	$\mu_{21} = 5$	$\mu_{22} = 10$	$\mu_{23} = 15$	$\mu_{2\cdot} = 10$
Column Totals		$\mu_{\cdot 1} = 10$	$\mu_{\cdot 2} = 10$	$\mu_{\cdot 3} = 10$	$\mu_{\cdot\cdot} = 10$

(a) Is $H_{0_1}: \mu_{1\cdot} = \mu_{2\cdot}$?
(b) Is $H_{0_2}: \mu_{\cdot 1} = \mu_{\cdot 2} = \mu_{\cdot 3}$?
(c) Is $H_{0_3}: \mu_{11} - \mu_{21} = \mu_{12} - \mu_{22} = \mu_{13} - \mu_{23}$?

16. Which hypotheses in question 15 pertain to main effects and which pertain to interaction?

ANSWERS TO MASTERY TEST

1. school level and ethnicity
2. attendance
3. three levels of ethnicity and three levels of school type
4. (c)
5.

ANOVA Summary Table

SV	SS	v	MS	F	p
School Level (S)	900	2	450	9.0	<.001
Ethnicity (E)	500	2	250	5.0	<.01
$S \times E$	1,200	4	300	6.0	<.001
Within Cell	45,000	900	50		

6. For $\alpha = .05$: $_{.95}F_{4,900} = 2.39$; $_{.95}F_{2,900} = 3.01$.
   For $\alpha = .01$: $_{.99}F_{4,900} = 3.36$; $_{.99}F_{2,900} = 4.65$.
   For $\alpha = .001$: $_{.999}F_{4,900} = 4.69$; $_{.999}F_{2,900} = 7.00$.
7. Yes, H_{0_1}: $\mu_E = \mu_J = \mu_H$ is rejected at $\alpha = .001$; $9.0 > 6.95$; $p < .001$.
   H_{0_2}: $\mu_I = \mu_{II} = \mu_{III}$ is rejected at $\alpha = .01$; $5.0 > 4.62$; $p < .01$.
8. Yes, $F = 6.0 > 4.65$; $p < .001$. The null hypothesis is rejected at $\alpha = .001$.
9. Only figure (c) is consistent with the ANOVA table. [Figure (a) has no main effects for factors S and E; figure (b) has no $S \times E$ interaction.
10. (a) True, although the numerator of the F-ratio would remain unchanged, the denominator of the F-ratio would be increased. Analyzed as a one-factor ANOVA:
    $MS_W = (500 + 1,200 + 45,000)/(2 + 4 + 900) = 51.55$; $F = 450/51.55 = 8.73$.
    (b) true
11. (b), (c), and (d)
12. (a) $SS_W = SS_{total} - SS_{b/cells} = 100 - 50 = 50$
    (b) $SS_{A \times B} = SS_{total} - SS_A - SS_B - SS_W = 100 - 50 - 25 - 10 = 15$
    (c) $(J - 1)(K - 1) = (2 - 1)(4 - 1) = 3$
    (d) $MS_{A \times B} = SS_{A \times B}/v_{A \times B} = 15/3 = 5.0$
13. The largest is $n_{..}$ since it is the total number of all observations, whereas $n_{.1}$ is the total from column 1 and $n_{1.}$ is the total in row 1.
14. No, the lines are parallel indicating that the differences between the methods are comparable for boys and girls. Either graph portrays this tendency.
15. (a) yes, (b) yes, (c) no
16. H_{0_1} and H_{0_2} pertain to main effects; the interaction null hypothesis is H_{0_3}.

PROBLEMS AND EXERCISES

1. Analyze the following scores on a 50-item vocabulary test administered to twenty-four students of high and average intelligence after one year of studying a foreign language under one of three methods with $\alpha = .10$.

	METHOD (FACTOR B)		
	Aural-Oral	Translation	Combined
High (IQ $\geq$ 115)	37	27	20
	30	24	31
	26	22	24
	31	19	21
FACTOR A			
Average (IQ $\geq$ 114)	32	20	17
	19	23	18
	37	14	23
	28	15	18

2. Use the Tukey multiple comparisons for the method effect in problem 1.
   (a) $s_{\bar{x}}$ for methods = $\sqrt{MS_W / nJ}$ = _____?_____
   (b) Which null hypotheses for differences in means can be rejected?

3. A group of twenty-four students was split at random into four equal groups, each of which is assigned to the four combinations of factor P, "position of question" (before vs. after the passage) and factor I, "type of question" (factual vs. thought-provoking). After ten hours of study

under these conditions, the students were given a test on the content of the materials. Perform a two-factor ANOVA on these data. Test the H_0's for both main effects and the interaction with $\alpha = .10$.

TYPE OF	POSITION OF QUESTION (P)			
QUESTION (T)	Before		After	
Fact	19	23	31	28
	29	26	26	27
	30	17	35	32
Thought-Provoking	27	21	36	29
	20	26	39	31
	15	24	41	35

4. High-ability (H) and low-ability (L) students were randomly assigned to three levels of the anxiety factor—(1) anxiety-producing (AP) conditions, (2) anxiety-reducing (AR) conditions, and (3) standard (S) conditions—and were administered the Academic Ability Test (AAT). Results from the 3 × 2 ANOVA are shown in the table below.

ANOVA Summary Table

SV	SS	v	MS	F	p
Anxiety Condition (C)	37.04	2	18.52	1.20	>.25
Ability Level (L)	796.69	1	796.69	51.43	<.001
C × L	7.48	2	3.74	.24	>.25
Within Cell	836.46	54	15.49		

(a) Do the ability level means differ significantly on the AAT?

(b) Did the anxiety-producing condition produce a significantly lower (or higher) mean than did either the anxiety-reducing or standard condition?

(c) Was there a trend for low-ability examinees to be affected more by the anxiety conditions than were the high-ability examinees?

(d) How many subjects ($n_{..}$) were there in the study?

(e) Was the difference between the means of the low- and high-ability groups significantly greater in certain of the anxiety conditions than in others?

(f) Which of the following interaction graphs is consistent with the results in the ANOVA table?

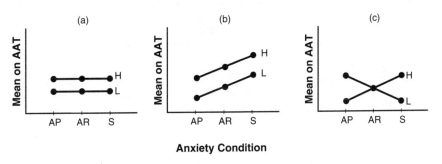

(g) Which graph conveys an interaction effect but no main effects?

ANSWERS TO PROBLEMS AND EXERCISES

1.

	METHOD OF STUDY			
	Aural-Oral	*Translation*	*Combined*	*Row Totals*
High IQ	$\overline{X}_{11} = 31$ $s_{11}^2 = 20.7$ $n_{11} = 4$	$\overline{X}_{12} = 23$ $s_{12}^2 = 11.3$ $n_{12} = 4$	$\overline{X}_{13} = 24$ $s_{13}^2 = 24.7$ $n_{13} = 4$	$\overline{X}_{1.} = 26$ $n_{1.} = 12$
Average IQ	$\overline{X}_{21} = 30$ $s_{21}^2 = 58$ $n_{21} = 4$	$\overline{X}_{22} = 18$ $s_{22}^2 = 18$ $n_{22} = 4$	$\overline{X}_{23} = 19$ $s_{23}^2 = 7.3$ $n_{23} = 4$	$\overline{X}_{2.} = 22$ $n_{2.} = 12$
Column Totals	$\overline{X}_{.1} = 30$ $n_{.1} = 8$	$\overline{X}_{.2} = 20.5$ $n_{.2} = 8$	$\overline{X}_{.3} = 21.5$ $n_{.3} = 8$	$\overline{X}_{..} = 24$ $n_{..} = 24$

Step 1. $MS_W = \Sigma\Sigma s_{jk}^2/JK = (20.7 + 11.3 + 24.7 + 58 + 18 + 7.3)/6 = 23.333$
$\nu_W = n_{..} - JK = 24 - 6 = 18 \ [SS_W = \nu_W(MS_W) = 18(23.333) = 420]$

Step 2. $SS_{b/cells} = n\Sigma(\overline{X}_{jk} - \overline{X}_{..})^2 = 4[(31 - 24)^2 + (23 - 24)^2 + \ldots + (19 - 24)^2] = 544$

Step 3. $SS_A = nK\Sigma(\overline{X}_{j.} - \overline{X}_{..})^2 = 12[(26 - 24)^2 + (22 - 24)^2] = 12(8) = 96$
$\nu_A = J - 1 = 1; \ MS_A = 96/1 = 96; \ F_A = 96/23.33 = 4.11$

Step 4. $SS_B = n_{.k}\Sigma(\overline{X}_{.k} - \overline{X}_{..})^2 = 8[(30 - 24)^2 + (20.5 - 24)^2 + (21.5 - 24)^2] = 436$
$\nu_B = K - 1 = 2; \ MS_B = 436/2 = 218; \ F_B = 218/23.33 = 9.34$

Step 5. $SS_{A \times B} = SS_{b/cell} - (SS_A + SS_B) = 544 - (96 + 436) = 12$
$\nu_{A \times B} = (J - 1)(K - 1) = 2; \ MS_{A \times B} = 12/2 = 6; \ F_{A \times B} = 6/23.33 = .26$

ANOVA Summary Table

SV	SS	ν	MS	F	p
Intelligence (I)	96	1	96	4.11	<.10
Method (M)	436	2	218	9.34	<.01
$I \times M$	12	2	6	.26	>.25
Within Cell	420	18	23.33		

Critical F-values: $_{.90}F_{1,18} = 3.01$; $_{.99}F_{2,18} = 6.01$

2. (a) $s_{\overline{X}}$ for columns (methods) $= \sqrt{23.33/8} = 1.71$

   (b) $H_0: \mu_A = \mu_T$ is rejected at $\alpha = .01$, since $q = (30 - 20.5)/1.71 = 5.56$ and $q > 4.70 = _{.99}q_{3,18}$.
   $H_0: \mu_A = \mu_C$ is rejected at $\alpha = .01$ since $q = (30 - 21.5)/1.71 = 4.97$ and $q > 4.70 = _{.99}q_{3,18}$.
   $H_0: \mu_C = \mu_T$ is tenable at $\alpha = .05$, since $q = (21.5 - 20.5)/1.71 = .58$ and $q < 3.61 = _{.95}q_{3,18}$.

3.

	FACTOR B		
	POSITION OF QUESTION		
FACTOR A	Before	After	Row Totals
Fact	$\overline{X}_{11} = 24$ $s_{11}^2 = 28$ $n_{11} = 6$	$\overline{X}_{12} = 29.8$ $s_{12}^2 = 11.8$ $n_{12} = 6$	$\overline{X}_{1.} = 26.9$ $n_{1.} = 12$
Thought-Provoking	$\overline{X}_{21} = 22.2$ $s_{21}^2 = 19.8$ $n_{21} = 6$	$\overline{X}_{22} = 35.2$ $s_{22}^2 = 21$ $n_{22} = 6$	$\overline{X}_{2.} = 28.7$ $n_{2.} = 12$
Column Totals	$\overline{X}_{.1} = 23.1$ $n_{.1} = 12$	$\overline{X}_{.2} = 32.5$ $n_{.2} = 12$	$\overline{X}_{..} = 27.8$ $n_{..} = 24$

Step 1. $MS_W = \Sigma\Sigma s_{jk}^2 / JK = (28 + 11.8 + 19.8 + 21)/4 = 20.15$

$v_W = n_{..} - JK = 24 - 4 = 20 \ [SS_W = v_W(MS_W) = 20(20.15)) = 403.]$

Step 2. $SS_{b/cells} = n_{jk}\Sigma(\overline{X}_{jk} - \overline{X}_{..})^2 = 6[(24 - 27.8)^2 + \ldots + (35.2 - 27.8)^2] = 627.5$

Step 3. $SS_A = nK\Sigma(\overline{X}_{j.} - \overline{X}_{..})^2 = 12[(26.9 - 27.8)^2 + (28.7 - 27.8)^2] = 18.4$

$v_A = J - 1 = 1; MS_A = 18.4/1 = 18.4; F_A = 18.4/20.13 = .91$

Step 4. $SS_B = n_{.k}\Sigma(\overline{X}_{.k} - \overline{X}_{..})^2 = 12[(23.1 - 27.8)^2 + (32.5 - 27.8)^2] = 532$

$v_B = K - 1 = 1; MS_B = 532/1 = 532; F_B = 532/20.13 = 26.4$

Step 5. $SS_{A\times B} = SS_{b/cells} - (SS_A + SS_B) = 627.5 - 18.4 - 532 = 77.1$

$v_{A\times B} = (J - 1)(K - 1) = 1; MS_{A\times B} = 77.1/1 = 77.1; F_{A\times B} = 77.1/20.13 = 3.83$

ANOVA Summary Table

SV	SS	v	MS	F	p
Type of Question (T)	18.4	1	18.4	.91	>.25
Position of Question (P)	532	1	532	26.4	<.001
$T \times P$	77.1	1	77.1	3.83	<.10
Within Cell	403	20	20.13		

Critical F-values: $_{.90}F_{1,20} = 2.97$; $_{.999}F_{1,20} = 14.8$

4. (a) Yes, $p < .001$; $F = 51.43 > 12.6 = _{.999}F_{1,54}$.

(b) No, $p > .25$; $F = 1.20 < 1.44 = _{.75}F_{2,54}$.

(c) No, $p > .25$.

(d) $n_{..} = v_{total} + 1 = 60$

(e) No; this question is the same as the question in option (c).

(f) graph a

(g) graph c

❖ Appendixes

Contents

❖ Appendix A

Math Notes

❖ MATH NOTE 1. *Multiples*

The multiples of a number, N, are N, $2N$, $3N$, $4N$, $5N$, etc. A multiple of N is a whole number times the value N. Multiples of $500 are $500, $1,000, $1,500, $2,000, etc.; multiples of 7 are 7, 14, 21, 28, etc.

Exercises	*Answers*
A. List the first six multiples of the number 9.	A. 9, 18, 27, 36, 45, 54
B. What is the largest number of which these numbers are multiples: 12, 15, 21, 30?	B. 3

❖ MATH NOTE 2. *Proportion and Percent*

A proportion is the ratio of a number, a, to another number, b (i.e., $\frac{a}{b}$), expressed as a decimal fraction. If, in a class of 20 students, 5 receive A's and 10 receive B's, the proportion who receive A's is found by reducing the $\frac{5}{20}$ to a decimal fraction—that is, by dividing 5 by 20: $5 \div 20 = .25$. The proportion receiving B's is 10 of 20 or $\frac{10}{20} = .50$. Proportion and percentage are alternative ways of conveying the same information:

$$\text{Proportion} = \frac{\text{Percentage}}{100}.$$

Exercise	*Answer*
A. If there are 10 girls in a class of 25 students, girls make up what proportion of the class?	A. $\frac{10}{25} = .40$

To find a given percent of any number, convert the percentage to a proportion and multiply this proportion by the number. For example, 60% of 35 is $.60 \times 35 = 21$; or 21 is 60% of 35.

Exercises	*Answers*
B. If 12% of the U.S. population of 250 million is black, how many Blacks are there in the United States?	B. $12\% = .12$; $.12 \times 250 = 30$ million
C. If, to receive an A on a test, 90% is required, how many items on a test of 60 questions must be answered correctly?	C. $90\% = .90$; $.9 \times 60 = 54$ items

❖ MATH NOTE 3. *Simple Summation*

The symbol Σ is the Greek capital letter *sigma*. Its conventional use in mathematics and statistics is to denote summation, and is read "the sum of ..." or "add up ..." The formula in Equation 3.1 indicates that the mean is "the sum of" the X's divided by n. Thus, ΣX means $X_1 + X_2 + ... + X_n$, where the subscripts 1, 2, ..., n serve only to identify specific observations. When the summation does not include all *n*-values of X, lower and upper limits of the summation would be required, but otherwise such limits are superfluous. That is, unless otherwise indicated, $\Sigma X = \sum_{i=1}^{n} X_i$, where the latter reads "the sum of X_i as i goes from 1 to *n*." If $X_1 = 5$, $X_2 = 9$, $X_3 = 7$, and $X_4 = 10$, then $\Sigma X = \sum_{i=1}^{n=4} X_i = X_1 + X_2 + X_3 + X_4 = 5 + 9 + 7 + 10 = 31$. But $\sum_{i=1}^{n=3} X_i = X_1 + X_2 + X_3 = 5 + 9 + 7 = 21$. In virtually all applications in this book, the summation is for all *n*-values; hence, the lower and upper limits will be eliminated from the summation sign, Σ.

Exercises	*Answers*
Suppose $X_1 = 2$, $X_2 = 1$, and $X_3 = 5$.	
A. Does $\Sigma X = \sum_{i=1}^{n} X_i = \sum_{i=1}^{3} X_i = X_1 + X_2 + X_3$?	A. yes
B. What is the value of ΣX?	B. 8
C. If $Y_1 = 10$, $Y_2 = 0$, $Y_3 = 4$, and $Y_4 = 6$, then $\Sigma Y = ?$	C. 20

❖ MATH NOTE 4. *Rounding*

For most purposes, answers with three of four figures convey the degree of precision needed. (Zeros to the left and right of the last nonzero digit are not counted.) If we round off 9.7354 to four figures, it becomes 9.735; to three digits, 9.74. Rules for rounding are as follows: (*a*) When the nonzero digit to be truncated is less than 5, simply drop it (as when 9.7354 was rounded to 9.735), (*b*) If the leftmost digit to be truncated is 5 or more, increase the preceding digit by 1. For example, in rounding to three figures, 7.5349 becomes 7.53, 93.05 becomes 93.1, .8996 becomes .900, and .103203 becomes .103. Do not round off to fewer than four figures until you get to the final answer.

Exercises	*Answers*
A. Round 1.0549 to three digits.	A. 1.05
B. Round .096 to two decimal places.	B. .10
C. Round 20.5% to the nearest whole percent.	C. 21%

❖ MATH NOTE 5. *Numerals*

Numerals are symbols for numbers. The symbols 4, IV, 2^2, $\sqrt{16}$, $\frac{4}{1}$, $\frac{8}{2}$, 4^1 and "four" are all numerals that represent the same number.

❖ MATH NOTE 6. *Simple Dot Notation*

When more than one mean is involved, to avoid ambiguity the grand mean of all observations is denoted by $\overline{X}_.$; the dot indicates that the mean is based on *all* observations in *all* groups. Likewise, $n.$ denotes the total number of observations from all groups. From Math Note 3, it should be evident that $n.$ is a simple way to express Σn or, more specifically, $\sum_{i=1}^{J} n_i = n.$

Exercises	Answers
A. If $n_1 = 100$ and $n_2 = 50$, $n. = ?$	A. $n. = n_1 + n_2 = 150$
B. Which symbol denotes the mean of all the 150 observations in exercise 1?	B. $\overline{X}.$

❖ MATH NOTE 7. *Multiplication Notation*

The expression $n \cdot \overline{X}, n \times \overline{X}, (n)\,\overline{X}, n(\overline{X}), (n)(\overline{X}), n[\,\overline{X}\,], [n][\,\overline{X}\,], (n)[\,\overline{X}\,]$, and simply $n\,\overline{X}$ are synonymous, and denote "n times $\overline{X}$." Parentheses and brackets are ordinarily not used unless needed for clarity. They explicate the *order* of operations $(\times, \div, +, -)$. If parentheses and brackets are given, one first finds the value within the parentheses, then within the brackets. For example, $[(4 - 2)(7 + 3)][4(6/2)] = [(2)(10)][4(3)] = [20][12] = 240$.

Exercises	Answers
A. $[(1 + 2) + (4 - 3)]/[4/(12 - 10)]$	A. $[3 + 1]/[4/2] = 4/2 = 2$
B. $[(4 \times 3)/(3 - 2)] - [6(4.5 - 2\frac{1}{2})]$	B. $[12/1] - [6(2)] = 12 - 12 = 0$

❖ MATH NOTE 8. *Absolute Values*

The absolute value of any number is simply its value irrespective of its sign, + or −. For example, the absolute value of −8 (or +8) is 8. Thus, the absolute value of $1 - 6$ and $6 - 1$ is 5 in each instance. The symbol $|X|$ means the absolute value of X. What are the absolute values of 3, −4, and −1.6? (*Answers:* 3, 4, 1.6)

Exercises	Answers
A. Give the absolute values of 1.5, −2.6, −3.0, .03, −1.	A. 1.5, 2.6, 3.0, .03, 1
B. Are the absolute values of 1.98 and −1.98 equal?	B. Yes, the absolute value of each is 1.98.
C. If $X_1 = 15$ and $\overline{X} = 20$, and $x_1 = X_1 - \overline{X}$, what is $|x_1|$?	C. $x_1 = X_1 - \overline{X} = 15 - 20 = -5;\ |x_1| = 5$

❖ MATH NOTE 9. *Squaring and Exponents of Positive Numbers*

The square of a number is simply the number times itself: 5^2 ("5 squared") is $5 \cdot 5 = 25$; X^2 ("X squared") is $X \cdot X$. The superscript "2" is used to indicate the square of a number: $4^2 = 4 \cdot 4 = 16$. Unlike subscripts, which are used only as "name tags" for observations, superscripts indicate the mathematical operation of squaring. Thus, X_3 by any other subscript would smell the same, but X^3 is $X \cdot X \cdot X$. If no superscript is specified, it is understood that it is "1"—that is, $X^1 = X$, or $3^1 = 3$. Superscript numbers are called *exponents*. An exponent indicates the number of times the base number is used as a factor; thus, $4^3 = 4 \cdot 4 \cdot 4 = 64$. (The expression X^3 is described as "X to the third power" or "X cubed.") Or, XY^2 means $X \cdot Y \cdot Y$; if $X = 3$ and $Y = 4$, the value of XY^2 is $3 \cdot 4 \cdot 4 = 48$. Note that exponents involve the operation of multiplication—for example, $X^2 = X \cdot X$—and unless otherwise indicated by parentheses, are performed first in an equation, *before* any other multiplication.

Exercises	*Answers*
A. If $\Sigma x^2 = \Sigma X^2 - n\bar{X}^2$, and if ΣX^2 = 30,000, $n = 10$, and $\bar{X} = 50$, what is Σx^2?	A. $\Sigma x^2 = 30{,}000 - (10)(50)^2$ $= 30{,}000 - 10(2{,}500)$ $= 30{,}000 - 25{,}000$ $= 5{,}000$
B. Equation 8.4: $s_{Y \cdot X}^2 = s_Y^2(1 - r^2)$. If s_Y = 10 and r = .6, what is $s_{Y \cdot X}^2$?	B. $s_{Y \cdot X}^2 = (10)^2[1 - (.6)^2]$ $= 100(1 - .36)$ $= 100(.64) = 64$

❖ MATH NOTE 10. *Order of Operations*

Unless indicated otherwise, multiplication is performed first in an equation, then division, then addition or subtraction. In other words, the numerator in Equation 3.2 could be written:

$$(n_A \bar{X}_A) + (n_B \bar{X}_B) + (n_C \bar{X}_C)$$

But with this conventional order of "**My D**ear **A**unt **S**ally," the additional parentheses are unnecessary. In other words, unless contraindicated by parentheses or brackets, multiplication and then division are conducted prior to addition and subtraction. (The division bar, like parentheses, brackets, etc., is one of those devices that "indicates otherwise"; i.e., *all* the operations in both the numerator and denominator—above and below the bar—should be performed before division.) For the equation, $Y = .5X + 50$, which of the following equations specifies the correct order: (*a*) $Y = .5(X + 50)$ or (*b*) $Y = (.5X) + 50$? Note that the correct order of operation (*b*) gives a very different answer for Y than the incorrect order of operation (*a*).

Exercises	*Answers*
A. In the equation $T = 10z + 50$, if $z = 1.5$, $T = $?	A. $T = 10(1.5) + 50$ $= 15 + 50 = 65$
B. The equation in exercise A can be expressed as $T = 10\left(\dfrac{x}{\sigma}\right) + 50$. If $x = 14$ and $\sigma = 7$, $T = $?	B. $T = \dfrac{10(\cancel{14})^2}{\cancel{7}^1} + 50$ $= 20 + 50 = 70$

❖ MATH NOTE 11. *Squaring Negative Numbers*

Recall that the product of any two negative numbers is a *positive* number. Since to square a number we multiply it by itself, the square of any positive or negative number is a positive number. For example, $5^2 = (5)(5) = 25$, but also $(-5)^2 = (-5)(-5) = 25$. In other words, the absolute value of the deviation score determines x^2; its sign is of no consequence, since all x^2-values are positive. If $x_1 = -9$, $x_2 = 8$, and $x_3 = 1$, what are the values of x_1^2, x_2^2, x_3^2, and Σx^2? Since $x_1^2 = (-9)^2 = 81$, $x_2^2 = (8)^2 = 64$, and $x_3^2 = (1)^2 = 1$, then $\Sigma x^2 = 146$.

Exercise	*Answer*
A. If $x_1 = -4$, $x_2 = -1$, and $x_3 = 5$, then $\Sigma x^2 = ?$	A. $\Sigma x^2 = (-4)^2 + (-1)^2 + (5)^2 = 42$

❖ MATH NOTE 12. *Square Root*

The square root of a number multiplied by itself equals the number. The square root of 16 is 4 since $4 \times 4 = 16$. The square root of A^2 is A because $A \cdot A = A^2$. The square root of B is $\sqrt{B}$; hence, $(\sqrt{B})(\sqrt{B}) = B$. We shall consistently use the symbol "$\sqrt{}$" (termed "radical") to denote square root. If $\sigma^2 = 144$, what does σ equal? (*Answer:* $\sigma = \sqrt{\sigma^2} = \sqrt{144} = 12$, because $(12)(12) = 144$.)

Exercises	*Answers*
A. If $N = 36$, then $\sqrt{N} = ?$	A. $\sqrt{36} = 6$
B. Satisfy yourself that $$\sqrt{\frac{A^2}{B^2}} = \frac{\sqrt{A^2}}{\sqrt{B^2}} = \frac{A}{\sqrt{B^2}} = \frac{\sqrt{A^2}}{B} = \frac{A}{B}.$$ Let $A = 8$ and $B = 2$.	B. $\sqrt{\dfrac{A^2}{B^2}} = \sqrt{\dfrac{8^2}{2^2}} = \sqrt{\dfrac{64}{4}} = \sqrt{16} = 4$; $\dfrac{\sqrt{A^2}}{\sqrt{B^2}} = \dfrac{\sqrt{8^2}}{\sqrt{2^2}} = \dfrac{\sqrt{64}}{\sqrt{4}} = \dfrac{8}{2} = 4$; $\dfrac{A}{\sqrt{B^2}} = \dfrac{8}{\sqrt{2^2}} = \dfrac{8}{\sqrt{4}} = \dfrac{8}{2} = 4$; $\dfrac{\sqrt{A^2}}{B} = \dfrac{\sqrt{8^2}}{2} = \dfrac{\sqrt{64}}{2} = \dfrac{8}{2} = 4$; $\dfrac{A}{B} = \dfrac{8}{2} = 4$.

❖ MATH NOTE 13. *Operations with Fractions I*

An example equation could be written as $z = \dfrac{7\frac{1}{2}}{2\frac{6}{10}}$. To divide a fraction (or a whole number) by a fraction, convert each fraction to a decimal number and proceed with the division. For example, $\dfrac{7\frac{1}{2}}{2\frac{6}{10}} = \dfrac{7.5}{2.6} = \dfrac{75}{26} = 2.884$ or 2.88. Or $\dfrac{71}{5\frac{}{11}} = \dfrac{71}{.4545} = 156.21$ or 156.2; or $\dfrac{3\frac{2}{7}}{13\frac{1}{4}} = \dfrac{(3+.286)}{(13+.250)} = \dfrac{3.286}{13.25} = .2479$ or .248.

Exercise	Answer

A. What is 111 divided by $2\dfrac{1}{6}$?

A. $\dfrac{111}{2\dfrac{1}{6}} = \dfrac{111}{2.167} = 51.22$

or 51.2

An alternative method is less time-consuming if a hand calculator is not available. This method is also useful for rearranging formulas. To divide by a fraction, simply invert ("turn upside down") the divisor and multiply. For example, $\dfrac{\dfrac{11}{5}}{11} = \dfrac{11}{1} \times \dfrac{11}{5} = \dfrac{121}{5} = 24\dfrac{1}{5}$

or 24.2; or $3\dfrac{2}{7} \div 13\dfrac{1}{4} = \dfrac{23}{7} \div \dfrac{53}{4} = \dfrac{23}{7} \times \dfrac{4}{53} = \dfrac{92}{371} = .24798$ or .248.

Exercise	Answer

B. What is $\dfrac{111}{\dfrac{13}{6}}$?

B. $\dfrac{111}{\dfrac{13}{6}} = \dfrac{111}{1} \div \dfrac{13}{6}$

$= \dfrac{111}{1} \times \dfrac{6}{13} = \dfrac{666}{13} =$

51.23 or 51.2

Bear in mind that the "bar" in a fraction means "divided by" (e.g., "$\dfrac{1}{2}$" means "one divided by two") and that to divide by a fraction, we invert the divisor and multiply. Using these procedures, one will be able to rearrange and simplify many formulas and to follow some simple derivations of formulas. For example, $\dfrac{A}{B} \div \dfrac{C}{D}$ can be rewritten $\left(\dfrac{A}{B}\right)\left(\dfrac{D}{C}\right) = \dfrac{AD}{BC}$.

Exercise	Answer

C. Divide both the numerator and the denominator of the fraction, $\dfrac{A}{B}$ by the fraction $\dfrac{1}{100}$. Is the value changed?

C. No; $\dfrac{A \div \dfrac{1}{100}}{B \div \dfrac{1}{100}}$

$= \dfrac{\dfrac{A}{1} \times \dfrac{100}{1}}{\dfrac{B}{1} \times \dfrac{100}{1}}$

$= \dfrac{\dfrac{100A}{1}}{\dfrac{100B}{1}} \div \dfrac{100B}{1}$

$= \dfrac{\cancel{100}A}{1} \times \dfrac{1}{\cancel{100}B} = \dfrac{A}{B}$

Operations with Fractions II

When fractions are multiplied by fractions, the product of the numerators is divided by the product of the denominators. For example, $\dfrac{A}{B} \times \dfrac{C}{D} = \dfrac{A \times C}{B \times D} = \dfrac{AC}{BD}$; or $\dfrac{A}{B} \times \dfrac{A}{C} = \dfrac{A^2}{BC}$;

or $\dfrac{A}{10}\times\dfrac{5}{B}=\dfrac{\cancel{5}A}{\cancel{10}B}=\dfrac{A}{2B}$; or $\dfrac{6}{A}\times\dfrac{5}{B}=\dfrac{30}{AB}$; or $\dfrac{1}{5}\times 7=\dfrac{1}{5}\times\dfrac{7}{1}=\dfrac{7}{5}=1\dfrac{2}{5}$ or 1.4.

Of course, if fractions to be multiplied are expressed as decimal fractions, then the product will also be a decimal fraction. Note also that $\dfrac{3}{10}\times\dfrac{2}{5}=\dfrac{6}{50}=.12$ is an alternative route to $.3\times\dfrac{2}{5}=\dfrac{.6}{5}=.12$, or $.3\times.4=.12$, or $\dfrac{3}{10}\times.4=\dfrac{1.2}{10}=.12$.

Exercises	*Answers*
A. Express the product $\dfrac{4}{7}\times\dfrac{8}{9}$ as a fraction.	A. $\dfrac{32}{63}$
B. Express the answer to exercise 1 above as a decimal fraction.	B. $\dfrac{32}{63}$ means 32 divided by 63 = .5079 or .508. Or, $\dfrac{4}{7}=.571$, $\dfrac{8}{9}=.889$, and $(.571)(.889)=.5079$ or .508.

Note that the procedure is the same if three or more factors are involved, that is, $\dfrac{A}{D}\times\dfrac{B}{E}\times\dfrac{C}{F}=\dfrac{ABC}{DEF}$, or $\dfrac{A}{B}\times\dfrac{A}{B}\times\dfrac{A}{C}=\dfrac{A^3}{B^2C}$, or $\dfrac{A}{\cancel{C}}\times\dfrac{B}{1}\times\dfrac{\cancel{C}}{D}=\dfrac{AB}{D}$. When performing hand computations, time can often be saved by "canceling" when a factor in the numerator and a factor in the denominator are both multiples of a given number. For example, $\dfrac{\overset{2}{\cancel{4}}}{\cancel{7}}\times\dfrac{\cancel{14}}{\cancel{2}}\times\dfrac{3}{\cancel{2}}=\dfrac{6}{1}$ or 6.

If one or more factors are mixed numbers (a whole number and a fraction, e.g., $3\dfrac{1}{6}$), convert the mixed number to an improper fraction (e.g., $3\dfrac{1}{6}=\dfrac{19}{6}$) by multiplying the whole number by the denominator and adding the product to the numerator of the fraction; the denominator remains unchanged. For example, $5\dfrac{3}{5}=\dfrac{25+3}{5}=\dfrac{28}{5}$, or $11\dfrac{1}{7}=\dfrac{77+1}{7}=\dfrac{78}{7}$. After the mixed numbers are converted to improper fractions, the multiplication proceeds as before. For example, $5\dfrac{1}{2}\times 4\dfrac{2}{3}\times\dfrac{4}{11}=\dfrac{^{1}\cancel{11}}{\cancel{2}_{1}}\times\dfrac{14}{3}\times\dfrac{\cancel{4}^{2}}{\cancel{11}_{1}}=\dfrac{28}{3}=9\dfrac{1}{3}$ or 9.33. With a hand calculator it is simpler to convert mixed numbers to decimals and multiply, that is, $5.5\times 4.667\times.3636=9.33$.

Exercises	*Answers*
C. Convert $6\dfrac{7}{9}$ to an improper fraction.	C. $6\times 9=54$, $\dfrac{54+7}{9}=\dfrac{61}{9}$

D. Find the product $3\frac{1}{5}\times 4\times \frac{3}{8}$.

D. $\dfrac{\overset{2}{\cancel{16}}}{5}\times\dfrac{4}{1}\times\dfrac{3}{\cancel{8}_1}=\dfrac{24}{5}=4\dfrac{4}{5}$

or 4.80

E. Work exercise D, using decimals.

E. $3.2\times 4\times .375 = 4.800$ or 4.8

❖ MATH NOTE 14. *Division and Multiplication by Reciprocals*

Division is simply multiplication by *reciprocals*. This fact is quite useful when using hand calculators. For example, $A\div B = \dfrac{A}{B}=(A)\left(\dfrac{1}{B}\right)$. Exchange the denominator and numerator of any number and you have its reciprocal. The reciprocal of $\frac{2}{3}$ is $\frac{3}{2}$; the reciprocal of $N\left(\text{or }\dfrac{N}{1}\right)$ is $\dfrac{1}{N}$. Hence, Equation 6.3 can be rewritten $s_{XY}\left(\dfrac{1}{s_X}\right)\left(\dfrac{1}{s_Y}\right)$. Since the product $a\cdot b\cdot c$ is the same regardless of the order of multiplication—that is, $a(bc)=(ab)c=b(ac)$—then $\dfrac{s_{XY}}{s_X s_Y}=\dfrac{s_{XY}}{s_X}\left(\dfrac{1}{s_Y}\right)$ or $s_{XY}\left(\dfrac{1}{s_X s_Y}\right)$ or $\dfrac{s_{XY}}{s_Y}\left(\dfrac{1}{s_X}\right)$ will all give the same answer. (The fact that the product of any number of factors is the same, irrespective of the order in which the factors are multiplied, is known as the *associative principle of multiplication*.)

Exercises	*Answers*
A. Is $\dfrac{\Sigma x^2}{N}=\left(\dfrac{1}{N}\right)\Sigma x^2$?	A. yes
B. Confirm exercise A with $\Sigma x^2 = 50$	B. $\dfrac{\Sigma x^2}{N}=\dfrac{50}{10}=5.0,$ $\left(\dfrac{1}{N}\right)\Sigma x^2 =\left(\dfrac{1}{10}\right)(50)$ $= .1(50) = 5.0$
C. Is $\dfrac{X-\mu}{\sigma}=\dfrac{1}{\sigma}(X-\mu)$?	C. yes

❖ MATH NOTE 15. *Addition, Subtraction, Multiplication, and Division with Equations*

Recall that the equal sign ("=") in an equation means that the two sides of the "scale" are balanced. Anything we do equally to both does not upset this balance.

    Addition and subtraction. If the same number is added to or subtracted from both sides, the balance remains intact. For example, if $2X = Y-4$, then $2X+4=Y-4+4$ or $Y=2X+4$. Or if $T = 10z+50$, then $T-50 = 10z+50-50$ or $10z = T-50$. Or if we subtract c from both sides of $\hat{Y}=bX+c$, then $\hat{Y}-c=bX$. Equation 8.4, which appears later in Chapter 8, can be expressed as $s_{Y.X}^2 = s_Y^2 - r^2 s_Y^2$.

Exercise	Answer
A. Rearrange the equation below to find $\hat{Y} = bX + c$.	A. $c = \hat{Y} - bX$ (Obviously, since the two sides of an equation are equal, they can change places without disturbing the equality.)

Division and multiplication. When "equals" (e.g., $A = B/D$) are multiplied by the same number (e.g., C) the two products will be equal: $A = B/D$, hence $CA = CB/D$. Suppose $A = 2$, $B = 6$, and $D = 3$: $A = B/D = 2 = 6/3 = 2$. If $C = 10$, then $CA = 20$ and $CB/D = 20$. Likewise, when "equals" are divided by the same number, the two quotients remain equal. If each side of Equation 8.1, $\hat{z}_Y = rz_X$, is divided by z_X, then $\dfrac{\hat{z}_Y}{z_X} = \dfrac{rz_X}{z_X}$ or $r = \dfrac{\hat{z}_Y}{z_X}$.

Exercises	Answers
B. Solve the equation $\sigma^2 = (\Sigma x^2)/N$ for Σx^2.	B. If each side is multiplied by N, then $N\sigma^2 = \Sigma x^2$.
C. What is n if $\overline{X} = 10$ and $\Sigma X = 250$?	C. Since $\overline{X} = (\Sigma X)/n$, if each side is multiplied by n, then $n\overline{X} = \Sigma X$. And if each side is divided by $\overline{X}$, then $n = (\Sigma X)/\overline{X}$; hence, $n = 250/10 = 25$.
D. Solve $T = 10z + 50$ for z.	D. If 50 is subtracted from each side, then $T - 50 = 10z$; if both sides are divided by 10 then, $\dfrac{T-50}{10} = z$ or $z = \dfrac{T-50}{10}$.
E. Can $z = \dfrac{T-50}{10}$ be written as $z = .1T - 5$?	E. Yes, $z = \dfrac{T-50}{10}$ $= \dfrac{T}{10} - \dfrac{50}{10} = .1T - 5$.
F. If $X = \sqrt{Y}$, does $X^2 = Y$?	F. Yes, each side is an "equal" that multiplied by itself yields "equals." Squaring each side of an equation is multiplying each side by the same value.

❖ MATH NOTE 16. *Algebraic Manipulations and Formula Rearrangement*

Note that Equation 6.3 can be rewritten:

$$r = \frac{s_{XY}}{s_X s_Y} = \frac{\dfrac{\Sigma xy}{n-1}}{\sqrt{\dfrac{\Sigma x^2}{n-1}}\sqrt{\dfrac{\Sigma y^2}{n-1}}} = \frac{\dfrac{\Sigma xy}{n-1}}{\dfrac{\sqrt{\Sigma x^2}}{\sqrt{n-1}}\dfrac{\sqrt{\Sigma y^2}}{\sqrt{n-1}}}$$

Since the square of a square root is the quantity itself, $(\sqrt{n-1})(\sqrt{n-1}) = n-1$. Recall Note 12 that $(\sqrt{A})(\sqrt{B}) = (\sqrt{AB})$; hence, $\sqrt{\Sigma x^2}\sqrt{\Sigma y^2} = \sqrt{\Sigma x^2 \Sigma y^2}$. Therefore:

$$r = \frac{\dfrac{\Sigma xy}{n-1}}{\dfrac{\sqrt{(\Sigma x^2)(\Sigma y^2)}}{n-1}} = \frac{\Sigma xy}{n-1} \div \frac{\sqrt{(\Sigma x^2)(\Sigma y^2)}}{n-1} = \left(\frac{\Sigma xy}{\cancel{n-1}}\right)\left(\frac{\cancel{n-1}}{\sqrt{(\Sigma x^2)(\Sigma y^2)}}\right)$$

$$= \frac{\Sigma xy}{\sqrt{(\Sigma x^2)(\Sigma y^2)}} \quad \text{since } n-1 \text{ can be canceled out.}$$

Exercises	*Answers*
A. Simplify the following equation: $$W = \frac{\dfrac{Z^2 Y}{X^2}}{\left(\dfrac{Y^2}{X}\right)\left(\dfrac{Z^2}{\sqrt{X}}\right)\left(\dfrac{V}{\sqrt{X}}\right)}$$	A. $W = \dfrac{\dfrac{Z^2 Y}{X^2}}{\dfrac{Y^2 Z^2 V}{X^2}} = \dfrac{\cancel{Z^2}\cancel{X}}{\cancel{X^2}} \cdot \dfrac{\cancel{X^2}}{\cancel{Y^2}\cancel{Z^2}V}$ $$= \frac{1}{YV}$$
B. Using Equation 6.3 find the covariance s_{XY}.	B. $s_{XY} = r s_X s_Y$

❖ MATH NOTE 17. *Factoring and Summation Signs*

The expression $aX + aY + a^2 Z$ can be simplified if the common factor, a, is factored out: $a(X + Y + aZ)$. Or the expression $6X^2 + 9Y + 30Z$ becomes $3(2X^2 + 3Y + 10Z)$ when 3 is factored out. $nd_1^2 + nd_2^2 + \ldots + nd_j^2 = n(d_1^2 + d_2^2 + \ldots + d_j^2)$; or, $n\Sigma d_j^2$.

Exercises	*Answers*
A. Simplify $6X^2 + 3XY + 3$.	A. $3(2X^2 + XY + 1)$
B. If c is a constant, does $c\Sigma x_i^2 = \Sigma c x_i^2$?	B. yes
C. If both x and y are variables (not constants), does $\Sigma xy = x\Sigma y$?	C. no

❖ MATH NOTE 18. *Dot Notation Exercises with Double Subscripts*

Given that $\overline{X}_{11} = 10$, $\overline{X}_{12} = 15$, $\overline{X}_{13} = 20$, $\overline{X}_{21} = 14$, $\overline{X}_{22} = 21$, $\overline{X}_{23} = 25$, and $n_{11} = n_{12} = n_{13} = n_{21} = n_{22} = n_{33} = 10$, answer the following questions.

Exercises	Answers
A. What is $\overline{X}_{1\cdot}$?	A. $\overline{X}_{1\cdot} = \dfrac{\overline{X}_{11} + \overline{X}_{12} + \overline{X}_{13}}{3} = 15$
B. What is $\overline{X}_{\cdot 1}$?	B. $\overline{X}_{\cdot 1} = \dfrac{\overline{X}_{11} + \overline{X}_{21}}{2} = 12$
C. What is $\overline{X}_{22}$?	C. $\overline{X}_{22} = 21$
D. What is $\overline{X}_{\cdot 2}$?	D. $\overline{X}_{\cdot 2} = \dfrac{15 + 21}{2} = 18$
E. What is $\overline{X}_{\cdot 3}$?	E. $\overline{X}_{\cdot 3} = 22.5$
F. Is there an $\overline{X}_{3\cdot}$ in this example?	F. No, there are only two rows.
G. What is $\overline{X}_{2\cdot}$?	G. $\overline{X}_{2\cdot} = 20$
H. What is $\overline{X}_{\cdot\cdot}$?	H. $\overline{X}_{\cdot\cdot} = \dfrac{\overline{X}_{1\cdot} + \overline{X}_{2\cdot}}{2}$, or
	$= \dfrac{\overline{X}_{\cdot 1} + \overline{X}_{\cdot 2} + \overline{X}_{\cdot 3}}{3}$, or
	$(\overline{X}_{11} + \overline{X}_{12} + \overline{X}_{13}$
	$+ \overline{X}_{21} + \overline{X}_{22} + \overline{X}_{33})/6$
	$= 17.5$
I. What is n_{11}?	I. $n_{11} = 10$
J. What is $n_{1\cdot}$?	J. $n_{1\cdot} = n_{11} + n_{12} + n_{13} = 30$
K. What is $n_{\cdot\cdot}$?	K. $n_{\cdot\cdot} = n_{11} + n_{12} + n_{13}$
	$+ n_{21} + n_{22} + n_{23}$, or
	$= n_{1\cdot} + n_{2\cdot}$, or
	$= n_{\cdot 1} + n_{\cdot 2} + n_{\cdot 3} = 60$

❖ MATH NOTE 19. *Logarithms*

There are two widely used logarithms. *Common logarithms* use the base number of 10, The *log* (logarithm) of a number, N, is the exponent or power of 10 that will equal that number. The log of 100 is 2 because $10^2 = 100$. The log of 1,000 is 3 because $10^3 = 1,000$. What is the log of 10? (*Answer:* 1, because $10 = 10^1$.) More generally, the log of a number, N, is p if $10^p = N$; that is, $\log N = p$. Common logs are designated by "log" or "$\log_{10}$"—for example, $\log 100 = 2$.

   Natural logarithms do not use 10 as a base but a natural number, "e," ($e = 2.718...$). Hence, the natural log ($\log_e$ or ln) of a number, N, is x if $N = e^x$, that is, $\ln N = x$. The natural log of 10 is $2.302...$ because $10 = e^{2.302...}$ or $10 = 2.718^{2.302}$. Note that the Fisher Z-transformation is one-half the natural logarithm of $\left(\dfrac{1+|r|}{1-|r|}\right)$. The natural logarithm, ln, of a number, N, is 2.303 times its common log—that is, $\ln x = 2.303 \log x$. Hence, Equation 13.4 using common logs becomes $|Z| = \dfrac{1}{2}\ln\left(\dfrac{1+|r|}{1-|r|}\right)$ or $|Z| = 1.15 \log\left(\dfrac{1+|r|}{1-|r|}\right)$.

Exercises	*Answers*
A. What is the common log of 10,000?	A. 4, because $10^4 =$ (10)(10)(10)(10) = 10,000.
B. If the common log of any number is greater than 1 but less than 2, the number is between ____ and ____.	B. 10 and 100, because $\log 10 = 1$ and $\log 100 = 2$.
C. Since $\ln N = 2.303 \log N$, what is the natural logarithm of 100?	C. $\log 100 = 2$; hence, $\ln 10 = 2.303 \times 2 = 4.606$.
D. What is the value of the Fisher Z that corresponds to $r = .8$, given $\ln 9 = 2.1972$?	D. $Z = \dfrac{1}{2}\ln\left(\dfrac{1+.8}{1-.8}\right)$ $= \dfrac{1}{2}\ln\left(\dfrac{1.8}{.2}\right)$ $= \dfrac{1}{2}\log 9 = \dfrac{1}{2}(2.1972)$ $= 1.0986$ or 1.099
E. Does the answer agree with the Z-value for $r = .8$ given in Table G?	E. Yes, within rounding error.

❖ Appendix B

Tables

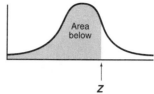

Z

❖ **TABLE A** Areas of the unit normal (z) distribution[a]

z	Area Below	z	Area Below	z	Area Below
−6.00	.000000001	−2.74	.0031	−2.38	.0087
−5.50	.0000001	−2.73	.0032	−2.37	.0089
−5.00	.0000003	−2.72	.0033	−2.36	.0091
−4.50	.0000034	−2.71	.0034	−2.35	.0094
−4.00	.0000317	−2.70	.0035	−2.34	.0096
−3.80	.0000723				
−3.719	**.0001000**	−2.69	.0036	−2.33	.0099
−3.60	.0001591	−2.68	.0037	**−2.326**	**.0100**
−3.40	.0003369	−2.67	.0038	−2.32	.0102
−3.29	.0005000	−2.66	.0039	−2.31	.0104
−3.20	.0006871	−2.65	.0040	−2.30	.0107
−3.090	.00100000				
−3.00	.0013	−2.64	.0041	−2.29	.0110
		−2.63	.0043	−2.28	.0113
−2.99	.0014	−2.62	.0044	−2.27	.0116
−2.98	.0014	−2.61	.0045	−2.26	.0119
−2.97	.0015	−2.60	.0047	−2.25	.0122
−2.96	.0015				
−2.95	.0016	−2.59	.0048	−2.24	.0125
		−2.58	.0049	−2.23	.0129
−2.94	.0016	**−2.576**	**.0050**	−2.22	.0132
−2.93	.0017	−2.57	.0051	−2.21	.0136
−2.92	.0018	−2.56	.0052	−2.20	.0139
−2.91	.0018	−2.55	.0054		
−2.90	.0019			−2.19	.0143
		−2.54	.0055	−2.18	.0146
−2.89	.0019	−2.53	.0057	−2.17	.0150
−2.88	.0020	−2.52	.0059	−2.16	.0154
−2.87	.0021	−2.51	.0060	−2.15	.0158
−2.86	.0021	−2.50	.0062		
−2.85	.0022			−2.14	.0162
		−2.49	.0064	−2.13	.0166
−2.84	.0023	−2.48	.0066	−2.12	.0170
−2.83	.0023	−2.47	.0068	−2.11	.0174
−2.82	.0024	−2.46	.0069	−2.10	.0179
−2.81	.0025	−2.45	.0071		
−2.80	.0026			−2.09	.0183
		−2.44	.0073	−2.08	.0188
−2.79	.0026	−2.43	.0075	−2.07	.0192
−2.78	.0027	−2.42	.0078	−2.06	.0197
−2.77	.0028	−2.41	.0080	**−2.054**	**.0200**
−2.76	.0029	−2.40	.0082	−2.05	.0202
−2.75	.0030				
		−2.39	.0084	−2.04	.0207

Note: As an example, .0100 (2%) of the area in a normal curve falls below z = −2.326.

[a]Exact value can be obtained using EXCEL's "NORMSDIST" function.

❖ **TABLE A** (Continued)

z	Area Below	z	Area Below	z	Area Below
−2.03	.0212	−1.61	.0537	−1.18	.1190
−2.02	.0217	−1.60	.0548	−1.17	.1210
−2.01	.0222			−1.16	.1230
−2.00	.0228	−1.59	.0559	−1.15	.1251
		−1.58	.0571		
−1.99	.0233	−1.57	.0582	−1.14	.1271
−1.98	.0239	−1.56	.0594	−1.13	.1292
−1.97	.0244	−1.55	.0606	−1.12	.1314
−1.96	**.0250**			−1.11	.1335
−1.95	.0256	−1.54	.0618	−1.10	.1357
		−1.53	.0630		
−1.94	.0262	−1.52	.0643	−1.09	.1379
−1.93	.0268	−1.51	.0655	−1.08	.1401
−1.92	.0274	−1.50	.0668	−1.07	.1423
−1.91	.0281			−1.06	.1446
−1.90	.0287	−1.49	.0681	−1.05	.1469
		−1.48	.0694		
−1.89	.0294	−1.47	.0708	−1.04	.1492
−1.881	**.0030**	−1.46	.0721	**−1.036**	**.1500**
−1.88	.0301	−1.45	.0735	−1.03	.1515
−1.87	.0307			−1.02	.1539
−1.86	.0314	−1.44	.0749	−1.01	.1562
−1.85	.0322	−1.43	.0764	−1.00	.1587
		−1.42	.0778		
−1.84	.0329	−1.41	.0793	−0.99	.1611
−1.83	.0336	−1.40	.0808	−0.98	.1635
−1.82	.0344			−0.97	.1660
−1.81	.0351	−1.39	.0823	−0.96	.1685
−1.80	.0359	−1.38	.0838	−0.95	.1711
		−1.37	.0853		
−1.79	.0367	−1.36	.0869	−0.94	.1736
−1.78	.0375	−1.35	.0885	−0.93	.1762
−1.77	.0384			−0.92	.1788
−1.76	.0392	−1.34	.0901	−0.91	.1814
−1.751	**.0400**	−1.33	.0918	−0.90	.1841
−1.75	.0401	−1.32	.0934		
		−1.31	.0951	−0.89	.1867
−1.74	.0409	−1.30	.0968	−0.88	.1894
−1.73	.0418			−0.87	.1922
−1.72	.0427	−1.29	.0985	−0.86	.1949
−1.71	.0436	**−1.282**	**.1000**	−0.85	.1977
−1.70	.0446	−1.28	.1003	**−0.842**	**.2000**
		−1.27	.1020		
−1.69	.0455	−1.26	.1038	−0.84	.2005
−1.68	.0465	−1.25	.1056	−0.83	.2033
−1.67	.0475			−0.82	.2061
−1.66	.0485	−1.24	.1075	−0.81	.2090
−1.65	.0495	−1.23	.1093	−0.80	.2119
−1.645	**.0500**	−1.22	.1112		
		−1.21	.1131	−0.79	.2148
−1.64	.0505	−1.20	.1151	−0.78	.2177
−1.63	.0516			−0.77	.2206
−1.62	.0526	−1.19	.1170	−0.76	.2236

❖ TABLE A *(Continued)*

z	Area Below	z	Area Below	z	Area Below
−0.75	.2266	−0.34	.3669	0.09	.5359
		−0.33	.3707	0.10	.5398
−0.74	.2296	−0.32	.3745		
−0.73	.2327	−0.31	.3783	0.11	.5438
−0.72	.2358	−0.30	.3821	0.12	.5478
−0.71	.2389			**0.126**	**.5500**
−0.70	.2420	−0.29	.3859	0.13	.5517
		−0.28	.3897	0.14	.5557
−0.69	.2451	−0.27	.3936	0.15	.5596
−0.68	.2483	−0.26	.3974		
−0.674	**.2500**	−0.25	.4013	0.16	.5636
−0.67	.2514	**−0.243**	**.4000**	0.17	.5675
−0.66	.2546			0.18	.5714
−0.65	.2578	−0.24	.4052	0.19	.5753
		−0.23	.4090	0.20	.5793
−0.64	.2611	−0.22	.4129		
−0.63	.2643	−0.21	.4168	0.21	.5832
−0.62	.2676	−0.20	.4207	0.22	.5871
−0.61	.2709			0.23	.5910
−0.60	.2743	−0.19	.4247	0.24	.5948
		−0.18	.4286	0.25	.5987
−0.59	.2776	−0.17	.4325	**0.253**	**.6000**
−0.58	.2810	−0.16	.4364		
−0.57	.2843	−0.15	.4404	0.26	.6026
−0.56	.2877			0.27	.6064
−0.55	.2912	−0.14	.4443	0.28	.6103
		−0.13	.4483	0.29	.6141
−0.54	.2946	**−0.126**	**.4500**	.0.30	.6179
−0.53	.2981	−0.12	.4522		
−0.524	**.3000**	−0.11	.4562	0.31	.6217
−0.52	.3015	−0.10	.4602	0.32	.6255
−0.51	.3050			0.33	.6293
−0.50	.3085	−0.09	.4641	0.34	.6331
		−0.08	.4681	0.35	.6368
−0.49	.3121	−0.07	.4721		
−0.48	.3156	−0.06	.4761	0.36	.6406
−0.47	.3192	−0.05	.4801	0.37	.6443
−0.46	.3228			0.38	.6480
−0.45	.3264	−0.04	.4840	**0.385**	**.6500**
		−0.03	.4880	0.39	.6517
−0.44	.3300	−0.02	.4920	0.40	.6554
−0.43	.3336	−0.01	.4960		
−0.42	.3372	**0.00**	**.5000**	0.41	.6591
−0.41	.3409			0.42	.6628
−0.40	.3446	0.01	.5040	0.43	.6664
		0.02	.5080	0.44	.6700
−0.39	.3483	0.03	.5120	0.45	.6736
−0.385	**.3500**	0.04	.5160		
−0.38	.3520	0.05	.5199	0.46	.6772
−0.37	.3557			0.47	.6808
−0.36	.3594	0.06	.5239	0.48	.6844
−0.35	.3632	0.07	.5279	0.49	.6879
		0.08	.5319	0.50	.6915

❖ **TABLE A** (Continued)

z	Area Below	z	Area Below	z	Area Below
0.51	.6950	0.94	.8264	1.37	.9147
0.52	.6985	0.95	.8289	1.38	.9162
0.524	**.7000**			1.39	.9177
0.53	.7019	0.96	.8315	1.40	.9192
0.54	.7054	0.97	.8340		
0.55	.7088	0.98	.8365	1.41	.9207
		0.99	.8389	1.42	.9222
0.56	.7123	1.00	.8413	1.43	.9236
0.57	.7157			1.44	.9251
0.58	.7190	1.01	.8438	1.45	.9265
0.59	.7224	1.02	.8461		
0.60	.7257	1.03	.8485	1.46	.9279
		1.036	**.8500**	1.47	.9292
0.61	.7291	1.04	.8508	1.48	.9306
0.62	.7324	1.05	.8531	1.49	.9319
0.63	.7357			1.50	.9332
0.64	.7389	1.06	.8554		
0.65	.7422	1.07	.8577	1.51	.9345
		1.08	.8599	1.52	.9357
0.66	.7454	1.09	.8621	1.53	.9370
0.67	.7486	1.10	.8643	1.54	.9382
0.674	**.7500**			1.55	.9394
0.68	.7517	1.11	.8665		
0.69	.7549	1.12	.8686	1.56	.9406
0.70	.7580	1.13	.8708	1.57	.9418
		1.14	.8729	1.58	.9429
0.71	.7611	1.15	.8749	1.59	.9441
0.72	.7642			1.60	.9452
0.73	.7673	1.16	.8770		
0.74	.7704	1.17	.8790	1.61	.9463
0.75	.7734	1.18	.8810	1.62	.9474
		1.19	.8830	1.63	.9484
0.76	.7764	1.20	.8849	1.64	.9495
0.77	.7794			**1.645**	**.9500**
0.78	.7823	1.21	.8869	1.65	.9505
0.79	.7852	1.22	.8888		
0.80	.7881	1.23	.8907	1.66	.9515
		1.24	.8925	1.67	.9525
0.81	.7910	1.25	.8944	1.68	.9535
0.82	.7939			1.69	.9545
0.83	.7967	1.26	.8962	1.70	.9554
0.84	.7995	1.27	.8980		
0.842	**.8000**	1.28	.8997	1.71	.9564
0.85	.8023	**1.282**	**.9000**	1.72	.9573
		1.29	.9015	1.73	.9582
0.86	.8051	1.30	.9032	1.74	.9591
0.87	.8078			1.75	.9599
0.88	.8106	1.31	.9049	**1.751**	**.9600**
0.89	.8133	1.32	.9066		
0.90	.8159	1.33	.9082	1.76	.9608
		1.34	.9099	1.77	.9616
0.91	.8186	1.35	.9115	1.78	.9625
0.92	.8212			1.79	.9633
0.93	.8238	1.36	.9131	1.80	.9641

❖ TABLE A *(Continued)*

z	Area Below	z	Area Below	z	Area Below
1.81	.9649	2.25	.9878	2.68	.9963
1.82	.9656			2.69	.9964
1.83	.9664	2.26	.9881	2.70	.9965
1.84	.9671	2.27	.9884		
1.85	.9678	2.28	.9887	2.71	.9966
		2.29	.9890	2.72	.9967
1.86	.9686	2.30	.9893	2.73	.9968
1.87	.9693			2.74	.9969
1.88	.9699	2.31	.9896	2.75	.9970
1.881	**.9700**	2.32	.9898		
1.89	.9706	**2.326**	**.9900**	2.76	.9971
1.90	.9713	2.33	.9901	2.77	.9972
		2.34	.9904	2.78	.9973
1.91	.9719	2.35	.9906	2.79	.9974
1.92	.9726			2.80	.9974
1.93	.9732	2.36	.9909		
1.94	.9738	2.37	.9911	2.81	.9975
1.95	.9744	2.38	.9913	2.82	.9976
		2.39	.9916	2.83	.9977
1.96	.9750	2.40	.9918	2.84	.9977
1.97	.9756			2.85	.9978
1.98	.9761	2.41	.9920		
1.99	.9767	2.42	.9922	2.86	.9979
2.00	.9772	2.43	.9925	2.87	.9979
		2.44	.9927	2.88	.9980
2.01	.9778	2.45	.9929	2.89	.9981
2.02	.9783			2.90	.9981
2.03	.9788	2.46	.9931		
2.04	.9793	2.47	.9932	2.91	.9982
2.05	.9798	2.48	.9934	2.92	.9982
2.054	**.9800**	2.49	.9936	2.93	.9983
		2.50	.9938	2.94	.9984
2.06	.9803			2.95	.9984
2.07	.9808	2.51	.9940		
2.08	.9812	2.52	.9941	2.96	.9985
2.09	.9817	2.53	.9943	2.97	.9985
2.10	.9821	2.54	.9945	2.98	.9986
		2.55	.9946	2.99	.9986
2.11	.9826			3.00	.9987
2.12	.9830	2.56	.9948		
2.13	.9834	2.57	.9949	3.09	.9990
2.14	.9838	**2.576**	**.9950**	3.20	.9993129
2.15	.9842	2.58	.9951	3.29	.9995000
		2.59	.9952	3.40	.9996631
2.16	.9846	2.60	.9953	3.60	.9998409
2.17	.9850			3.719	.9999000
2.18	.9854	2.61	.9955		
2.19	.9857	2.62	.9956	3.80	.9999277
2.20	.9861	2.63	.9957	4.00	.9999683
		2.64	.9959	4.50	.9999966
2.21	.9864	2.65	.9960	5.00	.9999997
2.22	.9868			5.50	.9999999
2.23	.9871	2.66	.9961	6.00	.999999999

❖ **TABLE B** Random digits

60	36	59	46	53	35	07	53	39	49	42	61	42	92	97	01	91	82	83	16
83	79	94	24	02	56	62	33	44	42	34	99	44	13	74	70	07	11	47	36
32	96	00	74	05	05	24	62	15	55	12	12	92	81	00	11	13	30	75	86
19	32	25	38	45	57	62	05	26	06	66	49	76	86	46	78	13	86	65	59
11	22	09	47	47	07	39	93	74	08	48	50	92	39	29	27	48	24	54	76
31	75	15	72	60	68	98	00	53	39	15	47	04	83	55	88	65	12	25	96
88	49	29	93	82	14	45	40	45	04	20	09	49	89	77	74	84	39	34	13
30	93	44	77	44	07	48	18	38	28	73	78	80	65	33	28	59	72	04	05
22	88	84	88	93	27	49	99	87	48	60	53	04	51	28	74	02	28	46	17
78	21	21	69	93	35	90	29	13	86	44	37	21	54	86	65	74	11	40	14
41	84	98	45	47	46	85	05	23	26	34	67	75	83	00	74	91	06	43	45
46	35	23	30	49	69	24	89	34	60	45	30	50	75	21	61	31	83	18	55
11	08	79	62	94	14	01	33	17	92	59	74	76	72	77	76	50	33	45	13
52	70	10	83	37	56	30	38	73	15	16	52	06	96	76	11	65	49	98	93
57	27	53	68	98	81	30	44	85	85	68	65	22	73	76	92	85	25	58	66
20	85	77	31	56	70	28	42	43	26	79	37	59	52	20	01	15	96	32	67
15	63	38	49	24	90	41	59	36	14	33	52	12	66	65	55	82	34	76	41
92	69	44	82	97	39	90	40	21	15	59	58	94	90	67	66	82	14	15	75
77	61	31	90	19	88	15	20	00	80	20	55	49	14	09	96	27	74	82	57
38	68	83	24	86	45	13	46	35	45	59	40	47	20	59	43	94	75	16	80
25	16	30	18	89	70	01	41	50	21	41	29	06	73	12	71	85	71	59	57
65	25	10	76	29	37	23	93	32	95	05	87	00	11	19	92	78	42	63	40
36	81	54	36	25	18	63	73	75	09	82	44	49	90	05	04	92	17	37	01
64	39	71	16	92	05	32	78	21	62	20	24	78	17	59	45	19	72	53	32
04	51	52	56	24	95	09	66	79	46	48	46	08	55	58	15	19	11	87	82
83	76	16	08	73	43	25	38	41	45	60	83	32	59	83	01	29	14	13	49
14	38	70	63	45	80	85	40	92	79	43	52	90	63	18	38	38	47	47	61
51	32	19	22	46	80	08	87	70	74	88	72	25	67	36	66	16	44	94	31
72	47	20	00	08	80	89	01	80	02	94	81	33	19	00	54	15	58	34	36
05	46	65	53	06	93	12	81	84	64	74	45	79	05	61	72	84	81	18	34
39	52	87	24	84	82	47	42	55	93	48	54	53	52	47	18	61	91	36	74
81	61	61	87	11	53	34	24	42	76	75	12	21	17	24	74	62	77	37	07
08	58	61	61	20	82	64	12	28	20	92	90	41	31	41	32	39	21	97	63
90	76	70	42	35	13	57	41	72	00	69	90	26	37	42	78	46	42	25	01
40	18	82	81	93	29	59	38	86	27	94	97	21	15	98	62	09	53	67	87

❖ **TABLE B** *(Continued)*

34	41	48	21	57	86	88	75	50	87	19	15	20	00	23	12	30	28	07	83
63	43	97	53	63	44	98	91	68	22	36	02	40	08	67	76	37	84	16	05
67	04	90	90	70	93	39	94	55	47	94	45	87	42	84	05	04	14	98	07
79	49	50	41	46	52	16	29	02	86	54	15	83	42	43	46	97	83	54	82
91	70	43	05	52	04	73	72	10	31	75	05	19	30	29	47	66	56	43	82

Source: A Million Random Digits With 100,000 Normal Deviates (New York: Free Press, 1955), by permission of the RAND Corporation

❖ **TABLE C** Critical values of $t^{a,b}$

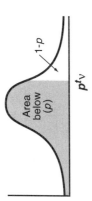

ν	$_{.75}t$	$_{.80}t$	$_{.90}t$	$\alpha_1=.05$ $\alpha_2=.10$ $_{.95}t$	$\alpha_1=.025$ $\alpha_2=.05$ $_{.975}t$	$\alpha_1=.01$ $\alpha_2=.02$ $_{.99}t$	$\alpha_1=.005$ $\alpha_2=.01$ $_{.995}t$	$\alpha_1=.001$ $\alpha_2=.002$ $_{.999}t$	$\alpha_1=.0005$ $\alpha_2=.001$ $_{.9995}t$	ν	Kurtosis γ_2
1	1.000	1.376	3.078	6.314	12.706	31.821	63.657	318.309	636.619	1	
2	.816	1.061	1.886	2.920	4.303	6.965	9.925	22.327	31.598	2	
3	.765	.978	1.638	2.353	3.182	4.541	5.841	10.214	12.924	3	
4	.741	.941	1.532	2.132	2.776	3.747	4.604	7.173	8.610	4	
5	.727	.920	1.476	2.015	2.571	3.365	4.032	5.893	6.869	5	6
6	.718	.906	1.440	1.943	2.447	3.143	3.707	5.208	5.959	6	3
7	.711	.896	1.415	1.895	2.365	2.998	3.499	4.785	5.408	7	2
8	.706	.889	1.397	1.860	2.306	2.896	3.555	4.501	5.041	8	1.5
9	.703	.883	1.383	1.833	2.262	2.821	3.250	4.297	4.781	9	1.2
10	.700	.879	1.372	1.812	2.228	2.764	3.169	4.144	4.587	10	1.0
11	.697	.876	1.363	1.796	2.201	2.718	3.106	4.025	4.437	11	.86
12	.695	.873	1.356	1.782	2.179	2.681	3.055	3.930	4.318	12	.75
13	.694	.870	1.350	1.771	2.160	2.650	3.012	3.852	4.221	13	.67
14	.692	.868	1.345	1.761	2.145	2.624	2.977	3.787	4.140	14	.60
15	.691	.866	1.341	1.753	2.131	2.602	2.947	3.733	4.073	15	.55
16	.690	.865	1.337	1.746	2.120	2.583	2.921	3.686	4.015	16	.50
17	.689	.863	1.333	1.740	2.110	2.567	2.898	3.646	3.965	17	.46
18	.688	.862	1.330	1.734	2.101	2.552	2.878	3.610	3.922	18	.42
19	.688	.861	1.328	1.729	2.093	2.539	2.861	3.579	3.883	19	.40
20	.687	.860	1.325	1.725	2.086	2.528	2.845	3.552	3.850	20	.38

| | | | $\alpha_1 = .10$ | $\alpha_1 = .05$ | $\alpha_1 = .025$ | $\alpha_1 = .01$ | $\alpha_1 = .005$ | $\alpha_1 = .001$ | $\alpha_1 = .0005$ | | Kurtosis |
| | | | | $\alpha_2 = .10$ | $\alpha_2 = .05$ | $\alpha_2 = .02$ | $\alpha_2 = .01$ | $\alpha_2 = .002$ | $\alpha_2 = .001$ | | |
ν	$_{.75}t$	$_{.80}t$	$_{.90}t$	$_{.95}t$	$_{.975}t$	$_{.99}t$	$_{.995}t$	$_{.999}t$	$_{.9995}t$	ν	γ_2
21	.686	.859	1.323	1.721	**2.080**	2.518	**2.831**	3.527	3.819	**21**	.35
22	.686	.858	1.321	1.717	2.074	2.508	2.819	3.505	3.792	**22**	.33
23	.685	.858	1.319	1.714	2.069	2.500	2.807	3.485	3.767	**23**	.32
24	.685	.857	1.318	1.711	2.064	2.492	2.797	3.467	3.745	**24**	.30
25	.684	.856	1.316	1.708	2.060	2.485	2.787	3.450	3.725	**25**	.29
26	.684	.856	1.315	1.706	2.056	2.479	2.779	3.435	3.707	**26**	.27
27	.684	.855	1.314	1.703	2.052	2.473	2.771	3.421	3.690	**27**	.26
28	.683	.855	1.313	1.701	2.048	2.467	2.763	3.408	3.674	**28**	.25
29	.683	.854	1.311	1.699	2.045	2.462	2.756	3.396	3.659	**29**	.24
30	.683	.854	1.310	1.697	2.042	2.457	2.750	3.385	3.646	**30**	.23
35	.682	.852	1.306	1.690	2.030	2.438	2.724	3.340	3.591	**35**	.19
40	.681	.851	1.303	1.684	2.021	2.423	2.704	3.307	3.551	**40**	.17
50	.680	.849	1.299	1.676	2.008	2.403	2.678	3.261	3.496	**50**	.13
60	.679	.848	1.296	1.671	2.000	2.390	2.660	3.232	3.460	**60**	.11
70	.678	.847	1.294	1.667	1.994	2.381	2.648	3.211	3.435	**70**	.09
80	.678	.847	1.293	1.665	1.990	2.374	2.638	3.195	3.416	**80**	.08
90	.678	.846	1.291	1.662	1.987	2.368	2.632	3.183	3.402	**90**	.07
100	.677	.846	1.290	1.661	1.984	2.364	2.626	3.174	3.380	**100**	.06
120	.677	.845	1.289	1.658	1.980	2.358	2.617	3.160	3.373	**120**	.05
200	.676	.844	1.286	1.653	1.972	2.345	2.601	3.131	3.340	**200**	.03
300	.676	.843	1.285	1.650	1.968	2.339	2.592	3.118	3.323	**300**	.02
400	.676	.843	1.284	1.649	1.966	2.336	2.588	3.111	3.315	**400**	.015
500	.676	.843	1.284	1.648	1.965	2.334	2.586	3.107	3.310	**500**	.012
1000	.675	.842	1.283	1.647	1.962	2.330	2.581	3.098	3.301	**1000**	.006
∞	.674	.842	1.282	1.645	1.960	2.326	2.576	3.090	3.291	**∞**	0

[a] Table C is adapted from Table III of Fisher and Yates: *Statistical Tables for Biological, Agricultural and Medical Research*, published by Oliver & Boyd Ltd., Edinburgh, and by permission of the authors and publishers. (Certain corrections and additions from Federighi (1959); other values were calculated by Geroge Kretke.)

[b] The lower percentiles are related to the upper percentiles which are tabulated by the equation $_p t_\nu = -_{1-p} t_\nu$. Thus, the 10th percentile in the t-distribution with $\nu = 15$ equals the negative of the 90th percentile in the same distribution, that is, $_{.10}t_{15} = -1.341$. *Critical values for nondirectional (α_2) tests are:* $|_{1 - \alpha_2}t|$; for directional (α_1) tests: $_{1 - \alpha_1}t$. Thus, with $\alpha_2 = .05$ and $\nu = 20$: $|2.086|$; for $\alpha_1 = .05$ and $\nu = 20$, $|t| = 1.725$.

❖ **TABLE D** Critical values of *chi*-square

Percentile: 50	75	90	95	97.5	99	99.9
v α: .50	.25	.10	.05	.025	.01	.001
1 .45	1.32	2.71	**3.84**	5.02	**6.63**	10.8
2 1.39	2.77	4.61	**5.99**	7.38	**9.21**	13.8
3 2.37	3.11	6.25	**7.81**	9.35	**11.3**	16.3
4 3.36	5.39	7.78	**9.49**	11.1	**13.3**	18.5
5 4.35	6.63	9.24	**11.1**	12.8	**15.1**	20.5
6 5.35	7.84	10.6	**12.6**	14.4	**16.8**	22.5
7 6.35	9.04	12.0	**14.1**	16.0	**18.5**	24.3
8 7.34	10.2	13.4	**15.5**	17.5	**20.1**	26.1
9 8.34	11.4	14.7	**16.9**	19.0	**21.7**	27.9
10 9.34	12.5	16.0	**18.3**	20.5	**23.2**	29.6
11 10.3	13.7	17.3	**19.7**	21.9	**24.7**	31.3
12 11.3	14.8	18.5	**21.0**	23.3	**26.2**	32.9
13 12.3	16.0	19.8	**22.4**	24.7	**27.7**	34.5
14 13.3	17.1	21.1	**23.7**	26.1	**29.1**	36.1
15 14.3	18.2	22.3	**25.0**	27.5	**30.6**	37.7
16 15.3	19.4	23.5	**26.3**	28.8	**32.0**	39.3
17 16.3	20.5	24.8	**27.6**	30.2	**33.4**	40.8
18 17.3	21.6	26.0	**28.9**	31.5	**34.8**	42.3
19 18.3	22.7	27.2	**30.1**	32.9	**36.2**	43.8
20 19.3	23.8	28.4	**31.4**	34.2	**37.6**	45.3
21 20.3	24.9	29.6	**32.7**	35.5	**38.9**	46.8
22 21.3	26.0	30.8	**33.9**	36.8	**40.3**	48.3
23 22.3	27.1	32.0	**35.2**	38.1	**41.6**	49.7
24 23.3	28.2	33.2	**36.4**	39.4	**43.0**	51.2
25 24.3	29.3	34.4	**37.7**	40.6	**44.3**	52.6
26 25.3	30.4	35.6	**38.9**	41.9	**45.6**	54.1
27 26.3	31.5	36.7	**40.1**	43.2	**47.0**	55.5
28 27.3	32.6	37.9	**41.3**	44.5	**48.3**	56.9
29 28.3	33.7	39.1	**42.6**	45.7	**49.6**	58.3
30 29.3	34.8	40.3	**43.8**	47.0	**50.9**	59.7
40 39.3	45.6	51.8	**55.8**	59.3	**63.7**	73.4
50 49.3	56.3	63.2	**67.5**	71.4	**76.2**	86.7
60 59.3	67.0	74.4	**79.1**	83.3	**88.4**	99.6
100 99.3	109.1	118.5	**124.3**	129.6	**135.8**	149.5

Source: Adapted from Table 8 in E.S. Pearson and H.O. Hartley (Eds.), *Biometrika Tables for Statisticians,* 3rd ed. (1966), by permission of the *Biometrika* Trustees.

Notes: 1. The α-values pertain to nondirectional hypotheses.

2. For $v > 30$, the central *chi*-square distribution is approximately normally distributed with a standard deviation of 1. Appendix Table A can be used for $v > 30$ using:

$$z = \sqrt{2\chi^2} - \sqrt{2v - 1}$$

❖ **TABLE E** Critical values of *r* for rejecting H_0: $\rho = 0$

n	α_1: .05 / α_2: .10	.025 / .05	.01 / .02	.005 / .01	.0005 / .001
3	.988	.997	.9995	.9999	.99994
4	.900	.950	.980	.990	.999
5	.805	.878	.934	.959	.991
6	.729	.811	.882	.917	.974
7	.669	.754	.833	.874	.951
8	.622	.707	.789	.834	.925
9	.582	.666	.750	.798	.898
10	.549	.632	.716	.765	.872
11	.521	.602	.685	.735	.847
12	.497	.576	.658	.708	.823
13	.476	.553	.634	.684	.801
14	.458	.532	.612	.661	.780
15	.441	.514	.592	.641	.760
16	.426	.497	.574	.623	.742
17	.412	.482	.558	.606	.725
18	.400	.468	.542	.590	.708
19	.389	.456	.528	.575	.693
20	.378	.444	.516	.561	.679
21	.369	.433	.503	.549	.665
22	.360	.423	.492	.537	.652
23	.352	.413	.482	.526	.640
24	.344	.404	.472	.515	.629
25	.337	.396	.462	.505	.618
26	.330	.388	.453	.496	.607
27	.323	.381	.445	.487	.597
28	.317	.374	.437	.479	.588
29	.317	.374	.437	.479	.588
30	.306	.361	.423	.463	.570
35	.282	.333	.391	.428	.531
40	.264	.312	.366	.402	.501
45	.248	.296	.349	.381	.471
50	.235	.276	.328	.361	.451
60	.214	.254	.300	.330	.414
70	.198	.235	.277	.305	.385
80	.185	.220	.260	.286	.361
90	.174	.208	.245	.270	.342
100	.165	.196	.232	.256	.324
150	.135	.161	.190	.210	.267
200	.117	.139	.164	.182	.232
250	.104	.124	.147	.163	.207
300	.095	.113	.134	.148	.189
400	.082	.098	.115	.128	.169
500	.074	.088	.104	.115	.147
1,000	.052	.062	.074	.081	.104
5,000	.0233	.0278	.0329	.0364	.0465
10,000	.0164	.0196	.0233	.0258	.0393

Source: Column entries for α_2 = .10, .05, .02, and .01 for *n* = 3 to *n* = 100 are taken from Table 13 in E.S. Pearson and H.O. Hartley (Eds.), *Biometrika Tables for Statisticians,* 2nd ed. (1962), by permission of the *Biometrika* Trustees. Other entries were obtained using Equation 13.3.

Note: If the value of an *r* from a sample of size *n* exceeds the tabled value for α and *n*, the null hypothesis that $\rho = 0$ may be rejected at the α-level of significance. For example, a sample *r* of .561 or more with *n* = 20 leads to rejection of the hypothesis $\rho = 0$ at α_2 = .01.

❖ **TABLE F** Critical values of *F*

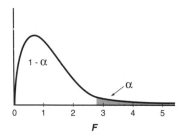

V for Denomi-nator	*α*	*V for Numerator*											
		1	*2*	*3*	*4*	*5*	*6*	*7*	*8*	*9*	*10*	*12*	*15*
1	.25	5.828	7.500	8.200	8.581	8.820	8.983	9.102	9.192	9.263	9.320	9.406	9.493
	.10	39.86	49.50	53.59	55.83	57.24	58.20	58.91	59.44	59.86	60.19	60.71	61.22
	.05	161.4	199.5	215.7	224.6	230.2	234.0	236.8	238.9	240.5	241.9	243.9	245.9
	.025	647.8	799.5	864.2	899.6	921.8	937.1	948.2	956.6	963.3	968.6	976.7	984.9
	.01	4052	4999	5404	5624	5764	5859	5928	5981	6022	6056	6107	6157
2	.25	2.571	3.000	3.153	3.232	3.280	3.312	3.335	3.353	3.366	3.377	3.393	3.410
	.10	8.526	9.000	9.162	9.243	9.293	9.326	9.349	9.367	9.381	9.392	9.408	9.425
	.05	18.51	19.00	19.16	19.25	19.30	19.33	19.35	19.37	19.38	19.40	19.41	19.43
	.025	38.51	39.00	39.17	39.25	39.30	39.33	39.36	39.37	39.39	39.40	39.41	39.43
	.010	98.50	99.00	99.16	99.25	99.30	99.33	99.36	99.38	99.39	99.40	99.42	99.43
	.001	998.4	998.8	999.3	999.3	999.3	999.3	999.3	999.3	999.3	999.3	999.3	999.3
3	.25	2.024	2.280	2.356	2.390	2.409	2.422	2.430	2.436	2.441	2.445	2.450	2.455
	.10	5.538	5.462	5.391	5.343	5.309	5.285	5.266	5.252	5.240	5.230	5.216	5.200
	.05	10.13	9.552	9.277	9.117	9.013	8.941	8.887	8.845	8.812	8.785	8.745	8.703
	.025	17.44	16.04	15.44	15.10	14.88	14.73	14.62	14.54	14.47	14.42	14.34	14.25
	.010	34.12	30.82	29.46	28.71	28.24	27.91	27.67	27.49	27.34	27.23	27.05	26.87
	.001	167.1	148.5	141.1	137.1	134.6	132.8	131.6	130.6	129.9	129.2	128.3	127.4
4	.25	1.807	2.000	2.047	2.064	2.072	2.077	2.079	2.080	2.081	2.082	2.083	2.083
	.10	4.545	4.325	4.191	4.107	4.051	4.010	3.979	3.955	3.936	3.920	3.896	3.870
	.05	7.709	6.944	6.591	6.388	6.256	6.163	6.094	6.041	5.999	5.964	5.912	5.858
	.025	12.22	10.65	9.979	9.604	9.364	9.197	9.074	8.980	8.905	8.844	8.751	8.657
	.010	21.20	18.00	16.69	15.98	15.52	15.21	14.98	14.80	14.66	14.55	14.37	14.20
	.001	74.13	61.25	56.17	53.43	51.72	50.52	49.65	49.00	48.47	48.05	47.41	46.76
5	.25	1.692	1.853	1.884	1.893	1.895	1.894	1.894	1.892	1.891	1.890	1.888	1.885
	.10	4.060	3.780	3.619	3.520	3.453	3.405	3.368	3.339	3.316	3.297	3.268	3.238
	.05	6.608	5.786	5.409	5.192	5.050	4.950	4.876	4.818	4.772	4.735	4.678	4.619
	.025	10.01	8.434	7.764	7.388	7.146	6.978	6.853	6.757	6.681	6.619	6.525	6.428
	.010	16.26	13.27	12.06	11.39	10.97	10.67	10.46	10.29	10.16	10.05	9.888	9.722
	.001	47.18	37.12	33.20	31.08	29.75	28.83	28.17	27.65	27.24	26.91	26.42	25.91
6	.25	1.621	1.762	1.784	1.787	1.785	1.782	1.779	1.776	1.773	1.771	1.767	1.762
	.10	3.776	3.463	3.289	3.181	3.108	3.055	3.014	2.983	2.958	2.937	2.905	2.871
	.05	5.987	5.143	4.757	4.534	4.387	4.284	4.207	4.147	4.099	4.060	4.000	3.938
	.025	8.813	7.260	6.599	6.227	5.988	5.820	5.695	5.600	5.523	5.461	5.366	5.269
	.010	13.75	10.92	9.780	9.148	8.746	8.466	8.260	8.102	7.976	7.874	7.718	7.559
	.001	35.51	27.00	23.71	21.92	20.80	20.03	19.46	19.03	18.69	18.41	17.99	17.56

Source: Critical values with *V* for numerator of 50, 100, 200, 500, and 1,000, or with *V* for denominators of 200, 500, and 1,000 determined via computer thanks to Frank B. Baker, James R. Morrow, and Gregory Camilli. Other values are reprinted from Table 18 in E.S. Pearson and H.O. Hartley (Eds.), *Biometrika Tables for Statisticians*, 3rd ed. (1966), by permission of the *Biometrika* Trustees.

❖ **TABLE F** (Continued)

20	25	30	40	50	100	120	200	500	1000	∞	α	ν for Denomi-nator
					ν for Numerator							
9.581	9.634	9.670	9.714	9.741	9.795	9.804	9.822	9.838	9.844	9.849	.25	1
61.74	62.05	62.26	62.53	62.69	63.01	63.06	63.17	63.26	63.30	63.33	.10	
248.0	249.3	250.1	251.1	251.8	253.0	253.3	253.7	254.1	254.2	254.3	.05	
993.1	998.1	1001	1006	1008	1013	1014	1016	1017	1018	1018	.025	
6209	6240	6260	6286	6302	6334	6340	6350	6360	6363	6366	.01	
3.426	3.436	3.443	3.451	3.46	3.47	3.47	3.47	3.47	3.48	3.48	.25	2
9.441	9.451	9.458	9.466	9.47	9.48	9.48	9.49	9.49	9.49	9.49	.10	
19.45	19.46	19.46	19.47	19.5	19.5	19.5	19.5	19.5	19.5	19.5	.05	
39.45	39.46	39.46	39.47	39.5	39.5	39.5	39.5	39.5	39.5	39.5	.025	
99.45	99.46	99.47	99.48	99.5	99.5	99.5	99.5	99.5	99.5	99.5	.010	
999.3	999.3	999.3	999.3	999.3	999.3	999.3	999.3	999.3	999.3	999.3	.001	
2.460	2.463	2.465	2.467	2.469	2.471	2.472	2.473	2.474	2.474	2.474	.25	3
5.184	5.175	5.168	5.160	5.155	5.144	5.143	5.139	5.136	5.135	5.134	.10	
8.660	8.634	8.617	8.594	8.581	8.554	8.549	8.540	8.532	8.529	8.526	.05	
14.17	14.12	14.08	14.04	14.01	13.96	13.95	13.93	13.91	13.91	13.90	.025	
26.69	26.58	26.50	26.41	26.35	26.24	26.22	26.18	26.15	26.14	26.13	.010	
126.4	125.8	125.4	125.0	124.7	124.1	124.0	123.7	123.6	123.5	123.5	.001	
2.083	2.083	2.082	2.082	2.082	2.081	2.081	2.081	2.081	2.081	2.081	.25	4
3.844	3.828	3.817	3.804	3.795	3.778	3.775	3.769	3.764	3.762	3.761	.10	
5.803	5.769	5.746	5.717	5.699	5.664	5.658	5.646	5.635	5.632	5.628	.05	
8.560	8.501	8.461	8.411	8.381	8.319	8.309	8.288	8.270	8.264	8.257	.025	
14.02	13.91	13.84	13.75	13.69	13.58	13.56	13.52	13.49	13.47	13.46	.010	
46.10	45.69	45.43	45.08	44.88	44.47	44.40	44.27	44.14	44.09	44.05	.001	
1.882	1.880	1.878	1.876	1.875	1.872	1.872	1.871	1.870	1.870	1.869	.25	5
3.207	3.187	3.174	3.157	3.147	3.126	3.123	3.116	3.109	3.107	3.105	.10	
4.558	4.521	4.496	4.464	4.444	4.405	4.398	4.385	4.373	4.369	4.365	.05	
6.329	6.288	6.227	6.175	6.144	6.080	6.069	6.048	6.028	6.022	6.015	.025	
9.553	9.449	9.379	9.291	9.238	9.130	9.112	9.075	9.042	9.032	9.020	.010	
25.39	25.08	24.87	24.60	24.44	24.11	24.06	23.95	23.85	23.82	23.79	.001	
1.757	1.753	1.751	1.748	1.746	1.741	1.741	1.739	1.738	1.737	1.737	.25	6
2.836	2.815	2.800	2.781	2.770	2.746	2.742	2.734	2.727	2.725	2.722	.10	
3.874	3.835	3.808	3.774	3.754	3.712	3.705	3.690	3.678	3.673	3.669	.05	
5.168	5.107	5.065	5.012	4.980	4.915	4.904	4.882	4.862	4.856	4.849	.025	
7.396	7.296	7.229	7.143	7.091	6.987	6.969	6.934	6.901	6.891	6.880	.010	
17.12	16.85	16.67	16.44	16.31	16.03	15.98	15.89	15.80	15.77	15.75	.001	

❖ **TABLE F** (Continued)

V for Denominator	α	V for Numerator											
		1	2	3	4	5	6	7	8	9	10	12	15
7	.25	1.573	1.701	1.717	1.716	1.711	1.706	1.701	1.697	1.693	1.690	1.684	1.678
	.10	3.589	3.257	3.074	2.961	2.883	2.827	2.785	2.752	2.725	2.703	2.668	2.632
	.05	5.591	4.737	4.347	4.120	3.972	3.866	3.787	3.726	3.677	3.637	3.575	3.511
	.025	8.073	6.542	5.890	5.523	5.285	5.119	4.995	4.899	4.823	4.761	4.666	4.568
	.010	12.25	9.547	8.451	7.847	7.460	7.191	6.993	6.840	6.719	6.620	6.469	6.314
	.001	29.25	21.69	18.77	17.20	16.21	15.52	15.02	14.63	14.33	14.08	13.71	13.32
8	.25	1.538	1.657	1.668	1.664	1.658	1.651	1.645	1.640	1.635	1.631	1.624	1.617
	.10	3.458	3.113	2.924	2.806	2.726	2.668	2.624	2.589	2.561	2.538	2.502	2.464
	.05	5.318	4.459	4.066	3.838	3.688	3.581	3.500	3.438	3.388	3.347	3.284	3.218
	.025	7.571	6.059	5.416	5.053	4.817	4.652	4.529	4.433	4.357	4.295	4.200	4.101
	.010	11.26	8.649	7.591	7.006	6.632	6.371	6.178	6.029	5.911	5.814	5.667	5.515
	.001	25.41	18.49	15.83	14.39	13.48	12.86	12.40	12.05	11.77	11.54	11.19	10.84
9	.25	1.512	1.624	1.632	1.625	1.617	1.609	1.602	1.596	1.591	1.586	1.579	1.570
	.10	3.360	3.006	2.813	2.693	2.611	2.551	2.505	2.469	2.440	2.416	2.379	2.340
	.05	5.117	4.256	3.863	3.633	3.482	3.374	3.293	3.230	3.179	3.137	3.073	3.006
	.025	7.209	5.715	5.078	4.718	4.484	4.320	4.197	4.102	4.026	3.964	3.868	3.769
	.010	10.56	8.022	6.992	6.422	6.057	5.802	5.613	5.467	5.351	5.257	5.111	4.962
	.001	22.86	16.39	13.90	12.56	11.71	11.13	10.70	10.37	10.11	9.894	9.570	9.239
10	.25	1.491	1.598	1.603	1.595	1.585	1.576	1.569	1.562	1.556	1.551	1.543	1.534
	.10	3.285	2.924	2.728	2.605	2.522	2.461	2.414	2.377	2.347	2.323	2.284	2.244
	.05	4.965	4.103	3.708	3.478	3.326	3.217	3.135	3.072	3.020	2.978	2.913	2.845
	.025	6.937	5.456	4.826	4.468	4.236	4.072	3.950	3.855	3.779	3.717	3.621	3.522
	.010	10.04	7.559	6.552	5.994	5.636	5.386	5.200	5.057	4.942	4.849	4.706	4.558
	.001	21.04	14.90	12.55	11.28	10.48	9.926	9.517	9.204	8.956	8.754	8.446	8.129
11	.25	1.475	1.577	1.580	1.570	1.560	1.550	1.542	1.535	1.528	1.523	1.514	1.504
	.10	3.225	2.860	2.660	2.536	2.451	2.389	2.342	2.304	2.274	2.248	2.209	2.167
	.05	4.844	3.982	3.587	3.357	3.204	3.095	3.012	2.948	2.896	2.854	2.788	2.719
	.025	6.724	5.256	4.630	4.275	4.044	3.881	3.759	3.664	3.588	3.526	3.430	3.330
	.010	9.646	7.206	6.217	5.668	5.316	5.069	4.886	4.744	4.632	4.539	4.397	4.251
	.001	19.69	13.81	11.56	10.35	9.579	9.047	8.655	8.355	8.116	7.923	7.625	7.321
12	.25	1.461	1.560	1.561	1.550	1.539	1.529	1.520	1.512	1.505	1.500	1.490	1.480
	.10	3.177	2.807	2.606	2.480	2.394	2.331	2.283	2.245	2.214	2.188	2.147	2.105
	.05	4.747	3.885	3.490	3.259	3.106	2.996	2.913	2.849	2.796	2.753	2.687	2.617
	.025	6.554	5.096	4.474	4.121	3.891	3.728	3.607	3.512	3.436	3.374	3.277	3.177
	.010	9.330	6.927	5.953	5.412	5.064	4.821	4.640	4.499	4.388	4.296	4.155	4.010
	.001	18.64	12.97	10.80	9.633	8.892	8.378	8.001	7.711	7.480	7.292	7.005	6.709
13	.25	1.450	1.545	1.545	1.534	1.521	1.511	1.501	1.493	1.486	1.480	1.470	1.459
	.10	3.136	2.763	2.560	2.434	2.347	2.283	2.234	2.195	2.164	2.138	2.097	2.053
	.05	4.667	3.806	3.411	3.179	3.025	2.915	2.832	2.767	2.714	2.671	2.604	2.533
	.025	6.414	4.965	4.347	3.996	3.767	3.604	3.483	3.388	3.312	3.250	3.153	3.053
	.010	9.074	6.701	5.739	5.205	4.862	4.620	4.441	4.302	4.191	4.100	3.960	3.815
	.001	17.82	12.31	10.21	9.073	8.355	7.856	7.489	7.206	6.982	6.799	6.519	6.231
14	.25	1.440	1.533	1.532	1.519	1.507	1.495	1.485	1.477	1.470	1.463	1.453	1.441
	.10	3.102	2.726	2.522	2.395	2.307	2.243	2.193	2.154	2.122	2.095	2.054	2.010
	.05	4.600	3.739	3.344	3.112	2.958	2.848	2.764	2.699	2.646	2.602	2.534	2.463
	.025	6.298	4.857	4.242	3.892	3.663	3.501	3.380	3.285	3.209	3.147	3.050	2.949
	.010	8.862	6.515	5.564	5.035	4.695	4.456	4.278	4.140	4.030	3.939	3.800	3.656
	.001	17.14	11.78	9.730	8.622	7.922	7.436	7.078	6.802	6.583	6.404	6.130	5.848

❖ **TABLE F** *(Continued)*

												V for
				V for Numerator								Denomi-
20	*25*	*30*	*40*	*50*	*100*	*120*	*200*	*500*	*1000*	*∞*	*α*	*nator*
1.671	1.667	1.663	1.659	1.657	1.651	1.650	1.648	1.646	1.646	1.645	.25	7
2.595	2.571	2.555	2.535	2.523	2.497	2.493	2.484	2.476	2.473	2.471	.10	
3.445	3.404	3.376	3.340	3.319	3.275	3.267	3.252	3.239	3.234	3.230	.05	
4.467	4.405	4.362	4.309	4.276	4.210	4.199	4.176	4.156	4.149	4.142	.025	
6.155	6.058	5.992	5.908	5.858	5.755	5.737	5.702	5.671	5.660	5.650	.010	
12.93	12.69	12.53	12.33	12.20	11.95	11.91	11.82	11.75	11.72	11.70	.001	
1.609	1.603	1.600	1.595	1.591	1.585	1.584	1.581	1.579	1.578	1.578	.25	8
2.425	2.400	2.383	2.361	2.348	2.321	2.316	2.307	2.298	2.295	2.293	.10	
3.150	3.108	3.079	3.043	3.020	2.975	2.967	2.951	2.937	2.932	2.928	.05	
3.999	3.937	3.894	3.840	3.807	3.739	3.728	3.705	3.684	3.677	3.670	.025	
5.359	5.263	5.198	5.116	5.065	4.963	4.946	4.911	4.880	4.869	4.859	.010	
10.48	10.26	10.11	9.919	9.804	9.572	9.532	9.453	9.382	9.358	9.333	.001	
1.561	1.555	1.551	1.545	1.541	1.534	1.533	1.530	1.527	1.527	1.526	.25	9
2.298	2.272	2.255	2.232	2.218	2.189	2.184	2.174	2.165	2.162	2.159	.10	
2.936	2.893	2.864	2.826	2.803	2.756	2.748	2.731	2.717	2.712	2.707	.05	
3.667	3.604	3.560	3.505	3.472	3.403	3.392	3.368	3.347	3.340	3.333	.025	
4.808	4.713	4.649	4.567	4.517	4.415	4.398	4.363	4.332	4.321	4.311	.010	
8.898	8.689	8.547	8.368	8.260	8.038	8.002	7.926	7.858	7.836	7.813	.001	
1.523	1.517	1.512	1.506	1.502	1.493	1.492	1.489	1.486	1.485	1.484	.25	10
2.201	2.174	2.155	2.132	2.117	2.087	2.082	2.071	2.062	2.059	2.055	.10	
2.774	2.730	2.700	2.661	2.637	2.588	2.580	2.563	2.548	2.543	2.538	.05	
3.419	3.355	3.311	3.255	3.221	3.152	3.140	3.116	3.094	3.087	3.080	.025	
4.405	4.311	4.247	4.165	4.115	4.014	3.996	3.962	3.930	3.920	3.909	.010	
7.803	7.604	7.469	7.297	7.192	6.980	6.944	6.872	6.807	6.785	6.762	.001	
1.493	1.486	1.481	1.474	1.469	1.460	1.459	1.455	1.452	1.451	1.450	.25	11
2.123	2.095	2.076	2.052	2.036	2.005	2.000	1.989	1.979	1.975	1.972	.10	
2.646	2.601	2.570	2.531	2.507	2.457	2.448	2.431	2.415	2.410	2.404	.05	
3.226	3.162	3.118	3.061	3.027	2.956	2.944	2.920	2.898	2.890	2.883	.025	
4.099	4.005	3.941	3.860	3.810	3.708	3.690	3.656	3.624	3.613	3.602	.010	
7.008	6.815	6.884	6.517	6.416	6.210	6.175	6.105	6.041	6.020	5.998	.001	
1.468	1.460	1.454	1.447	1.443	1.433	1.431	1.428	1.424	1.423	1.422	.25	12
2.060	2.031	2.011	1.986	1.970	1.938	1.932	1.921	1.911	1.097	1.904	.10	
2.544	2.498	2.466	2.426	2.401	2.350	2.341	2.323	2.307	2.302	2.296	.05	
3.073	3.008	2.963	2.906	2.871	2.800	2.787	2.763	2.740	2.733	2.725	.025	
3.858	3.765	3.701	3.619	3.569	3.467	3.449	3.414	3.382	3.372	3.361	.010	
6.405	6.217	6.090	5.928	5.829	5.627	5.593	5.524	5.462	5.441	5.420	.001	
1.447	1.438	1.432	1.425	1.420	1.409	1.408	1.404	1.400	1.399	1.398	.25	13
2.007	1.978	1.958	1.931	1.915	1.882	1.876	1.864	1.853	1.850	1.846	.10	
2.459	2.412	2.380	2.339	2.314	2.261	2.252	2.234	2.218	2.212	2.206	.05	
2.948	2.882	2.837	2.780	2.744	2.671	2.659	2.634	2.611	2.603	2.595	.025	
3.665	3.571	3.507	3.425	3.375	3.272	3.255	3.219	3.187	3.176	3.165	.010	
5.934	5.751	5.626	5.467	5.370	5.172	5.138	5.070	5.009	4.988	4.967	.001	
1.428	1.420	1.414	1.405	1.400	1.389	1.387	1.383	1.380	1.378	1.377	.25	14
1.962	1.933	1.912	1.885	1.869	1.834	1.828	1.816	1.805	1.801	1.797	.10	
2.388	2.341	2.308	2.266	2.241	2.187	2.178	2.159	2.142	2.136	2.131	.05	
2.844	2.778	2.732	2.674	2.638	2.565	2.552	2.526	2.503	2.495	2.487	.025	
3.505	3.412	3.348	3.266	3.215	3.112	3.094	3.059	3.026	3.015	3.004	.010	
5.557	5.377	5.254	5.098	5.002	4.807	4.773	4.707	4.645	4.625	4.604	.001	

❖ **TABLE F** (Continued)

V for Denominator	α	\multicolumn{12}{c}{V for Numerator}
		1	2	3	4	5	6	7	8	9	10	12	15
15	.25	1.432	1.523	1.520	1.507	1.494	1.482	1.472	1.463	1.456	1.449	1.438	1.426
	.10	3.073	2.695	2.490	2.361	2.273	2.208	2.158	2.119	2.086	2.059	2.017	1.972
	.05	4.543	3.682	3.287	3.056	2.901	2.790	2.707	2.641	2.588	2.544	2.475	2.403
	.025	6.200	4.765	4.153	3.804	3.576	3.415	3.293	3.199	3.123	3.060	2.963	2.862
	.010	8.683	6.359	5.417	4.893	4.556	4.318	4.142	4.004	3.895	3.805	3.666	3.522
	.001	16.59	11.34	9.335	8.253	7.567	7.091	6.741	6.471	6.256	6.081	5.812	5.535
16	.25	1.425	1.514	1.510	1.497	1.483	1.471	1.460	1.451	1.443	1.437	1.426	1.413
	.10	3.048	2.668	2.462	2.333	2.244	2.178	2.128	2.088	2.055	2.028	1.985	1.940
	.05	4.494	3.634	3.239	3.007	2.852	2.741	2.657	2.591	2.538	2.494	2.425	2.352
	.025	6.115	4.687	4.077	3.729	3.502	3.341	3.219	3.125	3.049	2.986	2.889	2.788
	.010	8.531	6.226	5.292	4.773	4.437	4.202	4.026	3.890	3.780	3.691	3.553	3.409
	.001	16.12	10.97	9.006	7.944	7.272	6.805	6.460	6.195	5.984	5.812	5.547	5.275
17	.25	1.419	1.506	1.502	1.487	1.473	1.460	1.450	1.441	1.433	1.426	1.414	1.401
	.10	3.026	2.645	2.437	2.308	2.218	2.152	2.102	2.061	2.028	2.001	1.958	1.912
	.05	4.451	3.592	3.197	2.965	2.810	2.699	2.614	2.548	2.494	2.450	2.381	2.308
	.025	6.042	4.619	4.011	3.665	3.438	3.277	3.156	3.061	2.985	2.922	2.825	2.723
	.010	8.400	6.112	5.185	4.669	4.336	4.101	3.927	3.791	3.682	3.593	3.455	3.312
	.001	15.72	10.66	8.727	7.683	7.022	6.562	6.224	5.962	5.754	5.584	5.324	5.055
18	.25	1.413	1.499	1.494	1.479	1.464	1.452	1.441	1.431	1.423	1.416	1.404	1.391
	.10	3.007	2.624	2.416	2.286	2.196	2.130	2.079	2.038	2.005	1.977	1.933	1.887
	.05	4.414	3.555	3.160	2.928	2.773	2.661	2.577	2.510	2.456	2.412	2.342	2.269
	.025	5.978	4.560	3.954	3.608	3.382	3.221	3.100	3.005	2.929	2.866	2.769	2.667
	.010	8.285	6.013	5.092	4.579	4.248	4.015	3.841	3.705	3.597	3.508	3.371	3.227
	.001	15.38	10.39	8.487	7.460	6.808	6.355	6.021	5.763	5.557	5.390	5.132	4.866
19	.25	1.408	1.493	1.487	1.472	1.457	1.444	1.432	1.423	1.414	1.407	1.395	1.382
	.10	2.990	2.606	2.397	2.266	2.176	2.109	2.058	2.017	1.984	1.956	1.912	1.865
	.05	4.381	3.522	3.127	2.895	2.740	2.628	2.544	2.477	2.423	2.378	2.308	2.234
	.025	5.922	4.508	3.903	3.559	3.333	3.172	3.051	2.956	2.880	2.817	2.720	2.617
	.010	8.185	5.926	5.010	4.500	4.171	3.939	3.765	3.631	3.523	3.434	3.297	3.153
	.001	15.08	10.16	8.280	7.265	6.622	6.175	5.845	5.591	5.387	5.222	4.967	4.703
20	.25	1.404	1.487	1.481	1.465	1.450	1.437	1.425	1.415	1.407	1.399	1.387	1.374
	.10	2.975	2.589	2.380	2.249	2.158	2.091	2.040	1.999	1.965	1.937	1.892	1.845
	.05	4.351	3.493	3.098	2.866	2.711	2.599	2.514	2.447	2.393	2.348	2.278	2.203
	.025	5.871	4.461	3.859	3.515	3.289	3.128	3.007	2.913	2.837	2.774	2.676	2.573
	.010	8.096	5.849	4.938	4.431	4.103	3.871	3.699	3.564	3.457	3.368	3.231	3.088
	.001	14.82	9.953	8.098	7.096	6.461	6.019	5.692	5.440	5.239	5.075	4.823	4.562
22	.25	1.396	1.477	1.470	1.454	1.438	1.424	1.413	1.402	1.394	1.386	1.374	1.359
	.10	2.949	2.561	2.351	2.219	2.128	2.060	2.008	1.967	1.933	1.904	1.859	1.811
	.05	4.301	3.443	3.049	2.817	2.661	2.549	2.464	2.397	2.342	2.297	2.226	2.151
	.025	5.786	4.383	3.783	3.440	3.215	3.055	2.934	2.839	2.763	2.700	2.602	2.498
	.010	7.945	5.719	4.817	4.313	3.988	3.758	3.587	3.453	3.346	3.258	3.121	2.978
	.001	14.38	9.612	7.796	6.814	6.191	5.758	5.437	5.190	4.993	4.832	4.583	4.326
24	.25	1.390	1.470	1.462	1.445	1.428	1.414	1.402	1.392	1.383	1.375	1.362	1.347
	.10	2.927	2.538	2.327	2.195	2.103	2.035	1.983	1.941	1.906	1.877	1.832	1.783
	.05	4.260	3.403	3.009	2.776	2.621	2.508	2.423	2.355	2.300	2.255	2.183	2.108
	.025	5.717	4.319	3.721	3.379	3.155	2.995	2.874	2.779	2.703	2.640	2.541	2.437
	.010	7.823	5.614	4.718	4.218	3.895	3.667	3.496	3.363	3.256	3.168	3.032	2.889
	.001	14.03	9.340	7.554	6.589	5.977	5.551	5.235	4.991	4.797	4.638	4.393	4.139

❖ **TABLE F** (Continued)

| | | | | | *v for Numerator* | | | | | | | *v for Denomi-* |
20	25	30	40	50	100	120	200	500	1000	∞	α	*nator*
1.413	1.404	1.397	1.389	1.383	1.372	1.370	1.366	1.362	1.360	1.359	.25	15
1.924	1.894	1.873	1.845	1.828	1.793	1.787	1.774	1.763	1.759	1.755	.10	
2.328	2.280	2.247	2.204	2.178	2.123	2.114	2.095	2.078	2.072	2.066	.05	
2.756	2.689	2.644	2.585	2.549	2.474	2.461	2.435	2.411	2.403	2.395	.025	
3.372	3.278	3.214	3.132	3.081	2.977	2.959	2.923	2.891	2.880	2.868	.010	
5.249	5.071	4.950	4.796	4.702	4.508	4.475	4.408	4.348	4.327	4.307	.001	
1.399	1.390	1.383	1.374	1.369	1.356	1.354	1.350	1.346	1.345	1.343	.25	16
1.891	1.860	1.839	1.811	1.793	1.757	1.751	1.738	1.726	1.722	1.718	.10	
2.276	2.227	2.194	2.151	2.124	2.068	2.059	2.039	2.022	2.016	2.010	.05	
2.681	2.614	2.568	2.509	2.472	2.396	2.383	2.357	2.333	2.324	2.316	.025	
3.259	3.165	3.101	3.018	2.967	2.863	2.845	2.808	2.775	2.764	2.753	.010	
4.992	4.817	4.697	4.545	4.451	4.259	4.226	4.160	4.100	4.080	4.059	.001	
1.387	1.377	1.370	1.361	1.355	1.343	1.341	1.336	1.332	1.330	1.329	.25	17
1.862	1.831	1.809	1.781	1.763	1.726	1.719	1.706	1.694	1.690	1.686	.10	
2.230	2.181	2.148	2.104	2.077	2.020	2.011	1.991	1.973	1.967	1.960	.05	
2.616	2.548	2.502	2.442	2.405	2.329	2.315	2.289	2.264	2.256	2.247	.025	
3.162	3.068	3.003	2.920	2.869	2.764	2.746	2.709	2.676	2.664	2.653	.010	
4.775	4.602	4.484	4.332	4.240	4.049	4.016	3.950	3.890	3.870	3.849	.001	
1.376	1.366	1.359	1.350	1.344	1.331	1.328	1.324	1.319	1.318	1.316	.25	18
1.837	1.805	1.783	1.754	1.736	1.698	1.691	1.678	1.665	1.661	1.657	.10	
2.191	2.141	2.107	2.063	2.035	1.978	1.968	1.948	1.929	1.923	1.917	.05	
2.559	2.491	2.445	2.384	2.347	2.269	2.256	2.229	2.204	2.195	2.187	.025	
3.077	2.983	2.919	2.835	2.784	2.678	2.660	2.623	2.589	2.577	2.566	.010	
4.590	4.418	4.301	4.151	4.059	3.869	3.836	3.770	3.710	3.690	3.670	.001	
1.367	1.356	1.349	1.339	1.333	1.320	1.317	1.312	1.308	1.306	1.305	.25	19
1,814	1.782	1.759	1.730	1.711	1.673	1.666	1.652	1.639	1.635	1.631	.10	
2.155	2.106	2.071	2.026	1.999	1.940	1.930	1.910	1.891	1.884	1.878	.05	
2.509	2.441	2.394	2.333	2.295	2.217	2.203	2.176	2.150	2.142	2.133	.025	
3.003	2.909	2.844	2.761	2.709	2.602	2.584	2.547	2.512	2.501	2.489	.010	
4.430	4.259	4.143	3.994	3.902	3.713	3.680	3.615	3.555	3.534	3.514	.001	
1.358	1.348	1.340	1.330	1.324	1.310	1.307	1.302	1.298	1.296	1.294	.25	20
1.794	1.761	1.738	1.708	1.690	1.650	1.643	1.629	1.616	1.612	1.607	.10	
2.124	2.074	2.039	1.994	1.966	1.907	1.896	1.875	1.856	1.850	1.843	.05	
2.464	2.396	2.349	2.287	2.249	2.170	2.156	2.128	2.103	2.094	2.085	.025	
2.938	2.843	2.778	2.695	2.643	2.535	2.517	2.479	2.445	2.433	2.421	.010	
4.290	4.121	4.005	3.856	3.765	3.576	3.544	3.478	3.418	3.398	3.378	.001	
1.343	1.332	1.324	1.314	1.307	1.293	1.290	1.285	1.280	1.278	1.276	.25	22
1.759	1.726	1.702	1.671	1.652	1.611	1.604	1.590	1.576	1.571	1.567	.10	
2.071	2.020	1.984	1.938	1.909	1.849	1.838	1.817	1.797	1.790	1.783	.05	
2.389	2.320	2.272	2.210	2.171	2.090	2.076	2.047	2.021	2.012	2.003	.025	
2.827	2.733	2.667	2.583	2.531	2.422	2.403	2.365	2.329	2.317	2.305	.010	
4.058	3.891	3.776	3.628	3.537	3.349	3.317	3.251	3.191	3.171	3.150	.001	
1.331	1.319	1.311	1.300	1.293	1.278	1.275	1.270	1.264	1.263	1.261	.25	24
1.730	1.696	1.672	1.641	1.621	1.579	1.571	1.556	1.542	1.538	1.533	.10	
2.027	1.975	1.939	1.892	1.863	1.800	1.790	1.768	1.747	1.740	1.733	.05	
2.327	2.257	2.209	2.146	2.107	2.024	2.010	1.981	1.954	1.945	1.935	.025	
2.738	2.643	2.577	2.492	2.440	2.329	2.310	2.271	2.235	2.223	2.211	.010	
3.873	3.707	3.593	3.447	3.356	3.168	3.136	3.070	3.010	2.989	2.969	.001	

❖ **TABLE F** (Continued)

V for Denomi- nator	α	\multicolumn{12}{c}{V for Numerator}
		1	2	3	4	5	6	7	8	9	10	12	15
26	.25	1.384	1.463	1.454	1.437	1.420	1.406	1.393	1.383	1.374	1.366	1.352	1.337
	.10	2.909	2.519	2.307	2.174	2.082	2.014	1.961	1.919	1.884	1.855	1.809	1.760
	.05	4.225	3.369	2.975	2.743	2.587	2.474	2.388	2.321	2.265	2.220	2.148	2.072
	.025	5.659	4.265	3.670	3.329	3.105	2.945	2.824	2.729	2.653	2.590	2.491	2.387
	.010	7.721	5.526	4.637	4.140	3.818	3.591	3.421	3.288	3.182	3.094	2.958	2.815
	.001	13.74	9.117	7.357	6.406	5.802	5.381	5.070	4.829	4.637	4.480	4.238	3.986
28	.25	1.380	1.457	1.448	1.430	1.413	1.399	1.386	1.375	1.366	1.358	1.344	1.329
	.10	2.894	2.503	2.291	2.157	2.064	1.996	1.943	1.900	1.865	1.836	1.790	1.740
	.05	4.196	3.340	2.947	2.714	2.558	2.445	2.359	2.291	2.236	2.190	2.118	2.041
	.025	5.610	4.221	3.626	3.286	3.063	2.903	2.782	2.687	2.611	2.547	2.448	2.344
	.010	7.636	5.453	4.568	4.074	3.754	3.528	3.358	3.226	3.120	3.032	2.896	2.753
	.001	13.50	8.930	7.193	6.253	5.657	5.241	4.933	4.695	4.505	4.349	4.109	3.859
30	.25	1.376	1.452	1.443	1.424	1.407	1.392	1.380	1.369	1.359	1.351	1.337	1.321
	.10	2.881	2.489	2.276	2.142	2.049	1.980	1.927	1.884	1.849	1.819	1.773	1.722
	.05	4.171	3.316	2.922	2.690	2.534	2.421	2.334	2.266	2.211	2.165	2.092	2.015
	.025	5.568	4.182	3.589	3.250	3.026	2.867	2.746	2.651	2.575	2.511	2.412	2.307
	.010	7.562	5.390	4.510	4.018	3.699	3.473	3.305	3.173	3.067	2.979	2.843	2.700
	.001	13.29	8.773	7.054	6.125	5.534	5.122	4.817	4.582	4.393	4.239	4.001	3.753
40	.25	1.363	1.435	1.424	1.404	1.386	1.371	1.357	1.345	1.335	1.327	1.312	1.295
	.10	2.835	2.440	2.226	2.091	1.997	1.927	1.873	1.829	1.793	1.763	1.715	1.662
	.05	4.085	3.232	2.839	2.606	2.449	2.336	2.249	2.180	2.124	2.077	2.003	1.924
	.025	5.424	4.051	3.463	3.126	2.904	2.744	2.624	2.529	2.452	2.388	2.288	2.182
	.010	7.314	5.178	4.313	3.828	3.514	3.291	3.124	2.993	2.888	2.801	2.665	2.522
	.001	12.61	8.251	6.595	5.698	5.128	4.731	4.436	4.207	4.024	3.874	3.643	3.400
60	.25	1.349	1.419	1.405	1.385	1.366	1.349	1.335	1.323	1.312	1.303	1.287	1.269
	.10	2.791	2.393	2.177	2.041	1.946	1.875	1.819	1.775	1.738	1.707	1.657	1.603
	.05	4.001	3.150	2.758	2.525	2.368	2.254	2.167	2.097	2.040	1.993	1.917	1.836
	.025	5.286	3.925	3.343	3.008	2.786	2.627	2.507	2.412	2.334	2.270	2.169	2.061
	.010	7.077	4.977	4.126	3.649	3.339	3.119	2.953	2.823	2.718	2.632	2.496	2.352
	.001	11.97	7.768	6.171	5.307	4.757	4.372	4.086	3.865	3.687	3.542	3.315	3.078
100	.25	1.339	1.406	1.391	1.369	1.349	1.332	1.317	1.304	1.293	1.283	1.267	1.248
	.10	2.756	2.356	2.139	2.002	1.906	1.834	1.778	1.732	1.695	1.663	1.612	1.557
	.05	3.936	3.087	2.696	2.463	2.305	2.191	2.103	2.032	1.975	1.927	1.850	1.768
	.025	5.179	3.828	3.250	2.917	2.696	2.537	2.417	2.321	2.244	2.179	2.077	1.968
	.010	6.895	4.824	3.984	3.513	3.206	2.988	2.823	2.694	2.590	2.503	2.368	2.223
	.001	11.496	7.408	5.857	5.017	4.482	4.107	3.829	3.612	3.439	3.296	3.074	2.840
120	.25	1.336	1.402	1.387	1.365	1.345	1.328	1.313	1.300	1.289	1.279	1.262	1.243
	.10	2.748	2.347	2.130	1.992	1.896	1.824	1.767	1.722	1.684	1.652	1.601	1.545
	.05	3.920	3.072	2.680	2.447	2.290	2.175	2.087	2.016	1.959	1.910	1.834	1.750
	.025	5.152	3.805	3.227	2.894	2.674	2.515	2.395	2.299	2.222	2.157	2.055	1.945
	.010	6.851	4.787	3.949	3.480	3.174	2.956	2.792	2.663	2.559	2.472	2.336	2.191
	.001	11.38	7.321	5.781	4.947	4.416	4.044	3.767	3.552	3.379	3.237	3.016	2.783
200	.25	1.331	1.396	1.380	1.358	1.337	1.319	1.304	1.291	1.279	1.269	1.252	1.232
	.10	2.731	2.329	2.111	1.973	1.876	1.804	1.747	1.701	1.663	1.631	1.579	1.522
	.05	3.888	3.041	2.650	2.417	2.259	2.144	2.056	1.985	1.927	1.878	1.801	1.717
	.025	5.100	3.758	3.182	2.850	2.630	2.472	2.351	2.256	2.178	2.113	2.010	1.900
	.010	6.763	4.713	3.881	3.414	3.110	2.893	2.730	2.601	2.497	2.411	2.275	2.129
	.001	11.15	7.152	5.634	4.812	4.287	3.920	3.647	3.434	3.263	3.123	2.904	2.672

❖ **TABLE F** *(Continued)*

				V for Numerator								V for Denomi-nator
20	25	30	40	50	100	120	200	500	1000	∞	α	
1.320	1.309	1.300	1.289	1.282	1.266	1.263	1.257	1.251	1.249	1.247	.25	26
1.706	1.671	1.647	1.615	1.594	1.551	1.544	1.528	1.514	1.509	1.504	.10	
1.990	1.938	1.901	1.853	1.823	1.760	1.749	1.726	1.705	1.698	1.691	.05	
2.276	2.205	2.157	2.093	2.053	1.969	1.954	1.925	1.897	1.888	1.878	.025	
2.664	2.569	2.503	2.417	2.364	2.252	2.333	2.193	2.156	2.144	2.131	.010	
3.723	3.558	3.445	3.299	3.208	3.020	2.987	2.922	2.861	2.840	2.819	.001	
1.311	1.299	1.291	1.279	1.271	1.255	1.252	1.246	1.240	1.238	1.236	.25	28
1.685	1.650	1.625	1.592	1.572	1.528	1.520	1.504	1.489	1.484	1.478	.10	
1.959	1.906	1.869	1.820	1.790	1.725	1.714	1.691	1.669	1.662	1.654	.05	
2.232	2.161	2.112	2.048	2.007	1.922	1.907	1.877	1.848	1.839	1.829	.025	
2.602	2.506	2.440	2.354	2.300	2.187	2.167	2.127	2.090	2.077	2.064	.010	
3.598	3.434	3.321	3.176	3.085	2.897	2.864	2.798	2.736	2.716	2.695	.001	
1.303	1.291	1.282	1.270	1.263	1.245	1.242	1.236	1.230	1.228	1.226	.25	30
1.667	1.632	1.606	1.573	1.552	1.507	1.499	1.482	1.467	1.462	1.456	.10	
1.932	1.878	1.841	1.792	1.761	1.695	1.683	1.660	1.637	1.630	1.622	.05	
2.195	2.124	2.074	2.009	1.968	1.882	1.866	1.835	1.806	1.797	1.787	.025	
2.549	2.453	2.386	2.299	2.245	2.131	2.111	2.070	2.032	2.019	2.006	.010	
3.493	3.330	3.217	3.072	2.981	2.792	2.760	2.693	2.631	2.610	2.589	.001	
1.276	1.263	1.253	1.240	1.231	1.212	1.208	1.201	1.193	1.191	1.188	.25	40
1.605	1.568	1.541	1.506	1.483	1.434	1.425	1.406	1.389	1.383	1.377	.10	
1.839	1.783	1.744	1.693	1.660	1.589	1.577	1.551	1.526	1.517	1.509	.05	
2.068	1.994	1.943	1.875	1.832	1.741	1.724	1.691	1.659	1.648	1.637	.025	
2.369	2.271	2.203	2.114	2.058	1.938	1.917	1.874	1.833	1.819	1.805	.010	
3.145	2.984	2.872	2.727	2.636	2.444	2.410	2.341	2.277	2.255	2.233	.001	
1.248	1.234	1.223	1.208	1.198	1.176	1.172	1.163	1.154	1.151	1.147	.25	60
1.543	1.504	1.476	1.437	1.413	1.358	1.348	1.326	1.306	1.299	1.291	.10	
1.748	1.690	1.649	1.594	1.559	1.481	1.467	1.438	1.409	1.399	1.389	.05	
1.944	1.869	1.815	1.744	1.699	1.599	1.581	1.543	1.507	1.495	1.482	.025	
2.198	2.098	2.028	1.936	1.877	1.749	1.726	1.678	1.633	1.617	1.601	.010	
2.826	2.667	2.555	2.409	2.316	2.118	2.082	2.009	1.939	1.915	1.890	.001	
1.226	1.210	1.198	1.182	1.171	1.145	1.140	1.129	1.118	1.114	1.109	.25	100
1.494	1.453	1.423	1.382	1.355	1.293	1.282	1.257	1.232	1.223	1.214	.10	
1.676	1.616	1.573	1.515	1.477	1.392	1.376	1.342	1.308	1.296	1.283	.05	
1.849	1.770	1.715	1.640	1.592	1.483	1.463	1.420	1.378	1.363	1.347	.025	
2.067	1.965	1.893	1.797	1.735	1.598	1.572	1.518	1.466	1.447	1.427	.010	
2.591	2.431	2.319	2.170	2.076	1.867	1.829	1.749	1.671	1.644	1.615	.001	
1.220	1.204	1.192	1.175	1.164	1.137	1.131	1.120	1.108	1.103	1.099	.25	120
1.482	1.440	1.409	1.368	1.340	1.277	1.265	1.239	1.212	1.203	1.193	.10	
1.659	1.598	1.554	1.495	1.457	1.369	1.352	1.316	1.280	1.267	1.254	.05	
1.825	1.746	1.690	1.614	1.565	1.454	1.433	1.388	1.343	1.327	1.310	.025	
2.035	1.932	1.860	1.763	1.700	1.559	1.533	1.477	1.421	1.401	1.381	.010	
2.534	2.375	2.262	2.113	2.017	1.806	1.767	1.684	1.603	1.574	1.543	.001	
1.209	1.192	1.179	1.162	1.149	1.120	1.114	1.100	1.086	1.080	1.074	.25	200
1.458	1.414	1.383	1.339	1.310	1.242	1.228	1.199	1.168	1.157	1.144	.10	
1.623	1.561	1.516	1.455	1.415	1.321	1.302	1.263	1.221	1.205	1.189	.05	
1.778	1.698	1.640	1.562	1.511	1.393	1.370	1.320	1.269	1.250	1.229	.025	
1.971	1.868	1.794	1.694	1.629	1.481	1.453	1.391	1.328	1.304	1.279	.010	
2.424	2.264	2.151	2.000	1.902	1.682	1.641	1.552	1.460	1.427	1.390	.001	

❖ **TABLE F** (Continued)

V for Denominator	α	\multicolumn{12}{c}{V for Numerator}
		1	2	3	4	5	6	7	8	9	10	12	15
500	.25	1.326	1.390	1.374	1.351	1.330	1.312	1.296	1.283	1.271	1.261	1.243	1.223
	.10	2.716	2.313	2.095	1.956	1.859	1.786	1.729	1.683	1.644	1.612	1.559	1.501
	.05	3.860	3.014	2.623	2.390	2.232	2.117	2.028	1.957	1.899	1.850	1.772	1.686
	.025	5.054	3.716	3.142	2.811	2.592	2.434	2.313	2.217	2.139	2.074	1.971	1.859
	.010	6.686	4.648	3.821	3.357	3.054	2.838	2.675	2.547	2.443	2.356	2.220	2.075
	.001	10.96	7.004	5.506	4.693	4.175	3.813	3.542	3.332	3.163	3.023	2.806	2.576
1000	.25	1.325	1.388	1.372	1.349	1.328	1.309	1.294	1.280	1.268	1.258	1.240	1.220
	.10	2.711	2.308	2.089	1.950	1.853	1.780	1.723	1.676	1.638	1.605	1.552	1.494
	.05	3.851	3.005	2.614	2.381	2.223	2.108	2.019	1.948	1.889	1.840	1.762	1.676
	.025	5.039	3.703	3.129	2.799	2.579	2.421	2.300	2.204	2.126	2.061	1.958	1.846
	.010	6.660	4.626	3.801	3.338	3.036	2.820	2.657	2.529	2.425	2.339	2.203	2.056
	.001	10.89	6.956	5.464	4.655	4.139	3.778	3.508	3.299	3.130	2.991	2.774	2.544
∞	.25	1.323	1.386	1.369	1.346	1.325	1.307	1.291	1.277	1.265	1.255	1.237	1.216
	.10	2.706	2.303	2.084	1.945	1.847	1.774	1.717	1.670	1.632	1.599	1.546	1.487
	.05	3.841	2.996	2.605	2.372	2.214	2.099	2.010	1.938	1.880	1.831	1.752	1.666
	.025	5.024	3.689	3.116	2.786	2.566	2.408	2.288	2.192	2.114	2.048	1.945	1.833
	.010	6.635	4.605	3.782	3.319	3.017	2.802	2.639	2.511	2.407	2.321	2.185	2.039
	.001	10.83	6.908	5.422	4.617	4.103	3.743	3.474	3.266	3.098	2.959	2.742	2.513

❖ **TABLE F** *(Continued)*

20	25	30	40	50	100	120	200	500	1000	∞	α	V for Denomi-nator
					V for Numerator							
1.198	1.181	1.168	1.149	1.136	1.103	1.096	1.081	1.062	1.055	1.045	**.25**	**500**
1.435	1.391	1.358	1.313	1.282	1.209	1.194	1.160	1.122	1.106	1.087	**.10**	
1.592	1.528	1.482	1.419	1.376	1.275	1.255	1.210	1.159	1.138	1.113	**.05**	
1.736	1.655	1.596	1.515	1.462	1.336	1.311	1.254	1.192	1.166	1.137	**.025**	
1.915	1.810	1.735	1.633	1.566	1.408	1.377	1.308	1.232	1.201	1.164	**.010**	
2.328	2.168	2.054	1.900	1.800	1.571	1.526	1.427	1.319	1.276	1.226	**.001**	
1.195	1.177	1.164	1.145	1.131	1.097	1.090	1.073	1.053	1.044	1.031	**.25**	**1000**
1.428	1.383	1.350	1.304	1.273	1.197	1.181	1.145	1.103	1.084	1.060	**.10**	
1.581	1.517	1.471	1.406	1.363	1.260	1.239	1.190	1.134	1.110	1.078	**.05**	
1.722	1.640	1.581	1.499	1.445	1.316	1.290	1.230	1.162	1.132	1.094	**.025**	
1.897	1.791	1.716	1.613	1.544	1.383	1.351	1.278	1.195	1.159	1.112	**.010**	
2.297	2.136	2.022	1.868	1.767	1.533	1.487	1.383	1.266	1.216	1.153	**.001**	
1.191	1.174	1.160	1.140	1.127	1.091	1.066	1.066	1.042	1.030	1.0097	**.25**	∞
1.421	1.375	1.342	1.295	1.263	1.185	1.130	1.130	1.082	1.058	1.0006	**.10**	
1.571	1.506	1.459	1.394	1.350	1.243	1.170	1.170	1.106	1.075	1.0007	**.05**	
1.708	1.626	1.566	1.484	1.428	1.296	1.205	1.205	1.128	1.090	1.0009	**.025**	
1.878	1.773	1.696	1.592	1.523	1.358	1.247	1.247	1.153	1.107	1.0010	**.010**	
2.266	2.105	1.990	1.835	1.733	1.494	1.338	1.338	1.207	1.144	1.0014	**.001**	

❖ **TABLE G**   Fisher's Z-transformation of r: $|Z| = \frac{1}{2}\ln\left(\frac{1+|r|}{1-|r|}\right)$.

r	Z	r	Z	r	Z	r	Z	r	Z
.000	.000	.200	.203	.400	.424	.600	.693	.800	1.099
.005	.005	.205	.208	.405	.430	.605	.701	.805	1.113
.010	.010	.210	.213	.410	.436	.610	.709	.810	1.127
.015	.015	.215	.218	.415	.442	.615	.717	.815	1.142
.020	.020	.220	.224	.420	.448	.620	.725	.820	1.157
.025	.025	.225	.229	.425	.454	.625	.733	.825	1.172
.030	.030	.230	.234	.430	.460	.630	.741	.830	1.188
.035	.035	.235	.239	.435	.466	.635	.750	.835	1.204
.040	.040	.240	.245	.440	.472	.640	.758	.840	1.221
.045	.045	.245	.250	.445	.478	.645	.767	.845	1.238
.050	.050	.250	.255	.450	.485	.650	.775	.850	1.256
.055	.055	.255	.261	.455	.491	.655	.784	.855	1.274
.060	.060	.260	.266	.460	.497	.660	.793	.860	1.293
.065	.065	.265	.271	.465	.504	.665	.802	.865	1.313
.070	.070	.270	.277	.470	.510	.670	.811	.870	1.333
.075	.075	.275	.282	.475	.517	.675	.820	.875	1.354
.080	.080	.280	.288	.480	.523	.680	.829	.880	1.376
.085	.085	.285	.293	.485	.530	.685	.838	.885	1.398
.090	.090	.290	.299	.490	.536	.690	.848	.890	1.422
.095	.095	.295	.304	.495	.543	.695	.858	.895	1.447
.100	.100	.300	.310	.500	.549	.700	.867	.900	1.472
.105	.105	.305	.315	.505	.556	.705	.877	.905	1.499
.110	.110	.310	.321	.510	.563	.710	.887	.910	1.528
.115	.116	.315	.326	.515	.570	.715	.897	.915	1.557
.120	.121	.320	.332	.520	.576	.720	.908	.920	1.589
.125	.126	.325	.337	.525	.583	.725	.918	.925	1.623
.130	.131	.330	.343	.530	.590	.730	.929	.930	1.658
.135	.136	.335	.348	.535	.597	.735	.940	.935	1.697
.140	.141	.340	.354	.540	.604	.740	.950	.940	1.738
.145	.146	.345	.360	.545	.611	.745	.962	.945	1.783
.150	.151	.350	.365	.550	.618	.750	.973	.950	1.832
.155	.156	.355	.371	.555	.626	.755	.984	.955	1.886
.160	.161	.360	.377	.560	.633	.760	.996	.960	1.946
.165	.167	.365	.383	.565	.640	.765	1.008	.965	2.014
.170	.172	.370	.388	.570	.648	.770	1.020	.970	2.092
.175	.177	.375	.394	.575	.655	.775	1.033	.975	2.185
.180	.182	.380	.400	.580	.662	.780	1.045	.980	2.298
.185	.187	.385	.406	.585	.670	.785	1.058	.985	2.443
.190	.192	.390	.412	.590	.678	.790	1.071	.990	2.645
.195	.198	.395	.418	.595	.685	.795	1.085	.995	2.994

Source: Values reported in this table were calculated by Thomas O. Maguire and are reproduced with his kind permission. Exact values can be obtaoned by EXCEL's "FISHER" and "FISHERINV" functions, and by most hand calculators with trigometric functions.

❖ **TABLE H** Critical values of the Studentized range statistic, $q = (\bar{X}_L - \bar{X}_S)/s_{\bar{X}}$.[a]

v for Denominator	α	2	3	4	5	6	7	8	9	10	11	12	13	14	15	16	17	18	19	20
																		J (Number of Means in Set)		
1	.10	8.93	13.4	16.4	18.5	20.2	21.5	22.6	23.6	24.5	25.2	25.9	26.5	27.1	27.6	28.1	28.5	29.0	29.3	29.7
	.05	18.0	27.0	32.8	37.1	40.4	43.1	45.4	47.4	49.1	50.6	52.0	53.2	54.3	55.4	56.3	57.2	58.0	58.8	59.6
	.01	90.0	135	164	186	202	216	227	237	246	253	260	266	272	277	282	286	290	294	298
2	.10	4.13	5.78	6.78	7.54	8.14	8.63	9.05	9.41	9.73	10.0	10.3	10.5	10.7	10.9	11.1	11.2	11.4	11.5	11.7
	.05	6.09	8.3	9.8	10.9	11.7	12.4	13.0	13.5	14.0	14.4	14.7	15.1	15.4	15.7	15.9	16.1	16.4	16.6	16.8
	.01	14.0	19.0	22.3	24.7	26.6	28.2	29.5	30.7	31.7	32.6	33.4	34.1	34.8	35.4	36.0	36.5	37.0	37.5	38.0
	.001	44.7	00.4	70.8	78.4	84.5	89.5	93.7	97.3	101.	103	106	108	110	112	114	116	117	119	120
3	.10	3.33	4.47	5.20	5.74	6.16	6.51	6.81	7.06	7.29	7.49	7.67	7.83	7.98	8.12	8.25	8.37	8.78	8.58	8.68
	.05	4.50	5.91	6.82	7.50	8.04	8.48	8.85	9.18	9.46	9.72	9.95	10.2	10.4	10.5	10.7	10.8	11.0	11.1	11.2
	.01	8.26	10.6	12.2	13.3	14.2	15.0	15.6	16.2	16.7	17.1	17.5	17.9	18.2	18.5	18.8	19.1	19.3	19.6	20.0
	.001	18.3	23.3	20.7	29.1	31.1	32.7	34.1	35.3	36.4	37.3	38.2	39.0	39.7	40.4	41.0	41.5	42.1	42.6	43.1
4	.10	3.01	3.98	4.59	5.04	5.39	5.69	5.93	6.14	6.33	6.50	6.65	6.78	6.91	7.03	7.13	7.23	7.33	7.41	7.50
	.05	3.93	5.04	5.76	6.29	6.71	7.05	7.35	7.60	7.83	8.03	8.21	8.37	8.52	8.66	8.79	8.91	9.03	9.13	9.23
	.01	6.51	8.12	9.17	9.96	10.6	11.1	11.5	11.9	12.3	12.6	12.8	13.1	13.3	13.5	13.7	13.9	14.1	14.2	14.4
	.001	12.2	15.0	16.8	18.2	19.3	20.3	21.0	21.7	22.3	22.9	23.4	23.8	24.2	24.6	24.9	25.2	25.6	25.9	26.1
5	.10	2.85	3.72	4.26	4.66	4.98	5.24	5.44	5.65	5.82	5.97	6.10	6.22	6.34	6.44	6.54	6.63	6.71	6.79	6.86
	.05	3.64	4.60	5.22	5.67	6.03	6.33	6.58	6.80	6.99	7.17	7.32	7.47	7.60	7.72	7.83	7.93	8.03	8.12	8.21
	.01	5.70	6.97	7.80	8.42	8.91	9.32	9.67	9.97	10.2	10.5	10.7	10.9	11.1	11.2	11.4	11.6	11.7	11.8	11.9
	.001	9.71	11.7	13.0	13.9	14.7	15.4	15.9	16.4	16.8	17.2	17.5	17.9	18.1	18.4	18.7	18.9	19.1	19.3	19.5
6	.10	2.75	3.56	4.07	4.44	4.73	4.97	5.17	5.34	5.50	5.64	5.76	5.88	5.98	6.08	6.16	6.25	6.33	6.40	6.47
	.05	3.46	4.34	4.90	5.31	5.63	5.89	6.12	6.32	6.49	6.65	6.79	6.92	7.03	7.14	7.24	7.34	7.43	7.51	7.59
	.01	5.24	6.33	7.03	7.56	7.97	8.32	8.61	8.87	9.10	9.30	9.49	9.65	9.81	9.95	10.1	10.2	10.3	10.4	10.5
	.001	8.43	9.96	11.0	11.7	12.3	12.8	13.3	13.6	14.0	14.3	14.5	14.8	15.0	15.2	15.4	15.6	15.8	15.9	16.1
7	.10	2.68	3.45	3.93	4.28	4.56	4.78	4.97	5.14	5.28	5.41	5.53	5.64	5.74	5.83	5.91	5.99	6.06	6.13	6.20
	.05	3.34	4.16	4.69	5.06	5.36	5.61	5.82	6.00	6.16	6.30	6.43	6.55	6.66	6.76	6.85	6.94	7.02	7.10	7.17
	.01	4.95	5.92	6.54	7.01	7.37	7.68	7.94	8.17	8.37	8.55	8.71	8.86	9.00	9.12	9.24	9.35	9.46	9.55	9.65
	.001	7.65	8.93	9.77	10.4	10.9	11.3	11.7	12.0	12.3	12.5	12.7	13.0	13.1	13.3	13.5	13.6	13.8	13.9	14.0

Source: Abridged from table 29 in E.S. Pearson and H.O. Hartley (Eds.), *Biometrika Tables for Statisticians*, vol. 1, 2nd ed. (1962), by permission of the *Biometrika* Trustees.

[a]In the one-factor ANOVA with n observations in each of J groups, $v_W = n, -J$. In general, v_W is the number of degrees of freedom for the mean square within (MS_W) in an analysis of variance.

❖ **TABLE H** *(Continued)*

								J (Number of Means in Set)											
ν for Denominator	α	2	3	4	5	6	7	8	9	10	11	12	13	14	15	16	17	18	19	20
8	.10	2.63	3.37	3.83	4.17	4.43	4.65	4.83	4.99	5.13	5.25	5.36	5.46	5.56	5.64	5.74	5.83	5.87	5.94	6.00
	.05	**3.26**	**4.04**	**4.53**	**4.89**	**5.17**	**5.40**	**5.60**	**5.77**	**5.92**	**6.05**	**6.18**	**6.29**	**6.39**	**6.48**	**6.57**	**6.65**	**6.73**	**6.80**	**6.87**
	.01	4.74	5.63	6.20	6.63	6.96	7.24	7.47	7.68	7.78	8.03	8.18	8.31	8.44	8.55	8.66	8.76	8.85	8.94	9.03
	.001	7.13	8.25	8.98	9.52	9.96	10.3	10.6	10.9	11.2	11.4	11.6	11.7	11.9	12.1	12.2	12.3	12.5	12.6	12.7
9	.10	2.59	3.32	3.76	4.08	4.34	4.55	4.72	4.87	5.01	5.13	5.23	5.33	5.42	5.51	5.58	5.66	5.72	5.79	5.84
	.05	**3.20**	**3.95**	**4.42**	**4.76**	**5.02**	**5.24**	**5.43**	**5.60**	**5.74**	**5.87**	**5.98**	**6.09**	**6.19**	**6.28**	**6.36**	**6.44**	**6.51**	**6.53**	**6.64**
	.01	4.60	5.43	5.96	6.35	6.66	6.91	7.13	7.32	7.49	7.65	7.78	7.91	8.03	8.13	8.23	8.33	8.41	8.50	8.57
	.001	6.76	7.77	8.42	8.91	9.30	9.62	9.90	10.1	10.4	10.6	10.7	10.9	11.0	11.2	11.3	11.4	11.5	11.6	11.8
10	.10	2.56	3.28	3.70	4.02	4.26	4.47	4.64	4.78	4.91	5.03	5.13	5.23	5.32	5.40	5.47	5.54	5.61	5.67	5.73
	.05	**3.15**	**3.88**	**4.33**	**4.65**	**4.91**	**5.12**	**5.30**	**5.46**	**5.60**	**5.72**	**5.83**	**5.93**	**6.03**	**6.11**	**6.19**	**6.27**	**6.34**	**6.41**	**6.49**
	.01	4.48	5.27	5.77	6.14	6.43	6.67	6.87	7.05	7.21	7.36	7.48	7.60	7.71	7.81	7.91	8.00	8.08	8.15	8.23
	.001	6.49	7.41	8.01	8.45	8.80	9.10	9.35	9.	9.77	9.95	10.1	10.3	10.4	10.5	10.6	10.8	10.9	11.0	11.0
11	.10	2.54	3.23	3.66	3.97	4.21	4.40	4.57	4.71	4.84	4.95	5.05	5.15	5.23	5.31	5.38	5.45	5.51	5.57	5.63
	.05	**3.11**	**3.82**	**4.26**	**4.57**	**4.82**	**5.03**	**5.20**	**5.35**	**5.49**	**5.61**	**5.71**	**5.81**	**5.90**	**5.99**	**6.06**	**6.18**	**6.20**	**6.27**	**6.33**
	.01	4.39	5.14	5.62	5.97	6.25	6.48	6.67	6.84	6.99	7.13	7.26	7.36	7.46	7.56	7.75	7.73	7.81	7.88	7.95
	.001	6.28	7.	7.69	8.10	8.43	8.70	8.93	9.14	9.32	9.48	9.63	9.77	9.89	10.0	10.1	10.2	10.3	10.4	10.5
12	.10	2.52	3.20	3.62	3.92	4.16	4.35	4.51	4.65	4.78	4.89	4.99	5.08	5.16	5.24	5.31	5.37	5.44	5.50	5.55
	.05	**3.08**	**3.77**	**4.20**	**4.51**	**4.75**	**4.95**	**5.12**	**5.27**	**5.40**	**5.51**	**5.62**	**5.71**	**5.80**	**5.88**	**5.95**	**6.02**	**6.09**	**6.15**	**6.21**
	.01	4.32	5.04	5.50	5.84	6.10	6.32	6.51	6.67	6.81	6.94	7.06	7.17	7.26	7.36	7.44	7.52	7.50	7.67	7.73
	.001	6.11	6.92	7.44	7.82	8.13	8.38	8.60	8.79	8.96	9.12	9.25	9.38	9.50	9.61	9.71	9.80	9.89	9.98	10.1
13	.10	2.51	3.18	3.59	3.89	4.12	4.31	4.46	4.60	4.72	4.83	4.93	5.02	5.10	5.18	5.25	5.31	5.37	5.43	5.48
	.05	**3.06**	**3.73**	**4.15**	**4.45**	**4.69**	**4.88**	**5.05**	**5.19**	**5.32**	**5.43**	**5.53**	**5.63**	**5.71**	**5.79**	**5.86**	**5.93**	**6.00**	**6.06**	**6.11**
	.01	4.26	4.96	5.40	5.73	5.98	6.19	6.37	6.53	6.67	6.79	6.90	7.01	7.10	7.19	7.27	7.37	7.42	7.49	7.55
	.001	5.97	6.74	7.23	7.60	7.89	8.13	8.33	8.51	8.67	8.82	8.95	9.07	9.18	9.28	9.38	9.47	9.55	9.63	9.70
14	.10	2.49	3.16	3.56	3.83	4.08	4.27	4.42	4.56	4.68	4.79	4.88	4.97	5.05	5.12	5.19	5.26	5.32	5.37	5.43
	.05	**3.03**	**3.70**	**4.11**	**4.41**	**4.64**	**4.83**	**4.99**	**5.13**	**5.25**	**5.36**	**5.46**	**5.55**	**5.64**	**5.72**	**5.79**	**5.85**	**5.92**	**5.97**	**6.03**
	.01	4.21	4.89	5.32	5.63	5.88	6.08	6.26	6.41	6.54	6.66	6.77	6.87	6.96	7.05	7.13	7.20	7.27	7.33	7.40
	.001	5.86	6.59	7.06	7.41	7.69	7.92	8.11	8.28	8.43	8.57	8.70	8.81	8.91	9.01	9.10	9.19	9.27	9.34	9.41
16	.10	2.47	3.12	3.52	3.80	4.03	4.21	4.36	4.49	4.61	4.71	4.81	4.89	4.97	5.04	5.11	5.17	5.23	5.28	5.33
	.05	**3.00**	**3.65**	**4.05**	**4.33**	**4.56**	**4.74**	**4.90**	**5.03**	**5.15**	**5.26**	**5.35**	**5.44**	**5.52**	**5.59**	**5.66**	**5.73**	**5.79**	**5.84**	**5.90**
	.01	4.13	4.78	5.19	5.49	5.72	5.92	6.08	6.22	6.35	6.46	6.56	6.66	6.74	6.82	6.90	6.97	7.03	7.09	7.15
	.001	5.68	6.37	6.80	7.12	7.37	7.59	7.77	7.92	8.06	8.19	8.30	8.41	8.50	8.59	8.68	8.76	8.83	8.90	8.96

ν for Denominator

		J (Number of Means in Set)																		
ν	α	2	3	4	5	6	7	8	9	10	11	12	13	14	15	16	17	18	19	20
18	.10	2.45	3.10	3.49	3.77	3.98	4.16	4.31	4.44	4.55	4.66	4.75	4.83	4.91	4.98	5.04	5.10	5.16	5.21	5.26
	.05	**2.97**	**3.61**	**4.00**	**4.28**	**4.49**	**4.67**	**4.82**	**4.96**	**5.07**	**5.17**	**5.27**	**5.35**	**5.43**	**5.50**	**5.57**	**5.63**	**5.69**	**5.74**	**5.79**
	.01	4.07	4.70	5.09	5.38	5.60	5.79	5.94	6.08	6.20	6.31	6.41	6.50	6.58	6.65	6.73	6.79	6.85	6.91	6.97
	.001	5.55	6.20	6.60	6.91	7.14	7.34	7.51	7.66	7.79	7.91	8.01	8.11	8.20	8.28	8.36	8.43	8.50	8.57	8.63
20	.10	2.44	3.08	3.46	3.74	3.95	4.12	4.27	4.40	4.51	4.61	4.70	4.78	4.86	4.92	4.99	5.05	5.10	5.16	5.21
	.05	**2.95**	**3.58**	**3.96**	**4.23**	**4.45**	**4.62**	**4.77**	**4.90**	**5.01**	**5.11**	**5.20**	**5.28**	**5.36**	**5.43**	**5.49**	**5.55**	**5.61**	**5.66**	**5.71**
	.01	4.02	4.64	5.02	5.29	5.51	5.69	5.84	5.97	6.09	6.19	6.29	6.37	6.45	6.52	6.59	6.65	6.71	6.77	6.82
	.001	5.44	6.07	6.45	6.74	6.97	7.15	7.31	7.45	7.58	7.69	7.79	7.88	7.97	8.04	8.12	8.19	8.25	8.31	8.37
24	.10	2.42	3.05	3.42	3.69	3.90	4.07	4.21	4.34	4.45	4.54	4.63	4.71	4.78	4.85	4.91	4.97	5.02	5.07	5.12
	.05	**2.92**	**3.53**	**3.90**	**4.17**	**4.37**	**4.54**	**4.68**	**4.81**	**4.92**	**5.01**	**5.10**	**5.18**	**5.25**	**5.32**	**5.38**	**5.44**	**5.49**	**5.55**	**5.59**
	.01	3.96	4.54	4.91	5.17	5.37	5.54	5.69	5.81	5.92	6.02	6.11	6.19	6.26	6.33	6.39	6.45	6.51	6.57	6.61
	.001	5.30	5.88	6.24	6.50	6.71	6.88	7.03	7.16	7.27	7.37	7.47	7.55	7.63	7.70	7.77	7.83	7.89	7.95	8.00
30	.10	2.40	3.02	3.39	3.65	3.85	4.02	4.16	4.28	4.38	4.47	4.56	4.64	4.71	4.77	4.83	4.89	4.94	4.99	5.03
	.05	**2.89**	**3.49**	**3.84**	**4.10**	**4.30**	**4.46**	**4.60**	**4.72**	**4.83**	**4.92**	**5.00**	**5.08**	**5.15**	**5.21**	**5.27**	**5.33**	**5.38**	**5.43**	**5.48**
	.01	3.89	4.45	4.80	5.05	5.24	5.40	5.54	5.65	5.76	5.85	5.93	6.01	6.08	6.14	6.20	6.26	6.31	6.36	6.41
	.001	5.16	5.70	6.03	6.28	6.47	6.63	6.76	6.88	6.98	7.08	7.16	7.24	7.31	7.38	7.44	7.48	7.55	7.60	7.65
40	.10	2.38	2.99	3.35	3.61	3.80	3.96	4.10	4.22	4.32	4.41	4.49	4.56	4.63	4.70	4.75	4.81	4.86	4.91	4.95
	.05	**2.86**	**3.44**	**3.79**	**4.04**	**4.23**	**4.39**	**4.52**	**4.63**	**4.74**	**4.82**	**4.91**	**4.98**	**5.05**	**5.11**	**5.16**	**5.22**	**5.27**	**5.31**	**5.36**
	.01	3.82	4.37	4.70	4.93	5.11	5.27	5.39	5.50	5.60	5.69	5.77	5.84	5.90	5.96	6.02	6.07	6.11	6.17	6.21
	.001	5.02	5.53	5.84	6.06	6.24	6.39	6.51	6.62	6.71	6.80	6.87	6.94	7.01	7.07	7.12	7.17	7.22	7.27	7.31
60	.10	2.36	2.96	3.31	3.56	3.76	3.91	4.04	4.16	4.26	4.34	4.42	4.49	4.56	4.62	4.68	4.73	4.78	4.82	4.86
	.05	**2.83**	**3.40**	**3.74**	**3.98**	**4.16**	**4.31**	**4.44**	**4.55**	**4.65**	**4.73**	**4.81**	**4.88**	**4.94**	**5.00**	**5.06**	**5.11**	**5.15**	**5.20**	**5.24**
	.01	3.76	4.28	4.60	4.82	4.99	5.13	5.25	5.36	5.45	5.53	5.60	5.67	5.73	5.79	5.84	5.89	5.93	5.97	6.02
	.001	4.87	5.37	5.67	5.86	6.02	6.16	6.27	6.37	6.45	6.53	6.60	6.66	6.72	6.77	6.82	6.87	6.91	6.96	7.00
120	.10	2.34	2.93	3.28	3.52	3.71	3.86	3.99	4.10	4.19	4.28	4.35	4.42	4.49	4.56	4.59	4.60	4.65	4.69	4.74
	.05	**2.80**	**3.36**	**3.69**	**3.92**	**4.10**	**4.24**	**4.36**	**4.48**	**4.56**	**4.64**	**4.72**	**4.78**	**4.84**	**4.90**	**4.95**	**5.00**	**5.04**	**5.09**	**5.13**
	.01	3.70	4.20	4.50	4.71	4.87	5.01	5.12	5.21	5.30	5.38	5.44	5.51	5.56	5.61	5.66	5.71	5.75	5.79	5.83
	.001	4.77	5.21	5.48	5.67	5.82	5.94	6.04	6.13	6.21	6.28	6.34	6.40	6.45	6.50	6.54	6.58	6.62	6.66	6.70
∞	.10	2.33	2.90	3.24	3.48	3.66	3.81	3.93	4.04	4.13	4.21	4.29	4.35	4.41	4.47	4.52	4.57	4.62	4.65	4.69
	.05	**2.77**	**3.31**	**3.63**	**3.86**	**4.03**	**4.17**	**4.29**	**4.39**	**4.47**	**4.55**	**4.62**	**4.68**	**4.74**	**4.80**	**4.85**	**4.89**	**4.93**	**4.97**	**5.01**
	.01	3.64	4.12	4.40	4.60	4.76	4.88	4.99	5.08	5.16	5.23	5.29	5.35	5.40	5.45	5.49	5.54	5.57	5.61	5.65
	.001	4.05	5.06	5.31	5.48	5.62	5.73	5.82	5.90	5.97	6.04	6.09	6.14	6.19	6.23	6.27	6.31	6.35	6.38	6.41

❖ **TABLE I** High School and Beyond (HSB) case study data

Case	Sex	Race	SES	School Type	Program Type	Read	Write	Math	Sci	Civics
#	M = 1 F = 2	H = 1 A = 2 B = 3 W = 4	L = 1 M = 2 H = 3	Pub = 1 Priv = 2	Gen = 1 Aca = 2 Voc = 3	T	T	T	T	T
001	2	1	1	1	3	34	44	40	39	41
002	2	1	2	1	3	39	41	33	42	41
003	1	1	1	1	2	63	65	48	63	56
004	2	1	1	1	2	44	50	41	39	51
005	1	1	1	1	2	47	40	43	45	31
006	2	1	1	1	2	47	41	46	40	41
007	1	1	2	1	2	57	54	59	47	51
008	2	1	1	1	2	39	44	52	44	48
009	1	1	2	1	3	48	49	52	44	51
010	2	1	2	1	1	47	54	49	53	61
011	1	1	2	1	2	34	46	45	39	36
012	1	1	2	1	3	37	44	45	39	46
013	2	1	2	1	3	47	46	39	47	61
014	1	1	3	1	2	47	41	54	42	56
015	1	1	3	1	3	39	39	44	26	42
016	1	1	1	1	3	47	31	44	36	36
017	2	1	2	1	2	47	57	48	44	41
018	1	1	2	1	3	50	33	49	44	36
019	2	1	1	1	1	28	46	43	44	51
020	1	1	3	1	2	60	52	57	61	61
021	1	1	2	1	1	44	44	61	50	46
022	1	1	2	1	3	42	39	39	56	46
023	2	2	1	1	2	65	65	64	58	71
024	1	2	2	1	2	52	62	66	47	46
025	2	2	2	1	1	47	44	42	42	36
026	2	2	3	1	2	60	59	62	61	51
027	1	2	2	1	2	53	61	61	57	56
028	2	2	2	1	1	39	53	54	50	41
029	1	2	1	1	1	52	44	49	55	41
030	2	2	3	1	2	41	59	42	34	51
031	2	2	2	2	1	55	59	52	42	56
032	2	2	3	1	3	50	67	66	66	56
033	2	2	1	1	2	57	65	72	54	56
034	2	1	3	2	2	73	61	57	55	66
035	2	1	1	2	1	60	54	50	50	51
036	2	3	1	1	1	44	49	44	35	51
037	2	3	1	1	3	41	47	40	39	51
038	1	3	1	1	2	45	57	50	31	56
039	2	3	3	1	2	66	67	67	61	66
040	1	3	1	1	1	42	41	43	50	41
041	1	3	2	1	2	50	40	45	55	56
042	2	3	2	1	3	46	52	55	44	56
043	2	3	1	1	2	47	37	43	42	46
044	2	3	1	1	3	47	62	45	34	46
045	2	3	1	1	3	34	35	41	29	26

❖ **TABLE I** (Continued)

Case	Sex	Race	SES	School Type	Program Type	Read	Write	Math	Sci	Civics
#	M = 1 F = 2	H = 1 A = 2 B = 3 W = 4	L = 1 M = 2 H = 3	Pub = 1 Priv = 2	Gen = 1 Aca = 2 Voc = 3	T	T	T	T	T
046	2	3	1	1	2	45	55	44	34	41
047	2	3	1	1	2	47	46	49	33	41
048	1	3	2	1	2	57	55	52	50	51
049	1	3	3	1	3	50	40	39	49	47
050	1	3	2	1	1	50	59	42	53	61
051	2	3	3	1	1	42	36	42	31	39
052	2	3	1	1	2	50	46	53	53	66
053	1	3	2	1	3	34	37	46	39	31
054	2	3	1	2	1	47	54	46	50	56
055	2	3	2	2	2	52	49	49	44	61
056	1	4	2	1	3	55	45	46	58	51
057	2	4	2	1	2	71	65	72	66	56
058	1	4	2	1	3	55	41	40	44	41
059	2	4	2	1	2	65	67	63	55	71
060	1	4	2	1	2	57	65	51	63	61
061	2	4	3	1	2	76	63	60	67	66
062	1	4	3	1	1	65	65	48	63	66
063	2	4	1	1	1	52	65	60	56	51
064	2	4	3	1	3	50	52	45	58	36
065	2	4	2	1	2	55	54	66	42	56
066	2	4	2	1	3	68	62	56	50	51
067	1	4	1	1	3	37	37	42	33	32
068	1	4	2	1	2	73	67	71	63	66
069	2	4	1	1	3	44	44	40	40	31
070	1	4	1	1	1	57	52	41	47	57
071	2	4	2	1	1	57	62	56	58	66
072	2	4	2	1	3	42	54	47	47	46
073	2	4	2	1	2	50	52	53	39	56
074	2	4	2	1	2	57	50	50	51	58
075	1	4	2	1	3	60	46	51	53	61
076	1	4	3	1	2	47	52	51	50	56
077	2	4	1	1	2	61	59	49	44	66
078	2	4	2	1	2	39	54	54	53	41
079	2	4	2	1	2	60	62	49	50	51
080	1	4	3	1	2	65	62	68	66	66
081	1	4	1	1	2	63	43	59	65	44
082	2	4	3	1	2	68	62	65	69	61
083	2	4	2	1	3	50	62	41	55	31
084	1	4	2	1	1	63	57	54	58	51
085	1	4	2	1	1	55	39	57	53	46
086	1	4	3	1	1	44	33	54	58	31
087	2	4	2	1	1	50	52	46	50	56
088	2	4	3	1	2	68	60	64	69	66
089	2	4	1	1	3	35	35	40	51	33
090	2	4	3	1	2	42	54	50	50	52

❖ **TABLE I** *(Continued)*

Case	Sex	Race	SES	School Type	Program Type	Read	Write	Math	Sci	Civics
#	M = 1 F = 2	H = 1 A = 2 B = 3 W = 4	L = 1 M = 2 H = 3	Pub = 1 Priv = 2	Gen = 1 Aca = 2 Voc = 3	T	T	T	T	T
091	2	4	3	1	3	50	49	56	47	46
092	2	4	3	1	1	52	67	57	63	61
093	2	4	3	1	2	73	67	62	58	66
094	1	4	3	1	2	55	49	61	61	56
095	1	4	3	1	2	73	60	71	61	71
096	2	4	3	1	2	65	54	61	58	56
097	1	4	3	1	2	60	54	58	58	61
098	2	4	1	1	3	57	60	51	53	37
099	2	4	3	1	1	47	59	56	66	61
100	2	4	3	1	2	63	65	71	69	71
101	2	4	3	1	2	60	62	67	50	56
102	1	4	3	1	2	52	41	51	53	56
103	1	4	3	1	2	76	52	64	64	61
104	1	4	3	1	2	54	63	57	55	46
105	2	4	2	1	2	50	41	45	44	56
106	2	4	2	1	3	36	44	37	42	41
107	1	4	1	1	3	47	39	47	42	26
108	1	4	2	1	1	34	33	41	36	36
109	2	4	2	1	1	42	39	42	42	41
110	2	4	2	1	3	52	55	50	54	61
111	2	4	1	1	1	39	54	39	47	36
112	2	4	2	1	2	52	59	48	55	61
113	1	4	2	1	2	44	52	51	63	61
114	1	4	3	1	2	68	65	62	55	61
115	1	4	1	1	1	42	49	43	50	56
116	2	4	2	1	2	57	59	54	50	56
117	1	4	3	1	3	34	49	39	42	56
118	2	4	2	1	1	55	62	58	58	61
119	2	4	1	1	1	42	57	45	50	43
120	2	4	3	1	2	63	52	54	50	51
121	2	4	2	1	3	68	59	53	63	61
122	2	4	2	1	2	52	59	58	53	66
123	1	4	3	1	1	68	59	56	63	66
124	2	4	1	1	3	42	54	41	42	41
125	2	4	1	1	2	68	65	58	59	56
126	1	4	2	1	1	42	31	57	47	51
127	1	4	3	1	2	63	59	57	55	56
128	1	4	3	1	2	39	33	38	47	41
129	2	4	1	1	1	44	44	46	47	51
130	2	4	3	1	1	43	54	55	55	46
131	2	4	3	1	2	65	59	57	46	66
132	1	4	2	1	2	73	62	73	69	66
133	1	4	2	1	3	50	31	40	34	31
134	1	4	1	1	1	44	44	39	34	46
135	2	4	1	1	2	63	60	65	54	66

❖ **TABLE I** (Continued)

Case	Sex	Race	SES	School Type	Program Type	Read	Write	Math	Sci	Civics
#	M = 1 F = 2	H = 1 A = 2 B = 3 W = 4	L = 1 M = 2 H = 3	Pub = 1 Priv = 2	Gen = 1 Aca = 2 Voc = 3	T	T	T	T	T
136	1	4	2	1	2	65	59	70	63	51
137	2	4	3	1	2	63	65	65	53	61
138	2	4	2	1	3	43	57	40	50	51
139	2	4	2	1	2	68	59	61	55	71
140	1	4	2	1	3	44	41	40	50	26
141	1	4	3	1	3	63	44	47	53	56
142	2	4	2	1	3	47	42	52	39	51
143	1	4	2	1	3	63	63	75	72	66
144	1	4	3	1	1	60	65	58	61	66
145	2	4	2	1	3	42	46	38	36	46
146	1	4	3	1	2	55	62	64	63	66
147	2	4	1	1	2	47	62	53	53	61
148	2	4	2	1	3	42	57	51	47	61
149	1	4	1	1	1	63	49	49	66	46
150	1	4	2	1	3	42	41	57	72	31
151	2	4	2	1	3	47	46	52	48	46
152	2	4	3	1	2	55	57	56	58	61
153	1	4	2	1	3	39	31	40	39	51
154	1	4	3	1	2	65	65	66	61	66
155	1	4	2	1	1	44	44	46	39	51
156	2	4	2	1	2	50	59	53	61	61
157	1	4	2	1	1	68	59	58	74	66
158	2	4	2	1	1	52	54	55	53	51
159	1	4	3	1	2	55	61	54	49	61
160	2	4	2	1	2	55	65	55	50	61
161	2	4	1	1	2	57	62	72	61	61
162	2	4	2	1	3	57	52	40	61	56
163	2	4	1	1	2	52	57	64	58	56
164	1	4	2	1	3	31	36	46	39	46
165	1	4	1	1	3	36	49	54	61	36
166	2	4	2	1	2	52	59	53	61	51
167	1	4	2	1	1	63	49	35	66	41
168	1	4	2	1	2	52	54	57	55	51
169	1	4	1	1	1	55	59	63	69	46
170	1	4	3	1	2	47	62	61	69	66
171	1	4	2	1	2	60	54	60	55	66
172	1	4	2	1	2	47	52	57	53	61
173	2	4	1	1	1	50	62	61	63	51
174	1	4	2	2	2	68	59	71	66	56
175	2	4	3	2	1	36	57	42	50	41
176	1	4	2	2	2	47	47	41	42	51
177	1	4	2	2	2	55	59	62	58	51
178	1	4	2	2	3	47	57	57	58	46
179	2	4	2	2	2	47	65	60	50	56
180	2	4	3	2	2	71	65	69	58	71

❖ **TABLE I** *(Continued)*

Case	Sex	Race	SES	School Type	Program Type	Read	Write	Math	Sci	Civics
#	*M = 1* *F = 2*	*H = 1* *A = 2* *B = 3* *W = 4*	*L = 1* *M = 2* *H = 3*	*Pub = 1* *Priv = 2*	*Gen = 1* *Aca = 2* *Voc = 3*	*T*	*T*	*T*	*T*	*T*
181	1	4	2	2	2	50	46	45	58	61
182	2	4	2	2	2	44	52	43	44	51
183	1	4	2	2	2	63	59	49	55	71
184	2	4	2	2	3	50	52	53	55	56
185	1	4	2	2	2	63	57	55	58	41
186	2	4	2	2	2	57	62	63	55	41
187	2	4	2	2	1	57	41	57	55	52
188	2	4	3	2	2	63	62	56	55	61
189	1	4	2	2	2	47	59	63	53	46
190	2	4	2	2	2	47	59	54	58	46
191	2	4	3	2	2	47	52	43	48	61
192	1	4	3	2	2	65	67	63	66	71
193	2	4	2	2	2	44	49	48	39	51
194	2	4	3	2	2	63	63	69	61	61
195	1	4	2	2	1	57	57	60	58	56
196	1	4	3	2	2	44	38	49	39	46
197	1	4	3	2	2	50	42	50	36	61
198	2	4	3	2	2	47	61	51	63	31
199	1	4	3	2	2	52	59	50	61	61
200	1	4	2	2	2	68	54	75	66	66

❖ Appendix C

Glossary of Symbols

1. Symbols introduced in Chapter 1, *Introduction and Overview*

   HSB   The High School and Beyond data pool, the course case study data

2. Symbols introduced in Chapter 2, *Frequency Distributions*

   f Frequency occurrence of a score

   n Number of scores in a sample

   N Number of scores in a population

   P_k kth percentile point

   Q_1 Quartile 1, the 25th percentile

   Q_2 Quartile 2, the 50th percentile

   Q_3 Quartile 3, the 75th percentile

   w Interval width for a grouped frequency distribution

   X, Y, Z Variables represented by italicized upper case letters

   X_i ith observation or score for variable X

   X_{max} Largest score in a set of data

   X_{min} Smallest score in a set of data

3. Symbols introduced in Chapter 3, *Central Tendency*

   $\overline{X}, \overline{Y}$ Sample means

   μ Population mean

   ΣX Sum of the scores for variable X

   $\overline{X}.$ Grand mean for combined samples

   Mo Mode for a set of observations

   Md Median for a set of observations

4. Symbols introduced in Chapter 4, *Variability*

x	Deviation score, difference from the mean
Σx^2	Sum of squares, sum of squared deviation scores
SS	Sum of squares, sum of squared deviation score
σ^2	Variance of a population
σ	Standard deviation of a population
s^2	Variance of a sample
s	Standard deviation of a sample

5. Symbols introduced in Chapter 5, *The Normal Curve*

z	Basic standard score with a mean of 0 and a standard deviation of 1
T	Standard score with a mean of 50 and a standard deviation of 10
Q	Quartile deviation, or semi-interquartile range

6. Symbols introduced in Chapter 6, *Correlation*

r	Pearson correlation coefficient of a sample
ρ	Pearson correlation coefficient of a population
s_{XY}	Covariance for variables X and Y

7. Symbols introduced in Chapter 7, *Interpreting Correlation Coefficients*

ρ_1	Correlation for a restricted segment of a population
ρ_U	Correlation for an unrestricted population
σ_1	Standard deviation for a restricted segment of a population
σ_U	Standard deviation for an unrestricted population

8. Symbols introduced in Chapter 8, *Prediction and Regression*

$\hat{z}_Y$	Predicted z-score on the criterion
$\hat{Y}$	Predicted criterion raw score
b	Regression coefficient in the raw score regression equation
c	Constant in the raw score regression equation
$s_{Y.X}$	Standard error of estimate
$R_{Y.XZ}$	Multiple correlation coefficient
$r_{YX.Z}$	Partial correlation coefficient

9. Symbols introduced in Chapter 9, *Sampling Distributions and Confidence Intervals*

$\sigma_{\bar{X}}$	Standard error of the mean
.95 CI	95% confidence interval
$s_{\bar{X}}$	An estimate of the standard error of the mean

10. Symbols introduced in Chapter 10, *Hypothesis Testing*

H_0	Statistical hypothesis, or null hypothesis
p	Probability of occurrence if H_0 were true

α Level of significance

β Probability of a type-II error (accepting a false H_0)

t Student t-ratio

ν Degrees of freedom

$_{.95}t_\nu$ 95th percentile of the t-distribution with ν degrees of freedom

11. Symbols introduced in Chapter 11, *Testing Hypotheses about the Difference between Two Means*

$\sigma_{\bar{X}_1-\bar{X}_2}$ Standard error of the difference between means

s_W^2 Pooled within—group variance based on both samples

MS_W Within—group variance, synonymous with s_W^2

Δ Effect size of the mean difference in σ-units

$\hat{\Delta}$ Estimate of effect size based on sample data

$s_{\bar{X}_1-\bar{X}_2}$ Estimate of the standard error of the difference between two means

12. Symbols introduced in Chapter 12, *Inferences about Proportions*

p Proportion or probability as inferred from context

π Proportion in a population

σ_p Standard error of a proportion for infinite populations

σ_{p_f} Standard error of a proportion for finite populations

χ^2 *Chi*—square statistic

o, ε Observed and expected frequency in χ^2 analyses

$_{.95}\chi_\nu^2$ 95th percentile of the χ^2 distribution with ν degrees of freedom

13. Symbols introduced in Chapter 13, *Inferences about Correlations*

σ_r Standard error of the Pearson correlation coefficient

s_r Estimate of σ_r

σ_Z Standard error of the Fisher Z-transformation

$\sigma_{Z_{r_1}-Z_{r_2}}$ Standard error of the difference between Fisher Z-transformations

Z_r Fisher Z-transformation of r

14. Symbols introduced in Chapter 14, *One-Factor Analysis of Variance*

J Number of groups in the independent factor

F F-ratio for ANOVA

MS_B Mean square between groups estimate of the population variance, σ^2

MS_W Mean square within groups estimate of σ^2

SS_B Sum of squares between groups

SS_W Sum of squares within groups

SS_{total} Total sum of squares

ν_B Degrees of freedom between groups

v_W Degrees of freedom within groups

$._{95}F_{v_1,v_2}$ 95th percentile of the F-distribution with v_1 and v_2 degrees of freedom

15. Symbols introduced in Chapter 15, *Multiple Comparisons*

MC   Multiple comparisons between group means

q Studentized range statistic

HSD   Honest significant difference

r Inclusive range in subset of ranked means

16. Symbols introduced in Chapter 16, *Two-Factor Analysis of Variance*

A, B Factors in two-way ANOVA

$A \times B$ Interaction of factors A and B

J Number of levels of factor A

K Number of levels of factor B

$SS_{A \times B}$ Sum of squares for interaction of factors A and B

$MS_{A \times B}$ Mean square for interaction of factors A and B estimate of σ^2

MS_W Mean square within cell estimate of σ^2

n Number of observations in each cell of a factorial ANOVA

$n_{j\cdot}$ Number of scores in row j in a two-way ANOVA

$n_{\cdot k}$ Number of scores in column k in a two-way ANOVA

$n_{\cdot\cdot}$ Total number of scores in a two-way ANOVA

$\overline{X}_{j\cdot}$ Mean score of row j in a two-way ANOVA

$\overline{X}_{\cdot k}$ Mean score of column k in a two-way ANOVA

$\overline{X}_{\cdot\cdot}$ Grand mean for the total sample in a two-way ANOVA

$\overline{X}_{jk}$ Mean score of the cell in row j and column k in a two-factor ANOVA

❖ Appendix D

Glossary of Statistical Formulas

Formulas introduced in Chapter 2, *Frequency Distributions:*

$$\text{range} = X_{\max} - X_{\min} \tag{2.1}$$

To determine the interval width to yield n_{c_i} class intervals:

$$w = \frac{\text{range}}{n_{c_i}} \tag{2.2}$$

Formulas introduced in Chapter 3, *Central Tendency:*

$$\overline{X} = \frac{\Sigma X}{n} \text{ and } \mu = \frac{\Sigma X}{N} \tag{3.1–3.2}$$

$$\overline{X}_{\bullet} = \frac{n_1\overline{X}_1 + n_2\overline{X}_2 + \ldots + n_j\overline{X}_j}{n_{\bullet}}, \text{ or } \overline{X}_{\bullet} = \frac{\Sigma X_1 + \Sigma X_2 + \ldots + \Sigma X_J}{n_1 + n_2 + \ldots + n_J} \tag{3.3}$$

Formulas introduced in Chapter 4, *Variability:*

$$x = X - \mu \tag{4.1}$$

$$\text{Sum of Squares} = SS = \Sigma x^2 = \Sigma(X - \mu)^2 \tag{4.2}$$

$$\sigma^2 = \frac{\Sigma(X - \mu)^2}{N} = \frac{\Sigma x^2}{N} = \frac{\text{sum of squares}}{N} = \frac{SS}{N} \tag{4.3}$$

$$\sigma = \sqrt{\sigma^2} = \sqrt{\frac{SS}{N}} \tag{4.4}$$

$$\text{Sampling error} = \text{the Statistic} - \text{the Parameter} \tag{4.5}$$

$$s^2 = \frac{\Sigma(X - \overline{X})^2}{n-1} = \frac{\Sigma x^2}{n-1} = \frac{\Sigma x^2}{v} = \frac{SS}{v} \tag{4.6}$$

$$s = \sqrt{s^2} = \sqrt{\frac{SS}{v}} \tag{4.7}$$

$$E(\text{unbiased statistic}) = \text{parameter} \tag{4.8}$$

$$E(s^2) = \sigma^2 \tag{4.9}$$

$$range = X_{\max} - X_{\min} \tag{4.10}$$

$$Q = \frac{Q_3 - Q_1}{2} \tag{4.11}$$

Formulas introduced in Chapter 5, *The Normal Curve:*

$$z = \frac{X - \mu}{\sigma} = \frac{x}{\sigma} = \frac{\text{deviation score}}{\text{standard deviation}} \tag{5.1a}$$

$$X = \mu + z\sigma \tag{5.1b}$$

$$A = \mu_A + z(\sigma_A) \tag{5.2}$$

$$T = 50 + 10z \tag{5.3}$$

Formulas introduced in Chapter 6, *Correlation:*

$$\rho = \frac{\Sigma z_X z_Y}{N} \qquad \textbf{(6.1)}$$

$$s_{XY} = \frac{\Sigma xy}{n-1} = \frac{\Sigma(X - \overline{X})(Y - \overline{Y})}{n-1} \qquad \textbf{(6.2)}$$

$$r = \frac{s_{XY}}{s_X s_Y} \qquad \textbf{(6.3)}$$

$$r = \frac{\Sigma z_X z_Y}{n-1} \qquad \textbf{(6.4)}$$

$$r = \frac{\Sigma xy}{\sqrt{(SS_X)(SS_Y)}} = \frac{\Sigma XY - n\overline{X}\overline{Y}}{\sqrt{(\Sigma X^2 - n\overline{X}^2)(\Sigma Y^2 - n\overline{Y}^2)}} \qquad \textbf{(6.5)}$$

Formulas introduced in Chapter 7, *Interpreting Correlation Coefficients:*

$$\rho_U^2 = \frac{\rho_I^2 \left(\dfrac{\sigma_U}{\sigma_I} \right)^2}{1 + \rho_I^2 \left(\dfrac{\sigma_U}{\sigma_I} \right)^2 - \rho_I^2} \qquad \textbf{(7.1a)}$$

$$\rho_U = \sqrt{\rho_U^2} \qquad \textbf{(7.1b)}$$

Formulas introduced in Chapter 8, *Prediction and Regression:*

$$\hat{z}_Y = r z_X \qquad \textbf{(8.1)}$$

$$residual = Y - \hat{Y} \qquad \textbf{(8.2)}$$

$$\hat{Y} = bX + c \qquad \textbf{(8.3a)}$$

$$b = r(s_Y/s_X) \qquad \textbf{(8.3b)}$$

$$c = \bar{Y} - b\,\bar{X} \tag{8.3c}$$

$$s_{Y.X} = s_Y \sqrt{1 - r^2} \tag{8.4}$$

$$R^2_{Y.XZ} = \frac{r^2_{YX} + r^2_{YZ} - 2r_{YX}r_{YZ}r_{XZ}}{1 - R^2_{Y.XZ}} \tag{8.5a}$$

$$R_{Y.XZ} = \sqrt{R^2_{Y.XZ}} \tag{8.5b}$$

$$r_{YX.Z} = \frac{r_{YX} - r_{YZ}r_{XZ}}{\sqrt{(1 - r^2_{YZ})(1 - r^2_{XZ})}} \tag{8.6}$$

Formulas introduced in Chapter 9, *Sampling Distribution and Confidence Intervals:*

$$\sigma_{\bar{X}} = \frac{\sigma}{\sqrt{n}} \tag{9.1}$$

$$.68 \text{ CI} = [\bar{X} \pm \sigma_{\bar{X}}] = [\bar{X} - \sigma_{\bar{X}},\ \bar{X} + \sigma_{\bar{X}}] \tag{9.2}$$

$$.95 \text{ CI} = [\bar{X} \pm 1.96\sigma_{\bar{X}}] \tag{9.3}$$

$$s_{\bar{X}} = \frac{s}{\sqrt{n}} \tag{9.4}$$

$$\text{CI} = [\bar{X} \pm ts_{\bar{X}}] \text{ or } [\bar{X} - ts_{\bar{X}},\ \bar{X} + ts_{\bar{X}}] \tag{9.5}$$

Formulas introduced in Chapter 10, *Hypothesis Testing:*

$$z = \frac{\bar{X} - \mu}{\sigma_{\bar{X}}} \tag{10.1}$$

$$t = \frac{\bar{X} - \mu}{s_{\bar{X}}} \tag{10.2}$$

Formulas introduced in Chapter 11, *Testing Hypotheses about the Difference between Two Means:*

$$z = \frac{(\text{observed statistic} - \text{hypothesized parameter})}{\text{standard error of the difference}} \tag{11.1}$$

$$z = \frac{(\overline{X}_1 - \overline{X}_2) - (\mu_1 - \mu_2)}{\sigma_{\overline{X}_1 - \overline{X}_2}} \tag{11.2a}$$

For H_0: $\mu_1 = \mu_2$,

$$z = \frac{(\overline{X}_1 - \overline{X}_2)}{\sigma_{\overline{X}_1 - \overline{X}_2}} \tag{11.2b}$$

$$\sigma_{\overline{X}_1 - \overline{X}_2} = \sqrt{\sigma_{\overline{X}_1}^2 + \sigma_{\overline{X}_2}^2} \tag{11.3}$$

$$t = \frac{\text{observed } (\overline{X}_1 - \overline{X}_2) \text{ difference} - \text{hypothesized } (\mu_1 - \mu_2) \text{ difference}}{\text{estimate of the standard error of the } (\overline{X}_1 - \overline{X}_2) \text{ difference}} \tag{11.4}$$

$$t = \frac{(\overline{X}_1 - \overline{X}_2) - (\mu_1 - \mu_2)}{s_{\overline{X}_1 - \overline{X}_2}} \tag{11.5a}$$

For H_0: $\mu_1 = \mu_2$,

$$t = \frac{(\overline{X}_1 - \overline{X}_2)}{s_{\overline{X}_1 - \overline{X}_2}} \tag{11.5b}$$

$$s_w^2 = \frac{SS_1 + SS_2}{v_1 + v_2} = \frac{SS_w}{v_w} = MS_w \tag{11.6}$$

$$s_{\overline{X}_1 - \overline{X}_2}^2 = s_w^2 \left(\frac{1}{n_1} + \frac{1}{n_2} \right) \tag{11.7a}$$

$$s_{\overline{X}_1 - \overline{X}_2} = s_w \sqrt{\frac{1}{n_1} + \frac{1}{n_2}} \tag{11.7b}$$

$$t = \frac{\overline{X}_1 - \overline{X}_2}{s_{\overline{X}_1 - \overline{X}_2}} = \frac{\overline{X}_1 - \overline{X}_2}{s_w \sqrt{\frac{1}{n_1} + \frac{1}{n_2}}}$$

(11.8)

$$F = \frac{s_{larger}^2}{s_{smaller}^2}$$

(11.9)

$$s_{\overline{X}_1 - \overline{X}_2}^2 = s_{\overline{X}_1}^2 + s_{\overline{X}_2}^2 - 2rs_{\overline{X}_1} s_{\overline{X}_2}$$

(11.10)

$$.95 \text{ CI for } (\mu_1 - \mu_2) = [(\overline{X}_1 - \overline{X}_2) + (_{.975}t_v) s_{\overline{X}_1 - \overline{X}_2}]$$

(11.11)

$$\Delta = \frac{\mu_1 - \mu_2}{\sigma}$$

(11.12)

$$\hat{\Delta} = \frac{\overline{X}_1 - \overline{X}_2}{s},$$

(11.13)

Formulas introduced in Chapter 12, *Inferences about Proportions:*

$$\sigma_p^2 = \frac{\pi(1 - \pi)}{n}$$

(12.1a)

$$\sigma_p = \sqrt{\sigma_p^2}$$

(12.1b)

$$\sigma_{p_f} = \sigma_p \sqrt{1 - (n/N)}$$

(12.2)

$$\chi^2 = \Sigma \frac{(o_j - \varepsilon_j)^2}{\varepsilon_j}$$

(12.3)

$$v = (J - 1)(K - 1)$$

(12.4)

$$\varepsilon_{jk} = \frac{(n_{j.})(n_{.k})}{n_{..}}$$

(12.5)

$$\chi^2 = \sum_j \sum_k \frac{(O_{jk} - \varepsilon_{jk})^2}{\varepsilon_{jk}} \tag{12.6}$$

Formulas introduced in Chapter 13, *Inferences about Correlations:*

$$z = \frac{r}{\sigma_r} = \frac{r}{\frac{1}{\sqrt{n-1}}} = r\sqrt{n-1} \tag{13.1}$$

$$t = \frac{r}{s_r} = \frac{r}{\sqrt{\frac{1-r^2}{v}}} \tag{13.2}$$

$$\text{Critical } r = \frac{\text{Critical } t}{\sqrt{(\text{Critical } t)^2 + v}} \tag{13.3}$$

$$|Z_r| = .5 \ \ln\left(\frac{1+|R|}{1-|R|}\right) \tag{13.4}$$

$$\sigma_z^2 = \frac{1}{n-3} \tag{13.5}$$

$$\sigma_z = \frac{1}{\sqrt{n-3}} \tag{13.6}$$

$$z = \frac{Z_{r_1} - Z_{r_2}}{\sigma_{Z_{r_1} - Z_{r_2}}} \tag{13.7}$$

$$\sigma_{Z_{r_1} - Z_{r_2}} = \sqrt{\sigma_{Z_{r_1}} + \sigma_{Z_{r_2}}} = \sqrt{\frac{1}{n_1 - 3} + \frac{1}{n_2 - 3}} \tag{13.8}$$

Formulas introduced in Chapter 14, *One-Factor Analysis of Variance:*

$$F = \frac{MS_B}{MS_W} \tag{14.1}$$

$$MS_B = ns_{\overline{X}}^2 \tag{14.2}$$

$$s_{\overline{X}}^2 = \frac{\Sigma_j (\overline{X}_j - \overline{X}_{\bullet})^2}{J - 1} \tag{14.3}$$

$$MS_B = \frac{SS_B}{\nu_B} \tag{14.4}$$

$$SS_B = \Sigma n_j (\overline{X}_j - \overline{X}_{\bullet})^2 \tag{14.5}$$

$$\nu_B = J - 1 \tag{14.6}$$

$$MS_W = \frac{\Sigma s_j^2}{J} = \frac{s_1^2 + s_2^2 + \ldots + s_J^2}{J} \tag{14.7}$$

$$MS_W = \frac{SS_W}{\nu_W} \tag{14.8}$$

$$SS_W = \sum_j SS_j = \sum_j \left(\sum_i X_{ij}^2 - n_j \overline{X}_j^2 \right) \tag{14.9}$$

$$\nu_W = n_{\bullet} - J \tag{14.10}$$

$$F = \frac{MS_B}{MS_W} \tag{14.11}$$

$$SS_{\text{total}} = \Sigma\Sigma (X_{ij} - \overline{X}_{\bullet})^2 \tag{14.12a}$$

$$SS_{\text{total}} = \Sigma\Sigma x_{ij}^2 = \Sigma\Sigma X_{ij}^2 - n_{\bullet} X_{\bullet}^2 \tag{14.12b}$$

$$SS_{\text{total}} = \Sigma\Sigma X_{ij}^2 - (\Sigma\Sigma X_{ij})^2 / n_{\bullet} \tag{14.12c}$$

$$SS_{\text{total}} = SS_B + SS_W \tag{14.13}$$

Formulas introduced in Chapter 15, *Multiple Comparisons:*

$$q = \frac{\overline{X}_i - \overline{X}_j}{s_{\overline{X}}} = \frac{\overline{X}_i - \overline{X}_j}{\sqrt{MS_w / n}} \qquad \textbf{(15.1)}$$

$$HSD = s_{\overline{X}}(\text{critical } q) \qquad \textbf{(15.2)}$$

Formulas introduced in Chapter 16, *Two-Factor Analysis of Variance:*

$$SS_{\text{total}} = SS_A + SS_B + SS_{A \times B} + SS_w \qquad \textbf{(16.1)}$$

$$MS_w = \Sigma\Sigma s_{jk}^2 / JK \qquad \textbf{(16.2)}$$

$$v_w = JK(n - 1) \qquad \textbf{(16.2)}$$

$$SS_{\text{b/cells}} = n\Sigma(\overline{X}_{jk} - \overline{X}_{..})^2 \qquad \textbf{(16.4)}$$

$$SS_A = nK\Sigma(\overline{X}_{j.} - \overline{X}_{..})^2 \qquad \textbf{(16.5)}$$

$$v_A = J - 1 \qquad \textbf{(16.6)}$$

$$MS_A = SS_A / v_A \qquad \textbf{(16.7)}$$

$$F_A = MS_A / MS_w \qquad \textbf{(16.8)}$$

$$SS_B = nJ\Sigma(\overline{X}_{.K} - \overline{X}_{..})^2 \qquad \textbf{(16.9)}$$

$$v_B = K - 1 \qquad \textbf{(16.10)}$$

$$MS_B = SS_B / v_B \qquad \textbf{(16.11)}$$

$$F_B = MS_B / MS_w \qquad \textbf{(16.12)}$$

$$SS_{A \times B} = SS_{\text{b/cells}} - (SS_A + SS_B) \qquad \textbf{(16.13)}$$

$$v_{A \times B} = (J - 1)(K - 1) \qquad \textbf{(16.14)}$$

$$MS_{A \times B} = SS_{A \times B} / v_{A \times B} \qquad \textbf{(16.15)}$$

$$F_{A \times B} = MS_{A \times B} / MS_W \qquad \textbf{(16.16)}$$

$$s_{\overline{X}_j} = \sqrt{\frac{MS_W}{nK}} \qquad \textbf{(16.17)}$$

$$s_{\overline{X}_k} = \sqrt{\frac{MS_W}{nJ}} \qquad \textbf{(16.18)}$$

❖ Appendix E

Glossary of Terms

ABSCISSA refers to the horizontal or x-axis of a graph.

ABSOLUTE VALUE is the numerical magnitude of a number without respect to its algebraic (+ or –) sign; for example, the absolute value of –3 is 3, symbolized by |3|.

ALPHA ERROR is a type-I error—rejecting a null hypothesis when it is true.

ALPHA (α) LEVEL or level of significance—a priori allowable risk of a type-I error, for example; $\alpha = .05$.

ANALYSIS OF VARIANCE (ANOVA) is a statistical procedure to determine whether two or more means differ significantly.

BALANCED DESIGN is a data set in which all subgroups have equal n's.

BAR GRAPH is comprised of bars whose lengths indicate the frequency or percentage for a score or category.

BELL CURVE refers to a bell-shaped or normal curve.

BETA (β) is the probability of making a type-II error, that is, failing to reject a false null hypothesis.

BETA ERROR is a type-II error—accepting a null hypothesis when it is false.

BIAS is a systematic tendency for an inferential statistic (e.g., s) to be consistently larger than or smaller than the corresponding population parameter (e.g., σ).

BIASED SAMPLES differ systematically from random samples—the differences are not due to just sampling error. Their characteristics differ markedly from those of the target population.

BIMODAL DISTRIBUTIONS have two distinct peaks, about which the observations tend to cluster.

BINOMIAL DISTRIBUTIONS comprise events having only two possible outcomes.

BIVARIATE DISTRIBUTIONS simultaneously display distributions of two variables, one along the x-axis and the other along the y-axis.

BIVARIATE NORMAL DISTRIBUTIONS have normally distributed Y-scores (or residuals) for each level (column) of X and the variances of the residuals are constant for all values of X.

BOX-AND-WHISKER PLOTS (or box plots) display a box with whiskers at opposite ends. The box represents the middle 50 percent of the distribution, a line within the box designates the median, and the whiskers portray the distance to the prescribed endpoints.

CATEGORICAL (or NOMINAL) DATA comprise variables in which observations have no inherent rank or order or underlying continuum, for example, gender, race, and job are categorical variables.

CELLS for a two-factor ANOVA or *chi*-square test of association refer to the subgroups formed when the rows and columns cross.

CENTRAL *F*-DISTRIBUTION is the distribution of *F*-ratios when samples come from the same population, that is, when the null hypothesis is true.

CENTRAL LIMIT THEOREM stipulates that the distribution of sample means ($\overline{X}$'s) approaches a normal distribution as the sample size, *n,* increases, regardless of the shape of the parent population.

CENTRAL *t*-DISTRIBUTION is the distribution of *t*-ratios when samples come from the same population, that is, when the null hypothesis is true.

CENTRAL TENDENCY of a distribution refers to the middle or typical or average score; the median, mode, and mean are measures of central tendency.

***CHI*-SQUARE** is a test statistic to determine if the obtained proportions in various categories differ significantly from the expected proportions, if the null hypothesis were true.

CLASS INTERVALS are formed when a specified range of adjacent scores are combined. These class interval frequencies can then be used to construct a grouped frequency distribution.

COEFFICIENT OF DETERMINATION equals r^2 and specifies the proportion of the variance in one variable that is predictable from the other variable.

COMMON LOGARITHM is the exponent or the power to which 10 must be raised to give *N*. For example, $\log_{10} 100 = 2$ since $10^2 = 100$.

.95 CONFIDENCE INTERVAL (or .95 CI) specifies a range of values within which the target parameter resides in 95 percent of the applications.

CONFIDENCE LIMITS consists of a lower limit and an upper limit between which the target parameter is presumed to fall.

CONSISTENCY is the statistical property of a statistic that insures that as the sample size increases the sampling error decreases.

CONSTANT, in contrast to a variable, is uniform for all units in the population. For example, the citizenship of the U.S. electorate is a constant since all the voters are U.S. citizens.

CONSTRUCT, an unobservable hypothesized variable theorized to explain a phenomenon. Intelligence and ego-strength are examples of constructs.

CONTINGENCY TABLES are two-dimensional arrays displaying the cell frequencies, that is, the number of observations falling in the subgroup categories formed by crossing the levels of the row variable with the levels of the column variable.

CONTROL GROUP is the group not receiving the special intervention (treatment); it is the group to be compared with the experimental group.

CORRECTION FOR ATTENUATION is a procedure to estimate the correlation between two variables if the measurement error in the two variables were eliminated.

CORRECTION FOR RANGE RESTRICTION is a procedure to estimate the correlation between two variables if the variability within the group were representative (or different from what was observed).

CORRELATED (or PAIRED) OBSERVATIONS occur when the scores comprising two sets of data are paired.

CORRELATION COEFFICIENTS are descriptive measures showing the direction and degree of the relationship between two variables.

COVARIANCE between two variables is the extent to which the two variables in question vary together. When divided by the product of the standard deviations of the two variables, the quotient is the Pearson correlation coefficient.

CRITICAL REGION refers to that portion of the sampling distribution of the test statistic that requires that the null hypothesis be rejected.

CRITICAL VALUE(S) of the test statistic is the point at or above which the null hypothesis can be rejected.

CUMULATIVE FREQUENCY of a point refers to the number of scores at or below that point.

CUMULATIVE PERCENTAGE CURVE, an ogive formed by graphing the cumulative percentage values of successive interval upper limits of a grouped frequency distribution and connecting them with line segments.

CURVILINEAR RELATIONSHIPS between pairs of variables are indicated when the swarms of points comprising the scatterplots tend to follow a curve, rather than a straight line.

DEGREES OF FREEDOM, v, is a mathematical property of a set of data that is related to the number of restrictions imposed on the data.

DEPENDENT VARIABLE is the outcome or criterion variable that is hypothesized to be related to changes in the independent variable.

DESCRIPTIVE STATISTICS is the branch of statistics that involves summarizing, organizing, and displaying data for a population.

DEVIATION SCORE is the result when the mean score is subtracted from a raw score. It reflects the distance from the mean to the raw score (i.e., $x = X - \overline{X}$).

DICHOTOMOUS VARIABLES are comprised of only two distinct categories.

DIRECTIONAL HYPOTHESES specify a priori the direction of a difference in a parameter. One-tail tests employ directional hypotheses.

DISTRIBUTION-FREE (or NONPARAMETRIC) STATISTICS make no assumptions concerning the distribution of observations in the population or its parameters.

EFFECT SIZE is the difference between two means, expressed in standard deviation units, for example, $\Delta = (\mu_E - \mu_C)/\sigma$ is an effect size.

EFFICIENCY of a statistic is related to the relative magnitude of sampling error expected in a statistic, for example, the same mean is more efficient than the sample median.

EMPIRICAL DISTRIBUTIONS are distributions based on actual observations.

ERROR OF ESTIMATE (or RESIDUAL) is the difference found by subtracting a predicted score from the subsequent obtained score.

ERROR OF MEASUREMENT is the difference between an obtained score and a true score due to uncontrolled factors.

ERROR TERM in ANOVA is the denominator of the F-test.

EXPERIMENT is a typical study in which subjects are randomly assigned to the experimental and control groups.

EXPERIMENTAL GROUP is comprised of subjects who receive the experimental treatment and who are compared to a control group.

EXPERIMENT-WISE (or FAMILY) ERROR RATE refers to the probability of making one or more type-I errors from the statistical tests of the entire set of null hypotheses in the data set.

F-**DISTRIBUTION** is described by the ratio of two variance estimates when sampling from populations with the same variance.

F-**RATIO** is the ratio of two independent variance estimates. It is the test statistic for ANOVA.

F-**TEST** is a test statistic that is used primarily to determine if two or more group means differ significantly. It is also used to determine if two sample variances differ significantly.

FACTOR in the ANOVA context refers to an independent variable.

FACTORIAL DESIGNS include two or more factors (independent variable) and allow, a test of the interaction effects between the factors.

FINITE POPULATION refers to populations with N elements where N is a definite number. Most statistical applications assume that N is infinite.

FISHER'S Z is a transformation of r that has an approximately normal sampling distribution regardless of ρ or n.

FREQUENCY is the number of times a score occurs in a category or set of data.

FREQUENCY DISTRIBUTION is an array of ordered scores in which the frequency of each score is reported or displayed.

FREQUENCY POLYGON is a graph formed by connecting the points representing the frequencies of the class intervals.

GENERALIZABILITY pertains to whether the findings based on the sample data can be applied to the population.

GOODNESS-OF-FIT TEST is a test to determine if an empirical distribution of observations differs significantly from a theoretical distribution. A test of normality is a goodness-of-fit test.

GRAND MEAN is the mean of all observations in a data set.

GROUPED FREQUENCY DISTRIBUTION is an array of ordered score intervals displaying the frequency of each interval.

H_0 **(or STATISTICAL HYPOTHESIS)** is a statement specifying a numerical value for a population parameter.

HETEROGENEITY OF VARIANCE indicates that the variances of the designated populations differ.

HISTOGRAMS are comprised of bars whose lengths indicate the frequencies or percentages of the score intervals.

HOMOGENEITY OF VARIANCE prevails when the population variances being compared do not differ.

HOMOSCEDASTICITY, a term to indicate uniform variability of the residuals about the regression line for all values of X.

HSD (honest significant difference) specifies the minimum difference in means required to reach statistical significance when the Tukey method of multiple comparisons is used.

HYPOTHESIS is a statement specifying a numerical value for a parameter.

HYPOTHESIS TESTING is a type of inferential statistics to assess the credibility of the null (statistical) hypothesis. It involves stating a null hypothesis and alpha level, computing a test statistic and its probability, and rejecting or retaining the null hypothesis.

INDEPENDENT DATA results when each observation is unaffected by and unrelated to any other observation in the data set.

INDEPENDENT VARIABLE is the variable manipulated (the predictor) to determine its effects (predictions) on the dependent variable.

INFERENTIAL STATISTICS is that branch of statistics that makes statements about population attributes using probabilities based on random samples.

INFINITE POPULATIONS are populations whose elements are large beyond number, that is, $N = \infty$.

INTERACTION between two factors exists when the effects of the levels of factor A depend upon the levels of factor B, that is, the effects of factors A and B are not additive.

INTERQUARTILE RANGE is the difference between the quartiles Q_3 and Q_1; it includes the middle 50 percent of the observations.

INTERVAL SCALES have an arbitrary zero point with equal units.

KURTOSIS describes the degree to which the observed proportions differ from those of the normal curve. Distributions with a greater proportion of extreme scores have positive kurtosis (leptokurtic); those with fewer extreme scores have negative kurtosis (platykurtic).

LEAST SQUARES CRITERION defines "best" as the statistic (or line) having the minimum value for the sum of the squared deviation scores (residuals).

LEPTOKURTIC DISTRIBUTIONS are symmetrical bell-shaped curves that have fatter tails and are more peaked than the normal curve.

LEVEL OF SIGNIFICANCE, or alpha level, is the risk of making a type-I error (rejecting a true null hypothesis).

LINEAR TRANSFORMATIONS are numerical changes in the observations that result from adding, subtracting, multiplying, or dividing by constants. These operations do not alter the shape of the distribution, and correlate 1.0 with the original scores.

LOGARITHM, COMMON is the exponent or the power to which 10 must be raised to give N. For example, $\log_{10} 100 = 2$ since $10^2 = 100$.

LOGARITHM, NATURAL ($\ln_e$) is the exponent or the power to which e ($e = 2.718 \ldots$) must be raised to give N. For example, $\ln_e 100 = 4.60517$ since $e^{4.60516} = 100$.

MAIN EFFECT in ANOVA is an effect attributable to a factor. A two-factor ANOVA has two main effects.

MATCHED PAIR DESIGN is one in which the observations comprising two arrays of data can be logically paired.

MEAN (or arithmetic mean) is the arithmetic average of a set of scores.

MEAN SQUARE is a variance estimate.

MEASUREMENT is a process by which numbers (or quantifications) are assigned to observations.

MEDIAN is the midpoint of a distribution of the scores—precisely one-half of the scores fall above the median; it is also called the 50th percentile, or Q_2.

MODE is the score (or category) with the greatest frequency of occurrence.

MU (μ) is the mean of the population.

MULTIPLE COMPARISONS is a procedure to identify which mean(s) differ significantly from which other mean(s).

MULTIPLE CORRELATION COEFFICIENT (R) describes the linear relationship between a criterion variable and a variable that results from an optimally weighted set of predictor variables.

MULTIPLE REGRESSION is a statistical procedure to predict performance on criterion variables from two or more predictor variables.

MULTIPLE t-TESTS is an unrecommended procedure using several nonindependent applications of the t-test to test pairwise null hypotheses.

NATURAL LOGARITHM is the exponent or the power to which e ($e = 2.718 \ldots$) must be raised to give N. For example, $\ln_e 100 = 4.60517$ since $e^{4.60516} = 100$.

NEGATIVE CORRELATION is indicated when observations above the mean of one variable tend to be associated with observations below the mean on a second variable, and vice versa.

NEGATIVE SKEW describes a symmetric distributions in which the median exceeds the mean; the tail of the distribution is toward the low scores.

NEWMAN-KEULS is a multiple comparisons procedure to identify significant differences between means using a contrast-based error rate.

NOMINAL SCALE of measurement uses numbers as labels or names. Categorical variables represent nominal scales.

NONDIRECTIONAL HYPOTHESES use two-tail inferential tests in which the null hypothesis can be rejected by any nonrandom outcome in either of two directions. (For a directional test, the null hypothesis can only be rejected if the difference is in the prespecified direction.)

NONLINEAR TRANSFORMATIONS, are mathematical conversions of the data that alter the shape of the distribution. If the X's are squared, or their square roots or logarithms are used, the transformation is nonlinear.

NONPARAMETRIC STATISTICS, in contrast to parametric statistics (like the t-test), make no assumptions concerning the population parameters, or of the shape of the distribution.

NORMAL DISTRIBUTION or normal curve is a symmetrical bell-shaped distribution that forms the basis for much of inferential statistics. A host of naturally occurring attributed and several sampling distributions approximate the normal curve.

NULL HYPOTHESIS, or statistical hypothesis, is a statement specifying a numerical value for a population parameter.

OGIVE is a cumulative percentage curve.

ONE-SAMPLE t-TEST is an inferential test to determine if a sample mean differs significantly from a stipulated value.

ONE-TAIL TESTS are associated with directional hypotheses and place the critical region (α) in the positive tail of the sampling distribution. When used properly, one-tail tests are more powerful than two-tail tests.

ONE-WAY ANOVA (one-factor or simple ANOVA) is used to determine if a set of two or more sample means differ by more than expected due to sampling error.

ORDINAL SCALE measurement assumes an underlying continuum and yields data in the form of ranks. This implies that a larger number indicates a greater amount or degree of the attribute measured than does a lower number, but differences between ranks may not be equal.

ORDINATE is the vertical or y-axis of a two-dimensional graph.

PAIRWISE COMPARISON is used in multiple comparisons techniques to determine if two means differ significantly.

PARAMETER is a characteristic or attribute of the population.

PARTIAL CORRELATION is a technique to assess the relationship between two variables after holding one (or more) variable(s) constant thus removing their effects from the obtained correlation coefficient.

PERCENTILE is one of 99 points along a distribution that partition the distribution into hundredths. For example, P_{28} is a point that separates the lower 28 percent of the distribution from the upper 72 percent.

PERCENTILE RANK of a score is the percent of the distribution that is at or below that score.

PIE CHART is a circular graph comprised of wedges or slices, the sizes of which are determined by the relative frequency (or percentage) of each segment of the variable.

POINT ESTIMATES are specific numerical estimates of population parameters. For example, $\overline{X}$ is a point estimate of μ.

POOLED VARIANCE (or within-group mean square) is the estimate of the population variance based on the weighted average of the subgroup variances.

POPULATION, all members, elements, observations or scores that fit a specific criterion.

POSITIVE CORRELATION describes a bivariate relationship between two variables in which subjects' scores tend to go together (to some extent); in general, those who score above the mean on one variable are also more likely to score above the mean on the second variable.

POSITIVE SKEW describes asymmetric distributions in which the mean exceeds the median; the scores "tail off" toward the higher scores.

POWER is the probability of rejecting a false null hypothesis; power equals $1 - \beta$.

PRACTICAL SIGNIFICANCE pertains to whether the observed finding is substantial enough to make a meaningful difference in practice. Statistical significance may, or may not, have practical significance.

PROBABILITY is the likelihood of occurrence, expressed as a proportion.

PROBABILITY OF A COMPUTED STATISTIC is the probability of obtaining a value as large as or larger than the computed statistic if the null hypothesis were true; it is denoted by the symbol, p. When $p < \alpha$, H_0 is rejected.

PROPORTION is the ratio of a part to the whole.

QUALITATIVE or nominal measurement occurs when the assigned numerals are used as labels or names rather than for quantification.

QUANTITATIVE measurement assigns numbers to the observations reflecting the amount or degree of the attribute possessed.

QUARTILE is one of three points (Q_1, Q_2, Q_3) which partition the distribution into four equal segments. Q_1 is the point that divides the lower fourth of the distribution from the upper three-fourths; $Q_1 = P_{25}$, $Q_2 = P_{50}$, $Q_8 = P_{75}$.

QUARTILE DEVIATION or semi-interquartile range is one-half the difference between Q_1 and Q_3: $Q = (Q_3 - Q_1)/2$.

RANDOM SAMPLING occurs when each unit of the population has an equal probability of being selected, and where this probability is independent (unaffected by the selection of any other unit).

RANGE is the difference between the least and greatest scores in the distribution.

RANKS are used to order a set of observations according to the criterion of "greater than."

RATIO SCALE of measurement is calibrated from an absolute zero point and successive numbers mark off equal amounts of the attribute being measured.

RAW SCORES are the original observations prior to any subsequent mathematical transformations.

REGRESSION is a statistical procedure to predict performance on criterion variables from one or more predictor variables.

REGRESSION COEFFICIENT is the multiplier of X (the predictor variable) in the regression equation to predict Y: $Y = bX + c$.

REGRESSION EFFECT refers to the phenomenon that subjects who deviate markedly from the mean, when retested, tend to regress or score closer to the group mean.

REGRESSION INTERCEPT is the additive constant in the regression equation to predict Y from X.

REGRESSION LINE is the straight line of "best fit" for predicting criterion (Y) scores. It bisects the swarm of points comprising the scatterplot, thus connecting the predicted criterion means for all values of X.

REPRESENTATIVE SAMPLE is one whose characteristics and attributes closely match those of the corresponding population.

RESIDUAL is the error of estimate—the difference between the obtained criterion score and the prediction.

RESTRICTED VARIABILITY occurs when the total range of scores is not included in the analysis and nonrepresentative homogeneity is affects. This condition has a spuriously depressing effect upon the value of the correlation coefficient.

RHO (ρ) is the parameter correlation coefficient.

ROBUSTNESS is the extent to which the probabilities associated with computed statistics are unaffected by whether or not the data fail to meet the mathematical assumptions required for the derivation of the statistical test.

SAMPLES are subsets of populations.

SAMPLING DISTRIBUTION is a theoretical distribution of an infinite number of replications of a sample statistic, each of which is based on a random sample of a given size.

SAMPLING ERROR is the difference between an obtained sample statistic and its corresponding population parameter.

SAMPLING FRACTION (n/N) is the ratio of the sample size to the population size.

SCATTERPLOT is a set of points in an XY-plane, each of which simultaneously indicates a subject's performance on both the horizontal or X-variable and the vertical or Y-variable.

SEMI-INTERQUARTILE RANGE (or quartile deviation) is one-half the difference between the 25th percentile (Q_1) and the 75th percentile (Q_3): $Q = (Q_3 - Q_1)/2$.

SKEWNESS describes the lack of symmetry in a distribution.

STANDARD DEVIATION (σ or s) is a measure of variability or individual differences among a set of scores. In a normal distribution, about two-thirds of the scores will be within one standard deviation of the mean.

STANDARD ERROR is the standard deviation of a theoretical sampling distribution.

STANDARD ERROR OF ESTIMATE ($\sigma_{Y \cdot X}$ or $s_{Y \cdot X}$) is the standard deviation of the errors of estimate (residuals) from the regression line.

STANDARD ERROR OF THE DIFFERENCE BETWEEN MEANS ($\sigma_{\bar{X}_1 - \bar{X}_2}$ or $s_{\bar{X}_1 - \bar{X}_2}$) is the standard deviation of the sampling distribution of the difference between two means.

STANDARD ERROR OF THE MEAN ($\sigma_{\bar{X}}$ or $s_{\bar{X}}$) is the standard deviation of the sampling distribution of the mean.

STANDARD SCORES are derived scores having a fixed (standard) mean and a fixed standard deviation. Common standard scores are z-scores, T-scores, and IQ scores.

STATISTICAL HYPOTHESIS or null hypothesis, is the hypothesis to be tested by the inferential technique.

STATISTICAL SIGNIFICANCE means that the probability of the obtained statistic, if the null hypothesis were true, is less than alpha ($p < \alpha$), the stated level of significance. Therefore, the null hypothesis is rejected as untenable and the findings are said to be statistically significant.

STATISTICS (or inferential statistics) are measures based on sample data; they are used to estimate the corresponding parameters for the population.

STUDENT t-TEST (or t-test) is hypothesis testing procedure to determine whether two group means differ significantly. It is also used to determine if a single mean ($\bar{X}$)

differs significantly from a stated value for μ or whether a correlation coefficient differs from zero.

STUDENTIZED RANGE STATISTIC is the sampling distribution of the ratio of the difference between a pair of means to the standard error of the mean when sampling from the same population: $q = (\overline{X}_i - \overline{X}_j)/s_{\overline{X}}$. It is used by the Tukey and the Newman-Keuls methods of multiple comparisons.

SUM OF SQUARES *(SS)* is the sum of the squared deviation scores, Σx^2.

SYSTEMATIC SAMPLING selects every kth name from a population listing after randomly selecting the starting point. Ordinarily, systematic samples tend to be comparable to simple random sampling in terms of representativeness.

*t***-DISTRIBUTION** is the sampling distribution of the t-ratio when H_0 is true.

*T***-SCALE** is a standard score scale with a mean of 50 and a standard deviation of 10: $T = 10z + 50$.

*t***-TEST** is a hypothesis testing procedure to determine whether two group means differ significantly. It is also used to determine if a single mean ($\overline{X}$) differs significantly from a stated value for μ or whether a correlation coefficient differs from zero.

TUKEY METHOD is a multiple comparisons procedure used to identify which pairs of subgroup means differ significantly, using a family α-error rate.

TWO-FACTOR ANOVA DESIGNS specify two independent variables (factors). The analysis of these designs yields not only tests for main effects from the two factors, but also a test for an interaction effect between the two factors.

TWO-TAIL TESTS are associated with nondirectional hypotheses and allow the null hypothesis to be rejected for any nonrandom outcome (whereas for a one-tail or directional test, the null hypothesis can only be rejected if the difference is in the previously specified direction).

TYPE-I ERRORS are made when true null hypotheses are rejected. The rate of type-I errors is controlled by adopting an appropriate alpha level.

TYPE-II ERRORS are made when false null hypotheses are accepted as tenable. The rate of type-II errors is decreased by increasing the sample size, increasing the value of α, and several other design considerations.

VARIABILITY pertains to the degree of heterogeneity in the data.

VARIABLES are characteristics or attributes which yield observations which differ.

VARIANCE (σ^2) or mean square *(MS)* is the average squared deviation score. The square root of the variance is the standard deviation.

*z***-SCORE** is the basic standard score with a mean of zero and a variance of 1: $z = (X - \mu)/\sigma$.

*z***-TEST** is a hypothesis testing procedure to determine if two statistics differ significantly. In contrast to the t-test, the z-test requires that the population variances be known.

Bibliography

Allison, D. E. 1970. "Test anxiety, stress, and intelligence performance," *Canadian Journal of Behavioral Science, 2,* 26–27.

Bashaw, W. L. 1969. *Mathematics for Statistics.* New York: John Wiley.

Bennett, G. K., H. G. Seashore, and A. G. Wesman. 1974. *Differential Aptitude Tests: Sixth Edition Manual.* New York: Psychological Corporation.

Boneau, C. A. 1960. "The effects of violations of assumptions underlying the *t*-test," *Psychological Bulletin, 57,* 49–64.

Borgatta, E. F., and G. Bohrnstedt. 1980. *Social Measurement.* Beverly Hills, CA: Sage Publications.

Box, G. E. P., W. G. Hunter, and J. S. Hunter. 1978. *Statistics for Experimenters.* New York: John Wiley.

Brinzer, R. J., and R. L. Sinatra. 1982. "Survey of statistics textbooks used by the top 100 American Educational Research Association contributors." Paper presented to the American Educational Research Association, New York.

Burstein, H. 1971. *Attribute Sampling: Tables and Explanations. Tables for Determining Confidence Limits and Sample Sizes Based on Close Approximations of the Binomial Distribution.* New York: McGraw-Hill.

Camilli, G., and K. D. Hopkins. 1978. "Applicability of *chi*-square to 2 × 2 contingency tables with small expected frequencies," *Psychological Bulletin, 85,* 163–167.

Camilli, G., and K. D. Hopkins. 1979. "Testing for association in 2 × 2 contingency tables with very small sample sizes," *Psychological Bulletin, 86,* 1011–1014.

Chambers, A. C., K. D. Hopkins, and B. R. Hopkins. 1972. "Anxiety, physiologically and psychologically measured: Its effects on mental test performance," *Psychology in the Schools, 9,* 198–206.

Cochran, W. 1977. *Sampling Techniques* (3rd ed.). New York: John Wiley.

Conover, W. J. 1980. *Practical Nonparametric Statistics* (2nd ed.). New York: John Wiley.

Conover, W. J., and others. 1974. "Some reasons for not using the Yates' Continuity Correction on 2×2 contingency tables," *Journal of the American Statistical Association, 69,* 374–382.

Cook, T. D., and D. T. Campbell. 1979. *Quasi-experimentation: Design and Analysis Issues for Field Settings.* Chicago: Rand-McNally.

Cronbach, L. J. 1982. *Designing Evaluation of Educational and Social Programs.* San Francisco: Jossey-Bass.

Dixon, W. J., and F. J. Massey. 1980. *Introduction to Statistical Analysis* (4th ed.). New York: McGraw-Hill.

Elmore, P. B., and P. L. Woehlke. 1988. "Statistical methods employed in *American Educational Research Journal, Educational Researcher,* and *Review of Educational Research* from 1978 to 1987," *Educational Researcher, 17,* 19–20.

Erlenmeyer-Kimling, L., and L. F. Jarvik. 1963. "Genetics and intelligence," *Science, 142,* 1477–1479.

Flexer, R. J. and A. S. Flexer. 1967. Six booklets: 1. *Fractions;* 2. *Linear and Literal Equations;* 3. *Quadratic Equations;* 4. *Exponents and Square Roots;* 5. *Logarithms;* 6. *Introduction to Statistics.* New York: Harper & Row.

French, J. W. 1962. "Effects of anxiety on verbal and mathematical examination scores," *Educational and Psychological Measurement, 22,* 553–564.

Ghosh, B. K. 1979. "A comparison of some approximate confidence intervals for the binomial parameter," *Journal of the American Statistical Association, 74,* 894–900.

Glass, G. V, and K. D. Hopkins. 1996. *Statistical Methods in Education and Psychology* (3rd ed.). Boston, MA: Allyn & Bacon.

Glass, G. V, B. McGaw, and M. L. Smith. 1981. *Meta-analysis in Social Research.* Beverly Hills: Sage Publications.

Glass, G. V, P. D. Peckham, and J. R. Sanders. 1972. "Consequences of failure to meet assumptions underlying the fixed-effects analysis of variance and covariance," *Review of Educational Research, 42,* 237–288.

Glass, G. V, V. L. Willson, and J. M. Gottman. 1975. *Design and Analysis of Time-Series Experiments.* Boulder: Colorado Associated University Press.

Goodwin, L. D., and W. L. Goodwin. 1985. "Statistical techniques in AERJ articles, 1979–1983: The preparation of graduate students to read the educational research literature," *Educational Researcher, 14,* 5–11.

Gullickson, A. R., and K. D. Hopkins. 1976. "Interval estimation of correlation coefficients corrected for restriction of range," *Educational and Psychological Measurement, 36,* 9–25.

Hald, A. 1952. *Statistical Tables and Formulas.* New York: John Wiley.

Hartshorne, H., and M. A. May. 1928. *Studies in the Nature of Character, I: Studies in Deceit.* New York: Macmillan.

Hays, W. L. 1988. *Statistics* (4th ed.). New York: Harcourt, Brace, Jovanovich.

Hedges, L. V., and I. Olkin. 1985. *Statistical Methods for Meta-analysis.* New York: Academic Press.

Heermann, E. F., and L. A. Braskamp. 1970. *Readings in Statistics for the Behavioral Sciences.* Englewood Cliffs, NJ: Prentice-Hall.

Hopkins, K. D. 1969. "Regression and the matching fallacy in quasi-experimental research," *Journal of Special Education, 3,* 329–336.

Hopkins, K. D. 1982. "The unit of analysis: Group means vs. individual observations," *American Educational Research Journal, 19,* 5–18.

Hopkins, K. D. 1983. "A strategy for analyzing ANOVA designs having one or more random factors," *Educational and Psychological Measurement, 43,* 107–113.

Hopkins, K. D., and E. G. Sitkie. 1969. "Predicting grade one reading performance: Intelligence vs. reading readiness tests", *Journal of Experimental Education, 37,* 31–33.

Hopkins, K. D., J. C. Stanley, and B. R. Hopkins. 1990. *Educational and Psychological Measurement and Evaluation* (7th ed.). Englewood Cliffs, NJ: Prentice-Hall.

Hsu, P. L. 1938. "Contribution to the theory of Student's *t*-test as applied to the problem of two samples," *Statistical Research Memoirs, 2,* 1–24.

Hsu, T. C., and L. S. Feldt. 1969. "The effects of limitations on the number of criterion score values on the significance of the *F*-test," *American Educational Research Journal, 6,* 515–527.

Jaeger, R. M. 1984. *Sampling in Education and the Social Sciences.* New York: Longmans.

Jeffrey, W. E., and S. J. Samuels. 1967. "Effect of method of reading training on initial learning and transfer," *Journal of Verbal Learning and Verbal Behavior, 6,* 354–358.

Kearney, P. A. 1970. *Programmed Review of Fundamental Mathematics for Elementary Statistics.* Englewood Cliffs, NJ: Prentice-Hall.

Kirk, R. E. 1982. *Experimental Designs for the Behavioral Sciences* (2nd ed.). Belmont, CA: Brooks/Cole.

Kish, L. 1965. *Survey Sampling.* New York: John Wiley.

Kramer, C. Y. 1956. "Extension of multiple range test to group means with unequal number of replications," *Biometrics, 57,* 649–655.

Kruskal, W. H. 1980. "A review of R. A. Fisher: The life of a scientist," *Journal of the American Statistical Association, 75,* 1019–1029.

Luce, R. D., D. H. Krantz, P. Suppes, and A. Tversky. 1990. *Foundations of Measurement Volume III.* New York: Academic Press.

Miller, R. G. 1966. *Simultaneous Statistical Inference.* New York: McGraw-Hill.

Miller, R. G. 1977. "Developments in multiple comparisons, 1966–1976," *Journal of the American Statistical Association, 72,* 779–788.

Mitchell, J. 1986. "Measurement scales and statistics: A clash of paradigms," *Psychological Bulletin, 100,* 398–407.

Mood, A., and F. A. Graybill. 1963. *Introduction to the Theory of Statistics* (2nd ed.), New York: McGraw-Hill.

Moore, D. S., and G. P. McCabe. 1993. *Introduction to the Practice of Statistics* (2nd ed.). New York: W. H. Freeman.

Newman, H. H., F. N. Freeman, and K. J. Holzinger. 1937. *Twins: A Study of Heredity and Environment.* Chicago: University of Chicago Press.

Pearson, E. S., and C. J. Clopper. 1934. "The use of confidence intervals or fiducial limits illustrated in the case of the binomial," *Biometrika, 26,* 404–413.

Pearson, E. S., and H. O. Hartley. 1966. *Biometrika Tables for Statisticians.* Cambridge: Cambridge University Press.

Porter, T. M. 1986. *The Rise of Statistical Thinking 1820–1900.* Princeton, N.J.: Princeton University Press.

Rock, D. A., T. L. Hilton, J. Pollack, R. B. Ekstrom, and M. E. Goertz. 1985. *Psychometric Analysis of the NLS and the High School and Beyond Test Batteries.* Washington, DC: U. S. Government Printing Office (NCES 85-218).

Roscoe, J. T., and J. A. Byars. 1971. "An investigation of the restraints with respect to sample size commonly imposed on the use of the *chi*-square statistic," *Journal of the American Statistical Association, 66,* 755–759.

Sachs, L. 1982. *Applied Statistics: A Handbook of Techniques Translated by Z. Reynarowych.* New York: Springer-Verlag.

Scheffé, H. 1959. *The Analysis of Variance.* New York: John Wiley.

Shepard, L. A., and K. D. Hopkins. 1977. "Regression and the matching fallacy in quasi-experimental research," *National Association for Business Teachers Education Review, 4,* 11–15.

Shepard, L. A., M. E. Graue, and S. F. Catto. 1989. "Delayed entry into kindergarten and escalation of academic demands." Paper presented to the American Educational Research Association, San Francisco.

Shlomo, S. S., and R. C. Blair. 1992. "A more realistic look at the robustness and type-II error properties of the *t*-test to departures from population normality," *Psychological Bulletin, 111,* 352–360.

Smith, M. L., and G. V Glass. 1986. *Research and Evaluation in Education and the Social Sciences.* Englewood Cliffs, NJ: Prentice-Hall.

Smith, R. A. 1971. "The effect of unequal group size on Tukey's *HSD* procedure," *Psychometrika, 36,* 31–34.

Snedecor, G. W., and W. G. Cochran. 1980. *Statistical Methods* (7th ed.). Ames: Iowa State University Press.

Tanur, J. M., F. Mosteller, W. H. Kruskal, R. F. Link, R. S. Pieters, G. R. Rising, and E. L. Lehmann. 1978. *Statistics: A Guide to the Unknown* (2nd ed.). San Francisco: Holden-Day.

Thorndike, R. L. 1949. *Personnel Selection.* New York: John Wiley.

Townsend, J. T., and F. G. Ashby. 1984. "Measurement scales and statistics: The misconception misconceived," *Psychological Bulletin, 96,* 394–401.

Tufte, E. R. 1983. *The Visual Display of Quantitative Information.* Cheshire, CN: Graphics Press.

Tukey, J. W. 1960. "Conclusions vs. decisions," *Technometrics, 2,* 423–433.

Tukey, J. W. 1977. *Exploratory Data Analysis.* Reading, MA: Addison-Wesley.

Velleman, P. F., and L. Wilkinson. 1993. "Nominal, ordinal, interval, and ratio typologies are misleading," *American Statistician, 47,* 65–72.

Wainer, H. 1992. "Understanding graphs and tables," *Educational Researcher, 21,* 14–23.

Wechsler, D. 1967. *Manual for the Wechsler Preschool and Primary Scale of Intelligence.* New York: Psychological Corporation.

White, K. R., and K. D. Hopkins. 1975. "The reliability of a self-report measure of socio-economic status, and the relationship of SES and pupil achievement in grades 2–6." Paper presented to the National Council on Measurement in Education, Washington, DC.

Willson, V. L. 1980. "Research techniques in AERJ articles: 1969 to 1978," *Educational Researcher, 9,* 5–10.

Winer, B. J. 1971. *Statistical Principles in Experimental Design* (2nd ed.). New York: McGraw-Hill.

Winer, B. J., D. R. Brown, and K. M. Michels. 1991. *Statistical Principles in Experimental Design* (3rd ed.). New York: McGraw-Hill.

❖ Author Index

❖ Subject Index

Tables

Disk Information

The enclosed diskette includes the HSB data set from the High School and Beyond Study; achievement and demographic data are given for a national representative sample of 200 high school seniors. These data are presented in three formats:

(1) ASCII (text) code: HSB200.TXT
(2) EXCEL format: HSB200.XLs
(3) SPSS for Windows format: HSB200.SAV

All spreadsheet and statistical packages for the PC can read one or more of the above formats. Experienced Macintosh users will be able to read the files and convert them to Mac format. Additional information is given in the diskette's README.TXT file.